SECOND WORLD

A N D

GREEN WORLD

STUDIES IN
RENAISSANCE
FICTION-MAKING

H A R R Y   B E R G E R,   J R.

Selected and Arranged, with an Introduction,
by John Patrick Lynch

UNIVERSITY OF CALIFORNIA PRESS

Berkeley, Los Angeles, London

University of California Press
Berkeley and Los Angeles, California

University of California Press, Ltd.
London, England

© 1988 by
The Regents of the University of California

Library of Congress Cataloging-in-Publication Data

Berger, Harry.
Second world and green world.

Includes index.
1. English literature—Early modern, 1500–1700—
History and criticism.   2. Shakespeare, William, 1564–
1616—Criticism and interpretation.   3. Renaissance.
4. Humanism.   5. Art, Renaissance.   6. Civilization,
Modern.   I. Lynch, John Patrick.   II. Title.
PR413.B47   1988   823'.3'09   87-10935
ISBN 0-520-05826-7 (alk. paper)

Printed in the United States of America

1   2   3   4   5   6   7   8   9

For Tommy

Thomas Harry Berger

FEBRUARY 27, 1948–JANUARY 16, 1965

Who that has sailed by star
on the light night-air,
first hand on the tiller,
second, the nibbling sheet,

who, looking aloft and then aback,
has not one moment lost
in the wind's still eye
his second world
and the bright star
before the long shudder fills on
                    the windward tack?

   R. P. Blackmur, "The Second World"

Mean while the Mind, from pleasure less,
Withdraws into its happiness:
The Mind, that Ocean where each kind
Does streight its own resemblance find;
Yet it creates, transcending these,
Far other Worlds, and other Seas;
Annihilating all that's made
To a green Thought in a green Shade.

           Andrew Marvell, "The Garden"

CONTENTS

ACKNOWLEDGMENTS

This volume would never have seen daylight if my good friends Professors Stephen Greenblatt, Thomas Vogler, and John Lynch hadn't prodded and cajoled me into doing something about it, hadn't assaulted and undermined my inertia by a variety of devious tactics that only a good friend could forgive. Lynch in fact took it on himself first to present me with a table of contents and then to go on to write an introduction. And as if that weren't bad enough, he conspired with Doris Kretschmer of the University of California Press, and between them they had the face to push me into a corner and make me go to work. Once in the corner I grew accustomed to their face and penetrated to its subtext, and I found there enough patience, dedication, loyalty, and affectionate concern to move me to forgive them their trespasses.

Yet when confronted by the actual prospect of going through old essays, checking old footnotes, and—even worse—adding footnotes that should have been there, a new set of waves washed over me: anxiety and helplessness cresting into anger, followed by long low quiet splashless swells of boredom. The whole project would assuredly have gone under had not my research assistant, Beth Pittenger, saved it with long low quiet splashless hours of hard work—hours I know she didn't have to spare. I am deeply grateful to her for the meticulous care with which she prepared the manuscript, helped me reconstruct the footnotes, and retyped them all in printer-ready form.

I have, in addition, a special bone to pick with Charlotte Cassidy, not because she has been typing and copyediting my manuscripts for twenty years but because the form of her fair copy was so much more beautiful than the content of my foul papers that I was often reluctant to disturb it with revisions that would undoubtedly have made this a better book. This is almost enough to keep me from expressing my thanks and gratitude for the skill, accuracy, and intelligence with which over the years she has made some thousands of pages more presentable than they deserved to be; almost, but not quite.

Because she made me think my prose immortal, Ms. Cassidy has to take responsibility for what Stephanie Fay did to it when, on behalf of the University of California Press, she copyedited the manuscript, which is a euphemism for her incessant and eager attacks on page after lovely page. By bullying puny passages, unpretzeling my prose, undangling my participles, penciling away at my particles, my prepositions, my appositions, my pronouns, my very periods, she drove me to those intense feelings of appreciation and worthlessness that always, sooner or later, prove salubrious to self-esteem. Her severity with the author is exceeded only by her kindness to the reader. I thank her for this and ask only that she leave the sentence in which I'm thanking her alone.

I should also mention that the writing has profited from the mop-up operations performed by Amy Klatzkin, Ms. Fay's successor. And I take pleasure in recording a more general debt to Barbara Ras not only for the care with which she oversaw these painful improvements but also for the patience with which—gently yet persistently, at times ingeniously, and at last successfully—she twisted a reluctant author's arm.

For a very long time the Committee on Research at the University of California, Santa Cruz, has responded generously to my annual cries for help. I take pleasure in recording my gratitude to them for their willingness to believe my promises and for their good sense in supporting my research.

I wish to thank the following editors, journals, and publishers for their permission to reprint these essays:

"The Renaissance Imagination: Second World and Green World," *Centennial Review of Arts and Sciences* 9 (1965): 36–78. Republished with restoration of footnotes excluded by the editorial practice of the journal.

"The Ecology of the Mind: The Concept of Period Imagination—An Outline Sketch," *Centennial Review* 8 (1964): 409–35; an earlier version of some of the ideas developed here was published as "Ecology of Mind," *Review of Metaphysics* 17 (1963): 109–34.

"Naive Consciousness and Culture Change: An Essay in Historical Structuralism," *Bulletin of the Midwest Modern Language Association* 6 (1973): 1–44.

"Theater, Drama, and the Second World: A Prologue to Shakespeare," *Comparative Drama* 2 (1968): 3–20.

"Troilus and Cressida: The Observer as Basilisk," *Comparative Drama* 2 (1968): 122–36.

"Miraculous Harp: A Reading of Shakespeare's *Tempest*," *Shakespeare Studies 5*, edited by J. Leeds Barroll (Dubuque, Iowa: Wm. C. Brown and Co., 1969), 353–83.

"Pico and Neoplatonist Idealism: Philosophy as Escape," *Centennial Review* 13 (1969): 38–83 (with footnotes restored).

"Utopian Folly: Erasmus and More on the Perils of Misanthropy," *English Literary Renaissance* 12 (1982): 271–90.

"Andrew Marvell: The Poem as Green World" contains three published essays which were parts of the original manuscript version. The chapter takes its title from the first essay, republished from *Forum for Modern Language Studies* 3 (1967): 290–309; the remaining pieces are republished as sections: "Marvell's 'Garden': Still Another Interpretation," *Modern Language Quarterly* 28 (1967): 285–304; and "Marvell's 'Upon Appleton House.'" *Southern Review* (Australia) 1, no. 4 (1965): 7–26.

"*Paradise Lost* Evolving, Books I–VI: Toward a New View of the Poem as the Speaker's Experience," *Centennial Review* 11 (1967): 483–531. Section IV has been added from "Archaism, Vision, and Revision: Studies in Virgil, Plato, and Milton," *Centennial Review* 11 (1967): 46–51.

"L. B. Alberti on Painting: Art and Actuality in Humanist Perspective," *Centennial Review* 10 (1966): 237–78 (with footnotes restored).

"Leonardo da Vinci: The Influence of World View on Artistic Style," *Centennial Review* 13 (1969): 241–67 (with footnotes restored).

"Conspicuous Exclusion in Vermeer: An Essay in Renaissance Pastoral," *Yale French Studies* 47 (1972): 243–65.

"Some Vanity of His Art: Conspicuous Exclusion and Pastoral in Vermeer," from a manuscript version. The first section was published under the same title in *Salmagundi* 44/45 (1979): 89–112.

For me, education in the humanities is education in the meaning and awareness of persons in both these dimensions—self and personality—and their works. This awareness develops hand in hand with the ability to interpret: to look, listen, and read with care and precision. We learn to hear people speaking to us, not through their mouths and bodies but through all the mediated forms—the media. The media are separated from bodies, and so they make it possible for selves and personalities to be present to us without the encumbrance—though without the immediacy—of their physical beings. . . .

. . . It bothers me that when students talk about the word "abstract" they usually mean boring, heavy. If you think about it not in terms of "abstraction"—a noun—but in terms of the activity of drawing out of, you see that "abstractive" or the verb "to abstract" is a very much better term than "abstract" or "abstraction." Essentially anything that gets done by man is done by drawing something out of the world into his head. To be abstracted is to be withdrawn. Artists when they're creating are abstracted from the world around them while they are abstracting—selecting—what they are doing. The central feature of all imaginative activity is abstracting. One thinks of something abstract as that which is colorless and gray and not concrete. But clock time is no more abstract than body time; it just involves a different kind of concreteness. It's been abstracted from the rhythms of life, the natural organic rhythms of life, and so we think of it as abstract, but what happens on the face of a clock is very concrete. One of the problems here is that anything that's abstracted is probably difficult. Something had to be there to begin with, and you have had to go through the whole activity of selecting and weeding out with a blueprint in mind, an idea—at least a vague idea. You're trying to discover what it is that you are trying to produce. In abstracting from what is there, you turn away from what is given in order to take something, to make something, to produce something. The process of abstracting from your impressions, abstracting from whatever is given you, and focusing actively, participatively, on a particular set of ideas or sentences is creative. You create by excluding; by excluding you produce, focus, shape, form, concentrate. The very existence of the medium of writing makes this not only possible but necessary; the writing experience is the source of the creation and discovery of new worlds.

Harry Berger, Jr., in *Why Read and Write?*
a conversation with Louis E. Haga

INTRODUCTION

by John Patrick Lynch

Harry Berger, Jr., is an American literary critic whose work has had a significant impact on certain specialists, particularly among Spenserians, scholars of Renaissance literature, and proponents of the so-called New Historicism.[1] He has also had a long-standing and loyal following as a teacher, a number of his students having gone on to accomplished careers in literary criticism and teaching. But in the judgment of many who have been his students and colleagues, Harry Berger's prolific, provocative, and wide-ranging critical writing has yet to reach the wide and more general audience that it deserves. The following selection of essays is an attempt to begin to correct that situation; addressed to students and scholars of the Renaissance, of cultural history, and of literary theory, this varied sample of Berger's adventurous criticism presents a microcosm of the prodigious interpretive program in which he has been engaged for the last thirty years.

This introduction is offered as a modest attempt to make Harry Berger's critical project a little more accessible to those not already familiar with his work. Since I am a classicist and a novice in Renaissance Studies, I have no credentials, qualifications, or expertise to justify my doing this, except for fifteen years of friendship and colleagueship with Harry, many hundreds of hours of conversation with him about literature, and several team-teaching experiences with him. I am proposing here to provide only an "outsider's view" on a subject, not a specialist's evaluation. I would like to thank all the friends and colleagues who have helped me, especially Tom Vogler, Michael Warren, Hayden White, and Andrew Wright.

[1]On the New Historicism see the exemplifications collected and edited by Stephen Greenblatt, *The Power of Forms in the English Renaissance* (Norman, Oklahoma, 1982). That collection and Greenblatt's stimulating book *Renaissance Self-Fashioning* (Chicago, 1980), particularly its Introduction, I found to be among the most instructive works that I consulted in preparing the present volume.

While Berger's essays are characterized by detailed textual analyses—close readings of individual paintings as well as literary works—his project goes far beyond explication as an end in itself and beyond reconstituting the text as a work of art. Berger's writing might better be understood as cultural history or literary anthropology rather than as literary or art criticism as it is usually practiced. For him texts, both verbal and visual, are a means of understanding the way cultures constitute themselves and change. These Renaissance studies are only a part of his attempt to develop a theory of culture, a totalizing perspective on the dynamics of cultures as revealed by individual products of the human imagination.

Like all theorists, Berger is interested in control and in developing a theory that controls as much as possible the phenomena with which it is concerned, in this case the phenomena of cultures and of culture. But at the same time he is keenly aware of the difficulty, and even perhaps the undesirability, of achieving the goal of a totalizing theory. He does not concern himself with the truth in interpretation but is after something more human in scale: an *adequate* theory, judged—as in the natural and social sciences—by its explanatory power rather than by its propinquity to godlike perspective. Unlike truth, adequacy as a concept necessitates flexibility, resourcefulness, and strategy as well as an openness and willingness to revise and improvise as one goes along. What prompts and animates Berger's inquiry, in fact, is a sense of the unfinished task as a stimulator and motivator of critical discourse; by contrast, the finished task—the magnum opus, the classic example, the model provided by the great practitioner—tends to inhibit and cut off the dialectic of critical debate.

A central element of Berger's critical agenda, therefore, subverts all manifestations of canonization in literary studies. He sees the tendency to canonize as an attempt to fence in both culture and interpretation, whereas the hydrokinetic movement of culture and interpretation as he understands them works through internal explosions, changing dynamically and dialectically. As a result, like other contemporary critics, Berger identifies himself not with the mainstream of interpretive discourse but with its margins—because the center will not hold, despite attempts to contain it by forming movements, institutions, schools, and canons. Berger has always been something of a maverick in literary studies, an "outsider" in temperament and orientation; but this standing is not so much a matter of personal choice, training, or force of circumstance as it is a deliberate philosophical position. For him, in contradistinction to the first generation of New Critics who were his teachers, the mind rages not for a settled order but for an emergent meaning.

Berger shares with almost every critical movement of the last fifty years the intent to subvert common-sense positivism in interpretation. That great Anglo-American philosopher Yogi Berra said, "You can observe a lot just by watching." Berger is almost an inverse Berra. The eyes do not tell the mind what it is thinking; the mind tells the eyes what they are seeing and, to complicate matters even further, the culture tells the mind a large part of what it is thinking. It is not simply that Berger is a complicated, highly abstract, and difficult writer and thinker. He programmatically resists simplification. For him interpretation penetrates to a level of reality not accessible to those who glide quickly to neat formulations, easy generalizations, and smooth presentations.

In some ways it has been an act of betrayal for me to put together a book like this—not a betrayal of a colleague and friend, who has been cooperative and encouraging throughout the project, but a betrayal of the essays themselves, their nature, spirit, and contents. Most of these pieces do not grow out of the state of the question in contemporary published criticism but rather out of the teaching situation. They are heuristic devices: attempts in some instances to bring clarity to dark and unexplored territory, in others to cast dark shadows over what seemed clear through inadvertence or force of habit. For Berger, despite the extent of his published (and even more numerous unpublished) writings, *teaching* literature has always been the primary activity, to which writing is secondary and subordinate. Though Berger himself would recoil from the comparison and neither his friends nor his foes would want to push it very far, teaching for him is Socratic rather than dogmatic—a searching, dynamic, and endless (though far from pointless) process, with hypotheses formulated not as ends but as stages to be transcended. Many of his published writings are indeed monographs and books in progress, with all the virtues and possibilities, as well as limitations, that attend methodologies provisionally suggested rather than ideologically dictated, problems identified more than resolved, questions posed rather than answered, and conclusions tentatively rather than definitely drawn. Compatible with the teaching situation out of which they grow, Berger's essays tend to be directed toward the process of uncovering rather than covering. They were never meant to be chapters in a conventional book of literary criticism, and they run the risk of defying a reader's expectations when set up that way. Even more troublesome, perhaps, much of what these essays contain would probably be disavowed now by Berger himself, and it may even be that the original act of writing them down was not so much a sign of conclusiveness as an act of disavowal.

Why then republish them in book form? Because Berger's *modus operandi* of constantly revising and seldom revisiting his thinking at a previous stage makes it unlikely that any of these essays—despite their critical energy, interest, and sophistication—will ever be developed into the books or monographs they individually prefigure. They are only preliminary explorations and propaedeutics in service of the larger theoretical project. But there is nevertheless an overriding value in these essays as they are presently formed: the strong challenge that they give to the canonized, the conventional, the accepted, the received in the area of Renaissance studies. They may not always be right "on target" in any ordinary sense, but they represent unique, original, and independent-minded syntheses that expand our notion of "the target" and our sense of how many targets there are.

The essays selected for this volume do, I believe, hang together and exhibit a unifying concern that illuminates Berger's larger project, namely, a working toward a comprehensive and integrated theory of culture change that would characterize the Renaissance in contradistinction to previous and subsequent cultural moments. Berger himself would probably now prefer the term "Early Modern Europe" to the more traditional name for the period; but part of my purpose in putting together the present volume has been to engage Berger's project with more traditional Renaissance studies, where I believe his work promises to have the most significant impact. What Berger calls the second world and green world are fictive attitudes that usefully characterize and illuminate the culture commonly called the Renaissance. In Berger's view, the cultural moment known as the Renaissance was characterized by the rediscovery of a belief in the human imagination and in the power of fiction to manipulate realities and to create a common ethos. The word *fiction* as Berger uses it in this theoretical context is a broad and not strictly literary term, denoting anything classified as human invention and therefore not considered to be "given," "natural," or "real"; it includes things or ideas "made up" *and* those "made by human art." This rediscovery during the Renaissance leads to the creation of a "second-world attitude," the desire to live in and therefore control a world made by human invention rather than in the "first world," the world as God, nature, or the gods have contrived it. The desire for a "green world"—a primeval world of innocence and shepherdlike existence—is a special instance of the second-world attitude, generating the mode of representing and understanding that we call pastoral. The second-world and green-world attitudes not only represent an aesthetic refinement of the first world but also strive to compete with the first world and in some ways to replace it with a world of greater clarity, complexity of order, and density of meaning. To quote Berger's own formulation, the second-world attitude represents "first and foremost . . . a commitment to the expressly fictive or imaginary dimension of experience in works of art and literature, and to the expressly hypothetical dimension in works of science and philosophy. . . . Whether or not it purports to resemble actual life, it is in that respect counterfactual—a world elsewhere, and otherwise, operating under its own rules of art, proclaiming by conspicuous artifice its differentness from the first world." In these intellectual developments Berger locates an important dynamic in cultural change, which he characterizes as "a dialectic of disenchantment, reenchantment, redisenchantment, re-rereenchantment, etc." Disenchantment with the traditional order controlled by knowledge of, and belief in, the power of the first world leads to the enchantment of the "subversive discourse" through which humans create an alternative attitude, a second world, in which the mind is not only freed from its subservience to nature and the divine but is also given new access to and power over "reality and nature." As Berger sees it, the second-world attitude questions knowledge and faith to make room for that most human of intellectual activities, interpretation. In locating this attitude more concretely within the Renaissance itself, Berger likes to quote the formulation of the seventeenth-century religious thinker and writer Thomas Traherne: "God hath made you able to create worlds in your own mind which are more precious unto Him than those which He created" (*Centuries of Meditations* II, 90).

In an unpublished—as yet untitled—essay that I have been quoting from, paraphrasing, and doubtless oversimplifying, Harry Berger describes himself as a "reconstructed old New Critic" and goes on to trace his own critical development in terms that parallel those of his own literary anthropology or cultural history of the Renaissance. New Criticism even turns out to be, in Berger's retrospect, a "heroic pastoral" or "green world" that aimed to "regreen a sense of value everywhere bleached out by the arid landscape of consumer capitalism." It is a detailed and fascinating account, one that makes an important contribution to understanding that protean phenomenon we call the New Criticism and—beyond that—provides considerable insight into the way American criticism has developed among practitioners like Berger who became progressively disenchanted with the heritage of New Criticism. The essay is unusual among Berger's voluminous writings since he rarely writes autobiographically about his critical theory or practice; I hope it will be published soon so that readers who desire to follow up on the present selection of essays can do so with more awareness of Berger's perspective on the fundamental issues of criticism.

Even allowing that New Critics exhibit essential theoretical differences among themselves, I would have difficulty sustaining Berger's own proposition that he "started out as a fairly conventional New Critic." True, there are many ingredients associated with New-Critical interpretation in Berger's writing from the first to the present, and no doubt one could document greater allegiance to basic New-Critical postulates in his early writing. Implicit in the way he continues to interpret is a tacit acceptance of some of the hallmarks of New-Critical practice; though he makes very little of any of these premises, he does seem to be careful to avoid all the Big Bad Wolves identified by the New Critics: the intentional fallacy, the biographical fallacy, the affective fallacy, and the heresy of paraphrase. Like the conventional New Critics, he shows little interest in traditional categories that classicists like myself, historically less affected by modern critical movements, continue to value in discussing literature: genre, character, and plot, to name a few obvious examples. But my own view of Berger's relation to the New Criticism is somewhat different from his. It seems to me that from the beginning of his career to the present Berger has been following his own critical agenda, not that of any contemporary critical movement, and he has been doing so by taking over and merging with his own conceptual vocabulary the language that emerges in the critical currents of the age. Berger is no eclectic of the sort Paul de Man once identified with American literary thinking and with the death of true criticism—that is to say, of the "Wimsatt has a point, Frye has a point, Derrida has a point" sort.[2] Rather I would characterize Berger as an appropriative critic: for him the interpretive strategies, vocabulary, and theoretical insights of New Critics, phenomenologists, structuralists, and deconstructionists—not to mention independents of various flavors—are all potentially useful in developing his own literary anthropology. But when he makes use of particular critics or schools of criticism, he is interested not in their agendas but in his own; he uses their ideas, vocabulary, or insights not their way but his own. Berger is a theorist of both theorists and practitioners: he eventually appropriates them all within his frame of reference or—to change the metaphor—makes them grist for his interpretive mill, a resolutely independent mill without ties to any franchise or chain, that he guards against obsolescence or archaism as new systems emerge and that therefore stays modern without losing its original character and purpose.

No one familiar with Berger's work would identify him with a large

---

[2] "The Crisis of Contemporary Criticism," a 1967 lecture republished as chapter 1, "Criticism and Crisis," of de Man's *Blindness and Insight,* 2d ed. (Minneapolis, 1983).

part of the agenda of the New Criticism—establishing the disinterested-ness of the critic or the essential organic unity, autonomy, and autotely of the work of art, for example; even less would one identify him with that movement's championing of formalism, aestheticism, literary democracy, and Christianity. What Berger does use from the New Criticism, he appropriates as postulates and reading strategies to serve his own agenda: New Criticism's concern for the tonal and linguistic quality of individual texts (especially through seizing on etymologies, verbal repetitions, and patterns of imagery); a tendency to see meaning emerging dramatically, even in nontheatrical texts; dissociating the points of view of the text from those of the author; a concern for ambiguity, tension, paradox, and irony in formulating interpretation; and the insistence on the fictiveness or imaginariness and the nonreferential separateness of the world of the text. But in each case one senses in Berger's writing a progressive radicalizing of these postulates and strategies, as well as an extension of them to forms of discourse other than traditional "fiction"—history, oratory, science, autobiography, even criticism itself, for example—and to nonverbal forms of discourse, in particular the visual arts. The radicalizing tendency is perhaps most evident in Berger's intensification of the categories of ambiguity, tension, and irony to duplicity, hypocrisy, and bad faith. In addition, Berger has progressively developed intertextual and interdisciplinary interests and perspectives in his writing, he has emphasized more and more the social and political backgrounds and implications of literary and artistic works, and he has always been primarily attracted not to "reading in" (in the style of the New Critics) but rather to "reading out"—to the larger cultural context. For him textual interpretation leads beyond the text to the mind that created the text and the culture that speaks through the mind. In the end literature and other modes of discourse stand not as aesthetic objects communicating their content and structure to a reader but as cultural documents charged with meaning about the mind and culture by which they were produced.

Berger's writing and his teaching significantly radicalize another feature of New Criticism—the insistence on the fictive otherness of poetic language, its connotative, metaphorical, and nonreferential character, in contrast to the language of the sciences. In Berger, this becomes a radical distrust of all surfaces, in all modes of discourse, whether or not they are poetic or even verbal. One of the commonest strategies that I see at work in Berger's interpretation of texts, paintings, and cultures—and this is certainly related to his rejection of positivism as well as to his own presentational style—is the radical suspicion of all externalized, obvious, or "on-the-face-of-it" meanings. In this he is by no means unique among modern critics—though his doubting of surface reality may be more intense. Berger's dialectical and dynamic theory of culture change leads him to an interesting interpretive pattern. Whereas other modern writers and teachers exhort their audiences to look under surface meanings, Berger continues to probe even the subtext—doubting equally the meaning underlying the surface. You can't trust the eyes, of course—but in Berger's interpretive universe you can't trust the mind's eye either, since there is a culture thinking through the mind. This process of radical doubt in Berger is often revealed on both sides of the text—in the creator, that is to say, as well as in the interpreter.

For me some of Berger's most striking interpretive insights have been an articulation of a pattern in which the artist (verbal or visual) creates a surface meaning that packages but is not to be taken as the "real" underlying meaning. The artist's own distrust of the surface created leads to a distrust of the subsurface that it is covering—that is to say, to a distrust of the whole creative act, its inner content as well as its outer form.

Berger's career and work challenge us to reevaluate what it means to profess literature and, in particular, to rethink the assumptions of New Criticism, which continues to be deeply embedded in American literary studies and in American ideology. At the same time his stimulating methods and ideas provide us with a way of saving what deconstructionists call the Humanist project, not by digging in our heels and reasserting older, more rigid, and often discredited arguments but by appropriating and often radicalizing useful concepts for literary study that reaffirm the essential continuity of Western tradition. Even if that continuity emerges in Berger's construct as fluvial, dynamic, and dialectically defined, his views lend support to those of us who are reluctant to accept that intellectual history and interpretation started all over in 1968. Berger's literary anthropology provides an option to playing out the latest version of the battle between ancients and moderns. He is a critic to disagree as well as agree with (and that mixed response is for him essential to learning); and he is a teacher from whom there is much to learn, who sees no need for and in fact discourages any ideological conversion during the learning process.

Even if I am only partially right about the nature and significance I have ascribed to the criticism of Harry Berger, I hope I have made a compelling case that his is an important voice in contemporary critical theory and practice. The essays I have chosen appear to me to be a coherent piece of his large, perhaps ultimately unfinishable, project; more important, they together constitute a significant contribution toward understanding Renaissance culture. The University of California Press is doing a notable service to literary studies by republishing these essays together and giving them the sequential organization, availability, and accessibility that they deserve. In no sense should this volume be regarded as a monument: monuments enclose, as canons do, and—as Berger helps us to see—interpretation more appropriately opens up and out.[3]

[3]To cite one interesting example of the way Harry Berger's kind of cultural history might influence and inform more general interpretive perspectives, see the provocative synthesis made by William J. Bouwsma in his presidential address before the American Historical Association (San Francisco, 1978), "The Renaissance and the Drama of Western History," published in the *American Historical Review* 84 (1979): 1–15.

The modern sense of the creative freedom of mankind now finds stimulating expression in a concept of culture that underlies the work of a group of distinguished contemporary anthropologists. According to this view of the human condition, the universe man inhabits is essentially a complex of meanings of his own devising; man, as Max Weber perceived him, is "an animal suspended in webs of significance he himself has spun." These webs make up his culture or, more exactly, since they are utterly various, his cultures. Furthermore, as philosophers and linguists have made increasingly clear, he spins these webs from language. Through language man orders the chaos of data impinging on his sensorium from, in a singularly mysterious and problematic sense, "out there," organizing them into categories and so making them intelligible, manageable, and useful. The human world might, therefore, be described as a vast rhetorical production, for the operations that bring it into existence are comparable to such basic rhetorical transactions as division and comparison, or metonymy and metaphor. This concept denies not that an objective universe exists but only that man has direct access to it or can know what it is apart from what he makes of it, out of his own limited perceptual and intellectual resources and for his own purposes, whatever these might be. (10–11)

Bouwsma's footnote at the end of this paragraph acknowledges his debt to "the theoretical essays of Harry Berger, Jr.," citing in particular Berger's "Outline of a General Theory of Cultural Change," *Clio* 2 (1972): 49–63, and "Naive Consciousness," *Papers on Language and Literature* 8 (1973): 1–44.

PART ONE

Theoretical Orientations

The Renaissance Imagination:
Second World and Green World

I

DURING AN ANALYSIS of Pontus de Tyard's *Premier Solitaire*, Frances Yates remarks in *The French Academies of the Sixteenth Century* on the "universal delight in the cryptic statement" characteristic of Renaissance culture:

> It was on the "image level" of the mind (if one may speak thus) that the Renaissance man achieved his unified outlook; and the philosophy of symbolism is intimately related to the religion of the Florentine Neo-Platonists, with its continual emphasis on the ability of man to reach heights of experience which are hidden in the sense of being so exalted as to be inexpressible save in the veiled form.

This is a revised and amplified version of a talk given at the New England Renaissance Conference at Brandeis University, May 4, 1963. I am grateful to my friend and colleague Professor Richard Sylvester for suggestions which led me to make numerous changes in the original essay and for the many casual conversations which have, over the last few years, provided me with an education in the character and problems of Renaissance humanism. We have hashed over so many Renaissance topics together that I often find it hard to define exactly where *our* thinking ends and *my* thinking begins. This is especially true of the section on More's *Utopia*, which is really the germ of a longer essay we had planned to write. I can only say, as one is expected to say, that he is neither to be blamed for any of the flaws nor praised for all the insights in what follows. (December 1963)

3

Yates goes on to suggest a progression from the exoteric level of popular handbooks through the more systematically organized level of the theoretical treatise toward the mythopoetic level of the image:

> The elaborate material concerning the Muses, the Graces, and Apollo which fills pages of Tyard's *Premier Solitaire* is lifted, in an almost raw state, from Gyraldi, and becomes part of the poetic dialogue between the solitary and Pasithee. One more step, and this mythology will be embodied in a creative work of art, a poem or a picture. The Apollo and Muses of the *Premier Solitaire* are half emerged from the mythological manual but not yet quite embodied in the work of art. Here one seems almost to catch the Renaissance man in the very act of "hiding" his meanings in the myth. The encyclopaedia which Tyard is expounding in his dialogue is also being concealed in the great encyclopaedic symbol of Apollo and the Muses. . . . The personal element in Tyard's mythology, the way in which he is adapting the raw material from Gyraldi to his own use, is shown in the prominence given to "Pasithee" . . . [who] is, for Tyard, a kind of reduction of the symbolism of Apollo and the Muses into a more condensed symbol . . . the symbol of the beginning of an intuitive grasp of the whole reached in the *furor poeticus*.[1]

Tyard's dialogue is not really a fiction but a rhetorical presentation of a theoretical program: it is *literary* rather than *literature*, and its vividness as experience is outweighed by its symbolic function as statement. Yates reads it as a fable about the aspirations of the Pléiade, "expressive of a spiritual journey from the study of the universal encyclopaedia to a state of mind symbolized by the union of Poetry and Music." Like the masque and other borderline forms, it is too closely bound to the historical conditions it elucidates to be imaginatively self-sufficient: we read it less for itself than for what it tells us about the intellectual atmosphere of the Pléiade. Yet the whole drift of the work is toward recognition of the primacy of poetry as the union of all disciplines in an inspired image.

Between the handbook and the poem: the continuum along which Tyard's dialogue is located admits of a number of different forms, and I should like to distinguish three:

1. Yates identifies the exoteric-esoteric spectrum with a movement from the discursive to the intuitive, and in Neoplatonic thought this is tantamount to climbing the ladder from lower to higher forms of knowledge. Tyard also appeals to a related Neoplatonic commonplace in treating his "more condensed symbol" or hieroglyph as a repository of hid-

---

[1] Frances A. Yates, *The French Academies of the Sixteenth Century* (London: Warburg Institute, 1947), 132–33.

den wisdom kept safely beyond the reach of the vulgar. The rejection of
popularism in thought and style stands in sharp contrast to a central
strategy of the medieval imagination. It points to a new emphasis on
mind—on a small closed society of interpreters who embody the forces
of intellect and preserve them from the ignorant passion-ridden many.

2. A similar movement has been explored in depth by Edgar Wind
as one manifestation of the process whereby the mind "unfolds" and "infolds" meanings—a process which Wind adapts from the *explicatio* and
complicatio of Cusanus. The termini of this process are, on the one hand,
a series of simple and unambiguous elements usually in disjunctive or
contrastive relation to one another and, on the other hand, a harmony
(rather than fusion) of elements, a paradox, a tensional reconciliation of
opposites, a mean which contracts the extremes within itself:

> In *The Choice of Hercules,* . . . which is the perfect instance of a popular
> moral, the terms of the argument are literal and fixed. Voluptas is appointed
> to tempt the hero with specious allurements, while Virtus acquaints him in all
> her austerity with the arduous prospect of heroic labours: and it may be ex-
> pected of a reliable Hercules that he will not remain suspended between them.
> The choice is clear because the two opposites, having been introduced in a
> complete disjunction, obey the logical principle of the excluded middle. . . .
> In Ben Jonson's *Pleasure Reconciled to Virtue,* a sequence of "knots" is intro-
> duced by the dancing master Daedalus, who interweaves the two opposites in
> a perfect maze; and his labyrinthine designs are accompanied by a warning
> that while the "first figure" should suggest the contrast of Virtue and Pleasure
> as in *The Choice of Hercules,* it is the purpose of the dance to "entwine" Plea-
> sure and Virtue beyond recognition:
>
> > Come on, come on! and where you go,
> > So interweave the curious knot,
> > As ev'n the observer scarce may know
> > Which lines are Pleasure's, and which not.
>
> In the course of tying the knot, the "unfolded" figures, which appeared fa-
> miliar because they were closer to exoteric terms, are united—"infolded"—
> in a mysterious cipher which comprises the contraries as one.[2]

Since the infolded figure offers itself for interpretation, asks to be puzzled
out, its particular form—its *image*—becomes important and relatively
independent. One may view this hermetically and feel the need of special

---

[2] *Pagan Mysteries in the Renaissance* (New Haven: Yale University Press, 1958),
168–69.

or prior knowledge to qualify as an interpreter, or one may adopt a more literary attitude and assume that the meaning is conveyed—perhaps created—by the sensuous form of the image. Such images are neither mere percepts, mere particulars, nor are they mere allegorical shadows, symbols *à clef*. If they call attention to themselves and invite serious interpretation, it is because whatever they "stand for" is inextricable from the concrete form which holds the various elements of meaning together. A familiar example of this doctrine is Sidney's insistence that the poetic image surpasses—because it synthesizes—the historical fact and the philosophical precept.

3. The third form of the continuum is for our purposes the most important and provides the subject of this essay: it is the movement from fact to fiction, from actuality to imagination, from life to art. This movement may be seen as parallel to, often inclusive of, the first two, though with a significant and problematical difference: if in each of the first two cases the *terminus ad quem* was more highly valued than the *terminus a quo*, here a question is raised by the close connection of fiction with fantasy, of make-believe with lying and illusion, of art with the deceptions or temptations of artifice. The result is that, as C. S. Lewis points out, the relation between fact and fiction may be felt more as a conflict than as a continuum:

> The defence of poetry . . . is a defence not of poetry as against prose but of fiction as against fact. The word *poetry* often covered all imaginative writing whether in prose or verse, and even those critics who did not so extend it thought of poetry primarily as invention. What is in question is not man's right to sing but his right to feign, to "make things up". . . . Our sixteenth-century critics are . . . contributing to, or concluding, an age-old debate; and that debate, properly viewed, is simply the difficult process by which Europe became conscious of fiction as an activity distinct from history on the one hand and from lying on the other.[3]

In the course of exploring or justifying the limits of fiction, poets and critics of this period found themselves flirting with the norms of the other two continua: the norm of an intuitive wisdom, a rare and ideal state of consciousness which transcends ordinary modes of experience, is to be sought through disciplined meditation, manifests itself in visionary symbols, and is best expressed in that form of cryptic image which the

[3] *English Literature in the Sixteenth Century* (Oxford: Clarendon Press, 1954), 318–19.

Neoplatonists called *hieroglyph;* and the norm of a complex harmony, an equilibrium in which opposites are at once distinct and reconciled, an experience in which the mind reveals not only the ability to organize the diversity of existence into a unified whole but also the ability to fix and vividly convey this whole in the immediacy of a visual or verbal or aural image.

Both these norms seem to presuppose a desire to move beyond the imperfections and unresolved tensions of actual life. "To move beyond," however, is an ambiguous phrase; does it mean, in any particular case, "to cope with and master," or "to escape from"? Is resolution achieved by true reconciliation, or by avoidance? Is the goal an ethical ideal (what *should* be) or a hedonist idyll (what *could* be)? It is tempting to construe a vision of the ideal or idyllic as a vision of the real. In the quest for God it may not always be easy to distinguish the urge to transcend oneself from the urge to get rid of oneself. The mind may visualize the condition to which it aspires as a perfect place—heaven, paradise, utopia, fairyland, arcadia—but this *locus amoenus* may be designed primarily as a mental hideout from one or another set of earthly imperfections. It is in dealing with dangers and temptations of precisely this sort that the techniques of fiction—fiction *as such*—reveal their usefulness.

The norms of Neoplatonic idealism and poetry (fiction) often were—and still are—confused with each other. It is not hard to see why. The idealist and the poet have in common a belief in the superiority of interpretations to appearances, of forms in the mind to forms in the actual world. Both admire and cultivate the norms of the second continuum with its *complicatio*, its *concordia discors*, its fulfillment in the vivid image or condensed symbol. Yet there are crucial differences between idealist and poet of which Renaissance, and especially English, poets were well aware. The gist of the difference lies in two related areas of connotation more evident in the word *fiction* than in the word *poetry: fiction* is etymologically and semantically related to terms meaning *invention, creation, construction,* and to terms meaning *illusion;* it suggests both *something made* and *something made up.* Where the idealist tends to minimize the second term in each set, the true poet makes the most of it. Thus Sidney, in what is perhaps the *locus classicus* of the true poet's credo in his *Apology for Poetry:*

> The Poet . . . nothing affirmes, and therefore never lyeth. . . . The Poet never maketh any circles about your imagination, to conjure you to beleeve for true what he writes. . . . What childe is there that, comming to a Play,

and seeing Thebes written in greate Letters upon an olde doore, doth beleeve that it is Thebes?[4]

He believes, that is, that he is watching a play in which he is being asked to make believe the action takes place at Thebes. He is both willing and able to take the action seriously on this level. He does not have to "suspend disbelief"; he merely, and as it were instinctively, makes believe. If the poet is ultimately to make truth-claims similar to those made by the Neoplatonist, he must do so under totally different conditions, within a frame of reference established by the awareness that "we are only playing, only making-believe." Such formulas as "once upon a time" imply a supposition: "Let us imagine that in some place and time, some world other than this . . . ," *this* being the actual place, time, and world in which we live. For Sidney, the logical first moment of fiction consists in a framing or bounding gesture of this sort, in which what I should like to call the *counterfactual* nature of fiction is clearly established. Thus to abandon adherence to factual or propositional truth—the truth of correspondence—is to disjoin the imaginary from the actual field of experience, to win for it greater freedom and autonomy.

But this is only a first moment, and if there were nothing more than this in the species of Renaissance poetics exemplified by Sidney, it would be thin and fanciful business indeed. What makes it worth attention is that this withdrawal from life to fiction is seen as fulfilled in a return to life which has two aspects: a return to the image of life within the play world of art and a return to life itself at the end of the fictional experience. For Sidney and his contemporaries, high seriousness and entertainment, the ideal and the artificial, the significant and the counterfactual, are indissolubly connected. The poet, in Sidney's words, "commeth unto you with a tale which holdeth children from play and old men from the chimney corner. And pretending no more, doth intend the winning of the mind from wickedness to vertue." To acknowledge that we are only playing, that this is only make-believe, is not only to safeguard the mind's activity by restricting its pretensions—"Your If," said Touchstone, "is your only peacemaker." It is also to proclaim the mind's peculiar excellence, which lies in its ability to interpret, its freedom to re-create, the world of the senses in its own image, an image at once closer to "noumenal" truth and more vivid than actual life. The Italian critic

---

[4]G. Gregory Smith, ed., *Elizabethan Critical Essays* (London: Oxford University Press, 1904), I, 184–85.

Mazzoni, in *On the Defense of the "Comedy,"* sees no contradiction between his exalted praise of Dante and his emphasis on poetry as a game:

> It is not forbidden to the poet to treat things pertaining to the sciences and to the speculative intellect, if only he treats them in a credible manner, making idols and poetic images, as Dante surely has done with marvelous and noble artifice, in representing with idols and beautiful images before the eyes of everyone all intellectual being and the intelligible world itself.
>
> . . . the civil faculty is that which considers the legality of actions; hence it is also that which considers the legality of cessation . . . [i.e.] all the actions done for the sake of pastime, to wit, all those done in play. . . . among all the recreations none is found more worthy, more noble, or more important than that which is made through the labor of poets.[5]

The pleasure, as Mazzoni and others note, may be uncontrolled, hedonist, or sophistical, but it may also be regulated, rational, and useful. And the pleasure may refer to the poet's recreative delight in making as well as to the response of his audience.

In this connection we would do well to view, with greater sympathy than critics have usually shown, the root metaphor of the sugar-coated moral pill. Where medieval theories of art are always conjunctive—pleasure *plus* profit—or disjunctive—pleasure, ornament, vividness *here*, allegory, philosophy, theology, worship *there*—the enlightened Renaissance understanding of the metaphor is *profit inside pleasure*. And if the metaphor itself stresses the medicinal reality under the delightful appearance, the better critics (e.g., Mazzoni, Tasso, Sidney) were deadly serious about their fictions. They spent so much time on formal and poetic issues that in a phrase like "fayning notable images of vertues," the profitable end ("notable images of vertues") is often identical with, sometimes subservient to, the pleasurable means ("fayning notable images"). *To fayne* requires its full range of meanings to do justice to the concept: to desire, pretend, imagine, devise, entemple.

The explicit affirmation that even the most important aspects of art have their roots in play, in controlled fantasy and artifice, is a historical novelty. Play means more to the Renaissance imagination than the mere exercise of lawful recreative activity. In its most significant form it is the act of the mind withdrawing to its happiness "from pleasure less," a "pleasure less" which springs from the deceptive image of the world

---

[5] Allan Gilbert, ed., *Literary Criticism: Plato to Dryden* (New York: American Book Company, 1940), 366, 374 (trans. Gilbert).

transmitted by the senses and surrounding, constricting, impinging on the mind. God expects the mind to explore itself as well as the appearances presented to it, and God therefore implants in the mind a desire for, a delight in, the exercise of its powers. Cervantes' canon expresses the common opinion when he praises books of chivalry because they offer "a good intellect a chance to display itself" and give an author "an opportunity of showing his talent" (*Don Quixote* I.47).

In the literature of periods previous to the fourteenth century, the counterfactual sentiment, "This is only make-believe," is seldom expressed as an important stylistic function intrinsic to the excellence of art or thought. Platonic dialogue, for example, is really a fictional form, but stylistically it is presented as a fusion of history and philosophy. Even Aristotle, whose literary theory is in many ways most "modern," defends the fictional and formal autonomy of drama only insofar as it has cognitive value—only, that is, insofar as the product of *mimesis* is felt to apprehend an objective pattern obscured by the flux of history or the recalcitrance of matter. For Aristotle, poetry is not creation, not even discovery, but something closer to *recovery*. The best gloss on this aspect of the *Poetics* is the theory of perception in *De Anima* ii.6–iii.2: what the psyche does by nature in the *De Anima*, the mind does by art in the *Poetics*. In Greek culture generally, legend, myth, history, philosophy, and poetry appear from our standpoint to intermingle. Greek genres mixed constitutive and imitative elements, fiction and fact, myth and history. This was not because the Greeks were naive about their emergent cultural forms but rather because of what in retrospect appears to have been their basic cultural situation. Reduced to the most central terms demanded by my topic, the great problem confronting classical thought was that it did not quite know how to keep the order it assumed as objective reality from looking like a projection. The Greek imagination never fully attained to the Christian solution it seemed to be groping for—belief in a divine creator, a source of world order wholly other, greater, and better than the self.

The Christian assignment of system building to God entailed sharper restrictions on the role played by the mind, but these very restrictions, with a gradual shift of value, became the source of power in Renaissance thought. For the Christian imagination up through the fourteenth century, the second nature or world made by the mind was second because the first world made by God (and transmitted accurately, if partially, through the senses) was better. If the Middle Ages, in Huizinga's words, "knew only applied art," this was largely because the first world was *the* unique creation, the only original work of art.[6] Fantasy and the counterfactual in themselves were, with few exceptions, treated as false, irresponsible, or unimportant. But this means that a region of autonomous imaginative activity was marked out and circumscribed more sharply than was possible in Greek thought. The clear idea of a fictional event, a bounded mind-made field, is ultimately the product of Christian epistemology. There are few poems before the *Divine Comedy* in which the author, first, gets the entire actual universe inside a fiction and, second, seems aware of this and deals with it as a problem.

The history of thought from the fourteenth to the late seventeenth century may be seen to turn on the shifting relations between the actual physico-spiritual universe in which God has placed man and the hypothetical or imaginary *kosmoi* posited by the mind. A simplified synoptic view of these centuries reveals that as nature loses its Aristotelian substantiality, as the lines between subjective and objective forms of phenomena become more sharply drawn, as physical reality becomes more closely identified with atoms, force, and mathematics—as, in general, man by retracting his projected self-images confers new otherness on both God and nature, the mind-made orders increase in dignity and importance. Late medieval thinkers like Petrarch, Boccaccio, Chaucer, Eckhart, and the scientists at Oxford and Paris displayed great interest in exploring their own private worlds, and they justified such personal ventures by framing them in an atmosphere of counterfactuality. The retraction, or palinode, allowed the mind to follow its own speculative and visionary concerns before it acknowledged the superior reality of the world ordered by God, the Church, and Aristotle. But by the time of Galileo, Descartes, Bernini, Milton, Leibniz, and Newton, the second world tends to be thought of as improving, superseding, or even replacing the first world. Actuality becomes a chaos or blueprint offered by God as raw material to the mind. Thus Traherne could say, "God hath made you able to create worlds in your own mind which are more precious unto Him than those which He created" (*Centuries* II.90).

Between the apologetic Dante and the oracular Traherne there emerges a technique of the mind centered on what I should like to call the idea of the *second world*. The second world is the playground, laboratory, the-

---

[6] *The Waning of the Middle Ages*, trans. F. Hopman (New York: Longman, Green, 1949), 224 and *passim*. Meyer Schapiro's attempt to isolate an autonomous esthetic attitude does not really affect this judgment, for what Schapiro means by esthetic is simply the gratuitous pleasure in beautiful things ("On the Aesthetic Attitude in Romanesque Art," in *Art and Thought*, ed. K. B. Iyer [London: Luzac, 1947], 130–50).

ater, or battlefield of the mind, a model or construct the mind creates, a time or place it clears in order to withdraw from the actual environment. It may be the world of play or poem or treatise, the world inside a picture frame, the world of pastoral simplification, the controlled conditions of scientific experiment. Its essential quality is that it is an explicitly fictional, artificial, or hypothetical world. It presents itself to us as a game which, like all games, is to be taken with dead seriousness while it is going on. In pointing to itself as serious play, it affirms both its limits and its power in a single gesture. Separating itself from the casual and confused region of everyday existence, it promises a clarified image of the world it replaces.

Of course any fiction is in effect a second world, and I am saying not that there was no fiction in the Middle Ages but simply that fiction then *tended* stylistically to present itself in the guise of history, actuality, philosophy, theology, etc.[7] Chivalric literature offers a good example: however fantastic and remote a romance adventure might be, its narrative was always open to some irrelevant interruption appealing to or reflecting the concerns of the feudal audience. The romance was a Hollywood idealization, a glamorized daydream version of feudal life, and the links were drawn more emphatically as the gap between the ideal and the actual increased. But the chivalry of Ariosto and Spenser is an entirely different matter. "The ducal court," as Charles Baldwin observed, "is distinct both from the idealized castle of the medieval romance and from the actual castle of the Middle Ages."[8] The vocabulary and imagery of Renaissance chivalry are patently noncontemporary and artificial. Like Uccello's St. George paintings, the fictions of Ariosto and Spenser proclaim their kinship to forms of art and play rather than forms of life and

---

[7] The significance of the emergence of fiction as a second world from the quite different matrix of medieval thought has been suggestively and thoroughly explored by C. S. Lewis in *The Allegory of Love* (London: Oxford University Press, 1948), *passim* but especially 82ff., and by André Malraux in *The Voices of Silence*, trans. Stuart Gilbert (New York: Doubleday, 1953), *passim* but especially 70ff. Lewis distinguishes three worlds, "the probable, the marvellous-taken-as-fact, the marvellous-known-to-be-fiction," as "the triple equipment of the post–Renaissance poet" and argues that the old gods were preserved in medieval culture "as in a temporary tomb, for the day when they could wake again in the beauty of acknowledged myth and thus provide modern Europe with its 'third world' of romantic imagining" (82).

A strikingly similar argument for the role of schematic form in medieval painting as a preparation for rational perspective has been advanced by Erwin Panofsky, *Early Netherlandish Painting: Its Origins and Character* (Cambridge: Harvard University Press, 1953), I, 12ff. See also M. S. Bunim, *Space in Medieval Painting and the Forerunners of Perspective* (New York: Columbia University Press, 1940), 175–76.

[8] *Renaissance Literary Theory and Practice* (Gloucester: Peter Smith, 1959), 11.

society—to fantasy, tapestry, masquing, and such recreative pageantry as the Accession Day tournament which Frances Yates attributes to the "imaginative refeudalization of culture" popular throughout Europe at the time.[9]

Some examples of the second world will suggest both its range and its frequency, but they may also suggest a basic problem of definition: More's Utopia, Sidney's golden world and Arcadia, Spenser's Faerie, Shakespeare's green world and stage world, Marvell's poetic gardens, Alberti's picture plane as a window, Leonardo's painted second nature, Filarete's Sforzinda, Castiglione's Urbino, Machiavelli's hypothetical state, Gilbert's magnetic terrella, Galileo's experiment world, the new world described in Descartes's *Discourse*. The problem is this: which are we to call the second world, Hythloday's island or More's treatise, Spenser's landscape or his poem, Shakespeare's green world or his stage world, Gilbert's earthlike magnet or the total situation of analogy denoted by his book on the magnet?

The essence of the question was raised and curiously begged by Northrop Frye in his essay "The Argument of Comedy" (1949), where he refers to the green world *as* a second world. He identifies a form of comic action which begins "in a world represented as a normal world, moves into the green world, . . . and returns to the normal world":

> The conception of a second world bursts the boundaries of Menandrine comedy, yet it is clear that the world of Puck is no world of eternal forms or divine revelation. Shakespeare's comedy . . . is an Elizabethan kind, and is not confined either to Shakespeare or to the drama. Spenser's epic is a . . . contrapuntal intermingling of two orders of existence, one the red and white world of English history, the other the green world of the Faerie Queene. The latter is a world of crusading virtues proceeding from the Faerie Queene's Court and designed to return to that court when the destiny of the other world is fulfilled. . . . Shakespeare too has his green world of comedy and his red and white world of history.[10]

Frye does not clearly distinguish the actual normal world from the fictional "world represented as a normal world," the actual red and white

---

[9] "Elizabethan Chivalry: The Romance of the Accession Day Tilts," *Journal of the Warburg and Courtauld Institutes* 20 (1957): 22.

[10] Leonard F. Dean, ed., *Shakespeare: Modern Essays in Criticism* (New York: Oxford University Press, 1961), 85, 87. Frye traces "the drama of the green world" to "the drama of folk ritual, of the St. George play and the mummers' play, of the feast of the ass and the Boy Bishop, and of all the dramatic activity that punctuated the Christian calendar with the rituals of an immemorial paganism." The theme of this drama is "the tri-

world of history from its image in fiction. There is a difference between the second world *in* a fiction and the second world *as* a fiction. There is also in Renaissance thought a significant ambiguity about this which is sometimes a source of confusion and sometimes a source of power: the qualities just listed may be referred either to the place of withdrawal *within* the work, or to the total work (play, poem, picture, book, etc.) as a place of withdrawal. It is, as we shall see, the dynamic and shimmering interplay between these two possibilities that makes the embodiments of Renaissance imagination so fascinating. But to have interplay required some awareness that there *were* two distinct possibilities, and this aware-ness has too often been slurred over in the work of modern literary scholars, whereas historians of art and science have shown themselves much more alive to the phenomenon.

The second world as the imaginary or hypothetical world of fiction has in fact been considered elsewhere by Frye,[11] and it has been discussed extensively and brilliantly by Meyer Abrams under the name of *hetero-cosm*, the second nature or second world "created by the poet in an act analogous to God's creation of the world." The idea of heterocosm was "originally developed to free a poem from conformity to the laws of this world by envisioning it as its own world." And as Abrams shows, the concept of the poem as "an object-in-itself, a self-contained universe of discourse"—a notion "at the heart of much of the 'new criticism'"—has its roots in the fifteenth and sixteenth centuries.[12] The novel and signifi-cant mark of the Renaissance imagination derives less from the idea of the green world per se than from the tendency first to separate, then to interrelate different fields of experience. The counterfactual emphasis on fiction as fiction implies a second world whose excellence resides as much in its being independent of actuality as in its being superior to it. The clarity and simplicity of the green world may be balanced by the variety

---

umph of life over the waste land, the death and revival of the year impersonated by figures still human, and once divine as well" (85). He also identifies the green world with a "world of fairies, dreams, disembodied souls, and pastoral lovers [which] may not be a 'real' world, but, if not, there is something equally illusory in the stumbling and blinded follies of the 'normal' world. . . . We spend our lives partly in a waking world which we call normal and partly in a dream world which we create out of our own de-sires. Shakespeare endows both worlds with equal imaginative power, brings them op-posite one another, and makes each world seem unreal when seen by the light of the other. . . . his distinctive comic resolution . . . is a detachment of the spirit born of this reciprocal reflection of two illusory realities" (88–89).

[11]See, e.g., "Levels of Meaning in Literature," *Kenyon Review* 12 (Spring 1950): 246–63, especially the discussion of the "second level" of meaning, 249–53.

[12]*The Mirror and the Lamp* (New York: Oxford University Press, 1953), 272, 327.

of an imaginary field in which a number of such worlds coexist, by the epistemologically complex ways in which they may be interrelated, by the equally complex and flexible modes of relation which may be established between the imaginary world and its audience. The particular virtue of the imaginary world lies in its being, since it is neither actual nor ideal, potentially an image of either or both. Thus it seems more accurate to apply the terms *second world* and *second nature* to the heterocosmic element than to what Frye has called the green world. As a sophisticated literary device, Frye's green world is not the peculiarly Elizabethan phenomenon he claims it to be, and it may have a dangerous or sinister side to it which he is inclined to play down in the Elizabethans, though he takes account of it in Blake.[13] The sophisticated notion of a green world, and of a problematical green world, goes back at least as far as Homer's Phaiakia.

In referring to Hamlet's famous definition, Frye cites only the second and third of its four parts, though his formula would seem to require all of them: "to hold . . . the mirror up to nature, to show virtue her own feature, scorn her own image, and the very age and body of the time his form and pressure."[14] The feature of virtue and image of scorn may be taken to refer to two sides of a green or golden world: pure good and pure evil, wish fulfillment and nightmare, abstracted from the smokier atmosphere of actual life in which they are deceptively mingled and but dimly visible; added to these is the very image of the smoky atmosphere itself. All together constitute the mirror—or, to put it in a way which emphasizes slightly different theoretical assumptions, all are included "in" the mirror. To hold the mirror up to nature is hardly possible unless we have first framed a reflecting or refracting surface which is different and at a distance from whatever nature we have in mind, a surface which can admit the image only on condition that it keep out the original. This condition was felt as a necessary defect in the medieval speculum, a reflector valued more for its likeness than for itself. But the Renaissance glass was invested with dioptric and prismatic powers deriving from the interpretive activity of the human mind. Its exclusiveness was therefore prized as a guarantee of the mind's freedom from the tyranny of the actual world.

This mirror corresponds to the second world, or heterocosm, and includes the green world. From a modern standpoint the difference be-

---

[13] See *Fearful Symmetry* (Princeton: Princeton University Press, 1947), e.g., 233–34, on Blake's Beulah. I am not sure whether Frye thinks of this as a green world, but his description identifies with some precision what I have in mind.

[14] "The Argument of Comedy," 83.

tween Frye's green world and Abrams's heterocosm is fairly sharp. As a place of withdrawal or experiment, an ideal of one sort or another, the green or golden world possesses determinate content. But insofar as the concept of heterocosm entails no assumptions about the quality of experience to be found in such a world, its content is neutral or indeterminate. Heterocosm in its barest and most generic sense is simply a *gestalt*, a unified field which—like any system—is coherent, self-sufficient, and finite. Modern thought commonly reserves the term *universe* for organized wholes of this sort and understands them as hypothetical in that they are constructed by thought rather than given in experience. As one cosmologist puts it, "the 'universe-as-a-whole' does not constitute a name for some object or entity which exists antecedently to or independently of our inquiry." [15] It is rather a frame of reference or coordinate system originally chosen with a view toward exploring a concrete problem or fulfilling a specific desire. Carried to an extreme, the modern view of *universe* extends to all mankind the apology Sidney reserves for poets: "The Poet . . . nothing affirmes, and therefore never lyeth." Every world is invented, none is discovered; every sentence is hypothetical, none is propositional. Thus all universes will be separate and equal; none will have priority over any other. In this radical context the term *heterocosm*, which literally means *other world*, will serve primarily to remind us that disjunction or difference is the basic relation between universes. The universe of biology differs from that of physics or of astronomy; the universe of science differs from that of art or of mathematics. Any element or set of elements, any appearance or set of appearances, may exist simultaneously in a number of such universes, and it may have a different function in each.

Though some of these properties are common to both modern and Renaissance concepts, the description just given depends heavily on post-Renaissance developments in thought and language. The Renaissance heterocosm was more literally a *second* world because it was conceived as being set over against not *an* other world or *a* first world but *the* first world. This first world is the actual universe of kingdoms, planets, stars, and angels. It comprises the natural, historical, and spiritual environments of man. Depending on one's viewpoint, one could ascribe its created structure to nature or God or both and its apparent character to perception or tradition or both. The general Renaissance attitude toward these worlds may be located, in historical terms, somewhere between the positions epitomized in the following two statements. First, St. Au-

[15] M. K. Munitz, *Space, Time, and Creation* (New York: Collier Books, 1961), 63.

gustine: "There is no principle of unity but that alone from which all unity derives," namely, God.[16] Second, Cassirer: "True unity is never to be sought in things as such, but in intellectual constructions, in frames of reference, which we choose according to the peculiarity of the field to be measured."[17]

The above distinctions between heterocosm and green world have been somewhat exaggerated to differentiate clearly concepts about which there has hitherto been critical confusion. In practice, as I have suggested, relations between green world and second world may become ambiguous and the ambiguous treatment is itself a source of richness and power in Renaissance works. The remainder of this essay will focus for the most part on two examples which illustrate various aspects of the relation. The first is more general, the second more concrete; the first will concern primarily the heterocosm and its relation to the audience, the second the relation between second and green worlds. The first example is the technique of perspective in painting; the second is More's *Utopia*.

II

What is variously called focused perspective, one-point (monocular) perspective, artificial perspective, or rational perspective—there are other methods—is in essence the geometrical projection of a three-dimensional space on a flat surface; the surface is construed as the transparent intersection of the visual pyramid whose apex is at the eye.[18] This

[16] *De Vera Religione*, xxxiv.64, trans. J. H. S. Burleigh, *Of True Religion* (Chicago: Henry Regnery, 1959), 60.

[17] *Substance and Function* and *Einstein's Theory of Relativity*, trans. W. C. Swabey and M. C. Swabey (New York: Dover, 1953), 361.

[18] This discussion summarily reviews familiar facts which have been presented and analyzed by many art historians, and here I can acknowledge only a small, if significant, part of my debt: G. C. Argan, "The Architecture of Brunelleschi and the Origins of Perspective Theory in the Fifteenth Century," trans. Nesca Robb, *Journal of the Warburg and Courtauld Institutes* 9 (1946): 96–122; Argan and J. Lassaigne, *The Fifteenth Century: From Van Eyck to Botticelli*, trans. Stuart Gilbert (New York: Skira, 1955); M. S. Bunim, *Space in Medieval Painting and the Forerunners of Perspective*; W. M. Ivins, Jr., *On the Rationalization of Sight* (New York: Metropolitan Museum of Art, 1938); T. K. Kitao, "Prejudice in Perspective: A Study of Vignola's Perspective Treatise," *Art Bulletin* 44 (1962): 173–94; Robert Klein, "Pomponius Gauricus on Perspective," *Art Bulletin* 43 (1961): 211–30; Richard Krautheimer, in collaboration with Trude Krautheimer-Hess, *Lorenzo Ghiberti* (Princeton: Princeton University Press, 1956); Luigi's Mallé's introduction to his edition of Leon Battista Alberti, *Della Pittura* (Florence: Sansoni, 1950); Erwin Panofsky, "Once More 'The Friedsam Annunciation and the Problem of the Ghent Altarpiece,'" *Art Bulletin* 20 (1938): 419–42, *The Codex Huyghens and Leonardo da Vinci's Art Theory* (London: Warburg Institute, 1940), *Early Netherlandish Painting,*

particular method differs from earlier empirical or specialized uses of perspective in that its practitioners do not look on it merely as a workshop technique for creating a convincing floor, ceiling, or solid; rather, it is consciously conceived as an intellectual method for creating a totally unified field, a field in which all lines perpendicular to the picture plane converge on a single vanishing point. Rational perspective is not necessary if the painter merely intends to imitate objects as they look in nature; its chief use is in the imitation and control of *visual relations among objects*. The perspective field exists, theoretically or ideally, before any objects are in it. It is potentially charged with vectors or directional lines of force which determine how objects are to look when they enter the field. Perspective anticipates and crudely exemplifies the more modern ideas of coordinate systems and superimposed frames of reference. In a single place we find two absolutely different and physically unrelated spaces, the three-dimensional field of the picture and the two-dimensional field of the surface. Insofar as a single geometrical system may be viewed ambiguously as a set of graphic lines *on* a plane and a set of visual rays cutting *through* the plane, perspective sharpens the artist's awareness that the claims of his medium tend to divide into two opposed stylistic categories, those of surface design and those of spatial recession. And though it took time to be mastered, this division was not simply a problem but a new possibility, and not simply a technical matter but the basis of a new way of seeing. It was the very consciousness of these rival claims, of their antipathies and of their common basis, which allowed the expressive interplay of space and plane to be brought more thoroughly under conscious control and to yield a brilliant new variety of effects in the painting of the fifteenth and sixteenth centuries. And once perspective was mastered as a factor in design, sophisticated departures or distortions could be used as stylistic interpretations of the subject—e.g., Masaccio's *Trinity*, Piero della Francesca's *Resurrection*, a number of works by Fra Angelico (e.g., the Cortona *Annunciation*, the San Marco *Descent From the Cross*, the Louvre *Coronation*) and Botticelli (oddest of which is the Washington *Adoration*). The significant development was not so much

---

Meaning in the Visual Arts (Garden City: Doubleday-Anchor, 1955), "Artist, Scientist, Genius: Notes on the 'Renaissance-Dammerung,'" in *The Renaissance: Six Essays*, W. K. Ferguson, R. S. Lopez, et al. (New York: Harper & Row, 1962); John White, *The Birth and Rebirth of Pictorial Space* (London: Faber & Faber, 1957); Rudolf Wittkower, "Brunelleschi and 'Proportion in Perspective,'" *Journal of the Warburg and Courtauld Institutes* 16 (1953): 275–92.

My discussion is necessarily oversimplified to emphasize those aspects relevant to my topic. At least a partial corrective may be supplied by John White, *Birth and Rebirth*, chapters 8, 13, and 14.

that artists acquired a new way of making a flat surface look three-dimensional—this was the recreative or play aspect—but rather that space became one of the technical elements of the medium along with pigment, one of the instruments of design along with line and color.

A perspective system is not confined to relations within the picture. More important for our immediate purposes is the fact that the system includes the eye of artist or observer, and that eye and picture exist in a double relation: (1) the picture is determined by the position of the eye, but (2) it also creates that position. The painter may, by raising or lowering the eye point, control the height of the vanishing point.[19] Construing a point as an eye, a geometric vertex as an optical focus, the artist may imaginatively convert a practical technique for organizing space from ouside the picture into a triumphant assertion of the eye's power. On the other hand, a properly focused picture, whether organized by perspective or not, creates its own audience. An observer standing in one space—that of an actual gallery—is simultaneously located in another space, the imaginary extension of the picture. And insofar as linear perspective is coordinated with the atmospheric diminutions of outline and color (the three systems described and integrated by Leonardo),[20] the consequent blurring of remote objects fulfills the actual conditions of seeing-from-a-distance so as to keep us optically out of the picture. It is a different matter with the painting of the van Eycks and their contemporaries, who focused scenes in a perspective which, however precise, was empirical: there the eye is drawn into the picture by the unnatural clarity of distant forms and is kept serially in motion by crowding and varying. At the same time Flemish painting is, for all its realism, an art of visual surfaces which does not invite kinesthetic entry or participation.[21] Kinesthetic exclusion is a negative rather than positive element of the esthetic experience—it is a by-product of such stylistic traits as the tipped-up

[19] This is most clearly and simply demonstrated in Piero della Francesca's *De prospectiva pingendi*, Book I. For a translation of the relevant passage, see Elizabeth Holt, *A Documentary History of Art* (Garden City: Doubleday-Anchor, 1957), I, 260.

[20] See Jean Paul Richter, *The Notebooks of Leonardo da Vinci* (New York: Dover, 1970), I, 25–65, 125–66.

[21] In Flemish painting a fixed glance takes in only a slice or portion of what is there to be seen; in Florentine perspective the whole picture is offered to the fixed glance. When in the *Purgatorio* Dante reaches the Terrestrial Paradise, he alludes frequently to problems of perspective—how something appears, by whom or from where it is seen, etc.—and these allusions remind us how little the human eye can take in of the symbolic landscape. The medieval point of view expresses the finitude of the human observer, whereas Renaissance perspective expresses his power. The medieval alternative is vicariously to adopt the viewpoint of God or angels, which produces a different situation from that of Renaissance perspective.

ground plane which makes the picture space uninhabitable, and as such
it is subordinate to, not in tension with, the invitation to the eye. But in
the line of Florentine and Roman development leading to what is called
High Renaissance style, the relation is reversed: the rendering of space
and architecture, the modeling of figures to emphasize volume and
weight, the interest in sculptural isolation and anatomical precision—
these invite our tactile and kinesthetic involvement in a visual world
which offers more than optical information to the eye, a self-contained
heterocosm which replaces nature and puts the whole range of sensuous
experience at the eye's disposal. Here optical exclusion is a primary and
positive element of the esthetic experience, and this distance or detachment is played off against the invitation to touch in such a way as to establish a tensional relation between the observer-here and the image-
there. This relation may be manipulated in either direction—one may,
as Robert Klein has observed, treat the picture plane as a door or as a
window[22]—but the point is that the more intimate modes of sensory perception are (1) vicarious and (2) given play within the dominant optical
context, therefore admitted as fictional or hypothetical aspects of a second
world.[23]

This sense of the self-sufficiency of the picture and of the fullness of
experience offered to and through the eye is well exemplified in Alberti's
treatise on painting. Alberti writes as if the picture plane were an architectural space and as if he wanted the painter not merely to "look
through the window" and paint but also to crawl inside the frame and
start building his world from the floor up. But it is not simply as a mathe-
matician, an architect, or a taxidermist that the painter is to function:
these activities are all by way of imitating nature, which to Alberti means
emulating and replacing *natura naturans:*

> On the pavement, drawn with its lines and parallels, walls and similar
> planes . . . are to be built. Here I will describe most briefly what I do. First
> I begin with the foundation. I place the width and the length of the wall and
> its parallels. In this laying out I follow nature.[24]

[22] "Pomponius Gauricus on Perspective," 228–29.
[23] Wölfflin long ago showed how Italian painting during the Quattrocento and Cinquecento moved toward a stylistic ideal in which the picture may be serially and "tactually"
explored *within* a controlling optical context, while this context presented a unified field
which the eye could fix in a single sustained glance.
[24] *On Painting*, trans. J. R. Spencer (New Haven: Yale University Press, 1956), 70.
Future page references are to this translation. Spencer's final sentence is a free rendering,
and the Italian, continuing into the next sentence, reads as follows: "in quale descriptione
seguo la natura in qual veggo che di niuno quadrato corpo, quale abbia retti angli, ad

. . . there is no more certain and fitting way for one who wishes to pursue this than to take them from nature, keeping in mind in what way nature, marvelous artificer of things, has composed the planes in beautiful bodies. (72)

. . . we ought to have a certain rule for the size of the members. In this measuring it would be useful to isolate each bone of the animal, on this add its muscles, then clothe all of it with its flesh. . . . Before dressing a man we first draw him nude, then we enfold him in draperies. So in painting the nude we place first his bones and muscles which we then cover with flesh so that it is not difficult to understand where each muscle is beneath. Since nature has here carried the measurements to a mean, there is not a little utility in recognizing them. (73)

By thus imitating the constructive activity of nature, the artist creates a second nature which is a projection neither of what the eye alone perceives (the visual field of Velázquez and later painters) nor of what the mind reflects and the hand adorns (the allegorical-decorative panel of earlier painting).[25] Nature is re-created in a new world whose visual laws are in fact different from those governing actuality—from the laws of natural or Euclidean optics—since, as we know, ordinary perception is neither monocular nor so rigorously geometrized. Alberti has in mind a world seen at a certain moment and from a certain distance, yet objectively unified and probable. It would be a failure "if in the same distance one person should appear larger than another, or if dogs should be equal to horses, or better, as I frequently see, if a man is placed in a building as in a closed casket." From the art which he saw about him in Florence and praised in his brief prologue he drew the stylistic elements of a significant second world: the expressive content of Donatello's human figures, the rationalized space of Brunelleschi, and Masaccio's fusion of both in the imaginary space of painting. What Berenson has identified as the "tactile" effect which makes the figures of Giotto and Masaccio "life-enhancing"; what Wölfflin has called "closed form," the tendency to order the picture according to the rectilinear axes of the frame so that the image has its own center of gravity and is cut off from the surrounding world;

---

uno tratto posso vedere dintorno più che due facce congiunte" (*Della Pittura*, ed. Mallé, 86; future page references are to this edition of the Italian text). In this context, "seguo la natura" seems to mean "I follow the way things actually look." Spencer's phrasing is deceptive.

[25] For Alberti's departure from the earlier "metaphysical" conception behind art theory, see Panofsky, *Idea: A Concept in Art Theory*, trans. J. J. S. Peake (Columbia: University of South Carolina Press, 1968), 57–59, 208–9.

what Wittkower has called "proportion in perspective," the attempt not simply to make an image correspond with its three-dimensional original but to create a coherent three-dimensional field on the flat intersection— all these tendencies which animate Alberti's treatise point to his central interest, the reality of make-believe.

Art historians sometimes speak as if perspective extends the observer's space into the picture, e.g., "the pictorial space illusionistically continues the actual space,"[26] but this is not an accurate way of expressing the situation, at least so far as Alberti is concerned. The lines of force move in the opposite direction: it is pictorial space which appears to extend beyond the frame and encompass the observer. This extension is seldom insisted on until a later period (e.g., in the art of Rubens), but it is there in principle. For Alberti, the lines of force from picture to observer serve a special function: they complete the dialogue taking place between painter and observer. This dialogue is arranged in a sequence which is all the more significant for being hypothetical. The centric ray shoots from the painter's eye and determines the centric point, is checked against "the height of the man I have to paint," and rebounds into the observer's eye. "Thus both the beholder and the painted things he sees will appear to be on the same plane." The lines of force having been thus geometrically established, they are reasserted at the level of *istoria:* "The *istoria* will move the soul of the beholder when each man painted there clearly shows the movement of his own soul." A movement of soul implies a *now*, a focused moment of imaginary experience which is, in this statement, coordinated with a *now* of seeing. A number of statements in the second book reveal Alberti's concern for the temporal focus or unity of the event:

> Provide that every member can fulfill its function in what it is doing. (73)
> . . . all bodies should harmonize in size and function to what is happening in the *istoria*. (75)
> Remember how man in all his poses uses the entire body to support the head. (79)

The climactic example of Alberti's interest in creating and controlling the hypothetical observer is his notion of the presenter or interlocutor:

> All the bodies ought to move according to what is ordered in the *istoria*. In an *istoria* I like to see someone who admonishes and points out to us what is happening there; or beckons with his hand to see; or menaces with an angry

---

[26] Kitao, "Prejudice in Perspective," 178.

face and with flashing eyes, so that no one should come near; or shows some danger or marvellous thing there; or invites us to weep or to laugh together with them. Thus whatever the painted persons do among themselves or with the beholder, all is pointed toward ornamenting or teaching the *istoria*. (78)

Iconographically, this figure seems a variant of the traditional *witness*— St. John, for example—who looks at others in the painted world and points to the significant event.[27] The apparently small matter of shifting the witness's gaze so as to establish ocular contact with observers outside the painted world embodies a radical change in attitudes toward painting—if not in contemporary paintings by themselves, then certainly within the intellectual ambience produced by this statement. Alberti's last sentence suggests that he is thinking of the presenter as, in part, a special representative of the painter who pictorially embodies and carries on the dialogue with observers. Firmly locked behind the picture plane, his presenter makes an ocular or gestural contact with living observers. He establishes, as it were, a third space, shifting and indeterminate, cutting through the picture plane as do the rays of the visual pyramid. He is in effect "aware" that he is part of a picture made and an event represented for the benefit of the audience. This means that the imaginary event is *labeled* imaginary by the very gesture which indicates its significance; the depicted event is recessed or framed in the presenter's space, which is still imaginary and not actual. By thus indicating its own limits as illusion, the space behind the picture plane becomes intellectually (if not sensuously) and mediately (if not immediately) more complex. It demands more careful attention from the observer and engages his participation in a more intimate manner. Yet at the same time the presenter helps to keep us out of the picture, for his "awareness" of the audience interposes a strange middle ground between the event and us— interposes, in G. C. Argan's words, "between the spectator and the action a mental distance . . . corresponding to the optical distance which perspective requires between the eye and the object."[28] We are not, for example, looking at or through a pictorial symbol of a holy event and relating ourselves directly to that unique event which happened or happens outside the picture. We are looking at *this reconstruction* of the event

---

[27] The interlocutor is discussed by Panofsky, *Early Netherlandish Painting*, 16; Spencer, *On Painting*, 26, and "Ut Rhetorica Pictura," *Journal of the Warburg and Courtauld Institute* 20 (1957): 42; Argan, "Architecture of Brunelleschi," 120; Klein, "Pomponius Gauricus on Perspective," 215.

[28] "Architecture of Brunelleschi," 120. See Panofsky, *Idea*, 50–51, for a discussion of distance as a means of freeing both subject and object.

or of its traditional image; we are directed to the response and interpretation of *this artist* as he selects and renders certain features of the event in the light of certain stylistic interests. The center of interest is not the *event* but the *event as image;* the implied Albertian premise—again hypothetical—is that the event behind (beyond, outside, above, etc.) the plane is to be reduced to a visual action which is best seen when "placed at a definite distance with definite lights and a definite position of centre in space and in a definite place in respect to the observer." The Albertian presenter, who links not only the event but also the painter with the observer, provides an intensified means of controlling this definiteness of position and distance.

It is thus clear that in Alberti's thought the idea of the second world is not confined to the objective work. The work as a cross section of the visual pyramid is the focal point of a system which includes the perceiving subject and the perceivable object. Subject and object are not merely presupposed as conditions which determine correct representation, conditions to be left behind once the proper method has been explained and followed. Rather, they are readmitted, re-created, as elements in the total hypothetical system, and they are no less imaginary, no less real, than the intersecting plane. As Alberti's treatment of composition and *istoria* shows, the painted surface is understood as a part whose function and meaning depend on the whole of which it is a part. That whole, the heterocosm, is a complicated unity of separate and relatively independent parts—painter, object behind the plane, painted image of the object on the plane, observer—and these parts seem bound together by temporal/causal as well as by spatial/simultaneous relations. Alberti wants the finished painting to reproduce these parts and represent these relations as well as it can.

The significance of the heterocosmic idea is not to be sought merely in notions of correction, abstraction, perfection, ideality, etc. These are of course involved: artificial perspective "abstracts from" and "corrects" the actual conditions of perception, freeing the painted world from these subjective limits; on the other side, the object is to be freed from natural limits: the painter is

> not only to make all the parts true to his model, but also to add beauty there. . . . Demetrius, an antique painter, failed to obtain the ultimate praise because he was much more careful to make things similar to the natural than to the lovely.
>
> For this reason it is useful to take from every beautiful body each one of the praised parts and always strive . . . to understand and express much loveliness. This is very difficult because complete beauties are never found in a

single body, but are rare and dispersed in many bodies. Therefore we ought to give our every care to discovering and learning beauty. (92–93)

Correcting, abstracting, and selecting are gestures of style—i.e., the painting is to reveal itself as offering a special experience so that, in spite of the criterion of verisimilitude, it is to assert its difference from actuality. The illusionistic treatment of solids and space in fact contributes to the self-sufficiency of the work and may thus harmonize with the seemingly opposed urge to artifice. These matters may be summed up in a formula which reflects attitudes explicit in Alberti's treatise: "To see a better thing and see it better." Here the idea of heterocosm is sustained, but slanted toward the idea of a golden world. But a more radical and significant idea is tacitly embodied in many of Alberti's practical descriptions of procedure: the notions of difference from and superimposition on actual experience are extended to matters of technique, to the relation between painter and observer, to the creation of a new world not simply on the picture plane but on both sides of it.

An experience of this sort can be conceived only by a sensibility conscious of a second, or hypothetical, audience set over against a second or hypothetical world. The resulting possibilities of interplay are inexhaustible. In Shakespeare, for example, the situation within the play world may be extended to the total theatrical situation containing the play world; at the same time, the total theatrical situation may be reflected or contained within the play world. Spectators may be treated as members of the play world, and members of the play world may be treated as members of the audience. Poets and painters may comment on their own powers and limitations by placing poet and painter figures in the second world. Thus poets may present antipoets who practice magic or escape from reality into worlds of their own making, and in this way they may deal with tendencies which they recognize in themselves. Painters may image themselves standing among their social or religious betters, reminding us that though they are masters of the second world, in the first they depend on patronage and inspiration.

III

In turning now from painting to our next example, the *Utopia*, I shall temporarily ignore the relation between heterocosm and artists or audience, and I would therefore like to suggest in advance that the control of this relation provides the most interesting feature of the relation between second world and green or golden world. The second world of the *Utopia* is the total work, while the green world is Hythloday's island. The total work is divided into three moments: the introductory letter to Peter Giles, written in the present tense of incomplete dialogue which characterizes the epistolary form; the narrative of the first book, which recounts the conversation in Antwerp; and Hythloday's Utopian monologue, which occupies nearly all of the second book.

The introductory letter not only anticipates the body of the work but also contains the past experience in miniature form. It reveals the continuing pressure of actual affairs on More, the insufficiency of time, the discordant claims of pleasure and business, desire and obligation. It portrays a world in which ideal conditions are something man may rather wish for than hope after:

> Howbeit to the dyspatchynge of thys so lytle busynesse, my other cares and troubles did leave almost lesse than no leasure. Whiles I doo dayelie bestowe my time aboute lawe matters: some to pleade, some to heare, some as an arbitratoure with myne awarde to determine, some as an umpier or a judge, with my sentence finallye to discusse. Whiles I go one waye to see and visite my frende: another waye about myn owne privat affaires. Whiles I spende almost al the day abrode emonges other, and the residue at home among mine owne; I leave to my self, I meane to my booke, no time.
>
> For when I am come home, I muste commen with my wife, chatte with my children and talk wyth my servauntes. All the whiche thinges I recken and accompte amonge businesse, forasmuche as they muste of necessitie be done . . . Emonge these thynges now rehearsed, stealeth awaye the daye, the moneth, the yeare.[29]

From this perspective More distances the Utopian state: it is another's discovery, not his own; he will render it in Hythloday's "homely plaine, and simple speche," the speech, as it turns out, of pastoral exclusion, of a simplicity which is escape.

At the same time, the letter ends with a purely evil image of actuality, a negative ideal which does not really disclose life as it is but shows rather a vision selectively controlled by a pessimism which borders on despair:

> the natures of man be so divers, the phantasies of some so waywarde, their myndes so unkynde, their judgementes so corrupte, that they which leade a merie and a jocounde lyfe, folowynge theyr owne sensuall pleasures and carnall lustes, may seme to be in a muche better state or case, then they that vexe

---

[29] Trans. Ralphe Robynson (1551), in *Three Renaissance Classics*, ed. B. A. Milligan (New York: Scribner, 1953), 106. Future page references are to this edition.

and unquiete themselves with cares and studie for the putting forthe and publishynge of some thynge, that maye be either profeit or pleasure to others: which others nevertheles will disdainfully, scornefully, and unkindly accepte the same. The moost part of al be unlearned. And a greate number hathe learning in contempte. The rude and barbarous alloweth nothing, but that which is verie barbarous in dede. (109)

And so More goes on for many more lines, arguing the futility of publishing his book, the little likelihood of its having any salutary effect on so corrupt a world.

My colleague Richard Sylvester, editor of the Yale edition of the *History of Richard III*, points out that More there uses the phrase "green world" to identify just this image of unmitigated and thus unreal brutality. It is an image similar to that produced by Machiavelli in *The Prince*. Like Shakespeare, Spenser, and many others, More points to this particular version of "green world" as an objectification of despair, of narcissism, of a too-absolute submission to the pleasure or power principle. Those who cannot accept the world as it is construe the Golden Age as more than imaginary and either bemoan its loss or long to recover it. The attitude More displays in the letter verges on Hythloday's pessimism, and when he ponders the futility of publication he displays a shadow of Hythloday's despair. Hythloday and his Utopia externalize an attitude existing in More and in every man. Within the second world of the imaginary experience More isolates this attitude, gives it play, copes with it, effectually contains it, and yet reveals its power even now, as he writes to Giles. Hythloday's radical idealism is that of a closed inner world: it is pure and monologic, not open to time, correction, compromise, or the interplay of perspectives made possible by dialogue and conversation.

Criticism of the *Utopia* has in the main recognized ambiguities in More's presentation of Hythloday but has tended to overstress the positive side, namely, that More places many of his own ideals in Hythloday's mouth. Yet as Sylvester has pointed out, if they agree about *ends*, the important issue is *means*, and here More differs radically from Hythloday on both esthetic and moral, pleasurable and profitable, grounds. The disagreement is not simply founded on the difference between the uncompromising character of Hythloday's "schole philosophye" and More's pragmatic civil philosophy "whyche knoweth . . . her owne stage . . . and . . . playethe her parte accordinglye with comlyenes." More important is that Hythloday is too earnest and intense, that he lacks the sense of play, musing and amused, by which a more tentative and self-conscious

mind remains negatively capable, alive to its own limits and to the
world's good. Unable to control his distance and detachment within the
world, he detaches himself from the world. (More, like Alberti and
other humanists, indicates this tendency by remarking Hythloday's preference for Greek over Latin.) Hythloday made his withdrawal easy by
getting rid of all natural and emotional attachments early in life:

> As concernyng my frendes and kynsfolke (quod he) I passe not greatly for
> them. For I thinke I have sufficiently doone my parte towardes them already.
> For these thynges, that other men doo not departe from, untyl they be olde
> and sycke, yea, whiche they be then verye lothe to leave, when they canne no
> longer keepe, those very same thynges dyd I beyng not only lustye and in
> good helth, but also in the floure of my youth, divide among my frendes and
> kynsfolkes. Which I thynke with this my liberalitie ought to hold them con-
> tented, and not require nor to loke that besydes this, I shoulde for their sakes
> geve myselfe in bondage unto kinges. (117)

He is a latter-day Odysseus (the analogues are numerous and pointed),
though somewhat in reverse: gladly leaving home, he steers toward
fabulous places which, for the Greek hero, were preparations for home-
coming. But if Hythloday would gladly remain in Phaiakia, at the other
end of the world from cyclopean actuality, More is truer to his model:

> He is in his talke and communication so merye and pleasaunte, yea and that
> withoute harme, that through his gentyll intertaynement, and his sweete and
> delectable communication, in me was greatly abated and diminished the fer-
> vent desyre, that I had to see my native countrey, my wyfe and my chyldren,
> whom then I dyd muche longe and covete to see, because that at that time I
> had been more than iiii. monethes from them. (112)

More is describing Peter Giles, though if Hythloday embodies an aspect
of More's mind, he certainly has this effect in a negative sense—to diminish "the fervent desyre, that I had to see my native countrey"—but
More has resisted the temptation to bear his unsullied ideals far off to
Nowhere. As in the case of that truly ideal idealist, Cardinal Morton,
visits from Hythloday—one might say "attacks" of Hythloday—are re-
served for after-dinner conversation, channeled into recreative occasions.
    Morton humors Hythloday as he humors the lawyer, friar, and para-
site—a Chaucerian gallery eminently qualified to bring on an attack. He
amuses himself with them, is amused by them, allows them to vent their
vanities and theories at his table, and dismisses them when it is time "to
heare his sueters." The Cardinal, controlling his guests as umpire but

encouraging them as host, seems in effect to be playing something like Cesare Gonzaga's game as reported by Castiglione:

> We have seen it happen in this house that many who were at first held to be very wise have been known, in the course of time, to be full of folly, and this came about through nothing save the attention we gave to it. . . . we, whenever we have detected some hidden trace of folly, have stimulated it so artfully and with such a variety of inducements . . . that finally we have understood what its tendency was; then, having recognized the humor, we agitated it so thoroughly that it was always brought to the perfection of an open folly. . . . wherein . . . we have had some wonderful entertainment. I hold this, then, to be certain: that in each of us there is some seed of folly which, once awakened, can grow almost without limitation.
>
> . . . each of us will profit from this game of ours by knowing his faults, the better thereby to guard against them.[30]

But unlike Castiglione's courtiers, the Cardinal is not seated in an ideal circle among trusted and intelligent friends. *The Courtier* describes how persons of spirit and consequence withdraw temporarily and guardedly from the untrustworthy world to the solidarity of that circle, there to seek both pleasurable relief and profitable self-knowledge. Disagreeing with conviction yet seldom with anger, encouraging criticisms and qualifications, they mutually refresh and hone themselves for the return to action. More's Cardinal is a lonelier, more embattled figure who "passed all his tyme in much trouble and busines, beyng continually tumbled and tossed in the waves of dyvers mysfortunes and adversities," by which "he lerned the experience of the worlde." He knows better than to hope by his reason, rather than by his status, to influence or improve the human specimens at his table; yet though Hythloday is near, he does not "leave and forsake the common wealthe" but continues his direction of the civil stage. Seated among "deaffe hearers," he is for the most part presented as silent and smiling, a giant "of a meane stature, and . . . stricken in age" who fills More's imagination as a model from the *illo tempore* of his childhood. What More admires most about him and sees as the secret of his endurance is his ability to *play*, his delight in experimental yet sympathetic engagement of other men:

> He had great delite manye times with roughe speache to his sewters, to prove, but withoute harme, what proper witte and what bolde spirite were in

---

[30] *The Book of the Courtier*, trans. C. S. Singleton (Garden City: Doubleday-Anchor, 1959), I.8, 20–21.

every man. In the which, as in a vertue much agreinge with his nature, so that therewith were not joyned impudency, he toke greate delectatyon. (120)

Morton is an anti-Hythloday, and More, if anything, is a lesser Morton, one who has greater need of friends and is more susceptible to attacks of Hythloday. His most severe attack is recorded in the second book of *Utopia*, and it is important that this withdrawal to a golden world was written first, to be qualified and contained only later by the return to actuality in Book I. But the second book itself gives witness to its author's essential detachment from the Utopian ideal. The very self-enclosed spatiality of Hythloday's green world is a criticism; it is a womblike retreat protected from the outside world. Since it is a triumph of human art, an ideal system, it is totally unified and homogenous, purged of that variety—more difficult to control—which springs from accidents of history and differences of individual perspective: "There be in the ilande liiii. large and faire cities, or shiere townes, agreyng all together in one tonge, in lyke maners, institucions and lawes. They all be set and situate alyke, as farforthe as the place or plot sufferethe." Broadest in the middle and narrowest at the ends, Utopia is turned "about a circuit or compasse" so that it bears ironically enough the shape of a new moon between whose points

the sea runneth in . . . and there surmountethe into a large and wide sea, which by reason that the land on every side compassethe it about, and shiltreth it from the windes, is not roughe, nor mounteth not with great waves, but almost floweth quietlye, not muche unlike a greate standinge powle: and maketh welneighe all the space within the bellye of the land in maner of a haven: and to the greate commoditie of the inhabitauntes receaveth in shyppes towardes everye parte of the lande. (155−56)

But More immediately intersperses a few faint signs of danger which remind us that Utopia may be a risky port to steer for and that Utopians, like Hythloday, jealously guard their purity and exclusiveness, their independence of weaker mortals:

The forefrontes or frontiers of the ii. corners, what with fords and shelves, and what with rockes be verye jeoperdous and daungerous. In the middle distaunce betwene them bothe standeth up above the water a greate rocke, which therfore is nothing perillous bycause it is in sight. Upon the top of this rocke is a faire and strong tower builded, which they hold with a garrison of men. Other rockes there be lyinge hidde under the water, which therfor be daungerous. The channelles be knowen onely to themselfes. And therfore it seldome chaunceth that anye straunger oneles he be guided by an Utopian can come in to this haven. In so muche that they themselves could skaselye entre withoute jeoperdie, but that their way is directed and ruled by certaine lande markes standing on the shore. By turninge, translatinge, and removinge thies markes into other places they maye destroye theire enemies navies, be they never so many. (156)

These hints are not developed until later in the second book, for More has given Hythloday's monologue a definite shape: its first half is relatively innocent; the criticisms of actuality are for the most part just, and the defects of Utopia barely touched on. The logic is that of satiric exorcism: "It would be nice if what is wrong with actuality could be screened out. We shall call the corrected image Utopia." The climax of this movement falls almost exactly at the center of the second book. Hythloday has been describing the facility with which the Utopians absorb the small library of humanist culture he has bestowed on them, and he remarks their special interest in the "phisike" of Hippocrates and Galen; even though "there be almost no nation under heaven that hath less nede of phisike then they, . . . phisike is no where in greater honour":

> For whyles they by the helpe of this philosophie searche oute the secrete mysteryes of nature, they thinke themselfes to receave therby not onlye wonderfull greate pleasure, but also to obteine great thankes and favour of the autour and maker therof. Whome they thinke, according to the fassion of other artificers, to have set furth the marvelous and gorgious frame of the world for man with great affection intentively to beholde. Whom only he hath made of witte and capacitie to considre and understand the excellencie of so great a woork. And therefore he beareth (say they) more goodwil and love to the curious and diligent beholder and vewer of his woork and marvelour of the same, then he doth to him, which . . . hathe no regarde to soo great and so wonderfull a spectacle. (199)

Two aspects of this passage deserve special attention. First, the Utopians' gratuitous and somewhat pompous use of "phisike" should be connected with Hythloday's frequent assertions that they are extraordinarily quick learners who "quickelye, almoste at the first meting, made their owne what soever is among us wealthelye devised." Utopia is a Platonic Garden of Adonis, a place without pain where everyone learns everything the short smooth way: "amonge the Utopians, where all thinges be sett in good order," time has no function and history no meaning. The hard-won accomplishments of Western culture are absorbed without sweat or struggle; Utopian logic and imagination replace the trial and error of human experience. The Utopians are handed the classical inheritance in the Aldine edition, untrammeled by the existential context of past-and-present, loss-and-recovery, which has made that inheritance so precious. That inheritance is to them as Ulysses' tale of painful voyaging was to the Phaiakians.

Second, Hythloday's praise of man is so close to Pico's in the *Oratio* as to seem like an echo or allusion: the divine artificer, having finished the creation of the world and wishing "there were someone to ponder the plan of so great a work, to love its beauty, and to wonder at its vastness," made man, placed him in the middle of the world, and addressed him thus:

> Neither a fixed abode nor a form that is thine alone nor any function peculiar to thyself have we given thee, Adam, to the end that according to thy longing and according to thy judgment thou mayest have and possess what abode, what form, and what functions thou thyself shalt desire. . . . We have set thee at the world's center that thou mayest from thence more easily observe whatever is in the world. We have made thee neither . . . mortal nor immortal, so that with freedom of choice and with honor, as though the maker and molder of thyself, thou mayest fashion thyself in whatever shape thou shalt prefer. Thou shalt have the power to degenerate into the lower forms of life, which are brutish. Thou shalt have the power . . . to be reborn into the higher forms, which are divine.[31]

Hythloday's echo may of course be a straightforward and conventional piece of *laus hominis*, but the context turns it slightly awry. There is something hermetic, something More might indeed have felt in Pico, in the detachment and gratuitous self-delight of curious Utopian observers. The Utopians observe whatever is in the world more easily because they are not located at its center but are safely removed to the periphery. Their naiveté about the psychological appeal of such vices as dicing, hunting, and love of jewels suggests how little experience they have of the mortal weaknesses from which they are remote. The long discourse on pleasure terminated by the *laus* is vaguely unsatisfying because Hythloday is so concerned to justify the Utopian delight not only in good health per se but in good health as a *feeling*, a state of consciousness. Similarly, of mental pleasures, "the chiefe parte of them they thinke doth come of the exercise of vertue, *and conscience of good life*" (italics mine). To the "delectation that commeth of the contemplation of treweth . . . is joyned the pleasaunte remembraunce of the good lyfe paste." That a man

---

[31]Trans. E. L. Forbes, in *The Renaissance Philosophy of Man*, ed. E. Cassirer, P. O. Kristeller, J. H. Randall, Jr., et al. (Chicago: University of Chicago Press, 1948), 224–25.

should remind himself of his mere humanity, should love himself and his neighbor for God's sake, should wear a hairshirt (and still be happy) is unthinkable:

> For a vaine shaddow of vertue, for the wealth and profite of no man, to punishe himselfe, or to the intente he maye be hable courragiouslie to suffer adversitie, whiche perchaunce shall never come to him; this to do they thinke it a point of extreame madnes, and a token of man cruellye minded towardes himselfe, and unkind towardes nature, as one so disdaining to be in her daunger, that he renounceth and refuseth all her benefites. (196)

As Florentine idealism is in one sense an escape from what man is to what he would like to be (which Ficino and Pico conflate with what he should be), so the preferred shape to which the Utopians have fashioned themselves leads them too often to exclaim, "Happy to be me!"

In the last half of the second book, the questionable aspects of Utopia emerge into full view. There are first such isolated instances as the praise of euthanasia and suicide; here the violation of divine law is subtly intensified by the previous discussion of pleasure. The urge to turn a critique whole-hog into a program—that primary manifestation of the political pleasure principle—makes itself felt in the Utopian trick of avoiding corruption in legal procedure by abolishing the procedure—throwing out the form of government because the party in power is corrupt. A similar attitude is displayed toward leagues, though the argument is more roundabout. There is first the bitter satiric inversion: "Here in Europa, and especiallye in these partes where the faith and religion of Christe reigneth, the majestie of leagues is everye where estemed holy and inviolable, partlie through the justice and goodnes of princes, and partly at the reverence and motion of the head bishops." Then follows the Utopian response: "In that newe founde parte of the world . . . no trust nor confidence is in leagues" because the neighbors of the Utopians always violate them. This is not the fault of human nature, for "men be better and more surely knit togethers by love and benevolence, then by covenauntes of leagues." The fault lies in human institutions, namely leagues, which cause men "to thinke themselves borne adversaries and enemies one to another." Thus the Utopian makes his pastoral withdrawal from the painful state of civilization to the ideal state of nature. More has placed the contrast to all these Utopian methods, and the criterion by which they are to be judged, in the figure of Cardinal Morton.

In the final two sections, on Utopian warfare and religion, the irony becomes massive, beginning with the Utopian use of cyclopean Zapoletes (the best using the worst, a figure of the end-means split) and end-

ing with the tepid panaceas of the Utopian faith. At the end Hythloday
unwittingly supplies an anatomy of the Utopian mind, for he shows how
withdrawal is founded on despair of things as they are. Actuality is reduced to the negative ideal: "When I consider and way in my mind all
these commen wealthes, which now a dayes any where do florish, so God
helpe me, I can perceave nothing but a certain conspiracy of riche men
procuringe theire owne commodities under the name and title of the
commen wealth." Hythloday's is a solution procured through the verbal
magic of personification by which complex issues are simplified for quick
disposal: do away with those two princesses, Lady Money and Lady
Pride. "How great an occasion of wickednes and mischiefe is plucked up
by the rotes!" The image recalls one of the more outlandish feats of Utopian husbandry mentioned shortly before Hythloday's praise of man—
the Utopians not only matched the farmers of other countries in craft
and cunning "to remedie the barrennes of the grounde," but they outdid
Macduff: "a whole wood by the handes of the people plucked up by the
rootes in one place, and set againe in an other place."

Thus More has so shaped Hythloday's account as first to draw us into
Utopia, then to push us away from it. This dynamic narrative pattern
works against the atemporal and ahistorical life of the island. What
seems most important is the narrative control of the audience. The relations which determine the overall structure of *Utopia* are after all primarily verbal, intelligible, and temporal: the three moments which unfold its experience are relatively discrete units, each more condensed and
immediate than those which follow it. The letter to Giles frames both
parts of the work within the present tense of the writer's experience,
whereas the first book frames Hythloday's monologue in the more realistic and inclusive context of European affairs. The openness and intimacy of More's address to Peter Giles establishes the proper distance for
the reader, who is in effect the addressee.[32] Such places of the mind as

----

[32] For a relatively unflattering interpretation of the role of Giles, see David M. Bevington, "The Dialogue in *Utopia:* Two Sides of the Question," *Studies in Philology* 58
(July 1961): 496–510, especially 499–501. Bevington, who treats Hythloday as something of a hero, seems to belittle Giles mainly to confirm a structural analogy between the
present and past triumvirates: in both, "the function of the third party . . . is to serve as
spokesman for the wrong point of view, and thus provide a basis of agreement between
the principal characters" (504).

Some interesting light on Giles and the epistolary convention is thrown by Peter R.
Allen in "*Utopia* and European Humanism: The Function of the Prefatory Letters and
Verses," *Studies in the Renaissance* 10 (1963): 91–108, especially 94–95.

On the implications of monologue and dialogue, see Father Surtz's introduction to
Utopia, vol. IV of the Yale Edition of the Complete Works, ed. E. L. Surtz, S. J. Hexter, and J. H. Hexter (New Haven: Yale University Press, 1964).

Hythloday's green world are best dealt with not in lonely voyages but in the friendly play of an afternoon's talk, in the good fellowship of men who love and trust each other, in the shared discourse which refreshes weary minds so that they can return to the stage of the actual world next morning. More exorcizes as a purely spatial nowhere the tendency, so obvious in Hythloday, to abolish time and chance.

We may be reminded here of a fact of which Plato was perhaps the first to make systematic use: insofar as landscape is symbolic—even the conversation of the first book of *Utopia* is symbolically placed in a garden, and in the garden of More's *temporary* lodgings—the dimension of space subserves the movement of words and the play of minds which shape and reshape themselves in time. Plato's unfinished utopian dialogue, the *Critias*, provides an instructive model and analogue of More's method, and I should like briefly to consider it. Critias locates ideal gardens of Adonis at the beginning of history in Atlantis and primeval Attica. He describes them as literal, not metaphoric, places—the state of nature, not the state of myth—and as such they embody Heraclitean ideals. His description emphasizes the great flux and variety of physical things. As their temporal location indicates, these are given rather than earned utopias, and the same fate of decline overtakes the physical luxuriance of Attica and the ethos of the men of Atlantis. The dialogue implies that their loss of self-mastery moved Zeus to put the Atlanteans to the test by sending them out to do battle. It was in the Atlantic invasion of the Mediterranean world that Athens proved her mettle: "When the rest fell off from her, being compelled to stand alone, after having undergone the very extremity of danger, she defeated . . . the invaders, and preserved from slavery those who were not yet subjugated, and generously liberated all the rest."[33] The corruption of Atlantis is made the occasion whereby the Athenian ethos is tested and proved heroic: if the Attic gardens decay, their inhabitants—losing the original state of nature—acquire the eros and inner strength through which the soul confronts and masters the experience. The Atlanteans apparently did not meet the test of experience, and when their island was submerged, their oceanic power never revived in its human form, whereas the Athenians, weathering cataclysm after cataclysm, still send roots into their rocky cliff. Their *aretē* was displaced from body to soul, and this is Plato's historical message: to convert a Heraclitean ideal into a Platonic vision, Athene must confront and defeat Poseidon. The mind must transfer its garden states from object to image, from perception to thought, from

---

[33] *Timaeus* 25c, trans. Jowett.

history to myth, from nature to spirit, from the beginning of experience to its end. Critias's narrative is presented as dogmatic rote work; his mind, resolved and inactive, passively reproduces the written Egyptian records as accurately as it can; similarly, he describes the laws of Atlantis as tyrannized by convention and the wisdom of the elders. In theme and treatment, Plato's position is diametrically opposed to that of Critias. By sharply outlining the backward-looking attitude which treats the story as literal while he himself presents it as myth or allegory, Plato conveys both the sense of loss and the act of recovery. This act consists in the dialogue itself: here the remembered image is valued not for its pseudo-historical accuracy but for its cognitive significance as an allegory of loss and recovery. The allegory implies that the soul can never simply return to the past or malinger in its green world but must go the long way around until the sense and image of loss have been transformed into the desire and vision of future fulfillment.

The green world seems to possess two essential qualities: first, since it is only metaphorically a place or space, it embodies a condition whose value should not remain fixed but should rather change according to the temporal process of which it is a part. It appears first as exemplary or appealing and lures us away from the evil or confusion of everyday life. But when it has fulfilled its moral, esthetic, social, cognitive, or experimental functions, it becomes inadequate and its creator turns us out. Those who wish to remain, who cannot or will not be discharged, are presented as in some way deficient. Thus the second quality of the green world is that it is ambiguous: its usefulness and dangers arise from the same source. In its positive aspects it provides a temporary haven for recreation or clarification, experiment or relief; in its negative aspects it projects the urge of the paralyzed will to give up, escape, work magic, abolish time and flux and the intrusive reality of other minds.

IV

Simply as a pattern of withdrawal and return, the shuttling between normal and green, or brazen and golden, worlds is of too widespread an incidence to be identified with the genius of a particular age and culture. The significant Renaissance contribution lies in the doubling of this pattern so that the second world, or heterocosm, assumes the status of a green world in relation to the first world of the audience. And it would be misleading to think of the pattern within the second world as an image of the larger dialectic between second world and audience; nature is better seen as imitating art in this situation; fiction provides actuality with its model. According to this model, the dialectic in which the artist or audience engages the second world seems capable of division into three hypothetical phases, and the division may throw some light on that often-maligned region of Renaissance poetics, the concern for pleasure and profit. There is, first, the artist's delight in making and the reader's or spectator's delight in the recreative occasion of entertainment; second, esthetic delight in the object for its own sake—exactness of limitation, coherence, beauty, etc.—a delight which is ideally fulfilled by the relevance and significance of the image, by the re-creation of the first world within the autonomous unity of the second; third, ethical delight in the content or "teaching," the phase in which the mind disengages itself from the second world and gathers up what it has made into the revised, the continually changing, context of its own concerns. In the transition from the second to the third phase we find both continuity and disjunction: continuity insofar as the moral return begins, so to speak, midway through the second world with the controlled readmission of life into the prepared space of art and is then carried beyond art out to life; disjunction in that the disengagement from art is usually effected by some gesture of release, some form of the technique which psychoanalysts call breaking the transference.

Familiar examples of this pattern occur when Rosalind and Prospero carry the return from Arden and island through the play world into their respective epilogues. The withdrawal has made everything clear: golden and brazen forms have been distinguished, are made to confront and reform each other. Now as the play world turns to artifice before our eyes, as the characters turn back into actors, we are asked to share the playwright's responsibility. It is up to us to respond to the words and images graven in our souls, to carry them home with us from the theater as Rosalind and Prospero did from their retreats, to transform the bounded moment of esthetic delight into a model or guide for moral action. What Rosalind and Prospero finally communicate as they fade is a lesson, a moral significance, which was rubbed vividly into the very grain of the fiction, which we can find there if we take the plays seriously enough to interpret them, and which those who do not submit to the plays as written do not see in the epilogues. This implies that profit is immanent in the very nature of artifice and fiction, but that fiction can fulfill itself only by going beyond itself and invading life. It does this through open gestures of self-limitation, as when, by revealing itself as mere make-believe, it seals off its image, breaks the transference, releases the audience, and consigns the fate of its rounded image to their wills.

The artist, philosopher, and scientist conceive of their second worlds as only temporarily self-sufficient and ultimately as interpretations which (they hope) will revise the first world. Similarly, the reader or observer, placed at a distance from the second world, is enjoined not to lose himself in the work but to interpret and move on. *Interpretation*, in its broadest aspect, is what the mind does to what it receives, or feels it receives—what the mind conceives as its original response to the data of appearance, its contribution to the discovery of the real. In the context under discussion, interpretation lies between pleasure and profit, between passive or tacit and active or articulate understanding. Between the first sight of affective delight and the second sight of moral understanding lies the insight of cognitive interpretation. In affective first sight the work is reduced to our responses and disappears in subjective appreciation. In cognitive insight the work demands that we separate it from ourselves, think about it in itself, and submit ourselves to its objective character. In moral second sight we place the work, so interpreted, over against ourselves, moving beyond it as it is in itself, catching it up in the context of our own concerns. To engage in this dialectic with the work, the interpreter frees himself by adopting what Hannah Arendt calls an "Archimedean point," a hypothetical position outside the field of inquiry, from which he may choose his frame of reference and control his involvement in the field.

Etymologically, an interpreter is a kind of price-fixer, a negotiator or go-between who assigns value to objects. Unlike his medieval predecessors, the Renaissance interpreter claims that his activity not only reflects but also *affects* the nature of the object submitted to his evaluation. The danger of this claim is that he may become a basilisk, that—as in Shakespeare's *Troilus and Cressida*—agents and actions may be corrupted by the "ill aspects," the vitiated perspectives of onlookers who are not up to their new responsibilities. The strength of the claim is that it produces belief in a genuinely creative process of *re-vision*, a more immediate commitment to the reality of time and the openness of the future which radically affects the sense of personal and historical experience. Behind this is the dim feeling that whatever reality is, it is neither exhausted by the medieval version nor exhaustible by any other human model of reality; this feeling need not be expressed only as pessimism or some secular form of chiliasm; it may, through the medium of that controlled skepticism which Keats called Negative Capability, encourage the belief that the real (whatever it is) is genuinely and continually altered, enriched, reconstructed by acts of interpretation. These two alternatives are ultimately focused in the Battle of the Books, but they exist side by side throughout the postmedieval centuries. The pessimistic response is often embodied in historical or sociological appeals to that form of green world known as the Golden Age; the more optimistic response is explicitly asserted as a form of *interpretation* by Pico, Leonardo, and Bacon, for all of whom the term has reference to the *here-now* of significant decision and revision.

In many strands of Renaissance thought the submission to ancient authority and to the wisdom of the Golden Age is construed as an expression of the pleasure principle. This holds true for the Reformation interest in reviving the simplicity and purity of the early Church, since ancient religion is approached in historical perspective and treated as a model providing lessons rather than dogmas for the present time: to the gratuitous or esthetic motive of slavish role playing, the Reformation sensibility opposes a moral attitude, a demand for correction and revision. The dialectician and the moralist are alike concerned mainly with the existential *now* of usage, of experiment and personal choice. They know that by attributing one's own ideal solutions to the ancient sages one simply denies the otherness of the past, substitutes fantasy for history, abolishes those salutary resistances and limitations which make thought responsible and remind it that it is only thought. Such a strategy tends to reduce present-tense experience to rote work which sustains the old wisdom or to an archaeological pedantry which fulfills itself in recovering the old wisdom. The underlying motive, if it is not exposed as sheer self-indulgence, is shown to be the fear of time and death, the belief that mutability is only negative and reality only mutable, the despair of finding any significant pattern in the apparent chaos of history or of contemporary life. Plato treats Critias and his Atlantis very much as More treats Hythloday and his Utopia, as Spenser treats Faerie, Sidney poetry, and Shakespeare the green world. All are useful only if they proclaim their hypothetical status and are understood to have literal existence not in space or time but solely, in Spenser's words, "deepe within the mynd." They should not be approached as exemplars to be copied but rather as hypothetical models—guides, not commanders, as Jonson put it. However much they attract us in and for themselves, their ultimate purpose is to lead us beyond them. Models exist to be emulated, not imitated; the interpreter aims to render his models in a sense obsolete by becoming a model himself. "For rightly," to conclude with Bacon's familiar words, "rightly is truth called the daughter of time, not of authority. It is no wonder therefore if those enchantments of antiquity and authority and consent have so bound up men's powers that they have been made impotent (like persons bewitched) to accompany with the nature of things."

The Ecology of the Mind:
The Concept of Period Imagination—
An Outline Sketch

I

THE FOLLOWING OBSERVATIONS and interpretations will try to make
sense and use of these three texts:

1. Ecology may be defined broadly as the science of the interrelation
   between living organisms and their environment . . . the *living organism* . . . is self-regulating . . . and is in process of equilibration
   with its environment. The *environment* of any organism consists, in
   final analysis, of everything in the universe external to that particular organism. (Allee, Emerson, Park, Park, and Schmidt, *Principles of Animal Ecology*, Philadelphia, 1949, p. 1).
2. "O blessed rage for order!" (Wallace Stevens)
3. Pride goeth before a fall. (Old Saying)

The first is a definition, the second an exclamation, the third a warning.
I want to make the exclamation put life into the definition and the warning take some of the steam out of the exclamation. The first step is to
twist and reapply the definition by substituting the word *mind* for the
phrase *living organism*. We then have a new field of inquiry: cultural
ecology or, more precisely, mental ecology, the study of the mind in relation to its environment. After this we may—by begging a few ques-

tions which embrace the whole of ontology and epistemology—roughly and tentatively identify mind with *self* and environment with *other*. We now have some opposites out of which, by careful handling, we can produce dialectic, tension, drama. If we naively and inadequately equate *mind* with whatever human consciousness conceives as belonging to itself, we shall have to make a slight alteration in the scope of our new field: cultural ecology must be phenomenological. It does not ask, "What *is* the relation . . ." but rather, "What does the mind *conceive* the relation to be between itself and its environment?" So general a question is entirely impracticable. We need a historical qualification to make it work, and this may be supplied in the appended phrase "at any given time or period, in any given work."

The next major move is to ascribe to the mind of our first statement the blessed rage for order of our second. We may then bring the exclamation and the warning into immediate play in the following manner: We assume that—at least so far as Western civilization is concerned— all periods of human culture arise as responses to a single perennial human need, namely, the mind's desire for order. But we remember that this desire is problematical. It is always threatened by two dangers between which the human enterprise steers a perilous course, a course which zigzags from one brink to another, driving men continually from one to another temporary solution, one to another cultural environment. The dangers are simple, constant, and recurrent, but the historical course is irreversible.

The first danger is the fear that man can know nothing of reality, or can do nothing about it, or both. The real is felt as inscrutable, powerful, indifferent or hostile, violent and alien. It impinges on our everyday life not only as death, weather, bad luck but also as human malice. Consciously or unconsciously man is compelled to cope with this risky universe by projecting an order which makes life possible, makes it tolerable—an order which will not work unless man accepts the equal reality of disorder, but an order which conforms as much as safety allows to man's wishes and hopes.

The second danger is that man presumes to such complete knowledge and power that he reduces the structure of reality to the structure of mind. Whether through fear, ignorance, or arrogance, he fails to curb his blessed rage, tries to rationalize himself into a dream world, a walled paradise where he thinks to escape from the terrors and uncertainties inherent in his condition. When this structure collapses, when it runs up against hard fact and is unveiled as fantasy, man's triumph may turn into despair—a despair whose intensity and sophistication make it harder to deal with than any vague primitive terror.

Thus a double obligation is imposed on the mind: to recognize the power of imagination and to recognize its limits. When the power of imagination is affirmed alone, we construct ideal worlds and engage in that withdrawal from fact or reality which Freud called the tendency of the pleasure principle—the urge to reduce pain and tension, to gratify desires as quickly and completely as possible, to go through life with minimal irritation from the outside world. And we should note that Freud assigns this tendency to an unconscious "drive" which he calls the death instinct. He describes this drive much as scientists describe the closed system, and he suggests that when an individual becomes—like Narcissus—locked within himself and his garden fantasies, he hastens that running-down process whereby the organism loses its power of self-regulation.

Fantasy becomes true creativity only when the limits of imagination are affirmed, when the mind opens itself to the forces that impinge from the outside and from the future as well as from within itself. Such an awareness corresponds to what Freud called the reality principle—the tendency to take note of one's surroundings, to accept pain and tension as the natural condition of life. The reality principle affirms the presence of forces over against the self, a reality about which the self can do nothing unless it first accepts its own powerlessness to escape—unless, indeed, it realizes not only the extent to which self projects itself on the otherness of environment but also the extent to which it discovers that otherness lurking within the structure of self. At one stage of his career Freud connected the reality principle with what he called the life instincts, related to reproductive processes. The life instincts are manifested in one's desire to join with and be fulfilled by another, the recognition of one's own insufficiency and the need for love. The obvious analogue in the domain of biology is the concept of the open system, which is renewed by energy from the outside, by a metabolic interchange between self and other.

This interchange is based on simple and familiar facts of mental topography which may be rapidly summarized. Consciousness tends to divide its experience into three categories: the appearances, consisting of relatively detailed information coming from outside the mind, to which we seem to respond passively; interpretations, which the mind is aware of adding or contributing to the information received; and the facts or realities, whatever they are, which the mind feels to be "out there" and to be attained by revelation or discovery. The data of appearance seem incomplete and demand that we do something about them. They function like codes to be cracked, cues demanding a response, clues to be followed up. They present themselves as congeries of isolated facts which want to be classified, ordered, numbered, or interpreted in some other way. The mind does not believe it *constructs* the appearance, if we understand the term *construct* to indicate a conscious, rational process. The appearance may differ from the real fact (as the appearance of the sun's motion differs from the physical fact which "causes" it), its form may owe largely to the character of our nervous system and gravitational situation, but in a basic sense the appearance feels as if it comes *from* the outside. It challenges us to deal with its otherness, to make sense of it, to cope with its chanciness or apparent disorder. What the mind originates within itself is a response to the challenge. Whether consciously or unconsciously, the mind fills out the information given, orders the appearances into classes, fields, systems, coherent universes. The felt insufficiency of data drives the mind to complete the picture by its own act of construction, and the current belief is that no system, no bounded and determinate whole, is ever given to us as information from the outside but is the product of interpretation.

The real is felt to be the goal, the answer, the first cause, the underlying x factor (whether permanently unknowable or temporarily unknown) which accounts for appearances. Like the appearance, the real is a given, an other; the mind does not believe that it constructs the fact or reality, for if it did, facts and realities would be reducible to fictions. We must think of the real as an objective something, but we need not identify it with a particular content. The real as such is indeterminate until the mind confronts it or feels that it is itself confronted, and the content is determined by what the mind is looking for in a particular case—it may be an atom, the prime mover, gravitation, a person, God, etc. Human beings seem on the whole to take the possibility of such a confrontation for granted. As a possible experience, the real is a fact of conscious life, although not a fact to be exhausted by any particular assigned value.

Yet there is a problem here, and it makes itself felt in the syntax with which I blandly describe the real: "We *must* think of the real as . . ." Recent cultural history tends to indicate that such a confrontation cannot be taken for granted, at least in official and articulate thought. The category of the real can be kept open to experience only by persistent and deliberate self-limitation. Kant did not discover, though he made explicit, the principle of self-limitation invoked and reinvoked in varying ways, with varying degrees of consciousness, during the course of Western (Greek, Hebraic, Christian) civilization: "Even the *assumption* . . . of *God, freedom* and *immortality* is not permissible unless at the same time speculative reason be deprived of its pretensions to transcendental insight . . . I have therefore found it necessary to deny *knowledge* in order to make room for *faith*." Hegel based this principle on dialectical necessity by insisting that *self* cannot exist without *other*, by systematically developing the concept of the other as indissoluble from the concept of the self: "Self-consciousness exists in itself and for itself, in that, and by the fact that it exists for another self-consciousness; that is to say, it *is* only by being acknowledged or 'recognized.'"

To create, to determine, to articulate an environmental other over against the self seems to be a primitive human need, a psychic reflex basic to survival. Men cope with themselves and their environments not simply by fighting, hunting, mating, eating, farming but also by exerting the equally active and equally primary forces of imagination whereby they construct the world in which they find themselves. Ritual is implicit myth making, magic implicit world making, prayer implicit god making. Self cannot act on or react to, cannot have dialogue with, a world felt as a terrifying negation of self (a not-self); it requires, to use Blake's term, a contrary, an other, a self-there which acknowledges the existence and hears the voice of self-here even if it does not fulfill its wishes. Such a relation could not be—and traditionally was not—felt as a reciprocal relation of equals on the model of Aristotle's theory of friendship. It was rather felt as an I-Thou situation in which self-here establishes a measure of control by voluntarily giving up power to self-there according to the process which Hegel has analyzed in his account of master and slave. Humility and self-abasement are among the strategies whereby man may avoid humiliation and helpless passivity. Thus any ecological inquiry must center on the Axiom of Self-Limitation, which states that human power, the possibility of creative and significant action, is open to the self only insofar as the mind commits the reality of world order to forces greater than self and over against self, forces whose limiting otherness will test, judge, restrain, answer, and reward the self.

II

Ecological theory is pragmatic. It has three phases—general hypotheses, historical application, particular interpretation—of which the second is more important than the first, the third most important of all. Its aim is to interpret the individual cultural object so that the living and dynamic act it embodies will leap forth from the relatively static or spatial form in which it is preserved. The hypotheses and constructs of the first two phases will not be judged by historical, not even by intellectual-historical, criteria but by the extent to which they prove operationally useful to interpretation. This caveat is especially pertinent to the second phase, historical application, with which the remainder of the discussion is concerned. The subject of this phase is the concept of period imagination, which must be distinguished from the concept of historical or cultural period. A historical period has a roughly datable beginning and end. It functions as a heterogeneous cultural matrix from which scholars selectively isolate the "background" appropriate to the cultural object being considered. But a period imagination is homogeneous in that all its scattered characteristics may be deduced from a few primary ecological and phenomenological conditions which are established according to the hypotheses outlined above. Ecological method substitutes hypothetical for historical causes because its aim is to describe cultural objects as phenomena in their own right rather than account for them as effects of the "background." The relation of mind to environment is explored only insofar as it belongs to the foreground of the concrete works in question. These works reveal the existence of a period imagination and make it a permanently available datum of experience. Since the forces and processes of thought engender the forms of cultural environment much as a living organism creates its own shell, the shell, once relatively complete, may be inhabited at any subsequent time. A period imagination, unlike a historical period, may be revived or revised, uncritically perpetuated or critically tested, during later historical periods.

Rather than try further to define what I mean by period imagination, I shall compare two types, medieval and Renaissance, using two illustrations as points of departure. It should be noted that the following pictorial comparison is rigged: the figures are used as models exemplifying the general characteristics of a period imagination rather than as instances embodying these characteristics. Figure 1 is a zodiacal diagram from a French manuscript of about 1400; Figure 2 is Leonardo da Vinci's famous man of perfect proportions (Accademia, Venice), often called Vitruvian Man.

Both images depict man as microcosm, but whereas this fact is immediately perceptible in the first figure, in Vitruvian man it is conveyed by geometrical symbolism which demands some interpretive activity from the mind. If both are also understood as *imagines Dei*, they give the phrase different connotations. Notice the looseness and flimsiness of the medieval *imago*, far from godlike, more like a rag doll whose limbs and

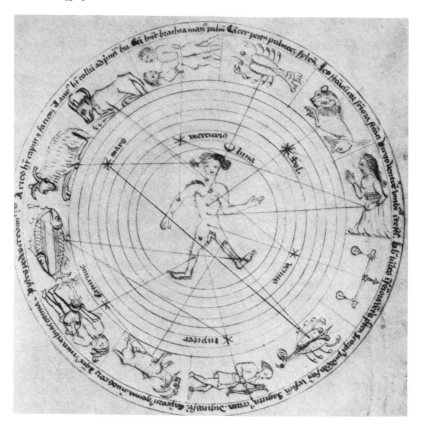

1. Zodiacal diagram from medieval French manuscript.

head are arranged so as to fit easily, concentrically, within the containing sphere. Notice also how the astrological forces home in like wasps, pin the poor soul down, make him dance. And yet, though he seems help-less, he does not look especially sad. One might in fact discern faint traces of a smile on the face, or at least a certain calmness—as if he knows that everything is under control in spite of appearances. If he is firmly bounded and determined from the outside, he nevertheless fills up a central and relatively large portion of a universe which directs all its attention to him. But there is an even simpler reason for his touch of complacency: although man depicts his own image in the humblest atti-tudes, the whole cosmic scheme is—to us—clearly a product of man-made lore. The projective and architectonic tendencies of the medieval imagination are never more in view than in its diagrams. Here we see

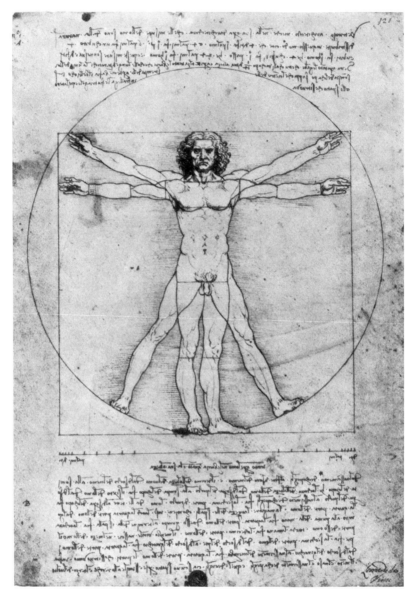

2. Leonardo da Vinci, *Vitruvian Man,* or *Study of Proportions of the Human Figure.* Accademia, Venice.

how the mind has organized and controlled the world in whose power man seems to be. The "causes in nature" have been named, rationalized, and visualized.

When we turn to Leonardo's man, we are immediately struck by the increased scale and solidity, the plastic assertion of the figure. And we are reminded of the Renaissance image—familiar since Burckhardt—of the overreacher, the fully self-sufficient hero playing the role of an incarnate god. Drawn in symmetric frontality, with athletic limbs in two positions as if doing the jumping jack, the hero marks the limits of circle and square. He seems virtually to hold them in place, to give dimension to these geometrical symbols of perfection as he lends his proportions to the universe.

But on the other hand, the heroic sternness of the face is creased with something like pain. The arms extended stiffly and uncomfortably recall, in one position, the crucified Christ and, in the other, Prometheus spread-eagled by Jove. The head pressed slightly by the upper horizontal of the square that confines it and the space vaulted by the top sector of the circle soaring freely above together reveal that the other side of the assertion of the mind's power is a painful awareness of insufficiency. Man, who feels himself to be godlike in form and power, knows himself to be mortal and finite, pressed as well as blessed by a longing that drives him continually to aspire beyond human limit and so continually to feel, to knock up against, that irrevocable limit. Man circles the universe yet is bound to his tiny planet. Because he can no longer intuitively believe in the scriptural revelation and its promise, he must bring himself around to the belief by a conscious, a deliberate and sophisticated, pressure of thought.

The cost of his new burden, his assumption of godlike powers of thought, is etched into every line of Leonardo's figure. Man is in two worlds, but they are no longer the medieval worlds of flesh and spirit or nature and grace which, even when antithetical, were hierarchically ordered in a single universe: now there is a world around man hemming him in and a world within pressing out from the center of self, and these two worlds are discontinuous, for the first is actual, the second imaginary or hypothetical. What is important here is the awareness that the first world must be articulated, the limit asserted, to make the second world significant. The mind cannot validly count itself king of infinite space unless it feels itself bounded in a nutshell. Nor can it affirm the power and responsibility of the thinking which makes things good or bad unless it does something about its bad dreams—not only those of

Hamlet but also those of Descartes, who kept protesting that a good God would not deceive us.

Both of our images, both of the ecological systems they exemplify, are man-made, but the first reflects a conscious denial of this fact, the second a conscious affirmation. Both may be seen as attempts to avoid the extremes of self-expansion and self-defeat, dogmatism and skepticism, pride and despair—extremes which are two sides of the same attitude. The difference between the two world views is carried into our images as a difference in pictorial style. Different forms of period imagination embody different *styles* of response to the perennial challenge, different ways of avoiding the ever-threatening extremes.

What I call the medieval imagination was first described with great precision and historical insight by St. Augustine, who saw where the pagans missed the mark and how Judeo-Christianity provided a solution to the problem dramatically embodied in the decline of Rome. Augustine criticized two aspects of pagan theology: (1) the gods were too often represented in evil and sinful attitudes which reflected corrupt human fantasies; this indicated that (2) the gods were too evidently the products of human imagination: "When the pagans made images of the gods that looked like men their idea was that the spirit of mortals which is in the human body is very like the spirit which is immortal . . . they imply that god (or the gods) is of the same nature as a rational soul." Augustine's criticism is practical as well as moral, for these two aspects, taken together, suggested to him that the failure of the pagan culture to survive resulted from the failure to honor the axiom of self-limitation. In projecting a divine order which clearly displayed the stamp of human thought and desire, the pagans failed to place the source of guidance and restraint securely above and beyond the vagaries of man's mutable will: "It was not the effigy [of Minerva] that guarded the men, but the men who guarded the effigy."

Augustine realized that it is not enough for man to disclaim any role in the making of world order; he has actually to *believe* that he is a passive vessel, acted on from the outside, filled with the presence of the Spirit. The Gospel tradition of active humility could promise more than the classical posture of heroic self-sufficiency. Armed with the Judeo-Christian doctrine of creation *ex nihilo*, Augustine saw that a solution to the pagan dilemma was built into the very tissues of the Christian faith: if man believes in a God who creates the world out of nothing and is totally responsible for it, man can attribute all schemes of order to him, can safely project this order beyond the mortal limits of human mind and will. The Christian God is a Thou, an Other who is both rational and superrational. By proclaiming the transcendent mystery of this rational Other, the Christian imagination limits the likeness between man and God. In the phrase *imago Dei*, the word *imago* connotes both difference and likeness: the difference precedes the likeness in Christian thought, for it is only by the miracle of grace and love through which God chooses to diminish his absolute otherness that human persons are created. Therefore the relation, unlike that in classical thought, is mutual. Aristotle and Plotinus may affirm, each in his own context, that man loves or should love God; Cicero may state, as he frequently does, that man needs *religio* properly to venerate a divine being; the Christian differs in believing that God speaks first, in Creation and through love, so that man's attitude is not simply a natural tendency of *nous* to expand or join forces with a similar power, not even a longing prompted by remoteness from the source. Man's attitude is a response to an Other with whom he is in direct communication. As Aquinas put it, "God is the object of faith, not only because we believe in a God, but because we believe God."

Greek thinkers tended to identify the source of order with whatever was conceived as self. Most typically, from the late fifth century on, this was *nous*, and from Plato on, cosmic *nous* was a projected version of human *nous*, the highest rational activity of *psyche*. Thus the irrational, the chaotic and hostile, the source of disorder, was inevitably located in an *other*—*moira, chaos, menos, ate, hyle*, etc. Whatever individual Greek thinkers may have believed, the main tradition of Greek thought does not reveal clarity or conviction about the objectivity of world order. Even Aristotle, having constructed his cosmos by projecting a geometer's hypothetical model onto the physical world, had no surefire way of burying the evidence, since his divinity was not a creator but something more like a disembodied human mind. Down to the end of the classical period, around the third century after Christ, the schemes which purported to describe the cosmos were projections or extensions of logical, geometrical, psychological, or political structures, but the trouble with late antique world views was that reality began to *look* man-made. When this is the case, the mind badly needs to convince itself that the picture of reality is not a mere figment of thought. There is always the danger that man will find himself once again in an essentially irrational and chaotic universe such as that which surrounded Homeric man, a universe which was only gradually rationalized during the succeeding centuries of Greek culture.

The tensions peculiar to the medieval imagination arise from the Christian way of limiting knowledge to make room for faith. "It is enough," Augustine asserts, "for the Christian to believe that the only cause of all created things, whether heavenly or earthly, whether visible or invisible, is the goodness of the Creator, the one true God; and that nothing exists but Himself that does not derive its existence from Him." The human imagination must give up any claim to creative powers: its role is that of a speculum, a glass or mirror which reflects what is already in the world. Its job is to discover, not to create; to imitate, not to invent. Yet, granted this continually avowed self-limitation, we are faced with the peculiar fact that at no time in our history did the human imagination so completely control the universe. The official or prevailing image of the world, from the time of the early Church Fathers up through the fifteenth century and after, was a completely organized and esthetically integrated system of projections—an artistic triumph rarely exceeded in history, characteristic in every way of the mind's processes, its interpretations and forms of thought. In fact, it had the qualities which Aristotle found praiseworthy in the drama: for example, spatially and temporally, its magnitude was such that the beginning and the end, the center and the circumference, were perceptible to all observers. The whole was unified by a coherent and symmetrical spatial order. Its temporal course had a true beginning, middle, and end, and it terminated in a definite issue for the characters concerned—happiness or unhappiness. The plot of history was not simply a random sequence of events, regardless of its appearance, but was fully meaningful and symbolic, the unfolding in time of God's plan or Idea. In the Bible, God was the maker of the plot, man the maker of verses. Thus all reality was artifact. And to keep it this way—to insure belief in its reality—it had continually to be credited to God. The medieval mind's faith in the rationality of God's world was only the overt side of a more obscure faith in man's architectonic power: in the exercise of the first faith, whereby man merely reflected what was *out there*, lay the justification of the concealed power whereby he was able continually to create what he supposed he reflected.

Given this paradoxical situation, it is clear that the mind must be careful about products and tendencies which explicitly proclaim its own creative function. It must be careful, for example, how it defines poetry, how it uses painting, how it approaches pagan mythology and any form of knowledge which does not bear the seal of God or his earthly representative, the Church. All attempts to create hypothetical or imaginary worlds must be tested by a single method: comparison and correspondence with God's universe and his Scriptures. The individual imagination remains as anonymous as it can. It appoints its monitors among the institutions or spiritual realities which are outside it: God, tradition, the Church. When socio-political and cultural upheavals demanded solutions, syntheses and visions which had to be hammered out by exceptional individuals, the very acts by which these individuals sustained the Christian imagination threatened its mode of existence.

To summarize, three beliefs about the world are crucial for the medieval imagination: first, an esthetic belief in the harmony and shapeliness of Creation, which was approached as a work of art, and second, a belief in the unity of the world which—since there is but one Creator—is inflected toward the idea of uniqueness: one God, one Creation, one Incarnation, one cosmos, one space-time. Augustine's trenchant assertion of this principle suggests why the medieval imagination can only be reflective, why human creation is easily construed as vanity and illusion:

> There is no principle of unity but that alone from which all unity derives . . . if there is only one Rome . . . that is a false Rome which I conjure up in my thoughts . . . I am one person, and I feel that my body is here, but in imagination I go where I like, and speak to whom I like. These imaginary things are false, and what is false cannot be known.

The third belief is that appearances, phenomena, are objective, meaningful, symbolic, and real. "To save the phenomena" is a program which means more to a Christian theologian than to the Greek philosophers and astronomers who formulated it. It is through the appearances that God manifests his effects and causes. This means that the locus of reality is in the external and given order, not in the order corrected by the human mind. Belief in the reliability of perception is probably the most important prerequisite for a cosmic order founded on such an I-Thou relation, because it guarantees a state of accurate receptivity.

III

The character of perception is such that it locates us in one environment, a single continuous, if finite, field of space to which there are really no perceptual alternatives. We can imagine different kinds of places, or more of the same, or life on other planets, but we cannot easily imagine a different *kind* of physical or perceptual experience, nor can we easily think of ourselves in a special space absolutely discontinuous and closed, with no precise physical relation to the actual space around us. It is easier to "perceive" an immaterial spirit somehow existing "in" material space than it is to think of ourselves as superimposed on a two-dimensional plane, or as moving ambiguously in two places at one moment, or as being related to other environments as a character in a novel is to the world of the author and his readers. Actual space is unambiguous and unique, and when a system of thought is so projected outward that it is felt to be part of that spatial actuality, there can be only one true universe. There may be different theories, but they will all reflect the same cosmos.

The problem which Renaissance thinkers discovered was that perception was badly misunderstood in classical and medieval epistemology. When Aristotle looked up into the sky, for example, he assumed that he saw the spherical heavens moving around him. This confusion between appearance and interpretation, observation and inference, survived for centuries and made it difficult for men to realize the extent to which they projected what they thought they received. It made it possible for perception to deliver phenomena, interpretations, and realities in a single package. Moving out from eye and self to the distant bound of the concave world, the whole universe was organized and systematized according to what was felt to be given in sense experience. This experience was completed and stabilized by geometrical theory, but elements of theory were often "perceived" as elements of phenomena.

The shift from medieval to Renaissance imagination may be detailed by a number of epitomes: from the mind as speculum to the mind as stage; from *imago Dei* to Vitruvian Man; from the criterion of dogmatic certainty based on authority and communal tradition to the criterion of probability based on hypothesis, experiment, internal and individual experience; from the emphasis on correspondence to the emphasis on coherence; from a metaphysics in which substance and essence have both logical and temporal priority over function and operation to a metaphysics in which they emerge as symbolic forms which are consequent on thought; from temporal process as the unfolding of a spatially conceived eternity and Form to visual images as the forms of temporal process and force; from attention to exemplary causes in the mind of God to attention to hypothetical causes in the mind of a particular scientific or philosophical investigator. Koyré's transition, from the closed world to the infinite universe, is but one side of a more basic shift, from the universe as an external and perceptual cosmos to the universe as an intellectual system. All these are examples of a single basic alteration which affected the way men tended to evaluate the three phenomenological categories. Where the medieval imagination would rank realities above appearances and appearances above interpretations, the Renaissance imagination ranks interpretations above appearances and usually, but not always, below realities.

In 1615, the year before Shakespeare's death, Galileo had occasion to defend the Copernican theory, and his defense fixes with great accuracy on the really new element in the Renaissance imagination: Copernicus knew, he remarks,

> the power over our ideas that is exerted by custom and by our . . . way of conceiving things since infancy. Hence, in order not to increase for us the confusion and difficulty of abstraction, after he had first demonstrated that the motions which appear to us to belong to the sun or to the heavens are really not there but in the earth, he went on calling them motions of the sun and of the heavens.

Galileo sees that what is significant is not that the content of the world picture has changed but that the new content, the true picture, no longer agrees with the evidence of the senses. To arrive at the true picture it was necessary to deny the appearances and to accredit an interpretation made by the mind. Awareness that the senses are untrustworthy puts us on a totally new footing, for we become more conscious of the mind's constructive power, we assert *that* the mind is an agent in creative collaboration with God, and we come to see this collaboration not only as a privilege but also as a responsibility.

What differentiates the Renaissance from the medieval imagination, what determines the specific qualities of Renaissance intellectual and imaginative style, what leads to peculiarly Renaissance strategies of self-limitation is this awareness that the mind need not consider itself passive to dogma, tradition, and perception; it may actively choose, and reveal itself as actively choosing, the elements of its environment. When Descartes said, as he often did, that a good God would not deceive us, he intended not to question the motives or character of the traditional God but to remind us that since our senses were faulty, God must want us to organize the appearances by a stronger effort of interpretation. Things are not known, he said, "from the fact that they are seen or touched, but only because they are understood." Thus what is called reality is what issues forth as the product of internal experience, controlled thought, scientific method, poetic creation.

As early as 1440, Nicholas of Cusa wrote that "no image will so faithfully or precisely produce the original as to rule out the possibility of an infinite number of more faithful and precise images," thus prophetically outlining the course of subsequent intellectual history. When the real is no longer accepted as the truth embodied in appearances, abstracted and reflected by thought, then the world of appearances must be left behind, reimagined, reconstituted in accordance with the mind's ideal. A major theme of Renaissance literature centers on the techniques of controlled and experimental withdrawal into an artificial world—a "second nature" created by the mind—where the elements of actuality are selectively admitted, simplified, and explored.

The method of withdrawal is directly related to another shared interest: the attention of artists, poets, scientists, philosophers, and mystics to the methods and techniques, the *how*, of their various disciplines. They pursued problems of theory and technique not simply under the aspect of craftsmanship but under the aspect of intellectual method. Withdrawal often consisted in turning away from life to art, playing with the conditions of the medium for their own sake, using the particular medium or discipline as a model with which to explore life, returning to actuality to apply the results of exploration. This new concern for the *how* of method has obvious connections with the stylistic emphasis on the introspective *now* of artistic, poetic, philosophic, or scientific experience. During the later Renaissance, the hypothetical *now* of image, lyric, plot, discourse, dialectic, and experiment is often oddly and closely interrelated with the actual *now* of the imaginative processes of production, performance, observation, interpretation.

The complex forces of a period imagination appear in such divergent tendencies as the humanist preference for images and the iconoclasm of many Reformation thinkers. The images of itself which the Renaissance imagination has left reveal that it was capable of considering the process whereby meaning was translated into image, Ideas into visual/verbal/material form, as experimental and creative. The image may not only express but also complicate and alter the idea it is intended to represent. The Aristotelian and Plotinian metaphor of the architect who merely copies or embodies a pre-existing Idea in matter became less and less applicable. Many Renaissance artists, architects, and poets display in their careers a development from a phase in which models are studied, measured, and scrupulously copied through a phase of variation and free, generalized expression of traditional motifs to a phase in which the models are left behind as obsolete or are drastically altered in form and content by the pressure of new vision. This development is no doubt natural and universal, but Renaissance artists were especially concerned with it and articulate about it. Furthermore, because of the peculiar relation of the Renaissance to classical culture, many aspects of Renaissance activity manifest this development as a cultural phenomenon. One aspect, for example, which Panofsky has traced in his *Idea* (Leipzig, 1924), is the changing status of the Idea from an objective and transcendent to a subjective and transcendental entity. Parallel to this was a changing attitude toward the meaning and function of the *model*, which was first conceived primarily as a normative exemplar, later as a convention, blueprint, or starting point which the creative process transforms into a richer and more personal expression of experience. In all these cases a concept of *image* is at work which differs sharply from that assumed by the medieval imagination. The medieval image, both as percept and as symbol, points beyond itself in an asymmetrical way toward a more real and significant referent. The Renaissance image reveals that the center of gravity has shifted to the here-now of its perceptual character; the asymmetrical pointing is present but diminished, since the meaning is to be sought by careful analysis of the form; the perceptual form is often expected to embody the psychic energy interposed between conception and creation.

The so-called iconoclasm of Calvin is based on similar assumptions. Calvin conceives of religious experience primarily in dynamic temporal terms. God and the Holy Spirit are envisaged as force rather than form, energy rather than stable substance. The divine energy of He Who Is About To Come draws us *toward* God and demands that we keep ourselves open to the future. Among the defects of icons, their spatial and static nature—they "merely exhibit bodily shapes and figures"—is a major cause of the distortion which freezes the mind within a present tense confined to the actuality of nature. A preferred style of imagery as well as a theory of genres is implicit in Calvin's, as in any other, set of epistemological beliefs: the baroque symbols of cloud, smoke, and fire are superior to more definite and linear images; representations of historical events are superior to representations of figures; the Baptism and Lord's Supper, "those living symbols which the Lord has consecrated by his own word" and which demand immediate, dramatic, personal participation, are best of all; finally, since Scripture is the chief interpreter of the Creator's presence in Creation, verbal images have priority over visual images, a speaking narrative allows for a more active and intimate dialogic relation than a speaking picture.

Calvin's concern over inadequate and deceptive images springs directly from the gap between symbols and realities, stressed with growing intensity in his cultural environment. What had been prescribed by centuries of hermeneutic interpretation as *the* authorized way of imaging the Other was now being rejected as anthropomorphic: the Papist or medieval imagination reduced the Other to "some figment like itself, with which it . . . vainly solaces itself as a representation of God." To secure the transcendence and otherness of God one must now stylistically affirm the difference between consciousness and Being. The rejection of the traditional iconography, which was primarily visual, seems connected to the more fundamental rejection, or decline, of the classical epistemology: there, the Other could be apprehended *as Other* through perceptual categories whose primarily visual or spatial implications reflected a view of God as unchanging substantial form. Here, any spatio-visual representation must proclaim its self-limiting difference: for a secular Renaissance imagination, this difference will consist chiefly in displaying artifice, which signifies the work of the human mind preserving in its own forms the wisdom it has received; for a religious Reformation sensibility, this difference resides in the inadequacy of the symbol to image a God whose essence is felt to conform more closely to the dynamic categories of what Kant called the internal sense. The active pressure, the motion, of an energy continually working on and modulating the soul is best envisaged under the aspect of temporal process. Time is viewed rather as a private and psycho-spiritual medium than as the public and historical medium through which the divine plan unfolds.

The cosmological assumptions apparent in the *Institutes* seem closer to a disjunctive Cartesian dualism than to a medieval hierarchy. Calvin admits no ladderlike gradations, no system of intermediaries, no support for faith *from* the medieval tradition or *in* the medieval cosmos, both of which interpose themselves from the outside between self and its experience of God. He returns rather to the early Gospel emphasis on testimony and witness, but he does so in moving away from the world view toward which Gospel thought tended and in which it was systematically unfolded. In Gospel thought the gap between man and God was felt as the primary condition which had to be "covered" by immediate testimony. In Calvin, one sees rather a systematic elaboration of the gap *for the sake of* affirming the need of inner testimony—i.e., the *Institutes* do not really ask, "Under what conditions can man and God, nature and grace, best be reconciled?" but, "Under what conditions can the criterion of subjective experience, the primacy and certainty of the here-now of illumination, best be justified?" And in this, as one scholar has recently shown (R. H. Popkin, *The History of Scepticism from Erasmus to Descartes*), the Calvinist reformation in theology anticipates the Cartesian reformation in philosophy.

IV

This sampling of the historical aspects of cultural ecology may have seemed more like old-fashioned description of the *Zeitgeist* than it really is. This is partly because the most important and extensive work, concrete interpretation, is far beyond the scope of an introductory sketch. It is therefore worth repeating that in addition to being more pragmatic, the method here illustrated (1) does not pretend to induce a general picture *from* the historical facts, (2) does not demand any dialectical necessity from cultural change beyond that of irreversibility, and (3) does not attempt to explain (away) the novelties of period style and imagination by typological classification. On the other hand, one of the virtues of this method is that it can critically use and unify the work of scholars in various fields, can suggest why so many similar conclusions have been reached independently in recent scientific, philosophical, literary, historiographical, and art-historical inquiries into the periods under consideration. The principle in which both primary and secondary sources of evidence are unified may be recalled by stating once again the leading ecological question: "What does the mind conceive the relation to be between itself and its environment, at any given time or period, in any given work?" From this I have tried to develop a speculative model rather than a method for describing historical background.

The consciousness, the heuristic situation, involved in model making and model using is closely bound up with the shift from medieval to Renaissance forms of imagination, and model making is one of the basic strategies of self-limitation. A model, as I am using the term, is neither an exemplar nor a copy; that the word has confusing relations to both concepts indicates its tensional and ambiguous character. A model is a hypothetical construct, image, world, etc., which may be interesting and informative in its own right but which also serves as a guide to something beyond it. If we treated a model either as an exemplar or as a dead image, then we should feel too sure of its referent—if the model is an exemplar, the mind has absolute control over the referent; if the model is a copy, the mind transparently imitates or reflects the referent. Where the referent is some aspect of the real as unknown or unknowable, the dangers are obvious. A model is best used when it is made to signify its own built-in limitations. The medieval imagination was, at best, interested in concealing the extent to which its world consisted of models projected from the mind and ascribed to God. The Renaissance imagination proclaimed with increasing clarity that God wanted man to make models, that the tentative and experimental creation of models and second worlds was the chief role of interpretation, the surest discovery procedure. One way to thrown off the onus of certainty, custom, atrophied tradition was to turn away and make a model, adopting a wait-and-see attitude. In this respect, Descartes's use of his models exemplifies an important peculiarity in the Renaissance attitude, one which placed the problem of self-limitation squarely before the men of his time.

In the fifth section of his *Discours* Descartes tells us that to philosophize without being burdened by traditional terms, concepts, and controversies he resolved to make a new start by creating as a second world his own hypothetical model of the universe: "I resolved . . . to speak only of what would happen in a new world if God now created, somewhere in an imaginary space, matter sufficient wherewith to form it, and if He agitated in diverse ways, and without any order, the diverse portions of this matter, so that there resulted a chaos as confused as the poets ever feigned, and concluded His work by merely lending His concurrence to Nature in the usual way, leaving her to act in accordance with the laws which He had established." And in the closing paragraphs of the same work he asserts that what he once called mere hypotheses have come to assume, through the coherence of his reasoning, the validity and certainty of systematic causal explanations. We know that this imaginary world resolved and composed within the controlled now of Descartes's thinking self ultimately issued forth as the reality whose creation Descartes assigned to God. God was not a final consequence of the Cartesian system but a rhetorical necessity required to reestablish the *otherness* of the world Descartes constituted. To the probability produced by the model's internal coherence Descartes wished to affix the certainty induced by the appeal to theological criteria of correspondence and divine creation.

The historical failure of this attempt is well known. The conception of God and of the "Wholly Other" had come to be identified with the dogmatic medieval world model and image of divinity. Though this identification was by no means necessary, the Wholly Other was to stand and fall with one particular version of the Wholly Other. It became increasingly difficult to accept this version as a datum, therefore increasingly necessary to seek new modes of conviction, proof, and certainty, new ways of limiting the self. The new modes were defined in terms of individual experience and experiment, internal quest and inquiry. A reality whose assigned form is felt to be consequent on controlled inner experience easily reveals its dependence on the antecedent activity of consciousness whereby the form was constituted. From this arises the problem, not posed for medieval thought, of explicitly affirming the otherness of reality to consciousness. Two familiar seventeenth-century embodiments of this problem are found in the flamboyant baroque and the neoclassic styles: The former localizes the self's experience of the other in the *now* of a transitory but life-changing Moment of Truth and in the *here* of intense, even exaggerated, psychological response. The neoclassic sensibility emphasizes the importance of following rules, which are created and projected, then obeyed, by the mind. Hence such well-known aspects of both styles as attention to Unities and genres, classification of the passions (*affetti*), and the structural importance of elements which echo, sustain, or diffuse the effects of the Moment—elements like landscape (Poussin) or the dénouement, the long vista which springs or uncoils from the richly compressed moment.

The attention to rules, the stylistic emphasis on rule following, indicates a failure to discover more truly objective restraints. The primary datum of experience is stated with increasing candor to be the self—genius, mind, sensibility, tabula rasa, Reason, a priori categories, the instrumentality of Consciousness. The problem becomes all the more urgently to create an Other, to find it, to prove its necessity or simply to get rid of it as a problem. Blake was especially sensitive to the situation, and two sentences from Harold Bloom's reading of romantic poetry (*The Visionary Company*) will place Blake's enlightened and romantic insights in sharp causal juxtaposition: (1) "Blake wishes to take away from our vision of divinity everything that would make God a 'wholly other.'" (2) "The most sublime act, Blake says, is to set another before you." Blake sees clearly that the Creator, the Other, is not as such the consequence or cause of any world system but is added as a subsequent limit and bound to validate what man has made. God is thus Nobodaddy. Since it is a man who makes his world, man should accept this fact, should openly recognize both the responsibility and the freedom which accompanies it. To sign one's name on the canvas, to take the blame, to assume the great burden of making up and then following one's own rules, to make and destroy models, to change the world every time one changes oneself, to follow the consequences of one's own creative energy as if it were an imposed fate—all this, which constitutes the Blakean annunciation, emerges as a statement of what was implicit in the developing thought and style of the preceding centuries. Blake belongs to the Enlightenment in providing a language, a level of rational discourse, which the Renaissance imagination lacked to describe what the Renaissance imagination was doing. What were intricate maneuvers and gestures in Renaissance style become the surface propositions of eighteenth-century style. But this change, as Hegel and the romantics realized, unleashes a whole new set of problems and is accompanied by new gestures. Blake's romantic insight is that all confrontation must be willed by the self; otherwise there can be no others. Selfhood is self-absorptive narcissism until its energy supplies its own limit.

Blake's thought, like that of Nietzsche and Yeats after him, centers on what might be called an ecological awareness produced in effect by the development I have just been tracing. The essence of this awareness is that self carries the world on its back as a turtle carries its shell, but that self and shell, unlike turtle, continually and mutually change as they inch through time. The great spokesmen for any period imagination always assume the mantle by proclaiming that what the previous period understood as other was really a projection of self. The Prolific requires the Devourer as self needs other. In their own way and for their own time they commit past shells to ritual fire, both asserting and enacting the phoenix life of imagination as it springs the real from the firetraps of its own past interpretations. Homer, as Yeats reminds us, "had not sung"

> Had he not found it certain beyond dreams
> That out of life's own self-delight had sprung
> The abounding glittering jet; though now it seems
> As if some marvellous empty sea-shell flung
> Out of the obscure dark of the rich streams,
> And not a fountain, were the symbol which
> Shadows the inherited glory of the rich.

And in a later, more synoptic and dynamic, utterance:

> Civilization is hooped together, brought
> Under a rule, under the semblance of peace
> By manifold illusion; but man's life is thought,
> And he, despite his terror, cannot cease
> Ravening through century after century,
> Ravening, raging, and uprooting that he may come
> Into the desolation of reality:
> Egypt and Greece, good-bye, and good-bye, Rome!
> Hermits upon Mount Meru or Everest,
> Caverned in night under the drifted snow,
> Or where that snow and winter's dreadful blast
> Beat down upon their naked bodies, know
> That day brings round the night, that before dawn
> His glory and his monuments are gone.

Naive Consciousness and Culture Change: An Essay in Historical Structuralism

IN A RECENT issue of *Clio* I outlined the rudiments of a general theory of culture change, a theory which might be able to provide an integrative but noncoercive setting for modes of interpretation in a variety of disciplines.[1] The thematic center of the theory is the ecological interaction between *homo faber* and his environment—that is, the conscious and nonconscious productive processes by which man makes his history and by which he continually re-creates himself and the world in which he finds himself. I tried in that essay to convert the theme into a set of working definitions and axioms and from that set to derive a hypothetical model in which processes of culture change were arranged in a probable sequence. One of the obvious requirements of such a theory is that it distinguish cultural from biological, or historical from evolutionary, considerations and try at least to interrelate the areas of consideration so distinguished. My purpose in the present essay is to meet this requirement by suggesting how a sequential model of culture change may be generated from, and related to, a hypothesis about the character and prejudices of human perception. Before beginning, however, I should offer a brief structural description of the general theory.

The thematic center cited above seems innocuous enough if it refers

---

[1] "Outline of a General Theory of Culture Change," *Clio* 2 (1972): 49–63.

only to man as *a* creator *in* his environment and not to man as *the* creator *of* his environment: when we call the world real, more than mere fantasy, we generally mean it has been and continues to be shaped by extra-human as well as human forces. One of the significant gradients of history, in contemporary opinion, is the changing proportion of the creative mix: what we call reality appears to us to have been increasingly affected by human forces, and especially by consciously directed productive processes. This opinion must be differentiated from the recognition that postmedieval society has increasingly *proclaimed* the role played by human forces in the constitution of reality. But the two propositions are functionally interdependent, and they suggest some lines of inquiry that articulate what men do with how they perceive what they do. For example, you might explore the interplay—at any given time or for a given period of time—between the following two relations: (1) between man's conscious and nonconscious productive processes and (2) between what appears to man to have been produced by himself and what appears to him to be given, that is, created by nonhuman or transhuman forces. You are then likely to discover a considerable overlap between (1) and (2) because historically much of what has appeared to men to be transcendent in origin has in fact been a human product nonconsciously created by man.

At this point, and on the basis of this example, let me introduce the basic terms of the theory. When I speak of "a human product nonconsciously created by man," I refer to such culturally imposed structures as kinship, cosmos, the natural order, divisions of time, and social organization and to such cognitively or perceptually imposed structures as space, time, objects, and the various categories and relations in which they are ordered. I group all the nonconscious processes by which such structures are generated under the term *transposition*. *Transposition* may be defined as the nonconscious transfer of structures from man to world so that they appear to be transcendent elements in and of the world. *Transcendence* in this context refers to whatever appears to man to owe its origins and being to nonhuman sources. *Transposition* and *transcendence* are two of the three basic terms that carry the weight of the two relations mentioned in the previous paragraph. The third term, *technology*, embraces the sum total of consciously directed productive processes, or *techniques*. Extending the term beyond its normal range, I use *technology* to refer to all arts and skills of mind or hand—crafts, philosophy, music, law, commerce, war, sciences, art, etc.—and all activities aimed at affecting economic, social, and political conditions. Technology and transposition are thus the complementary modes of human creation, while transposition and transcendence have a historically defined affinity since so many structures which in traditional societies were perceived as transcendent have subsequently been redefined as products of transposition. To return to our two relations, we may now substitute the three basic terms: (1) is the relation between technology and transposition, (2) is the relation between technology and transcendence, and the link between (1) and (2) is the relation between transcendence and transposition.

Having defined these terms, I begin with the postulate that technology and transposition are complementary modes of adaptation in man's struggle for existence, and on this basis go on to generate a dynamic model from the changing interplay of the three terms.[2] For example, when technology is in its rudimentary stages, transposition is necessarily the dominant adaptive mode by which early man transforms his environment to be able to cope with it more adequately. By transposition he restructures "brute nature," metamorphosing its blank features to a source of recognition and communication and thus establishing the form and context of reality—social, cosmic, divine—within which traditional techniques receive their particular characters and functions. As human techniques develop, the burden of adaptation gradually shifts from transposition to technology, with two significant and interrelated consequences: (1) the evidence of technical human mastery becomes more conspicuous, encouraging further technological effort and, always in conjunction with that, criticism of technology as ultimately hubristic and futile; (2) the transpositions generated in earlier technical adaptations and ascribed to transcendent forces are jeopardized by skeptical critiques—charges of archaism, anthropomorphism, and projection necessitate defenses and revisions of traditional "reality."[3] Without going into further detail, I shall simply note that one of the aims served by this dynamic model is the articulation of a set of hypothetical structures which I call forms of cultural and period consciousness. I have discussed some of these in earlier studies,[4] and the formulation of the general model allows me to trace the historical careers of these structures as manifestations of the changing interplay of basic terms.

Consciousness is currently an overworked and badly abused word, but

[2] For a somewhat more detailed (though still cursory) sketch of this interplay, see "Outline of a General Theory," *Clio,* 56–61.

[3] Cf. the four axioms of culture change, "Outline of a General Theory," *Clio,* 61.

[4] See the following essays in this volume: "The Renaissance Imagination: Second World and Green World," 3–40; "The Ecology of the Mind: The Concept of Period Imagination—An Outline Sketch," 41–62. See also "Ecology of the Medieval Imagination: An Introductory Overview," *Centennial Review* 12 (1968): 279–313.

like *instinct* it can, if carefully employed, provide some useful heuristic services. I don't propose at this juncture to define it except in a vaguely ostensive manner by indicating three contexts in which it is conventionally viewed. First, consciousness may be studied in the individual. You can explore the consciousnesses of actual persons, and you can also construct hypothetical models of individual consciousness to help in that exploration. Second, consciousness may be studied as a cultural configuration imposed on individuals, as the prevailing set of internalized values, norms, assumptions, prejudices, customs, etc., and—among other things—attitudes toward transcendence, technology, and transposition. Third, consciousness may be studied at the level of the species: as members of *homo sapiens* we all share a single basic perceptual apparatus determined by the neurophysiological makeup of the human organism. Presumably we shall continue to do so as long as the species endures in its current form. I shall refer to this as *naive consciousness*.

Any actual individual consciousness is partly conditioned and shaped by the structures of cultural and naive consciousness, since culture and species are defining aspects of the individual. For purposes of interpretation, cultural consciousness and naive consciousness may be abstracted from the context of the actual individual and considered in relation to each other. The remainder of this essay will be devoted to this task. In the following section I shall summarize some familiar facts about perception, the basis of naive consciousness, to identify those preferences and biases which have a bearing on various cultural configurations of the three basic terms. After that I shall describe two basic structures of cultural consciousness and suggest how their historical relations are influenced by the structure of naive consciousness. In my *Clio* essay I referred to these cultural forms as *traditional* and *modern*, for the sake of simplicity. As the following discussion will show, these terms are misleading and inadequate, and will be replaced by what I hope are more accurate descriptive terms.

The Prejudices of Naive Consciousness

I take as my point of departure Husserl's classic description of the *natural standpoint*, or *natural attitude:*

> I find continually present and standing over against me the one spatio-temporal fact-world to which I myself belong, as do all other men found in it and related in the same way to it. This "fact-world," as the world already tells us, I find to be *out there*, and also *take it just as it gives itself to me as something*

that exists out there. All doubting and rejecting of the data of the natural world leaves standing the *general thesis of the natural standpoint.* "The" world is as a fact-world always there; at the most it is at odd points "other" than I supposed . . . but the "it" remains . . . a world that has its being out there.[5]

Phenomenology has illuminated the more or less systematic character of the natural attitude by taking its stand outside the frame of reference of that consciousness and conceiving it not merely as an attitude but as a *standpoint,* a *thesis*—a coherently organized set of tendencies and prejudices whose structural order may be made explicit by description. This order is nevertheless rooted in the neurophysiological structure of the body via our perceptual systems, and because it is an order which frames all our experience and awareness, I shall henceforth refer to it as naive consciousness.

The reliance on perception should not merely be noted and then ignored. We should view it as the first and most basic prejudice of naive consciousness: *it commits itself to perception.* (It might have been otherwise; human perception and consciousness are products of natural selection.) Merleau-Ponty speaks of the primacy of perception and identifies as its most significant effect *perspectivism:* both in space and in time the incarnated perceiving consciousness is *positional*—restricted to a certain point of view—and therefore its experience is perspectival. Consciousness is aware, or may easily be made aware, that it is limited by its bodily standpoint to only a partial view of its objects, that there is always more than is seen in any perception, always other points of view from which to apprehend the object. The object is thus experienced as transcending the perceiver, whose perceptual experience includes at least latent awareness of the object's independent otherness:

> The "things" in naive experience are evident as perspectival *beings:* it is essential to them . . . to reveal themselves only gradually and never completely . . . I grasp *in* a perspectival appearance, which I know is only one of its possible aspects, the thing which transcends it. A transcendence which is nevertheless open to my knowledge. . . .[6]

Perspectivism and its consequences may also be illuminated by reference to perceptual evolution. James Gibson has observed that many fishes

---

[5] *Ideas,* trans. W. R. Boyce Gibson (1931; New York: Collier, 1962), 96.

[6] Maurice Merleau-Ponty, *The Structure of Behavior,* trans. A. L. Fisher (1963; Boston: Beacon Press, 1967), 187.

and animals possess something like panoramic eyes and therefore have no need of the exploratory eye movements involved in scanning because they have "no especially acute foveal areas in the retinas and no centers of clear vision to correspond. They see equally well in all directions, and they do not have to 'look' in order to see." But since certain directions may have more importance than others, depending on the creature's way of life, "evenly dispersed panoramic vision in all directions is . . . wasteful, and some animals adapted to this fact by concentrating the resources of each eye, that is, by a tendency toward foveation." For example, primates developed accurate depth perception (through binocular vision), especially for nearby objects. Frontal foveal development "must be accompanied by the development of the ability to *look*—that is, to explore . . . by scanning."[7]

Because man has a fovea, a concentrated center of clear vision on the retina, he can register detail with considerable precision and discrimination. Because his eyes are directionally oriented, he can comprehend the ambient world only by successive fixations in time. Because more precise detail is available to him, the awareness of scanning per se is likely to be more conspicuous—he may have to select or inhibit, and at any rate, he has actively to guide his looking. Greater reliance on active and controlled detection would seem to be accompanied by greater differentiation and intensity of proprioceptive awareness. Our experience of scanning in time, for example, is separated from our experience of the stable and enduring world. This separation ultimately leads to reciprocal enhancement of the differences between subjective and objective poles of experience and, at a more "philosophical" level, between self and other.

Man differs from other animals whose visual systems have evolved in this direction because his proprioceptive awareness is at once more intense and more differentiated. If in certain respects he does not see as much or as well as other animals, he is aware of the limitation and consequently aware, so to speak, of what he is *not* seeing. This perspectival awareness is reinforced by the different senses that not only cooperate in enhancing perception but also cooperate in telling tales on each other—in making each other's limitations available to general awareness: sight tells us what touch fails to perceive, taste and smell tell us what sight fails to perceive, etc. Thus the senses inform us simultaneously about their own limitations and the transcendence of their objects.

In committing itself to perception, naive consciousness therefore com-

[7] *The Senses Considered as Perceptual Systems* (Boston: Houghton Mifflin, 1966), 170, 175.

mits itself to transcendence. By this I mean that it prefers to experience the structure and order of the perceived world as given to it rather than as constructed by it. Since we tend to accept perceptual experience as accurate most of the time, we normally feel ourselves to be in direct sensory contact with a real world of space-time, objects, persons, and events and with the sights, sounds, smells, tastes, and touches they give off. And since we experience very little of the mechanical operations of perception additional to perceiving itself, we take it for granted that perceiving is a passive activity. Our commitment to what we feel is a passive and accurate process of receiving information from "out there" in the world encourages us to take for granted the reality and transcendence of the external sources of information. In this sense the commitment of naive consciousness to perception reveals a preference for a transcendent world and a preference for having one's experience of that world automatically determined from outside. This provides something like a sense of security in our relation to the world: perception is something we don't have to be anxious about; it comes naturally and easily; it is automatic and inborn—*naive*.

When we are told by phenomenologists, psychologists, and others that all this is at best only partly true, then we are pushed to the same conclusion even more forcefully: naive consciousness reveals a *bias* toward belief in the automatic passivity and accuracy of perception, toward belief in the transcendence of the perceived world, toward belief that the forms and structures of that world determine the way we perceive them. These beliefs do not square with the facts revealed by sophisticated students of perception (including poets). Perception is much more active, selective, and constructive than it appears to normal consciousness. Perception not only receives data but also transposes them, and perceptual or cognitive transposition is basic to all other forms of transposition. A bias against recognizing this seems to have been built into naive consciousness during the evolutionary development of perception to its present form. We might have been made to perceive otherwise and to experience perception differently.

Naive consciousness commits itself to a perceptual system which in turn prefers to rely heavily on the distance senses, sight and hearing (especially the hearing of speech), for its most important information. This extends its grasp not only of space but also of time. Seeing a star, for example, *contemporizes* two *now*'s, or moments of present actuality—the star's and the observer's—eons apart in time. We have to remember what we were taught in order to frame that percept in the awareness that the farther away a light source is, the longer ago it was. Visual perception is always perception of the past, however minute the time lag is, yet the percept itself abstracts from the reference to time and nullifies the temporal divergence between the two moments. "Sight is *par excellence* the sense of the simultaneous or coordinated, and thereby of the extensive."[8] In his primeval orientation toward the heavens man had, without knowing it, altered the global structure of space-time.[9] Though it would take millennia to bring that knowledge to light, the solar-stellar orientation itself greatly extended man's control over the local and diurnal organization of experience (as is the case with the polarization of light in bees). And because beyond a certain distance our seeing diminishes in precision as it gains in comprehensiveness, the possibility existed from the start that man would articulate and domesticate the distance through transposition.

Though the perception of stars is an extreme example, the same abstractive character of vision is manifest in other ways and dominates man's engagement with the world. Vision abstracts from physical process—the temporally ordered transmission-of-energy events that underlie seeing—and is thus a relatively quiescent form of experience. As in scanning, vision also abstracts from the temporal sequence of sensations, allowing the identity of the scene or object to be preserved through the succession of changing fixations. In these ways sight differs from hearing, which is more like touch in including physical and mechanical events as components of the percept. Our auditory system is made to feel the pressure of sound waves as vibrations at the tympanic membrane, whereas vision screens out the perception of light waves, which travel at much higher frequencies. Thus hearing, unlike sight, has a dynamic vector character; sound is experienced as coming-from-out-there-toward-us.[10]

---

[8] Hans Jonas, *The Phenomenon of Life* (1966; New York: Harper & Row, 1968), 136.

[9] Cf. Erwin W. Straus, "The Upright Posture," in *Essays in Phenomenology*, ed. Maurice Natanson (The Hague: Nijhoff, 1966), 164–92.

[10] Hearing is a mechanical event which seem to have evolved from the basic orienting system—the primitive *statocyst* (a sac filled with fluid; ciliary, or hairlike, receptors; and lime or sand granules serving as a weight—a *statolith*—which may be displaced relative to the sac) which functions in certain invertebrates as the organ of balance and equilibrium. The human statocyst is the inner ear, and like it the outer ear "responds to being shaken, although the shaking is only the minute vibrations of the air." The inner ear "picks up forces of acceleration" and cooperates with touch in registering "the direction of gravity," while the input to the auditory system "specifies the nature of vibratory events in the world" and their direction (Gibson, *Senses*, 53). This imposes a physical limit on the distances of auditory sources and situates us in a directional field of spatial forces which are both gravitational and sonic. Transcendence as a criterion of *provenance*—reality as that which moves from there to here—is perceptually embodied in the pressures and vectors of auditory experience.

But to the extent that our perceptual field is dominated by the influences of visual structuring, it gives priority to space over time.

Primarily through the overlapping distribution of automatically imposed stimuli over the basic orienting system (the statocyst), the haptic system, and occasionally the auditory system, external reality communicates its pressure, its insistence and resistance.[11] But vision is different, and Hans Jonas describes three characteristics which give it a peculiar form of objectivity and make it more abstract: "(1) *simultaneity* in the presentation of a manifold, (2) *neutralization* of the causality of sense-affection, (3) *distance* in the spatial and mental senses." The first is exemplified by scanning and the second by the absence of radiant vibration from the visual percept: "Effacement of causality means disengagement from it. . . . From the onrush and impact of reality, out of the insistent clamor of its proximity, the distance of appearance is won," and *effect* is replaced by *image*. Distance involves abstraction in the sense of detachment or disengagement, and not merely at the conscious level proposed by Jonas: "We consciously stand back and create distance in order to look at the world, i.e., at objects as part of the world."[12] But the possibility of distance is preconsciously inherent in the amplitude of the perceptual field made available by radiant energy, and this possibility is actualized through transposition in "a world," a structured cosmos whose primary sources of stimulation occupy its outermost reaches. At varying depths in the concavity of that world, things *appear* with what Whitehead called "presentational immediacy"; the appearance as such contains no reference to causal relations either among objects or between itself and the perceiver, and in itself it tells us very little about the "intrinsic characters" of the things perceived—that is, about their intentions, forms of activity, histories, possible effects on us, and so forth. If there is no pure appearance—no "presentational immediacy"—in the sense just described, it is because we transpose intrinsic characters and thus, through psycho-cultural conditioning, perceive them as transcendent.[13] This pro-

---

[11] Though the interaction between touch and sight is complex, and influential on both, the experiences of "objectivity" provided by touch and sight are opposed in nature: touch gives proximate and pressure-laden experiences of objects, and its information is transmitted through tactile sensations, while vision gives distant and pressure-free experiences of objects, and visual sensations play little or no role in transmitting visual information. When we perceive through sensations, as in touch, subject and object are intermingled in a more intimate manner. But when the object is abstracted from subjective sensations, as in vision, the object is more easily distinguishable from the subject and thus more "impersonal."

[12] Jonas, *The Phenomenon of Life*, 136, 131, 150.

[13] Cf. A. N. Whitehead, *Symbolism: Its Meaning and Effect* (Cambridge: Cambridge University Press, 1928).

cess is concealed and therefore supported by the abstractive detachment of vision which, in its self-awareness, contributes to the perspectival character of "objectivity":

> *Eidos*, "appearance," is an object of sense, but not its whole object. In perception external objects are apprehended not merely as "such," but also as "there." . . . Perception is intrinsically awareness of such self-giving presences—the experience of the reality of the object as co-existing with me here and now and on its own determining my sensory condition. . . .
>
>   But there is this paradox to sense perception: the felt affectiveness of its data . . . must in part be canceled out again in order to permit the apprehension of its "objectivity." . . . Some sort of disengagement from the causality of the encounter provides the neutral freedom for letting the "other" appear for itself.[14]

The peculiar characteristics of visually dominated perception—distance, abstraction, objectivity, extensive organization of space-time, causal neutrality—make it an ideal vehicle through which to transpose into the world the structures of meaning and causality without which we could not have the orientation presupposed by elective and effective action. It is fashionable nowadays to speak of the brain as a quasi-computer. But it seems just as helpful to think of *the world* as a computer programmed by nonconscious operators working in perceptual and cultural fields of activity. We feed information into the world and receive messages from it. Our aim is to reduce uncertainty and "noise" by setting up a restrictive code of symbols designated according to some previous tacit understanding. Through perceptual transposition we apprehend reality as a significant world which communicates messages that we can read and understand. And in the earlier phases of human experience, long before the computer analogy was available, man transposed message senders, or a Sender, so that he could engage in genuine two-way communication with his computer.

The terms of this analogy remind us not to overestimate the contributions of sight to perceptual experience, for only in certain respects may it be called the king or queen of the senses. It shares this dominance with the auditory system because of language, and though language may be a second-order phenomenon owing to its conventional or symbolic character, there are two familiar reasons for taking seriously the possibility that its role in perception may be more direct and primitive: (1) it demands and presupposes extremely refined acoustic precision within a narrow

[14] Jonas, *The Phenomenon of Life*, 167–68.

range, and therefore (2) it must have influenced the character of hearing and its functions vis-à-vis the other senses during the millennia in which language developed into rudimentary systems for organizing information. Hearing and vision may be considered dialectical foci of human perception, a view set forth by Walter Ong in *The Presence of the Word* (1967) and other studies. The following brief paragraph is based on a selective distillation of Ong's views.

Where sight perceives *surfaces* of objects, hearing and sound offer clues to *interiors*—physical as well as psychological interiors. Sound communicates interiors revealing themselves; sound is a function of the resonance produced *inside* the things that resonate. Sound as the spoken word moves from one human "interior" to another and opens them to each other without physical violation or intrusion. Human encounter is achieved largely through voice. The combination of vision, hearing, and the spoken word produces a greater awareness both of *objective others* and of *subjective others* in the world. This too intensifies our sense that something within others is held in reserve, that we don't make it all out, that there are puzzles in what we see and hear. It makes us want to find out more, to seek security in the belief that we are perceiving what is in fact the case.

This underlying urge for security seems connected to the theory that certain functional preferences for socialization may be genetically programmed into perceptual attention: babies display an apparent preference for facelike objects, which may indicate a tendency to look toward particular forms as cues to the sources of security and pleasure. We seem quite early in life to divide *others* into those like us and those unlike us. From time immemorial, man has divided the world into *persons or presences* and *objects;* into those who speak, hear, and understand his language and those who don't. We seem intuitively to gravitate toward the former; we fasten on selflike others as most important to our welfare. Naive consciousness tends toward collective life, seeks the solidarity of shared awarenesses, and reaches through perception and communication toward community. It prefers a world of facelike personlike motherlike fatherlike womblike objects, places, and spaces. And because of our early helplessness, it prefers to commit its future to them, to allow itself passively to be determined from the outside by others.

The urge for security and control is manifested in other abstractive preferences of naive consciousness. It may be that the three-tense structure of time governs all life and existence, but it is peculiarly explicit and important for man. Our past and future are clearly demarcated parts of the present. We act directly and indirectly out of habit or because of memory, foresight, and expectation. We thus widen and deepen the present tense of existence; past and future permeate our consciousness in the present tense, enabling us to abstract ourselves from the immediate present and to control our consciousness of time, keeping us from being trapped in a sequence of vanishing-pointlike instants, a narrow one-way tunnel to death. By coordinating the tenses, by storing past and future experience in images, we can *spatialize* our awareness of time. In this respect our three-dimensional experience of time has a *countertemporal* character.

This tendency also informs the preference of naive consciousness for repetitive experience. We learn by imitating, remembering, repeating, and generalizing. The educative value of these processes leads naive consciousness to commit itself to a present tense dominated by the past, and dominated by others—those others who were there when each of us was born, and who were initially our models, protectors, and punishers. Any culture can either encourage or inhibit this conservative preference built into naive consciousness.

The movement from repetition to generalization is a movement from many similar individual experiences to the single class of which they are all instances, and this is another abstractive process: abstraction from a world of sheer individual, eccentric, unduplicated, and unrepeatable experiences or events, from a world of chaotic flux with which we could not cope. Naive consciousness tends to escape from this possibility of chaos by generalizing and typifying experience—that is, by organizing its data into classes, sets, and categories.[15] It further consolidates its experience by committing itself to perceive *physical objects* rather than dynamic patterns of energy or scattered sense events (the chaotic flux of sense data and sensations). These preferences for repetition, typification, and objectivity disclose a tendency to simplify, organize, and order experience so as to make it more manageable. Repetition and typification also interlock with another preference of naive consciousness: its gravitation toward collective life.

The need to transpose meaning and simplify experience seems to be

[15] Aristotle long ago discussed typification under the aspect of the universal, the mental correlate of the class nature or substantial form embodied in the individual members of any class or species. In the *Posterior Analytics* he remarks that "though the act of sense-perception is of the particular, its content is universal—is man, for example, not the man Callias" (100a17). Recent accounts of typification have replaced the objectivist by a phenomenological standpoint, but they approach the process in essentially the same way, as an originary process shaping perception and not an abstraction from prior experience. Cf. Maurice Natanson, "The Phenomenology of Alfred Schutz," *Inquiry* 9 (1966): 150ff.

connected with the sensitivity of our perceptual apparatus. Human sense receptors pick up a rich input of patterned energy from the environment—radiant, mechanical, and chemical patterns in great varieties—and recent experimental work in perceptual psychology suggests that there is something like "stimulation overload."[16] There appear to be distinct limitations on the ability of perceptual systems to handle, process, and interpret the data available to them—to turn stimulus energy into information. Every increase in the range and reach of discriminative receptivity entails an increase in the need to simplify and organize the rich input so as to realize its informational value. Between the initial reception of any stimulus and the final percept, a great deal of unconscious filtering, classifying, and reorganizing goes on, the aim of which is to enhance clarity and accuracy and to reduce ambiguity.

Both as a patterned system—a grammar—and as a system of signs, language influences the unconscious processing of perceptual input. It helps simplify and recode an input which might otherwise be a source of confusion and uncertainty. But language is double-edged: in its potential complexity and richness it is the source of new confusions. Vision and hearing, because they are highly developed and specialized senses, are also potential sources of confusion. The vividness yet muteness of visual objects and the indefinite "etcetera" of the visual field stretching away from the eye—these invite more strenuous efforts to improve object recognition. The richness of the auditory field, enhanced by myriad voices of men, forces the perceiver continually to impute meanings to their patterned murmurs and motives to their ingathered presences. Such ever-present sources of uncertainty lead to more drastic strategies of clarification. Confronted with both possibilities—chaos and order—naive consciousness inclines toward order and clarity, not only because they reduce anxiety but also because they seem gratifying in themselves.

In all these ways, then, perception is not only a passive receiver but also an active transposer. Yet, as I noted earlier, naive consciousness prefers not to notice the margin of transposition. It ignores the contributions of the brain and central nervous system to the structure of sense data. It takes no account of the fact that our perceiving is significantly modified by neurophysiological processes. It overlooks the cognitive influence of intelligence—logical, linguistic, mathematical, and symbolic structures—on the form of our perceptions. It attributes the forms of

---

[16] See George A. Miller, "The Magical Number Seven, Plus or Minus Two," in *Readings in the Psychology of Cognition*, ed. R. C. Anderson and D. C. Ausubel (New York: Holt, Rinehart & Winston, 1965), 241–67.

perceiving to the structure of the transcendent world and objects which are perceived. It commits itself, once more, to the primacy of the world outside the self, to others, to external influence. This relieves it of uncertainty, of the need to make up its own mind and make its own interpretations, of the need to take its destiny in its hands and be responsible for its own survival. It gravitates toward an external collectivity—a culture—which will satisfy these needs. Thus it gravitates toward *culture*, as embodied in the social world in which it first finds itself.

All the characteristics I have described in the preceding pages suggest to me that naive consciousness is the product of adaptive development *toward* a particular, coherently organized set of tendencies and capacities. This means that we may conjecture another set of possibilities which it avoids or denies. The emphasis here is on *conjecture*, for I take my cue from some speculations by Freud which are explicitly mythical, or should be seen as such. Consider, for example, the following two evolutionary events: (1) the evolution of perception toward a system dominated by the special features of sight, hearing, and language and (2) the evolution of a hominid toward *homo sapiens*, a creature who not only lives and dies but also has a conception of life and death; who not only lives in the world but is what he is because, in Wilfrid Sellars's words, "he has a conception of himself as man-in-the-world." These two events have one pattern in common: a shift of the center of gravity from "behind" or "beneath" consciousness to "within" and "beyond" consciousness.

Freud has focused on this tendency of man to *externalize*—to widen and deepen the objective space perceived by consciousness and to find his orders and solutions there. He posits a view of development based on differentiation of a secondary outer-directed ego from the primary inner-directed id. And he speculates that this differentiation is partly a response to external pressure but partly also an escape from internal pressure. Hence it is both a facing outward toward "nature" and a defensive flight toward "culture." Behind this flight is the specter of a psyche with only an id, driven only by death instincts and the pleasure principle, largely cut off from the external world, dominated by kinesthetic and tactile affect, unable to distinguish clearly between objects and states of feeling, fixed in its singular existence, less cognizant of space than of time—or rather of the duration measured by its affective oscillations. In this creature, even the instincts of self-preservation, should they exist, would serve the death instincts by helping "to assure that the organism should follow its own path to death, and to ward off any possible ways of returning to inorganic existence other than those which are immanent in the organism itself," for this creature—following the pleasure principle which is a function of the death instincts—strives to regain the inorganic state, unconscious and therefore pain-free, from which it originally arose, and "wishes to die only in its own fashion."[17]

In the Freudian myth, this truncated psyche is what perception "fears," as the ego fears the id. All the biases built into the structure of naive consciousness are biases against mortality, finitude, and death, and against an experience of time as mere disappearing flux, an entropic tide carrying us swiftly and helplessly to the appointed end. There is a bias against the prison of inwardness or pure subjectivity, against a consciousness held captive within the body, blind to the world and slave to its own sensations and feelings. There is a bias against a state of perpetual anxiety caused by dim and vague experiences of what moves, presses, or threatens the self from beyond it. There is a bias against a life which can command only two forms of behavior, advance and retreat, and two forms of response, attraction and repulsion. The preferences of perception seem to deny or avoid this mythical idlike existence as if it existed within or beneath consciousness, as if it was perception's constant shadow, the nightmare from which it is always struggling to awaken. To be the slave of destructive time, pure inwardness, and absolute singularity; to be blindly driven by fatal forces always close as touch yet never known: from this nightmare, perception and naive consciousness embody in their evolved structure a perpetual escape toward space, toward the sun, toward others, toward a changeless or repeatable present, toward community, toward a secure, familiar, comprehensible, smiling, cradling, mothering, fathering world. Therefore naive consciousness reduces its fundamental anxiety at the cost of uniqueness and freedom, and it does so by committing itself to culture which is—like any antidote to anxiety—not merely an *order*, but an *overorder*.

The Ontogenetic Hypothesis

What would be required of a culture which would help naive consciousness fulfill its desires and avoid its anxiety? It would have to assert the primacy of the past over the present; of space over time; of patterns of recurrence over the meaningless and fortuitous flux of history; of the collective over the individual; of selflike presences over hostile, threatening, nameless forces; of gods over men. It would have to rely heavily on transposition, denying creative responsibility, so that the world order

---

[17] *Beyond the Pleasure Principle*, trans. James Strachey (New York: Liveright, 1950), 51.

it constructs would appear to it as transcendent rather than constructed. In defending against anxiety (and also, in exercising a tendency toward creative play) naive consciousness would demand of its culture two characteristics:

The first characteristic is the ability to produce *overorder,* to make the universe into an absolutely comprehensible and poemlike unity, make it intellectually satisfying—even logical, mathematical, and geometrical in its perfection of form. What *we* think of as the peculiar characteristics of man-made structures in art or science, this culture would display as the marks of transcendent reality. What for us are the conscious achievements of human intelligence, this culture would present as the work of the gods. The same human intelligence is at play in both their world and ours, but in the former its creative activity is primarily nonconscious: it conditions the character of perception and passes directly into the world. Second, the less man is aware of such creative activities, the more he is controlled by them and passive to them, and the more he feels determined by the structures he has transposed. The second characteristic demanded by naive consciousness of its culture is the ability to implant a sense of passivity and determinism in its members. Since naive culture has to do the work done by "instinct" in other species, since it has to replace the genetic programming built into individual organisms in other species but not in man, it must close down very tightly on its members.

The culture of naive consciousness would have to apply the criteria of overorder and determinism to whatever forms of social organization it might develop. Human institutions would have to appear given and inevitable, natural and unalterable. Every man would have to be assigned his appropriate status and role in the social system so as to feel that it was his by nature, part of his being, the essence that identifies him and gives him his place in the world. In sociological jargon, all roles, statuses, and functions should be *ascribed* rather than *achieved,* by encouraging belief in the *embeddedness* of society in the real ("natural" or "divine") order and by cloaking political, social, and economic relations in the forms and idioms of kinship. The architecture of kinship, one of the most elemental cultural transpositions, satisfies a number of requirements. It gives the appearance of transcendence; it is, in its formal elegance and logical symmetry, a model of overorder; it is adaptable to a variety of ecological situations; it features the conservatism of relationships dominated by parents and elders, by ancestors and spirits of the dead, by the gods and the natural universe to which blood relationship (real or fictive) belongs. Through kinship the social ego may be welded to the individual as his inmost being and may be saturated with all the values, beliefs, customs, behavior patterns, and techniques of the culture: the whole of the culturally transposed world may bear in on the ego/self and cling to it. Thus culture may come to have the force and inevitability of the instinctual, the natural, and the sacred.

Since the socio-political order of naive culture should not appear either created or alterable by man, it must not be presented as the product of intelligence, intellectual systematizing, or philosophical conceptualizing, or of social contracts and constitutional conventions. Men should learn that it is divinely and naturally instituted—conferred by divinity and rooted in the biological order of family, blood, and generation. Social institutions, as they change or develop, should be presented as imitating and fulfilling a preordained pattern, a principle of order existing before and outside the society in the sacred origins of nature. Such beliefs may be reinforced by a familiar form of transposition and over-order: extending the society's particular model of organization to the world and the gods, so that they appear organized in families, lineages, tribes, states, and other socio-political hierarchies. Note the reversal produced by transposition: the copy and the original change places; the transposed copy becomes the transcendent paradigm from which the human society derived its patterns.

A culture such as I have just described is logically constructed to realize the partly adaptive and partly escapist preferences of naive consciousness.[18] It is the hypothetical ideal toward which naive consciousness, as I have depicted it, would aspire. It is therefore logically and ideally the first position in any putative cultural sequence. For this reason it may as well be called *primitive culture*. As a hypothetical model it has many characteristics ordinarily associated with the great variety of actual cultures which anthropologists subsume under the term *primitive* or *tribal*.

---

[18] And also to reinforce its dogmatism. Infallible authority and certainty "are psychologically much stronger in their appeal than any other criteria of belief, for all others suggest caution, some degree of doubt, and some insecurity. An ultimate appeal to authority takes all responsibility off the mind of the knower and affords him a feeling of protection. . . . It is worth noting that all, or practically all, the knowledge of primitive societies is based on authority either in the form of mythology or of practical skills passed along as cultural tradition. The strength of tradition, and the feeling of security which it assumes, could hardly be immediately supplanted by anything so delicately balanced and apparently so flimsy as a hypothesis or a probability estimate" (Stephen Pepper, *World Hypotheses* [1942; Berkeley: University of California Press, 1961], 17–18). The last two sections of this chapter, beginning on p. 87, discuss the transition to culture dominated by hypothetical thinking.

Though I clearly had some of these in mind—I might otherwise have deduced an entirely different set which could equally well have met the requirements—my point is that *they can be deduced as if they were logical consequences of the structure of naive consciousness.* They can also be derived from my hypothesis about the early configuration of the three basic terms—that is, the set of the characteristics that define a culture as primitive most completely and explicitly displays the interwoven primacy of transposition and transcendence as the basis of adaptation.

But this is only the beginning. How do we get from there to here, from primitive to modern? Is it simply by the more or less mechanical or pseudodeductive process of working the transformations on the basic terms, superimposing the derived sequence on selected historico-cultural cavalcades, and exclaiming at the results? Can any appeal be made beyond the primitive terms and axioms of the theory, either to some empirical basis or to some different theoretical matrix? If naive consciousness is by definition unchanging (and thus conservative) throughout the epoch of Man on earth, and if cultural consciousness is defined by the general theory as constantly changing, how can these two models be mediated? I see two possible sources of enlightenment here, and two related formal patterns which the sources can yield. The sources are (1) individual consciousness or some model of it and (2) the dynamic structure of naive consciousness, whose equilibratory stability seems polarized between its preferred self-image and its unperceived processes. The formal patterns are (1) developmental and (2) dialectical, the former generated from the study of models of individual consciousness, the latter from the polarity of naive consciousness. In this section and the next, I shall explore the developmental pattern, and in the final section of the chapter, the dialectical pattern. Behind this procedure is the assumption that only some such complementary yoking of disparate perspectives can do justice to the complex phenomena which the theory aspires to illuminate.

In establishing a link between naive and cultural consciousness, I should note that my account of the former was elaborated with reference to the species and was therefore concerned with a static description of structure. But in any hypothetical model of *individual* consciousness, naive consciousness is subject to processes of development, and—though we can never be precise or certain about this—it would appear that the crucial early phases of development are, in their general structural outlines, generic to the species. I mean no more by this statement than E. H. Lenneberg means when he observes that all language systems, however diverse, display three common features which may be posited as biologically (rather than culturally) determined possibilities and preferences: phonology, concatenation, and grammaticality.[19] The distinction is between biologically determined structuring tendencies and the particular structures elaborated in cultural contexts.

The developmental model I choose to employ is Piaget's, mainly because it is in many respects isomorphic with the transposition-to-technology pattern which I have been exploring. The basic concept binding the two is the relation of abstraction to developed consciousness. *Abstraction* is used here in an active sense, that is, *abstractiveness. Ab-* + *trahere* bears connotations not only of activity but of deliberate activity. To abstract is to abstract *from* something else; something else had to be there before you began abstracting. And in Piaget's perspective, abstraction is not only an act of consciousness, a special focusing of attention, but also a *bringing into consciousness.* What was *there* before the bringing into consciousness? Something there in the world but not *here* in consciousness. Yet not merely and only there in the world but placed there by transposition and therefore *here* "beneath" consciousness as well. Abstractiveness, which is already an originary tendency of naive consciousness (see the remarks on visual perception above), is the basis for all consciously guided processes of thought and action from which issue the products of human technology.[20]

Piaget teaches that the earliest activities of behavior and perception are vitally affected by formal—that is, form-producing—processes of intelligence.[21] These processes are essentially logical and mathematical: intelligence not only distinguishes objects from each other, numbers them, serializes them, and combines them in classes or sets but also constructs the objects themselves, as well as the system of space, time, and matter in which objects are perceived. But unlike logic and mathematics, these primary processes of intelligence are not the objects and instruments of

---

[19] "Language, Evolution, and Purposive Behavior," in *Culture in History: Essays in Honor of Paul Radin,* ed. Stanley Diamond (New York: Columbia University Press, 1960), 875–83.

[20] The whole of Jonas's discussion of relations among perception, vision, abstraction, and human freedom is illuminating (*The Phenomenon of Life,* 135–82).

[21] This account of Piaget's theory will of course be grossly oversimplified, centering only on those themes relevant to the present discussion. In certain respects, the oversimplification has advantages, because it allows me to avoid special problems raised by Piaget's approach and experimental method and because it identifies a general developmental thesis about which there is some consensus among psychologists. I would have preferred to use the developmental concepts and terms of L. S. Vygotsky as expressed in *Thought and Language,* but it is a skeletal and too restrictively cognitive presentation: not enough of Vygotsky's work is yet available either in published or translated form. For Piaget's ideas I have drawn chiefly on *The Psychology of Intelligence, The Origins of Intelligence in Children,* and selected essays (see next note).

conscious thought; through transposition, their structures travel unnoticed from the psyche to find lodgings in the world. With the help of parents, naive consciousness assures children that the results of these transpositions are transcendent and real.

At a certain phase in his growth, the child develops, and begins to master, such *concepts* as time, space, number, and causality. These concepts are conscious, but still bound to sensory experiences, to concrete acts and situations, and therefore Piaget calls the processes that produce them *concrete operations* of intelligence. Children who perform them "are usually incapable of them when they cease to manipulate objects and are invited to reason with simple verbal propositions." These operations are constantly tied to particular actions and emerge as reactions to or reflections of them. Hence they are not yet fully abstract: concrete thinking is imitative and reactive, rooted in perceptual experience of the world, confined within the categories and images of naive consciousness. Though formal intelligence has not yet become fully aware of itself, its constructive processes shape the world which conditions concrete behavior and thought.

Thought becomes abstract when it breaks free from this concrete dependency, becomes self-conscious and liberated—abstracted—from the limits imposed by perception. Piaget's term for this level of thinking is *formal operations*, but since I want to distinguish more clearly between conscious and nonconscious formal processes, I shall substitute the term *abstract thought*.

> What . . . are the conditions for the construction of abstract thought? The child must not only apply operations to objects—in other words, mentally execute possible actions on them—he must also "reflect" these operations in the absence of objects. . . . This "reflection" is thought raised to the second power. Concrete thinking is the representation of a possible action, and abstract thinking is the representation of a representation of possible action. . . . Abstract operations . . . are applied to hypotheses or propositions . . . and provide thinking with an entirely new ability that detaches and liberates thinking from concrete reality and permits it to build its own reflections and theories.[22]

Withdrawing from concrete actuality into its own domain, abstract thought is not restricted to logical, analytical, and mathematical activity; it is more generally *hypothetical* in that it concerns itself with alternatives

---

[22] *Six Psychological Studies*, trans. Anita Tenzer, ed. David Elkind (New York: Vintage, 1968), 63.

to the actual world in the realms of possibility. Abstract thinking embraces the exploration of the possible; not only in the experimental "If . . . then" of science and philosophy, but also in the fictional "If" and "As-if" of art. At its highest levels, abstract thinking frees itself from the concrete particularity of perception and from the prejudices of naive consciousness by moving toward systems of greater generality which contain the world given in perception as only one among a number of possible systems; and on this basis it may turn back to restructure, reimagine, or re-cognize concrete experience in new and different worlds in art as well as in science, mathematics, and philosophy.

Development, as Piaget traces it, is thus a process of continuous abstraction in which self-conscious intelligence is drawn out of its hiding places in naive consciousness and the world, a process in which the objects of abstract thought are disengaged from the concrete conditions of space, time, and the external world. Piaget remarks that intelligence is initially "entangled in a network of relations between the organism and the environment" and does not at first "appear as a power of reflection." Abstraction proceeds by differentiation: the activity of intelligence "progresses simultaneously in the conquest of things and reflection on itself," and it may ultimately become the most immediate factor of conscious life: "Physiological and anatomical organization gradually appears to consciousness as being external to it and intelligent activity is revealed for that reason as being the very essence" of the self's existence.

To discuss abstraction in the context of developmental psychology is to discuss it out of the context of history. But this brief outline generates some painfully obvious inferences which will lead us back toward the relation of naive consciousness to the sequential model of cultural consciousness. The first two inferences are virtually tautological. Since abstraction by definition presupposes something prior *from which* one abstracts, it must follow its antecedent chronologically as well as logically. And since abstract thought frees itself from concrete experience and transcends the influence of perception, it must be *counterperceptual*—just as abstract systems of quantum physics and relativity physics are counterperceptual. The most advanced stages of conscious formal intelligence radically challenge the biases of naive consciousness. Finally, abstraction, especially in its advanced stages, demands effort, discipline, and skill. For these reasons abstract thought so refined as to be historically significant is bound to be an improbable phenomenon, a rare and late cultural manifestation, achieved by relatively few members of most societies, and dominating very few societies in history.

I have simplified Piaget's model to restrict attention only to the two levels of formal intelligence—concrete and abstract thought—which will be applicable to a developmental view of culture change. On this basis, we may posit the following analogy between individual and cultural development: individual and cultural forms of consciousness both begin their careers under the aegis of naive consciousness, and both develop along similar lines through a concrete toward an abstract phase. To distinguish the two contexts let me arbitrarily assign names to the cultural versions of concrete and abstract thought, calling the former *empirical* and the latter *hypothetical*; the reasons for using these terms will be given in the next section. Following Piaget's developmental logic, we can describe empirical cultures as those which are more firmly rooted in naive consciousness and which represent structured extensions of its prejudices. Their world views, institutional orders, and technologies may be expected to reveal the characteristics of concrete behavior and thought. Advanced abstract thought, always centered in the minds of individual men, is likely to be a threat to the collective unity and security, the traditional authority and continuity, which the culture preserves in order to maintain itself. On the other hand, hypothetical cultures may be described as those which reveal the dominance of advanced abstract thought in the structure of world views, institutions, and technologies. These cultures (a) must be assumed to have encouraged abstract thought by allowing greater freedom to, and by placing higher value on, individual self-assertion and development. We may also assume that (b) their institutional structures and technologies will be reciprocally affected by that development: (a) and (b) are functionally interdependent. The cultural extensions of naive consciousness and its prejudices will be challenged; continual pressure will be exerted on the norms that encourage the individual to adopt a relatively passive stance toward the linked authorities of perception and tradition.

But this way of translating Piaget's developmental phases into cultural attitudes can't be right: if concrete = empirical and abstract = hypothetical, then I am saying that a culture, like a person, moves from infancy to maturity and that in its earlier phases it is childlike in being determined by the processes of concrete thought and behavior. This transfer of concepts from the individual to the collective structure, and from "nature" to culture, produces the ontogenetic fallacy: that we can study development in culture as if it were a large-scale version of development in the individual, and that this study is justified on the principle that "ontogeny recapitulates phylogeny," or in this case that "phylogeny recapitulates ontogeny." Many so-called primitive and archaic societies have been called childlike because the surviving evidence suggests that they were dominated by intuitive and concrete behavior, and this assumption sometimes crops up in its debased form: not only the cultures of such societies but all their members must be victims of arrested development.

This error can be avoided by taking Piaget's model into account in a negative manner, that is, by asserting its inapplicability. We have to begin by assuming that the individual members of any society have completed each his own personal progress through Piaget's stages of development and that there is no reason a priori why we shouldn't find either highly developed individuals or highly developed cultures at all times in history. Concrete behavior is not freely adopted but deterministically shaped—chiefly by psychophysical mechanisms and processes—during a relatively early phase in the progress of formal intelligence from its unconscious to its fully conscious states. But *empirical* refers to a culturally imposed attitude which presupposes full development in the individual and may involve conscious control of cognitive techniques characteristic of abstract thought. The empirical attitude is a general way of looking at things, that is, a world view. Thus we must assume *two* forms and levels of abstract thought, empirical and hypothetical. The former bears structural resemblances to concrete thought and behavior in the relations between transposition and the forms of conscious thought and technology which characterize the attitude. But the individual's reactions to this particular set of relations may vary from the most rudimentary to the most sophisticated, and from unthinking acceptance to ideological assertion.[23] Abstracted from the tissues of cultural forms and considered by itself, the empirical attitude is a philosophically respectable mode of conscious thought and behavior influenced but not inexorably determined by the same structural conditions that confine concrete thought and behavior in a more rigorous fashion.

Piaget's model is both structural and chronological: it consists of a sequence of overlapping but analytically separable structures, each of which has its own generalized and definable character, for example, sensory-motor, intuitive, concrete, and abstract structures of behavior and thought. It also consists of rough age sequences to which the structures

---

[23] It may be useful to set forth the following presuppositions to forestall misunderstanding: I assume that at any time in history and in any culture there will be both kinds of thinkers, empirical and hypothetical (and in any individual, both kinds of thought, depending on the contexts or objects of thought); that cultures may discourage or encourage advanced abstract thought by the structure of their institutions; and that in some cultures advanced abstract thinking may be institutionally inhibited yet developed and expressed by rare individuals. In *Saving The Appearances* (London: Faber & Faber, 1957), Owen Barfield has described two similar levels of abstraction as alpha-thinking and beta-thinking.

are correlated. Piaget treats these correlations flexibly, but more important, he assumes that the two sequences may be uncoupled so that the structural sequence can be examined apart from actual chronological sequence. The significant factors of growth lie less in the younger-older relations of actual childhood than in the before-after relations that lead one structure to be transformed into the next. This suggests how we can convert the ontogenetic fallacy to an ontogenetic hypothesis: we do not posit a two-term analogy between a child and a culture but rather an isomorphism between two models—child and culture—mapping out a structure of relations common to both. The common structural features center on the degree to which formal operations of intelligence are consciously or unconsciously exercised, the degree to which they are embedded in or abstracted from concrete experience—that is, the degree to which thought and technology are conditioned by the cooperating influences of perceptual and cultural transpositions.

For example, the sequential structures grouped together under the label *childhood* are characterized by the primacy of transposition and therefore by the transcendence of the structures of order that shape the child's world. Unaware of the extent to which he has contributed to that order, the child experiences it as real, accepting it with certainty and conviction. Similarly, the members of a society may be culturally encouraged to accept the reality of their world with "childlike" certainty and conviction. In both cases, the prejudices of naive consciousness are reinforced by the agents of authority and legitimized as the conditions of life. Experience is dominated by norms which bear the authority of the past and of some legislative source transcending the human agents. The authority of the norms is taken for granted even if the human agents of authority may be challenged. Since the influence of transposition dominates, technology will be governed by the empirical attitude (see below). But as technology develops and takes over creative functions of formal intelligence initially exercised through transposition, the emergence of the hypothetical attitude as a significant cultural force becomes more probable. And as the institutions of culture begin to encourage the development of advanced abstract thought, they gradually come to receive its imprint.

Yet anyone looking back through recorded history must be struck by the extreme rarity of that development. For we find in cultures of the most varied sorts a widespread tendency to inhibit or discourage the hypothetical attitude so that although it may be developed and expressed by individuals, it does not gear functionally into the institutional order. The most significant processes of classifying, organizing, systematizing, etc., tend either to be carried on primarily through transposition or to be carried on as technical efforts to imitate, reflect, and analyze those structures given through transposition. Thus genuine alternatives to the existing order are not easily envisaged. Because of this, and because of the inherent difficulty of advanced abstract thought, a culture dominated by the hypothetical attitude is an improbable phenomenon.

The basic cultural sequence elaborated here may seem to have no foundations in experience and to be generated entirely in the fairly arbitrary set of definitions and hypotheses which constitute the general theory. The ontogenetic hypothesis, however, provides a partial remedy by suggesting a ground in the relation between individual development and cultural change. Following Piaget, I have distinguished empirical from hypothetical structures as embodiments of two degrees of abstraction, the first clearly more subordinate and responsive to concrete experience, the second more removed from it. Piaget's model allows us to posit as a constant of human experience the priority in time of transpositional to technical influences, of concrete to abstract behavior and thought, and of empirical to hypothetical degrees of abstraction. This sequencing in the individual seems generically determined. In cultural sequence it is not. Yet something similar seems to happen, since in cultures, as in individuals, the functional dominance of hypothetical abstraction is a late and improbable event. The ontogenetic hypothesis, then, asserts that since this sequence is always the case for individuals, we can expect it to influence the pattern of cultural change and thus can expect the empirical attitude to precede the hypothetical in time as the dominant cultural factor.

The Empirical and Hypothetical Attitudes: A Developmental Perspective

In the *Clio* essay I sketched an epitome of the general model of culture change as a shift from *traditional* to *modern* attitudes, noting that those terms meant little beyond their reference to one attitude preceding and generating the other. I can now replace *traditional* by *empirical* and *modern* by *hypothetical*. *Empirical* is already laden with connotations which have little to do with the way I want to use the word, but I have decided to risk employing it here because its earlier history yields precise indications of the attitude I wish to describe. The term derives from a Greek word for *experience*, and there is also an archaic sixteenth-century English word, *empiric*, which refers to a quack doctor who depends on observation and experience to the exclusion of science and theory. Leibniz criticized men who, he said, behave like animals insofar as the sequence of their perceptions and actions is determined only by what they have observed and remembered; in this they resembled the empirical physicians who practice without any theory. And, he goes on to say, we are all empiricists in three-fourths of our actions. Leibniz is critical because he was a hypothetical thinker in an age when the empirical attitude was being defined in historical perspective and challenged. But stripped of their pejorative tone, his remarks pinpoint the meaning I want to emphasize: a mode of thought, a general attitude, a form of cultural consciousness which is empirical begins and ends with the world as experienced in naive consciousness. Unlike quack doctors, empirical thinkers may be exceptionally scientific and theoretical; but even their science and theory is ultimately determined by the concrete structure of what they have transposed, observed, and remembered.

The word *hypothetical* suggests in general that something is a mind-made construct, a product or process of conscious deliberation. But the term has various shades of meaning. It may be viewed at one extreme as *counterfactual*—unquestionably fictional, imaginary, or make-believe, as when we dismiss someone by saying, "That's a hypothetical question," that is, not worth asking because it refers to a state of affairs that couldn't possibly exist. It may mean *conjectural, uncertain*, with the implication that doubts outweigh assurances: "That's pretty hypothetical; what's your evidence?" It may mean *conditional*—experimental, provisional, tentative—with the implication that it is open to future determination and may be positively resolved: "Teachers operate on the hypothesis that the student may be stirred into useful mental activity by having his opinions challenged." And it may mean *inferred*, posited, laid down as a premise, supposed or presumed from other actual evidence (or, in deductive thinking, from other premises) to be really the case. "My hypothesis is that when the sun goes down it will be dark"; "If all men are mortal, and Socrates is a man, then Socrates is mortal." The first example implies that it is not yet the case but that it almost certainly will be the case; the second, that if you adopt *these* premises, *that* one must certainly follow. Yet even these inferential hypotheses imply a conditionality. These premises need not be adopted, and in fact there are alternatives to a logic based on a transitivity which verges on tautology. Furthermore, the *if-then* reminds us to take into account the "conditionality" of relevant conditions. In the first of the two inferential examples, the phrase "My hypothesis is that . . ." effectively pushes the conditionality of *when* toward that of *if*: "If the sun goes down it will be dark." We might conceive of alternatives in which the sun does not go down, or in which it will remain light after the sun goes down. We know too that "the sun goes down" expresses our perceptual response to the counterperceptual fact, "the earth turns round." Hobbes's statement about the conditionality of knowledge may be exaggerated by its nominalistic context, but it helps us drive the wedge between the absolute or dogmatic "tone" of the knowledge based on empirical "fact"—on observation and memory—and the tone of that based on hypothetical reasoning:

> No discourse whatsoever, can end in absolute knowledge of fact, past, or to come. For, as for the knowledge of fact, it is originally, sense; and ever after, memory. And for the knowledge of consequence, . . . it is not absolute, but conditional. No man can know by discourse, that this, or that, is, has been, or will be; which is to know absolutely: but only, that if this be, that is; if this has been, that has been; if this shall be, that shall be: which is to know conditionally.[24]

To exemplify how these two modes—empirical and hypothetical—may be transferred from the ontogenetic to the cultural model, I shall describe two familiar forms of abstraction, the first of which is more responsive, the second less, to concrete experience.[25] In the first, you abstract the "essence," or basic idea, of anything to understand it better; you eliminate irrelevant or accidental aspects. Thus Aristotelian-Thomistic epistemology holds that the mind abstracts the essence of a perceived object from the concrete image presented to the senses, drawing a universal *concept* out of a particular *percept*. The theory further assumes that the concept is automatically registered, passively received and abstracted. This makes it possible to view all simple concepts as accurate copies of essences in the real world. These concepts supply the raw data for the more complex and conscious mode of abstraction that characterizes reasoning: the activity of *judgment*, in which concepts are defined, separated, and combined. The aim of judgment is to produce knowledge of the object as it truly is—that is, to return to the perceived individual with an understanding of its form and matter, its essential and accidental structures, and the relations between them.

This theory presents knowledge as a sophisticated extension of the abstraction Piaget assigns to the level of concrete thought. However creative and independent the activity of judgment is, it remains an articulated reflection of something already in the world—and the most comprehen-

---

[24] *Leviathan*, ed. Michael Oakeshott (Oxford: Blackwell, 1960), 40. See also Oakeshott's introduction, xxiii–xxiv.

[25] For a related discussion to which I am obviously indebted, see Lewis Mumford, *Technics and Civilization* (1934; New York: Harcourt, Brace, World, 1963).

sive and summary judgment is the cosmological dogma, "There is one real world." The intellect may selectively abstract a variety of perspectives on the world, or theories about it, but all are understood as parts abstracted from a prior and transcendent whole; all are contained and fulfilled in the one reality that environs the mind of man. From the formula, "Nothing is in the intellect which was not first [deposited] in the senses," another (medieval) formula logically follows: "Truth is the adequation of thought to thing": what the mind conceives is valid to the extent that it corresponds to the given structure of the world outside the mind. By this theory, the prejudices of naive consciousness are both confirmed and reinforced.[26]

The second kind of abstraction is an act of fictive construction. As opposed to the *concept*, the abstract *construct* does not mirror preexisting essences or qualities in nature. It disengages abstract objects from the empirical conditions of space, time, and the external world, redefines them in logical, imaginary, or quantitative terms, and relocates them in a purely hypothetical space or world different from the world given in experience. The aim of construct formation is to investigate, discover, or invent something which was *not* first in the senses, because it is felt either that the senses are basically unreliable—active and creative rather than passive and mimetic—or that genuine understanding can be reached only by choosing frames of reference which entail rejection (or reconstruction) of the given.

Once thought has thrown off the yoke of naive consciousness, it tends to disengage itself from the "monocosmic" environment of empirical culture and organize its life situation into a set of *heterocosms*, whose hypothetical and disjunctive character I have discussed elsewhere.[27] Such studies as *World Hypotheses*, by Stephen Pepper, are paradigms, or perhaps caricatures, of the viewpoint of hypothetical culture. Pepper reduces the variety of world theories to four basic kinds, each generated from a particular root metaphor and each developed by constructive abstraction to "the highest available degree of structural corroboration." And Pepper testifies to the skepticism with which the hypothetical atti-

---

[26] While Platonic and illuminationist epistemologies explicitly rely less on the senses and more on the activity of mind, their principles are (1) permeated by perceptual (chiefly visual) terms and metaphors and (2) expressly mimetic in their dependence on a transcendent order which provides the paradigms and, in some theories, the motive force of thought, reflection, and noetic vision. For a concise and stimulating account of medieval theories, see M. H. Carré, *Realists and Nominalists* (Oxford: Oxford University Press, 1946).

[27] See "Outline of a General Theory," *Clio*, 53–56; "Renaissance Imagination," 3–40.

tude views the transcendence or givenness of "facts" when he notes, "The better a world theory, the less we are able to tell fact from theory, or pure fact from the interpretation of fact." A good world hypothesis "is not clearly distinguishable from much of the evidence it organizes, and the more highly developed it is, the less can the distinction be made."[28] Pepper's four basic theories are heterocosmic in that they differ from one another yet are all of equal explanatory power: they cannot be resolved into a single ultimate theory which can claim to reflect reality through conceptual abstraction. Each remains explicitly a construct, and each is autonomous: "If two or more world hypotheses handle their facts with the same degree of adequacy . . . and there is no world hypothesis of greater adequacy available, then there is no appeal beyond these hypotheses and each must be held as reliable as the other" (p. 98).

As Pepper notes that the facts of a world theory are not clearly distinct from the theory, so Ernst Cassirer identifies the "objects" of the sciences with constructs. Such constructs "as those of mass and form, the atom or the ether, the magnetic or electrical potential . . . are no simple thing-concepts, no copies of particular contents given in perception." They are, on the contrary, "theoretical assumptions and constructions, which are intended to transform the merely sensible into something measurable, and thus into an 'object of physics,' that is, into an object *for* physics."[29] And as hypothetical thought extrapolates from the one world of naive consciousness a universe of physics, so also it produces worlds of biology, religion, art, society, mathematics, politics, etc.: "True unity is never to be sought in things as such, but in intellectual constructions, which we choose according to the peculiarity of the field to be measured, and which are thus in principle possessed of an unlimited variability" (p. 361). Constructive abstraction is *disjunctive* because it involves the choice and selection of a particular frame of reference, which means the exclusion of others. The awareness of disjunction and exclusion contributes to the hypothetical (nondogmatic) character of constructive thought: it knows itself as limited in scope, and it further knows that its heterocosms are subject to verification or falsification by experience.

These characteristics of hypothetical culture are not limited to the intellectual sphere. It is a commonplace of sociology that modern experience is characterized by heterocosmic organization at the institutional level. Following Weber, modern sociology correlates the increasing rationalization of experience—that is, the increasing dominance of tech-

---

[28] *World Hypotheses*, 81–82.
[29] *Substance and Function* and *Einstein's Theory of Relativity*, trans. W. C. Swabey and M. C. Swabey (1923; New York: Dover, 1953), 357.

nology—with what is called the *structural differentiation* of various orders (social, economic, political, cultural) from each other. On the other hand, the concept of "embeddedness" is used to describe the relation of these orders to each other in traditional or empirical institutional organization: thus in tribal cultures, economic institutions are embedded in religious institutions; in traditional civilizations, technologies are embedded by custom or ideology in transcendent structures. Sociologists associate the emergence of modern culture with the period during which these orders leave their common transcendent bed and separate, and if we trace this process from the late Middle Ages, we can easily correlate it with the epistemological and scientific revolutions and with the other manifestations of the radical shift from transposition to technology which marks the emergence of the modern age.

It is important at least to note this change of institutional structure—the limits of space prevent further discussion—because it points to a peculiarity of hypothetical thought which the intellectualist emphasis of my previous discussion may have obscured. Its constructiveness extends to practical existence and is in fact defined by such familiar slogans as "conquest of nature," and by organized movements of reform and revolution. It not only abstracts from the world of naive consciousness more radically than empirical consciousness; it also returns to that world more aggressively. Constructive abstraction developed, after all, in a specific historical context which entailed the critique of conceptual abstraction and the awareness that man has been more responsible for the changing shape of his environment than he had hitherto known or was willing to recognize. The hypothetical attitude involves more than a new orientation of theory; it involves a new understanding of what theory is, what practice is, and how they are related; in fact, it involves a new conception of theory-and-practice as a single, dialectical, self-transforming activity.

Archimedes was said to have remarked that if he had a lever long enough, a place far enough away to exert sufficient pressure, he could move the earth. The Archimedean point is sometimes used to refer to the withdrawal of man to a standpoint from which he may explore the whole world and see it in a new perspective. Both empirical and hypothetical thinkers withdraw in this manner. But there are two essential differences between them. (1) Empirical withdrawal may be characterized by the term *speculation*, with its connection to *specula* (observation tower) and *speculum* (mirror). It is a mode of philosophical thinking whose relation to vision suggests that what it apprehends is already actualized: its object is the transcendent world or some part of it. But the hypothetical thinker exchanges the standpoint given by naive consciousness for another standpoint which is contrary to or at least different from the biologically and ecologically determined one in terms of which we usually view the world. When the astronauts reached the moon, they did not simply externalize the Archimedean process; that ancient empirical dream could be actualized only by a very different hypothetical journey whose itinerary may have been charted when we first took seriously the difference between seeing the sun go round the earth and knowing the earth goes round the sun. (2) In his return to the given world, the empirical theorist does not dialectically engage the practical technology around him. The social and intellectual reasons for this are familiar and need not concern us here except to the extent that we note that the empirical attitude could be expected to encourage a technology whose speculative and practical branches would be largely isolated from each other. *Making*, in the empirical attitude, tends to be tectonic rather than architectonic—based on traditional recipes, transmitted techniques, rote learning, and imitation. Only when (social conditions permitting) speculators become interested in machinery and get new ideas from mechanical models and when craftsmen become interested in theory and use or construct machines for experimental purposes—only then does the empirical begin to give way to hypothetical technology. For the hypothetical thinker, the first part of the Archimedean analogy—withdrawal, or (as Herbert Butterfield has put it) "putting on a different kind of thinking cap"—is only half the story. He entertains counterperceptual and heterocosmic alternatives not merely as speculative visions but also as programs for action; theoretical and practical technology develop hand in mind.

The new divergence in hypothetical culture is not between theory and practice but between science and common sense. The world familiar to naive consciousness has been reduced in modern culture to a much smaller portion of total reality than ever before. The environment within which naive consciousness finds itself is largely an alien one, no longer dominated by the transcendent cosmos which it had created through transposition. Empirical technology is suffering the same ecological fate as the wild animals, and its recent revival has been taking place in a golden, or Californian, atmosphere of nostalgia.

The divergence between science and common sense may be viewed in its sociological dimension as a split between a "high tradition" of experts, technicians, and theoreticians and a "low tradition" of laymen, naively conscious, uneasy, and anti-intellectual. And as in ancient Rome the equestrian order gradually developed "between" the patricians and plebeians, so in modern culture a "middle tradition" of organizers, managers, and others has emerged. But when this split was first socially encouraged by the sixteenth- and seventeenth-century organization of technology in science, law, art, administration, music, war, etc., it assumed a dialectical or complementary form: theory and practice, theoreticians and practitioners, for the first time in history began to cooperate in continuous and mutually transforming interaction. Metaphysics and natural philosophy moved "down" toward practice, and in consequence, empirical practice diverged from its traditional lines of organization (crafts, arts, guilds) and moved "up" toward modern technology. Subsequently, the "low tradition" divided into workers and technicians, the former replacing guilds with unions, the latter gravitating toward professionals, managers, and intellectuals. The dialectic between theory and practice itself moved upward, to be appropriated by the significant minority as the possession of a new elite. This minority may be considerably larger, in proportion to the total populace, than earlier historical elites, but it is still relatively small. The important difference is that it operates in a different mental world. Earlier historical elites maintained and exercised their power primarily by their ability to appeal to the traditional order and to draw sanction from criteria, beliefs, ideals, etc., which reflect the prejudices of naive consciousness and its socio-political institutions. But the modern elite receives its power and legitimacy from its control of the new counterperceptual environment, the new technology, developed by the radical abstraction of postmedieval thought and culture.

This new division in society reflects the fundamental dialectic of hypothetical thought between theory and practice. If social, political, and economic change made the hypothetical attitude dominant, the change could nevertheless not have taken place unless there were individuals, like Galileo and Newton, in whom the theoretician and the practitioner were combined. And as I have suggested, the basis *and* outcome of this dialectic is the organization of experience into heterocosms, separate and alternative universes and systems. For the method of empirical, or Aristotelian, abstraction, you need only one world. For the kind of abstraction employed by Galileo and Newton, you need at least two. Those hypothetical technicians who have changed the world we live in, and who continue to control it, have done so by hitching their technology to a star: by abandoning the geocentric viewpoint and withdrawing mentally to a "distance" from which the universes of man could be moved, *unhinged*, as by the lever of Archimedes. In *The Human Condition* Hannah Arendt sees this as the touchstone of the modern. It is, she writes, as if "the worst fear and the most presumptuous hope" of man could "only come true together": "the ancient fear that our senses, our very organs for reception of reality, might betray us" and, together with that, "the Archimedean wish for a point outside the earth from which to unhinge the world." It is as if the desire of Archimedes for a lever long enough, a pressure point far enough away, "would be granted only provided that we lost reality" as we had known it when naive consciousness was king and as if man could compensate for this loss only by acquiring "supramundane powers."[30]

The Empirical and Hypothetical Attitudes: A Dialectical Perspective

I have been constructing this model with reference to one great cultural sequence, the one we generally call Western civilization, originating in the Near East and extending from Neolithic times to the present. In this sequence the pattern of transformations appears to have been most fully played through, and thus it provides a paradigm against which to articulate the patterns of other cultures. The significant aspect of the Western pattern for the present discussion is the set of historical conditions in which the hypothetical attitude assumed cultural dominance. For although I have been presenting it in developmental perspective, the conditions provided by the transition from medieval to modern culture display little of the sense of "natural growth" or unfolding we may associate with developmental concepts. The Renaissance manifestation of hypothetical consciousness emerged in problematic circumstances and assumed a radically antithetical stance: it defined itself by its opposition to its predecessor, at first finding its roots in classical antiquity but soon preferring to see itself as revising, superseding, or "overgoing" classical culture. Even if this form of consciousness would prefer a stable and orderly world, that was not what it found in those centuries. In part, hypothetical culture was generated through force of circumstances by the gradual breakdown of the empirical world view. Renaissance consciousness developed in a contentious and competitive atmosphere by manifestly asserting its counterperceptual, countertraditional, and countermedieval character.

A structural account cannot remain satisfied with a description of external historical factors. It asks whether something inherent in the structure of the hypothetical attitude produces this aggressive character. And if we are to explore this question, we have to depart from the developmental perspective and turn from the ontogenetic model to the basic

[30] *The Human Condition* (Garden City: Doubleday, 1959), 237–38.

model of naive consciousness to seek there an alternative pattern of description. In postulating a Freudian myth to "explain" the preferences of naive consciousness, I emphasized the defense against anxiety as a primary factor revealed in the structures of both naive consciousness and primitive culture. The myth attributes the source of anxiety not merely to brute environmental challenges but also to vague psychic threats that may have some evolutionary basis. In *The Phenomenon of Life,* Jonas describes the "precarious and exposed mode of living" characteristic of animal life and affecting animal consciousness: a mode which commits the animal

> to wakefulness and effort, whereas plant life can be dormant. Responding to the lure of the prey, of which perception has given notice, alertness turns into the strain of pursuit and into the gratification of fulfillment; but also knows . . . hunger, . . . fear, . . . flight. . . . The suffering intrinsic to animal existence is thus primarily not that of pain . . . but that of want and fear. . . .
> . . . In its greater exposure and the pitch of awareness that goes with it, its own possible annihilation becomes an object of dread just as its possible satisfactions become objects of desire. (105, 107)

The human development of powers of memory and anticipation that accompany the enlarging of the brain may well allow some rude generalization of experiences of hunger, fear, and flight, of danger and malice, of perceived or possible death. What Freud called life and death *instincts* are better seen as life and death *concepts* or *images*, images first internalized in the dimmer affective awareness of animal sensibility.

Yet man's naive consciousness seems to have attained to its present structure by adaptive modifications which respond to the anxieties and pressures of animal consciousness in a manner that markedly differs from the adaptations of animals. "Where man differs from animals—so far as we yet know—is that throughout as much of his evolution as is known to us he has not normally remained supine but has striven to take a positive attitude and assume a definite line of conduct" toward the more incomprehensible processes of life and death which affect his survival. "What he says and does rests on the assumption that the secret workings of nature are capable of being influenced by his actions, and commonly on the further assumption that those secret workings are due to forces which operate in virtue of wills and emotions comparable with those which prompt his own operations."[31] I quoted this passage in my *Clio* essay while discussing the functions of transposition and technology and

---

[31] A. D. Nock, *Conversion* (1933; Oxford: Oxford University Press, 1961), 1.

in a context which the above account of naive consciousness as a response to anxiety virtually ignored: the context of *homo creator*. Anxiety is insufficient as a motivational hypothesis; *creativity* must be added. If there were only anxiety, it would be difficult to explain how human culture ever left its overordered primitive Eden to embark on its historical journey.

As soon as we add creativity, however, we introduce a complication into our account of the source of anxiety. This becomes clear if we consider modern views of perception as a transposer—a selective, creative, probing activity which not only helps determine the information it receives from the environment but also uses this information to suggest and test hypotheses about the environment. Naive consciousness may be imagined to have suppressed awareness of this active and creative character because of the difficulty and uncertainty of a life in which survival depended less on "instinct" and more on conscious processes of attention, interpretation, problem solving, and decision making. This, then, is a second source of anxiety, different from that postulated in the Freudian myth.

Some combination of both sources finds its way into the existentialist notion that man's fundamental anxiety is occasioned perhaps more by himself than by the world, and that this anxiety is the dread of human freedom, the dread of the discovery that man's fate is in his own hands— the dread of the freedom which resides in the unique human power of creativity. Consciousness of such freedom would impose an intolerable and paralyzing burden on a creature technologically incapable of using that freedom and directing those creative processes. Thus naive consciousness gravitates toward transposition as its chief creative process and toward a culture which would in effect exchange freedom for the minimal security required to allow man to develop his technology. Freedom in that sense is "sacrificed" by the individual to the culture, which will preserve it in a safe place until individuals become culturally enabled to accept it. In its more critical moods, existentialism fails to appreciate the survival value of cultural innocence and the importance of a quasi-deterministic overorder, but it has helped us appreciate the radical and irrepressible creativity of man which history has dragged out into the open over the objections of naive consciousness.

Following a respectable primitive model, I shall order the Freudian and existentialist notions into a set of binary opposites in the following arbitrary manner: man has two primal needs. First is a need for order, peace, and security, for protection against the terror or confusion of life, for a familiar and predictable world, and for a life which is happily more of the same. Thus the structures of naive consciousness and primitive culture answer to this Freudian need. But the second primal impulse is contrary to the first: man positively needs anxiety and uncertainty; thrives on confusion and risk; wants trouble, tension, jeopardy, novelty, mystery; would be lost without enemies; is sometimes happiest when most miserable. Human spontaneity is eaten away by sameness; man is the animal most expert at being bored. Restless and playful, he perpetually uproots himself from the soil in which he has been planted, reaches always beyond himself toward some dim and never fully actualized differentness, some mystery or transcendence which must be sustained as well as approached. To borrow an image from the painter Albert Ryder: "Have you ever seen an inch worm crawl up a leaf or twig, and then clinging to the very end, revolve in the air, feeling for something to reach something? That's like me. I am trying to find something out there beyond the place on which I have a footing." Plato has Meno ask Socrates, "How on earth are you going to set up something you don't know as the object of your search?" The implicit Platonic response is that the problem is precisely "*to* set up something you *can't* completely know," a transcendence which sustains as a perpetual possibility man's primal need for uncertainty, risk, mystery, and creative search. Plato's term for this need is *eros* and his critique of the polis is founded on the awareness that in its proper concern for order, peace, and security, it fails to discriminate between the impulses: its institutions fear and frustrate the existentialist *eros* as well as allaying the Freudian need.[32]

These two mythic impulses, which I shall distinguish as *need* and *eros*, are contrary in their modes of assertion: *need* is essentially passive, *eros* active; *need* is a condition, *eros* a process; *need* shrinks from the future, *eros* reaches toward it. *Need* is rooted in biological existence and its rhythms are periodic and recurrent. Without *eros* it would know only two primitive reflexes, approach and avoidance, and it would be locked into the ebbs and flows of *apprehension*—the desire to take, the fear of being taken. The threat to existence—whatever form it takes—produces signals of pain which indicate impending emptiness, shrinkage of being, life losing ground to death. These signals of disturbed equilibrium work like negative feedback mechanisms: they prompt irritable responses to *restore* the past state and extend it into the future.

The responses may be positive in the sense of being cooperative: need evokes not only the activities that protect, feed, or perpetuate the organism and its kind but also the variety of attentive acts implied in the

---

[32] This conception of *eros* has nothing in common with either Freud's myth of the instincts or Marcuse's transformed and utopian libido.

terms *care* and *consideration* and associated with *philia*, or "family feeling." Grooming, education, and sex are responses to need no less than the more negative responses by which the organism strives to ease its craving or diminish its anxiety and emptiness: the acts by which the *otherness* of a threatening or alluring object is destroyed, that is, aggression or the assimilation which replenishes the self. The objects of needy consciousness have no *otherness* in the sense of meaning in and for themselves which is recognized as valuable, as something to be preserved and enhanced in its distance and differentness from the self. In the context of need, even the generating and educating of a new creature are acts intended to produce an extension of self. The latent function of cooperative acts—care and consideration—is to tighten the solidary bonds that preserve the group. Need-dominated behavior is thus conservative in the basic sense of that term. It tends to restore an earlier condition, revive an earlier satisfaction, or produce more of the same. Its decisions about the future are copies of decisions made in the past. Its response to anxiety may be summarized in the formula "pairing and repairing."

The term that best describes *eros*, on the other hand, is *revising*, and the etymological suggestions are important: seeing again, seeing better, seeing more—though *not* more of the same but seeing differently, seeing anew. *Seeing* implies that properly speaking *eros* is a consciously directed mode of response. But historically the first and most radical appearance of revision was in the activity of transposition by which man created a transcendent *world* for himself. Perhaps we can speak of transposition as proto-erotic, and in this covert form the activity of *eros* is ancillary to need. *Eros* comes to consciousness as dissatisfaction with the world it had unknowingly structured in fulfilling the demands of *need*. It responds in *ennui*, in *annoyance*, to the suffocating fullness, the stultifying overorder, the seeming permanence of *what already is*. Where *need* speaks in answers, *eros* speaks in questions. Its questions challenge the answers it had provided for *need* or dig beneath them to lay open and resurrect earlier questions buried under those answers. It seeks what Robert Frost has called "the wonder of unexpected supply" and Wordsworth "something evermore about to be," something perpetually beyond—*evermore*, or *never now*. Where *need* involves an urge to incorporate something missing into the self, *eros* involves an urge to create an emptiness, a sense of something missing, and project it toward the future. *Eros* aspires to sustain the otherness of its objects and keep them from collapsing into the self. Unlike nature, *eros* demands a vacuum, a permanent *tohu bohu* without which no new creation or revision would be possible.

We may assume that there are as many configurations of these two impulses as there are individuals. But if, for the sake of analysis, we separate the impulses to articulate the dispositions and preferences characteristic of each in its pure form, we can construct two puppets, a man of
need and a man of *eros*. In this model the man of *need* gravitates toward
the consolations of naive consciousness and its preferred form of culture.
He is pious, conservative, and anti-intellectual. Clearly he prefers a
stable, typical, and orderly world and tries to keep it the way he finds it.
He learns and teaches that this world was created or is sustained by some
transcendent power(s) more durable and authoritative than man yet in
some ways similar to and aware of man. Thus he believes he can influence the power(s), which he finds at work in society as well as in nature.
He learns and teaches that the world has had this order for as long as it
has existed; that it offers its inhabitants favored directions—a center,
perhaps an outside, an above, a below, a past (*in illo tempore*). He further learns and teaches, as perception informs us, that there is only one
such world. It may have different regions and be articulated into different zones, but these will be related to each other in geography as well as
value. The usually invisible presences inhabiting that world are all to be
found, along with visible things, within its various zones. If the spiritual is invisible (or the invisible is spiritual), it must be in the same way
that air is invisible. And like air, the spiritual/invisible exists within the
one world available to perception—may be felt or heard, may enter
dreams—and its energies may flow like air currents through the world.

The man of *eros*, on the other hand, is a man against naive consciousness. In certain ways he is less independent than the man of *need:* he
needs his predecessor as he needs naive consciousness—not only, however, because he needs his five senses but also because he defines himself
by his opposition to his contrary. He does not teach that there is only one
world, that society is natural or divine, that the world always was and
will be the way it is. He does not take it for granted that society is more
real or valuable than the individual, does not prefer collective over singular norms of behavior, activity, and authority. He challenges every
source of givenness and transcendence which he has been told to accept:
memory, the past, tradition, time-honored customs and institutions, the
wisdom of the elders. He decides which to accept and which to throw
away; which to exalt and follow as paradigms, and which to consign
to flames.

For the man of *eros*, the real is what he decides it is after deliberation;
it issues forth as the product and fulfillment of his questing consciousness. And this quest is not something to be undertaken in some ritual or

otherwise collectively organized and shared experience; he prefers to work by himself, in a corner. There he can replace the one world given by perception with others which he imagines and constructs; and he may find these possible worlds more satisfying, comprehensible, and orderly than the given world. But it isn't enough for him to invent other worlds and stay in his corner. He is more contentious, restless, and ambitious. He notes with distaste his opponent's desire to keep the world the way he found it and decides thereupon that it should be changed. His ultimate aspiration is to make his view of the world *the world*. Within this grandiose hope he harbors a more modest scheme, based on his disagreement with the man of *need* over the origins of society and the state: he postulates that in the past men created their social systems without knowing it (that is, by transposition) and legitimized their man-made political systems by embedding them in the transcendent order; men should wake up to their power, shift from nonconscious to conscious creation, and take the shaping and changing of socio-political order into their own hands. Men should thus withdraw into themselves and their corners, muse out their plans and visions, and then, returning to the world, act to make them come true.

These two caricatures are familiar, and it must be apparent that the man of *need* symbolizes empirical consciousness while the man of *eros* symbolizes hypothetical consciousness. *Need* and *eros* are affective equivalents to those cognitive attitudes. And yet, however apparent it seems, this can hardly be true. It is at best, stated this way, trivial. It can't be true because the cognitive structures are developmentally related while the structures of *need* and *eros* are dialectically related. And it remains trivial until we sort out the referents of *need* and *eros*—that is, the species, individuals, forms of cultural consciousness. Naive consciousness reveals its responsiveness to need in the style of perception—passive, automatic, accurate—and in the qualities of transposed structures—over-ordered, determining, transcendent. Creative *eros* is present in the primordial mode of transposition; in this mode—the psychic unconscious and cultural nonconscious—it is the servant of *need*. As the condition of anxiety produced by organic *ananke* and its varied threats to existence, *need* arouses a dormant *eros* and puts it to work under the banner or yoke of necessity.

This *corvée* arrangement is basically tense and unstable, leading first to the tyrannic assertion of *need's* authority and ultimately to its loss. For in stimulating the proto-erotic activity of transposition, *need* makes it possible for consciousness to discover its creative power: this can happen only if it finds its products outside itself—in the world toward which naive consciousness gravitates—and intuits some reflection of that power in the products. The latter appear first as transcendent models to be imitated, as forms and powers that legitimize further technology, and as sources of authority, for example, welded to political institutions and wielded by political technicians—kings and priests—so as to intensify the output of *corvée* labor. But as the mark of human thought and power grows clearer—even if expressed only in such hubristic perversions of eros as lust, repression, and force—man's confidence in technology increases. And as creative eros finds expression in conscious forms and generates new technical structures, the old transpositions become problematic, open to doubts or criticism, perhaps obsolescent. If their validity is to be sustained and renewed, they must be defended—possibly revised—by means which are usually technical: ideology and speculative thought. These means remain in the service of *need:* they justify and are justified by transcendent sources of authority; they help preserve the transpositional (and usually the political) status quo. But *eros* is now less the slave of the divine king than a member of his city-state. It is beginning its long journey toward the time of partnership when, surrounded by the heavens and pantheon and polities it has made, *eros* discovers and flaunts its power and claims for technology a share in God's work. It is thus by the foresight of a nonconscious providence that early man in his need transposes his creations to the transcendent field where alone they may be "discovered," and from whence they may be repossessed, refined, and transformed. Auden's whimsical question, "How can I know what I think till I see what I say," may with slight alteration serve as a formula for this dialectical process in which first *need* and then *eros* is dominant: how can man know what he thinks and creates till he sees what he has made?

We may now correlate the affective structures of *need* and *eros* with the two basic forms of cultural consciousness by postulating that (a) since *need* and *eros* exist together in each individual, and (b) since *need* and *eros* are dialectically interactive in cultural as well as individual consciousness, and (c) since by virtue of their relation to naive consciousness *need* is initially the dominant condition and the empirical attitude the dominant form, then (d) the development of culture from its empirical to its hypothetical mode is congruent with the changing course produced by the dialectic postulated in (b): *need* dominating and challenged by *eros* is the affective structure of the empirical attitude, and when the challenge succeeds, this leads to the affective structure of the hypothetical attitude, *eros* dominating and challenged by *need*.

For the sake of convenience, let our two puppets, the man of *need* and the man of *eros*, be called Consciousness 1 (Cs 1) and Consciousness 2 (Cs 2); and let any lingering echoes of Charles Reich be dissolved like morning mist. In the empirical attitude, Cs 1 is the prevailing cultural mode; Cs 2 may be called its counterculture. The structure of the empirical attitude may be expressed as Cs 1 $\leftrightarrow$ > (Cs 2): > = "is greater than," or "includes," while $\leftrightarrow$ = "interacts in tensional opposition with." The structure of the hypothetical attitude may be expressed as Cs 2 $\leftrightarrow$ > Cs 1. In the first formula, Cs 2 is in parentheses to indicate that it has not yet emerged as the dominating mode. Cs 2 became the dominating mode by reacting against the already actualized structure dominated by Cs 1, which persists as a counterculture and retains its influence (supported by naive consciousness) in the hypothetical attitude. The difference between the formulas expresses the irreversible or developmental character of culture change.

These formulas are deficient in that they fail to express the calculus of transformations which, as a function of the interplay between Cs 1 and Cs 2, gives each of the two attitudes a definite and irreversible temporal profile. Empirical and hypothetical cultures are not static, monolithic forms. The career of the first is shaped by its gravitation toward Cs 2 and its attempts—increasingly technological and thus self-defeating—to resist that tendency and maintain Cs 1 in power. The career of the second is shaped by the gravitational force exerted by Cs 1 and leading to continuously changing modulations of the two affective structures. This can hardly be demonstrated without exploring the historical manifestations of these changes in considerable detail. For the present, I can do no more than conclude with an impressionistic description of each of the two careers. And first I would like to restate the two paradoxes with which I concluded the *Clio* essay: (1) the paradox of transcendence: the creature becomes the creator of the creation in which he is a creature, but he retains this power only on condition that he continue to think of himself as creature, not creator; (2) the paradox of technology: the creator becomes the creature of his creation, and this happens because he continues to think of himself as creator, not creature, as master, not servant of his creation and because he aspires to give it the independence and self-regulating character that will enable it to transcend the limits of his own fallible nature.[33] The first paradox epitomizes the dynamics of the empirical attitude, the second that of the hypothetical attitude.

(1) The empirical attitude may be conceived as sustaining its original

---

[33] Cf. "Outline of a General Theory," *Clio*, 61–62; this is a slightly modified formulation of the second paradox.

value structure, derived from naive consciousness, through a sequence of historical periods in the same way as a soaring hawk sustains its apparently calm, effortless stability and equilibrium: by continual fibrillating readjustments, microchanges, tiny compensatory motions that enable it to ride the shifting currents of environment—sometimes opposing, sometimes assisting the flows and ebbs and eddies of environmental energy. But this analogy will not explain those shifting currents that derive from the dialectic of Cs 1 and Cs 2 within the structure of period consciousness itself; currents produced when an emergent technology, manifesting and stimulating the exercise of man's conscious creative powers, increases the probability of more radical efforts to master or transform the world.

For example, in ancient conquest empires the political elites appropriated the god-power of the transcendent order and expropriated the man-power of the masses (in ancient bureaucratic empires, the same pattern took a more benign and effective form). The rulers desired an essentially heterocosmic situation—one world for the rulers and another for the ruled—and their reliance on political techniques approximated tendencies I have associated with Cs 2. But if they would continue as rulers and not reduce themselves to the helpless position of mere exterminators, they had to appeal with special force to the values espoused by Cs 1, for only the ideology provided by that model could justify their power and prolong their repression of the masses: it is more acceptable to rule in the god's name than in one's own. Another example: the first serious challenge to archaic transpositions was posed by classical technology, chiefly in politics, social and economic organization, natural philosophy, critico-speculative thought, and engineering. But this challenge led ultimately to the failure of Rome, the failure of the City of Man, and produced the sophisticated reaction of Christian culture. Christianity did not simply revive a more primitive culture; it strove to reinstitute a primitive configuration of relations between transposition and transcendence, transcendence and technology. The programmatic aspect of this enterprise— "*striving* to *re*-institute"—was historically a new manifestation of *eros;* this aspect became conspicuous during the high and late Middle Ages and took on the pale cast of human thought in scholastic and political technology.

The difference between these two examples suggests the difference between two phases of empirical culture in Western history. In the earlier phase, efforts to challenge the value structure of Cs 1 are overcome or must be kept latent through displacement. Such efforts may arouse strong conservative countermeasures or a variety of accommodations which may be transpositional or ideological. The resultant changes will derive in part from the subversive activities of the erotic counterculture, and the reaction of Cs 1 may successfully restore or maintain the original structure, but it will do so only by driving the actual configuration of culture into a new historical phase. Both examples make clear the role of the counterculture in sustaining the paradox of transcendence: though it is partly through the efforts of Cs 2 that the creature becomes the creator of the creation in which he is a creature, it is essential that he continue to see or to present himself as creature, not creator. The dominance of transposition, and of Cs 1, is thus paradoxically what *enables* the underground activity of Cs 2.

(2) The second example reveals the ultimate failure of empirical culture to honor the terms of this paradox. This made it possible for post-medieval men to proclaim, positively or critically, that man, by taking thought, was able to change himself, his history, and his world. Taking thought, placing the erotic mark of technology on the world, led to the revolutions associated with Copernicus, Galileo, Newton, Kant, America, France, Industry, and Marx. The scientific, epistemological, and political revolutions challenged the primacy and passivity of perception, the transcendent provenance of its data, and the metaphysical priority of space over time (that is, the superior symbolic efficacy of spatial categories as signifiers of transcendent "form"). They initiated a sustained critique which threatened the validity of transcendence as a significant *genetic* category providing the basic criterion of reality, and this critique succeeded because so much of what had traditionally been considered transcendent had gradually been revealed over the centuries as the effect of transposition. This critique was accompanied by the dual emergence of modern technology with the first clearly counterperceptual culture in history. At the same time, the career of hypothetical culture takes a peculiar direction: noting the nonconscious and thus automatic character of transposition, the modern critique of empirical culture left that character standing as a new criterion of reality validating such strange bed-fellows as the unconscious and the systematic, the psychic and the cybernetic, the realm of the transpersonal and the realm of the impersonal, E.S.P. and servomechanical sense organs.

Here we see the predicament and instability of Cs 2, the influence of Cs 1, and the dynamics of the paradox of technology. Hypothetical culture would like to convert its technical achievements into realities that have the same status as that previously possessed by transcendent forces; it would like to create structures or systems which not only change the world but may be depended on—through self-regulation—to continue changing it for the better. And in this impulse, at the heart of the most aggressive and power-seeking urges of Cs 2, lies the enemy agent working for Cs 1. In his drive to convert technology to a source of transcendence—to a transcendent force itself—the man of *eros* restores to *his* reality the independence and power it had for the man of *need*. If technology replaces transposition, it continues the work of transposition. Thus the Frankenstein paradox of technology presides over the dialectical career of a culture dominated by Cs 2.

Hypothetical culture as the product of the gradual undermining of the empirical dominance of naive consciousness: it is in this oversimplified—but comprehensive and economical—perspective that we may integrate the myriad utterances in our century of the sort of commonplace I am stating here. The discovery of man's radical creative power is the discovery of transposition (whether by this or any other name), and the significance of this discovery—going on over the last four centuries—is suggested in the slightly pejorative and also, perhaps, slightly nostalgic connotations of the term *naive* consciousness. Such terms as *rationalism* and *intellectualism* may be assimilated to the broader category of "distrust of transposition and reliance on technology."

Our ambivalence toward the historical fate of naive consciousness as a cultural form sometimes divides into the polar opposites of romanticism and technocracy, but it is better represented by more integrated attitudes, such as Max Weber's ambivalence toward what he calls "the disenchantment of the world." Weber asks whether the processes of rationalization and structural differentiation "which we have been undergoing for thousands of years" mean that we today "have a greater knowledge of the conditions of life under which we exist" than did early man. Answering in the negative, he notes that the savage "knows incomparably more about his tools" than we know about our instrumental systems. Therefore this "intellectualist rationalization, created by science and scientific technology," means something else:

> It means . . . the knowledge or belief that if one but wished one *could* learn it at any time. Hence, it means that principally there are no mysterious incalculable forces that come into play, but rather that one can, in principle, master all things by calculation. This means that the world is disenchanted. One need no longer have recourse to magical means in order to master or implore the spirits, as did the savage, for whom such mysterious powers existed. Technical means and calculations perform the service. This above all is what intellectualization means.[34]

[34] H. H. Gerth and C. Wright Mills, eds., *From Max Weber: Essays in Sociology* (1946; New York: Oxford University Press, 1958), 138–39.

Amplifying a similar theme, Jacques Ellul modifies Weber's insight with the notion that transcendence has not disappeared but has been displaced—in my terms—from transposition to technology:

> Nothing belongs any longer to the realm of the gods or to the supernatural. The individual who lives in the technical milieu knows very well that there is nothing spiritual anywhere. But man cannot live without the sacred. He therefore transfers his sense of the sacred to the very thing which has destroyed its former object: to technique itself. In the world in which we live, technique has become the essential mystery. . . . Those who have preserved some of the notions of magic both admire and fear technique.[35]

[35] *The Technological Society*, trans. John Wilkinson (New York: Vintage, 1964), 143.

PART TWO

Shakespeare

Theater, Drama, and the Second World:
A Prologue to Shakespeare

BY USING AS touchstone the idea of the second world—that is, the model or construct which the mind creates in order to withdraw from the actual environment, thus to offer a clarified image of the world it replaces— one can discern identifying marks of two sets of assumptions and world views, which I have called medieval and Renaissance.[1] My aim here is to describe two structurally different forms of drama which are parallel to those world views yet more specific: church ritual and Shakespearian play. These labels remind you that the forms are historical—they are embedded in historical circumstance, and have histories which helped shape them. But I am not now going to approach them in their historical context, or in their historical relation to each other, except perhaps to relate each very briefly to some of the inferences about intellectual history already put forth. The present discussion is primarily structural.

I

The fundamental distinction to be made is that between *drama* and *theater*. A play is both drama and theater, and we must understand the way

[1] Fuller discussions of the concept of the second world are available in two earlier essays of mine, both in this volume: "The Renaissance Imagination: Second World and Green World" and "The Ecology of the Mind: The Concept of Period Imagination— An Outline Sketch."

111

these two contexts interact and affect each other. *Drama* is a Greek word for action, acting, doing, performing. As Aristotle pointed out, drama is primarily a temporal rather than a spatial event, though the terms *drama* and *dramatic* tend to fall into two families of reference—when they are not used simply as synonyms for *theater* and *melodramatic*. We think first of shaped and significant conflict—of a dialectical action, an interaction, an agon; its module, its purest or most rudimentary form, is unmediated dialogue. But I think a second set of associations directs us toward the sense of the dramatic action as something externalized and viewed, or imagined, from outside the agonists. Even inner human action, to be made dramatic, has somehow to be externalized, socialized, made visible, asserted over against an *other*, exacting a response, or itself a response. Drama as action seems to require a co-presence of agents, and as performance it implies the additional presence of spectators or readers. Dramatic action is thus interaction.

Theater comes from a Greek word which denotes a place for seeing, displaying, and, again, performing. Where drama demands agents, theater demands actors. Where drama is an action capable of representation in a variety of media, theater is a particular medium—primarily visual (not primarily verbal)—which embraces the network of actual circumstances and participants who cooperate in representing and observing a particular action.

The theatrical situation is itself inherently dramatic: a play is immediately related to, directly performed before, an audience. The playwright is on the other side of the medium—behind it, not in front of it as in other *literary* forms. His disappearance behind the play leads to a more intense encounter of audience with play world, a more complex interaction among players, characters, and spectators. And since the main fact of the theater is the visual presence of actors playing usually predetermined roles before spectators, the playwright is in a paradoxical position. On the one hand, he has more power than the poet, because his vision is imposed on producers, directors, players, and spectators. On the other hand, and for exactly the same reason, he is much more at the mercy of others. He can invent plots, set the scene, and stand behind the arras, but because he has committed his work to the free wills of other interpreters, he cannot control their onstage behavior. The theatrical occasion may tempt the actor to subordinate the demands of the script and role to his own ego. The play as a whole may be reduced to a review, a background for the expression of individual personalities. The creator's more comprehensive idea may be frustrated, and his imaginary world may have to share the stage with the rhetorical self-concern of actors.

A struggle may thus arise between the author, with his central consciousness, and his interpreters, each of whom is potentially a central consciousness.

From the distinction between theater and drama, a number of others may be generated. First and most important is that between *actual space-time* and *dramatic space-time*—I find myself forced to use and to repeat this ungainly term, *space-time*, only in part because of an undernourished or overcherished vocabulary; the more justifiable reasons will, I hope, emerge later. In the category of the *actual* I include ritual or ecclesial space-time, civic space-time, and theatrical space-time—in other words, the actual duration of any performance, the actual place in which it occurs, and the actual conditions of representation. *Dramatic* space-time obviously refers to the represented event: this may include the presumptively real action of divine history symbolized by church ritual and the presumptively imaginary or fictional action of a play. Actual space-time is the here-now of congregation or audience, church or theater, priests or actors, altar or stage. Dramatic space-time is the here-now of biblical or Shakespearian characters and events.

A second distinction may be made on the basis of relations between actual and dramatic space-time: at one extreme of this spectrum of relations we have symbolic performance, and at the other extreme, realistic performance. The symbolic relation is such that the actual is more immediate than the dramatic; dramatic space-time is stylistically distanced or excluded from the plane of direct representation; it is rendered in symbolic or hieratic shorthand, and this demands that the observer try by some act of mental transformation to diminish the felt distance between the nonrepresentational formality of an actual event like ritual and the dramatic events to which ritual refers. I call this general range of distanced relations symbolic because a symbol is by definition something that stands for something else, therefore something that directs your attention beyond itself. And I would like further to divide symbolic reference into two kinds on the basis of the degree to which any symbol claims attention for its own sake rather than for the sake of its referent: an *iconic* symbol moves you beyond itself with relatively greater speed because it is simpler and less conspicuous—perhaps more stylized—as an immediate form; an *imagistic* symbol encourages you by its formal interest to linger awhile and pay more attention to it. This distinction has some points in common with that made by Francis Bacon between *cipher* and *hieroglyph* and other points in common with that made by Susanne Langer between *sign* and *symbol*. Icon, cipher, and sign are more transparent and self-transcending.

At the other end of the spectrum, actual space-time is largely, if not entirely, transformed into, therefore identifiable with, dramatic space-time. It is suppressed as much as possible, and its immediacy is assimilated by the dramatic event. Now you can think about theatrical space-time whenever you want during the course of a play; you never really forget about it, so there is no question of illusion, even in the most realistic stage drama; this drama asks you to bracket off actual space-time temporarily, to suspend it from consideration as of no relevance to this play.

Another distinction is demanded by the dramatic space-time of ritual, which differs in mode from that of the secular theater: the first is *real*, the second *fictional*. The dramatic events symbolically indicated by church ritual are real in that they are felt to be contained within the first world we inhabit. Though they are remote and must be brought closer by ritual evocation, they are temporally and spatially continuous with our world. Sacred history extends our time line to the Beginning and the End; therefore its *then* lies behind and ahead of us with reference to our *now*. The same is true of spatial relations: vaguely adumbrated during the earlier Middle Ages, developed more fully later, is the ancient image of a spherical universe which, in its dominant vertical organization of low and high, near and far, dense and rare, earthly and celestial, embodies the internal modes and hierarchies of relation joining creatures to each other and to God. At the same time, this cosmological organization is understood as mystically coordinated with its inversion in the series of relations whose model is that of outside to inside (surface to core, qualities to substance, phenomenon to reality, body to spirit). Such a model epitomizes the incarnational movement of God down into the core of human life and history and also into the core of the human soul. Late medieval poets, mystics, and theologians, accepting the spherical universe as the real picture of the world, felt that to move *inward* in contemplation, to withdraw mentally from the everyday world, was to move *upward*. Withdrawal was not to a radically discontinuous second world, another frame of reference; therefore *upward* was not construed as a metaphoric but as a symbolic adverb: the inward/upward movement of the spirit in contemplation was imagined to be a real *ascensus* of thought through the hierarchies, prefiguring the literal ascent of the saved soul after death. Any true inner withdrawal had to be conceived in a correspondence relation to some aspect of real space or time.

The dramatic space-time of ritual is *real* not only in being part of the first world, but also in the specially heightened sense that term assumes when set over against the everyday, the ordinary, or the merely actual. (Here I use *actual* to mean one thing in opposition to *dramatic*, and another in opposition to *real*.) At least through the sixteenth century, the relation of *actual* to *real* could be specified along the lines of the following examples: the relation of the profane or secular to the holy, the surface to the core, the effect to the cause, the natural and historical to the supernatural, normal perception to mystic or apocalyptic vision, and so forth. Within this framework, special requirements govern the way the actual forms of ritual symbolize the real events of sacred history. It is a commonplace among theorists of religious symbolism that any image, symbol, or copy must be shaped as an oblique or deficient representation to keep alive its inferiority to that which it represents. Thus Plato has Parmenides ask, "If a thing is made in the image of the Form, can that Form fail to be like the image of it?" (*Parm.* 132d). The implication is that the Platonic Forms may not be prior and transcendent but rather man-made copies of images which have been etherealized, distanced, and endowed with higher value. To claim perfect accuracy or identity is to threaten with collapse the necessary distinctions of level between Being and Becoming, divine referent and earthly symbol, the transcendent reality and the visible images by which it is shadowed.

The problem for church ritual was to bring near the far, to fill the worshipping self with the presence of the Wholly Other without jeopardizing that Other's existential distance and superiority, i.e., its otherness. This problem has consequences both for the inner structure of ritual and for the affective structure of its relation to the worshipper. O. B. Hardison's scrupulous and provocative analyses of various forms of liturgical drama allow us to isolate three planes which the ritual performance coordinates. The first is the plane of original sacred history, revealed in the Incarnation, fixed and preserved in Holy Scripture. The second is the plane of ritual itself, which not only commemorates but also revives the mysteries of God's earthly career and re-creates their eternal power to save and heal, along with their message of salvation.[2] The primary function of ritual is thus not—as least ideally—knowledge, edification, or consolation; it is communion, participation in the mystical body which is eternally present in absolute time and which recurs in different modes throughout the Church Year, and annually, in cyclical time.

The esthetic character of ritual performance is thus neither imaginary nor self-sufficient. It is *actual* and *real: actual* in being iconic, in referring to the reality for which it stands and of which it is the vehicle; *real* in being *sacramental*, which means that the ritual performer hopes his

---

[2] O. B. Hardison, Jr., *Christian Rite and Christian Drama* (Baltimore: Johns Hopkins University Press, 1965). Future references are to this edition.

act will be answered by God's filling the present moment with himself and his renewing power. *Sacramental efficacy* is therefore the fundamental objective of ritual, and it presupposes *belief* on the part of the worshipper—belief that if man beseeches in the prescribed form and proper spirit, God will respond. To encourage, renew, or sustain this belief is the next objective, so that the esthetic character of ritual must be partly controlled by the affective criterion of *psychological efficiency*.

The third plane is the hermeneutic plane of subsequent interpretations, aimed at explaining or adjusting the relations binding ritual to sacred history and dogma. These are the products of exceptional individuals, gifted and learned men, though their effectiveness depends on the anonymity which preserves any sacred phenomenon from the suspicion of merely human parentage. The interpreter articulates and makes explicit what was at first implicit in the revelation received by the relatively simple and naive souls of the gospel age; in a historical sense, he tries to bring the remote nearer, to make it more understandable to the present generation of simple souls.

Hardison describes the modifications and variations in liturgy as the effects of continual interaction between existing ritual forms and new interpretations. This dynamics is determined partly by the needs of sacramental efficacy and partly (perhaps more) by those of psychological efficiency. Ceremonies centered on mystical renewal and participation require symbolic distance between actual and dramatic space-time; they also require closer involvement of the congregation in the hieratic reenactment of the mysteries. On the other hand, there are sacred events which are not mystical in the above sense, but simply historical. These events occur in *linear* time; hence they are fixed in the past and are revived for purposes of commemoration rather than participation. They will be represented with greater verisimilitude because their primary aim is not to fulfill sacramental efficacy but to induce the proper devotional attitude in the congregation by an affective technique which later mystics called the composition of place (*compositio loci*). Apart from doctrinal requirements, the extent to which sacramental efficacy does or does not induce the proper psychological response would seem to be (at least partly) responsible for the changes produced by new interpretation in the representational or nonsymbolic elements of ritual performance, changes also in the ratio of iconic to imagistic elements of symbolism.

Problems of this sort do not affect the treatment of fictional space-time in theatrical drama (secular). The contrast might be focused by the following example: While *actual* and *real* refer to aspects of the first world, they may also be represented within a dramatic space-time which is explicitly fictional in mode. The dramatic space-time of church ritual is real in two senses—real rather than merely actual in the quality of the represented plane of existence and real rather than fictional in the mode of dramatic space-time. On the other hand, in a play like *Dr. Faustus*—to take a more blatant example—aspects of reality appear in a fictional world. The difference between these two situations is clearcut and has something to do with the structure of belief presupposed by each form: in ritual you are expected *to believe in* the reality of dramatic space-time; in the play you are expected *to make believe that* fictional space-time contains spiritual substances.

In the play situation, there is no continuity, no rational relation, between fictional and theatrical space-time. It is a situation very much like that of a perspective painting, in which two entirely different frames of reference—a three- and a two-dimensional field—are superimposed. And this relation cannot be affected by the particular content of any play: the history play and British king do not adumbrate a more actual space-time than does the Bohemian romance or the enisled magician. We do not make believe by degrees in such a way that once we get beyond a certain degree we start believing. We do not, therefore, make believe less when seeing *Henry V* and more when seeing *The Tempest*. A change in subject matter—from history to romance—influences our particular response to theme and character, but this is not the same as a change in dramatic mode; it does not make us change our basic mental set toward the performance from make-believe to belief. I have used the rather awkward locution *space-time* rather than *event* to handle this distinction: it suggests a container within which any number of event types may unfold without affecting the character of the dramatic mode.

Shakespeare's use of the medium goes far beyond this dialectical encounter between drama and theater (or, to put the emphasis on a slightly different, though related, theme, between verbal and visual presentation). The convergence of his art with the theater in which it developed produced the following consequences: his drama is not distanced by symbolic or ritual techniques; on the other hand, it does not often tend toward simple realism by ignoring the conditions of theater. His characteristic procedure is rather *to re-create aspects of theatrical space-time within fictional space-time*. The various relations among spectators, actors, playwrights, directors, stage, theater, and the world outside the theater: these are readmitted into the second world in various ways, with varying degrees of emphasis and openness. At one extreme we find casual verbal references to the play metaphor; generalized analogies to the effect that the world is a stage and its people players; and relatively vague statements about the similarities to or contrasts between art and life, imagination and actuality. Moving toward the other extreme, we find implicit behavioral analogies, as when a king, villain, or magician takes upon himself the creator's role (god or playwright) and tries to cast other characters as the puppets in his own play. We see this, for example, in Richard III, whose shadow lengthens in the sun as he converts the actual world into his own creation. Gradually his shadow world grows real, becomes independent of him, external to him. Having committed himself to it, he is trapped within it as one of its characters, forced to accept the consequences of the role he has shaped for himself. This process reaches its climax when real ghosts return to plague him the night before the battle. Richard's is only one of many kinds of role playing, from simple hypocrisy and disguise to the more complex and experimental forms demanded of figures like Richard II and Lear by the failure of an order in which roles were assured and could be spontaneously assumed. Questions of self-presentation—"What's my role?" "How shall I stage myself?"—presuppose more basic questions about the nature of the world, the real or fictional status of world views, the extent to which man makes, can make, or must make the world he lives in, and so forth.

The theatrical experience is more openly represented in plays which feature prologues, choruses, and epilogues to set up analogies between the experience of characters *in* the play and that of the audience *at* the play. I touched on this earlier when I mentioned the doubling of the withdrawal-return pattern in green world and second world. The audience a player addresses is given a role (*as* audience) within the play. Just as the observer of a perspective painting stands in both the actual space of the gallery and the extension of the three-dimensional picture space, so by direct address the audience is doubled, re-created, given a fictional role. Certain plays in fact have their own audiences built into them, connected as special attachments, and when the company unpacks the play it rolls out its portable audience like a carpet. The direction of influence here moves *from* fiction *to* audience, so that the fictional world may be extended beyond the stage into the pit and galleries, and beyond the theater to readers. This directionality is contrary to that which characterizes religious drama, whether ecclesiastical or secular, and since this contrariety is the symptom of an important structural difference, I should like to return to the earlier forms and embark on my Short History of Drama.

II

A Short Course in the History of Drama may be found in a large number of handbooks and textbooks. This course propels the drama from the church to the church porch to the city streets and innyards and finally drops it into the theater. In brief, it transports the drama from the first to the second world and from the God-made globe to the man-made Globe. Since this itinerary nicely fits some of the patterns I have been sketching out, it is something of a disappointment to me that there is no corresponding itinerary in the real world. Studies by Hardison, V. A. Kolve, Glynne Wickham, and others have rendered this short course obsolete. They have demonstrated the futility of presuming to trace the career of the drama as if it were a person taking a walk. I am nevertheless reluctant to give up the idea of transition from the first to the second world, and therefore I would like to see if there is another approach to the history of drama, another frame of reference which may perhaps allow us to save appearances which I find attractive. I have neither the time nor the competence to undertake such an approach in detail, but I can at least offer a rough and summary sketch which may suggest the lines such an approach might take. This approach, very briefly, consists in examining and comparing the structure and visible intentions of particular kinds of drama in the light of the distinctions developed in the previous section. First, then, a quick review of some of the more familiar facts of early stage history.

During the breakup of the Roman Empire, and in the early period of Christianity, drama suffered the same fate as other expressions of human imagination: it virtually disappeared as an independent art form, to be integrated into a new context in the first world as a form of applied art, an ancilla to religion, one of the many forms of *reductio* by which man could be drawn closer to God. Some of the reasons for this were briefly touched on in my earlier work on the esthetic, epistemological, and stylistic criteria required by the medieval imagination. The theatrical and dramatic impulses were transformed so as to serve God and his first world; drama was absorbed into the forms of Christian worship.

Hardison notes that as early as the ninth century writers were aware of the usefulness of allegorical interpretation which "can be appreciated by the illiterate and semi-literate, for whom historical details and theological subtleties are meaningless." They needed "a vivid, dramatic understanding of the Roman rite" (38–39). This need increased "as the separation between the clergy and the laity became more pronounced and as the language of the church became ever more remote from the vernacular" (39). The separation was architecturally intensified when the basilica form gave way to the cathedral: changes of scale and dimension and also a more emphatic dividing line between nave and altar placed greater distance between performers and worshippers. The congregation became, in effect, an *audience;* this made ritual participation more difficult and hence led to more reliance on the techniques of representational drama (cf. Hardison, Essay VI). Here we might briefly note another factor which led toward the same tendency: over the centuries, it became harder to sustain naive belief in, wholehearted assent to, the principle of sacramental efficacy. Belief and assent had therefore to be encouraged by various forms of persuasion, among them the rhetorical and visual heightening which could best be provided by representational techniques.

Such developments suggest a gradually deepening rift between church ritual and dogma, on the one hand, and the psychological needs of the laity, on the other. They suggest that to continue to produce its desired effects, religious drama would have to commit itself to extra-liturgical and extra-ecclesiastical modes of presentation. They suggest not a cause but a reason for the growing social and cultural prominence of non-liturgical drama, culminating in the mystery cycles. In short, they suggest that religious drama had to get closer to the people. And as we know, the English craft or mystery plays managed to do this in a number of ways. They were composed by laymen (probably) *for* lay amateur actors, and not for priests. They were explicitly invented as plays (*ludi*). The repertory of events was extended, the theatrical and dramatic styles changed, to encourage identification between contemporary Englishmen and the ancient characters of the drama. They aimed at a powerful and complete response, in which recreation and edification were one.

Most of these cycles seem to have been staged in wagons, with different plays being acted out by different craft unions in different parts of the city. Records show that they took up to seven days and used multiple casts. V. A. Kolve attributes the subject and form of these cycles to "the decision to honor the Corpus Christi feast with religious plays."[3] This feast was not a normal liturgical event; it had no traditional ritual to depend on for expression of its meaning; therefore it required a more complete and self-sufficient dramatic context. Kolve describes the two main features of the cycles as follows: First, the esthetic organization of these plays reflected various medieval theories about the shape of universal

[3] *The Play Called Corpus Christi* (Stanford: Stanford University Press, 1966).

history, the seven ages of man, the typological or figural anticipations and imitations of Christ in the Old and New Testaments. We see the persistence here of the plane of interpretation which Hardison has analyzed. Second, the Corpus Christi drama contains a good deal of local color and idiom, and some humor and parody (or what is sometimes referred to as realism). "By means of a pervasive anachronism and anglicization," Kolve writes, this drama "furnished a critical image of moral and social life as lived in the later middle ages. It is possible that these cycles felt no need to stage actions from present time because they staged all past actions as if they were of the present" (104).

This emphasis on the critical image of contemporary life is the central thesis of an earlier study by Eleanor Prosser.[4] She succeeds in showing, through sensitive interpretation, the extent to which the esthetic quality of the plays is intimately involved with a homiletic intention: the plays which are best as drama are effective "because the religious point is clearest, because doctrine and drama are carefully fused" (189). The attempt vividly to embody and communicate such a doctrine as, e.g., repentance, is identical with the attempt to put on a convincing and compelling play. She also remarks that by the fourteenth century, "biblical figures had become homiletic symbols" (42), so that the anachronism extensively discussed by Kolve helped sharpen the didactic effect.

I particularly want to stress in connection with these studies the effect on dramatic structure of the secularization of actual space-time. Psychological efficiency is now correlated not to sacramental efficacy but to the artistic persuasiveness—the vividness, probability, and coherence—through which the message is impressed on the audience. *Make-believe* becomes much more important, but it becomes important as an instrument in arousing or enlivening *belief*. And this leads me to the significant new feature characterizing the structure of the mystery play. Dramatic space-time is divided into two levels: as spectators, we *make believe* that we are beholding the real Isaac, Noah, or angel. In other words, we understand ourselves to be watching an explicit fiction—the first level—which imitates figures and events we believe to be historical—the second level; and, as historical, they are also real, visible embodiments which figurally and mystically convey the invisible truth. A symbolic relation remains between fictional space-time in the wagon and the obviously different, therefore relatively remote, real space-time of Scripture. The

[4]*Drama and Religion in the English Mystery Plays* (Stanford: Stanford University Press, 1961). Future references are to this edition.

second level has the effect of an encircling horizon: it embraces past and future history, the fiction, the actors, and the audience, all within the compass of the one real universe.

Let me sharpen the distinction between this kind of performance and ritual: in church ritual, the priests can represent sacred events and figures only on condition that they first of all represent themselves—that is, play the sacerdotal role in the ritual performance which takes place in actual space-time. The iconic reference to other places, times, and persons tends naturally to be a doctrinal and hermeneutic more than a presentational and histrionic matter—though, as we have seen, the ratio varies. But the cycle players do not represent themselves in the same way. Only by imitating biblical characters do they indirectly reveal something about themselves, as mortals, sinners, and Christians.

And yet, if on the one hand the cycle players are not priests, on the other hand they are not among the Lord Chamberlain's Men—not Kemp, or Burbage, or Armin. To see your neighbor playing Noah is a different experience from seeing Robert Armin play Feste. In the first case, you are involved in a more personal, social, and actual way, which tends to make the theatrical elements obtrude on the fictional elements. But professionalism separates and bounds off the actor-role relation. It lends itself more easily to the autonomy of the whole theatrical experience, to the removal of that experience from your personal and social context, and to its closer association with, its greater subordination to, the make-believe world. Such autonomy does not suit the purposes of the cycle play, whose fictional space-time works best when it is, so to speak, shallow, relatively artificial. It is not meant to be withdrawn or distinct from actual life. And in fact, far from enforcing the difference between play world and audience, the cycle play aims at obliterating this difference. You see your neighbor playing Noah and Mrs. Noah acting like your neighbor's wife; this is effective, not merely as comic realism or relief but as making immediate the behavior or condition to which the play on all its levels speaks. Sometimes audience, actors, and characters may all be treated as English townspeople, sometimes as Christian sinners. The role explicitly assigned to the actor, and implicitly to the spectator, is a role he already plays in life. The common address by God or prophets to ancient Israelites and modern Englishmen means that both play world and audience world are apprehended as contained within the encircling horizon of reality. And to the extent that biblical figures were seen as homiletic symbols, as mirrors of or models for the spectator, the dependence of fiction on actuality increases.

In all these respects, the cycle remains a medieval phenomenon. It would not be accurate, for example, to say that the plane of fictional space-time (what is represented in the wagon) may be extended beyond the wagon in such a way as to re-create and resituate the audience in a counterfactual second world. The influence moves in the other direction: *from* the audience world, into and through fictional space-time, toward reality, and thus back into the audience world. Fictional space-time is an extension of the actual frame of reference of the spectators standing in the city street and Christian world. And insofar as this is the case, insofar as fiction is subordinate to actuality and the first world, the art of the mystery cycle no less than the art of ritual is what Huizinga calls "applied art": both have their function and existence entirely within the first world.

Nevertheless, I think we can discern in all this a complication, which indicates a move away from the earlier medieval assumptions and toward the Renaissance: the fictional space-time of the cycle play is related to reality not as an icon but as an image; it is (however limited) a representation calling attention to itself, capable of being enjoyed for its own sake. The normative character of most symbol-referent relations, certainly of medieval Christian symbols, is asymmetrical: you are expected to move *from* the relatively inferior symbol *toward* its referent. But in the cycle play, the spectator may be inclined to move in the other direction: he may be thoroughly familiar with the biblical and even doctrinal treatments of the Flood, and he may thus be attentive primarily to this year's production of the episode. The divided structure of dramatic space-time makes it easier for him to move from holy day to holiday, to take the reality for granted and to focus not only on the didactic but also on the recreative function of make-believe. In this connection, the esthetic influence on the cycle plays exerted by sacred history is double-edged: the domain of the religious, the horizon of reality, surrounds and permeates the plays with its atmosphere; at the same time, it leads to more complex and self-sufficient esthetic arrangements—to contrasts, analogies, and allusions (e.g., the organic function of subplots)—and these invite greater attention to the total theatrical experience per se. The spectator is as likely to be stirred by compositional ingenuity or spectacle as by the mystery. A fifteenth-century eye witness account of a religious play, for example, displays wonder not that angels descend to man, but that the wires holding them up are not visible. A conflict thus emerges between the two levels of dramatic space-time; attention may be lured away from doctrine and toward the combined elements of fiction and spectacle. This tension may be expected to increase when the second level of dramatic space-time is not sacred or historical.

In the morality play we are asked to see the fictional event as the symbolic image of an actual state of affairs lying "beyond" or "outside" it (or, if you will, *within* the main character and, by implication, within each spectator). In *Everyman* there is symbolic reference to a psychological event which occurs primarily within one soul, and which—as an admonitory exemplum—is to be understood as typical of too many (if not all) souls in actual life. But the first or fictional level of dramatic space-time is external and social; centered on a particular group of individuals, it contains a number of nonsymbolic touches of local realism in language and character portrayal. In a play of this kind we find an unresolved struggle taking place, within a clearly fictional space-time, between the interest in representational immediacy and the interest in symbolic reference. The power of such a play, its ability to move or to moralize the audience, derives mainly from the first (the integration of theatrical and fictional space-time, of the story and its staging); yet the formal and esthetic implications of this are not fully realized, and fictional space time has not been fully liberated from extra-fictional restraints. The morality play is still erected on a medieval scaffold, an esthetic of A + B, pleasure plus profit, ornament plus argument, sensuous image plus allegorical message, play plus seriousness. And this is different from the Renaissance structure of A *in* B, seriousness *in* play, image *as* message; a structure in which pleasure and profit, withdrawal and return, may be dialectically related *within* the rhythm of the make-believe experience.

Before moving on to the Elizabethan theater, I would like at least to mention another kind of street theater which, whether stationary or mobile, was part of city life. Its main function was to celebrate the visit of royalty, to "catch the attention and interest of the prince" with pageants and tableaux.[5] Such street productions used a traditional inventory of emblems or symbolic devices: garden, fountain, cave, mountain, rock, boat, castle, and the arch representing the city. These are shorthand symbols, artificial props which—by their very artificiality—tend to exclude what they represent. Keeping dramatic space-time at a distance, they draw attention to theatrical space-time, to the recreative occasion and the rhetoric of sheer spectacle going on in the actual world.

The different examples I have discussed suggest the following generalization: When the drama moves from a sacred to a secular environment and its purposes change accordingly, emphasis tends to shift from

---

[5] George Kernodle, *From Art to Theater* (Chicago: University of Chicago Press, 1944), 64. Chapter 2 (52–111) studies *tableaux vivants* as links between civic and theatrical space.

holy day toward holiday; from the religious toward the recreative; from attention to the cosmic and historical context of the present moment to a more restricted concern with local—civic and psychic—actuality. Dramatic space-time divides into two levels: a fictional plane closely interwoven with theatrical space-time, and comparatively limited as representation by its various allegorical and theatrical functions, and a second plane which may be sacred or secular, real or actual. I think it is roughly true that when this plane is understood as real, it may tend to recede from the fictional plane, and when actual (as in the morality), it may interfere with the expressiveness of the fiction. In all these cases, the basic situation remains the same: these forms reflect the subordination of fictional space-time to the actual (and real) space-time in which the audience lives. In that sense they are, once again, examples of what Huizinga has called "applied art."

III

To establish the primacy of imaginary space-time, and prepare the way for the second world, one must mark off an area, wall out the rest of the world, and sell tickets—i.e., create a situation in which an audience is brought into a theatrical enclosure for the express purpose of seeing a play. And this brings me at last to the Elizabethan theater. The only contemporary sketch we have of such a theater is unfortunately drawn from a second-hand report. But there have been many attempts at reconstruction, and I find myself most persuaded by the theories of A. M. Nagler and C. W. Hodges.[6] There were in fact two types of Elizabethan stage, the court theater and the public theater, and the court theater itself existed in an earlier and a later form. "The hall or court drama in its most primitive form was probably acted simply on the floor of a hall with the more noble guests looking down on it from a raised platform, while the inferior guests moved aside to make room for the performance."[7] Similar methods of staging seem to have been used in productions put on in the courtyards of Italian *palazzi*. The boundary between audience and play space must have been extremely flexible in this form of staging, and the play world would no doubt have been firmly subordinated to the ambience of the actual, or audience, world. Such a situation

[6] Nagler, *Shakespeare's Stage* (New Haven: Yale University Press, 1958); Hodges, *The Globe Restored* (London: E. Benn, 1953). Future references are to this edition of Hodges's work.

[7] Hardin Craig, ed., *Complete Works of Shakespeare* (Chicago: Scott, Foresman, 1951), 30.

is ideal for the masque, which "is not an art that has emerged but an art that is emerging from life."[8] That is, the masque would typically be performed before a royal person and would make artfully indirect or direct references suitable to the occasion; the hero is not an autonomous fictional character in the dramatic world but the king or prince in the audience. The masque was ordinarily intended to do no more than state "in symbolic form and action, the truth of an actual political situation."[9] The later court stage, on the other hand, derives from the Italian perspective stage, whose playing area was recessed behind the proscenium. This stage encourages little or no interplay between actors and audience.

The Elizabethan public theater is a compromise between these two: its raised and protruding apron stage allows the play world greater independence than the early court stage and more flexible interplay with the audience than the later court stage. The effects of this arrangement have been well described by Anne Righter:

> The construction of the playhouse . . . allowed the spectators to impinge upon the world of the drama from almost all sides, and to share a common daylight, a common weather, with the stage. This audience could no longer be regarded as an actor, in the medieval sense [as in the mysteries and moralities, in which the spectator was asked to imagine himself the object of the play's message]. But neither could it be entirely ignored. Elizabethan dramatists were still obliged—and privileged—to associate their patrons with their characters, to define the relationship of the actual world [of the audience] . . . with the illusory country of the play.[10]

According to many stage historians, the apron is simply the transplanted trestle stage of the street and innyard theaters. But its new location makes an important difference: the trestle stage was originally not isolated from actual and civic space—this was appropriate to the decorative, political, recreative, or allegorical character of theatrical functions concerned chiefly with actual and civic occasions (the masque, the pageant, the civic reception or celebration, royal visit, etc.). To place this stage within a theater is to remove it from actuality—at least to the extent of providing a special atmosphere, a circumscribed arena which heightens the independence of both stage and audience, which separates them from the everyday world.

[8] Enid Welsford, *The Court Masque* (Cambridge: Cambridge University Press, 1967), 361.

[9] Welsford, 372.

[10] *Shakespeare and the Idea of the Play* (London: Chatto & Windus, 1962), 59–60.

The Elizabethan stage, with its canopy or "heavens"—a fixed central motif—did not look like any one place because it had to stand for so many different places. Yet its unrealistic architecture always confronted the spectator beneath the various names and places of dramatic space-time. He could easily be made to see the canopy as more immediate than the heavens, the platform as more immediate than the rich variety of earthly places, the cellarage as more immediate than hell. And this is not to be misconstrued as a "throwaway of dramatic illusion" (a popular phrase), first, because there is no illusion in make-believe and, second, because the theatrical elements are introduced within the fictional world; this world is being extended, not thrown away. It is Hamlet, not Burbage, who points to the "majestical roof fretted with golden fire" or refers to the distracted globe. Fictional space-time need not be rational or realistic; it may include the world and problems of theater—and of contemporary English theater—as well as the world and problems of ancient Denmark, if thinking makes it so.

In theatrical drama of this sort, the physical definition and dramatic function of *locale* raises important problems. The debate over the degree of spectacle in the Elizabethan theater seems for the time being to have been resolved in favor of a theater which, in Hodges's words, was "violent, ornate, fantastic, emblematic . . . and very noisy . . . far from . . . plain and simple" (77, 81). Shakespeare has been called exceptional in his restraint, but to see what this means we have to distinguish among the elements of spectacle, at least to the extent of sorting out the chiefly decorative enhancements of the stage setting; those elements which contribute to local realism, like bleeding and most sound effects; and those that comprise the use of costumes, physical gestures, and descriptive language. Though in scenes of action (battles) and pageantry Shakespeare seems to have indulged the popular taste, he was just as likely to make fun of it and to limit the function of spectacle in stage decor. On the other hand, there is evidence that he favored vivid and elaborate costumes. This transfer of spectacular elements from props to costume and language produces a shift of attention from the stage to the players, and from the containing world to the characters.[11] Combined with the neu-

---

[11] M. C. Bradbrook, *Themes and Conventions of the Elizabethan Tragedy* (Cambridge: Cambridge University Press, 1960), 7–8: "The chief characteristic of the Elizabethan stage was its neutrality and its corresponding virtue, flexibility. There was no inevitable scenic background, or any other localising factor, such as a Chorus provides. It followed that far more weight attached itself to the persons and movements of the actors . . . [who] were the really important means of locating the scene. They were not set against a background real or imaginary; the audience did not visualize a setting for them."

tral and multivalent stage space, this shift encourages us to feel that the dramatic world is defined by its characters, that the environment is not fully established until it has been caught up within the tissue of motives, perceptions, and responses of the individuals in conflict.

Hardison refers to "the Protean stage of the Elizabethans, which can be a palace one moment, a tavern the next, and the rebel camp a few moments later" (272), and he contrasts this to the fixed localities, or mansions, around which the twelfth-century Anglo-Norman stage seems to have been built (*Adam* and *Resureccion*). Prosser finds a similar flexibility in the amphitheater which Richard Southern reconstructed as the possible setting for the Cornish mystery plays. The unlocalized central area, or *platea*, "is now Jerusalem, now the outskirts of the city, now the entrance to Gethsemane" (51). Yet the overall effect is radically different from that produced by Shakespeare's use of the stage. In the earlier theater, the places are preestablished by a variety of factors: tradition; reference to localized stations apparently situated above the audience (like broadcast booths); the facts of sacred history and doctrine. With two of its stations labeled Heaven and Hell, Southern's theater was an iconic symbol of the containing world, a world whose places were already plotted along historical and cosmological axes. Stage flexibility is thus primarily a matter of theatrical convenience and convention. The cycle play does not bring it before your attention as a *dramatic* problem or an open question.

But Shakespeare does. To me the most interesting and important quality of his art lies in his peculiar way of relating theatrical and dramatic space-time. First, he very often uses dramatic locale as the raw material of symbolic and metaphoric atmosphere, and the conspicuous presence of theatrical space-time is essential to this effect. Characters may use dramatic locale to express or extend their conflicts, their points of view, their momentary attitudes, their habitual states of mind, or the conditions of society. Some examples: Rome and Egypt, Venice and Belmont, the Tower of London, court and tavern, court world and green world, the stormy heath, the sterile promontory, the confined deep, the remote magic island, and so forth. In figurative description, words may transform the public stage not merely into an objective and visualizable landscape but into the external correlatives of the speaker's character, concerns, or world view. Things "seen" will then be inseparable from the way they are seen. To describe in this manner is to interpret, and the world a character lives in and "sees" is subjective to the extent that it has been so interpreted. Here the presence of the nonrealistic stage in itself is of crucial importance. We are not free to imagine that which we see before us. A character describing landscape in detail does not neutralize the quite different theatrical scene in which he stands. The very absence of the scene we hear about may enforce our attention to the scene we see.

To *read* Shakespearian drama as theater is to visualize the conventional stage in which the describer stands as well as the place and world he projects in language. And when descriptive language contains a high percentage of figurative elements, the presence of this theater and stage intensifies the dramatic and subjective effect: we become more aware of characters trying each to impose *his* perspective on stage and world, whether in the interests of greed and power or of idealism and love. When Shakespeare classed the poet with the lover and lunatic, therefore, he did not intend an unqualified compliment: "of imagination all compact" describes an unrealistic stance, an absoluteness, an excess of *feigning* which is neither possible for the theatrical, nor healthy for the human, imagination.

Troilus and Cressida:
The Observer as Basilisk

THE MOOD ESTABLISHED by the opening speech of *Troilus and Cressida* may be discerned more clearly if we approach it by way of a contrasting example, the use of the choral speaker in *Henry V*. There the problems inherent in the theatrical conditions of representing are placed side by side with the problems inherent in the fictions represented. The relation of speeches to battle scenes, of boasting to defeat and wary modesty to triumph; the particular quality of Henry's triumph at Agincourt; his famous soliloquy on ceremony (IV.i.242); the motif of the epitome, i.e., the single hero who embodies, directs, and exalts in his little space the virtue of a nation and the forces of history—these analogues of the play's main theme are paralleled by the utterances of the choral presenter. Thus at the beginning of Act III, his appeal to the spectator's historical imagination is placed beside the king's appeal to the soldier's theatrical imagination:

> CHOR.: Thus with imagined wing our swift scene flies
> In motion of no less celerity
> Than that of thought. Suppose that you have seen
> The well-appointed king at Hampton pier
> Embark his royalty; and his brave fleet
> With silken streamers the young Phoebus fanning:
> Play with your fancies, and in them behold

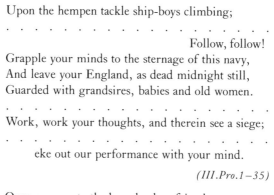

Upon the hempen tackle ship-boys climbing;

. . . .

                     Follow, follow!
Grapple your minds to the sternage of this navy,
And leave your England, as dead midnight still,
Guarded with grandsires, babies and old women.

. . . .

Work, work your thoughts, and therein see a siege;

. . . .

      eke out our performance with your mind.

(III.Pro.1–35)

K. HEN.: Once more unto the breach, dear friends, once more;
Or close the wall up with our English dead.
In peace there's nothing so becomes a man
As modest stillness and humility:
But when the blast of war blows in our ears,
Then imitate the action of the tiger:
Stiffen the sinews, summon up the blood,
Disguise fair nature with hard-favoured rage;
Then lend the eye a terrible aspect:
Let it pry through the portage of the head
Like the brass cannon. . . .

(III.i.1–11)

While one plays Samuel Eliot Morison, the other plays Stanislavsky. But which plays which? The roles seem interchangeable. The success of spectator and soldier alike depends on force of imaginative thought. As the spectator's imagination succeeds, he becomes the soldier. And since every spectator is in reality a potential English soldier, the play claims to be a kind of war game, a patriotic exercise carried on within the modest and relatively humble "girdle of these walls."

But Shakespeare does not simply run these two worlds together: the main significance of the parallel lies in the *contrast* between history and drama, between political and theatrical involvement. Because it is not history, drama can re-create the diffuse events of history in the unified significant *now* of the theatrical occasion. The play places before the English audience an ideal image of itself and then exhorts it to live up to that image. But, confined within the wooden O, the play—being only a play—can do no more unless the audience assists:

O England! model to thy inward greatness,
Like little body with a mighty heart,

What mightst thou do, that honour would thee do,
Were all thy children kind and natural!

                              (II.Pro.16–19)

A model identical to that of the England represented is provided by the
stage on which it is represented:

                                        pardon, gentles all,
        The flat unraised spirits that hath dared
        On this unworthy scaffold to bring forth
        So great an object; can this cockpit hold
        The vasty fields of France? . . .

        . . . .

        O pardon! since a crooked figure may
        Attest in little place a million;
        And let us, ciphers to this great accompt,
        On your imaginary forces work.

                              (I.Pro.8–18)

        Thus far, with rough and all-unable pen,
            Our bending author hath pursued the story,
        In little room confining mighty men,
            Mangling by starts the full course of their glory.
        Small time, but in that small most greatly lived
            This star of England.

                              (V.Ep.1–6)

The final lines blur the small time of the historical king's life with the
small time of the drama in which alone the *ideal prince* lives.

   By directing his plain British modesty to the stage, by saying, "This is
a poor imitation of the truth," Shakespeare glorifies that truth and places
it safely beyond the limits of theatrical visualization even while asking us
dramatically, imaginatively, to visualize. This strategy kills two birds
with one stone: on the one hand, the poor imitation is made more important by the subject matter which transcends it. Theater can press beyond
the limits of its medium only if it claims to be nothing but theater. On
the other hand, Shakespeare overgoes Holinshed in significance as well
as vividness. Distanced by the Chorus, the true facts of history take on
force and glamour without having their factuality jeopardized. And at
the same time, the very limits which make the stage a mockery are those
which best convey the truth *in* history. This is the truth not of outward
degree but of inward greatness, the inner force of a single man. Whatever ironies there may be in *Henry V* as a whole, to whatever degree it is

meant as a wish-fulfilling image, a garden spot in England's history offered to a more precarious contemporary world, the theatrical occasion established by the Chorus is a celebration, a ceremonial tribute to the old order in which the audience is asked to participate.

I

When the Prologue of *Troilus and Cressida* steps forward, his opening lines project a sense of epic distance and heroic scale which promises a mythic successor to the pageantry of *Henry V*:

> In Troy there lies the scene. From isles of Greece
> The princes orgulous, their high blood chafed,
> Have to the port of Athens sent their ships,
> Fraught with the ministers and instruments
> Of cruel war. Sixty and nine, that wore
> Their crownets regal, from th'Athenian bay
> Put forth toward Phrygia; and their vow is made
> To ransack Troy, within whose strong immures
> The ravished Helen, Menelaus' queen,
> With wanton Paris sleeps; and that's the quarrel.

The promise of ceremony is quickly dissipated. In *Henry V*, the movement from history to drama is effected in a way calculated to enforce the distinctions between them. But these lines lead us to expect that the stuff of poetry will be put directly on the stage. The difference between the myth and its dramatic representation is obscured by the reportorial tone and the high rhetoric of the description. And as Harry Levin has remarked, "To convert myth into explicit drama was to break its spell." Translated to the stage, the epic is jeopardized by lack of distance and by the presence of merely life-size actors. The rhetoric of the *Henry V* Chorus is used not so much to set the scene as to sustain the ceremony of the theatrical relation, e.g., the "If I only . . . (but I don't)" of the opening lines:

> O for a muse of fire, that would ascend
> The brightest heaven of invention,
> A kingdom for a stage, princes to act
> And monarchs to behold the swelling scene!
>
> *(1.Pro.1–4)*

By contrast, the tenses of the Prologue to *Troilus and Cressida* bring the epic there-then of the Trojan war rapidly into the theatrical here-now: *there* lies the scene, the princes *have sent* their ships, "their vow is made / To ransack Troy," "and that's the quarrel. / To Tenedos they *come*"; "*now* on Dardan plains" they pitch their tents, "*Now* expectation, tickling skittish spirits, / On one and other side, Trojan and Greek, / Set all on hazard." *Hither*

> am I come
> A Prologue arm'd, but not in confidence
> Of author's pen or actor's voice, but suited
> In like conditions as our argument,
> To tell you, fair beholders, that our play
> Leaps o'er the vaunt and firstlings of those broils,
> Beginning in the middle, starting thence away
> To what may be digested in a play.
> Like or find fault; do as your pleasures are:
> Now good or bad, 'tis but the chance of war.

Brusque, impersonal, and indifferent, the Prologue comes forward simply to expedite the performance. The play will stand on its own merits. Beyond his expository function, he and the audience have nothing to do with each other. The opening chorus of *Henry V* concludes with the opposite effect:

> Admit me Chorus to this history;
> Who prologue-like your humble patience pray,
> Gently to hear, kindly to judge, our play.

The history is thus acted out within the fictional ambience of a theater and world where trust, cooperation, ceremony, and order are assured; an occasion in which an ideal moment of history is shared and celebrated. The values safeguarded in that moment are reaffirmed now in the very relation of Chorus to audience.

The armed Prologue of *Troilus* does away with all this. There are no kindly judges watching this play. His final couplet anticipates Troilus's famous "What is aught but as 'tis valued?" but does so in a more cynical and unconcerned tone. He assumes nothing about, and demands nothing from, the audience. He suggests that their characters will determine their responses and their responses reveal their characters. In effect, then, he presents the play as an inkblot test. Throughout the play the audience is given a number of perspectives on, or theories about, the action. The views of Troilus and Hector, Agamemnon and Nestor, Cressida, and Ulysses all place the action within the framework of different theories.

One of these is elaborated in the famous speech by Ulysses (I.iii.83–124), which has been held up as a paradigm of lingering medieval influences in the Elizabethan world picture. A closer consideration of that speech, however, should direct us toward the play's center. If taken in a straightforward way as the utterance of commonplaces, Ulysses' lines refer to a natural system in which self and value, rights and duties, depend on one's fixed position relative to others in a hierarchic universe: "Take but degree away, untune that string, / And, hark, what discord follows!" (I.iii.109–10). The organization of this universe is felt to be real because made by God rather than by man; felt also to be perceptibly embodied in the spatial order of the cosmos, and to be reflected in the microcosmic structures of man and his immediate environment. Selves are defined by their place in an established public order; and since the order *is* hierarchic, it provides fixed vertical perspectives—above and below—in which one's nature and position may be established.

Ulysses' speech, however, is also susceptible to a different and more modern interpretation, which centers on his use of optical imagery. You should, in the first place, be put on your guard by a peculiar pull between geocentric and heliocentric pressures in the imagery, between the earthy object at the center and the light-giving subject in the middle of the order. A closer glance at lines 83–92 will suggest the alternative: As a "medicinable eye," the sun actively "communicates his parts to others": it provides its own light; it can perform operations on what it sees and make its objects better than they are. This may have the positive effect of keeping order by controlling the influences of evil planets; since what they are in themselves is less important than what they do to and for others in the system to which they belong, making them keep up appearances has some substantive value. But to correct the external aspects of evil objects may also be to vizard their true quality so that they become (in Thersites' words) "gilt counterfeits." And since *aspect* may also bear the transitive implication of *viewing*, we are reminded that evil gazers, like basilisks (and like Thersites), may with a noxious eye injure an object by projecting on it the poison of their inferior natures. These suggestions extend the range of the word *observe* at line 86: in the traditional reading, the heavens, planets, and earth observe degree, priority, etc., simply in the sense of fulfilling assigned roles and functions. But *observe* often means *conform to* or *comply with* in a negative sense—i.e., to pay lip service in merely formal celebration, to do what has to be done though it does not agree with one's nature, to subordinate private will to public weal (not a negative implication), or to mask one's true intentions in order to get what one wants.

There may finally be a vague sense in which *observe* means *see:* "Planets and men see this orderly system all around them; therefore they follow it as the best way to get things done." The motive here is not ethical and cosmological but practical and procedural; this accords with the purpose of the speech as a whole, which, after all, is not a hymn to cosmic order but a periphrastic way of analyzing a local problem. And the interpretation reflects back into the opening lines on degree—"Degree being vizarded, / The unworthiest shows as fairly in the mask." Given a certain view of nature, this can be a useful if not a good thing; the issue may be that of practical control rather than that of moral hypocrisy. For if we follow the second interpretation through as the play in fact urges us to do, we come to feel that appetite, the universal wolf, is the true nature of things, that degree is a lid shakily imposed on nature, an artificial system of distinctions and constraints which rubs against the grain of reality.

In typical Tudor fashion, Ulysses seems to be applying the hierarchic principle as a practical or rhetorical stopgap. Shakespeare does not have him question the cosmological and ontological status of degree—it had already been dubious for some time—but the phenomenological character of the belief in degree as an element of consciousness. Awareness of degree should be a given and unquestioned fact of mental life which imposes rules from within, inhibits the universal wolf, serves as a means of identification and a guide to action. But what made it a given and unquestioned fact was precisely that belief in its external and objective reality which had been jeopardized by developments in astronomy and by other cultural changes. When there is no single cosmic topography in which to locate, identify, and evaluate selves, then relative perspectives become positive influences: *What is seen* comes more to depend on *how it is seen,* and the inherent quality of self may depend as much on attribution as on objective value.

To summarize this discussion, the first and more traditional meaning of Ulysses' speech stresses an objective world order whose creatures have place, motion, and function in the ambience of a visible hierarchy. But the second meaning stresses the subjective agency of seers as they influence their objects by the way they see. Degree becomes a matter of perspective, and perspective entails an optical situation in which one judges or sees only at a distance and from the outside. This is the moral of the familiar dialogue on "reputation" (III.iii). Ulysses remarks that a man, no matter how virtuous,

> Cannot make boast to have that which he hath,
> Nor feels not what he owes but by reflection;

> As when his virtues aiming upon others
> Heat them, and they retort that heat again
> To the first giver.
>
> *(98–102)*

Achilles agrees that speculation, the power of sight, "turns not to it-self / Till it hath travelled and is married there / Where it may see it-self" (109–11). And Ulysses continues:

> no man is the lord of anything—
> Though in and of him there be much consisting—
> Till he communicate his parts to others;
> Nor doth he of himself know them for aught
> Till he behold them formed in th' applause
> Where they're extended. . . .
>
> *(115–20)*

With the failure of degree as a reliable criterion of value, a greater bur-den is imposed on *performance* as external display of self and on inter-pretation, in which the beholder must infer from the visible clues to the inner quality of the performer. This means that we cannot be sure to what extent our interpretation apprehends something already there, in-trinsic to the object, and to what extent it alters the object by communi-cation of the interpreter's parts.

II

The problem Shakespeare raises in *Troilus* is that the nature, value, and rewards of performance are too little in the power of agents and too much under the control of observers. And unfortunately the observers are not up to their responsibility. The character of Pandarus, the motives of Achilles and Cressida, the viewpoints of Cressida and Thersites reveal the primacy of interpreters who strip the action of its possible richness and reduce it to what may be digested by the sensibility of the cynical modern playgoer. And yet I think the point of the play is that this did not *have* to be the case: Thersites' view that all the argument's a cuckold and a whore is pushed in our faces as if it were the only moral to be drawn from the action, but Shakespeare has in fact provided an alternate read-ing, the center of which lies in the Trojan debate over Helen (II.ii), and for which Hector is the main spokesman.

When Troilus makes his famous statement, "What is ought but as 'tis valued?", Hector responds as follows:

> value dwells not in particular will:
> It holds his estimate and dignity
> As well wherein 'tis precious of itself
> As in the prizer: 'tis mad idolatry
> To make the service greater than the god;
> And the will dotes that is attributive
> To what infectiously itself affects,
> Without some image of th'affected merit.
>
> *(II.ii.53–60)*

This has sometimes been interpreted as a slap at Troilus. Hector, as Ellis-Fermor puts it, is "making it clear that the sense of value depends for its stability upon something outside itself, objective and absolute, inherent in the object."[1] But I think Hector is doing something else: his use of the word *image* is clearly a subjective use, for the image is a reflection of what the prizer wants. The phrase "wherein 'tis precious of itself" seems to refer either to an object *or* to a value, a standard of judgment. Hector's emphasis is still on the individual will and its attributive power, and he says to Troilus, "Value holds its estimate and dignity not only in the prizer but also 'wherein 'tis precious of itself'; it is silly to project value on a thing simply because you desire it; you ought to look for evidence in the object of the quality you value. You ought, in brief, to build a good case to justify your spending so much effort on the object." The scene is focused less on Helen than on Hector's attempt to make Troilus work out more rationally the position he shares with him. He does not air Menelaus's side of the argument as something intrinsically or objectively more "right": natural law and honor are poised against each other as two ways of attributing value to the object. Menelaus can make a good case for his criterion, which has nothing whatsoever to do with Helen's intrinsic merit. Can Troilus make a better case? He does, after Hector gives him a clue:

> She is a theme of honour and renown,
> A spur to valiant and magnanimous deeds,
> Whose present courage may beat down our foes,
> And fame in time to come canonize us. . . .
>
> *(II.ii.199–202)*

---

[1] Una Ellis-Fermor, "The Universe of *Troilus and Cressida*," in *Frontiers of Drama* (New York: Methuen, 1946), 65.

Hector would agree with Ellis-Fermor and others that the universe of the play reveals no fixed intrinsic value in objects. But this does not mean it is neutral; it simply means that it is ambiguous, a chaos packed with possibilities and alternatives. Value is what subjects must therefore create by their imagination and activity. A value is sufficiently objective or real if it makes demands on the prizer, imposes restraints, requires consistency of behavior, elicits noble action, and—most important—converts a world of indifferent objects into a significant field worthy of one's trouble and attention. Helen is a case in point: if women are whores, are they not accorded generous treatment in being considered pearls? If Thersites is right, do not Hector and Troilus improve Helen by making her a symbol of their own noble urges? One might even say that Helen's shortcomings offer a challenge to the heroic imagination, that a proof of its force lies in its ability to shape such recalcitrant material to its own higher uses. It is therefore necessary to *assert* Helen's intrinsic worthlessness or irrelevance and also to assert opposing claims like that of Menelaus and natural law. Only in this way can the heroic imagination test its premises and set about finding the proper grounds of quarrel in a straw. This attitude may be generalized to include the response to action, as when Troilus says "we may not think the justness of each act / Such and no other than event doth form it" (II.ii.119–20). *Event* becomes relevant only in supplying an outcome whose catastrophe may be heroically ignored as irrelevant.

The play's corrosive pattern of events ultimately makes fools of the Trojans. But it does not negate the logic underlying the idealistic Trojan theory. For if life is such that trial necessarily frustrates the "unbodied figure of thought," Trojan idealism could—in the right hands—become a practical as well as a noble posture: by expecting no reward from the "universe of event," by expecting rather that idealism best reveals its nature in becoming slave to the limits of action, one might be in the position to safeguard both expectation and value. But such a stance requires a tougher-minded hero than either Troilus or Hector. The Trojan way explored by Shakespeare, as one of a number of perspectives in this play, is established as the central method of imagination in the play and character of Hamlet.

Their nobility of thought and speech is rhetorically pitched at a level which makes the Trojans look a little fusty or archaic. Yet in this they are not singled out; most of the characters are allowed, indeed encouraged, to indulge the oratorical inclination. One of the most salient qualities of this play is the large scope it gives to noble thought and speech. In the long run these may suffer from the way the play's action tends to bear out Thersites' cynicism. But they are impressive when we hear them, and they are by no means all to be taken as hypocrisy or pure bombast, even though it is clear that most of the major characters, and especially Ulysses, will swing into a lecture at the drop of a hat. The point, though, is that the distribution of wisdom speeches among the different characters prevents us from easily accepting Thersites' opinion that everyone onstage is either a fool or a knave. On the other hand, he stands closer than most of the other characters to the audience, in part because his language is that of the contemporary stews. Therefore, his importance as an interpreter and his nearness to the audience seem calculated to lend his perspective more cogency than it deserves. I think Shakespeare intends us to move toward agreement with Thersites, but to do so unwillingly, to feel or discover that this was not the only possible perspective, merely the one to which we seem—a little reluctantly—to find ourselves disposed.

As the main soliloquist and interpreter of the action, Thersites with theatrical gusto assimilates everything to the expanding core of his self-proclaimed envy. He brings the heroes up to date and cuts them down to less than life size. His argument opposes itself to the heroic nostalgia for a vanished age of better men, since it assumes that only the haze of distance and patina of time impart the illusion of superiority. Seen close up and in the flesh, the antique heroes resemble us in our more unguarded moments. This remorseless attention—aimed not merely by Thersites at everyone else but by a majority of the characters at each other—lends the play world the atmosphere of a Hollywood night club. The spirit of gossip, whispering and staring, verges on the salacious. And this puts the characters on the spot. Cressida's phrase "minds swayed by eyes" refers to her own mind led into error by her own eyes, but it can be reinterpreted to refer also to one character's mind affected by the eyes of others, which is the way Ulysses and Achilles see it in their famous remarks on reputation.

And this meaning accurately describes the theatrical dilemma imposed on Shakespeare's heroic and romantic characters by their deportation from the remote and wide-open epic spaces to the more crabbed and exposed confines imposed by the visual context and physical stage of a play. Most of them seem somehow conscious of performing, observing, and being observed. Their uneasy awareness of being constantly on display, living a theatrical existence, renders them more complex and less stereotypical as characters. This is especially true when we see them occasionally living up to, or treating others as, their stereotypical images:

the wise counselor, the noble warrior, the loyal and betrayed lover, the braggart soldier, the ancient, indeed doddering, voice—indeed windbag—of experience. One is almost inclined to believe that if some of the nobler figures display nostalgia mixed with their self-consciousness, this is not simply a desire to revive the old order but a yen to return from exile and get safely back into the protective volume of an old epic poem.

That Thersites displays himself as an envious have-not makes the job of evaluation more difficult: On the one hand, we are tempted to feel that things must somehow be better than he says they are, since his viewpoint is so clearly vitiated by the "ill aspects" of his self-devouring nature. But on the other hand, his railing does not fall short of most of his targets. He has to *claim* envy because it is often so hard to see what he *does* envy in the parodies of Greek heroism around him. In one sense, the missing beauty in Achilles' stage life is what makes Thersites ugly, and this sense gives his railing its point and draws him closer to the audience.

Thersites' soliloquies have the effect of addresses to the audience; therefore they work to extend the logic of the play from the relations among characters to the relations between characters and audience. If Thersites continually says during the course of the play, "The men on stage are not heroes, but fools and knaves," Pandarus, turning toward the audience at play's end, adds, "And so are you." The syphilitic go-between steps forward to become the epilogue, the intermediary between play world and spectators. His poor entertainment, his bad jokes, strained doggerel, and elbow-digging topical allusions reflect not only on himself but on the audience he now serves:

> A goodly medicine for my aching bones! O world! World! thus is the poor agent despised! O traitors and bawds, how earnestly are you set a-work and how ill requited! why should our endeavor be so loved and the performance so loathed! (V.x.35–40)

If there is any truth to the rumor that the phrase in the preface to the 1609 reissue, "neuer clapper-clawd with the palmes of the vulgar," alludes to the audience *Troilus* was put on for (at the Inns of Court) rather than the reception it received, this device must have taken on the immediacy of a special joke. But its general function would thereby only have been sharpened. The epic vistas promised by the Prologue have been dissipated. The play ends still *in medias res*, having digested its "ample proposition" until, in the fifth act, nothing remains but the "fragments, scraps, the bits and greasy relics" (V.ii.159) of the battle scenes, with their rapid syncopated flicker of unfinished actions, their hurried vignettes of characters swerving from one to another object or intention,

their sudden collisions of epic and prosaic, heroic and comic moments.
All this presses into Troilus's final speech:

> I do not speak of flight, of fear, of death,
> But dare all imminence that gods and men
> Address their dangers in. Hector is gone:
> Who shall tell Priam so, or Hecuba?
> Let him that will a screech-owl aye be call'd,
> Go in to Troy, and say there, Hector's dead:
> There is a word will Priam turn to stone;
> Make wells and Niobes of the maids and wives,
> Cold statues of the youth, and in a word,
> Scare Troy out of itself. But, march away:
> Hector is dead; there is no more to say.
> Stay yet. You vile abominable tents,
> Thus proudly pight upon our Phrygian plains,
> Let Titan rise as early as he dare.
> I'll through and through you! and, thou great-sized coward,
> No space of earth shall sunder our two hates:
> I'll haunt thee like a wicked conscience still,
> That mouldeth goblins swift as frenzy's thoughts.
> Strike a free march to Troy! with comfort go:
> Hope of revenge shall hide our inward woe.
>
> *(V.x.12–31)*

The texture of this speech is identical with that of the battle scenes, alternating heroic phrases and images with colloquialisms. The rhetoric of
the Prologue is deliberately echoed to emphasize its remoteness and artifice: Troilus in effect consigns the heroic life to ancient statuary, where
alone it may be preserved from the tooth of time and fortune. The shift
from Niobe and Titan to goblins, who will do the Furies' work, moves
abruptly from classical to native mythology.

It is difficult to determine exactly what Troilus means—the tone of
"with comfort go," for example, is perplexing. His main intention is
apparently to vaunt, and this is the clue to the most evident quality of the
speech, a quality which could have been suggested by Chaucer: Troilus
seems self-consciously to be making his exit speech. We sense his awareness of being onstage and his reluctance to leave without a good conclusive rant. As the matter of the play is distanced, the extant moment of
playing receives the spotlight, all the more brightly in that Troilus's
hope of a resounding exit is frustrated:

[*As* Troilus *is going out, enter, from the other side* Pandarus.]

PAN.: But hear you, hear you!

TRO.: Hence, broker-lackey! ignomy and shame
Pursue thy life, and live aye with thy name!

(*V.x.32−34*)

Coming so suddenly on the heels of his bombast, this has the effect of offstage muttering: we seem to be reminded not only of Pandarus's role in the action but also of how inappropriate it is for Troilus to have such a man break in at such a moment.

Shakespeare's reason for assigning the epilogue to Pandarus may be suggested by the main difference between his and Chaucer's treatment of the go-between. Chaucer had carefully given his Pandarus motives of compensation—he is a frustrated lover who enjoys intrigue, derives vicarious pleasure from the affair he is arranging, and occasionally reveals his privation in vague suggestions of lust or prurience. Shakespeare discards all this. The motive of compensation is shifted to Thersites, and no reasons at all are given for Pandarus's behavior. He appears simply as a go-between, a performer serving bored or amorous Trojans, a courtly "straight man," or butt, who causes wit in others and sings an occasional song. He is the paradigm of pure external agency, a communicator of the parts of others with no privacy or privation of his own. Placing himself at their service, or rather mercy, he has no control over the significance and value of his own activity. He is not a trader "in the flesh" until Cressida's behavior has made him so. His contracting syphilis has an uncomfortable farcical quality to it, but it is entirely appropriate in that it connects his helplessness to what Cressida has made of him.

As a true go-between, he projects on the audience the condition to which the play has reduced him, and the implication is that they have seen and liked "as their pleasures are." Depending for its value on the way it is used, and on "the applause / Where it's extended," the play concludes in the climate of a contemporary off-color review. The audience which the play has "created" is the audience to whose pleasures it now pretends that it must pander. This fictional or second-world audience is finally called onstage from the stews and the pit, and there it plants the flag of a worsening world on the former ground of Troy.

The limitations on inwardness, the oppressive pressure of spectators, the clash of perspectives and interpretations to which the characters are subject are built into the staging which the play demands—for example, when Cressida first enters:

CRES.: Who were those went by?
ALEX.:   Queen Hecuba and Helen.
CRES.: And whither go they?
ALEX.:   Up to the eastern tower,
        Whose height commands as subject all the vale,
        To see the battle. . . .

                                                    (I.ii.1–4)

The audience watches people watching people watching people. The technique of multiple perspectives is sustained in the dialogue which follows by the difference between Alexander's straight epic answers and the quick nervous questions, the wry comments of Cressida. This is a mild instance because the figures indicated are not onstage and are suitably veiled by Alexander's rhetoric.

Late in the same scene, Pandarus and Cressida move to an observation point from which they view the heroes marching across the stage while Pandarus tells "them all by their names as they pass by"—Antenor, Hector, and Paris. We first *see* actors dressed according to some director's or designer's conception, and they are then introduced in the racy idiom of characters whose sensibilities are close to ours. When Troilus appears and Cressida asks, "What sneaking fellow comes yonder?" (I.ii.245), we realize that she is also "observing" Pandarus, that the chief value of the heroes in this scene is the ammunition they provide for the battle of wits. Technically, the problems of staging this scene could have been covered by the conventions of stage whisper and aside, but Shakespeare emphasizes the problems by having Cressida caution Pandarus, "Speak not so loud" (201). This focuses the atmosphere of gossip and publicity to which heroes are exposed, and in which Cressida's predilection for cabaret intrigue flourishes.

A final instance of this exposure and the self-consciousness it produces may be seen in the following dialogue between Achilles and Hector:

            Now, Hector, I have fed mine eyes on thee;
            I have with exact view perused thee, Hector,
            And quoted joint by joint.
HECT.:   Is this Achilles?
ACHIL.: I am Achilles.
HECT.:   Stand fair, I pray thee: let me look on thee.
ACHIL.: Behold thy fill.
HECT.:   Nay, I have done already.
ACHIL.: Thou art too brief: I will the second time,
         As I would buy thee, view thee limb by limb.

> HECT.:   O, like a book of sport thou'lt read me o'er;
>   But there's more in me than thou understand'st.
>   Why dost thou so oppress me with thine eye?
>
> *(IV.v.231–41)*

Achilles' "quick sense" is satisfied by the verbal aggression which Hector describes: "to prenominate in nice conjecture / Where thou wilt hit me dead" (249–50). To view Hector is to interpret him as a book, buy him as a morsel. Later on, the sword's "dainty supper" simply repeats, in a less rich and gratifying form, this extant moment of sensing. We sympathize with Hector's uneasiness—"there's more in me than thou understand'st"—because we realize how irrelevant that *more* becomes under the pressure of a perspectivism to which he, in his own way, subscribes. The plot texture of discrete inconsequential moments scarcely allows that *more* to be communicated by any act which does not threaten to make it hang "Quite out of fashion, like a rusty mail / In monumental mock'ry" (III.iii.152–53).

III

In conclusion, I should like to remark that the problems on which *Troilus and Cressida* centers may be specifically located in a historical or cultural framework. They belong to a peculiarly Renaissance set of problems. Yet at the same time they are problems Shakespeare could have found, and did find, by exploring the nature and limits of his medium. For inherent in the structure of theatrical experience are the limits of optical perception, the phenomena of distance and externality which are the essence of the relation between the seer and the seen. Since theatrical action is to be displayed before an audience, it is natural for the dramatist to create actions which can at the same time be displayed before characters onstage, and just as natural to create characters who are aware of, and exploit, this fact. Where characters are aware of acting and speaking before other characters, "sincerity" cannot be assumed automatically: the other characters, as well as the audience, may be placed in the position of spectators who can see only from the outside and who are thus forced to infer or interpret from limited evidence.

The *Troilus* is one of a number of plays in which Shakespeare makes pervasive use of theatrical space-time either openly or tacitly to present the conditions of life in the fictional world on the model of the conditions of theatrical life, or of the conditions inherent in the character of theatrical performance (*Hamlet*, *Measure for Measure*, and *The Tempest* are others).[2] In various ways, such plays ask a fundamental question: "What view might be developed by taking the nature and techniques of theatrical drama seriously as models of world order, and of human motivation and behavior?" The question arises in response to a critical Shakespearian and Renaissance concern which lies at the thematic center of many plays: the declining efficacy of an old order once felt to be objective and real, now requiring either to be discarded or, if accepted, placed on an entirely new footing. At whatever level, and in whatever form, this order is depicted (the cosmos, the state, the family, the traditions of culture, the conventions of literature, etc.), the problem remains the same: when beliefs, assumptions, or attitudes can no longer be taken for granted, they must be argued and revised if they are not to be given up. Their life depends more than ever on the wills and words of men. They must therefore be *staged*, played out, and tested by the mind. For example, it is one thing to have medieval ideas without looking at them as medieval, another thing to look at them as medieval and try to bring them up to date.

The *Troilus*, like *Hamlet*, *Lear*, and other plays, subjects traditional views of order to the controlled conditions of theatrical experiment and accords them, at best, qualified approval if and when they have met the test of the playwright's dramatic scrutiny. The Elizabethan stage may—as many scholars have affirmed—be a mirror of the traditional cosmos if it is a mirror of anything. But whether it is a mirror, whether there is a cosmos to be mirrored, and how it is to be mirrored—these are the problems rather than the givens of Shakespearian theater. And as I have tried to show here and in the previous essay, they are problems with which we can grapple only by correlating a number of different modes of inquiry—e.g., intellectual history, theatrical history, and the esthetics of theatrical drama—into a single hypothetical framework for interpretation.

[2] See the preceding essay in this volume.

Miraculous Harp: A Reading of Shakespeare's *Tempest*

ANTONIO: His word is more than the miraculous harp.
SEBASTIAN: He hath rais'd the wall, and houses too.
ANTONIO: What impossible matter will he make easy next?
SEBASTIAN: I think he will carry this island home in his pocket, and
            give it his son for an apple.
ANTONIO: And, sowing the kernels of it in the sea, bring forth
            more islands.

(Tempest II.i.83–89)

I

IN MANY OF the later plays, some analogue of dramatic control is imposed—and conspicuously imposed—on action which would otherwise get out of control, action which indeed in earlier tragedies did get out of control.[1] The echoes of, or allusions to, earlier tragic patterns in such plays as *Measure for Measure, Pericles, Cymbeline, The Winter's Tale,* and

---

[1] This is a revised and amplified version of a Bergen Lecture delivered at Yale University on November 13, 1967. I would like to thank my students in the 1966–67 graduate seminar in the Renaissance at Santa Cruz and Father James Devereux, S.J., of the Department of English, University of North Carolina, Chapel Hill, for many helpful discussions which affected my thinking about *The Tempest*.

The Tempest have often been remarked. The modes of resolution seem deliberately strained, unnatural, artificial, or unrealistic in these plays, especially since they resonate with allusions to earlier tragedies where resolutions were not forthcoming. This pattern emphasizes a crucial difference between life and theater: in art, life's problems are displayed and then resolved, perhaps displayed in order to be resolved, perhaps resolved so that people can get up and go home. Yet on the other hand— and this distinguishes many of the later plays from the earlier festive comedies—the spectators do not want to go home, sometimes because we are surprised by the unexpected and abrupt happy ending; sometimes because the play, fading into a golden past, makes us yearn after it; sometimes because the action is protracted, the ending delayed, by characters who themselves seem reluctant to leave the play world and return to actuality. The plays often present themselves as temporary and all-too-fragile hiding places in, or from, the worsening world.

Such qualities of the last plays have evoked criticism of the sort leveled by Madeleine Doran at the earlier problem plays:

> They do not seem to us to be satisfactorily resolved in the conventional happy ending of comedy. . . . [and this is so] because of the working out of a serious moral problem in an action built of improbable device and lucky coincidence. The result is only too often to make the solutions seem trivial or forced.
>
> The difficulty with these plays is that the problems are realistically viewed, the endings are not. . . . the manipulation of intrigue and lucky chance to bring about the conventional happy ending gives the effect of an evasion of the serious moral issue of the play.[2]

The main difference between the problem plays and the last plays is that in the latter not even the problems are realistically viewed: Shakespeare would want us to distinguish the grim actuality of Vienna from the pasteboard villainies of Cymbeline's court. Though Professor Doran's remarks are helpful as guides to description and interpretation, her intention to criticize detracts from their value. The critical mood is wrong mainly because Shakespeare has anticipated her by building her criticisms into the plays themselves. And in fact the burden of the present

---

My quotations of the play are from Frank Kermode's Arden edition of *The Tempest* (New York: Random House, 1964), which I found extraordinary for the density, range, and intelligence of its documentation, even though my reading of the play is very different from Kermode's.

[2] *Endeavors of Art* (Madison: University of Wisconsin Press, 1964), 366–67.

essay will be to suggest that Shakespeare would or could or did level Professor Doran's criticism toward her own reading of *The Tempest:* "The action of the play is Prospero's discovery to his enemies, their discovery of themselves, the lovers' discovery of a new world of wonder, Prospero's own discovery of an ethic of forgiveness, and the renunciation of his magical power" (327). This is, in epitome, perhaps the most commonly accepted view of the play,[3] and the best defense of this sentimental reading known to me has been made by Stephen Orgel,[4] who claims that from the first long dialogue with Miranda in I.ii, "Prospero's suffering . . . is essentially behind him," and therefore he "leads the play . . . through suffering to reconciliation and a new life." Orgel goes on to cite the pattern of the masque of Ceres as evidence that "the play is at this point moving away from the island and back to civilization" (127): "The conclusion of the revels, the vision of the masque as an 'insubstantial pageant,' and all that that vision implies for Prospero, provide a vital transition in the play to the renunciation of extraordinary powers and the return to the ordinary world." Orgel admits that "the transition is a painful one for Prospero" (130), but his major emphasis is on the magician's return and on his preparing to reassume his old job.[5]

[3] The hard-nosed view which centers on disapproval of Prospero is much rarer. W. H. Auden's "The Sea and the Mirror" is perhaps the most famous example. Its most engaging advocate is Clifford Leech, who in *Shakespeare's Tragedies* (London: Chatto & Windus, 1950), 142–58, describes Prospero as flawed by his embittered and slightly sadistic puritanism, a flaw Leech ascribes to the growing bitterness and puritanism of Shakespeare's own sensibility in his later years. Leech makes many acute observations, but his essay is subject to the same criticism as that I have just leveled at Madeleine Doran: his criticism of Shakespeare is actually Shakespeare's criticism of Prospero. While rejecting the pious reading of the play, Leech sneaks it in by attributing it to Shakespeare as the message Shakespeare wanted to convey but could not, e.g., in his remark that the songs and the musical sweetness of the verse "show a glimpse of the purified world which Shakespeare the puritan might reach out to in his dreams. But the play as a whole shows also how the world looked to him awake" (158). The remark can be changed from a faulty judgment to a useful interpretive insight by substituting "Prospero" for "Shakespeare." Page references of future citations from Leech are to this volume.

[4] "New Uses of Adversity: Tragic Experience in *The Tempest*," in *In Defense of Reading*, ed. Richard Poirier and Reuben Brower (New York: E. P. Dutton, 1962), 114, 125. Page references of future citations from Orgel are to this volume.

[5] The sentimental reading underlies a wide range of interpretations. Some examples: Reuben Brower, *The Fields of Light: An Experiment in Critical Reading* (New York: Oxford University Press, 1962), 95–122; Una Ellis-Fermor, *The Jacobean Drama* (London: Methuen, 1953), 266–71; Northrop Frye, *A Natural Perspective* (New York: Columbia University Press, 1965), 151–59 (but see also his more tempered account in the introduction to the Pelican Shakespeare edition of *The Tempest* [Baltimore: Penguin Books, 1959], 15–26; Frank Kermode, introduction to the Arden edition, xxiv–lxiii; Derek Traversi, *Shakespeare: The Last Phase* (London: Hollis & Carter, 1954), whose

I find it hard to accept this reading as it stands, not because it is wrong but because it does not hit the play where it lives. The renunciation pattern is there, but only as a general tendency against which the play strains. Too many cues and clues, too many quirky details, point in other directions, and critics have been able to make renunciation in this simple form the central action only by ignoring those details. Some of the puzzling items may be listed here. First, Prospero's language in describing the usurpation to Miranda encourages us to believe that he is partly responsible for what happened, yet he never seems to take this into account; throughout the course of the play, he acts the part of the good man wronged by villains, and he is not above an occasional reference to his injured merit. Second, Gonzalo, for all his goodness, was in effect Antonio's accomplice; as Alonso's counselor he mitigated the harshness of Prospero's exile, but the fact remains that he was master of the design, responsible for its execution. Furthermore Gonzalo, for all his goodness, is just a bit of a fool—maybe not as much as his knavish companions make him out to be, but a fool nonetheless. And yet the affinities between Gonzalo and Prospero are curiously insisted on in a number of verbal and ideological echoes. One more detail about Gonzalo: in any good romance his final speech would be the concluding sentiment; what ancient Gower is to *Pericles* Gonzalo would be to *The Tempest*. Only it is not that kind of play, and his epilogue is badly timed, preceding the end by 113 lines.

Third, an important set of questions emerging from the exposition in I.ii have never, to my knowledge, been pursued: What are we really to do with Ariel, Sycorax, and Caliban? Why was Ariel punished by being stuck in a tree, why does he continually ask for his freedom, why the names Sycorax and Caliban, why the business about the witch's exile from Africa with its obvious echoes of Prospero's exile from Europe? What to make of the difference, which many readers have noticed, between Prospero's view of Caliban and ours? Why do we respond to

---

long and influential essay (193–272) is thematically outlined on 194, 206, and 254–55. For other examples, see the concise summaries in Kermode, lxxxi–lxxxviii. A different set of problems and classifications vis-à-vis *Tempest* criticism has recently been considered from a logical and analytical standpoint by A. D. Nuttall in *Two Concepts of Allegory* (New York: Barnes & Noble, 1967). Nuttall's examination of some of the conceptual bases and presuppositions of allegoristic criticism and allegorical poetry sometimes reads like a parody of British analytical style, but it is flawed chiefly by the author's lack of experience of, or ability in, literary interpretation. More is to be learned about the play from the pragmatic, often impressionistic, effort at allegorical interpretation by D. G. James in his suggestive and beautifully distilled study, *The Dream of Prospero* (London: Clarendon Press, 1967).

qualities in Caliban which Prospero ignores, and why are we made to feel that the magician is more vindictive than he needs to be? Why the full sense Shakespeare gives us of life on the island before the ship sailed in from Tunis, where Alonso had just married off his daughter Claribel to the Prince? In this connection, what are we to do with the odd set of references and allusions to Africa and Carthage, and especially to episodes from the first half of Virgil's *Aeneid?* These references prod us into remembering Aeneas's journey from Troy to Italy, from an old to a new world; they offer that journey as a shadowy resemblance to the various voyages and themes of the plot action, and they ask us to make some sense of the resemblance, or at least not to ignore it.[6] Finally, why the twenty-line epilogue, in which Prospero asks the audience for applause, sympathy, and release?

I shall consider these questions within the framework of my disagreement with the sentimental reading I summarized earlier. The center of disagreement lies in the way I conceive the relation of Ariel and Caliban to Prospero. I want to begin, therefore, with something like an allegorical sketch of each of the first two characters.

II

To run through some preliminary and elemental distinctions, Ariel is air and fire to Caliban's earth and water. He is, in David William's words, "'an airy spirit,' once imprisoned in a pine, and aspiring towards total liberty." Caliban, on the other hand, "is capable of not a few human conditions . . . so that his appearance, however brutal, must indicate an aspiration towards human nature, whereas Ariel's is away from it."[7] Ariel's vision of freedom is to fly merrily after summer on the bat's back, to live in the blossom that hangs on the bough, to spend his life far from the pains and labor of humanity, pleasuring himself in a green and garden world. He is not so much a spirit of nature as a spirit for nature. He looks forward to a time when the last vestiges of man will have enriched nature's strange treasuries and traceries, bones into coral and eyes into pearls. But Ariel is also gifted with magical powers, with theatrical and rhetorical talents. And though he demands his freedom, his powers are recreative in that their exercise affords him delight. His last song—

[6] Frye (*A Natural Perspective*, 156) vaguely connects the Virgilian allusions to the theme of initiation and lists a few analogues in his introduction to the Pelican *Tempest*, 23.

[7] David William, "The Tempest on the Stage," in *Jacobean Theatre*, ed. John Russell Brown and Bernard Harris (New York: St. Martin's Press, 1960), 151.

"Where the bee sucks, there suck I"—reminds me of Plato's familiar comparison of the poet to a honey-gathering bee in the garden of the muses. Like Plato's poet, Ariel is a winged thing whose art is magically inspired, therefore brought forth without labor. He bears a light and melodious burden, a far cry from firewood. As a figure of the idyllic fancy, he is at once pleasure seeking and detached, a cool narcissist and a spirit of play.[8] He plans to retire in a delicate and diminutive green world where he may compute his thyme among flowers, securely separated from the baser elements of man. He acknowledges as his own no things of darkness but owls and bats.

Ariel, then, is a recreative and self-delighting spirit whose art and magic are forms of play, a spirit freed by a magician whose presence on the island owes not a little to his own self-delighting recreative impulse, his own playing with arts and magic. Spirit and master have much in common: each has both a histrionic and a rhetorical bent which he delights to indulge, and each savors his performances to the full. In the case of Ariel, this is perhaps unambiguously clear only in his opening speech, but it is marked enough there to set up the analogy. Notice, in the following lines, how his obvious delight in magical performance is doubled by his pleasure in describing it, how his speech builds up to its final heroic period, changes from past tense to the more vivid present, and pushes beyond descriptive report to a high-toned epic personification. "Hast thou," asks Prospero, "Perform'd to point the tempest that I bade thee?" And Ariel answers:

> To every article.
> I boarded the king's ship: now on the beak,
> Now in the waist, the deck, in every cabin,
> I flam'd amazement: sometime I'd divide,
> And burn in many places; on the topmast,
> The yards, and boresprit, would I flame distinctly,
> Then meet and join. Jove's lightnings, the precursors
> O' th' dreadful thunder-claps, more momentary

---

[8] D. G. James remarks of Ariel that "in the end the world of humanity bores him . . . but it is also true that the lineaments of his mind are all too human" (*The Dream of Prospero*, 68), anticipating what I am about to suggest about Ariel's relation to Prospero's mind. Frye describes Ariel as an Eros-Narcissus figure, a self-contained polymorph, and though his discussion of this figure is suggestive, it has nothing to do with Ariel (*A Natural Perspective*, 82–83). Some of the Roman influences on Shakespeare's treatment of Ariel and Caliban are discussed by Bernard Knox, "The Tempest and the Ancient Comic Tradition," in *English Stage Comedy*, ed. W. K. Wimsatt, Jr. (New York: Columbia University Press, 1955), 52–73.

And sight-outrunning were not: The fire and cracks
Of sulphurous roaring the most mighty Neptune
Seem to besiege, and make his bold waves tremble,
Yea, his dread trident shake.
PROSPERO: My brave spirit! . . .

(I.ii.193–206)

No doubt, as we learn a moment later, Ariel's enthusiasm owes something to his eagerness to get out from under and be free. Yet at the same time we respond to his gratuituous delight in putting on a good show and describing it in brave rhetoric. That this speaks to an answering delight in Prospero is evident throughout the play, most clearly in the two masques. At the end of the masque of judgment, he commends Ariel for performing "bravely the figure of this harpy" but also for following the script: "Of my instruction hast thou nothing bated / In what thou hadst to say" (III.iii.85–86). And the script contains far more than is necessary to induce fear and contrition. As the majority of onstage responses indicate, it is for the most part a bravura display of hocus-pocus and spectacular effects mixed with a learned allusion in the imitation and adaptation of the *Aeneid*, Book III. John Cranford Adams's remark that Prospero did not have to be present up top throughout the show only reinforces my feeling that he is there so that we can watch him enjoy his god's-eye view as he sees his work performed and observes the audience reaction—a little like Tom Sawyer at his funeral. If he missed the first spectacle reported by Ariel, he is not going to miss this one.

In this connection, his way of announcing the wedding masque is a little odd:

                                                    I must
Bestow upon the eyes of this young couple
Some vanity of mine Art: it is my promise,
And they expect it from me.

(IV.i.39–42)

He says this to Ariel, who doesn't seem to have known about it before (and therefore answers, "Presently?"—"right away?"). He may well have promised it to Ferdinand and Miranda, but there is no previous mention of it. "Some vanity of mine Art," uttered after his previous *tours de force*, has about it a comic note of Chaucerian self-deprecation, stressed immediately by his sense of his own image—"I must live up to their expectations." Shortly after, Ferdinand rises to the occasion by asking, "May I be bold / To think these spirits?" Prospero then willingly explains: "Spirits, which by mine Art / I have from their confines call'd to enact / My present fancies" (IV.i.119–22). The masque reveals much about his present fancies, and more is revealed by its having been rather suddenly and gratuitously conceived.

Ariel and Prospero thus share a delight in art, one which continually distracts Prospero from his ethical purpose and in one famous instance leads him to forget what goes on around him. His ingenuous pleasure makes him sacrifice plot to spectacle and drama to theater. David William remarks that "in no play is the visual trap more tempting or more dangerous," but he directs this criticism toward "producers [who] offer a visual accompaniment that more often than not distracts from the action instead of illuminating it."[9] I think we can also read this as part of Shakespeare's portrayal of Prospero, a part intimately connected with the presence and meaning of Ariel, who—like Lear's fool—reflects his master's mind.[10]

It may be pedantic to load theological symbolism onto the tree in which Ariel was trapped, but I shall do so for heuristic purposes, viz., let Ariel trapped in the tree of fallen human nature (*in medio ligni*) be an emblem of Prospero's Milanese experience. From the beginning, the Duke's own airy recreative impulse asserted claims that made him view his social and political circumstances as unduly burdensome. He neglected worldly ends for the seclusion in which he bettered his mind, made the liberal arts all his study, and allowed himself to be transported and rapt in secret studies, claiming indeed that withdrawn exclusiveness made these studies "o'erprize all popular rate." Thus he was easily deceived, betrayed, and exiled by the brother he trusted with "a confidence sans bounds," and to whom he committed his government.[11] Prospero no less than Ariel might be deemed "a spirit too delicate / to enact . . . [the] earthy and abhorred commands" not of Sycorax but of government in a world full of Antonios, Sebastians, and Alonsos. It may also be

---

[9] "The Tempest on the Stage," 133. Cf. also G. B. Harrison, "The Tempest," in *Stratford Papers 1962*, ed. B. W. Jackson (Toronto: W. J. Gage, 1963), 215–16.

[10] Traversi notes that Ariel symbolizes "the imaginative power, the fancy which now finds liberty and integration in Prospero's own spiritual vision," but his interest in the antithesis between "superior spirituality" and "material confinement" leads him to give higher marks to Prospero's spiritual vision than I think Shakespeare does (*Shakespeare: The Last Phase*, 229).

[11] James's long chapter on the occult and hermetic background leading from antiquity through Renaissance cabalism and Neoplatonism to Prospero is useful, but he does not make it pay off (*The Dream of Prospero*, 44–71): on the one hand, he places too great an allegorical burden on Prospero, making him represent Shakespeare's farewell, on behalf of the European imagination, to centuries of "illusions about magical beliefs and prac-

owing to Ariel that the former Duke of Milan has an unhealthy attitude toward labor—toward good clean manual work. We hardly expect him, as an aristocrat, to wash his own dishes and light his own fires. But he seems to have an ethical as well as a practical and social aversion to labor: Caliban and Ferdinand do not simply do his chores for him; he makes it clear that they do them as punishment and as an ordeal of degradation. Work is the evil man's burden, a cavalier attitude I find consonant with Prospero's general lack of interest in the active and common life, consonant also with his Neoplatonic preference for the more refined labors of the contemplative life. For Prospero's secret study pretty clearly springs from and leads to a particular view of man. The curriculum consists of two courses, magic and liberal arts, a combination familiar to anyone acquainted with the optimism or meliorism of the Florentine Neoplatonists. The Duke of Milan may well have trusted his brother so much because his studies led him to envisage a brave new world peopled with noble creatures, a world purified of the baser strains of human nature, the more mundane problems of social order, which he seemed inclined to avoid. On the other hand, Prospero's boundless confidence and careless trust in Antonio suited his impulse to retirement. His ethical idealism and esthetic or hedonistic idyllism tend to reinforce each other, tend in fact to converge.

As an emblem, the freeing of Ariel suggests that Prospero's exile was for him—whether or not he was aware of it—a liberation. Alonso, Antonio, and Gonzalo simply accomplished externally what he would wish—what he already wished—for himself. He had renounced the dukedom in his mind before handing it over to Antonio. His being set adrift on the ocean, committed to a course which washed away the old burdensome world of civilization and translated him magically to a new world, unpeopled and unreal—this removal and isolation fulfill the process by externalizing his self-sufficient insularity. Shakespeare presents in Prospero the signs of an ancient and familiar psychological perplex connected with excessive idealism and the longing for the golden age; a

---

tices" (68); on the other hand, he fails to draw the simple broad-planed thematic implications of Shakespeare's critical image in which this background is brought to life as a major function of Prospero's unwillingness to put up with life. See Traversi's comparison of Prospero and the duke of Vienna (*Shakespeare: The Last Phase*, 201ff). In his life of Sidney, posthumously published in 1652, Fulke Greville has a passage on the *Arcadia* which contains some remarks as applicable to Prospero as to Basilius (*The Life of the Renowned Sir Philip Sidney*, ed. Nowell Smith [Oxford: Clarendon Press, 1907], 11ff.). See also the beautifully apposite remarks of Frazer quoted by James in *The Dream of Prospero*, 128.

state of mind based on unrealistic expectations; a mind therefore hesitant to look too closely at the world as it is. Under the pressure of actual life, so unguardedly sanguine a hope dialectically produces its opposite, extreme disillusionment with things as they are. This in turn sometimes leads to the violent repressiveness of iron-age justice, vaguely hinted at in Prospero's attitude toward Caliban; and it sometimes generates the wish to escape back into a paradisaic state of nature. Wish fulfillment and nightmare are simple contraries, twinned and mutually intensifying impulses, neither of which is more realistic than the other, both of which seize the mind they possess and carry it out of the world.

Freed from the mortal coil and body politic of Milan, the Ariel within Prospero finds and releases its double in the outside world. That no one else knows of Ariel's existence testifies to the peculiar inwardness and privacy of Prospero. Ariel, the picture of Nobody, the secret who embodies Prospero's detachment and isolation, is his only confidant. And Ariel's persistent push toward absolute freedom from humanity exerts a corresponding pressure on Prospero. I read his desire for liberty as allegorically related to the central action of the play, Prospero's reinvolvement with human beings after twelve years of magic for magic's sake. This action produces within the enchanter a conflict between his recreative and ethical, his egocentric and social, concerns—between the pleasure and power of his art, on the one hand, and, on the other, the claims of revenge or forgiveness, his obligations and privileges as a father, a fellow man, a ruler, and a victim. He feels the freedom of the inward Ariel jeopardized; he knows he cannot easily return while still possessing, or being possessed by, a spirit which prefers coral to bones and pearls to eyes. Ariel's demands are therefore the other side of Prospero's decision to reenter the riven wood of humanity, and this decision is confirmed in action when Prospero splits the ship which will ultimately bear him to Milan. By the time of the epilogue, the two will have all but changed the places they occupied when Prospero first came to the island: Ariel will move from the tree trunk to his flowery Eden, Prospero from his magic hideaway to the bare platform surrounded on three sides by Englishmen—most of whom, we may imagine, might correspond to Trinculo's holiday fools who "will not give a doit to relieve a lame beggar" but "will lay out ten to see a dead Indian" and probably more to see a live savage.

Caliban and Sycorax throw another kind of light on Prospero. The name Sycorax means, among other things, "hooped together": "with age and envy grown into a hoop," as Prospero says. Turned in upon herself with envy, raven black with malice, exiled for "mischiefs manifold and

sorceries terrible," she appears to be Prospero's antithesis—the nightmare which complements his wish fulfullment—and this contrast is emphasized by their parallel situations.[12] Both owe their banishment to motives which lead them to the study or practice of magic. Though Sycorax
is motivated by pure evil and Prospero's motives by contrast seem good,
both are antisocial, both have withdrawn into themselves and have
proved unfit for, or inadequate to, social and political existence. If Prospero withdrew for traditional reasons—extreme idealism and idyllism,
contemplation and recreation—Sycorax embodies some of the features of
a contrary, though equally traditional, form of withdrawal: the plaintive
withdrawal of the have-not, those figures of envy and malice whose dissatisfaction with their lot produces hatred of self and others; who long
for the beauty they lack and hate it in others; who spend their time trying
to violate others either to possess their beauty and otherness or simply for
the temporary relief and communion gained by seeing them suffer.

Something of this disposition has been transmitted to Caliban. To the
familiar etymological interpretations of his name—*cannibal* and *blackness*
(Romany, *cauliban*, E. K. Chambers)—I would add *Kali* (beauty) +
ban or bane, and I would translate it in two ways: first, and most simply,
"the bane of beauty," which is the way Prospero comes to see him. The
second translation is a little more complicated, and it refers to what
we—as opposed to Prospero—see in Caliban: "banned from beauty,
beauty is his bane." Many critics have observed that he has areas of feeling and sensitivity of which Prospero is unaware. Stephen Orgel remarks on his rich fantasy and his concrete sense of the island's natural
resources (123–24). Clifford Leech notes that although there is "no
moral good in him," "Caliban speaks throughout the play in blank verse:
he is aware of beauty, whether in Miranda or in the fair features of the
island or in music or his dreams."[13] But these awarenesses lead only to
frustration. And since he is only, so to speak, a first-generation human
being, his desire apprehends limited forms of beauty—money, wine,
woman, and song; his impulses to love and worship are moved by brave
and fine appearances when they are not moved by mere alcohol and lust.

---

[12] Traversi draws the comparison (*Shakespeare: The Last Phase*, 228–29) but treats it
as too simply a case of black against white (see notes 5 and 10).

[13] *Shakespeare's Tragedies*, 150. Cf. also G. Wilson Knight, *The Shakespearian Tempest*
(London: Methuen, 1953), 258–63. Frye describes Caliban as "full of original sin" but
"likeable" (*A Natural Perspective*, 110).

James's description of Caliban is perhaps the most eloquent and revealing: "'the thing
itself', divided, in the encompassing darkness, between terror and love, despair and adoration, and aware, above all, of a transcendent, supernatural world. . . . What is pri-

The important point about Caliban is that he can by no means be reduced to a figure of pure evil, the antithesis of Miranda or Ariel, the
counterpart of Antonio. His baseness is shot through with gleams of aspiration, though the mixture is unstable and the diverse motives often
undifferentiated. He displays the most transcendent, the most poignant,
and the most natural urges of man as well as the most foolish and mur-
derous and disloyal. Critics have noted in the nature-nurture theme persistent parallels between Caliban and Miranda, but there is no reason to
stop with these. Situational parallels exist to Ferdinand (the log bearing), to Antonio (the plot), and to Prospero (who supplanted him on the
island). His longings appear, modulated into ideal civilized form, in
Miranda's capacity for wonder and Ferdinand's for worshipful service;
his visions of riches are sublimed in Prospero's insubstantial pageant and
cloud-capped towers. Prospero's original openness and subsequent antipathy to Antonio are reflected by both Prospero and Caliban in their island relationship. Finally, though it may seem odd, Caliban is not unlike Gonzalo, both in his attitude toward the island and in the way
his simpleminded good will is abused by Stephano and Trinculo (as
Gonzalo's is by Sebastian and Antonio). Childlike in his fears and passions, ingenuous in the immediacy of his responses to nature and man,
open in the expression of feeling, Caliban at his most evil and traitorous
shows up as a mere puppy, a comic Vice, a crude conspirator in the
pointed contrast to Antonio established by their plots.

He is thus a moonlight distortion not only of the villains but of all the
figures who have come to the island from the daylight world of civilization. In this sense he stands for the world; a handy and compact symbol
of human nature, not as we know it but as we might have found it at the
beginning of time, in the prehistory of civilization, when Carthage,
Tunis, and Troy were no more advanced than the Bermudas or Americas.
We see in him all man's possibilities in their undeveloped form, and this
means that we see the longing for brightness and beauty as no less real,
no less rooted and persistent, than the tendency to darkness and evil.
This is not what Prospero sees. Caliban is his epitome of human degra-

---

mordial in man's nature is forced back by nature, culture, and authority; but the deep
thing remains, however obscured" (*The Dream of Prospero*, 113–14). The ease with
which Caliban finds or makes gods, his preference of dreaming to waking, and his desire
to return to sleep (echoed by Prospero in his moment of disillusionment) are familiar
phenomena of the primitive and childlike mind. For a more extended discussion of this
paradoxical relation between archaic man and god—the distance between them at once
too little and too great—cf. my "Archaism, Vision, and Revision: Studies in Virgil,
Plato, and Milton," *Centennial Review* 9 (1967): 45ff.

dation: he is Milan without Prospero and Miranda; the cloven tree without Ariel; man as he really is and has become rather than man as he could or should be—man, in short, as Antonio, spreading his poison from the top of civilized Italy down to its boot and root.[14]

But Caliban in fact differs radically from his European counterpart. The difference is intimately bound up with the new world Prospero has created on the island, and to understand this we have to take seriously Shakespeare's many efforts in the play to direct our glance backward to the history of the island before the play begins. This early history discloses an edifying transition from evil to good and the emergence of a mythic, or romance, order. In his best of all impossible worlds, Prospero sees himself as the new god who has displaced the old, therefore the hero and savior as well as the king of his island universe.[15] The only ripple of disorder is caused by a difference between the old and new generations of evil. Sycorax, who died before Prospero reached the island, belongs to the archetypal past and is therefore an absolute or pure figure of evil. She may also be Prospero's archetype, his figment of evil, a relief from the various shades of human gray in Europe. She was, or would have been, easy to identify as the enemy. There would have been no such complicating factors as love, or trust, or kinship, or hypocrisy. She could have been dealt with by force alone, and Caliban comforts us on this point by suggesting that Prospero's magic is stronger than his mother's.[16] Thus no problem about Prospero's dealings with Caliban

---

[14] Harrison's comments epitomize the attitude of critics who view Caliban through Prospero's eyes: "Caliban . . . is no grotesque mockery, but real, dangerous beyond hope of reclamation, a devil, a born devil . . . *The Tempest* is a play of bright light and sinister darkness. We mistake its meaning if we regard Caliban and his confederates merely as comic accessories to a fairy tale" ("The Tempest," 233). James, while responding fully to Caliban's mixed nature, justifies Prospero's harshness as the function of superior insight into the dangers of that mixed nature and suggests, as have others, that in punishing Caliban he is punishing the dark possibilities within himself from the standpoint of what appears to be an enlightened Christianity (*The Dream of Prospero*, 120–21).

[15] As a character, Ariel owes little to the Bible, to put it mildly; still, the name Lion of God may be felt to have some ironic point with reference to Prospero; as an epithet for the tricksy spirit it is sheer burlesque, on the model of the heroic epithets applied by Spenser to his butterfly Clarion in *Muiopotmos*. See Kermode, Arden *Tempest*, 142–45.

[16] Frye, Kermode, Orgel, and others who worry over the distinction between white and black magic in their efforts to justify Prospero miss the more important distinction between magical and nonmagical (ethical, rhetorical, etc.) modes of response to life's problems. In his appendix on Ovid, Golding, and Medea (Arden *Tempest*, 147–50), Kermode's distinctions verge on hairsplitting; his evidence suggests that Shakespeare's use of Medea's speech as Prospero's farewell to magic might indicate another contrast: in this particular speech Medea is anticipating the magical business which will lead to the restoration of Aeson's youth and the betrayal of Pelias, on whom she avenges herself for

could develop were Caliban identical in these respects with Sycorax. What initially confused Prospero was the ambivalence and instability, the mixture of human motives we have already seen in Caliban. Unlike his mother, he offered Prospero a chance to exercise his more humane gifts in the liberal arts. When this failed, Prospero consigned him to the category of pure evil, alongside Sycorax and Antonio. The interesting thing about this whole episode is its resemblance to the Milanese experience, of which it is a modified repetition. Caliban claims that the island was taken from him by Prospero, and Prospero complains in return that he tried to be kind to Caliban, that he lodged him in his cell and gave him lessons. Like Hamlet's "Mousetrap," the situation admits of role switching: either character in the island drama can be seen as playing both parts, loser and winner, in the Milanese coup. Caliban is "all the subjects that he (Prospero) has," and in kicking him about, Prospero may continually, and securely, reenact his failure in Milan. The analogy also points in the other direction: Prospero's ethical and symbolic reduction of Caliban to a figure of pure evil may suggest his share of guilt in encouraging Antonio to his crime; for unwittingly he did everything he could to cultivate whatever dram of evil his brother may have been heir to; in that sense, he—no less than Antonio—new-created the creatures that were his and gave them the occasion to say, with Caliban, "have a new master; get a new man."

The magic circle is a pastoral kingdom, a simplified and more controllable analogue of Prospero's former situation.[17] It is a version of what Erik Erikson calls the microsphere, "the small world of manageable toys" which the child establishes as a haven "to return to when he needs to overhaul his ego." There he constructs a model of his past painful experiences, which will allow him to "play at doing something that was in reality done to him." In this way he "redeems his failures and strengthens his hopes."[18] The actual demands of Caliban's role in the

---

past wrongs; Prospero, on the other hand, is trying hard to give up his rough magic, forswear vengeance, and renew life for the next generation by less occult methods. The contrast is all in his favor, not because he is white and Medea black, but because she gives herself increasingly to her passion and art, while he fights against them.

[17] See Parry's description of the island Eden quoted by Harrison, "The Tempest," 220–21.

[18] *Childhood and Society* (New York: Norton, 1963), 217, 222. This is an amplified and somewhat modified version of Freud's discussion of repetition-compulsion in children's play, *Beyond the Pleasure Principle*, trans. James Strachey (New York: Liveright, 1950), 12–17.

microsphere differentiate him from the civilized force of evil he symbolizes to Prospero. His value as a scapegoat exceeds his usefulness as a
handyman. Continued in his helplessness, he stands as a token of his
master's victory and power; continued in his boorish ingratitude, he is a
constant reminder of Prospero's beneficence and patience. And to attenu-
ate the tedium of the island's perfect bliss, his surliness no doubt gives
Prospero a legitimate excuse for periodically venting his spleen and
clearing his complexion. As a scapegoat and member of Prospero's microsphere, Caliban is bound by two basic conditions. First, he can always be
controlled; this is guaranteed by the pleasant coupling of his general in-
efficiency with Prospero's magic. Second, so clearcut a case of villainy
sets Prospero's mind permanently at ease; there will be no deception, no
misunderstanding of motives, no need to worry about Caliban's soul or
conscience; he can be counted on to behave in a manner deserving only
of righteous anger, discipline, and punishment. Poor Caliban is a Platonist's black dream: Prospero feels he has only to lay eyes on his dark
and disproportioned shape to know what Evil truly Is, and where.

III

In William Strachey's letter describing and commenting on the 1609
Bermuda shipwreck and the expedition's subsequent fortunes in Vir-
ginia, there is a passage which supplies a close analogue to Prospero's
experience with Caliban. Sir Thomas Gates, one of the leaders of the
expedition and Lieutenant Governor of the colony, had sent a man out on
a mission, and the man was killed by Indians. Strachey reports that "it
did not a little trouble the Lieutenant Governour, who since first landing
in the Countrey . . . would not by any meanes be wrought to a violent
proceeding against them, for all the practises of villany, with which they
daily indangered our men; thinking it possible, by a more tractable
course, to winne them to a better condition: but now being startled by
this, he well perceived, how little a faire and noble intreatie workes upon
a barbarous disposition, and therefore in some measure purposed to be
revenged" (quoted in Kermode, 140). Strachey's letter is dated 1610, and
Shakespeare could have seen it in its unpublished form, but my interest
is in something he could not have seen, a marginal comment in *Purchas
His Pilgrimes* (1625), in which the letter was first published: "Can a
Leopard change his spots? Can a Savage remayning a Savage be civill?
Were not wee our selves made and not borne civill in our Progenitors
dayes? and were not Caesars Britaines as brutish as Virginians? The Ro-

mane swords were best teachers of civilitie to this & other Countries neere us."[19]

With this hardheaded historical perspective we may contrast another view of the—or *a*—New World and a different idea of the acquisition of civility. Imagine Prospero's delight were he to find himself translated to the island of Utopia where

> the people in general are easygoing, good-tempered, ingenious, and leisure-loving. They patiently do their share of manual labor when occasion demands, though otherwise they are by no means fond of it. In their devotion to mental study they are unwearied. . . .
>
> . . . after a little progress, their diligence made us at once feel sure that our own diligence would not be bestowed in vain. They began so easily to imitate the shapes of the letters, so readily to pronounce the words, so quickly to learn by heart, and so faithfully to reproduce what they had learned that it was a perfect wonder to us.[20]

Here all things have been set in good order from the beginning. Within the scope of a single regime and lifetime, the first king "brought the rude and rustic people to such a perfection of culture and humanity as makes them now superior to almost all other mortals" (60). In that island, which is Nowhere, Truth is not the daughter of Time. Time has no utility there, history no meaning. The hard-won accomplishments of Western civilization have been handed to the Utopians in the Aldine edition, so that they can quickly and painlessly riffle through two thousand years of culture during study hour (106–7).

Shakespeare's image of unspoiled man lies somewhere between Prospero's view of him as a born devil and the vision Thomas More assigned to the professional traveler Raphael Hythloday (which means "well trained in nonsense"). But I think it is Hythloday's vision rather than the more hardheaded attitude recorded by Purchas which lurks behind Prospero's rejection. Prospero's phrase "the dark backward and abysm of time" has a rich and profoundly resonant ring to us, but to him it signifies the space of twelve years, not the incredible vast of time which separates us from our progenitors. Shakespeare would have us remember that we cannot new-create Caliban from savagery to civility in twelve

---

[19] In Kermode, Arden *Tempest*, 139–40. Cf. James, *The Dream of Prospero*, 120, where the passage is applied to Prospero and Caliban in a manner similar to my own.

[20] St. Thomas More, *Utopia*, ed. Edward Surtz, S.J. (New Haven: Yale University Press, 1964), 103–4. Future page references are to this edition.

years, any more than we can new-create unregenerate Europeans in three hours, except in the world of romance.

The dark backward and abysm of time: Purchas gives us a better clue to its resonance than Hythloday or Prospero, and this clue leads to the dominant atmospheric effect of the play. Let me repeat David William's remark that Caliban's appearance "must indicate an aspiration towards human nature, whereas Ariel's is away from it." The two figures are separated by the whole of human history, civilization, and development. In Ariel alone, all Calibanic urges except the desire for freedom have been transcended, sublimed away, become pure esthetic play. In the insistently noted limits of an afternoon and a small island are compressed not only twelve years of experience but the beginning and the end of civilized man, the New World and the Old World, Africa and Europe, the travels of Aeneas and those of Sir Thomas Gates, the golden age and an earnest of apocalypse.[21] Similarly, our sense of spatial scale varies from the miniworld of elves and mushrooms through oceans and continents to the great globe itself; from unplummeted depths of earth and ocean through the green sea and cloud-capped towers toward the moon and the azure vault of heaven. The archaic world of folklore and superstition, the world of the mythy mind, is set beside the ultimate refinements of literary artifice and the marvels of theatrical and hermetic thaumaturgy.

These spatial and temporal coordinates are significantly distinguished by Prospero's being aware of the first but not of the second. Until he has bad dreams in the fourth act, his magic allows him to command infinite space while bounded in the nutshell of his microsphere. Yet his view into the distant past extends only half a generation. Milan seems long ago because he has spent his time in so different a world and because there are no clocks on the island; in the romance milieu, it would make little difference whether Ariel howled away in his tree for one, twelve, or twelve hundred years. But there is another measure in the play which magnifies the dark backward and downward of time, a scale of which neither Prospero nor the other characters are seriously cognizant: we, however, may remember that Amphion's miraculous harp raised the Theban wall in the fabled age of gods and heroes; that in what seems like the dawn of history Dido came to Carthage from Phoenicia, and Aeneas, relinquishing his first wife with his first civilization, passed through Carthage on his way to Italy; that his settlement was to become the high

---

[21] G. Wilson Knight documents the play's emphasis on ample distances (*The Shakespearian Tempest*, 254, 262–63).

and palmy state of Rome; that he abandoned his former home at the behest of the gods and for reasons of state; that the Trojans did not bring forth islands by sowing kernels in the sea—they ploughed the ocean to plant a difficult harvest they would not live to enjoy.

These echoes vibrate with the sense of history; they stretch out the expanse of time separating Caliban from the play's modern characters. And they provide us with a vantage point from which to view with detachment as well as sympathy the turning point of the play—the moment during which Prospero suddenly recalls Caliban's conspiracy, interrupts the masque of Ceres, and delivers his elegy on the end of the revels and the end of the world.

The action beginning with the tempest and culminating in this moment saves Prospero from becoming, or rather remaining, another Raphael Hythloday. Until his disenchantment, he too fits the image of the colonizer as frustrated idealist, wishing for and therefore finding himself in a new world, unhampered by decadent fellow Europeans; eager to start over from the beginning and project a golden age of towers, palaces, temples, and theaters—a culture brought forth not through centuries of "sweat or endeavor" but, like nature's foison, perhaps by "sowing kernels of it in the sea."

The source of his disenchantment is the same as the cause of his original abdication, and here again we find a close analogy in More's Utopia. Hythloday had also "devoted himself unreservedly to philosophy" (*Utopia*, 12); he had left his patrimony to his brothers and voyaged to the New World where, like Jaques in *As You Like It*, he begged to remain rather than return to the worldly stage. He considered service to king or commonwealth a futile disturbance of his own peace and quiet. More had lectured him on his disinterest and disillusion, saying, "If you cannot pluck up wrongheaded opinions by the root, if you cannot cure according to your heart's desire vices of long standing, yet you must not on that account desert the commonwealth. You must not abandon the ship in a storm because you cannot control the winds" (49–50). This reproof follows the famous passage in which More criticizes Hythloday's Platonic disdain of the real world. Hythloday wants to free himself of that world because it neither listens nor lives up to his utopian philosophy: There is no room, More says, for this scholastic philosophy which would impose itself absolutely and rigidly on life's situations without regard to the needs, differences, and limits of particular contexts:

> But there is another philosophy, more practical for statesmen, which knows
> its stage, adapts itself to the play in hand, and performs its role neatly and

appropriately. This is the philosophy which you must employ. . . . Would it not . . . [be] preferable to take a part without words than by reciting something inappropriate to make a hodgepodge of comedy and tragedy? You would have spoiled and upset the actual play by bringing in irrelevant matter—even if your contribution would have been superior in itself. Whatever play is being performed, perform it as best you can, and do not upset it all simply because you think of another which has more interest. (49)

Prospero thought of another play. In this, he and Hythloday differ from the old counselor Gonzalo. Gonzalo performs the play in hand as well as he can, but not quite well enough. He is the man Hythloday refuses to be, the well-intentioned advisor who remains haplessly in the world. He believes in, or at least clings to, the happy solutions wherever they may be found; he tries to ease matters when it is possible to do so without causing trouble. Shakespeare places in his mouth the famous, if muddled, speech about the golden age (some of it borrowed from Montaigne's essay on the cannibals), and even though Gonzalo claims he uttered it merely to make the king feel better, it accords with the sentiments he expresses elsewhere in the play. "Had I plantation of this isle . . . and were [I] the King on it," I would admit "no kind of traffic,"

> no name of magistrate;
> Letters should not be known; riches, poverty,
> And use of service, none; contract, succession,
> Bourn, bound of land, tilth, vineyard, none;
> No use of metal, corn, or wine, or oil;
> No occupation; all men idle, all;
> And women too, but innocent and pure:
> No sovereignty;—

SEBASTIAN: Yet he would be King on't.
ANTONIO: The latter end of his commonwealth forgets the beginning.
GONZALO: All things in common Nature should produce
> Without sweat or endeavour: treason, felony,
> Sword, pike, knife, gun, or need of any engine,
> Would I not have; but Nature should bring forth,
> Of it own kind, all foison, all abundance,
> To feed my innocent people.
> .   .   .   .
> I would with such perfection govern . . .
> T' excel the Golden Age.

(II.i.139–64)

This kind of pastoral wish fulfillment was a cliché in Shakespeare's time—getting rid of all problems by getting rid of civilization, throwing the baby out with the bath, letting Nature and the gods do with greater ease and certainty what men try to do and always bungle. The interesting thing is that the speech is echoed in some of the significant details and themes of Prospero's masque of Ceres, put on in Act IV as a betrothal celebration for the benefit of Ferdinand and Miranda. Gonzalo's speech is simple and simpleminded, direct and unreflective, inconsistent but well intentioned. Prospero's masque is an artful, sophisticated, and refined—not to mention magically induced—expression of the same pastoral escapism. The affinities between counselor and magician are stressed in a number of ways: First, Prospero is obviously fond of Gonzalo. Second, both assume that the masque of judgment has produced the desired feelings of contrition in Alonso, Sebastian, and Antonio, though we see nothing in the sinners' behavior to justify this assumption. Third, both seem to have suppressed or ignored the question of their own contribution to the Milanese coup. Both characters thus share equally in a refusal to look too closely at the actual state of affairs and, more generally, at the world they live in.

But here the resemblance stops. The same attitude which is highstrung, sharply pitched, in Prospero is loose and jangly in Gonzalo, who is marked by intellectual and moral slackness. What Gonzalo naively accepts, Prospero tries to re-create by his art; he has come during the course of the action to suspect that this is the only way in which things can be made to happen as he would like them to happen. Gonzalo expresses and embodies the attitude Prospero left behind him the other side of romance from disenchantment.[22] As he favors Gonzalo, so he clings to the sentimental attitude he no longer believes and tries briefly to evoke it by the techniques of magic and theater. Gonzalo's closing speech is in fact a statement of the usual sentimental reading of *The Tempest:*

> O, rejoice
> Beyond a common joy! and set it down
> With gold on lasting pillars: in one voyage
> Did Claribel her husband find at Tunis,
> And Ferdinand, her brother, found a wife
> Where he himself was lost, Prospero his dukedom

---

[22] Cf. Traversi's helpful comments on Gonzalo, "a personage satirically conceived," in *Shakespeare: The Last Phase,* 224ff. The relation between Gonzalo and Prospero is interestingly pointed up by Gonzalo's chief service in the plot: to give Prospero his precious books.

In a poor isle, and all of us ourselves
When no man was his own.

(V.i.206–13)

To which we may imagine Prospero's unheard reply: "'Tis so to thee." In one respect, the two characters are diametrically opposed: In my ideal kingdom, Gonzalo affirms, "letters should not be known," and this bears out our own suspicion about his literacy. His knowledge of the classics is a little shaky, and Antonio justifiably refers to him as "a lord of weak remembrance." He confuses Carthage with Tunis and tries to console Alonso by comparing Claribel to the notable Carthaginian widow and suicide. "His word," Antonio jeers, "is more than the miraculous harp" of Amphion, who raised the walls of Thebes by music. And then he and Sebastian finish off poor Gonzalo:

SEBASTIAN: He hath rais'd the wall, and houses too.
ANTONIO: What impossible matter will he make easy next?
SEBASTIAN: I think he will carry this island home in his pocket,
        and give it his son for an apple.
ANTONIO: And sowing the kernels of it in the sea, bring forth more
        islands.

(II.i.84–89)

More than the miraculous harp: in a way, the last laugh is on Antonio, since his own plans are about to be foiled by something like a miraculous harp. But the phrase ripples outward beyond its context. It is the harp of convenient forgetfulness and the sweet air of fantasy rearranging history, fact, and life to accord with one's wish. And it is also the miraculous harp of romance and magic, theater and art, raising Gonzalo's untutored hopes and evasions to the level of man's highest accomplishments, raising within the brief compass of island and stage—the brief space between afternoon storm and dinner—the wall, houses, towers, palaces, and temples of the great globe new-created.

The opposing music, the resonance which makes *The Tempest* more (that is, less) than the miraculous harp, is heard most clearly in the Virgilian echoes which are thrown away by the flippancy of the ignorant villains no less than by the happy vagueness of Gonzalo. The way of Virgil and of Thomas More is felt in the specter of Aeneas, who played the part handed him by the gods, from the chaos of his first tempest through the threats and temptations of Celaeno and Dido to the final victory, if one can call it that, over Turnus. The endurance of Aeneas suggests something also about the endurance of civilization, especially when we place his encounter with the Italic New World beside the play's image of the American New World. The presence in *The Tempest* of Troy, Italy, and Bermuda provides a sense of rhythmic recurrence, a ground bass to the elegiac burden of the revels speech. There will always be new worlds both behind us and ahead of us, and it is not likely that the work of twelve years or three hours will finally jeopardize the good or uproot the evil of the ancient globe we inherit and transmit.

Yet on the other hand, the Virgilian echoes do establish a measure of the condition of present-day Naples, once part of Aeneas's new world. Alonso left Naples to marry his apparently unwilling daughter Claribel to the Prince of Tunis. For reasons which strike me as worth looking into, but which I have not yet been able to puzzle out, Africa has lost a Sycorax and gained a Claribel. Claribel's pale romance name pushes her toward the status of a personification, and if we put this together with the questionable nature of the marriage, the oddly inappropriate analogy to the widow Dido, and the confusion of Tunis with Carthage, we may be willing to entertain one more allegorical fantasy, in which Alonso's voyage is a reflection of his state: the civilized European soul compromising with darkness, surrendering its clear beautiful ideals for the sake of expediency and thereby reversing the forward direction of Western man's arduous Virgilian journey. The voyage does not begin but ends, at least temporarily, with a Virgilian storm, and the angry divinity is not Juno but Prospero.

IV

Prospero's twelve years of romance, following Ariel's release from the cloven tree, seem to have consisted mainly of shadow boxing. Perhaps by the time he releases the Italians from the cloven ship, he is ready for a real enemy. During the early scenes he is clearly intent on and excited by his project. He has already made and confirmed his decision in raising the tempest; and in his speeches to Miranda, Ariel, and Caliban, he seems on the verge of packing. In all three interchanges he has the air at once of summarizing the past and looking toward the future. And one of his chief concerns is to impress his image on his auditors. "Look what they have done to us," he says to Miranda. "Beware of my power and remember what you owe me," he says to Ariel and Caliban. Staging himself in roles designed to evoke sympathy, fear, or guilt; working on them by rhetoric rather than by magic; reviewing the past to place it in clear perspective: these aspects of his behavior reveal Prospero going through a test run, a dress rehearsal, preparatory to his confrontation with Alonso and Antonio.

As he moves from Miranda to Ariel to Caliban, his tone and bearing undergo significant changes. He is least easy and assured with Miranda, most with Caliban. It seems harder for him to deal, or know how to deal, with the daughter he loves than with his pet monster. He chooses his words carefully; his sentences are at first disordered, his thoughts rambling, his narrative hesitant and digressive. Only gradually and with effort does he find the didactic handle and gain confidence that he is producing the desired effect.[23] To evoke the proper moral feelings in Miranda, he presents the past as a didactic romance, a parable of good and evil brothers. The interjections with which he punctuates his story—his "*attend*'s" and "*mark me*'s"—serve in every case to underline Antonio's perfidy.[24] At the same time, they betray a rhetorical nervousness: he wants to make sure he is getting his message across. This is apparently not the sort of thing he has had much practice in during the last twelve years.

The homiletic impulse gains force with Ariel, to whom he speaks in terms of hellfire, purgatory, and redemption, using—or rather creating—the pretense that Ariel has forgotten the causes and nature of his debt to Prospero. Critics have mistakenly assumed that Prospero is angry in this scene (I.ii).[25] No doubt he feels some impatience at first, since Ariel's demand for freedom delays his project. But he immediately warms to the chance to stage himself in a moralizing vein, and I think he relishes the display of righteous anger through which he dramatizes for Ariel the latter's ingratitude and his own Powerful Goodness. This is characteristic of Prospero as of other Shakespearian figures: his delight in the present moment of playing, speaking, or performing distracts him from his larger purpose, leads him momentarily to digress and indulge the immediate impulse. The pleasure of his little scene with Ariel gives him the idea of trying a repeat performance on wretched

[23] Cf. Traversi's detailed analysis in *Shakespeare: The Last Phase*, 195ff.

[24] Here I differ with Traversi, who thinks Prospero is explicit about his own share of the guilt when he speaks of his "'closeness,' his 'neglect' . . . of the ends of government" (*Shakespeare: The Last Phase*, 201). Prospero is in fact praising his noble disdain of mundane considerations: "I, thus neglecting worldly ends, all dedicated / To closeness and the bettering of my mind." Similarly, Traversi accepts at face value the happy ending Prospero gives his account, and the providential language with which he reinforces it, whereas this seems to me to be another instance of Prospero's relief at having got rid of the real world.

[25] This was also my assumption until the students in my seminar (see note 1) corrected me.

Caliban. Clifford Leech, who is not overly fond of Prospero, amusingly points up this motive: "After he has told Miranda his story and given Ariel his instructions and his morning lesson in obedience, he awakens Miranda . . . and oddly suggests: 'We'll visit Caliban my slave, who never / Yields us kind answer'. Miranda is reluctant to join in this kind of sport, but she is easily overridden" (*Shakespeare's Tragedies*, 147). Prospero has already settled Caliban's ethical hash and knows that he is a much better prospect for the role of ingrate than Ariel, whom he had to interrupt to keep him from yielding a number of kind answers not in the script. In contrast to his arduous effort with Miranda, the dialogue, or flyting match, with Caliban is released like a coiled spring.

These different styles of behavior evoked by Miranda and Caliban establish the problem of the play. Even as Prospero begins to set his plot machinery in motion, he is confronted by two alternatives: in consoling Miranda over the shipwreck, he says, "I have done nothing but in care of thee." The implications of this care reach beyond Ferdinand to Naples and Alonso. If he is going to do right by Miranda as well as himself, it will not be enough to discipline Ferdinand, to save the younger generation while their elders sink in the slough. The more difficult and humane course entails reconciliation with Alonso, but this in itself would be hollow unless preceded by "heart's sorrow / And a clear life ensuing" on the King's part. And since Antonio now infects Alonso's presence, Prospero perhaps hopes that he may influence even him to repent. In this way he might make all of them find themselves "when no man was his own," and he might restore the world to that brave and new condition he seems to have implanted as a prospect in Miranda's mind. This, I think, is one alternative, the favored one, entertained by Prospero. It is involved with his concern for Miranda and her future, it demands a delicacy and tact he has not had to exercise for years (if ever), and its various issues are by no means easily predictable. The other, much simpler, alternative, suggested by Caliban, is vengeance, discipline, servitude, and liberal doses of magic. The choice is complicated by Prospero's interest in putting on impromptu amateur theatricals.[26] He is obviously more at home in roles allowing him to cleave the ear with horrid speech, make mad the guilty, and appall the free. All these pressures are at work in the last part of I.ii, the scene with Ferdinand. Prospero's eagerness to unite Alonso's son with Miranda is balanced by his natural desire to try Ferdi-

---

[26] Prospero prefaces Miranda's first view of Ferdinand by saying, "The fringed curtains of thine eye advance, / And say what thou seest yond" (I.ii.411–12), which suggests that Miranda's eyes open on Prospero's play world.

nand and assess his quality (to make the swift business uneasy). But the balance is upset by the carryover of the theatrical anger generated in the previous scenes with Ariel and Caliban. The situation is at once funny and a little unpleasant: Miranda puzzled and upset, Ferdinand confounded, Prospero carried away by the chance to play at being the local constabulary, all the while chortling happy asides to Ariel and to himself. The scene reveals the extent to which his reliance on his various arts allies itself with his tendency to swerve toward the easier alternative. His use of theatrical indirections—eavesdropping, role playing, hiding his true feelings from others—is intimately connected with his habitual isolation, his aversion to social intercourse and consequent inexperience in dealing with others. He seems reluctant to confront people directly, to trust his spontaneous reflexes, or to commit himself to the normal channels of communication.

And yet I think that at the outset he would prefer the more difficult alternative, Miranda's way not Caliban's. Prospero would like to undo Antonio's evil and new-create the others by making them feel the inward pinches of conscience, rather than—as with Caliban—the merely physical pinches inflicted by his spirits. He would like to awaken and quicken them to their stagnancy, their ebbing reason mudded in spiritual ooze, so that the cleansing tide will return and purge them of their foul weather. This, rather than dunk them by magic force in some "filthy mantled" horse-pond and send them off punished, impressed by his power, but otherwise unchanged—like Caliban, who leaves the stage muttering a travesty of the sentiment Prospero would like to hear: "I'll be wise hereafter, / And sue for grace."[27]

What happens to Prospero's intentions during the play is a modified repetition of what happened when he swerved from Miranda through Ariel to Caliban in I.ii; and of what happened after he tried to deal humanely with Caliban; and of what happened after he entrusted Milan to Antonio.[28] Only this time the effect cuts much deeper. For of all Shakespeare's human characters he is the only one to have become a god of power, to have attained to Hamlet's kingdom of infinite space in the nutshell of his microsphere, to have entered and passed through pure

---

[27] As Traversi has noted, "all Prospero's efforts to regenerate Caliban have failed" (*Shakespeare: The Last Phase*, 264), and Prospero himself seems finally aware of the limits of punitive magic.

[28] The radical shift from the closely observed storm scene in I.i to the idyllic opening of I.ii, in which the storm is distanced (framed like an idealized painting) and ascribed to magic, anticipates this swerving from normal to magical ways of dealing with experience. Cf. Traversi, *Shakespeare: The Last Phase*, 194–95.

romance, to have achieved the dearest wish of hermetic sage or mage. His must therefore be the greatest disenchantment. He finds that magic cannot save souls, cannot even pinch the will. More than this, he finds that magic is the only effective policeman, and perhaps he comes to feel that there is very little to look forward to in a world without magic, the world to which he has committed himself to return. This mood has been well described in a recent study by Robert Hunter, who discusses the play's insistence on the inveteracy, the indestructibility of evil. "Only a rigid and unceasing control of the sort that Prospero had exercised over Caliban and . . . Antonio, can keep good in its . . . ascendancy." Prospero's pardoning of Antonio lacks any feeling, Hunter observes, because he knows that "to forgive unregenerate evil is safe only when . . . the good are in firm and undeceived control."[29] But *control* here should be understood in a more restrictive sense than Hunter intends it; only in the never-never land of magic and romance is such a control exerted. This is why Prospero connects despair to his lack of "spirits to enforce, art to enchant" in the epilogue.[30]

The role and function of Caliban in this process are peculiar. Everything that rendered him psychologically useful in the microsphere as a model and scapegoat contributes to Prospero's disenchantment during the course of the play. The reduction of Caliban or man to a devil was the easier way out when Prospero wanted to banish moral complexity, protect himself from humane attachments, maintain his psychic distance and mastery in his withdrawn world; but it is no help when he is preparing himself to return. Caliban's ineffectiveness now sets him apart from evil man and links him more closely to those ideal conditions of the microsphere which Prospero is about to renounce—there are, after all, no mooncalves in Milan. I can see no evidence for the view that Caliban is a real threat who keeps Prospero on edge, or for the pietistic reading of the subplot as moral parody—e.g., the idea that Caliban's plot to murder Prospero, as a comic analogue to the crimes of Alonso, Antonio, and Sebastian, reduces the pretensions of the latter by linking their behavior

[29] *Shakespeare and the Comedy of Forgiveness* (New York: Columbia University Press, 1965), 241, 240.

[30] Bonamy Dobree finds "a somewhat nasty taste about the quality of Prospero's forgiveness," which is Senecan rather than Christian: "'It is one kind of revenge to neglect a man as not worth it [forgiveness].' This seems to me exactly Prospero's sentiment with regard to Alonso. It is Ariel who has to remind him of pity and tenderness, and even then Prospero appeals to his 'nobler reason,' and rather priggishly performs what he thinks is a 'rarer' action. And after all, it is easy enough to forgive your enemies when you have triumphed over them" ("The Tempest," in *Shakespeare: The Comedies*, ed. Kenneth Muir [Englewood Cliffs: Prentice-Hall, 1965], 165–66).

"to the deformed and drunken idiocies of the clowns" (Hunter, 231). On the contrary, the analogy stresses the difference between the unreal symbol and what it represents—between the comic helplessness to which Prospero has reduced his symbol and the insidious craft which would have succeeded anywhere but on the island. It is only in respect of the rootedness of evil that symbol and referent, Caliban and Antonio, coincide. And this coincidence, intensifying through the play since the murder attempt in the second act, is surely on Prospero's mind when Ariel tells him that the three drunkards are "bending / Towards their project." He exclaims:

> A devil, a born devil, on whose nature
> Nurture can never stick: on whom my pains,
> Humanely taken, all, all lost, quite lost!
>
> *(IV.i.188–90)*

He is deeply troubled, as Ferdinand and Miranda had noticed, but not because of the external plot, the threat on his life, such as it is.

He is troubled because at this moment the meaning he has read into Caliban and the way represented by Caliban become for him the meaning and the way of reality. The series of reenactments of the same pattern of betrayal persuades him to generalize and validate his disillusion as the one abiding truth of life. The radical persistence of evil which he validates for himself at this moment is only the objective consequence of another persistence—his idealistic separation of Ariel from Caliban; of Ariel from the cloven tree; of liberal arts from servile labor; of the vanished age of gold, which must be restored, from the present age of iron, which must be either repressively disciplined or willfully ignored. The implied validation of Caliban as the real model of man is matched by the equally hasty act of generalization which connects the dissolving masque first to a dissolving culture, then to a dissolving world. I think we are meant to note the suddenness, the violence and facility, with which this reversal of his divided values takes place. What he feels this time, and for the first time, is that everything golden, noble, beautiful, and good— the works of man, the liberal arts, the aspirations variously incarnated in towers, palaces, temples, and theaters—is insubstantial and unreal compared to the baseness of man's old stock. And not merely as vanities but as deceptions, fantasies which lure the mind to escape from its true knowledge of darkness and which, dissolving, leave it more exposed, more susceptible, more disenchanted than before.

Here and now, Caliban becomes most truly Prospero's bane of beauty,

the catalyst leading him, in his revels speech, to criticize as groundless
the arts and projects, the beliefs and hopes by which he had ordered his
life. The crux of his self-criticism lies in the phrase "the baseless fabric
of this vision," especially in the word *baseless*. *Baseless* means insubstantial, not firmly based, without proper grounds but also not base, not
evil, too purely beautiful, excluding the dark substance of man and
therefore, once again, without grounds. "We are such stuff / As dreams
are made on"—*on* as well as *of:* the evil matter or basis, the Calibanic
foundation on which our nobler works are built, which they deceptively
cover over or from which they rise as in escape. Prospero would say, as
Spenser said of the golden House of Pride, "full great pittie, that so
faire a mould / Did on so weake foundation ever sit" (*Faerie Queene*
I.iv.5). And man's works are dreams not only in being vanities, fragile
illusions, but also in being—as Freud called them—the guardians of
sleep protecting the mind in its denial of or flight from reality. Feeling
this, Prospero might well envy his actors for being spirits who can melt
into thin air after their performance. The best the vexed and aging mortal creature can hope for is to have his little life rounded—*crowned*—
with sleep.

The perspective of the revels speech is itself a form of escape from
mortality. It is the god's-eye view and therefore identical to that which
dominated the masque of Ceres, even though the content of the masque
was pastoral and that of the revels speech is heroic. Pastoral and heroic
perspectives may be used indifferently, as here, to distance or diminish
the immediate problems of real life. The masque is in every respect an
exorcism of evil. It was arbitrarily introduced as a distraction, a vanity
of Prospero's art. "Some vanity of mine art" (IV.i.41) is meant to sound
self-deprecating: "Just a little something extra, and I'm doing it only
because they expect it of me."[31] But it also sounds apologetic, for he is
asking Ariel to bear with him while he puts on one more show, and the
revels speech shows him to have become aware of his self-indulgence. At
any rate, his spirits enact his "present fancies" and thus reveal the state
and tendency of his mind: by incantation and evocation they dispel not
only the foul plot but also the thoughts of lust, intemperance, and dis-
loyalty which had occupied him in his previous conversation with Ferdinand and Miranda.

Stephen Orgel makes the important point that the masque pictures an
idyllic nature, winterless, moving directly from harvest to spring (125–

---

[31] Traversi notes the irrelevance (*Shakespeare: The Last Phase*, 261) but blames it on
Shakespeare rather than Prospero.

28). It begins when Iris calls Ceres away from a less ideal and very English nature whose character—"thy sea-marge, sterile and rocky-hard"—communicates itself to the conventional woes imposed on lasslorn bachelors by cold nymphs crowned for chastity (IV.i.64–69)—as if Prospero sees only untempered chastity or intemperate lust, one or another kind of nunnery, possible in the actual world; the extremes may be tempered nowhere but on the magic island and in the masque where love is guided by gods. Married fertility is praised on the model of the securely determined round of nature. The imagery of this improved cycle seems to me a deliberately simplified and purged image of the human contract it celebrates, for it avoids those very problems of trust and self-discipline which Prospero himself had earlier raised with Ferdinand. At the same time the more unpleasant themes on Prospero's mind resonate even in their exclusion: the possibilities fulfilled in the fourth book of the *Aeneid* are carefully exorcised (IV.i.87–101), though just as carefully mentioned. Iris, announcing Juno's command to the Naiads, "temperate nymphs" of "windring brooks," warns them to "be not too late." The celebration of married sex is depicted by a conventional image of harvest dancing, yet even in their displacement to natural and collective activity the details echo Prospero's concerns: "You sunburned sicklemen, of August weary, / Come hither from the furrow and be merry" (IV.i.134–35). The passage of time, the brevity of holiday, the weariness of laborers, and the sexual associations all press into the couplet. Finally, Prospero's desire to protract the entertainment and delay the return to actuality is evident in the rhetoric of the masque, with its catalogues, its clustering adjectives, its appositions, and its "windring" sentences. The masque is thus a brief withdrawal into the golden age, Gonzalo's dream as magical theater, yet the realities of life which it evades are woven into its texture, revealing those pressures which now distract Prospero and become explicit in the revels speech.[32]

The play does not end with the revels speech, however, any more than the epilogue ends with the word *despair*. The consequence of this private recognition scene are odd. In fact there do not seem to be any consequences at first. Caliban and his new friends come onstage, freshly pickled, following Ariel's display of "glistering apparel." Caliban is here at his most cunning and Antonine. But shortly after, the plotters are put to rout. Prospero, to quote Leech once more, "turns his canine spir-

---

[32] Cf. the more sentimental interpretation in Frye, *A Natural Perspective*, 157ff. For a sensitive reading of Prospero's changing moods during the revels speech, see James, *The Dream of Prospero*, 134ff.

its on Caliban and his companions" and "bids Ariel see that the torment-
ing is done soundly" (148). It clearly relieves him from his attack of
Weltschmerz to get back into the role of punishing magician and have his
egregious culprit handy. But Ariel's description of the plotters preceding
their arrival onstage had made them look like helpless idiots, unworthy
of Prospero's fury. No such anger or vengeance is directed toward Antonio because Prospero deeply senses the futility of such responses, not
because his intentions are more humane where evil men are concerned.
With Caliban, he retreats temporarily into the microsphere, where punishment had therapeutic value, and relieves himself once more at the expense of his scapegoat. The exigencies of the subplot, the demands of
immediate physical danger, the rewards of an immediate physical solution, the panacea of magic: all these are now a positive diversion because
they have so little relation or correspondence to the subtler and less effective, the more difficult and less satisfying modes of activity to be encoun-
tered in the macrosphere.

The diversion continues on another, more significant, level in Act V,
during which Prospero relies heavily on magic and spectacle, giving
free expression to his love of theatrical display. At the conclusion of Act
IV he is in better spirits. "At this hour," he crows, "Lie at my mercy all
mine enemies." In this mood he retires and emerges to open the fifth act
in the same frame of mind, but all dressed up in his magic robes: "Now
does my project gather to a head, / My charms crack not, my spirits
obey, and time / Goes upright in his carriage." The words have the ring
of incantatory self-persuasion. No doubt he feels to some extent the exhilarated sense of approaching triumph, but he is also intent on keeping
himself keyed up for the performance which lies ahead.

Ariel reports that the king, Sebastian, and Antonio, "abide all three
distracted, / And the remainder mourning over them," but chiefly good
old Gonzalo, whose "tears run down his beard." It is important to notice
just how much or little Ariel says here. He continues:

> Your charm, so strongly works 'em,
> That if you now beheld them, your affections
> Would become tender.
> PROSPERO: Dost thou think so, spirit?
> ARIEL: Mine would, sir, were I human.
> PROSPERO: And mine shall.
> Hast thou, which art but air, a touch, a feeling
> Of their afflictions, and shall not myself,

> One of their kind . . .
>   be kindlier mov'd than thou art?
> Though with their high wrongs I am struck to th' quick,
> Yet with my nobler reason 'gainst my fury
> Do I take part: the rarer action is
> In virtue than in vengeance: they being penitent,
> The sole drift of my purpose doth extend
> Not a frown further. Go, release them, Ariel:
> My charms I'll break, their senses I'll restore,
> And they shall be themselves.
>
>   *(V.i.18–32)*

Ariel has said nothing about their being penitent; he said they were distracted, that is, enchanted, which made the others, chiefly Gonzalo, "brimful of sorrow and dismay." His phrase "your charm so strongly works 'em" may suggest the inner effect on their souls, but Ariel's context throughout is visual and seems to mean, "if you saw how uncomfortable and helpless they appeared, and if you saw how sorry this made the others, you would have pity on them." (*Them* may refer to Gonzalo and the rest of the entourage as well as the distracted trio.) So far as we know, only Alonso has displayed anything resembling remorse, and his feelings are by no means clear: his final words in the masque of judgment scene suggest that he feels himself involved in some retributive action connected with Prospero's old grievance, an action which has taken his son from him and which therefore impels him, in his grief for Ferdinand, to contemplate suicide. Sebastian and Antonio respond to the masque with two lines of foolish bravado before leaving the stage, and it is Gonzalo who makes the interpretation preferred by Prospero:

> All three of them are desperate: their great guilt,
> Like poison given to work a great time after,
> Now 'gins to bite the spirits.
>
>   *(III.iii.104–6)*

In view of what we have just seen, I do not think this is, or is meant to be, an accurate inference. It is of a piece with Gonzalo's other perceptions and judgments on the island and conveys more information about him than about his companions.

Prospero's "they being penitent" is also an unwarranted inference which tells us less about the inner state of his enemies than about the state he wants to produce in them by his magical spectacles and illusions. The masque of judgment, with Prospero occupying the god's position on top, was intended not simply to offer his courtly spectators roles, like an ordinary masque, but to assign them changes of heart, to catch their consciences. It was his major attempt to follow Miranda's alternative. And in the present speech Prospero is not considering a change of heart in himself but a change, a slight adjustment, of role which will make his part in the recognition scene more effective. Thus the deliberate and detached tone of the phrase "with my nobler reason 'gainst my fury / Do I take part" suggests to me that he is selecting, rather than experiencing, his response. And the next statement is not so much a sententious commonplace as it is the critical musing of an artist or playwright aiming at the right touch: "The rarer action is / In virtue than in vengeance." The sentiment accords with his deeper feeling that both vengeance and forgiveness are futile, but his attention here is to the dramatic moment: the effect will be better, because unexpected, if he reacts to their contrition with a display of divine forbearance, if he shows himself trying to fight down his just anger and offer them more leniency than they deserve. Therefore—and he is still thinking of theatrical effects—"therefore, not a *frown* further." Throughout the speech he holds his image at arm's length to apply the finishing touches before going onstage.

He does not go onstage, however, until he has delayed the action once again in the nostalgic summary of past magical achievements over which he lingers before threatening to drown his book (V.i.33–57). As the speech dramatizes his growing reluctance to rejoin humanity, so the rough magic he fondly recalls was practiced in a world devoid of any other human presence. The use of pastoral and heroic perspectives which characterized the masque of Ceres and the revels speech is repeated here: His former playgrounds were scaled to sub- and superhuman dimensions: the world of elfin pastoral and the cosmic arena where he played a game anticipating Milton's War in Heaven. His elves rejoice to hear the curfew, they work when people sleep, and they leave the sands printless. These insubstantial spirits were his assistants, his "weak masters," in staging wars fought not by men or angels but by the elements in the empty space "twixt the green sea and azure vault." The two details which do not square with the desert island locale are both relevant to his preference for a world without living or conscious men: the solemn curfew and the graves which Prospero commanded to open. And the remark about the elves who "chase the ebbing Neptune, and do fly him / When he comes back" (V.i.35–36) is oddly echoed forty-five lines later when he observes that his charmed victims are returning to their senses:

> Their understanding
> Begins to swell, and the approaching tide
> Will shortly fill the reasonable shore,
> That now lies foul and muddy. . . .
>
> *(V.i.79–82)*

The elfin instruments of his magic will fly the swelling tide of reason in a more permanent manner when the world of ordinary daylight and common recognition returns. And as far as Prospero is concerned, it would be better if the sinners could remain asleep; in restoring them to their sinful waking selves, he forces himself away from the magic island and closer to the real world.[33]

Two interrelated factors contribute to his growing pessimism about human nature and his increasing reluctance to abjure his self-delighting magical existence. First, with the exception of Alonso, none of the characters undergoes substantive changes as a result of Prospero's actions. Neither Antonio nor Sebastian gives any sign of remorse. Ariel's efforts to please his master spring, in spite of Prospero's affection for him, chiefly from his eagerness to be free. Second, I think we are meant to notice that he displays a limited knowledge of human nature. This is most evident in relation to Miranda and Ferdinand. They are so obviously pure and good, so obviously literary stereotypes of youthful love and virtue, that his "trials" of Ferdinand's love and his warning about temperance seem excessive and unnecessary.[34] The trial itself is peculiar: it amounts to proving oneself a true and faithful lover by carrying some thousand logs of wood and not behaving like Caliban in the process. We may justify Prospero's obtuseness in discerning or trusting apparent virtue on the grounds of his own betrayal by Antonio. But there is a more general reason: "the liberal arts," not people, politics, or society, were all his study. Neglecting worldly ends for the seclusion in which he bettered his mind, how could he be expected to have normal acquaintance with concrete human motives, character, and behavior? Like the Duke of Vienna, he seems to have been incapable of coping with, much less ruling, his fellow men in the normal ways and in direct encounter.

His inwardness and privacy are sustained throughout the play. We

---

[33] "Behind this speech lies the thought that nothing but such magic could have overcome the evil of Prospero's enemies" (Harrison, "The Tempest," 234).

[34] It is clear that Ferdinand is, in Dobree's words, "a very ordinary nice young man" ("The Tempest," in Muir, 169).

hardly ever see him engage others in the easy or open way of friendship. I do not mean this statement to be understood in the context of actual life, which would make such an observation ridiculous. Rather I have in mind the relations of other Shakespearian heroes to their fellows. Most of them have at least one companion whom they love or trust or with whom they deal openly, very often the opposing voice or foil which Maynard Mack has remarked as a characteristic feature of the tragedies.[35] Prospero is much more the complete loner than these heroes, closer in this respect to the wicked characters who keep their own counsel. He combines motives typical of the magician and the actor: like the first, he prefers the security of the one-way window relation in which he may observe without being observed and may work on others from a distance. Like the second, his reticence to expose himself in spontaneous or unguarded dealings blends with a love of the limelight, a delight in shows and performances, and a desire to impress others. Thus he hides either behind a cloak of invisibility or behind a role, a performance, or a relation which has been prepared beforehand. He is unguarded only when his attention is reflexively fixed on some aspect of his own art.

Prospero's farewell to magic is followed by what seems to me the strangest and most revealing scene in the play. He assembles the still-charmed Europeans in the magic circle, and before they have been allowed to regain their senses, he preaches to them. After some words of praise and promises of reward for Gonzalo, he turns to Alonso and the others:

> Most cruelly
> Didst thou, Alonso, use me and my daughter:
> Thy brother was a furtherer in the act.
> Thou art pinch'd for 't now, Sebastian. Flesh and blood,
> You, brother mine, that entertain'd ambition,
> Expell'd remorse and nature; whom, with Sebastian,—
> Whose inward pinches therefore are most strong,—
> Would here have kill'd your King; I do forgive thee,
> Unnatural though thou art. . . .

(V.i.71–79)

No one hears this but Ariel; it is, in effect, a soliloquy. It is as if Prospero hesitates to put on the real scene without one more dress rehearsal, or as if he is primarily aiming the words at himself, reminding himself of the part he has decided to play and of the parts he has written for them

---

[35] The Jacobean Shakespeare," in Brown and Harris, *Jacobean Theatre*, 15–19.

as penitents. He seems less concerned about Alonso here and more concerned about Sebastian and Antonio; he has fewer doubts about Alonso, but he has no reason to think that the others have been or could be pinched in any world but the world of his morality play; only when they stand distracted in the magic circle of the microsphere will he trust them to follow his script.

When they return to their senses a few moments later, his actual playing of the recognition scene is inflected very differently. The final act has little to do with disenchantment, with morality, forgiveness, and contrition. Or at least if these occur—as Prospero himself seems to know—they do so only in a play he puts on. This situation develops logically from his feeling that he cannot in any real sense new-create souls or catch consciences unless the others play the moral parts he has written for them. Therefore, he runs back into magic and art. In the play's final 214 lines, one sentence is devoted to gently pinching Alonso's conscience, followed later by 32 lines of cat-and-mouse about Ferdinand's supposed death, which has less to do with arousing contrition than with what Clifford Leech irritatedly calls the "celestial stage-manager at work once again, . . . the almighty contriver [who] must be allowed his thrill in building up his effect" (147). Prospero allows himself four and a half lines to warn Sebastian and Antonio of his power over them through his knowledge of their conspiracy, five and a half to throw Antonio a cold pardon—really a contemptuous dismissal—and reclaim his dukedom. For the rest, morality, contrition, and forgiveness take a back seat to the miraculous return of the lost prince, the subtleties of the island, and the theatrical *chef d'oeuvre* of the genius at the magic console. In his finest hour, he hogs the stage as actor, director, and hero; as the official greeter welcoming the visitors aboard; as the presenter supplying explanations and promising more entertainment after dinner; as the impresario busily pouring wonders, surprises, and reunions out of his baroque bag of tricks.

This is so clearly his last fling that I find it hard to accept the sentimental interpretation which centers on Prospero's renunciation and return. At the end he seems more unwilling to leave than ever. The closer he gets to leaving, the more Shakespeare shows him protracting and delaying the inevitable conclusion. Four times, beginning with "our revels now are ended," he bids farewell to his art and island, and prepares to leave (IV.i.148; V.i.29, 34, 64). Four times he reminds Ariel that he will soon be free (IV.i.261; V.i.5, 95, 241). On three different occasions he promises to tell his story later (V.i.162, 247, 302), which is a way of attenuating the absoluteness of the break and extending the experience into the future. Throughout the fifth act his attention is centered on the present enjoyment of his magic and his theatrical triumph. Finally, with the air of one winding things up, he looks forward to his return to Milan, promises good sailing on the morrow, and—at long last—frees Ariel. At this point, the audience begins to think of leaving. But not Prospero: his momentum carries him *through* the end of the play. Before we can flex a muscle or raise hands in applause, before the other characters can have vacated the stage, he has moved toward us; stopped us with "Please you draw near"; and in the tuneless, oddly skewed cadences of the epilogue, has asked us to release him too from "this bare island"— bare of magic, of other characters, of the play itself—a no man's land between conclusion and egress, now an apron in the theater more than an island in the sea:

> Now my charms are all o'erthrown,
> And what strength I have 's my own,
> Which is most faint: now, 'tis true,
> I must be here confin'd by you,
> Or sent to Naples. Let me not,
> Since I have my dukedom got,
> And pardon'd the deceiver, dwell
> In this bare island by your spell;
> But release me from my bands
> With the help of your good hands:
> Gentle breath of yours my sails
> Must fill, or else my project fails,
> Which was to please. Now I want
> Spirits to enforce, Art to enchant;
> And my ending is despair,
> Unless I be reliev'd by prayer,
> Which pierces so, that it assaults
> Mercy itself, and frees all faults.
>   As you from crimes would pardon'd be,
>   Let your indulgence set me free.

This is his final and most telling gesture, not only of delay but also of scene stealing. Yet its mood is in sharp contrast to the theatrical *carpe diem* of the previous scene.[36] The first impression is that of drained en-

---

[36] The most peculiar, perverse, and aberrant interpretation of the ending is surely that of Nevill Coghill, "In Retrospect," in Jackson, *Stratford Papers 1962*, 193–99. For other discussions of Elizabethan and Shakespearian uses of prologues, choruses, and epi-

ergy, literally of collapsed spirits. And this is essential to bring out the true strain of feeling under his exhilaration in the final act, a strain which might otherwise have been visible only in his aside to Miranda's "brave new world": "'Tis new to thee." But the epilogue is not easy to make out, because so much of what has happened is packed into it. Voicing his plea in the situational metaphors generated by the play—magic, performance, sailing, and pardon—he asks the help of the spectators' "good hands," first in applause and then in prayer. The interesting thing about this is that in asking to be freed, asking for auspicious winds and pardon, he places himself in the same relation to the audience as previously Ariel, the Italians, and also Caliban had stood to him. If we think of him as Ariel, then he is asking to vanish into thin air, or into a cowslip's bell, or wherever he may be far from humanity; for he has, he hopes, done his spriting correspondently, has answered to the spectator's higher and more disengaged pleasures in art. As Caliban, asking to be released from his laborious service, seeking a new master or simply grace from his present master—as Caliban he asks the audience to pray for him, pardon him, and release him from a bondage which comes to sound more ethical than theatrical toward the end of the epilogue. He may indeed claim to have been a scapegoat for the audience, to have taken their sins upon himself and reflected their true nature or true longings; to have lived their idyllic urges for them and so, perhaps, to have helped them stay in the world; to have kept them from his crime, which consisted of asking too much of that world and giving too little. Finally, he may, as the reinstated Duke of Milan, be begging *them* to help *him* return to the world.

And yet this is not all. The other side of this closing performance is that it is gratuitous; it keeps him from returning to Milan and from leaving the stage; it momentarily frees him from rounding out his little life, and it allows him to solicit a further range of spectators. He has tried to work on the souls of others; he has at least produced the expected happy ending; and now he moves toward us, as if he is not really at ease about that accomplishment. He wants to be reassured about the success of his project, "which was to please." To the end he continues to play on the spectators as he had on the characters, trying out his new role as mere fellow mortal, testing the audience response. An indecisiveness domi-

---

logues, see Anne Righter, *Shakespeare and the Idea of the Play* (London: Chatto & Windus, 1962); and my "Theater, Drama, and the Second World: A Prologue to Shakespeare" and "*Troilus and Cressida:* The Observer as Basilisk" in this volume, pp. 111–29 and 130–46.

nates the tone and rhythm of the epilogue almost to the end; it leaves us
wondering whether Prospero is sincere in claiming that his project was
to please:

> my ending is despair,
> Unless I be reliev'd by prayer,
> Which pierces so, that it assaults
> Mercy itself, and frees all faults.
> As you from crimes would pardon'd be,
> Let your indulgence set me free.

Here, as throughout the speech, the reference hovers uncertainly between the options of applause and prayer, the plight of the entertainer
and of the sinner, the spectator's concern for pleasure and for moral
profit. The lines which introduce the request can go both ways: "release
me from my bands / With the help of your good hands." And the final
line may mean no more than "be kind to the player and at least indulge
him to the extent of *showing* your enjoyment." If we take these words as
the utterance of the character and entertainer Prospero rather than of
Burbage or Shakespeare, then we are obliged to reconcile this sense with
the other one.

The same words may offer the audience a share in Prospero's mood of
weariness and in his growing conviction that it will take more than human magic to work any changes in our old stock.[37] The point of these
two levels of reference, working together and at cross-purposes in the
same set of words, is that Prospero is not sure of his audience. He
knows—or suspects—that there are more Trinculos and Antonios than
there are Gonzalos and Alonsos among the spectators. He offers them
two responses: one for those who may be moved by an appeal to common
humanity and sympathy, and who may have received the play and its
message at the level of conscience, but another for observers who may be
more cynical, or more disillusioned, or merely more casual, and who
have for this variety of reasons come to the theater to be entertained, to
be briefly transported to another world, to be spellbound by the combined magic and machinery of the spectacle, and to be released new-
created at play's end. Yet this is not all. The end is a final attempt to
reestablish mastery. The closing couplet has too much bite and sweep to

[37] James observes that our sense of Prospero "as signifying a superhuman Providence
is very strong in our minds" during the opening scenes, "but . . . later in the play
our sense of him as merely human, in spite of all his magical powers, grows steadily
stronger" (*The Dream of Prospero*, 163). This could also describe Prospero's sense of the
changes affecting him throughout the play.

it to be characterized as expressing weariness alone. It points the finger; it does not simply play on the spectator's sympathy but reminds him of the bond of common humanity which obliges him to assist Prospero. He has shifted his role slightly but significantly in the final couplet from that of fellow sinner to that of homilist, the voice of conscience. It is part of his refusal to vanish that at the very end, before losing all his strength and art, he *wills*, he ritually bequeaths, his role to the audience. And at the same time this effort at mastery, like those which preceded it during the play, is a dress rehearsal. It is our first view of Prospero in the real world, standing beyond the confines of his magic circle, preparing to confront life with only the ordinary means of persuasion. The epilogue is thus another prologue; he is still tentative and still experimental, still unresolved and still on the verge of a new phase of life. Although he knows his word is less than the miraculous harp, he lays the harp aside.

PART THREE

Renaissance Humanists

Pico and Neoplatonist Idealism: Philosophy as Escape

IN A SERIES of three essays published in the *Centennial Review* I have attempted to define a hypothesis based on the concept of *period imagination*, a hypothesis which might serve as an approach to the more detailed and concrete interpretation of specific works.[1] The second and third essays center on a subject of great interest to the Renaissance imagination, the *second world*, or *heterocosm*, and its relation to the concepts of *play* and *fiction*, to developments in perspective, and to humanist attitudes toward art. The aim of the present essay is to suggest what in retrospect appears to be a defective embodiment of the Renaissance imagination, defective primarily because of its failure to take these relations sufficiently into account. My discussion will focus on Pico della Mirandola but will extend to other figures in an effort to characterize the limits of the particular Neoplatonism associated with the Florentine Academy. In the first section I shall describe some of the essential features of Pico's thought and world view, in the second I shall briefly criticize them, and in the third I shall hazard some general critical conclusions.

---

[1] See the following essays in this volume: "The Renaissance Imagination: Second World and Green World," "The Ecology of the Mind: The Concept of Period Imagination—An Outline Sketch," and "L. B. Alberti on Painting: Art and Actuality in Humanist Perspective."

I

In the second proem to his *Heptaplus,* Pico divides the universe into three worlds, supramundane, celestial, and terrestrial, bound to one another by the various modalities of logical connection. Man, the fourth world, contains within himself all the aspects of the first three as possibilities, and we may assume that man's very indeterminacy raises him, for Pico, above the determinate universe. Within man all things lose their fixed outlines and are open to whatever new destiny man in his metamorphic freedom may achieve for them. But this achievement takes place *here* in the soul, not *there* in the world, and its validity depends for Pico on an explicit boundary-marking gesture, "Here, not there." For man is somehow in two places at once: *here* he is a frail dweller in the terrestrial world of mortal bodies (*caduca corporum substantia*), sharing with animals a single situation—"unprotected by cover or shade, exposed to rain, snow, sun, heat and cold" and, whether pure or impure, sacred or profane, subject to "the perpetual alternation of life and death." [2] *There* the all-things-in-all-things of the occult and Neoplatonic literatures are tempered by the fixed hierarchic topography of the essentially Aristotelian world model on which Pico superimposes them.

The two worlds are further distinguished, though not consciously, by a difference of inflection based on what Kant later analyzed as the difference between the external and internal forms of intuition: Pico conceived the *there* in primarily spatial terms, the *here* in temporal terms. *There* is a *where,* but *here* is a *now.* Man must see himself not only in both places but also in two relations: as a fixed object occupying a predetermined *place* in that medieval cosmos where time is a defective image of eternity and where the eternal is felt primarily in visual or spatial terms but also as an experiencing subject who occupies a span of time and within whom space and time emerge as modes whereby consciousness conceives its objects. If the language I am using sounds too modern, the distinction can be put this way: a determinate and hierarchic cosmos is one which has been spatially actualized and localized; an indeterminate creature whose central faculties are *ratio* and *voluntas* is a power performing serial operations whose aim is to determine the self by catching the dispersed Many of the cosmos into itself; this process of self-determination involves not only the imaging of the already actualized cosmos but also the

---

[2] *Heptaplus,* Pr. 2, in *De hominis dignitate, Heptaplus, De ente et uno e scritti vari,* ed. Eugenio Garin (Florence: Vallechi, 1942), vol. I, 186. Future references to the Latin text are to this edition.

acts of exploring and asserting its inner relations through the dialectical employment of symbol, metaphor, and allegory. Though Pico describes man as a fourth world in the *Heptaplus*, in the *Oratio* he treats him as a second creation, a new being and a new mode of existence placed over against the first and distinguished by his *consciousness* (*ratio*) of his situation.

In positing a disjunctive relation between world and man, Pico in effect lays stress on the second world taken by the mind. When God finished the first work of Creation, he "kept wishing that there were someone to ponder the plan of so great a work, to love its beauty, and to wonder at its vastness." Therefore, having made the finite universe perfect in plenitude, order, and diversity, he created man "as a creature of indeterminate nature" and placed him at the world's center so that "thou mayest from thence more easily observe whatever is in the world" and so that "with freedom of choice and with honor, as though the maker and molder of thyself, thou mayest fashion thyself in whatever shape thou shalt prefer." [3] The initial assignment of limits is crucial to Pico's position and consistent in his thought. One finds in Ficino many praises of *homo faber*, [4] and these are intended, as André Chastel has observed, "to fix by the analogy of art the manner in which God is present in his creation" and to suggest the comparable dignity of man, *deus in natura:* "His creative activity has its metaphysical justification in the fact that it extends the divine act which makes a perfect masterpiece of the universe." [5] But Pico stresses *homo speculator* rather than *homo faber.* Man is praised for making himself rather than for making things, and he makes himself by his acts of observation, contemplation, and interpretation. Man is like an artist and beholder standing before a perspective picture. The human eye, situated at a proper distance from the object—the universe— sees the whole from a particular subjective viewpoint which is at once ideal and true, a viewpoint which man can vary according to his choice. Placed at a distance which will best allow him *to see*, man's field of activity lies within himself. But this new privilege has as its counterpoise a new distance from God. In his *Commento* on Benivieni's poem, Pico takes issue with Ficino's concept of the beautiful (II.3.8) mainly because he wishes to separate God more cleanly from the realm of Ideas than

[3] "Oration on the Dignity of Man," trans. E. L. Forbes, in *The Renaissance Philosophy of Man*, ed. E. Cassirer, P. O. Kristeller, J. H. Randall, Jr., et al. (Chicago: University of Chicago Press, 1948), 224–25. Future references to the English translation are to this volume.
[4] E.g., *Theologia Platonica*, III.i, X.14, XIII.iii, the latter being the best known.
[5] *Marsile Ficin et l'art* (Geneva: E. Droz, 1954), 66.

Ficino does. At the same time, he makes this realm a more self-sufficient goal, for in knowing Ideas man somehow truly knows God and possesses the good, and yet, as Cassirer has shown, that is only the truth, knowledge, and possession of symbolic form. Cassirer goes on to draw the consequences:

> Pico is no longer trying to exhibit the Many as the *effect of* the One, or to deduce them as such from their cause, with the aid of rational concepts. He sees the Many rather as *expressions*, as *images*, as *symbols* of the One. And what he is trying to show is that only in this mediate and symbolic way can the absolutely One and the absolutely unconditioned Being manifest itself to human knowledge. . . . There are only different symbols and different interpretations of one and the same meaning, which is the foundation of them all, but which is not capable of being grasped by us as it is in itself, without any symbolic intermediary. . . . he maintains that our thinking and conceiving, in so far as it is directed toward the Divine, can never be an adequate expression, but only an image and a metaphor.[6]

And yet in the merely metaphoric, the merely imaginative, lies man's preeminent power of transforming reality as he can. Taking his stand within the relatively limited domain of *poetic* theology, implicitly revising the very significance of the term *ontological*, Pico is able to make and to some extent validate greater claims on man's behalf.

The new position assigned to man is discussed by Pico as that of a *magus* and *interpres*. Distinguishing the good from the bad form of magic, he remarks that the former "is nothing else than the utter perfection of natural philosophy," and he derives the word, on Porphyry's authority, from the Persian *magus*, which "expresses the same idea as 'interpreter' and 'worshiper of the divine' with us."[7] The magus "is the servant of nature and not a contriver," one who

> does not so much work wonders as diligently serve a wonder-working nature. . . . [H]aving clearly perceived the reciprocal affinity of natures, and applying to each single thing the suitable and peculiar inducements . . . [he] brings forth into the open the miracles concealed in the recesses of the world, in the depths of nature, and in the storehouses and mysteries of God, just as if

[6] "Giovanni Pico della Mirandola," *Journal of the History of Ideas* 3, no. 2 (1942): 138–39.

[7] Forbes, 247. For a more extended discussion, see *Apologia de magia*, fifth discussion, *de magia naturali*. . . . Compare P. O. Kristeller's account of Ficino's ideas about magic, *Philosophy of Marsilio Ficino*, trans. V. Conant (New York: Columbia University Press, 1943), 314. The subject has been treated at length by D. P. Walker in *Spiritual and Demonic Magic from Ficino to Campanella* (London: Warburg Institute, 1958).

she herself were their maker . . . [and] he weds lower things to the endow-
ments and powers of higher things.[8]

Sorcery or witchcraft is a presumptuous assertion of power which betrays itself as weakness: the attempt to be a contriver or wonder-worker
"makes man the bound slave of wicked powers" and subjects him to the
"enemies of God."[9] Its motivation seems connected with the uncontrolled desire of the lower faculties, the urge of the pleasure principle to
do away with all difficulty and obstacles to ease. The sorcerer is a false
god trying to create a false nature, bypassing the discursive questing of
natural philosophy to attain the false image of that peace which can be
granted only by theology:

> For if you see one blinded by the vain illusions of imagery, as it were of
> Calypso, and softened by their gnawing allurement, delivered over to his
> senses, it is a beast and not a man you see.[10]

> Why should we not call the hands of the soul its irascible power, which
> struggles on its behalf as the champion of desire and as plunderer seizes in
> the dust and sun what desire will devour in the shade?[11]

> Natural philosophy will allay the strife and differences of opinion which vex,
> distract, and wound the spirit from all sides. But she will so assuage them as
> to compel us to remember that, according to Heraclitus, nature was begotten
> from war, that it was on this account repeatedly called "strife" by Homer,
> and that it is not, therefore, in the power of natural philosophy to give us in
> nature a true quiet and unshaken peace but that it is the function and privi-
> lege of her mistress, that is, of holiest theology.[12]

If we consider Pico's attitude toward astrology, we may infer that interpretation, or natural magic, is the normative mean between two forms of
surrender: astrological determinism, which would do away with the responsibility of the thinking creature *now* (*here*), and utopian magic,
which would wish away the natural limits of the human animal *there* in
the terrestrial world.

This process of interpretation may be concretely illustrated on a small

---

[8] Forbes, 248–49.

[9] Ibid.

[10] Forbes, 226. The mention of Calypso in this Circe function is not really surprising,
and it may have been prompted by the derivation of the name Calypso from *Kaluptō*, to
veil or cover over—as the vain illusions of sorcery would veil true nature and screen out
natural strife.

[11] Forbes, 229–30.

[12] Forbes, 231.

scale by a passage from the *Oration* in which Pico considers how man may return to the divine source; the passage begins with an exhortation:

> Let us disdain earthly things, despise heavenly things, and finally, esteeming less whatever is of the world, hasten to that court which is beyond the world and nearest to the Godhead. There, as the sacred mysteries relate, Seraphim, Cherubim, and Thrones hold the first places; let us, incapable of yielding to them, and intolerant of a lower place, emulate their dignity and their glory. If we have willed it, we shall be second to them in nothing.
>
>   But how shall we go about it, and what in the end shall we do? Let us consider what they do, what sort of life they lead. If we also come to lead that life (for we have the power), we shall then equal their good fortune.[13]

The key word here is *emulate—aemulemur*. Emulation is aggressive imitation, an agon between the emulating self and its exemplar. The method of emulation about which Pico asks is most fully demonstrated at the level of style, by the grammatical and rhetorical strategies of his answer. The angels are first treated as exemplars at a distance from the self, superior and independently real—"*There*, as the sacred mysteries relate, they are. Let us observe them, imitate them, make ourselves their equals":

> The Seraph burns with the fire of love. The Cherub glows with the splendor of intelligence. The Throne stands by the steadfastness of judgment.[14]

Their reality is grammatically affirmed in the true Aristotelian manner: the angelic substance is the subject; the predicate includes its *energeia* in the mode of essential attribute. By imitating the activity, man may come to share in the attribute:

> If, in giving ourselves over to the active life, we have after due consideration undertaken the care of the lower beings, we shall be strengthened with the firm stability of Thrones. If, unoccupied by deeds, we pass our time in the leisure of contemplation, considering the Creator in the creature and the creature in the Creator, we shall be all ablaze with Cherubic light. If we long with love for the Creator himself alone, we shall speedily flame up with His consuming fire into a Seraphic likeness.[15]

---

[13] Forbes, 227.

[14] Forbes, 227. "Ardet Saraph caritatis igne; fulget Cherub intelligentiae splendore; stat Thronus iudicii firmitate" (Garin, I, 110).

[15] Forbes, 227–28. "Si actuosae addicti vitae inferiorum curam recto examine susceperimus, Thronorum stata soliditate firmabimur. Si ab actionibus feriati, in opificio opificem, in opifice opificium meditantes, in contemplandi ocio negociabimur, luce cherubica undique corruscabimus. Si caritate ipsum opificem solum ardebimus, illius igne, qui edax est, in saraphicam effigiem repente flammabimur" (ibid.).

The situation calls for metaphor only in its Aristotelian sense of the transfer of quality. But in the next two sentences the relation between angel and man becomes more fluid, more symmetrical:

> Above the Throne, that is, above the just judge, God sits as Judge of the ages. Above the Cherub, that is, above him who contemplates, God flies, and cherishes him, as it were, in watching over him.[16]

Here the attribute is focused as a genus of which angels and men may be species—the class of just judges, or of contemplative creatures—while the angelic title seems to be transferred from its proper reference to this genus. In effect Pico has replaced the substance with the power as the subject of thought. This leads to the following statement, whose syntax may allow us to see the Seraph reduced to a vehicle or symbol of man as lover:

> Whoso is a Seraph, that is, a lover, is in God and God in him, nay, rather, God and himself are one. Great is the power of Thrones, which we attain in using judgment, and most high the exaltation of Seraphs, which we attain in loving.[17]

Thus Pico has converted the Seraph from reality to metaphor, from angelic substance to human operation, from remote exemplar to indwelling attribute.

In the next passage, the Cherub as contemplation seems at first to have the status of a mere emblem:

> Moses loved a God whom he saw and, as judge, administered among the people what he had first beheld in contemplation upon the mountain. Therefore, the Cherub as intermediary by his own light makes us ready for the Seraphic fire and equally lights the way to the judgment of the Thrones. This is the bond of the first minds, the Palladian order, the chief of contemplative philosophy.[18]

Pico will later convert Moses in the same way, but here the historical figure provides an exemplar: man as complex embodiment of the simple

---

[16] Forbes, 228. "Super Throno, idest iusto iudice, sedet Deus iudex saeculorum. Super Cherub, idest contemplatore, volat atque eum quasi incubando fovet" (ibid.).

[17] Forbes, ibid. "Qui Saraph, idest amator est, in Deo est, et Deo in eo, immo et Deus et ipse unum sunt. Magna Thronorum potestas, quam iudicando; summa Saraphinorum sublimitas, quam amando assequimur" (Garin, I, 112).

[18] Forbes, ibid. "Amavit Moses Deum quem vidit, et administravit iudex in populo quae vidit prius contemplator in monte. Ergo medius Cherub sua luce et saraphico igni

qualities abstractly signified by "angels." Yet from this point on, Pico stylistically suggests a return of the Cherub to his original reality. At first this is merely implicit in the Cherub's reoccupation of the grammatical subject; he is still treated as an artificial model:

> This is the one for us first to emulate, to court, and to understand; the one from whence we may be rapt to the heights of love and descend . . . to the functions of active life. But truly it is worth while, if our life is to be modeled on the example of the Cherubic life, to have before our eyes and clearly understand both its nature and its quality and those things which are the deeds and the labor of Cherubs.[19]

But Pico then asserts man's insufficiency and interposes the mystical tradition between himself and the angels:

> But since it is not permitted us to attain this through our own efforts, we who are but flesh and know of the things on earth, let us go to the ancient fathers. . . . Let us consult the Apostle Paul, the chosen vessel, as to what he saw the hosts of Cherubim doing when he was himself exalted to the third heaven. He will answer, according to the interpretation of Dionysius, that he saw them being purified, then being illuminated, and at last being made perfect. Let us also, therefore, by emulating the Cherubic way of life on earth . . . cleanse our soul.[20]

We can know about real Cherubs only through the rare testimonies of God's chosen vessels; it is the human testimony, the symbolic form rather than the reality itself, which provides the model.

In the process of emulation embodied in this passage, boundaries are marked, dissolved, reasserted between the mind and the reality which is its model and object. The *ascensus* of the mind is thus unequivocally internal, poetic, metaphoric—the movement "upward" is diagrammati-

---

nos praeparat et ad Thronorum iudicium pariter illuminat; hic est nodus primarum mentium, ordo palladicus, philosophiae contemplativae praeses" (ibid.).

[19] Forbes, ibid. "Hic nobis et aemulandus primo et ambiendus, atque adeo comprehendendus est, unde et ad amoris rapiamur fastigia et ad munera actionum bene instructi paratique descendamus. At vero operae precium, si ad exemplar vitae cherubicae vita nostra formanda est, quae illa et qualis sit, quae actiones, quae illorum opera, prae oculis et in numerato habere" (ibid.).

[20] Forbes, 228–29. "Quod cum nobis per nos, qui caro sumus et quae humi sunt sapimus, consequi non liceat, adeamus antiquos patres. . . . Consulamus Paulum apostolum vas electionis, quid ipse cum ad tertium sublimatus est caelum, agentes Cherubinorum exercitus viderit. Respondebit utique Dionysio interprete: purgari illos, tum illuminari, postremo perfici: ergo et nos cherubicam in terris vitam aemulantes . . . animam purgemus" (Garin, I, 112–14).

cally conceived as a movement inward. The Piconian metamorphoses through which "man becomes all things" and so creates his own nature are processes of imagination. They are neither magical nor merely fictional: not magical because the word *becomes* really means, for Pico, "plays the roles of"; not fictional because the transformational activity of mind which his language mirrors is part of the growth of a real self and adumbrates a reality *an sich*. The very passage, as an *aemulatio*, is a historic moment in the development of Pico della Mirandola. The process whereby angels are converted to abstractions or hypothetical figures thus has ontological significance. But the reference of *ontological* is in transit here, for the domain of objective spirit is less congruent with *cosmos* and more with *homo* than it is even in Ficino. Where Ficino usually speaks of *anima*, Pico usually addresses or speaks of *homo*. This is significant since there is a World Soul but not a World Man. The individual soul may easily be envisaged as in or part of the universe, a portion of the World Soul, its epistemological counterpart, etc. But *man* is a self-contained unit whose body and soul may be set over against the world as well as envisaged within it. *Spiritual* tends in its connotations to move toward "psychological," "mental," "imaginative"; therefore the play of metaphor becomes a more substantial activity so long as it is circumscribed as such:

> In the medium of this symbolic form of knowledge the fixed dogmatic content of the Church's teaching begins in some measure to grow fluid. Whatever is substantial and sacramental is dissolved and becomes intimation, an image of something purely spiritual. Neither word nor picture, neither rite nor any other external action can exhaust the deepest meaning of the religious.[21]

But an image becomes an image-of, a noumenon, only through that final self-limitation whereby the mind bounds the area in which it has given play to its constitutive power and distinguishes that area from the transcendent realm where Cherubs are ineffable. Pico's seems a casual or conventional rather than a felt gesture of limitation. The dominant vector of his thought is from world to self, from reality/history/nature to mind, from mystery to metaphor. This becomes clearer if his treatment of the angels is compared to that of others. St. Augustine, for example, is definite on the subject of angelic emulation:

[21] Cassirer, "Pico," 139.

Those who seek God by way of the spiritual powers set over the world or its parts, drift far away from him—separated not by space but by difference of affection. They strive towards the eternal, and desert what lies within them, though God is more inward than the innermost. They may have heard or conceived of some holy celestial power; but what draws them is the admiration that human weakness feels for the works of such a power, rather than the model of reverent submission which attains to the rest of God. They choose rather the pride of angelic potency than the devotion of angelic being. No holy person rejoices in his own power, but in the power of him from whom is derived all potency for fitting action.[22]

For the saying "Know thyself" has a different sense from a saying like "Know the Cherubin and Seraphim": our knowledge of them is belief concerning beings not present to us, based on the statement that they are a kind of heavenly power.[23]

Much later, after God was understood to have revealed knowledge through the agency of Pseudo-Dionysius, one could say more precise things about angels—so long as it was *revealed* knowledge about heavenly powers whose reality *extra nos* was unquestioned: "God loves in the Seraphim as charity, knows in the Cherubim as truth, resides in the Thrones as equity."[24] By the time of St. Bonaventure, who cites this passage from St. Bernard in the *Itinerarium mentis in Deum* (IV.4), there was an empyrean at the circumference of the actual world in which to situate the angels, and the common opinion was that if ever men could truly be like angels, it would be only in the next life. Before the literal ascent of the blessed soul through the spheres, likeness was restricted to proportional analogy, as when, for example, the soul is ordered in a way which *corresponds* to the nine angelic orders.

In all this, the functions of self, mind, and metaphor were exercised in place—place being defined by two coordinates, the earthly center of the cosmos and the human middle of the hierarchy of creatures. The point of invoking angelic exemplars lay in the presupposition of their greater perfection and higher reality. When St. Bonaventure has symbolic recourse to the Seraph, it is the six-winged figure seen by St. Francis in the vision of Alverna, and when he writes, "*si . . . Cherub es essentiala Dei contemplando*" (*Itin.* VI.5), he is not thinking of a real an-

---

[22] *De Trinitate* VIII.11 (vii), trans. John Burnaby, *Augustine: Later Works*, Library of Christian Classics, vol. VIII (London: SCM Press, 1955), 51.

[23] Ibid., X.12 (ix), 84.

[24] St. Bernard, *De consideratione* V.12 ("Deus in Seraphim amat ut caritas, in Cherubim novit ut veritas, in Thronis sedet ut aequitas").

gel but of the symbolic figures on the tabernacle (*Itin.* V.1): to the placing of man in the spatial and vertical hierarchies of cosmology and mystical theology, these usages add a historical-figural ambience which firmly, if implicitly, controls and defines the experience being described. The two *viae* to God—rational and mystical or philosophical and theological—could still be related to each other as complements or alternatives, and the particular tension between them discloses what was *not yet* problematical: the otherness of and distance between God and man; consequent acceptance of the information conveyed by different external intermediaries (Scripture, Church, tradition, perception); the ability to let the qualities of the information (facts, dogmas, symbols, images) rub off on the mystical objects to which they were extended without jeopardizing the "ineffable" and transcendent otherness of such objects. Thus, on the one hand, St. Bonaventure can elaborate correspondences with abandon to bring near what is presupposed as remote and dissimilar; on the other hand, he can resolve the tension between inward and outward itineraries by applying the principle of hierarchic subordination, which presupposes the unity of the one true world.[25]

By Calvin's time, those things which St. Bonaventure could presuppose *had* become problematical: the relations between consciousness and Being, hierarchy and unity, interpretation and reality. Calvin's so-called iconoclasm is an attempt to evolve a less isomorphic style of reference, one which by revealing its difference from its transcendent referents increases their distance. In the course of articulating this program Calvin mentions the Cherubim of the tabernacle, using them in a way which clearly reveals his departures from both St. Bonaventure and Pico:

> God sometimes appeared in the form of a man, but this was in anticipation of the future revelation of Christ, and, therefore, did not give the Jews the least pretext for setting up a symbol of Deity under the human form. The mercy-seat, also . . . where, under the Law, God exhibited the presence of his power, was so framed, as to intimate that God is best seen when the mind rises in admiration above itself; the Cherubim with outstretched wings shaded, and the veil covered it, while the remoteness of the place was itself a sufficient concealment. It is therefore mere infatuation to attempt to defend images of God and the saints by the example of the Cherubim. For what, pray, did these figures mean, if not that images are unfit to represent the mysteries of God, since they were so formed as to cover the mercy-seat with

---

[25] This resolution can be seen most conveniently by conflating *Breviloquium* II with the *Itinerarium:* the *corporalis mundi machina tota* exists not merely in and for itself but also in itself and for man.

their wings, thereby concealing the view of God, not only from the eye, but from every human sense, and curbing presumption.[26]

To this we may compare Pico's treatment of the tabernacle, as well as his use of the historical figure Moses:

> Let us also cite Moses himself . . . proclaiming laws to us who are dwellers in the desert loneliness of this body: "Let those who, as yet unclean, still need moral philosophy, live with the people outside the tabernacle under the sky, meanwhile purifying themselves like the priests of Thessaly. Let those who have already ordered their conduct be received into the sanctuary but not quite yet touch the holy vessels; let them first like zealous Levites in the service of dialectic minister to the holy things of philosophy. Then when they have been admitted even to these, let them now behold the many-colored robe of the higher palace of the Lord, that is to say, the stars; let them now behold the heavenly candlestick divided into seven lights; let them now behold the fur tent, that is the elements, in the priesthood of philosophy, so that when they are in the end, through the favor of theological sublimity, granted entrance into the inner part of the temple, they may rejoice in the glory of the Godhead with no veil before his image." This of a surety Moses commands us.[27]

It is worth noting that the difference here is not located in Pico's confident allegorizing as opposed to Calvin's meek submission to the text. Calvin allegorizes as much and as confidently as Pico. But the *style* of allegorization differs: Pico gives play to metaphoric fancies because his main interest is in the possibilities of the symbolic form; Calvin asserts its limitations by stressing its inadequacy. Pico had previously introduced Moses in a more historical perspective, but here he uses him as a mouthpiece. This is not Moses, but Pico playing the role of Moses. Where Calvin enforces the historical autonomy of scriptural events and figures as a guarantee of true interpretation, Pico revises Moses according to the rationale of *aemulatio*, which involves transforming literal fact to metaphor, theological "poetry" to poetic theology, a *then* to a *now*, a historical to a mental occasion. And this revision raises some important questions about the relation between his aims and his accomplishment. For if his definition and program of interpretation are novel, they are embodied too seldom in his practice to be adequately represented, much less *enacted*.

---

[26] *Institutes of the Christian Religion* I.xi.3, trans. H. Beveridge (London: James Clarke, 1953), vol. I, 92–93.
[27] Forbes, 232–33.

II

In moving from description to critique, we have to keep in mind the difference between Pico's stated intentions and those "motives" which a later interpreter elicits from his work. The present essay is concerned primarily with the life, thought, personality, motives, and in general the "activity of spirit" which the work itself renders. With Pico, as with Ficino, Bruno, and many others loosely called Renaissance Neoplatonists, we are confronted with a body of work which is second-rate from a literary or philosophical point of view but of great significance to the history of culture and ideas. Nesca Robb, whose judgments are always shrewd and perceptive, has summed it up this way:

> There are writers who live though their works die, and Pico is one of them. . . . it is Pico himself rather than his work that is still vital. He was the raw material of a poet, lacking in literary gift yet possessed of an inherent poetry of mind and character that illumines his life and breaks in veiled flashes through the inchoate clouds of his learning.[28]

In exploring this gap between the man *behind* the work and the man *in* the work, we may most profitably direct our attention toward the formal, structural, and stylistic exigencies which are entailed but not realized by Pico's "philosophy."

The assumptions and motives of Pico the man are familiar and may be set forth briefly: he believes that God's language is the language of symbol—"hieroglyph"—and that divine symbols display their transcendent origin by being hermetically obscure; they hide their meanings and thus spur the mind of man to interpretation. The cosmos is the greatest symbol, and the Mosaic Scripture—especially Genesis—is its preeminent verbal representation. Moses is a model for all writers because he was inspired to set down in a single synoptic text a vision of the cosmos which infolded all possible interpretations. Pico treats the inspired account of Creation as the product of intuitive or noetic thought—having received the Word from the same Spirit who presided over Creation, Moses is called *aemulator naturae*.[29] Less fortunate interpreters who are not thus inspired must fall back upon discursive modes of apprehension normal to fallen man. Pico resorts to *ratio*, to philosophy and discursive interpretation, to get beyond them and attain to a simultaneous intuitive vision of God. Though his often labored pursuit of correspondences ap-

---

[28] *Neoplatonism of the Italian Renaissance* (London: Allen & Unwin, 1935), 60–61.
[29] Garin, I, 182, 194.

pears nothing if not rational, the context of pursuit is an emotive and mystical quest. His interpretive exercises may seem little more than a game, yet they have a serious psychological function: through them he hopes to work himself up to a state in which the vision will (seem to) flood his mind with its light. He is of course aware that man is not and cannot become God, that human dignity entails the tragic limitation, that if man could literally become a god he would lose the essential mark of his greatness, that is, the impulse to transcend a condition of mortality which in one sense cannot ever be transcended.

The distinction between discursive and noetic knowledge, between the human and angelic forms of apprehension, is very old, but Pico's concern with it derives immediately from Ficino. In *Theologica Platonica* III.1 Ficino cites the field seen and painted by Apelles:

> It is the field which gives Apelles' soul at one and the same moment the perception of the view and the desire to paint it, but if Apelles sees and paints one blade of grass, then another, in successive moments, this is no longer an effect of the field but of Apelles' soul, which by nature is capable of seeing and performing things not simultaneously but successively.[30]

As André Chastel remarks, the example is intended to distinguish "the normal modes of our inner activity from the operations aroused by the intervention of God and the angelic world, where intuitions are given as simultaneous wholes; and it is precisely toward the splendors of the superior vision and its symbols that Ficino's curiosity tends."[31] Ficino's conception derives from Plotinus's famous misinterpretation of the hieroglyph:

> The sages of Egypt . . . in order to reveal to us their wisdom . . . symbolized objects by hieroglyphs, and in their mysteries symbolically designated each of them by a particular emblem. Thus each hieroglyphic sign constitutes a kind of science or wisdom; and without discursive conception or analysis places the thing under the eyes in a synthetic manner.[32]

But Ficino passed on to Pico an interest not so much in the mystical character of the symbol as in the discursive content and the process lead-

---

[30] "Pratum profecto facit ut anima Apellis videat ipsum, & appetat pingere, sed ut subito. Quod autem per diversa temporis momenta nunc herba una, nunc alia videatur, & similiter exprimatur, non ipsum efficit pratum, sed Apellis anima: cuius ea natura est, ut non simul inspiciat varia, referatque, sed paulatim" (*Opera omnia* [Basel, 1576], 118).

[31] *Marsile Ficin et l'art*, 65.

[32] *Ennead* V.viii.6, *Works*, trans. K. S. Guthrie (Alpine, N.J.: The Platonist Press, 1918), vol. II, 560.

ing up to the intuition embodied in the image: "Unless one knows what a hieroglyph means, one cannot see what it says. But once one has acquired the relevant knowledge, 'unfolded' by more or less exoteric instruction, one can take pleasure in finding it 'infolded' in an esoteric image or sign."[33] To see the whole universe as a radiant hieroglyph, or rather to strip away the veil and see it all at once in angelic vision, was the goal of Ficino's philosophic quest. His spiritualization of the humanist praise of man was ambiguous to the extent that this goal made him sensible of the life in time as fragmentary and unsatisfactory, an exile from man's true home. Time, itself like a hieroglyph, existed to be transcended. The particular symbol Ficino uses in his gloss on Plotinus is curiously emblematic of his central concern:

> Your thought of time . . . is manifold and mobile, maintaining that time is speedy and by a sort of revolution joins the beginning to the end. It teaches prudence, produces much, and destroys it again. The Egyptians comprehend this whole discourse in one stable image, painting a winged serpent, holding its tail in its mouth.[34]

The emblem *visualizes* the prior acts of thought whereby the mind came to the intuition the image represents. It is not *time*, but *the thought of time* which the symbol infolds. The interest in the discursive process thus leads the mind, whether consciously or not, to symbolize its own interpretation rather than the object giving rise to the interpretive impulse.

This tendency is more assertive in Pico. He strives to establish in the object of his attention some *otherness* which is to be overcome—or more precisely, to establish it *in order to overcome it*. This otherness may be something exemplary, or neutral, or recalcitrant, or partial, or defective, but whatever it is, its function is to stimulate him to confront it, transform it, assimilate it—in short, to dissolve the world into the self as a first phase in the process of self-transcendence, a first step on the ladder to God. When we turn our attention from the man and his motives to the work and its character, we may locate one important cause of failure in this tendency, for it produces an unbalanced interest in the subject, the self, and tends to dissipate the very sense of otherness which makes self-

---

[33] Edgar Wind, *Pagan Mysteries in the Renaissance* (New Haven: Yale University Press, 1958), 170.

[34] *Commenturia in Platonem, Opera omnia*, 1768. Translated by George Boas in his introduction to *The Hieroglyphs of Horapollo* (New York: Pantheon Books, 1950), 28. See Cassirer, *The Individual and the Cosmos in Renaissance Philosophy*, trans. M. Domandi (New York: Harper & Row, 1964), 69–70.

transcendence possible. In his polemic against astrology, for example, he distinguishes natural (physical and spiritual or intelligible) causes from occult causes in the cosmos: the former influence nature but not man, the latter are not astral or demonic forces but human fictions, symbols, projections. But Pico's aim, as Cassirer has shown, is the liberation of man, not the objective revaluation of nature. Unlike the cosmologists and scientific philosophers of the later Renaissance, his attempt to improve human power does not proceed by freeing nature from human idols, striving to make it more independent and real so that it may be confronted as it is in itself. His attempt proceeds rather by freeing man from nature and restricting all nonhuman influences. The result, as Cassirer says in *Individual and Cosmos*, simply extends the thesis introduced in the "Oration": "not a new way of conceiving nature, but a new way of conceiving man's worth. Now, against the power of 'Fortuna' is opposed the power of 'Virtus'; against destiny, the will conscious of itself and trusting in itself."[35]

Cassirer remarks that Pico sees in man's sinfulness "nothing but the correlate and counterpart to something other and higher":

> Man must be capable of sin, that he may be capable of good. For this is just Pico's underlying idea, that in good as in evil man is never a completed being, that he neither rests ever securely in good, nor is ever a hopeless prey to sin. The way to both lies ever open before him—and the decision is placed within his own power. . . . Hence however high he may rise, man must always expect a Fall: but at the same time no Fall, however deep, excludes the possibility of his rising and standing erect once more.[36]

Pico's main interest is in the rising vector: sin and evil are less real to him than human power; they are dialectically necessary rather than existentially present in his writing. That is, they function as alien obstacles to be overcome so that man may fulfill the main tendency of his nature, which is to keep moving.[37] Thus, if natural philosophy reminds us that it is not in her power "to give us in nature a true quiet and unshaken peace," this is not because of human limits but simply because of the limits of natural philosophy, which passes the baton to "holiest theology."[38]

Even when God is the object of inquiry, the same tendency to estab-

---

[35] Cassirer, *Individual and Cosmos*, 120.

[36] Cassirer, "Pico," 229–30.

[37] See "Oration" 4–14 (Forbes, 225–32) for a series of rising vectors in which evil, discord, lust, etc. are treated as chaos-functions or matrices which the soul overcomes in its rise to peace. The emphasis is not on conflict but on ascent.

[38] Forbes, 231.

lish and then dissipate the otherness of the object makes itself felt. In the longest and most important chapter of the *De ente et uno* (chapter 5), Pico leans heavily on Pseudo-Dionysius's negative theology to characterize God as "the being who infinitely transcends all that can be imagined." [39] The purpose of the chapter is "to show that not only with the Platonists and Peripatetics, who disagree with one another, but often in the same single writer, there can be, with respect to the divine attributes, many affirmations and many negations equally just" (20). The argument exemplifies Pico's attitude as described by Cassirer (see p. 192): "Our thinking and conceiving, insofar as it is directed toward the Divine, can never be an adequate expression, but only an image and a metaphor." Pico arranges the quest for knowledge of God in four degrees, in the third of which God is conceived as superior to whatever is signified by the transcendental terms (the one, the true, the good, and being). "In the fourth degree, finally, we know Him as superior not only to these four transcendentals, but also to every idea which we could form, to every essence which we could conceive Him to be" (26). After two short chapters disposing of Platonist difficulties in regard to prime matter and multiplicity, Pico devotes the eighth chapter to showing how "being, unity, truth, and goodness, are present in all that exists beneath God" (28). This leads to a curious reversal in Chapter IX, "in which it is indicated how these four attributes pertain to God," for they can be referred to him not only—as we might expect—"as He is the cause of other beings," but also "as He is taken absolutely in Himself" (32). The tone of the discourse at this point makes it difficult for us to believe that Pico has taken seriously his own strictures on the limits of attribution, for he seems to have shifted in an unqualified manner from negative to positive theology:

We conceive God first of all as the perfect totality of act, the plenitude of being itself. It follows from this concept that He is one, that a term opposite to Him cannot be imagined. See then how much they err who fashion many first principles, many gods! At once it is clear that God is truth itself. For, what can He have which appears to be and is not, He who is being itself? It follows with certainty that He is truth itself. (32) [40]

---

[39] *Pico della Mirandola: Of Being and Unity*, trans. Victor Hamm (Milwaukee: Marquette University Press, 1943), 26. Future page references are to this translation.

[40] "Deum primitus sic concipimus, ut sit universitas omnis actus, plenitudo ipsius esse. Quam intelligentiam ita subsequitur ut sit unus, ut neque oppositum concipi possit. Vide quantum aberrent qui plura principia fingunt, plures deos. Statim et verissimum est. Quid enim habet quod appareat esse et non sit, qui est ipsum esse? Consequens certe ut sit et ipsa veritas" (Garin, I, 434–36).

We cannot tell whether Pico has lowered God or whether he has simply given up God-as-He-is and retracted his discussion to the symbolic form of God, God-as-He-is-conceived. In the tenth and final chapter, at any rate, he draws a moral from the treatise by using the transcendentals as the ground of an *aemulatio Dei*, for example:

> Let us, lest we speak more of other things than of ourselves, take care that, while we scrutinize the heights, we do not live too basely, in a manner unworthy of beings to whom has been given the divine power of inquiring into things divine. . . . The best precept . . . which this discussion can give us, seems to be that, if we wish to be happy, we ought to imitate the most happy and blessed of all beings, God, by establishing in ourselves unity, truth, and goodness. . . .
>
> Let us therefore fly from the world, which is confirmed in evil; let us soar to the Father in whom are the peace that unifies, the true light, and the greatest happiness. But what will give us wings to soar? The love of the things that are above. . . . If . . . by grace of truth, we do not fall beneath our model, we have only to move towards Him who is our model, through goodness, in order to be united with Him in the afterworld.
>
> Since, finally, these three attributes: unity, truth, and goodness, are united to being by a bond which is eternal, it follows that, if we do not possess them, we no longer exist, even though we may seem to do so; and although others may believe we exist, we are in fact in a state of continuous death rather than of life. (33–34)

It is not God's love for us but our love of higher things, not the grace of God but the grace of truth, which will urge us upward.

The treatise in this fashion ultimately reduces God to a terminus for man, and even the remoteness of the God of mystical theology may serve chiefly to indicate how high man can soar by the proper use of his own powers. There is little feeling in Pico of human action as a *response* to divine pressure, as part of a dialogue with a God who is both present in the soul and wholly other. The God who cannot be determined as an object exists indeed as a noumenon for Pico, but as such is of little functional or methodological importance.

It may be argued that the *De ente et uno* is not meant as mystical theology, but this is the point: Pico uses the strategy of the *via negativa* merely to respond "to the arguments which the Platonists invoke to sustain against Aristotle . . . the superiority of the one over being" (20). The chapter is an episode in his unfinished attempt to reconcile Aristotle and Plato, and at its conclusion the brief essay into theology is abruptly terminated:

From all this we conclude that God is . . . the being who infinitely transcends all that can be imagined, as David the prophet put it in the Hebrew:
"Silence alone is Thy praise."

So much for the solution of the . . . difficulty. The window is now wide open
for a true understanding of the books composed by Denys the Areopagite on
Mystical Theology and *The Divine Names*. Here we must avoid two mistakes:
either to make too little of works whose value is great, or, seeing that we
understand them so ill, to fashion for ourselves idle fancies and inextricable
commentaries. (26–27)

Since Pico does not avail himself of the newly opened window, his
Q.E.D. would be a non sequitur except that it underlines his main
theme, which has less to do with God and Denys than with trying to
solve old problems in new ways. Here as in the envoi of the final chapter, with its somewhat inconsistent and irrelevant though characteristically Piconian attention to the rising vector, we cannot be sure whether
Pico is more serious about the body of the argument or about the reflective envelope in which he has placed it.

It is something of a jolt to see the transcendental terms used in the
tenth chapter in a purely figurative manner, after they had been treated
with scholastic seriousness in previous sections. The tenth chapter has
ostensibly the structural function of a return—from God to man, from
contemplation to action, from intellectual withdrawal to moral application. But in fact it seems to display itself chiefly as a rhetorical triumph:
the topics previously referred to God have now been neatly transferred
to man; the subject of the *De ente et uno* has been verbally assimilated to
the familiar assertions about the dignity of man. There is a "return" in
name only, since the areas of mystical, metaphysical, and ethical discourse are but nominally distinct. And the "return" is itself an exhortation to renewed withdrawal: "Let us fly from the world and soar to the
Father, imitating Him by becoming unified, true, and good; since these
three attributes are united to being, we do not exist if we do not possess
them, and are in a state of continuous death." The notions of nonexis-
tence and death aroused here are no less imprecise, no less hyperbolic,
than the image of soaring, which means—reduced to literal terms—retiring within oneself and meditating on the Neoplatonic ascent.

III

From this examination of Pico it seems legitimate to draw some general
critical conclusions which I think apply as well to Ficino, to Bruno, and

to other thinkers influenced by Florentine Neoplatonism. In brief, it might be said of them that they go up without coming down, they withdraw without returning, their going up is a form of withdrawal, and not withdrawal *with* but withdrawal *from* their problems. Some of the causes, qualifications and ramifications of the dilemma follow:

1. In the case of the three figures, especially Bruno and to a lesser extent Ficino, withdrawal or escape is projected into the *work*, while their *lives* in different ways exemplify courage, will, and endurance. Nesca Robb's judgment that the man is better than the work applies to Ficino and Bruno as well as to Pico. Speaking of Ficino's protracted period of melancholia, she remarks that "little is known of this episode," and certainly very little of it is felt in his formal work as a scholar and "philosopher."[41] The *opera* seem to represent not the pressure but the purging of the problem. If he "carried on his work unflinchingly through a lifetime of ill health,"[42] this is precisely what the work leaves behind in its often enthusiastic optimism. Ficino gave his depression a traditional intellectual focus by viewing it as a conflict between his faith and his philosophy, and it was essentially this conflict which produced a body of work most notable for the quality of reconciliation. Relatively late in his life he became a priest, and this may suggest that the *opera* provided him with the *locus amoenus* in which problems were worked out and resolved, if not transcended.

While Ficino remained very much in the world as a priest, Pico, who had fewer personal problems, was fascinated in a more or less esthetic way by the idea of fleeing the world. However seriously he intended it, the interest in asceticism which became marked in his last years seems in retrospect to have been pursued as a game. Though he came under Savonarola's influence during this period, he was unable to make a *real* renunciation—he could only speak and write of it, and perhaps this was a way of putting off the real thing. At any rate, his renunciation was put off until *after* death—he was buried in the habit of a Dominican monk. The act of writing and philosophizing may thus function as an expression of the pleasure principle, and the work may become a green world. The will to do away with an imperfect actuality leads the serious Neoplatonist to convert his *wish* to a *hope*, to confuse the ideal with the idyllic and project them not only "upward" but also "outward" as presumptive reality.

[41] *Neoplatonism of the Italian Renaissance*, 58.
[42] Ibid., 59.

This will, or wish, helps to condition the treatment of, and attitude toward, immortality. For many reasons it was no longer easy to presuppose this doctrine as revealed fact and man's true end. By 1513 it had to be dogmatically reaffirmed by the Lateran Council, and Pomponazzi's famous critique appeared in 1516. It may seem that Florentine Neoplatonism was one of the strongholds in which this dogma was sustained, but in fact Ficino gave the concept a strong this-worldly orientation which influenced Pico and many others. Castiglione's Bembo brings this out clearly when he says, "Let us die a happy death *in life*" (italics mine). In his *Renaissance Thought*, Kristeller, who has frequently and thoroughly discussed the question, reveals this orientation as much in his phrasing as in his explicit analysis:

> Ficino does not condemn or minimize the practical activities of life, but he states with great emphasis that the main purpose of human life is contemplation. By contemplation he understands a spiritual experience which begins with a detachment of our mind from the outside world, which then proceeds through various degrees of knowledge and desire, and finally culminates in the immediate vision and enjoyment of God. Since this final union with God is rarely attained during the present life, Ficino postulates a future life in which this aim will be attained in a permanent fashion by all those who made the necessary effort during the present life. The immortality of the soul thus becomes the center of Ficino's philosophy, because *immortality is needed to justify his interpretation of human existence as a continuing effort of contemplation*. Without immortality, that effort would be vain, and human existence would be without any attainable end.[43]

Immortality is important not as a truth of revelation and dogma but as a dialectical or systematic (or perhaps rhetorical) function which reinforces the value of special experiences attainable in this life. This reverses the emphasis of Christian mystics from the Gospel Age through the fifteenth century, for whom the moments of vision in this life were merely pledges of the more abiding bliss to come.

It does not seem that Ficino was aware of these implications, partly, perhaps, because of a semantic confusion inherent in his work. For example, he frequently affirms that the soul needs to separate itself from matter to fulfill its longing, return to its natural place, and see God. But this idea of separation is also applied to a different process: when the soul

[43] *Renaissance Thought* (New York: Harper, 1961), 129–30; italics mine. See also the same author's *Philosophy of Marsilio Ficino*, 324, and "Renaissance Platonism," in *Facets of the Renaissance*, ed. W. H. Werkmeister (New York: Harper & Row, 1963), 117–18.

internalizes the universe, it separates lower things from their material bondage by converting them to mental images, then to symbols of higher things. The first is a mystical, the second an epistemological statement, and it is hard to avoid the feeling that the first is developed by metaphoric extension from the second. Thus the following passage seems susceptible of either interpretation:

> [A]nimus . . . investiget quoque supernas causas, earumque effectus: item ab effectibus inferioribus per medias causas usque ad causam supremam ascendat: atque vicissim a suprema causa usque ad infimos eventus circulo remeet.[44]

He may have in mind simply the theory that the soul possesses all things as objects of thought, a power accounted for not only by reflection but also by innate *"imagines . . . divinorum, a quibus ipsa dependit,"* and *"inferiorum rationes & exemplaria: quae quodammodo & ipsa producit."*[45] But he may also have in mind a more literal ranging of the sort suggested in such phrases as *"transit in omnia"* and *"dum in alia migrat, non deserit alia: sed migrat in singula: ac semper cuncta conservat."*[46] These claims sound Hermetic, and it is not easy for us to take them seriously when we compare them to the more modest, because more explicitly metaphoric, statements which derive from the assumptions of earlier epistemology. The point is that Ficino seems to be more serious and literal about epistemology than about ontology, mystical theology, and eschatology, even though he does not think this is the case; he seems to be concerned mainly and primarily with the processes of consciousness, even though his avowed interest is directed toward, and phrased in the language of, more traditional and metaphysical topics.[47] Thus he frequently speculates about the vision *after* life when man, like the angels, will view the whole at once, freed from the limitations of temporal duration and mortal perspective. But his own philosophic activity suggests that he is really more concerned with the vision produced *in this life* when after restless striving the philosopher's *ratio* embraces the universe, reconciles different points of view, and completes the harmonious world picture unfolded in his discursive record, the *Theologica Platonica* and the *Opera omnia*. In this context, to make the soul "return to" God is a program

---

[44] *Theologia Platonica*, IX.6, *Opera omnia*, 218.
[45] Ibid., III.2, 121.
[46] Ibid.
[47] See Michele Schiavone, *Problemi filosofici in Marsilio Ficino* (Milan: Mazorati, 1957), 259ff.

which may be satisfied when the soul's highest power, *speculatio*, which operates without the help of bodily instruments, is given full play, since *speculatio* resembles the activity of the divine mind. This semantic confusion, which approaches magic, seems clearly to have been shared by Pico and Bruno and to be connected with what can only be called the green-world idealism of the Renaissance Neoplatonists.

2. Renaissance Neoplatonists, for various reasons, lack a true dialogic sense; their work spreads out from the self in a dominantly unidirectional manner, as exemplified above in the case of Pico. This becomes explicit and self-conscious in Bruno, for whom the individual philosophic quest had priority over anything which might be received, whether from tradition, antiquity, the church, or God.[48] In Bruno the monologic pressure toward "infinite Being" becomes a program which, separated from his life, loses the realistic or tragic dimension which might have rendered the *oeuvre* significant in its own right. The work, standing alone, projects the image of the Overreacher in caricature form. There is more conflict, more confusion, between the intentions and the accomplishments of Ficino and Pico; had they evolved different strategies of language and thought, had they adequately embodied their intentions in their work, their achievement might have been as rich in itself as it was in its historical influence. Both required, and both lacked, methods of "otherating" the divine, methods which would allow them to approach God without diminishing his transcendence. One has the odd feeling in reading Ficino and Pico that while they imagine themselves to be climbing up the ladder to God, God is actually lowering the ladder while they climb in place. Methodological slogans like "becoming God by becoming all things" too often lead their proponents to cross the insufficiently defined boundary separating metaphor or analogy from theological fact.

This monologal tendency has interesting effects in other contexts. There is, for example, a wide gap between Ficino as translator and as commentator and virtually no gap between Ficino as commentator and as philosopher. He has not achieved the middle way of historical perspectivism which was to mark the origins of modern scholarship. He extends his own syncretic thought uncritically back into his sources. If this is in itself a medieval failing, there is a crucial difference in the historical circumstances: Ficino possessed new sources, complete texts, the materials for a more objective history of thought. The question of the

---

[48] See J. C. Nelson, *Renaissance Theory of Love* (New York: Columbia University Press, 1958), 263–64.

relation between ancient and modern, sources and self, arises for him as it did not for earlier thinkers, but he does not come to grips with it. The most familiar and influential instance of this failure is his commentary on Plato's *Symposium*, known as *De amore*. Here Ficino plays the roles of his friends who "explain" (*exponerent*) the speeches of the seven participants in the original dialogue. All the "explanations" in fact develop Ficino's own version of the philosophy of eros, which draws more from Plotinus than from Plato.[49] Though he makes a pretense of recording and interpreting the ideas of others, he reads his own viewpoint into the utterances of his friends and back into "Plato." The peculiar quasi-actual status of Ficino's banquet produces an effect different from that of the quasi-historical status of the symposium which Plato's speaker "recalls."

Ficino's monologal tendency is most tellingly revealed in his theory of friendship, which I should like to contrast to an example of a truly dialogal theory, that of St. Thomas Aquinas. The latter's three questions on the nature, cause, and effects of love in the *Summa theologica* (I–II, 26–28) are chiefly concerned to show how there can be a union which does not destroy but, on the contrary, enhances the otherness and independence of persons in love. Statements about union are always qualified, and even when they appear in the objections to be answered, the replies do not question the qualification:

> Love is a kind of union. . . . But a union or bond is not a passion, but rather a relation. Therefore love is not a passion. (26, 2, obj. 2)

> Union belongs to love in so far as by reason of the complacency of the appetite, the lover stands in relation to that which he loves, *as though* it were himself or part of himself. Hence it is clear that love is not the very relation of union, but that union is a result of love. (Ibid., *ad* 2, italics mine)

> But love does not cause union of essence; else love could not be between things essentially distinct. (28, 1, obj. 2)

> But the lover in act is not the beloved in act. Therefore union is the effect of knowledge rather than of love. (Ibid., obj. 3)

> There is a . . . substantial union, as regards the love with which one loves oneself; while as regards the love wherewith one loves other things, it is the union of likeness. . . . There is also a union which is essentially love itself. This union is . . . *likened* to substantial union, inasmuch as the lover stands to the object of his love, as to himself. . . . Again there is a union, which is the effect of love. This is real union, which the lover seeks with the object of his love. Moreover this union is in keeping with the demands of love: for as

[49] E.g.: "Deum . . . pro homine fieri [amans] cupit, atque conatur. Quis autem pro Dei hominem non cummutet" (*De amore* II.6).

the Philosopher relates . . . , *Aristophanes stated that lovers would wish to be united both into one, but since this would result in either one or both being destroyed,* they seek a suitable and becoming union;—to live together, speak together, and be united together in other like things.

Knowledge is perfected by the thing known being united, through its likeness to the knower. But the effect of love is that the thing itself which is loved, is, *in a way,* united to the lover. . . . Consequently the union caused by love is closer than that which is caused by knowledge.[50]

The second reply is especially interesting for the echo of the *Symposium* transmitted through Aristotle.[51] Aquinas cites as evidence precisely that seriocomic myth of the divided sexes which the remainder of the dialogue resolves in a typically Platonic way, that is, by climbing up the ladder.

Even more peculiar is the hint that the love in question is between man and woman; no doubt St. Thomas did not read the passage in this way. In discussing the sacraments he adopts the normal medieval attitude toward marriage: "Matrimony . . . a remedy against concupiscence in the individual, and against the decease in numbers that results from death" (*S.T.* III, 65, 1 *resp.*). As its Latin roots suggest, *matrimony,* or marriage, refers less to a relation between persons than to the maternal (material) function of the female and the generative (form-giving) function of the male (*mas, maris; maritus*). The discussion of love, on the other hand, has to do with a relation between equals, a communion between independent persons in which the other is loved as a "second self." For this Aquinas naturally relies on Aristotle's theory of friendship. The respect and disinterested love of friends has nothing to do with sexual love; more important, it is treated as an end in itself; one's friendship for another person may be proper or improper, may be a figure of one's love for God (*S.T.* II–II, 23, 1), but it is never treated as a rung on the Neoplatonic ladder. Friendship as Ficino treats it in *De amore* has mistakenly been read as homosexual, on the other hand, because it is described in erotic metaphors; but their purpose is to express the power of God's attraction, the frustration produced by any earthly attachment in the lover who has once taken the bait of Beauty.[52]

---

[50] All passages are from the *Summa theologica* in the authorized translation by the Fathers of the English Dominican Province (New York, 1947).

[51] In *Politics* II.4 Aristotle mentions the *Symposium* not in a sexual or erotic context but as a comparison to the state which tends toward too great unity, not enough differentiation of parts.

[52] See *De amore* II.6 and VII.4–14, and Kristeller's excellent discussion, *Philosophy of Marsilio Ficino,* 276–88.

Aristotle's theory allows St. Thomas to distinguish between two kinds of attraction which are blurred in the *De amore*. There is desire, which implies something lacking and which draws one toward the thing desired in the hope of making that other a part of the self; but there is also friendship, which is based not primarily on longing for an unpossessed object but on love of the self.[53] So, after describing the various sentiments that comprise friendship, Aristotle concludes:

> It is . . . because the good man has these various feelings towards himself, and because he feels towards his friend in the same way as toward himself (for a friend is another self), that friendship . . . is thought to consist in one or other of these feelings, and the possession of them is thought to be the test of a friend.

The self-love in friendship differs from the self-love of desire, for in the first the other is treated as self; in the second the other is reduced to an object:

> The movement of love has a twofold tendency: towards the good which a man wishes to someone,—to himself or to another, and towards that to which he wishes some good. Accordingly, man has love of concupiscence towards the good that he wishes to another, and love of friendship, towards him to whom he wishes good . . . that which is loved with the love of friendship is loved simply and for itself; whereas that which is loved with the love of concupiscence, is loved, not simply and for itself, but for something else. (S.T. I–II, 26, 4, *resp.*)

The clarity of the distinction depends, for Aquinas, on avoiding any suggestion of erotic desire, which belongs to the class of desires directed toward inferior things. There can be "no friendship for wine and suchlike things," as he remarks in the *sed contra* of the same article, after quoting Aristotle: "A man is said to love wine, on account of its sweetness which he desires." The analysis of the relation between lovers is kept in the masculine gender, and this emphasizes the attachment based on equality as against that based on want and inclination. "One kind of likeness arises from each thing having the same quality actually," and this causes "love of friendship or well-being":

---

[53] "In love of concupiscence, the lover is carried out of himself, in a certain sense; in so far, namely, as not being satisfied with enjoying the good that he has, he seeks to enjoy something outside himself. But since he seeks to have this extrinsic good for himself, he does not go out from himself simply, and this movement remains finally within him. On the other hand, in the love of friendship, a man's affection goes out from itself simply; because he wishes and does good to his friend, by caring and providing for him, for his sake" (*S.T.*, I–II, 28, 3, *resp.*).

For the very fact that two men are alike, having, as it were, one form, makes them to be, in a manner, one in that form: thus two men are one thing in the species of humanity. . . . Hence the affections of one tend to the other, as being one with him; and he wishes good to him as to himself.

In such love, which is by analogy or proportion, each friend loves by remaining within himself yet being aware that *what* he loves is a person other than himself. But a second likeness "arises from one thing having potentially and by way of inclination, a quality which the other has actually," as when wine possesses the sweetness desired by taste, or a woman "possesses" the imagined pleasure promised by her beautiful appearance:

The second kind of likeness causes love of concupiscence, or friendship founded on usefulness or pleasure: because whatever is in potentiality, as such, has the desire for its act; and it takes pleasure in its realization, if it be a sentient and cognitive being. (I–II, 27, 3, *resp.*)

Both kinds of love or likeness belong to the actual relation of friendship, as we see when Aquinas discusses "mutual indwelling"—that is, the way in which love causes separate persons to be "within" each other:

The object loved is said to be in the lover, inasmuch as it is in his affections . . . because the complacency in the beloved is rooted in the lover's heart. . . . On the other hand, the lover is in the beloved, by the love of concupiscence and by the love of friendship, but not in the same way. For the love of concupiscence is not satisfied with any external or superficial possession or enjoyment of the beloved; but seeks to possess the beloved perfectly, by penetrating into his heart, as it were. Whereas, in the love of friendship, the lover is in the beloved, inasmuch as he reckons what is good or evil to his friend, as being so to himself; and his friend's will as his own, so that it seems as though he felt the good or suffered the evil in the person of his friend. (I–II, 28, 2, *resp.*)

By making it clear that the oneness of two lovers is metaphorical rather than metaphysical, sentimental rather than substantial, Aquinas shows how love derives its origin and its very meaning from the irrevocable distinctness of persons; he also shows how through the complicated psychic process of mutual indwelling, each lover can be "alone together," can sustain a "dialogue of one."

In the *De amore*, Ficino also discusses likeness and mutual indwelling, and devotes most of the fourth speech to Aristophanes' myth of the demi-men. Though many of his individual conceptions are naturally similar to those of St. Thomas, the context of thought shows them to be working toward—or from—an opposite set of principles. Where

Aquinas is concerned to keep lovers apart, Ficino's aim is to dissolve the otherness of a beloved self by reducing it to an object of thought. Since the lover's basic urge is for absolute union with God, the theory of friendship has to serve this end: respect and love cannot be for the self, the person, of the beloved so much as for something separable from him and much more important than his individual existence:

> The passion of a lover is not quenched by the mere touch or sight of a body, for it does not desire this or that body, but desires the splendor of the divine light shining through bodies. . . . For this reason lovers never know what it is they desire or seek, for they do not know God Himself. . . .
>
> . . . It . . . often happens that the lover wishes to transform himself into the person of the loved one. This is really quite reasonable, for he wishes and tries to become God instead of man; and who would not exchange humanity for divinity? . . .
>
> . . . If we love bodies, the Soul, or the Angelic Mind, we do not really love these, but God in them. . . .[54]

This means that the love of friendship, the idea of twin selves "horizontally" related, is of much less consequence than the sharp vertical inclination which moves the mortal creature toward the potential immortality, the permanent union with God, which he lacks on earth. And such an ascent abolishes the need for a concept of twin selves: when the individual mind attains to the level of its objective correlate, the Angelic Mind (*Nous, Mens Mundana*), it apprehends the single exemplar not yet divided into the subsequent multiplicity of individual forms.[55]

The aim of likeness and reciprocity in love, the abstraction of one form from two bodies, is thus contrary to that of the Aristotelian theory of friendship. The axis of ascent is located within each lover by virtue of the innate formulas which, since they are Ideas, are much purer than their inferior counterparts in the concrete world. This adds a certain inequality to the attraction through likeness: love—the mean between Poverty and Plenty—is always of the beautiful. The old man is the lover of the young, the less beautiful of the more beautiful, because the lover sees reflected in the external form what he is trying to find and see in his own soul. Thus the concrete forms of nature provide merely the first step (though it is an important step) in the reflexive act of recollection. In describing the self-sufficiency of the lover, Ficino models his advice on

[54] II.6 and VI.19, trans. Sears R. Jayne, *Marsilio Ficino's Commentary on Plato's Symposium*, Univ. of Missouri Studies, vol. 19, no. 1 (Columbia: University of Missouri Press, 1944), 140–41 and 215.

[55] See *De amore* VI.13.

the classical principle of artistic selection, familiar through the often-repeated anecdote of Zeuxis and the Crotonian virgins. But he gives it what might be called a Mannerist twist because the selection does not perfect what was immanent, though incomplete, in nature; on the contrary, it arouses and unfolds an object peculiar to the order of mind:

> If you observe men individually, you will praise none of them in every detail. Whatever is right anywhere you will gather together and you will make up a whole figure in your mind from the observation of all . . . so that the absolute beauty of the human species, which is found here and there in many bodies, will be gathered together in your soul in the conception of one image. You value little the beauty of each man . . . if you compare it with your Idea. You possess that (Idea), not thanks to bodies, but thanks to your own soul. *So love that image which your soul created and that soul itself, its creator,* rather than that crippled and scattered exterior.[56]

3. In the first two chapters of his study of Renaissance philosophy, Cassirer has described with great force the historical significance of Cusanus and some of the main connections between his thought and that of the Florentine Neoplatonists. Cassirer's interest in the development of early modern idealism, however, leads him to move *from* Cusanus's emphasis on self-limitation *toward* those more optimistic theses about the nature and power of man which were embraced by Ficino and Pico. Since what is new is the attention given to the mind's self-sufficiency, its germinal possession of all things and its ability to unfold them through experience, the form of Cassirer's exposition is itself naturally impelled along the rising vector. For example:

> The proof of the mind's specific perfection consists in its refusal to stand still at any attained goal and in its constant questioning and striving beyond the goal. . . . In this thought, perhaps, the basic Faustian attitude of the Renaissance received its clearest philosophical expression and its deepest philosophical justification. The striving for the infinite, the inability to stop at anything given or attained is neither a fault nor a shortcoming of the mind; rather, it is the seal of its divine origin and of its indestructibility . . . this basic and characteristic Renaissance motif . . . is at the centre of Leonardo's theory of art, and at the centre of Ficino's philosophical doctrine of immortality.[57]

For the purposes of the present discussion it will be useful to reaffirm here the context of self-limitation within which Cusanus developed his more "Faustian" ideas. This may be done by citing three methodological

[56] VI.18, Jayne, 213, italics mine.
[57] Cassirer, *Individual and Cosmos*, 69.

axioms which guided his thought: (a) between the absolute maximum (God) and the relative maximum (the universe), between the infinite and the finite, the creator and the created, there can be no mean except that which God himself chose to create in Jesus (*Docta ignorantia* and *De pace seu concordantia fidei*). Since no human image of the divine can leap the gap and reproduce the original, (b) the mind must begin by acknowledging the perspectivist character of its relation (*De visione Dei* and *De beryllo*):

> As everything appears red to the physical eye when it looks through a red glass, so the spiritual eye, in its limitedness, sees you, the goal and object of the mind's observation, according to the nature of its own limitation. Man is capable only of human judgment. . . . Ah, God, how wonderful is your face: the youth, if he would conceive of it, must imagine it as young, the man as male, the old man as old. In all faces the face of faces appears, veiled, as in an enigma—but it cannot be seen uncovered unless it be when we go beyond all faces to that secret, dark silence, wherein nothing remains of the knowledge and the concept of face.[58]

If this passage, especially in its final sentence, reveals its debt to the *devotio moderna* of earlier German mystics, it also points toward the Neoplatonists. For Pico, as we have seen, the limits of perspectivism exist to be overcome, though the darkness of the *via negativa* tends to be dispelled by a relatively anthropomorphic brightness.

(c) The third and perhaps most significant axiom, Edgar Wind has described in *Pagan Mysteries* as *serio ludere:* "In order to guide the mind toward the hidden God, Cusanus invented experiments in metaphor, semi-magical exercises which would solemnly entertain and astonish the beholder. These serious games consisted in finding within common experience an unusual object endowed with the kind of contradictory attributes which are difficult to imagine united in the deity."[59] One of Wind's major concerns in *Pagan Mysteries* is to show the extent to which the men of letters who revived the pagan mysteries in the Renaissance "had learned from Plato that the deepest things are best spoken of in a tone of irony" (189). He distinguishes three meanings of the term *mysteries* available to these men, the "ritual," the "figurative" and the "magical": (1) "The first and original meaning of mysteries, which is exemplified by the festival of Eleusis, is that of a popular ritual of initiation. In it the neophytes were purged of the fear of death and admitted

---

[58] Cited in Cassirer, ibid., 32–33.
[59] *Pagan Mysteries of the Renaissance*, 179.

into the company of the blessed, to which they were bound by a vow of silence" (13). (2) Plato is chiefly responsible for making "figurative use of terms and images which were borrowed from the popular rites but transferred to the intellectual disciplines of philosophical debate and mediation. In a half-serious, half-playful appraisal of himself the philosopher took on the attitude of a new hierophant" (14–15).

> (3) the adoption of a ritual terminology to assist and incite the exercise of intelligence proved exceedingly useful as a fiction, but ended, as such fictions are likely to do, by betraying the late Platonists into a revival of magic. . . . If the soul could be induced by a certain kind of poetic hymn to rise to a state of philosophic enthusiasm in which it could commune with the Beyond, then a similar force might be claimed also for the magical skills of incantation, for the art of invoking sacred names or numbers, or of . . . casting spells by drawing figures or by manipulating magical tools. (15–16)

Though "in the literature transmitted to the Renaissance the three phases were already thoroughly mixed," Wind finds that "among the great Renaissance antiquaries . . . the figurative understanding was upheld . . . as basic," and he attributes this to the naiveté with which they projected their own preferences back into the ancient sources:

> Whenever "the mysteries of the ancients" were invoked by De Bussi, Beroaldo, Perotti, or Landino, not to mention Ficino or Pico della Mirandola, their concern was less with the original mystery cults than with their philosophical adaptation. Good judgment alone did not impose the restriction; it was largely a case of good luck, for it derived from a historical misconception: they mistook the figurative interpretation as inherent in the original mysteries. . . . Plato appeared to them not as a critic or transposer of mysteries, but as the heir and oracle of an ancient wisdom for which a ritual disguise had been invented by the founders of the mysteries themselves. (16–17)

It seems clear, however, that Ficino and Pico did not understand the implications of *serio ludere* as well as Cusanus or Plato did. They did not, at least, see how its consequences could be fruitfully translated into a method of production, formally and structurally embodied in their *opera*. Like so many of their contemporaries, they took an essentially Roman and medieval view of the concept of the *poetic*, which they identified with the *rhetorical* or *metaphoric*—Pico's well-known censure of ornamental style as merely man-made (in contrast to divine symbols) is a case in point. What they failed to appreciate was the potential usefulness of the poetic as fictional, counterfactual, hypothetical, heterocosmic. Properly understood, *serio ludere* protects the mind from slipping into magic by keeping it aware of its symbols as only symbols, its fictions only fictions. *Serio ludere* also entails taking whatever game one plays *very* seriously, both for its own sake and as a model of activities which may be more general or significant. The game, that is, is pleasurable in itself and profitable as an analogy. So long as these two functions are clearly distinguished from each other, so long as the player recognizes the game is only a game and stays within its prescribed limits, he may concentrate all the more intently on mastering its techniques and exploring its possibilities. Yet at the same time he may with equal fervor climb the ladder and pursue the ideal, the utopian, the "supersensible" or "supramundane" without deceiving himself as to the nature of his accomplishment. The problem, in Wind's terms, is thus to unmix the three phases of the mysteries, to establish the figurative as distinct from the ritual or magical, to acknowledge it as basic precisely because *figurative* means "confessedly fictional," "artificial," "mind-made." What is required is not Pico's syncretic goal of a Poetic Theology; this is a dialectical halfway house which, by exposing the full force and weakness of its green-world idealism, leads through critique toward a more tensely articulated concord: Poetry *and* Theology (or Mysticism), each knowing itself distinct from the other and thus able without confusion to utilize the disciplines of the other.

The attitude of *serio ludere* might well be posited as the impulse behind much that is new and historically significant in Renaissance thought: the reorganization of relations between understanding and doing, contemplation and action, theory and practice; the greater dignity and emphasis accorded to method and technique, to technology and experiment, to the possibilities of a particular discipline or a particular medium, etc.; the development of the heterocosm as the playground or questing ground which the individual mind circumscribes both to pursue its inquiries and to manifest in formal and structural terms its experience of pursuit. To cite a few examples, such an attitude at work in the visual and literary arts informs the theory—Alberti, Pico, Leonardo, Mazzoni, Tasso, Sidney, Spenser, Shakespeare, Cervantes, Jonson—as well as the practice of the period. *Serio ludere* might well be the slogan not only of Montaigne but also of Castiglione, whose *Book of the Courtier* is concerned less with the Neoplatonic seriousness of Bembo's discourse than with a Machiavellian seriousness which sees games as essential to survival. Castiglione's purpose is reflected more clearly in the words of Cesare Gonzaga than in those of Bembo:

We have seen it happen in this house that many who were at first held to be very wise have been known, in the course of time, to be full of folly, and this came about through nothing save the attention we gave to it. . . . whenever we have detected some hidden trace of folly, [we] have simulated it so artfully . . . that finally we have understood what its tendency was; then . . . we agitated it so thoroughly that it was always brought to the perfection of an open folly . . . wherein, as you know, we have had some wonderful entertainment. . . .

Hence, I wish that for this evening our game might be a discussion of this matter, and that each would say: 'In case I should openly reveal my folly, what sort mine would be and about what . . .'; and let the same be said of all the others, keeping to the order of our games, and let each one seek to base his opinion on some real sign and evidence. Thus, each of us will profit from this game of ours by knowing his faults, the better thereby to guard against them.[60]

Like the games it represents, Castiglione's book is by no means an elegant image of escape *from* actuality—the attention critics have given to Bembo's Ficinian speech has been both excessive and inaccurate—but a controlled withdrawal, allowing its participants to perfect their defenses within the pleasant, secure, and temporary green world of their friendly circle. What is most important to Castiglione is not the mere image of the ideal courtier, not the various theories about proper behavior, not even the individual parcels of instruction but rather the whole method which the book exemplifies as well as demonstrates. *The Book of the Courtier* is usually misunderstood because its readers take its literary form, its concrete presence as a work, less seriously than did Castiglione. As his prefaces make clear, the friendly circle survives for the author only in *il libro*, the circle of his memory and imagination to which he himself manifestly withdraws.

The achievement of Ficino and Pico stands in relation to the great monuments of Renaissance imagination as prefaces do to great works. It is easy enough to state the new aims and new programs in fine prefatory rhetoric, more difficult to demonstrate them in the processes of thought, style, and experience—that is, in the works which embody these processes. Modern historians of ideas are sometimes cavalier about this distinction, and they might well profit from Leibniz's acute remarks about Patrizzi:

a man of admirable views . . . who lacked the learning necessary to pursue them. He wanted to correct the ways of demonstrating things in Geometry,

[60] I.8, trans. Charles S. Singleton (Garden City: Doubleday-Anchor, 1959), 20–21.

he had indeed seen that there was something lacking in them, and he wanted to do something also for Metaphysics, but he lacked the strength. The preface of his New Geometry, dedicated to the Duke of Ferrara, is admirable, but the contents are pitiful.[61]

Cassirer applies the same distinction positively to Kepler and relates it to the astronomer's own awareness of the importance of *serio ludere:* Kepler's esoteric beliefs and Neoplatonic speculations may have been important from the standpoint of psychological motivation, but

> none of this is really significant. The real emancipation is accomplished in Kepler's *work*. And it could be accomplished there only because Kepler stood for a new and stricter *ideal of truth*. Kepler himself tells us that in his first studies of planetary motion he had arrived at an hypothesis which formulated all his observations with sufficient accuracy: the error amounted to only eight minutes. . . . But he was not satisfied, and went further: "Those eight minutes," he himself says, "became the beginning of the whole new astronomy." It was thus a new demand for "precision" which gave birth to Kepler's laws. And so there grew up a new and stricter scientific critique of all pictorial and symbolic ideas, a clearer recognition of what symbols can and cannot do. *"Ludo quippe et ego symbolis,"* Kepler says in a letter, *"sed ita ludo, ut me ludere non obliviscar. Nihil enim probatur symbolis; nihil abstrusi eruitur in naturali philosophia per symbola geometrica."* [62]

Not only his accidental interest in two different modes of activity but his self-consciousness about it, his ability to shift back and forth between them, to honor their differences yet make use of them, sets Kepler apart from what in comparison is the merely prefatory work of Bruno and Fludd.

As A. C. Crombie has pointed out, it was not the gratuitous interest in experiments but the felt scientific value of this interest which set apart the scientists of the sixteenth and seventeenth centuries from their medieval predecessors:

> Undirected experiments and simple everyday observations abound in the work of medieval scientists. Certainly there was no general movement to conceive of experimental inquiry as a sustained testing of a series of precisely and quantitatively formulated hypotheses, pressing on to the reformulation of a whole area of theory. The examples of experimental inquiries, even the

---

[61] *Selections*, ed. and trans. Philip Wiener (New York, 1951): 53.

[62] "Some Remarks on the Question of the Originality of the Renaissance," *Journal of the History of Ideas* 4, no. 1 (January 1943): 53.

best of them, remained isolated without general effect on the accepted doctrines of light or of cosmology. They were thought sufficient to illustrate the method, and methodology was an end to itself. It would have become a dead end had not Galileo and his contemporaries, with a new direction of interest, pursued the subjects of the examples for their own sakes. It was through taking these seriously, through paying attention to the detailed facts of experiment and measurement and mathematical functions actually exemplified in nature, that the 17th century scientists were led to their radical revolution.[63]

Thus, early in the first day of the *Dialogues Concerning Two New Sciences*, Galileo has Sagredo use the *serio ludere* argument to encourage Salviati to digress:

SALV.: To solve the problems which you raise it will be necessary to make a digression into subjects which have little bearing upon our present purpose.

SAGR.: But if, by digressions, we can reach new truth, what harm is there in making one now, so that we may not lose this knowledge, remembering that such an opportunity, once omitted, may not return; remembering also that we are not tied down to a fixed and brief method but that we meet solely for our own entertainment? Indeed, who knows but that we may thus frequently discover something more interesting and beautiful than the solution originally sought?[64]

The openness which marks the apparent structure of the treatise is analogous to the open and tentative method whereby Galileo again and again withdraws to a hypothetical play world which he recognizes at once as counterfactual and as the only way to arrive at the reality behind phenomena. For example:

SALV.: . . . If therefore this experiment is to be made with accuracy it should be performed in a vacuum where every heavy body exhibits its momentum without the slightest diminution. If then, Simplicio, we were to weigh a portion of air in a vacuum would you then be satisfied and assured of the fact?

SIMP.: Yes truly: but this is to wish or ask the impossible. I grant that . . . conclusions proved in the abstract will be different when applied to the concrete and will be [to some extent] fallacious.[65]

[63] *Medieval and Early Modern Science* (Garden City: Doubleday-Anchor, 1959), II, 117–18.
[64] Trans. H. Crew and A. De Salvio (New York: Dover, 1914), 7–8.
[65] Ibid., 81, 251.

Salviati asks his companions to visualize not the situation in nature but the situation in a controlled experiment: "Imagine this page to represent a vertical wall, with a nail driven into it."[66] Experimental withdrawal, however, can be justified only by the phase of *return* to actual nature, which for Galileo means applying the principle of *correction:*

> If we consider only the resistance which the air offers to the motions studied by us, we shall see that it disturbs them in an infinite variety of ways . . . hence, in order to handle this matter in a scientific way, it is necessary to cut loose from these difficulties; and having discovered and demonstrated the theorems, in the case of no resistance, to use them and apply them with such limitations as experience will teach. . . . I now proceed to the consideration of motions through the air.[67]

As a final example of *serio ludere* in the field of scientific inquiry, we may glance at Gilbert's method of withdrawal through the eyes of Sir Kenelm Digby who, in 1658, acutely discerned its significance:

> All the knowledge he got of this subject, was by forming a little loadstone into the shape of the earth. By which means he compassed a wonderfull designe, which was, to make the whole globe of the earth maniable: for he found the properties of the whole earth, in that little body; which he therefore called a Terrella, or little earth; and which he could manage and try experiments upon, at his will. And in like manner, any man that hath an aim to advance much in natural sciences, must endeavor to draw the matter he inquireth of, into some small model, or some kind of manageable method; which he may turn and wind as he pleaseth.[68]

As demonstrated by the sixth book of the *De magnete,* of course, Gilbert's return to actuality was inadequate, since the principle of correction was not applied rigorously enough, but Digby's statement heads us in the right direction.

Serio ludere, in whatever field it exerts force as a motive, demands primarily a commitment to *the work*—both process and product—and to whatever "truth" emerges from this commitment. Commitment to

[66] Ibid., 170.

[67] Ibid., 252–53. The subject has been extensively treated. See, for example, Herbert Butterfield, *The Origins of Modern Science* (New York: Free Press, 1965), chapter one and *passim;* I. B. Cohen, *The Birth of a New Physics* (Garden City: Doubleday-Anchor, 1960), 95–129; A. R. Hall, *The Scientific Revolution, 1500–1800* (Boston: Beacon Press, 1956), 168–77.

[68] *Two Treatises . . .* [on] *The Nature of Bodies . . .* [and] *The Nature of Man's Soul* (London, 1658), 225.

one's work must be greater than, or at least equal to, commitment to one's life but not greater than commitment to life. The specialization involved in mastering a particular set of techniques and methods conditioned by the particular medium of work one chooses—this specialization itself should become a moment of consciousness leading beyond itself. Thus, for example, a more intense concentration on literary, artistic, philosophical, or scientific technique should theoretically produce a more intense awareness *that* one is specializing, that whatever "truth" or "reality" one apprehends is limited by the conditions which the work imposes. This implies a formal exigency, namely, that the work ought to display this awareness; in order to effect this, one must learn the various techniques of closure or circumscription whereby the work suggests its limits and points beyond itself. Furthermore, the work, like a picture plane, must be structured so as to draw into its field what is initially "on both sides" of it, that is, subject and object, or self and other. It is at this point that the *serio ludere* axiom makes close contact with the conditions and imperatives of a true perspectivism. I would like to illuminate this contact with two modern statements drawn from different contexts, statements whose juxtaposition may suggest something about the close relation between formal and intellectual imperatives. The first is by Richard Rorty and the second by W. K. Wimsatt, Jr.:

> The "subjectivist bias of modern philosophy" can only be reconciled with realism if we can find a way of reconciling the fact that all knowledge is *perspectival* with the fact that knowledge is about objects distinct from and independent of the experiencing subject. . . . it is logically impossible that there should be a description of reality which is not a description from a perspective which is one among alternative perspectives—[this fact] does not involve a surrender to idealism. To grant this consequence . . . to show that it is compatible with the claim that reality remains distinct from, and independent of, our knowledge about it is to defeat [the idealist] . . . our knowledge may be about an independent reality without its being the case that it is even logically possible that this reality should be described independently of the observer's perspective.[69]

> Poetic symbols . . . call attention to themselves as symbols and in themselves invite evaluation. What may seem stranger is that the verbal symbol in calling attention to itself must also call attention to the difference between itself and the reality which it resembles and symbolizes. . . . In most discourse we look right through this disparity. There is one-way transparent intellectual

[69] Richard N. Rorty, "The Subjectivist Principle and the Linguistic Turn" in *Alfred North Whitehead*, ed. G. L. Kline (Englewood Cliffs: Prentice-Hall, 1963), 153.

reference. But poetry by thickening the medium increases the disparity between itself and its referents. Iconicity enforces disparity. The symbol has
more substance than a noniconic symbol and hence is more clearly realized as
a thing separate from its referents and as one of the productions of our own
spirit.[70]

I submit these statements as commonplaces of modern thought. When
Cusanus made a statement similar to Rorty's (see p. 000) it was not a
commonplace, and the various consequences to which it could lead had
not been explored. If one such consequence is embodied in the above
statement, another appears in the neo-idealism of Cassirer. My own feeling is that the more adequate perspectivism is first chiefly worked out in
the practical domain of the various arts and sciences and also in the
broader context of the Reformation seen as a movement which fulfills or
sublates the Renaissance thought identified with Ficino and Pico. It
might be noted in passing that the idea of commitment is caught up and
modified in the important Reformation concept of *the calling*.

Language, poetry, philosophy, and scientific inquiry may be seen primarily under the aspect of *statement* or primarily under the aspect of *action*. That is, each may be viewed as a mold into which one puts one's
experiences, ideas, images, etc., and therefore as a medium which expresses and communicates a finished product; or, on the other hand, each
may be viewed as the record of the process through which one arrived at
the finished product. Doing philosophy, for example, may be conceived
as working out *and then* presenting to an audience one's philosophical
views or system; or it may be conceived as presenting to an audience the
image of oneself working out one's philosophical views or system. The
latter, with its self-reference, is the Platonic way in which philosophy
cannot be separated from philosophizing. Modern perspectival realism
would seem to entail a return to this Platonic way, and I think it is clear
that Ficino and Pico follow Cusanus in taking a first step along this
way—the way of perspectival idealism in which the role of the self is
stressed at the expense of the phenomenological reality of the other. But
the step they take has itself the quality of a preface or a programmatic
statement rather than the quality of action.

A program for experience is not the same as the experience; a program for contemplation or meditation differs from contemplative or
meditative action; descriptive or methodological assertions about climb-

---

[70] W. K. Wimsatt, Jr., "Verbal Style: Logical and Counterlogical," in *The Verbal Icon*
(Lexington: University of Kentucky Press, 1954), 217.

ing the ladder are not the same as climbing the ladder. Pico tends to conflate program with action and to confuse talking about philosophy with doing philosophy. The central image which emerges from Pico's *opera*—with the possible exception of the *In astrologiam*—is not the world view which Pico sets forth but rather Pico setting forth his world view. The man-centered character of his philosophy and the self-centered character of his method are in a peculiarly accurate way projections of this failure to keep his eye on the object, to sustain the independence and otherness of the reality outside mind or beyond self, whether this reality be natural, cultural, or divine. This failure is intimately bound up with what is new and significant in Pico's thought, which—as Cassirer has so persuasively argued—is the relocation of culture- and world-making activity within the now of the thinking self, the establishment of epistemology as the basic point of departure for the elaboration of *Weltanschauung*. But, apart from any personal failings, there is a formal exigency in a relocation of this sort which Pico misses and which perhaps he could not be expected to note except in historical retrospect: when philosophy is understood as the experience of philosophizing, when the criteria of certainty or objectivity shift from tradition and dogma to controlled inner experience, when the limitations on what the mind can do and make are no longer presupposed as the beginning and end of its activity, then it must *reconstruct* criteria and limitations on a new model. Intellectual, volitional, and emotional strategies of self-limitation must be newly elaborated along with a style through which they may be expressed. If Pico is one of the protogenitors of symbolic-form philosophy, if he anticipates Montaigne's conscious analyses of the concrete now and Descartes's formulation *Cogito ergo sum*, it makes all the difference in the world that he did not restrict his focus as Montaigne did, that he did not utter to himself the magic Cartesian formula. Descartes ended up roughly where Pico did in his attempt to objectify his own system and attribute it to a God who must thereby be no other than a projected Cartesian system builder. Descartes *faced* the problem of reconstructing the real within the limits of a method restricted to subjective certainty, and he unfortunately overcame the restriction by an arbitrary act of will, a fiat. But the immediate and positive result of his confrontation was that both in method and in world view, he analyzed experience into a number of clear and distinct areas, each with its own character and procedures, each imposing a unique set of rules on the mind, rules determined by the nature of the constructed—or reconstructed—object. Descartes's method and philosophy are thus deliberate *externalizations* of his attempt to meet the problem posed by the *cogito*, whereas Pico's are more or less intuitive *projections* of his ignorance of the fact that the problem confronted him. The result in Pico's work is a habitual conflation of areas originally clear and distinct, a continual metamorphosis in mental and verbal style whereby theology, philosophy, poetry, and magic restlessly exchange places and natures.

Utopian Folly: Erasmus and More on the Perils of Misanthropy

IN THEIR DIFFERENT ways both *The Praise of Folly* and *Utopia* drama- tize the same vitiated attitude toward life and explore its consequences. Both undertake an analysis of what I shall call misanthropy and depict the structures this condition erects to protect itself from life. Erasmus's emphasis is primarily psychological, More's political. Erasmus shows how a cultural system may be mobilized to serve the interests of mis- anthropic self-deception. More imagines a society performing the same service. The two works may be distinguished, somewhat artificially, as enacting different phases of the pattern of withdrawal and return—with- drawal in the pastoral misanthropy envisaged by Erasmus, false return in the utopian misanthropy portrayed by More. The two versions of misanthropy are embodied in the characters of Folly and Hythloday. Be- fore discussing the works, I shall try to describe the condition of mis- anthropy by reflecting on a classical figure, Anaxagoras—not the histori- cal Anaxagoras, but the Anaxagoras mentioned a number of times in Plato's dialogues, with an array of details which suggest that he repre- sents precisely this condition.

Anaxagoras

Diogenes Laertius, that notable hack, collected the following bits of rumor about Anaxagoras:

He was eminent for wealth and noble birth, and furthermore for magna-
nimity, in that he gave up his patrimony to his relations. For, when they
accused him of neglecting it, he replied, "Why don't you look after it then?"
And at last he went off and studied natural philosophy without troubling
himself about the affairs of the polis. When someone asked, "don't you care
about your fatherland?" he replied, "easy, there, I care a great deal about my
fatherland," and he pointed to the sky.[1]

Much of this could have come from Plato, and in this compact form it
may very well have offered More some suggestions for the character of
Hythloday. In the *Greater Hippias*, Socrates mentions Anaxagoras among
those figures of the past who are famous for their wisdom and who made
a habit of taking no active part in politics. A little later he observes that
Anaxagoras's wisdom was so mindless (his theory and treatise, according
to Diogenes, earned him the nickname Mind) that when he inherited a
large fortune, he neglected it and lost it all. This may be related to his
being—as we learn in the *Cratylus*—the authority for the opinion that
justice is mind, for mind has absolute power, and mixes with nothing,
and orders all things, and runs through all things. Socrates tells Phaedrus
that Anaxagoras helped Pericles cultivate natural philosophy and *ado-
leschia*, which can mean either "keen thought," "subtle reasoning," or
"idle talk," "garrulity." It made Pericles *hypsēlonoun*, "filled him with
high thoughts [*meteōrologia*] and taught him the nature of mind and lack
of mind, subjects about which Anaxagoras was in the habit of discours-
ing." Anaxagoras put his Mind at Pericles' disposal, and may eventually
have lost control of it, according to a tradition that he was prosecuted for
impiety to discredit Pericles.

There is a nice fit in this doxography between the pattern of Anaxagoras's life and the pattern of his thought. As we know from the famous
passage in the *Phaedo*, his theory of mind is ideally despotic and utopian.[2] If carried through, it should postulate a rational principle governing a universe of inert substances organized and changing according to
two laws: the attraction of like to like and the tendency of the heavy to
move toward the center. Perhaps in his high-minded disdain of practical
and political affairs Anaxagoras gave up his patrimony, escaped from
local constraints and commitments, and began to dream of a fail-safe
world peopled by obedient substances, programmed by Mind, and running in good order forever. But in fact he seems to have ascribed to

---

[1] *Lives of Eminent Philosophers*, trans. R. D. Hicks, Loeb Classical Library (London:
William Heinemann, 1938), I, 134. I have modified Hicks's translation.
[2] These references to Anaxagoras may be found at *Greater Hippias* 281c and 283a,
Cratylus 413c, *Phaedrus* 270a, and *Phaedo* 97b–99c.

Mind only the initiation of world order, and then, attracted to matter, he went on to explain things in terms of physical causes and processes. He lost control of the theory, abandoned Mind too soon, and surrendered to the forces of mechanism. In life, after losing control of his fortune he went to Athens, committed his thought and his fate to Pericles' hands, and surrendered to forces of machination.

I can imagine that when Anaxagoras's high mind confronted experience, he became embittered because he expected too much for too little. Perhaps Socrates had him in mind at *Phaedo* 89d when, after the argument for immortality founders, he warns his auditors about the dangers of misology and misanthropy: if one uncritically believes in the impossible ideal of a world where there is no evil and everyone is necessarily good, experience will quickly produce the disenchantment of the other extreme. One will come to "dislike everybody and suppose that there is no sincerity to be found anywhere" and, further, "that there is nothing stable or dependable either in facts or in arguments, and that everything fluctuates . . . and never stays at any point for any time." Just so, Anaxagoras, flying too high, was bound to melt his wings and, wherever he dropped, was bound to find himself among ordinary folk who struck him as disorderly, unappreciative, and self-interested, to be entrusted with nothing except a clog and a muzzle. From the perspective of Mind, which enjoys contemplating heavenly bodies, most human beings appear beneath contempt. The only thing one could do—if one was forced to do anything—would be to refashion humanity into a world of tractable, obedient, mindless, reverent, sincere citizens. And this is what Folly and Hythloday, having inhaled the Anaxagoras spirit, set out to do.

The Praise of Folly: *Pastoral Misanthropy*

Folly is the voice of that familiar schismatic illness in which the dream of life as golden ease is coupled with the nightmare of life as sheer misery. Her birth and parentage signify the moment when the golden fantasy so captivates the mind as to canker its prospect of mortal existence. The presence of plants like nepenthe, panacea, and lotus among the flora of the blessed isles implies that the birth of folly may be recurrent, a moment not merely of origins but also of return and escape from the cankered world.[3] Folly is neither the fantasy nor the nightmare in itself but the obsessional dialectic between the two, the fantasy continually

---

[3] Erasmus, *Praise of Folly and Letter to Martin Dorp*, trans. Betty Radice, introduction and notes by A. H. T. Levi (Baltimore: Penguin Books, 1971), 71–72. Future page references are to this translation.

reanimated by contempt, the contempt exacerbated by fantasy. Her idyllism is a wax-winged flight. It arcs beyond the moon toward the fastness of the theologian's third heaven or the Olympian heights from which spectator gods look down and laugh, and thus, expecting too much, it generates its own Icarian plummet to the hard, cynical ground: "If you could look down from the moon, as Menippus once did, on the countless hordes of mortals, you'd think you saw a swarm of flies or gnats quarrelling amongst themselves, fighting, plotting, stealing, playing, making love, being born, growing old and dying. It's hard to believe how much trouble and tragedy this tiny creature can stir up, short-lived as he is, for sometimes a brief war or outbreak of plague can carry off and destroy many thousands at once" (143).

The argument of Folly is that the examined life is not worth living, the examined self not worth knowing. In this gloomy cave of Trophonius the body is disgusting, the soul hateful, our fellow human beings to be neither trusted nor endured. The only glue that holds society together is the complicity whereby we deceive ourselves and each other. Folly is the sole alternative to anarchy. Her birth is the nepenthe that puts us to sleep or the dream that sustains us in our divine lethargy. She promises to restore the Golden Age by building a Babel of innocents (112), masking universal paranoia behind universal harmony. She offers us *Kolakia* and *Philautia* as guides. Following the first, we increasingly scorn those we flatter because of their gullibility. Following the second, we accept their flattery while remaining insensible of their scorn. Folly as a cultural system obviates the more painful and futile exercise of wisdom and virtue.

But Folly does not, cannot, simply persuade us to accept her remedy. Like one of Plato's sophists, she has first to persuade us that we need it—i.e., that the misanthropy she induces fits the facts of life. She does this by appropriating and misusing the powers of Momus. Her specific criticisms and analyses cannot easily be dismissed, not only because they flatter our sense of our worldly wisdom but also because they seem to hit their targets. Her targets may be easy, but this only leads us to agree all the more and to second her moral rebukes. And here lies the danger of her attitude and program: she speaks to our need for indignation and our capacity for self-deception but also, and more profoundly, to our underlying feelings of self-contempt and helplessness. Some examples will suggest the range of strategies by which she tries to establish her dominion and will lead us beyond her toward a glimpse of her creator.

Discussing insanity in chapter 38, Folly directs our attention to what is apparently an innocent dieretic exercise:

The nature of insanity is surely twofold. One kind is sent from hell by the vengeful furies whenever they let loose their snakes and assail the hearts of men with lust for war, insatiable thirst for gold, the disgrace of forbidden love, parricide, incest, sacrilege, or some other sort of evil, or when they pursue the guilty, conscience-stricken soul with their avenging spirits and flaming brands of terror. The other is quite different, desirable above everything, and is known to come from me. It occurs whenever some happy mental aberration frees the soul from its anxious cares and at the same time restores it by the addition of manifold delights. (120–21)

This is much more than a simple classification. The message of the first part is that we are neither responsible for the evil we think and do nor capable of dealing with the mental punishment that results from it; in both cases we are the victims of supernatural agencies whose powers we—with our meager spiritual resources—are unable to resist or fend off. No merely human ally can protect us from the furies, and the message of the second part is that we must throw ourselves on the mercy of our divine protectress, Folly. The second insanity is the only cure for the first.

Erasmus's readers may glimpse an alternative explanation in the devious redundancy of "pursue the guilty, conscience-stricken soul with their avenging spirits and flaming brands of terror": if we take the allegorical snakes and brands not as reifications but as metaphors of the soul's evil desires and guilt, we may ascribe both evil and guilt to an inner energy—the first to the energy of "that old earthly Adam" within us, the second to the ethical energy that stabs us with the pain of our willed betrayal of the Christ who died for us. Both Folly's analysis and her antidote evoke the message of the *Enchiridion Militis Christiani*, which they distort:

Hence, therefore, the outcome . . . is not at all doubtful, for the reason that victory in no wise depends upon fortune, but all this lies in the hand of God, and, through Him, also in our hands. Here no one has failed to conquer unless he did not want to conquer. . . . He will fight for you . . . not without your own effort. For He who said, "Trust in me, for I have conquered the world," wishes you to be of a great, not a secure, mind. . . . Wherefore we ought to steer a middle course between Scylla and Charybdis, so that we neither act too securely because we rely on Divine Grace nor cast away our mind with our arms because we are dispirited by the difficulties of war.[4]

---

[4]*Enchiridion*, I.1, from *The Protestant Reformation*, ed. Lewis W. Spitz (Englewood Cliffs: Prentice-Hall, 1966), 29.

Folly proposes eschewing the middle course and moving from the Charybdis of the furies to the Scylla of divine folly, for the human mind, lacking greatness, can only hope for the security of the happy aberration.

The same exclusion of the Christian middle informs her concluding meditation on the folly of the Cross. This section is generally taken straight as expressing Erasmus's—and not merely Folly's—view of Christian piety. In arguing for the integrity of the *Praise*, Wayne Rebhorn and Richard Sylvester have recently defended this view.[5] Their account of the work's reflexive structure and movement is persuasive: Folly's "metamorphosis from ironist to satirist to Christian mystic," as Rebhorn puts it (463), articulates the three basic divisions of the *Praise*, and the final "vision of Christian folly" transcends

> the illusory hope of the first section and the horrifying "reality" of the second. Note that Folly no longer claims man's worship, for Christian folly clearly means worship of God. . . . Folly defines what she calls the doctrine of Christ and what elsewhere Erasmus labeled the "Philosophia Christi," insisting that it involves mildness, tolerance, charity, and most significantly, contempt for the life of this world. (471)

But of course Folly's version of contempt in the previous section of the *Praise* is a misanthropic perversion of Christian contempt as Erasmus has discussed it, e.g., in the *Enchiridion*, while "mildness, tolerance, charity" are not her trump cards. The Rebhorn/Sylvester argument for the consistency of the work may possibly be extended to the consistency of the speaker's character, and I think a small change in their reading of the last section will strengthen their reading of the whole.

There is much in what the Penguin annotator calls "the praise of evangelical folly" which strikes a true chord—the themes of spiritual ignorance and simple piety associated with the *devotio moderna*—but this only adds to the strength, that is, the dangerousness, of Folly's argument. She pushes the power and virtue of ignorance through the middle course of the *Enchiridion* and toward the extreme of the foolish insanity discussed above. Her distortions of the handbook are subtle but significant. She notes of the "sword of the spirit" that it penetrates the bosom and "cuts out every passion with *a single stroke*, so that nothing remains in the heart but piety" (193). But the idea of a one-battle victory, a once-

---

[5] Wayne A. Rebhorn, "The Metamorphoses of Moria: Structure and Meaning in *The Praise of Folly*," *PMLA* 89 (1974): 463–76; Richard S. Sylvester, "The Problem of Unity in the Praise of Folly," *ELR* 6 (1976): 125–39.

and-for-all encounter is a mirage: the dagger, the handbook, is a way of life, and the battle must be fought until the very end. Folly interprets piety as an absolute rejection of intellectual effort and wisdom, a return to childhood and natural instinct; this is the way to be "free from care or purpose." But in the *Enchiridion*, Erasmus counsels the necessity of weaning ("to remain like an infant is unfortunate"), and although he criticizes modern theologians, he recommends reading the Fathers because "their very thoughts constitute a prayerful meditation."

Folly's praise of simplicity continues the praise of irresponsibility that dominated the first division of her speech. Like the bad interpreters she castigated in the second division, she marshals up texts from the Old and New Testaments to support a specious notion of divine mercy: "When men pray for forgiveness, though they may have sinned in full awareness, they make folly their excuse and defence. . . . What else is acting ignorantly but acting foolishly, with no evil intent?" (199–200). By the end of the passage, the excuse has become the reality, while divine mercy has drawn closer to the folly of bad faith.

The uncompromising rejection of the body, its senses, and its affections is also suspect. It is a viewpoint which Folly shares with the Stoic censor she condemns, and the Christian critique of this viewpoint, deriving chiefly from St. Augustine, is familiar: since the body no less than the soul is God's creation, and since the soul is responsible for the body, it is both "angelic" presumption and ethical evasion to make the body the scapegoat for spiritual weakness; it is directly a slander of the body and indirectly a slander of the ethical will. Folly's hatred of creation, her contempt of ethical consciousness and effort, are still felt in the final section, which testifies not so much to a metamorphosis as to the ultimate *hybris*, the effort to use the Gospel message as a vehicle for the pastoral misanthropy which constitutes a perversion of the Gospel spirit. Thus, for example, the divine madness may be an even better antidote than *philautia* for the self-hatred which in Folly's eyes is inevitably conjoined to self-knowledge: "Anyone who loves intensely lives not in himself but in the object of his love, and the further he can move out of himself into his love, the happier he is," and a few sentences later Folly places the emphasis of this triumph not on union with God but on escape from self: "When the whole man will be outside himself, and be happy *for no reason except* that he is so outside himself, he will enjoy some ineffable share in the supreme good which draws everything into itself" (206–7).

Folly promotes an ideal of piety which stands in direct contrast to Erasmian watchfulness, an ideal of self-forgetfulness which entails throwing away the Christian soldier's dagger or handbook. Those who try to achieve that ideal and return to the state of infancy will be precisely those least able to distinguish the Erasmian message of the *Praise* from its misanthropic inversion. As she describes the final rapture, it is not a refreshing of the spirit which renews the soldier's dedication to his earthly mission. Rather it is a repetition of the dialectic between fantasy and contempt that constitutes the anti-Christian condition of Folly. The ecstasy, which produces in pious fools the same symptoms as those displayed by theologians in scholastic disputes, sends them back to waking life freshly disgruntled: "All they know is that they were happiest when they were out of their senses in this way, and they lament their return to reason, for all they want is to be mad forever with this kind of madness" (208). After this Folly resumes in her exordium the tone of flippant contempt for the audience that marked her "ironic" performance in the first section of the *Praise:* she can be as illogical and inconsistent as she pleases, for the fools who swallow her sophistries will believe anything that promises to dull their sense of the ugly truth about life and themselves.

The basis of the condition embodied as Folly, the source both of the golden-age fantasy and the *saeva indignatio* dialectically coupled with it, is hatred of self. Folly's contempt for her fools clearly displaces and relieves her contempt for herself. She operates on the principle that misery loves company. In flaying the grammarians, theologians, and ecclesiastics she practices the very abuses she condemns. The finest dramatic irony of this mirror relationship is not, however, to be located in the displacement of Folly's hatred from self to others. That irony lies in the underlying reversal of Folly's displacement, and it can be grasped only after we consider the fictive rhetorical situation of the work as a whole. It is only a partial truth, and a distracting one at that, to see Erasmus behind the mask of Folly. He shares his act of creation with others. For just as Folly creates fools, so fools create Folly. She does not appear before us with her hegemony already established. In fact, the occasion of her appearance is her effort to secure her regime. She comes to the podium knowing she is still in poor repute, an orator wearing an unaccustomed garb, a shadow in search of an embodiment and apotheosis long overdue. We ungrateful mortals do not yet appreciate her and have not yet granted her independent existence.

The point of her appearance, the reason for her oration, is that only her "subjects" can transfer to Folly the power she claims she already has. For she is our creation, our Daedalian puppet, at once our slave and our divinity (cf. *Meno* 97d ff.). We alone can enthrone her over ourselves by persuading ourselves of our helplessness and passivity, by throwing away the Christian dagger and acknowledging our inability to confront life with mere ethical armor. Her being is in our hands. Her insistence that she is compact of nature and spontaneity reflects our desire to animate and reify our self-deception so that we can forget we are responsible for it. She has to encourage us to keep up the illusion, act out the farce, because her life depends on it. She is the voice within us asking to be released from our self-control. But her appearance gives us the chance to reject her. It testifies that the ultimate complicity is still unrealized. We are not yet fully confirmed in our bad faith. Recognizing that her true face is worn by each of us, we remain free to reach for a different enchiridion.

Utopia *and Utopian Misanthropy*

We should not expect to find that handbook in More's—or rather Hythloday's—Utopia, for, although Raphael's method of healing differs from that of Folly, his basic sense—nonsense—of human nature is much the same. The society he idealizes is another Daedalian project, aspiring to reduce human beings to walking statues confined in a carefully carpentered world of labyrinthine rationalizations and fortified institutions. Utopian misanthropy has given up the hope that human beings can be trusted to solve their problems through the ordinary informal activity of self-regulation and self-criticism, persuasion and argument, cooperation and compromise. The means of order must be alienated from their separate wills and securely vested in the mechanisms of a coercive or cooptative social system. Since ethical reform is beyond attainment, institutional reform is the only alternative. But this statement of the case is not quite accurate, for utopian misanthropy is self-fulfilling: it creates the condition it contemns. We may see this process at work on the institutional level in its treatment of the family and on the ideological level in its hedonistic morality.[6]

---

[6] This exploration of certain themes in the *Utopia* extends and somewhat modifies the general interpretation briefly outlined in my "Renaissance Imagination: Second World and Green World," in this volume, see especially 25–36. It is also heavily indebted to Richard S. Sylvester, "'*Si Hythlodaeo Credimus*': Vision and Revision in Thomas More's *Utopia*," *Soundings* 51 (1968): 272–89, reprinted in *Essential Articles for the Study of Thomas More*, ed. Richard S. Sylvester and Germain Marc'hadour (Hamden, Conn.: Archon Books, 1977), 290–301; future citations give the *Soundings* pagination. My debt over the years to Professor Sylvester far exceeds what I have learned from him about *Utopia* and Thomas More.

This section on *Utopia* takes into account the helpful criticism which Robert Martin Adams and others have made of my sketch in "Renaissance Imagination." Professor Adams thinks that the effect of my argument is "to soften the book's sharp and authentic note of

In his introduction to the Yale edition of *Utopia*, J. H. Hexter stresses the structure and central importance of the monogamous and patriarchal Utopian family organization:

> The authority of parents over children, of husbands over wives, and of the eldest, the patriarch . . . over all is affirmed again and again in *Utopia* and tightly woven into the fabric of Utopian institutions. . . . The family provides a powerful cohesive force for the whole commonwealth both as a coercive institution and as a training place for citizens. It is one of the means by which Utopians counteract the possible disruptive effects of their egalitarianism.[7]

Hexter argues that since More borrowed from Plato's republic the community of property and goods but not the community of wives and children, his rejection of the latter "could hardly have been the result of anything but conscious choice" (xliv).

The problem with this argument is that while the patriarchal family is present in Utopia, it is embedded in a network of customs and institutions which put considerable pressure on it and which cast its hierarchic relations of authority, obedience, deference, and reverence in a curious light. The second sentence of Hythloday's account of social relations seems to bear Hexter out: "Since the city consists of households, households as a rule are made up of those related by blood" (134). But the "as a rule" (*ut plurimum*) quietly opens a loophole which gets larger as the account continues. The sequel removes the domestic unit progressively further from the household as we know it, or even as Peter Laslett knows it. If the urban domestic unit is an extended household, it is hard to see

---

social protest" and "reduce it to a mere *jeu d'esprit*" (*Sir Thomas More, Utopia: A New Translation, Backgrounds, Criticism*, trans. and ed. Robert M. Adams [New York: Norton, 1975], 202; future citations of Adams's comments or glosses on the text will be to this edition). While that was not my intention, I can see how my emphasis on the green-world aspects of Book II could easily generate this impression. My point was that Hythloday, Utopia, and Europe were the objects of More's protest, that Hythloday and Utopia represent inadequate, indeed perverse, responses to the European problems which Hythloday accurately (if simplistically) perceives, and that the *Utopia* offers a dramatic analysis of the ethico-psychological roots of those responses. Hythloday and Utopia are nowhere if not in European society and in the minds and hearts of its inhabitants. I argued in that essay that More, in protesting Hythloday's social protests, was to some extent dramatizing his own susceptibility to attacks of Hythloday. The present essay centers on More's critique of the misanthropic dark world under the green world, and I am grateful to Adams's criticism because in forcing me to clarify my position, he has helped me revise it.

[7] Vol. 4 of the *Yale Edition of the Complete Works of St. Thomas More*, ed. Edward Surtz, S.J., and J. H. Hexter (New Haven: Yale University Press, 1965), xlii; future citations of introduction and text are from this edition.

how it could remain an extended family for very long, since adults frequently shuttle in and out of the household. Hythloday had already detailed the two-year urban/rural cycle and told us that there is no private
property, that all houses on a city block share a single back yard, and that
homes are exchanged every year; now he goes on to describe the procedure for keeping population stable by moving individuals from block to
block, city to city, or island to mainland.[8]

Robert M. Adams notes that the housing lottery, complicated by the
agricultural cycle, "seems likely to create as many problems as it solves,"
which leads us to ask why they should go to all this trouble—i.e., what
problems are they trying to solve? Adams thinks the purpose is "to keep
people from getting attached to things" (38), and I would add two further considerations, the first supplied by Hythloday himself. (1) The
"system of changing farmers" aims at preventing "any individual's
being forced against his will to continue too long in a life of hard work,"
although it is not imposed on those "who take a natural pleasure in agricultural pursuits" (115). There is a problem about the attitude toward
labor in Utopia; people work when they have to but seem generally
averse to it. Scholarly prowess is rewarded by "perpetual freedom from
labor" (131). (2) Demographic control is a symptom of apprehen-
siveness, and as a public policy it is an excuse to keep people from getting attached to each other—as they are, for example, in More's household (depicted in the letter to Peter Giles). Adams infers from the
system that unless Utopian houses are unusually large, they are likely to
get crowded (45), and even if nuclear families remain together—even
though the urban/rural cycle makes this questionable—the collection of
several families in a single house is likely to diminish privacy and inhibit

---

[8] Hythloday's remarks on the fondness of Utopians and their founder for gardens
(121) suggest once again the green-world symptom of the misanthropic mind. In an interesting essay, Wayne Rebhorn suggests that "in depicting Utopia as a walled garden,
More deliberately invokes comparisons with the earthly paradise"; that "Utopia is an
immense Renaissance garden where man's art has civilized and domesticated practically
every aspect of the natural world"; and that "Utopia totally separates itself from that
world and sets up barriers of racks and fortresses to prevent any intrusion of vice or
disease or filth from its neighbors" ("Thomas More's Enclosed Garden: *Utopia* and Renaissance Humanism," *ELR* 6 [1976], 143, 155). Rebhorn is concerned to show how
More embodies humanist ideals in a positive utopian vision, but his concluding description reminds one more of the Skinnerian paranoia which More could have found—and
appreciated—in (what I take to be) Plato's ironic presentation of the guardian polis in
the *Republic*, in many ways a model for More's insights into the relation between misanthropic anxiety and dystopia. The image of society as a garden, the idea that human
beings can be cultivated and weeded like plants, must be as frightening to the potential
plant population as it is mollifying to the insane gardener who thinks to preserve himself
by this metamorphosis and control of his fellow beings.

intimacy. I would like to suggest that the patriarchal family as a functioning unit is present in Utopia for the most part in name only; that it is, if anything, an arm of the civil government; and that its peculiar arrangements have a specific aim: to redirect from family and household to larger, more public, units and ultimately to the political tribe as a whole the essential affective quality of *philia*—the deep bond of friendship and family feeling that leads people to care for each other, the source of the diffuse and particularistic attachments that guarantee reciprocity and cooperation. What bothers the government, in my view, is the privacy and intimacy, the loyalty, solidarity, and mutuality of interests encouraged by sustained family life. Like the founders of Plato's guardian polis, the Utopian mentality treats the private family space as a potential seedbed of conspiracy against the state, a place in which the constant face-to-face relations enable people to keep their backs to the world, confide in each other, share secrets, and hatch plots. As Hexter observes (xlii), the patriarch is his wife's penitential and penal officer (191, 233).

The campaign to displace *philia* from private to public institutions is exhibited in another feature of Utopian social life, the transfer from the household of two of its most essential solidary functions, meals and the care of the sick. I think Hexter misunderstands the meaning of this when he says that the order of the patriarchal family is maintained in the common meals (xlii). On the contrary, the family's autonomy is subtly undermined by them and its discipline replaced by the elaborate safeguards which the essentially military arrangement makes possible. Groups of thirty "families" are assigned to the halls of resident officials, summoned at fixed hours by a bugler, seated in prescribed order, and overseen by the officials and elders from their strategically raised table. The meal provides one of the most important vehicles of socialization and scrutiny. The big brotherhood of officials and elders, occasionally assisted by priests, implants proper attitudes in the young by example, by tactfully brief moral readings, by drawing out their charges in "approved subjects of conversation," and by unremitting surveillance. It has become clear by the end of the account that the domestic unit is no more than a nominal family and that most of its functions have been preempted by the *magna . . . familia* (148) of the commonwealth. It may be that the "blood" by which household members are related is Utopian "blood."

The mode of preemption is not coercive—indeed, it is studiedly noncoercive—but cooptative. No ill person is sent to a public hospital "against his will," but "there is hardly anybody in the whole city who . . . does not prefer to be nursed there rather than at home" (141). And "though nobody is forbidden to dine at home, yet no one does it willingly since the practice is not considered decent [*honestum*] and since it is foolish to take the trouble of preparing an inferior dinner when an excellent and sumptuous one is ready at hand in the hall nearby," where slaves perform all "menial offices" which involve "heavy labor or soil the hands" (141). The appeal to morality need not be distinguished from the appeal to ease and pleasure since, as we shall see, the two are identical. Hence in the statement "the reading which is conducive to morality [*ad mores faciat*] . . . is brief so as not to be tiresome" (145), the concluding adjectival phrase contributes much to the definition of *ad mores faciat*. The young are put at their ease ("in the relaxed atmosphere of a feast") so that their ability and character may be more readily manifested, or betrayed, to their guardians, who are less relaxed: "Nothing can be done or said at table which escapes the notice of the old present on every side" (143–45).

In Book I Raphael had criticized the English because "they first create thieves and then become the very agents of their punishment" (71). He might well direct the same criticism at his Utopians: their campaign to inhibit long-term intimate domestic relationships ironically enfeebles the one institution which can be counted on to give positive direction to relations between sexes, between generations, between persons. Utopians act as if they believe human nature incapable of companionly love. But it is they who have created or confirmed this incapacity. Distrusting whispers that cannot be overheard, they cut back the institutional ground of the bond of *philia*. The effects are clearly shown in their attitude toward marriage. The harsh punishment of premarital sex and adultery is based on the assumption that "unless persons are carefully restrained from promiscuous intercourse, few will contract the tie of marriage, in which a whole life must be spent with one companion and all the troubles incidental to it must be patiently borne" (187). This cynicism informs the bizarre procedure by which mates are selected. Choosing a wife is compared to buying a colt; since there is no reason to trust the seller, a complete physical examination is prescribed to assuage the fear that, e.g., "some sore lies concealed under these coverings" (189). As we shall see, this is not the only passage in which Utopian sensitivity to the body's offensiveness is depicted.

The animal analogy deserves closer scrutiny. Early in Book II Hythloday had informed us that Utopians use horses "for no other purpose than for exercising their young men in horsemanship" (whence the concern for hidden saddle sores) and that they prefer oxen for "the labor of cultivation and transportation" because they surpass horses "in staying power and endurance and are not liable to as many diseases" (115). In Utopia women are among the human and animal beasts of burden that lighten a man's labor. Richard Sylvester notes the unconscious irony produced when Hythloday juxtaposes "an account of slavery with an account of marriage" ("'*Si Hythlodaeo Credimus*,'" 288), and Professor Adams finds More (i.e., the Utopians) "rather less than generous to women, who, in addition to selecting, preparing, and cooking the family food, doing the family laundry, making the family clothes, cleaning the house, and doing a thousand other routine tasks of domestic drudgery, were responsible for taking care of the children, and were also 'blessed with a full-time trade'" (42). One can understand why Utopians departed from the Platonic scheme in instituting monogamy. Plato's guardians are members of a warrior class whose needs are tended by craftsmen and farmers. Since virtually all Utopians are craftsmen and farmers, their needs are tended by wives.

While Utopia does not have a special warrior class, its citizens are, after a manner of speaking, guardians. They are a cunningly aggressive, well-fortified, and defensive people, whose self-protective instinct is never more clearly in evidence than in the premarital inspection. And while the Platonic community of wives is rejected, some of its dangers linger on as residues in the Utopian attitude toward marriage and women. Socrates' discussions in the fifth and eighth books of the *Republic* suggest (1) that "marriage" is exclusively a sexual relationship aimed at controlled eugenic reproduction, and that sexual eros is aroused and manipulated not only toward this end but also as a stimulus to valor (458e ff., 468a ff.); and (2) that the failure of the polis derives primarily from a failure in eugenic control, the implication being that the institutional constraints on "marriage" were not as effective as the institutional promotion of promiscuity (546b ff.). Utopian monogamy is, among other things, a defense against the social disorders rooted in promiscuity. But the uneasy voyeurism of Utopian bridegrooms, their fear of a hidden sore, implies that promiscuity exists and that they continue to be anxious about it. This passage quickly shifts from mention of mutual inspection to the man's suspicious scrutiny of the woman's body, his concern for *his* future "pleasure or disgust," and his wish to be protected by law "from being entrapped by guile" should any "foul deformity" (189) be hidden. More makes Utopian males intensely unpleasant in this episode—morbidly prurient, suspicious, self-righteous. Fear of disgust, the other side of the high value they set on their own sexual pleasure, increases our sense that their horse-trader's interest in the feminine body is unhealthy, and that men are in less danger of being entrapped by guile than women are of being entrapped by law. These are, after all, the men who will be their prospective wives' judges, confessors, disciplinarians, and masters. No wonder wives are enjoined to recommend themselves to their husbands by their probity, reverence, virtue, and obedience (193). It it as if they must spend their married lives continually proving that the suspicion formalized in the betrothal procedure is unfounded.

It is neither sentimental nor anachronistic to speak of loveless relationships, of the absence from the family of *philia* and genuine conjugal affection. We do not have to go beyond the text to find a contrast that enables us to assess the impoverishment of Utopian family life. More presents it in his letter to Peter Giles:

> When I have returned home, I must talk with my wife, chat with my children, and confer with my servants. All this activity I count as business [*omnia inter negocia numero*] when it must be done—and it must be unless you want to be a stranger in your own home. Besides, one must take care to be as agreeable as possible to those whom nature has supplied, or chance has made, or you yourself have chosen, to be *the companions of your life*, provided you do not spoil them by kindness, or through indulgence make masters out of your servants. (39–41, my italics)

This concern is extended, a few sentences later, to his pupil-servant John Clement, and we are reminded of it in the first book—shortly before hearing of Raphael's eagerness to abandon his home and patrimony for the world—when More remarks that in Antwerp Giles's conversation "took away my nostalgia and made me less conscious than before of the separation from my home, wife, and children to whom I was exceedingly anxious to get back, for I had then been more than four months away" (49).

This sentiment should prevent us from misreading More's reference to the *negotium* of family life as a sign of chilliness. The point is rather that his life at home is as difficult, and at least as important, as his public affairs. Unlike Folly, he has no illusions about *philia;* it is not imbibed with mother's milk. It entails what Robert Frost has nicely expressed in the phrase "weary of considerations." *Considerations* is the right word: it suggests attentive thought, looking at or worrying about problems, taking things into account, having regard for other people, and also payments, remunerations for services. Family life is *negotium* in the sense that it is not, should not be expected to be, an idyll of pastoral *otium*. The labor of love acknowledges the weariness of considerations. If labor in both senses is dirty and arduous business, it is also creative, and if it is not in itself fulfilling as an experience, it may still be suffused with the importance of the ends it serves. More's brief passage on his family life suggests that *negotium* begins at home, that domestic *philia* and *cura* provide the energizing center of devotion to public life, and that the private and public aspects of human concern are mutually reinforcing. There will be less *cura* abroad if there is less *negotium* at home.[9]

If Utopians differ from Plato's founders in their attitude toward the family, it is only in being more devious: they promote its ideology while destroying its structural underpinnings. The animal-farm aspects of Plato's guardian polis appear explicitly here only in the raising of chickens (115), but this brief reference to the expropriation of the brooding function from hens to farmers prefigures the actual technique disingenuously concealed by the more discreet Utopian maintenance of a superficial family system. In this fashion More depicts the double bind of utopian misanthropy. Utopia diminishes the possibilities for *philia* in the family and further weakens its power in transferring it to larger public communities. Hence it creates the untrustworthiness it fears, and it devotes all its institutional energy to controlling or pacifying its monster. For *philia* is the affective source of genuine ethical feeling and commitment. Perpetual vigilance is its uneasy replacement, forced into service as the watchword not only of familial, parochial, municipal, ecclesiastical, and national inspectors but also of ancestors,[10] God, and the tenets of Utopian religion.

The central cultural instrument of control and pacification is the one religious belief strictly enjoined on all Utopians: that the soul is immortal and will be punished or rewarded in the afterlife provides Utopia with both its stick and its carrot. It anchors both sides of their hedonist ideology, fear of pain and pursuit of pleasure. The statements explaining its importance also reveal Utopia's faith in its citizenry. Only fear of eternal punishment keeps the citizen from treating as worthless the laws and customs of the commonwealth: "Who can doubt that he will strive either to evade by craft the public laws of his country or to break them by violence in order to serve his own private desires when he has nothing to fear but laws ond no hope beyond the body?" (221–23).[11] The justifi-

---

[9] The same message is dramatically conveyed in the account Hythloday gives in Book I of dinner at Cardinal Morton's (see my "Renaissance Imagination," 28–29, for a brief discussion of this episode). Hythloday's version of the message is that no one listens to him, but the scene he describes discloses to More's readers that he has had a very good audience indeed. Cardinal Morton's dinner table also provides a contrast to dinner in the syphogrant's hall (see further, note 12 below).

[10] Utopians are taught to believe that "the personal presence of their forefathers keeps men from any secret dishonorable deed" (225).

[11] These sentiments should be set beside the explanation of the harsh laws against extramarital intercourse (see p. 241 above).

cation of hedonism begins by asserting the same principles of immortality and judgment (but with the rhetorical emphasis falling on happiness and rewards) and moves to a direct expression of Utopian cynicism: "Once the principles are eliminated, the Utopians would have no hesitation in maintaining that a person would be stupid not to seek pleasure by fair means or foul, but that he should only take care not to let a lesser pleasure interfere with a greater nor to follow after a pleasure which would bring pain in retaliation" (163). Assent to the principles inhibits the employment of foul means but leaves the hedonistic calculus operative (cf. 167, 177).

The Utopians "define virtue as living according to nature," which is in turn defined as obeying "the dictates of reason." Reason "first of all inflames men to a love and veneration of the divine majesty, to whom we owe both our existence and our capacity for happiness"; and second, "it admonishes and urges us to lead a life as free from care and as full of joy as possible and, because of our natural fellowship, to help all other men, too, to attain that end" (163). In the succeeding paragraphs the appeal to altruism is converted into a rationalization for pursuing one's own pleasure. Throughout this section the tone is argumentative and defensive and the arguments slippery and often sophistical, even though the concept of pleasure they advocate appears relatively benign. It is as if Utopians have a guilty conscience about this advocacy but find it essential to civil order—as if they (and Hythloday with them) want to be persuaded, but do not quite believe, that the pursuit of virtue can be pleasurable and the pursuit of pleasure virtuous. They do not expect human beings to inconvenience themselves for the sake of virtue, or the good, or God, or their fellow mortals. Their emphasis, therefore, is on pleasurable states of consciousness; these are both the touchstone and the end of virtue. They include the feeling of good health, "the pleasant recollection of a well-spent life and the sure hope of happiness to come" (173), and the mental pleasure obtained "from the practice of the virtues and the consciousness of a good life" (175). The hedonist ideology induces smugness, complacency, self-satisfaction—in a word, *philautia*.

Yet surely the very attempt to make themselves feel better about pleasure, and therefore about themselves, must make them feel worse by stirring up precisely those feelings of worthlessness the ideology is intended to overcome. For their hedonism, with its religious anchor, is fastened to their knowledge that without it they would be likely to break the law and to their opinion that it would be stupid not to do so if it served their "own private desires." The arguments for pleasure and *philautia* are discharged from an underground launching pad of anxiety and *misautia*, which may account for their occasional stridency of tone. The basis of the hedonist calculus is *apprehension*, which is a form of self-knowledge—the knowledge of one's desire to *take* and the corresponding fear of *being taken*. The worthy protophylarch knows that *au fond* he is a *tranibor* (*tranēs* + *boros*, "plainly or distinctly gluttonous"); perhaps the reverend phylarch whose culinary blandishments have helped render the household meal obsolete dreams at night that his powers ascend from his *syphograncy*, the venerable pigsty or "foul rag-and-bone shop of the heart." Their older names and natures persist in the reformed language. So, to paraphrase Socrates (confecting misanthropic fantasies from Simonides' innocent verse), the best thieves make the best guardians (*Rep.* 334a).[12]

Their apprehension may be glimpsed in the uncertain Utopian attitude toward bodily functions. Although these are distinguished from false pleasures and classified among the genuine physical pleasures, they are not embraced without a gingerly aversion of the nose. The sense is filled "with clearly perceptible sweetness" which sometimes

> comes from the renewal of those organs which have been weakened by our natural heat. These organs are then restored by food and drink. Sometimes it comes from the elimination of things which overload the body. This agreeable sensation occurs when we discharge feces from our bowels or perform the activity generative of children or relieve the itching of some part by rubbing or scratching. (173)

The emphasis on pleasurable sensation is belied by the unpleasant linkage of copulation with defecation and scratching; since these are identified as ways "of eliminating anything that causes distress," one wonders whether childbirth (if it were pleasant) would also belong to this cate-

---

[12] Lupton speculated that *sypho-* alluded to *sypheos*, "pigsty" (with a possible pun, according to the Yale editors, on *syphos*, an Aeolic form of *sophos*). But *-grant* is not so clear. The Yale suggestion, *gerontes*, "old men," "elders," seems reasonable, though a word with an *alpha* would be lexicographically more agreeable—perhaps *geraios*, "ancient," *graias*, "old," or even *geras*, which has the added advantage of meaning "the cast skin, serpent slough," as well as "old age." Professor Adams may well be right to reject such guesses (39), but I remain attracted to the implications generated by (a) the coupling of "gluttonous" with "pigsty" and (b) the irony generated by keeping before us the older uncomplimentary titles rather than their political transformations. It emphasizes the Utopian assumption that man is at heart (in his former nature, in the old man) distinctly a glutton who would be content to root about in a pigsty world if his life were not totally reorganized and institutionally controlled. It also suggests that those with the largest appetites will have the energy to make the most effective political officials, once they have pledged allegiance to the hedonist ideology and its religious foundation. This interpretation lends support to Professor Adams's own astute characterization of the Utopians in Machiavellian categories (194–95).

gory. And conversely, one wonders whether making war—since it fits the category—is a form of pleasure.

Such pleasures are despised as much as enjoyed. Even food and drink suffer a decline in status after a page or two, when hunger and thirst are labeled diseases: a life given over to the pleasures of "eating, drinking, scratching, and rubbing" is "not only disgusting but wretched" because "they never occur unless they are coupled with the pains which are their opposites" (177). Intercourse takes on the vile, vaguely aggressive, and autoerotic associations of its neighbors: discharging semen into a woman is like discharging feces into a chamberpot—and a chamberpot made of gold. If we remember that the account of Utopian marriage occurs not long after this passage, we shall feel more keenly the extent to which mysogynist disgust and aggression infect the institution of premarital voyeurism.

The connection of these activities to war, by no means casual, is not difficult to make, requiring only the addition of gold as a middle term. The Utopians show their contempt for gold by using it to make chamberpots and fetters for slaves and to pay mercenaries or corrupt enemies. This scrupulously perverse employment, however, betrays both their continuing fascination with it—their awareness of its powerful attractiveness to them—and the high value they set on defecation, slavery, and the defeat or exploitation of enemies. Slavery and warfare (direct or indirect) bring pleasure because they eliminate things that cause distress—painful labor and foreign foes. Excess population is discharged into mainland colonies, and if the native inhabitants of the colonies refuse to submit to Utopian laws, they are in turn expelled (137).

These affections and customs must make the self-deception of *philautia* hard to achieve, since the Utopians continually find themselves attracted to and engaged in activities they loathe. War, which is no exception, is perhaps their salvation in this respect, enabling them to discharge their self-hatred into foreign foes. Though Hythloday reports that the Utopians regard war with utter loathing, his portrait of them reveals an obsessively contentious, cunning, unscrupulous, and mean-minded people. Their only two games are war games (129), they "assiduously exercise themselves in military training" (201), they are expert strategists and fortifiers, they prefer battle-axes to swords at close quarters because "their sharp point and great weight" make them "deadly weapons, whether employed for thrusting or hacking," and "they are very clever in inventing war machines," which they hide "with the greatest care" (213–15). The account of Utopia is immured in military parentheses: Hythloday begins the second book by describing their ingenious device for destroying an enemy's fleet (111), and he concludes his account by remarking that after prayer and dinner on religious holidays they devote the remainder of their time to "games and . . . exercises of military training" (237).

Having sacrificed *philia*, Utopia has not succeeded in replacing it with *philautia*. Its *enchiridion* of pleasure is more a dagger than a handbook. Its system of institutional reform routinizes, and thus preserves, the underlying distrust and disgust that mark the Utopians' hatred of life. It is a monument to their sense that their desire for pleasure is as powerful as it is base; that it is the foe of love, amity, and community; that it cherishes its narcissistic secrecy and encourages the paranoia of apprehension. Utopian polity is, in sum, a poor supplier of lotus, nepenthe, and panacea. It wants a better pharmacopoeia, a bigger chamberpot, for the expelling of poisons. Utopia is a community in search of, badly in need of, Folly.

PART FOUR

Marvell and Milton

Andrew Marvell: The Poem
as Green World

The Nymph, the Dewdrop, and the Horatian Ode

Critics have often acclaimed Marvell's exploration of the dialectic of withdrawal and return and his lyric ventures into what I have elsewhere called the green world ("The Renaissance Imagination," reprinted in this volume). The green world is an imaginary place into which the mind may withdraw for a variety of reasons, good and bad: escape, recreation, clarification, experiment. It is only metaphorically a "place" or "space"; actually the green world projects a condition or frame of mind which consciousness may court in a tentative and temporary manner, a condition to which it should not permanently surrender. "In its positive aspects it provides a temporary haven . . . in its negative aspects it projects the urge of the paralyzed will to give up, escape, work magic, abolish time and flux and the intrusive reality of other minds" (p. 36). The present essay will focus on three poems which not only consider aspects—good and bad—of the green-world sensibility but which in varying degrees *enact* these aspects. The first poem I wish to consider is the *Nymph Complaining for the Death of Her Faun*, and the approach to this poem has been made easier by two suggestive general statements.

Don Cameron Allen offers us probably the best description of the poem's subject:

[The nymph] is a young virgin, who lives in a world of pastoral innocence different from the world of "cruel men". Into this "little Wilderness" . . . has come a man . . . who has won the girl's love. The fawn, which Sylvio gives the girl as a token of love becomes, when he abandons her, a *surrogatus amoris;* in fact, it becomes something like the child that might have been hers had Sylvio not proved "counterfeit". The poem is . . . a sensitive treatment of the loss of first love, a loss augmented by a virginal sense of deprivation and unfulfillment. The nymph has brooded so much over losing her lover that she has enlarged the token of love into a life symbol.[1]

That the poem is a monologue whose plot lies in the present tense of the nymph's utterance has been remarked by Leo Spitzer. Spitzer sees it "as a structured whole whose parts correspond to the phases of the psychological development of the nymph. . . . The delicate art of the poet has so willed it that, in the inner monologue of the Nymph that is the poem, the description of her pet reflects on her own character in indirect characterization, the increasing idealization of the fawn allowing inferences about the maiden who so idealizes it."[2] As the following interpretation may suggest, Spitzer's inferences are too grandiose and high-toned, while Allen's inferences are too sparse;[3] neither shows sufficient awareness that the poet's playful attitude toward the green-world sensibility goes hand in hand with his serious attitude toward the poetic art.

The nymph's career more or less reverses that of Pygmalion's beloved as described by Orpheus in Ovid's *Metamorphoses* X. Marvell's character concludes by imagining herself in a statuary condition, but the idea behind both episodes is similar: the nymph partially renounces—she will not go so far as to die—a world whose entanglements oppress her. The incident of Pygmalion, whose ideal was externalized as a statue and transformed by Venus to a woman, is given its point by the various instances of perverted and frustrated love which surround it: Orpheus and Euridyce, Cyparissus and his stag, Phoebus and Hyacinthus, the Propoetides, Myrrha and Cinyras, Atalanta (whom Apollo advises to avoid the experience of men and remain her own woman), Venus and Adonis.

[1] *Image and Meaning* (Baltimore: Johns Hopkins University Press, 1960), 93–94.

[2] "Marvell's 'Nymph Complaining,'" in *Seventeenth-Century English Poetry*, ed. W. R. Keast (New York: Oxford University Press, 1962), 306.

[3] Spitzer has raised the same objection to Allen's reading: "He [Allen] fails to follow through in detail the development of the motif in the poem and rather concentrates on the history of the topoi that went into its composition" (306). However this may be, I find Allen's rare individual comments more useful and more on target than Spitzer's.

Only a projection of one's own ideal, an artifact come to life, a love essentially narcissistic, could remain secure and free from pain in such a world. The artist as lover could not actualize his wish, either by poetic or erotic power, without the help of a miracle, but the lover as artist—as Ovid or Orpheus—may withdraw to a world of literary fantasy where in his supreme power he commands the appearance of the *dea ex machina*. Allen's remarks on the end of the *Nymph Complaining* confirm the analogy to Ovid: "The flight from the realities of love to an ideal of love, Marvell seems to be saying, may be the course of caution, but even here the idea can be permanently fixed only by the hand of the artist."[4]

The nymph's escapist perspective is roughly equivalent in function to that of More's Hythloday in *Utopia*. Marvell, so to speak, *stages* the escapist sensibility and tries it out within the controlled context of poetry. The nymph begins with the cruel fact:

> The wanton Troopers riding by
> Have shot my Faun and it will dye.
> Ungentle men! They cannot thrive
> To kill Thee. Thou neer didst alive
> Them any harm: alas nor cou'd
> Thy death yet do them any good.
>
> *(1–6)*

She tries first to do something about her own feelings and the senselessness of the world by appealing to religion; here Marvell smilingly watches her strike a forgiving pose and project her harsher feelings onto divine justice:

> But, if my simple Pray'rs may yet
> Prevail with Heaven to forget
> Thy murder, I will Joyn my Tears
> Rather than fail. But, O my fears!
> It cannot dye so. Heavens King
> Keeps register of every thing:
> And nothing may we use in vain.
> Ev'n Beasts must be with justice slain;
> Else Men are made their *Deodands*.
> Though they should wash their guilty hands
> In this warm life-blood, which doth part

---

[4] *Image and Meaning*, 114.

> From thine, and wound me to the Heart,
> Yet could they not be clean: their Stain
> Is dy'd in such a Purple Grain.
> There is not such another in
> The World, to offer for their Sin.
>
> *(9–24)*

It is hard to agree with Spitzer that the nymph is here "considering her own death, a death of expiation which she, however, seems to reject at this time because of her unworthiness."[5] She seems rather to be magnifying the crime, turning the troopers into Christ killers, to make their act commensurate with her excessive feelings.

Having thus stigmatized the troopers, she transforms the fawn from a symbol of Christ to a symbol of her lover:

> Unconstant Sylvio, when yet
> I had not found him counterfeit,
> One morning (I remember well)
> Ty'd in this silver Chain and Bell,
> Gave it to me: nay and I know
> What he said then; I'me sure I do.
> Said He, look how your Huntsman here
> Hath taught a Faun to hunt his *Dear.*
> But Sylvio soon had me beguil'd.
> This waxed tame, while he grew wild,
> And quite regardless of my Smart,
> Left me his Faun, but took his Heart.
>   Thenceforth I set myself to play
> My solitary time away,
> With this: and very well content,
> Could so mine idle Life have spent.
> For it was full of sport; and light
> Of foot, and heart; and did invite,
> Me to its game: it seem'd to bless
> Its self in me. How could I less
> Than love it? O I cannot be
> Unkind, t' a Beast that loveth me.
>
> *(25–46)*

The flashback tells us something about her animus against ungentle men, about the reason for the fawn's value, about the helplessness of the

---

[5] "Marvell's 'Nymph Complaining,'" 308.

gentle feminine sensibility to cope with the actual vicissitudes of love and war on their own grounds. Sylvio's statement is ironically true in retrospect, and the Faun who hunts his Dear may be momentarily imaged as a wanton goat-man.[6] *Then*, in the past, the nymph gave up the world of normal experience and withdrew to a relation which was in hand and controllable—an appropriate pastoral response. *Now*, in the present tense of her monologue, the act of dwelling on the past temporarily consoles her, though it gives way briefly to a new doubt and a new generalization about the actual world dominated by men:

> Had it liv'd long, I do not know
> Whether it too might have done so
> As Sylvio did: his Gifts might be
> Perhaps as false or more than he.
> But I am sure, for ought that I
> Could in so short a time espie,
> Thy Love was far more better then
> The love of false and cruel men.
>
> *(47–54)*

The doubt may have been produced by her previous description of the fawn as "full of sport; and light / Of foot, and heart": the fawn is a perfect symbol of what was wrong with her false lover, who also invited her to his game and *seemed* to bless himself in her. But transposed to the innocent world of nymphs and fawns, this recreative love may well be the only kind such a nymph could enjoy—one which she can control, one in which she need not be asked to give too much.

Thus the shift from third person ("it" and "his") to direct address— "*Thy* Love"—tends to separate fawn from cruel men and move him, as a symbol, closer to the nymph. "Thy Love" may refer to her self-love as easily as to the fawn's love for her. Divesting the fawn of its unpleasant associations, her thought withdraws more radically into the green world. She remembers the fawn as a literal pet; the *surrogatus amoris* becomes a surrogate child and a paragon of feminine properties, a *speculum nymphae*:

> With sweetest milk and sugar, first
> I it at mine own fingers nurst.
> And as it grew, so every day
> It wax'd more white and sweet than they.
> It had so sweet a Breath! And oft

---

[6] The suggestion is Spitzer's, 308.

> I blusht to see its foot more soft,
> And white, (shall I say then my hand?)
> NAY any Ladies of the Land.
>
> *(55–62)*

The fawn is then remembered as an ideal playmate whose coy animal games were harmless vestiges of man's inconstancy:[7]

> It is a wond'rous thing, how fleet
> 'Twas on those little silver feet.
> With what a pretty skipping grace,
> It oft would challenge me the Race:
> And when 'thad left me far away,
> 'Twould stay, and run again, and stay.
> For it was nimbler much than Hindes;
> And trod, as on the four Winds.
>
> *(63–70)*

The nymph's consciousness reduced to, or displaced by, that of a hind: a solution she entertains only briefly because, as we shall see, she prefers to have psychological or figurative rather than actual metamorphoses; this way she can stage and savor herself in thought.

In the next phase of withdrawal the nymph identifies the fawn with her garden which (as Allen has pointed out) is easily identifiable with herself.[8] Here child, lover, and self, virginity, eroticism, and death, merge in a passage whose octosyllabic lightness of tone makes it even more compelling—the nymph with her childlike voice and sensibility projecting her narcissism, her desire for and fear of love, life, and death, into the image of casual play:

> I have a Garden of my own,
> But so with Roses over grown,
> And Lillies, that you would it guess
> To be a little Wilderness.
> And all the Spring time of the year
> It onely loved to be there.
> Among the beds of Lillyes, I
> Have sought it oft, where it should lye;
> Yet could not, till it self would rise,
> Find it, although before mine Eyes.

---

[7] See Spitzer, 310.
[8] *Image and Meaning,* 107–8.

For, in the flaxen Lillies shade,
It like a bank of Lillies laid.
Upon the Roses it would feed,
Until its Lips ev'n seem'd to bleed:
And then to me 'twould boldly trip,
And print those Roses on my Lip.
But all its chief delight was still
On Roses thus its self to fill:
And its pure virgin Limbs to fold
In whitest sheets of Lillies cold.
Had it liv'd long, it would have been
Lillies without, Roses within.

(71–92)

Spitzer remarks a little solemnly that

> this last "witty" identification may have its origin in the Song of Songs, but
> its function here is the metamorphosis of the animal into a paragon of virtues
> that are not found combined even in a human being: the coolness of virginal
> chastity and the flame of ardent love. . . . Wit . . . suggests the possibility of
> a miracle: the possibility of moral or spiritual qualities becoming sensuously
> perceptible as though they were objects in outward nature.[9]

But the point about both the Song of Songs and the paragon of virtues is
the inverted use: the object of the nymph's ardor is herself; the metamorphosis is a result of projection; the miracle is simply the wish-
fulfilling "all things here and now" of the green-world sensibility; the
fawn, replacing the human satyr, plays his role. Furthermore, the fawn
is not really a paragon: safe and secret within the nymph's *hortus conclusus*, it behaves a little like the poet in the fifth stanza of *The Garden* or
the Dionysiac stanzas of *Upon Appleton House* (71–81). Ensnared with
flowers, falling on the bank, bleeding and bold with the wine of crushed
roses, indulging its chief delight—"On Roses thus its self to fill"—the
fawn epitomizes the "wond'rous Life" of *The Garden* or the nymph's
ideal of an "idle Life . . . full of sport"—the passive surrender to the
senses as an escape from care, thought, effort, and the perils of an actual
society. "Society" means the difficulty of a life shared with others, a life
in which one's security is constantly threatened by one's own passion as
well as by theirs. Snug within the "whitest sheets" of herself, with only
her pet as consort, the nymph may give rein to her fantasy without the

---

[9] "Marvell's 'Nymph Complaining,'" 311.

expense of consideration. If her withdrawal is innocent rather than perverse, it yet has affinities to the retreat of the nuns in the "Virgin Buildings" of Appleton House:

> "What need is here of Man? unless
> These as sweet Sins we should confess.
>
> "Each Night among us to your side
> Appoint a fresh and Virgin Bride;
> Whom if *our Lord* at midnight find,
> Yet Neither should be left behind.
> Where you may lye as chast in Bed,
> As Pearls together billeted.
> All Night embracing Arm in Arm,
> Like Chrystal pure with Cotton warm."
>
> *(Upon Appleton House 183–92)*

During the course of the monologue the nymph has, by her control of
memory and image, dispelled her doubt:

> Had it liv'd long, I do not know
> Whether it too might have done so
> As Sylvio did . . .
>
> *(47–49)*
>
> Had it liv'd long, it would have been
> Lillies without, Roses within.
>
> *(91–92)*

Having replaced Sylvio with herself as the referent of the symbolic
fawn, she is now prepared to let the animal die, all the more moved because the death she stages is her own:

> O help! O help! I see it faint:
> And dye as calmely as a Saint.
> See how it weeps. The Tears do come
> Sad, slowly dropping like a Gumme.
> So weeps the wounded Balsome: so
> The holy Frankincense doth flow.
> The brotherless Heliades
> Melt in such Amber tears as these.
>   I in a golden Vial will
> Keep these two crystal Tears; and fill
> It till it do o'reflow with mine;
> Then place it in Diana's Shrine.

> Now my Sweet Faun is vanish'd to
> Whither the Swans and Turtles go:
> In fair Elizium to endure,
> With milk-white Lambs, and Ermins pure.
> O do not run too fast: for I
> Will but bespeak thy Grave, and dye.
>
> *(93–110)*

As a fitting conclusion to mock elegy, this is not too far in tone from Tom Sawyer's funeral. The nymph celebrates the solemn moment with a brief salvo of similes comparing the fawn to a wounded, mourning Nature[10]—no doubt the imagined audience of her own elegant swan song.

One source of the wry, even amusing, tone which Marvell manages in this final section may be the shift of verb tense from the past, which had dominated the poem from the opening strophe on the troopers, to the present and future. The nymph had previously tried to control her feelings and situation by withdrawing from the present and reworking what she remembers. Now she is not merely reflecting (as with the troopers) or remembering, but doing and planning.[11] The classical and pastoral motifs she invokes are like stage props helping to amplify the performance of which she is both stage directress and chief actress. The costume she dons is that of Niobe, a little too large for her and not entirely appropriate, except as she has adopted the role of mother: after she has consigned the fawn to an Elysium populated with nymph symbols (dying swans, mourning turtledoves, sacrificed lambs, and chaste ermines), she concludes the poem with a set of mortuary instructions which bespeak her own grave more than that of the fawn:

> First my unhappy Statue shall
> Be cut in Marble; and withal,
> Let it be weeping too: but there
> Th'Engraver sure his Art may spare;
> For I so truly thee bemoane,
> That I shall weep though I be Stone:
> Until my Tears, still dropping, wear
> My breast, themselves engraving there.

---

[10] Possibly we are to think of Orpheus assembling his grove of trees for his recital, *Met.* X, 86–106; the Heliades are here as well as in *Met.* II, 338–41. See Allen, 113, note 57, for other analogues.

[11] Her plans for crying into a bottle seem an especially wry effect on Marvell's part. Allen remarks that the fawn's "medicinal tears" are "famous in the Renaissance pharmacopaeia" (112), but unless nymphs' tears are equally medicinal, she devotes a watered-down solution to Diana.

> There at my feet shalt thou be laid,
> Of purest Alabaster made:
> For I would have thine Image be
> White as I can, though not as Thee.
>
> *(111–22)*

The finest and most satisfying escape the nymph can imagine is to be thus merged with her statue: there, safely encased in stone, she may be proof against passion and the world; but there also she may perhaps enjoy the admiration of spectators who behold the touching and melodramatic pose in which she will be memorialized. She avails herself of that primitive notion in which the burial stele contains the life of the departed. Her splendidly obsessive grief will be commemorated and at the same time drawn out; her consciousness, en-graved and immarbled, will be undying, or at least it will weather more slowly. At the same time this image, as seen by Marvell and us, is a figure of her emotional paralysis—that impossible state of half-renunciation in which she is unwilling to cope with life and consciousness, yet unwilling to give them up.

The concluding disjunction suggests that the memorial group will include the actual nymph but only the image of the fawn. Since the final *Thee* is capitalized, this may indicate that the nymph apotheosizes the fawn; her pet, now her god, is too good for this world and she has safely stowed the original in a remote Elysium. Allen's idea about this is helpful:

> The fawn's affection, which might have passed, is now assured by its death. Love, which she found to be false in her own one encounter with it in the real world; love, which was even uncertain in the garden, in the *hortus mentis*, is safe, unchanging, and everlasting only in the world of art. In this new world the nymph and the fawn are united eternally.[12]

But they are united on the nymph's terms. Allen closes his essay with the statement that in the statuary state "whiteness alone remains; the red of sentient life is gone";[13] the nymph, however, imagines herself as taking her sentience with her. The peculiar drift of the conclusion, i.e., that only the nymph will inhabit the memorial which is mainly in her honor, expresses her narcissism. It may be that she does not need the real fawn any more, having by the poem's end totally absorbed it into a figure of herself. The real fawn has done its work in providing her with an object

[12] *Image and Meaning*, 113.
[13] Ibid., 114.

of meditation to which she may attribute various symbolic values and thus control her feelings if not her experience. There is an instant of doubt at line 119 whether the dead animal is to be laid as an offering at the living statue's feet, and though it is immediately resolved, it casts a slightly ironic reflection on the final line: the image will be more durable than the original on the one hand, less vivid on the other.[14] The effect of these last four lines is concisely to summarize all her fears and all her desires—her fear, for example, of an inclination she might not be able to control for an object whose will and stability or mortality she cannot control; her desire for a one-way relation in which she is queen, goddess, saint, creatrix. A world proportioned to her sensibility and power of love ("White as I can") may admit no life but her own, except, of course, the life of worshipful passersby admiring the new Niobe. A pet is easier to love than a man and a statue easier than a pet, for hers is a monologic world. At the end of the monologue she sees herself standing alone, accompanied by the dead image of her symbolic fawn, an artifact ordered from "th'*Engraver*" but designed by herself.[15] Thus she works a refinement on the escape artistry of the Ovidian sculptor, for she has become Pygmalion as well as his statue.

Marvell's experiments with the green-world sensibility are frequent and diversified. One example, interesting because its context seems so different, is the meditation *On a Drop of Dew*. The two major strophes of this poem amplify a single comparison: "Just as a dewdrop . . . so the soul. . . ." The dewdrop is literally observed but described in terms that convert it to a symbol of something more important; the soul is then described metaphorically on the model of the dewdrop. But as Marvell develops each side of the analogy, the inherent disparity between dewdrop and soul leads him to two different interpretations. The dewdrop begins "careless of its Mansion new," enclosing itself round "For the clear Region where 'twas born," framing "as it can its native Element." But it quickly becomes restless, insecure, and fearful: "gazing back upon the Skies," it

[14] The reference to alabaster may well be straightforward and honorific, but Marvell may have known that it is ordinarily used for work on a smaller scale and that it is much less durable than marble; its translucence, on the other hand, allows for a greater effect of realism. These facts are not entirely irrelevant to the way the nymph conceives of the image in relation both to her statue and to the original fawn.

[15] After the first verse paragraph, and except for lines 53–54, the nymph has aimed her monologue at some general audience, but beginning at line 109 ("O do not run too fast"), the fawn is addressed in the vocative. If talking to a live fawn is a form of talking to oneself, talking to a dead fawn would seem to be even more so.

> Shines with a mournful Light;
>   Like its own Tear,
> Because so long divided from the Sphear.
>   Restless it roules and unsecure,
>   Trembling lest it grow impure:
>   Till the warm Sun pitty it's Pain,
> And to the Skies exhale it back again.
>   *(12–18)*

The soul, on the other hand, remains self-assured, coy, and disdainful throughout the second strophe. "Remembering still its former height," it shuns the leaves and blossoms of the human flower and recollects "its own Light, / . . . in its pure and circling thoughts":

> In how coy a Figure wound,
> Every way it turns away:
> So the World excluding round,
> Yet receiving in the Day.
> Dark beneath, but bright above:
> Here disdaining, there in Love.
> How loose and easie hence to go:
> How girt and ready to ascend.
> Moving but on a point below,
> It all about does upwards bend.
>
>   *(27–36)*

The firmly repeated tetrameter (six seven-syllable and four eight-syllable lines) stresses, or perhaps deliberately overstresses, the confidence of tone; its slightly obsessive drumbeat stands in sharp contrast to the staggered meter of the preceding passage.[16]

By thus differentiating the terms of the comparison, Marvell suggests how two opposed forms of response lead in the same direction: the sense of helplessness and the sense of superior value, of exclusiveness, both prompt the soul to depreciate earthly existence; fear of the world and contempt of the world share equally in the gnostic rationalization by which the urge to withdraw is treated as the desire of heaven. The comparison, with its "metaphysical" tension, its emphasis and reliance on the poet's reconciling wit, is itself an experiment using gnostic premises, for it seems to assume a violent opposition between heaven and earth. Yet

---

[16] The lines are, respectively, six, four, ten, eight, seven, eight, and ten syllables long—"restless . . . and unsecure."

this logic is qualified by the imagery of the poem—by the fondly observed minutiae of nature in the garden, the sweetness and beauty of the green world, which here includes the human flower. The motive of rejection is thus complicated by a hint of excessive attraction, and the fear may be in part the fear of loving what passes away, loving what is perhaps unworthy and illusory. This is the green-world fear influenced by the pleasure principle: a reluctance to open oneself to experience, give oneself to life, because of the risk of pain, frustration, and loss.

In the poem's final quatrain Marvell appears to abandon his experiment; he turns to a different tradition and finds there another answer:

> Such did the Manna's sacred Dew destil;
> White, and intire, though congeal'd and chill.
> Congeal'd on Earth: but does, dissolving, run
> Into the Glories of th' Almighty Sun.
>
> *(37–40)*

These lines are complicated on the one hand because they seem to continue the main analogy—"as the soul . . . so manna"—and on the other they introduce the new idea of a gift to the soul and a new biblical perspective which works as parable and allusion rather than as a simile. In the first context, Marvell shifts the soul model from dew to manna,[17] and this makes a considerable difference: unlike the soul-as-dew, the soul-as-manna is created by a special act of God *for* an earthly function, a particular historical mission; its relation to body is more Aristotelian than Neoplatonic, since soul-as-manna is congealed to an earthly form—in Aristotle's phrase, it is "the act of the body"—whereas the dewdrop clings to its pristine element. It is also unlike the dew in that what happens to it after dissolution does not merely fulfill a predetermined cycle; therefore its earthly existence will have made a difference.

The second context, that of parable and allusion, is perhaps more immediate in its effect on the reader. The conceits of the previous strophes are sustained but transformed by the scriptural atmosphere, for all the implications of the quatrain run counter to the green-world tendencies described above: the manna typologically prefigures the Eucharist which, together with the Incarnation and Sacrifice, validates both the goodness of earthly life and its suffering; added to this are the notions of divine assistance, of grace and promise, of a single great historical (and trans-

---

[17] "And when the dew that lay was gone up, behold, upon the face of the wilderness there lay a small round thing, as small as hoar frost on the ground" (Exodus 16:14).

historical) enterprise which binds together individuals and communities, lending both richness and significance to the temporal unfolding
of experience within the life of the individual as of the culture. The
gnostic view of a hostility between nature and spirit is replaced by the
mediating perspective of sacred history. Here the biblical situation
throws light on the failure of will which leads to withdrawal: the Israelites, complaining about their lot, longing for Egyptian luxuries (Numbers 11:5−6), are ready to give up the difficult journey when God revives them with manna. St. John draws the typological consequences in
his Gospel:

> For the bread of God is he which cometh down from heaven, and giveth
> life unto the world.
> Then said they unto him, Lord, evermore give us this bread.
> And Jesus said unto them, I am the bread of life: he that cometh to me shall
> never hunger; and he that believeth in me shall never thirst. . . .
> For I come down from heaven, not to do mine own will, but the will of him
> that sent me.
> And this is the Father's will which hath sent me, that of all which he hath
> given me I should lose nothing, but should raise it up again at the last day.
> And this is the will of him that sent me, that every one which seeth the Son,
> and believeth on him, may have everlasting life: and I will raise him up at
> the last day. (6:33−40)

Marvell's concluding pun brilliantly fuses all analogues: the Old Testament experience and the New Testament figural interpretation along
with his own images of natural and spiritual cycle run "Into the Glories
of th'Almighty Sun."[18]

This use of sacred doctrine and history is characteristic of Renaissance
and post-Renaissance culture. It is not important to ascertain whether
Marvell really believed in a particular dogma or legend per se. More
important is its dialectical function as a kind of argument which may
lend support to the poet's enterprise, and also to the more general,
though related, effort of the mind to face life. On a larger scale the final
two books of *Paradise Lost* and the final three cantos of the *Faerie Queene*
Book I work in a manner similar to Marvell's quatrain. In each case
there is a return from fiction to some form of reality as reflected in a
historical, cultural, or theological medium; a return, in other words,

---

[18] His handling of the rhythm lends the quatrain the force of a new idea: slow and
halting at first, as if considering the possibilities of the image. The alliterated "does,
dissolving," loosens up the meter and the final enjambed clause springs it free for the
triumph fulfilled only in the last word.

from poetry as myth or metaphor or fantasy to poetry as history or sacred legend or an analogue of revelation. Taking advantage of the Protestant emphasis on personal, inward experience of the Word, the poet may directly confront scriptural archetypes and engage them in what may be called an act of reciprocal interpretation: Scripture is the provisional interpreter between God and the poet, while the poet revives and revises his source, makes it current and persuasive, by interpreting between Scripture and his audience. Here there is also reciprocal justification of fiction by history and history by fiction, of man by God and God by man. The last two books of *Paradise Lost*, for example, justify the first ten books in that every historical action is shown to embody the archetypal pattern of behavior which Milton has so finely and exhaustively imagined in the body of his fiction. The first ten books are thus a hypothetical explanation of what happens in history. And *that* it happens over and over again, that history assumes a pattern and direction in the Adam-Christ polarity—this comes to justify not only the ways of God and history but also the ways of Milton and poetry. The poem re-creates the great sacred event of the Fall but does so in an entirely new form, converting the event to a psychological model of recurrent human action, correcting and clarifying the event to adapt it to the modern sensibility of Milton's audience.[19]

On a small scale something like this happens in Marvell's *Drop of Dew*. The poem begins as a recreative exercise of wit, the mind amusing itself in the play of analogy. The development of the image in the first strophe seems self-conscious enough to make this activity as conspicuous a subject as the dewdrop. It is hard to feel that we have a serious meditation on the soul's dilemma from the very beginning; this seriousness seems rather to grow through the second stanza and reach a climax in the quatrain; the decasyllabic structure of the last four lines helps to set them

[19] Milton as poet is an apologist or interpreter reviving ancient wisdom not only as a vision of a divinely ordered cosmos but also as an *argument*—a manifestation of causes (which may very well be hypothetical)—making sense of disjointed modern times. His version of Ramist logic throws light on the conception of an argument which seems applicable to his as to Marvell's practice: "*An argument is that which has a fitness for arguing something* . . . that is for showing, explaining, or proving something . . . the proper and primary potency of a simple argument is to explain and prove how one thing follows or does not follow from another; that is, it is judged that when one thing has been laid down as true something else is or is not laid down originally. Our Bacon . . . rightly suggests the same thing about induction: 'By one and the same operation of the mind the thing in question is both invented and judged.' . . . An argument in the proper sense of the word is not a word or a thing, but a certain fitness of something for arguing; this . . . can be called reason" (*The Art of Logic* 1.2, trans. Allan Gilbert, in *The Works of John Milton* [New York: Columbia University Press, 1935], XI, 23–25).

off as more sober and meditative. The concluding pun indeed solves the play problem at the level of imagery and wit, but as we have seen, it also solves a good deal more.

There is another factor to be considered in this as in so many poems of the period. The poem as we have it *displays* a distinction between those aspects of it which belong to planning and those which seem to emerge during the course of translating the plan to a lyric experience. We are confronted with a clearly and firmly prearranged syntactical structure which carries definite logical implications: the framework of the poem is a comparison which tells us that the soul is like a dewdrop because both originate above, are unhappy about descending to an alien state, and can scarcely wait to run back home. This framework is present in the poem and we must construe it as an element of the "beginning," i.e., as what the poet appears to start with. But the framework is subject to subtle and continuous dislocation, qualification, and even contradiction throughout the poem. We have seen this to occur in the garden imagery, which emphasizes the sweetness of life; in the different directions taken by the two strophes, which tend toward disparity between the objects compared; and finally in the way the quatrain rejects the premises which generated the comparison. If we consider plan and experience together—and I think the poem demands that we do this—then the plan has the status of a blueprint, a preliminary and provisional argument, while the experience is an interpretation and revision of the plan. The plan is obviously there to set the mind in motion, but the experience—the *now* of lyric utterance—produces something new, something not anticipated in the mental preparations, something truer and more important than the plan, something which in effect seems to have been discovered in the act whereby the plan becomes a poem. If we conceive this poetic process as a model and transfer it to the processes of mind and soul in general, we have still another rejection of the original premises: the plan is made for the poem as manna is made for earth; it must open and yield itself to the test of experience and it becomes significant only as it is "thrown away," transcended, altered, and outmoded during the course of its "earthly" career. In one sense we may view the plan as withdrawal and contemplation, the poem as return and action; moving beyond this, we may posit a similar relation between the mind pleasuring itself with "the pure and circling thoughts" of poetry as idyll or escape and the mind submitting its self-delighting poetic power to the perennial problems of life in history and society.

The gnostic oppositions of the two strophes appear freer of complication in two poetic dialogues which are chiefly versified plans: *A Dialogue Between the Soul and Body* is a complaint in which each member feels itself the prisoner of the other, though what disturbs both is nothing more than the threat to inertial pleasure. The soul is unhappy because it must employ all its care

> That to preserve, which me destroys:
> Constrain'd not only to indure
> Diseases, but, whats worse, the Cure:
> And ready oft the Port to gain,
> Am Shipwrackt into Health again.
>
> *(26–30)*

The body is tormented by loss of vegetable repose and unconsciousness:

> A Body that could never rest,
> Since this ill Spirit it possest.
>
> *(19–20)*

The soul is responsible for having taught it "the Cramp of Hope," "the Palsy Shakes of Fear," "The Pestilence of Love," and the other passions "Which Knowledge forces me to know; / And Memory will not forgoe" (39–40):

> What but a Soul could have the wit
> To build me up for Sin so fit?
> So Architects do square and hew,
> Green Trees that in the Forest grew.
>
> *(41–44)*

Marvell assigns the body an attitude occasionally represented by the figure of the mower who prefers the easy life, the "wild and fragrant Innocence" of Nature "plain and pure," to the complexities of love or art. The pastoral rationale—"Follow nature and keep free of worldly entanglements; everything will work itself out"—which Marvell here recognizes as based on fear of effort and pain, easily shades over into his own famous rationalization:

Whether it be a war of religion or of liberty, is not worth the labour to enquire. Whichsoever was at the top, the other was at the bottom; but upon considering all, I think the cause was too good to have been fought for. Men ought to have trusted God; they ought and might have trusted the King with that whole matter. . . . For men may spare their pains where nature is at work, and the world will not go the faster for our driving. Even as his present Majestie's happy Restauration did it self, so all things else happen in their best proper time, without any need of our officiousness.[20]

The same rationale is also behind the paean to Hesperian primitivism which Marvell places in the mouth of religious refugees in *Bermudas*. One feels that if Marvell sounds the depth of this rationalization, it is mainly because he has himself heard, and wanted to heed, the body's counsel.

In this dialogue, the mutual effect of the opposition is to make both soul and body "restless . . . and unsecure," each trembling because it feels it has already grown impure—an attitude which corresponds to that in the first strophe of *On a Drop of Dew*, which is perhaps why the body has the last word. In the second dialogue, *Between The Resolved Soul and Created Pleasure*, the last word is uttered by the disdainful soul; its rejection of the pleasures of passive repose (the senses, or the flesh) and active conquest (the world) corresponds to the attitude depicted in the second strophe. Marvell's attitude toward the resolved soul may be a little wry, but there is no indication that in this context he thinks of its triumph as a bad thing in itself.[21] Still it is clear that insofar as consciousness is divided into attitudes toward the world which Marvell labels "soul" and "body," these attitudes are partial at best and at worst capable of lending themselves to perverse rationalizations. He associates them variously with traditional formulas of withdrawal—ascetic, contemplative, epicurean, pastoral, etc.—and he shows that the main trouble with attitudes which have crystallized into Soul or Body is that they are *too* resolved: too fixed, exclusive, and coy. Though like plans they are prior "mental sets," they are not open to chance or choice, and they resist exposure to

---

[20] "The Rehearsal Transprosed," *Works*, ed. A. B. Grosart ([1873]; New York: AMS Press, 1966), III, 212–13.

[21] Its self-satisfaction makes the Soul faintly insufferable: it is impervious to Created Pleasure mainly because its own Uncreated Pleasures are so much more delicious. Thus it will not sup or rest below because it already sups and rests above (lines 17–18, 23–24). Its smugness reaches an ironic climax in the final rejoinder: "None thither mounts by the degree of Knowledge, but Humility." See F. H. Bradbrook, "The Poetry of Andrew Marvell," in *From Donne to Marvell*, Pelican Guide to English Literature, vol. 3, ed. Boris Ford (Baltimore: Penguin Books, 1960), 194; Isabel G. MacCaffrey, "Some Notes on Marvell's Poetry, Suggested by a Reading of His Prose," *Modern Philology* 61 (May 1964): 264; on this poem, and more generally on Marvell's treatment of withdrawal, see Harold Toliver, *Marvell's Ironic Vision* (New Haven: Yale University Press, 1965).

the vagaries of social and political life. Socio-politico-historical actuality is man's given and proper home, yet these attitudes project each its own environment by way of justifying its retreat: Soul aspires to the glories of Heaven; Body retires to the luxuriant nirvana of vegetable Nature.

Marvell's fascination with Cromwell seems connected with the fact that as regards these tendencies Cromwell is—to use Yeats's term— Marvell's Mask; the opposition between them is a less absolute version of the archetypal extremes of the Nymph and the wanton Trooper. Marvell appears initially and intuitively to view Cromwell as a political animal, also as an embodiment of heavenly and natural forces, an instrument through which they work their wills *in* human affairs. But there are other dispositions to which the tendencies of withdrawal are more congenial and, as the terms *Body* and *Soul* suggest, these may be innate, the raw psychological material with which reason and will must struggle. Utilizing an ancient and honorable pairing which I imagine Marvell had in mind, we might see the poet distinguished from the politician by this awareness of the inward division, and of the constant need to cope with oneself to make oneself cope with the world—and, further, by the resulting ironic awareness that each type is essential to the other, both within the individual and in the society. In this light, the pleasures of poetry are problematical: they may be merely recreative and harmless, or they may be dominated by the motives of Soul and Body; a peculiar combination of the two is represented in the figure of Fleckno, for whom verse equals universe; the gaunt "half transparent" poetaster's obsession annihilates himself as well as everything else that's made.[22] Clearly, the poet, unlike the politician, must overcome his inclination to remain in the green world of the Muses and to treat the first world as an alien place or as a domain which man by his officiousness cannot affect.

But this view of the politician and Cromwell is itself presented as a schema to be modified, and the modification worked out in the *Horatian Ode* is one which simultaneously affects (and justifies) politician and poet. We shall see Marvell achieve this by an interchange of politician and poet tendencies in which the poet moves beyond the schema and beyond partisan feelings in the course of rendering Cromwell more human. My reading will lean heavily on John Wallace's scrupulous and perceptive elucidation of the political function and historical background

---

[22] The opposite extreme is represented by the poet Tom May (*Tom May's Death*), whose poetry is totally in the service of Getting Ahead.

of the ode,[23] though the emphasis will be complementary, since I am
concerned more with the poetic than with the rhetorical context of
the ode.

The opening lines seem more applicable at first to Marvell, especially
since their reference to Cromwell is held in abeyance:

> The forward Youth that would appear
> Must now forsake his *Muses* dear,
>   Nor in the Shadows sing
>   His Numbers languishing.
> 'Tis time to leave the Books in dust,
> And oyl th'unused Armours rust:
>   Removing from the Wall
>   The Corslet of the Hall.
> So restless *Cromwel* could not cease
> In the inglorious Arts of Peace.

The lines justify not only Cromwell but also the poem Marvell is about
to write.[24] As there is perhaps a little of Cromwell in Marvell, so there
ought to be a little of Marvell in Cromwell. Thus both compliment and
exhortation look two ways. For example:

> Much to the Man is due.
> Who, from his private Gardens, where
> He liv'd reserved and austere,
>   As if his highest plot
>   To plant the Bergamot,
> Could by industrious Valour climbe
> To ruine the great Work of Time,
>   And cast the Kingdome old
>   Into another Mold.
>
> *(28–36)*

Cromwell surges forth into politics and Marvell into a political poem.[25]
But the image of Cromwell Marvell develops seems to be affected by

---

[23] "Marvell's Horatian Ode," *PMLA* 77 (March 1962): 33–46. See also Joseph
Mazzeo, *Renaissance and Seventeenth-Century Studies* (New York: Columbia University
Press, 1964), 166–83 and 183–209.

[24] This and other ideas in the present reading have developed out of discussions
with my friend, Michael Holahan, to whom I am indebted for many stimulating
suggestions.

[25] See Wallace, "Marvell's Horatian Ode," 35.

Marvell's own sense of the difficulty of public life. Cromwell is at first identified with the omnipotence of the force ("angry Heavens flame") using him as an instrument, yet Marvell no sooner utters that phrase than he distinguishes the mere man from the force ("And, if we would speak true, / Much to the man is due," 27−28).

Neither Brooks nor Bush seems to understand the drift of this distinction, though it is central to the poem: Marvell is not simply praising Cromwell's manliness,[26] nor is he merely defining the "actual person . . . who was an instrument of Providence";[27] rather he is suggesting how difficult it is to fulfill so awesome a role. His limits as a man are a measure of his excellence: "What Field of all the Civil Wars, / Where his were not the deepest Scars?" (45−46). He cannot simply sweep through history like a naked force but must study the "wiser Art" of letting the enemy make its own mistakes (47ff.); he must have enough patience to remain in the background and wait his time while the king has his day on the tragic stage; he must also, like Charles, learn to be aware of his public image and audience. The peculiar lines on Irish praise of the conqueror (73−80) may be explained in a similar manner. If, as Brooks thinks, they contain "some inflection of grim irony,"[28] this points up the entanglements—ethical and otherwise—into which even a righteous cause plunges the man saddled with the execution of divine plan. If, on the other hand, we maintain with Bush either that this attitude was typically English or that Marvell was "indulging in some wishful thinking,"[29] we may still be meant to feel the extent to which a partisan cause involves God's human agent in a delicate, if not problematical, situation.

The final forty lines extend this treatment of Cromwell in two directions. First, Marvell meditates on the paradox that Cromwell's power is increased in his voluntary submission to the will of the people ("How fit he is to sway / That can so well obey," 83−84). Second, the poem concludes on a note of grim determination to keep Cromwell marching whether he wants to or not:

[26] Cleanth Brooks, "Marvell's 'Horatian Ode,'" in Keast, *Seventeenth-Century English Poetry*, 329−30.

[27] Douglas Bush, "Marvell's 'Horatian Ode,'" in Keast, 345−46. This famous argument has always seemed both pompous and pointless to me. Brooks is right in seeing Marvell's attitude as ambiguous, though I think he misses the particular reasons for the ambiguity, reasons thoroughly adduced by Wallace. Bush is perhaps right to quarrel with the "sinister" implications of Brooks's reading, though he unbalances and distorts that reading to have something new-critical to criticize.

[28] Brooks, 334.

[29] Bush, 349−50.

> thou the Wars and Fortunes Son
> March indefatigably on;
> And for the last effect
> Still keep thy Sword erect:
> Besides the force it has to fright
> The Spirits of the shady Night,
> The same *Arts* that did *gain*
> A *Pow'r* must it *maintain.*
>
> *(113–20)*

The tone here seems to me far from that with which Marvell introduced his hero:

> So restless *Cromwel* could not cease
> In the inglorious Arts of Peace,
> But through adventrous War
> Urged his active Star.
>
> *(9–12)*

Now, however, Cromwell had better not cease and cannot afford to rest or drop his guard; his problems are subtler and more trying than those of martial adventure.[30] There will be no time for "inglorious Arts of Peace," though the "three-fork'd Lightning" will have to utilize other preparatory arts, perhaps inglorious in a different way.

There is a peculiar vibration here, if we remember that the inglorious arts of peace must include the pleasures of poetry. One reason the politician is being urged to his indefatigable defense of the commonwealth may well be to free the poet so that he may return in security to the commonwealth of the Muses. Thus after making the image of Cromwell increasingly sympathetic because he has transferred to the politician

---

[30] Brooks is aware of this tone but avoids dealing with it. He remarks that for Cromwell "any other course of action is positively unthinkable" and that "it will not be enough to hold the sword aloft as a ritual sword. The naked steel will still have to be used against bodies less diaphanous than spirits" (335; Wallace, 44, sees the first sentence as a misreading). Brooks apparently treats all this as part of Marvell's critical and ambivalent attitude, but it can more easily be seen as growing sympathy for the hero who must bear such a burden. The present interpretation, which bases itself on Wallace, makes more sense of Brooks's reading, for it allows the note of warning as part of the sympathetic awareness of Cromwell's difficult position. It also makes sense of Brooks's reading of line 113, "thou the Wars and Fortunes Son," since it suggests how Cromwell at this point of the poem is seen not only as the agent but also as the slave of the situation. I see no warrant for Bush's blanket rejection of Brooks here (Keast, 351); he gives no reasons and fails to supply his own justifying interpretation.

something of the poet's concern for human weakness, Marvell, as it were, breaks the transference: the gesture of the concluding lines signifies a parting of the ways temporarily joined in the political poem. This renders Cromwell a lonelier and more moving figure, while allowing us at the same time a brief glimpse of the poet's own complexity of attitude. And we may also see something else: Wallace suggests that the decorum of *An Horatian Ode* prescribes a relatively impersonal tone, the voice of a public person;[31] insofar as it is occasional and, at least on the surface, laudatory, a narrative about another rather than about the self, this may be so. Yet in this medium Cromwell becomes, if not more individual, certainly more a human being and less an abstract symbol of power as the poem develops.

The symbiosis of poet and politician could not be better enacted than by such an interchange: the poet leaves his "private Gardens" to make public his special ennobling insight into the hero who, like himself, knows the value of the withdrawal he must perforce sacrifice. The insight is that this side of Cromwell makes him less—and more—than an unthinking elemental force or "angry Heavens flame." He has studied the "wiser Art" and tried the tolerance of aspiration so that he knows when to submit, forbear, impose limits on himself. Marvell shadows the motif of retirement in a series of gestures which reveal how "much one Man can do, / That does both act *and know*" (75–76, italics mine):

> Nor yet grown stiffer with Command,
> But still in the *Republick's* hand:
> > How fit he is to sway
> > That can so well obey.
> He to the *Commons Feet* presents
> A *Kingdome*, for his first years rents:
> > And, what he may, forbears
> > His Fame to make it theirs:
> And has his Sword and Spoyls ungirt,
> To lay them at the *Publick's* skirt.
> > So when the Falcon high
> > Falls heavy from the Sky,
> She, having kill'd, no more does search,
> But on the next green Bow to pearch;
> > Where, when he first does lure,
> > The Falckner has her sure.
>
> *(81–96)*

[31] Wallace, 45.

In this ode, and on a much larger scale in *The First Anniversary*,[32] we see a development much like that discussed above as a shift from plan to experience. Here the "plan" may be equated to the abstract figure, Cromwell as impersonal scourge, while the poetic development gradually qualifies the simple stereotype of Politician until it is humanized by contamination with elements of Marvell's Poet.[33] If, in spite of its remaining unpublished, the ode was intended, as Wallace has argued, "to persuade readers of Cromwell's vocation,"[34] this pattern serves the apologetic function. By presenting the most troublesome side of Cromwell first, Marvell effectually outfaces those in doubt. The Protector's more dangerous characteristics are closely bound up with the role imposed by Providence, while his more sympathetic qualities emerge as human responses to the role so imposed. The violence of Cromwell may be absorbed into the positive and traditional idea of the violence of divine grace. Marvell's echoes of Lucan and Cromwell's likeness to Caesar, persuasively detailed by Wallace, work in the same direction:

> Marvell might be, like Lucan, the laureate of a madman he detested as the disturber of the peace, but on the other hand he is also writing an ode, the conventional vehicle of praise for victorious generals. The title of the poem suggests that Marvell is to be another Horace to Cromwell's Augustus, while the exordium could imply the poet's hostility towards his subject. Subsequently, the parallel with Lucan is seen to function as a means of establishing the poet as a just and thoughtful man: he knows that Cromwell appears to some men to be a tyrant, and it is at once plain that the ode is not to be a piece of panegyric flattery.[35]

On the other hand, the divine sanction implied in the concept of the *dux bellorum* elevates the Protestant deliverer far above the founder of the Roman Empire—here, in the polemical context of the ode, the negative aspects of the Caesar analogy are admitted and turned, whereas in *The First Anniversary* Marvell appeals to the less ambiguous analogies pro-

---

[32] There we see the same gradual shift from the image of all-powerful Cromwell (lines 1–116) to a Cromwell whose coach was overturned (175ff.), who resigned his "Privacy so dear, / To turn the headstrong Peoples Charioteer" (223–24), whom Marvell compares to a mate struggling to save a foundering ship while the passengers "grumble discontent" (265–78), and finally imagines as almost submerged in a chaotic sea of domestic and foreign foes (293–402).

[33] Wallace discusses a different plan-experience pattern in distinguishing the politico-rhetorical structure and formal intention of the ode from "the verbal detail by which a simple intention is sustained within a complex variety of ideas and feelings" (44).

[34] Wallace, 44.

[35] Wallace, 35.

vided by the Old Testament kings.[36] Thus Marvell's apology does not deny or ignore the standard objections against Cromwell; it admits and contains them, but it does so in a sequential pattern which might suggest that Brooks had read only the first half and Bush the second half of the ode. Wallace, who has read it through, does more justice to Marvell's image of

> the relationship between Cromwell as Christian hero and Cromwell as usurper: no critic would want to explain away altogether the "ambiguities" in Marvell's view of him. Many of the familiar taunts against Cromwell find their way into the ode . . . to Marvell Cromwell is still a bird of prey, but one who has shown latterly that he can behave like an obedient falcon.[37]

And in commenting on Marvell's Horatian tone as one which rises above faction and party-colored minds, Wallace remarks that "the people of England, like the poet, must learn to forget themselves and their prejudices, and to mark the signs God has given."[38] What we should note about this is the way in which the poem as an act exemplifies such disciplined impartiality by giving play to attitudes which are opposed, too simplistic or pure, and reconciling them in a richer perspective. While adhering to the demands of his formal scheme and rhetorical purpose, Marvell manages to convey the sense of a dynamic experience, of attitudes being qualified during utterance, similar to that produced in *The Nymph Complaining* and the *Drop of Dew*.

Marvell's Garden:
Still Another Interpretation

My excuse for revisiting Marvell's garden, if I need one, is simply that the interpretation offered here differs from any I have seen. The difference, in broadest perspective, is produced by an approach to the interpretation of lyric or first-person poetry which I have discussed and exemplified elsewhere,[39] and which is based on the familiar premise that a good deal of poetry in the first person is to be understood as a presenta-

---

[36] For a clear and brief statement of Marvell's critical or revisionist attitude toward the use of ancient history as example, see *Tom May's Death*, 39–54.

[37] Wallace, 44.

[38] Wallace, 45.

[39] E.g., "Spenser's Gardens of Adonis: Force and Form in the Renaissance Imagination," *University of Toronto Quarterly* 30 (1961): 128–49; jacket essays on R. P. Blackmur and Stanley Kunitz in the Yale Series of Recorded Poets; "Spenser's *Prothalamion:* An Interpretation," *Essays in Criticism* 15 (1965): 363–80.

tion of consciousness in action. This approach demands that we locate the "plot" and central action of a lyric poem in the *now* of utterance and treat the poem as a significant moment in the personal life the poem itself creates or implies. Directing this approach toward *The Garden*, I hope to show that Marvell's vaunted wit has an entirely different character and purpose when viewed as a form of phenomenological *action* than it has when viewed as a form of "metaphysical" *statement*.

In the first section of this essay I discussed the dialectic between two attitudes, which I called the voice of the Body and the voice of the Soul. The continually shifting tension and interplay between these attitudes provide the psychological drama of *The Garden*. The voice and attitude of the Body dominate the poet's consciousness during the first five stanzas, and I should like to begin with the famous fifth stanza which celebrates the Body Triumphant, recumbent in fruits and flowers:

> What wond'rous Life in this I lead!
> Ripe Apples drop about my head;
> The Luscious Clusters of the Vine
> Upon my Mouth do crush their Wine;
> The Nectaren, and curious Peach,
> Into my hands themselves do reach;
> Stumbling on Melons, as I pass,
> Insnar'd with Flow'rs, I fall on Grass.
>
> *(33–40)*

The best glosses on this are the fawn tripping, or perhaps reeling, to kiss the nymph, the Bermudan dreamworld, and, above all, the false retreat of the nuns in *Upon Appleton House:*

> "Within this holy leisure we
> Live innocently as you see.
> These Walls restrain the World without,
> But hedge our Liberty about.
> These Bars inclose that wider Den
> Of those wild Creatures, called Men.
> The Cloyster outward shuts its Gates,
> And, from us, locks on them the Grates.
>
> "Here we, in shining Armour white,
> Like *Virgin Amazons* do fight.
> And our chast *Lamps* we hourly trim,
> Lest the great *Bridegroom* find them dim.
> Our *Orient* Breaths perfumed are
> With insense of incessant Pray'r.

And Holy-water of our Tears
Most strangly our Complexion clears.

"Not Tears of Grief; but such as those
With which calm Pleasure overflows;
Or Pity, when we look on you
That live without this happy Vow.
How should we grieve that must be seen
Each one a *Spouse*, and each a *Queen*;
And can in *Heaven* hence behold
Our brighter Robes and Crowns of Gold?"

(97–120)

"Nor is our *Order* yet so nice,
Delight to banish as a Vice.
Here Pleasure Piety doth meet;
One perfecting the other Sweet.
So through the mortal fruit we boyl
The Sugars uncorrupting Oyl:
And that which perisht while we pull,
Is thus preserved clear and full.

"For such indeed are all our Arts;
Still handling Natures finest Parts.
Flow'rs dress the Altars; for the Clothes,
The Sea-born Amber we compose;
Balms for the griv'd we draw; and Pasts
We mold, as Baits for curious tasts.
What need is here of Man? unless
These as sweet Sins we should confess.

"Each Night among us to your side
Appoint a fresh and Virgin Bride;
Whom if *our Lord* at midnight find,
Yet Neither should be left behind."

(169–88)

The nuns exclude from their idyll all things that have the power to hurt
or tyrannize, but the pleasures associated with these things are revived
by surrogate objects; as the nun's language shows, their fancies metaphorically and their activities literally procure the sensations associated
with war, love, cosmetics, dress, cookery, arts, and crafts. Indeed, their
fantasies are domestic rather than merely sexual, and what they conjure
up is the whole context of married life, purged of the one relationship
that renders it both precarious and rewarding. Marvell is not so far gone

in the wondrous life of his fifth-stanza garden, but the rationalization
involved has the same end: the fruits grow tropical and sinister as, for all
their solid juiciness, they become more than fruits; animated with siren
purpose, they offer the pleasures without the dangers of feminine involvement; as objects to be plucked, enjoyed, devoured, and indolently
cast aside, they suggest how the green-world sensibility views women
and all other goods. The fruits replace "the Palm, the Oke, or Bayes" as
rewards of the idle consciousness; like daydreams, they become firmly
independent of their dreamer, usurp his will, and destroy his desire to
leave, his ability for further action. Possibly it is his turning into a
happy vegetable that causes the mutation of fruits to sirens.

The gifts these trees and plants press on the poet are hardly "in strong
contrast to those of the libertine garden," as Frank Kermode would have
it.[40] The suggested attitudes, if not the gifts, seem to me to have something in common with such Spenserian motifs as Clarion the butterfly in
the garden of *Muiopotmos* or Cymochles in the Bower of Bliss (*Faerie
Queene* II.v). If Marvell's attitude toward his fifth-stanza garden is not
so positive as Kermode makes out, it is also not so abandoned as that of
the nuns or of Spenser's Cymochles. His flowery fetters and vegetable
vamps weave a snare from which we may expect him to escape without
too great difficulty. Among the reasons for this, perhaps the most obvious is the tone of voice produced by his witty and elegant octosyllabic
verse: given the conventions of third-person narrative and dialogue (as
in the case of the nun), this is not a contributory effect, but in the lyric
situation, when the poet as such is describing himself, it compels us to
distinguish the speaker as subject from the image of himself which is the
object described. We do not directly confront Andrew Marvell in orgy;
rather, we stand beside the amused poet as he creates or imagines himself
in orgy. The saying of the poem is an aspect of the poetic experience
which interposes itself between us and the image. Seen this way, the
poem as it unfolds becomes an experimental staging of the green-world
sensibility. The central stanza turns the action of the poem, for it simultaneously concludes the movement of retreat and initiates a series of perspectives on life in the garden.

The first five stanzas are all given from a single perspective, that of
the fifth: the poet imagines himself already in the garden at the outset;
the arguments for going and staying there seem initially dominated by the
voice of the Body. From the standpoint of a consciousness "Insnar'd with

[40] Kermode, "The Argument of Marvell's 'Garden,'" in Keast, *Seventeenth-Century
English Poetry*, 298.

Flow'rs" and desiring "the Garlands of repose," the men who vainly "amaze" themselves to win fame, whose labors are ceaseless, are caught in another kind of snare, the "Toyles" of aspiration. But since the whole argument is an outlandish joke, the Body's counsel is not only being given play but is also mocked. "The joke is in the substitution of the emblem of victory for its substance" (Kermode, 296), and the point of the joke lies in the Body's literalism, its characteristic preference for that which is sensuous, palpable, and close at hand. The symbol is desired for itself, not for what it represents. This immediacy is realized in the fifth stanza, where something like the opposite of symbolism occurs, i.e., plants are magically more than plants. The five stanzas regress wittily from a highly civilized emblem style to a mock-primitive *participation mystique*.

The extent to which Marvell is deliberately staging this movement may be suggested by a glance at some phrases in the second, third, and fourth stanzas:

(1) "Society is all but rude, / To this delicious Solitude." That society is barbarous compared with his refined solitary pleasures seems like a complaint of the coy and disdainful Soul; that it is rude and impinges on his privacy is, on the other hand, a sentiment ascribable to the "restless . . . and unsecure" part of consciousness.

(2) "When we have run our Passions heat, / Love hither makes his best retreat." The retreat may be negative, as in a martial retreat, or positive, as in a religious retreat. Empson and Kermode stress the former and see the qualifying first line as a sign that the getaway is not a rout but an orderly withdrawal: "It is only for a time, and after effort among human beings, that he can enjoy solitude."[41] "Love enters this garden, but only when the pursuit of the white and red is done, and we are without appetite" (Kermode, 298). The important point is that the lines register the attraction of passion, and though passion immediately signifies love, it may be generalized to include the worldly passions of vain men in the first stanza—i.e., "Passions heat" may be the race to win the palm or oak. In its reference to love, the couplet also suggests that relations with women should be restricted to those that gratify passion; anything more serious, permanent, or entangling is to be avoided by withdrawing one's love to oneself, as in the case of the nuns and the nymph. A religious retreat, on the other hand, is the hope of the resolved (or perhaps, in this couplet, exhausted) Soul transferring its contemplation and desire from earthly to heavenly things.

---

[41] William Empson, *Some Versions of Pastoral* (London: Chatto & Windus, 1950), 131.

(3) "The *Gods*, that mortal Beauty chase, / Still in a Tree did end their race." The first line by itself inverts the idea of religious retreat (man pursuing heavenly beauty) and reminds us again of the dangerous appeal of what the retiring Soul gives up. This makes the willful misinterpretation of the following lines more comic: Apollo and Pan "pursued women not as women but as potential trees" (Kermode, 298). If, as Kermode insists, the gods desire only literal plants—the laurel and the reed—then the joke about escaping to vegetable nature is continued: in helping to reforest the earth, which has too many "busie Companies of Men" and too few trees, the gods are making more gardens available. But the sense of the poem makes it equally possible that the gods want not only plants but also what they stand for—poetry and music—in which case they are helping the disdainful Soul by transforming lower beauties to higher. The classic Empsonian analysis of *feigning* (137ff.) seems to apply here, since the gods are making the process of sublimation or substitution easier, and the singing Soul of stanza seven could profit from such activity.[42]

The extravagant arguments which Marvell adduces betray the real motive for retirement: not renunciation of the world or the flesh; certainly not the mere "study of right reason; the denial of the sovereignty of sense; the proper use of created nature"—the themes identified by Kermode (296). He withdraws because he wishes to savor all the pleasures offered by society and love in an undilute and immediate form, without let from others or effort on his own part. The point about the verbal play described above is that in the first half of the poem at least, the most divergent tendencies of mind may collaborate to urge this withdrawal: "religious" or contemplative and perhaps artistic motives are thoroughly entwined by the puns with "lower" impulses of pleasure and fear; we are not encouraged to evaluate motives or to distinguish good motives from bad. The immediate goal of these urges is the state embodied in the fifth stanza, at once exhilarated and languorous, passionate and passive; on the one hand, a fantasy, on the other, a hyperintense moment

---

[42] One might attempt to force the following couplet into an interpretation of this sort by leaning on the possible syntactical inversion: "Little, Alas, they know, or heed, / How far these Beauties Hers exceed!"—"Fond Lovers who roam the woods cutting names in trees little know or heed how superior their Lady's beauty is to that of plants." I think that this is straining some, although it accords with Marvell's ambiguous attitude toward the objects from which he withdraws and also with the farcical character of some of the arguments—"Well! If they love a lady in town, why are they out here courting trees?" is no more outlandish than "Prefer Ladies to trees? Incredible!"

of sensing and perceiving.[43] Commentators have been unable to resist the simultaneous presence of apples, wine, and a fall in a single stanza, but if these things seem portentous, I think it is again part of the same pattern: all levels of experience, including those presumably left behind, are telescoped into this sensuous climax and reduced to or by the perspective of the Body.[44]

We are not, as I mentioned before, to read *The Garden* as a poem about Andrew Marvell in a garden; it is a poem about Andrew Marvell imagining himself in a garden, staging or trying out—indeed evoking—the impulses to withdrawal. The tone of the first four stanzas is for the most part detached—by which I mean objective, not *cool*, for Marvell obviously enjoys the exercise of wit, and I think we sense that he is *watching himself* go through his paces. The sudden proximity and involvement of the fifth stanza suggest that Marvell now abandons himself to the image he has evoked. The garden image has become palpable; like the nectarine and curious peach, it insinuates itself into his consciousness, and this suggests that for the moment he succumbs to his creation. Active wit yields to emotional response so that here, in the middle of the poem, he has given himself to his green world. So Empson:

> The first four [stanzas] are a crescendo of wit, on the themes "success or failure is not important, only the repose that follows the exercise of one's powers" . . . he seems in this next verse to imitate the process he has described, to enjoy in a receptive state the exhilaration which an exercise of wit has achieved. (130–31)

The point I wish to make is that we cannot appreciate the poem unless we take into account something which is too often ignored because it is so obvious: Marvell withdraws in, and into, a poem, not a garden. Poetry allows him to withdraw in the image and not in the flesh, in a verbal and not an actual surrender. Since the poem is his garden and green world, he may all the more securely give vent to the pleasure principle. Nothing is more obvious in Marvell's work than that the poetic exercise of wit is his chief pleasure and self-delight. The corollary is that he takes seri-

---

[43] Empson calls the stanza Keatsian (131); I am reminded of a similarly fantastic effect produced by Frost in "After Apple-Picking": "And I could tell / What form my dreaming was about to take. / Magnified apples appear and disappear, / Stem end and blossom end" (*Complete Poems of Robert Frost* [New York: Holt, Rinehart & Winston, 1949], 88).

[44] Kermode's point is good: "The difference between this and a paradise containing a woman is that here a Fall is of light consequence and without tragic significance" (299).

ously the need to justify the pleasure: if withdrawal is to poetry as recreation, return must be to poetry as a useful or significant act.

One of the real puzzles about the mind's famous withdrawal in the next stanza has been slighted by commentators for the flashier multiple meanings: when did the mind begin to withdraw "into its happiness" and how does the stanza fit where it does in the meditative sequence? It is sharply set off from stanza five, not only in topic and tone but also in the shift from the poet's exulting identification with the "I" of the fifth stanza to the more abstract and musing focus on "the Mind" in the sixth.[45] Does the mind withdraw *from* what it conceives to be the "pleasure less" of the fifth stanza and, in general, from the retreat supervised by the Body throughout the first five stanzas? Or does it withdraw along *with* the Body?

The phrase "Mean while the Mind, from pleasure less, / Withdraws . . ." suggests a back-at-the-ranch situation which may be very simple if we include the information offered in stanza seven: "While in fantasy I sink to the grass at 'the Fountains sliding foot, / Or at some Fruit-trees mossy root,' my mind withdrawing creates other worlds, and my Soul gliding into the boughs sits and sings like a bird." But the "Mean while" gives the verb a progressive force: "the mind has been withdrawing since the beginning of the poem, though it is only now that I turn and attend to it." The effect is that of a stage direction and, as such, of a sudden shift from one to another level of consciousness. The poet severs his close involvement with the garden image and steps back, framing the first five stanzas in the two interpretations of stanzas six and seven. We can hardly help feeling that the end of the fifth stanza marks a caesura in the poem's rhythm. Before, the poet was participating with his happy wit in the pleasant process of withdrawal; from the sixth stanza to the end of the poem, he stands outside that process and characterizes it in a series of definitions and figures—the mind as ocean, the green thought, the birdlike Soul, the impossible longing for Eveless Eden, the gardener, the dial, and the bee. This act of introspection may be seen as a more radical mode of withdrawal: during the process of retreat, attention was primarily on the world and the garden, but in stanzas six and seven the focus has shifted to the retreating self apart from the world. Yet this very introspection, insofar as it creates a distance between the

---

[45] The opening line of the fifth stanza, by repeating the final rhyme of stanza four (*Speed—Reed—lead*), tends to bind those strophes more closely, a device that accelerates the tempo at that point and diminishes the peculiarly paratactic relation that the stanzas of *The Garden* have with each other.

speaker and the process, would seem to indicate that in the present tense
of lyric utterance, he has entered a phase of return.

Since the refinements of the sixth stanza have been discussed by Empson (124−26), I shall add to his account only the sense gained when the
fourth line is accented as follows: "that Ocean where each kind / Does
streight *its own* resemblance find." Within the mind, each kind locates
its own image more quickly than the images of others.[46] This idea of
narcissistic withdrawal may entail the notion that the images are thereby
straitened, lacking in richness or substance, like mirror images. The oceanic mind shares some of the ambiguous characteristics of the meadow
and flooding river in *Upon Appleton House:*

> To see Men through this Meadow Dive,
> We wonder how they rise alive.
> As, under Water, none does know
> Whether he fall through it or go.
>
> *(377−80)*

> *Denton* sets ope its *Cataracts;*
> And makes the Meadow truly be
> (What it but seem'd before) a Sea.
>
> *(466−68)*

> For now the Waves are fal'n and dry'd,
> And now the Meadows fresher dy'd.
>
> *(625−26)*

> as a *Chrystal Mirrour* slick;
> Where all things gaze themselves, and doubt
> If they be in it or without.
> And for his shade which therein shines,
> *Narcissus* like, the *Sun* too pines.
>
> *(636−40)*

Behind the *Garden* stanzas we may feel the deluge motif at work; the
mind diving into itself plays all roles: God, Noah, ark, flood, even—in
the next stanza—the symbolic bird. Both deluge and withdrawal aim at
the obliteration of evil in the first world and at a second, a fresher and
better, creation. But the second world may be either the one the mind

---

[46] Or "each kind finds within the mind forms peculiar to all members of that species."
The statement sounds as though it may carry the weight of an observation like that of
Xenophanes: if cows had gods, their gods would be cows.

finds within itself or the one to which it returns. It may be an underwater fantasy, not only offering us clarified images of ourselves but also tempting us with what we lack in actuality; the sun pines for cooling shade as well as for his unreal double; the flowers which the diver finds at the bottom may ensnare him. The flood must be made to recede, the diver to "rise alive," bearing his flowers to the surface.

The stanza brilliantly enacts this dilemma, for we see Marvell's mind contemplating the mind contemplating itself. The opening stage direction is followed by two couplets which seem parenthetical as the poet withdraws from the immediate situation to define two aspects of mind in general: first its passive function—"that Ocean where each kind / Does streight its own resemblance find"; then its creative activity—"Yet it creates, transcending these, / Far other Worlds, and other Seas." The final couplet, in Marvell's frequent paratactic manner, seems to follow from any or all of the three preceding couplets, thereby placing the burden of interpretation on the reader: "Annihilating all that's made / To a green Thought in a green Shade." Empson properly observes that the lines mean "either contemplating everything or shutting everything out" (119), but he then goes on to turn a problematical either/or into a triumphant (i.e., paradoxical) both/and:

> Evidently the object of such a fundamental contradiction (seen in the etymology: turning all *ad nihil*, *to* nothing, and *to* a thought) is to deny its reality. . . . This gives its point . . . to the other ambiguity, clear from the context, as to whether the *all* considered was *made* in the mind of the author or the Creator; to so peculiarly "creative" a knower there is little difference between the two. Here as usual with "profound" remarks the strength of the thing is to combine unusually intellectual with unusually primitive ideas; thought about the conditions of knowledge with a magical idea that the adept controls the external world by thought. (119–20)

There is nothing difficult or contradictory in saying that you have to shut out the world—free yourself from its distractions—to contemplate it or re-create it as the mind wants it. The stanza seems to balance the cost of destruction against the value of creation, and the final couplet is weighted toward the privative rather than positive opinion.[47] This being the case, it makes a good deal of difference whether the *all* was made "in the mind of the author or the Creator," for the mind's transcendent worlds and

---

[47] The final couplet reverses or opposes the sense of the preceding couplet: "The mind creates . . . but to do so it annihilates." For a different view, based on the positive use of *annihilate* by mystical writers, see Louis Martz, *The Meditative Poem* (Garden City: Doubleday-Anchor, 1963), 548.

seas are depicted only in monochrome. Because the poet is thinking hard "about the conditions of knowledge" in this stanza, he presents the "magical idea" in an ironic light; control of the external world by thought, so that the godlike mind fills its own place, is seen as a childlike or regressive way of responding to life. Joseph Summers's rhetorical question catches Marvell's tone and alternatives with some precision:

> Does "The Garden" . . . by exaggerating its claims for the perfect and simultaneous ecstasies of the body, mind, and soul in a world without women or effort . . . show the retired life as pleasant for "sweet and wholesome hours" but as dangerous if not absurd as an image for all of life?[48]

However one relates the seventh stanza to the sixth, it seems like a response that registers and comments on this dangerous tendency of mind. It is more detached and playful, its image is at once more artificial and intellectually complex—it is not, in fact, a mere image (like the fifth stanza) or statement (like the sixth) but an emblematic conceit. To shift from the mind as universe, creator, and destroyer to the Soul as delicate, birdlike creature within a world not of its own making is to shift to a more modest view of consciousness. Consciousness as mind can only dive within its own green depths, but consciousness as soul-bird can bask and play and fly away. This sense of ironic detachment is enhanced if— as seems allowable—we supply a colon after "green Shade" and read the seventh stanza as the next green thought. The Bermudan God of the Soul and its garden will then be the creative mind of stanza six:

> Here at the Fountains sliding foot,
> Or at some Fruit-trees mossy root,
> Casting the Bodies Vest aside,
> My Soul into the boughs does glide:
> There like a Bird it sits, and sings,
> Then whets, and combs its silver Wings;
> And, till prepar'd for longer flight,
> Waves in its Plumes the various Light.
>
> *(49–56)*

If we see this as an emblematic visualization of the state which is produced by the mind's previous activity, then these two stanzas seem not only to recapitulate but to reinterpret the experience of the first five stanzas. In the first version of that experience, the vegetable urges were

---

[48] Introduction to *Marvell*, Laurel Poetry Series (New York: Dell, 1961), 14–15.

satisfied by allowing the flesh to gorge itself into unconsciousness, to return to life's mossy root and melt in its sliding stream. Marvell may have thought of the "Vest" as a loose-fitting robe associated with Near Eastern dress, a symbol of perhaps needless opulence which the Soul has now left in a relaxed heap on the ground. After the flesh has run its passion's heat and found flowery repose, it no longer distracts the spirit from "worthier" pursuits. Insofar as we take the movement through the sixth to the seventh stanza as both an echo and a revision of the movement through the first four stanzas to the fifth, vegetable repose appears not as the goal of withdrawal but simply as a necessary first phase. As we have seen, the mind has been in charge of the operation from the beginning; if at first it seemed to give play to the voice and tendency of the Body, it now becomes clear that its real aim was to put the Body to sleep so that the disencumbered Soul could sing.

In depicting a sustained rather than a momentary fulfillment, an aloof rather than an engaged sensibility, an effortlessly active rather than a fainting consciousness, a "various light" rather than a green thought, the seventh stanza is a consummate image of self-delight. The soul-bird preens and pleasures itself as a true Epicurean, an "easie philosopher," not as a sensualist. Its tastes are refined, esthetic, and intellectual, though, unlike the occasionally hyperactive mind, it pursues its happiness with aristocratic *sprezzatura*. I know of nothing which more closely resembles this process and state of consciousness as described by Marvell than Yeats's account of the transition from the twelfth through the fifteenth lunar phases in *A Vision:*

> Thought and will are indistinguishable, effort and attainment are indistinguishable; and this is the consummation of a slow process; nothing is apparent but dreaming *Will* and the Image that it dreams. Since Phase 12 all images, and cadences of the mind, have been satisfying to that mind just in so far as they have expressed this converging of will and thought, effort and attainment. The words "musical," "sensuous," are but descriptions of that converging process. Thought has been pursued, not as a means but as an end—the poem, the painting, the reverie has been sufficient of itself . . . the *Creative Mind* . . . has more and more confined its contemplation of actual things to those that resemble images of the mind desired by the *Will*. The being has selected, moulded and remoulded, narrowed its circle of living, been more and more the artist, grown more and more "distinguished" in all preference. Now contemplation and desire, united into one, inhabit a world where every beloved image has bodily form, and every bodily form is loved. This love knows nothing of desire, for desire implies effort, and though

there is still separation from the loved object, love accepts the separation as necessary to its own existence. . . . All that the being has experienced as thought is visible to its eyes as a whole, and in this way it perceives, not as they are to others, but according to its own perception, all orders of existence.[49]

Yeats could not have come closer to Marvell—allowing for the striking differences between their poetic personalities—if he had had *The Garden* before him while writing this passage. The Yeatsian images expressive of this phase include such "self-born mockers of man's enterprise" ("that all heavenly glory symbolise") as the singing golden bird of Byzantium.

If we read the seventh stanza in the light of this passage, with its more explicit attention to the imaginative and poetic act, it may occur to us that singing and waving plumes are Marvell's allusions to such an act. The reflective and fantastic, creative and destructive processes attributed to "*the* Mind" of stanza six are generic, but stanza seven is about "*My* Soul," and the poet here seems to be acknowledging his own urge to pursue poetry "not as a means but as an end." Writing poetry, weaving his art, waving the various light of experience in his plumes, enjoying the exercise of a craft of wit and word which has attained to the spontaneous ease, the sureness, of a reflex act: this is his supreme pleasure, and because it is presumptively worthier and richer than the ecstasy described in stanza five, it is potentially a more dangerous temptation. An activity that is both contemplative and creative, a life passed in delicious solitude making oneself and one's surroundings beautiful, is surely entitled to be judged as "sufficient of itself." Marvell clearly recognizes both the truth and the seductiveness (increased by its truth) of the claim. The Soul, so engaged, is not yet "prepar'd for longer flight," and this situation is rendered more ambiguous by the flexibility which the whole context gives to "longer flight." This may indeed be a Platonic flight to heaven, in which case Marvell shows his poetic Soul to be coy but still not firmly resolved. The phrase may also signify a flight out of the garden, in the sense of a return to the world of busy men; the Soul refreshes itself with poetry either as a prelude and stimulus to return, or else as an amusement which diverts him while he is not yet prepared to return. But "longer flight" permits of a third meaning, a more complete or drastic *escape:* if the garden fails, one can always resort to heaven; if

[49] London: Macmillan, 1937, 135–36. For our purposes, Yeats's special interpretation of "*Creative Mind*"—a Kantian matrix of a priori categories or general forms— may be ignored.

the tempered withdrawal to poetry fails to persuade or satisfy the self, there is always the firmer sanction and more absolute strategy of religious retreat.[50]

As a moment in the meditative sequence, the seventh stanza embodies a gesture of detachment from the garden and return to the world. Its "Here-There" structure suggests that Marvell steps out of the garden experience which had in effect possessed him in stanza five; he steps back from the total process and projects it into an emblematic image, that of the ascending Soul divesting itself of the falling Body.[51] In the first five stanzas, the process was enacted; in the sixth, it was described; and now it is externalized so that the poet, as if before a painting, may confront, interpret, and evaluate his earlier experience. This disengagement continues, and the distance increases, in the eighth stanza, for the garden is suddenly removed to the past tense of prehistory:

> Such was that happy Garden-state,
> While Man there walk'd without a Mate:
> After a Place so pure, and sweet,
> What other Help could yet be meet!
> But 'twas beyond a Mortal's share
> To wander solitary there:
> Two Paradises 'twere in one
> To live in Paradise alone.
>
> *(57–64)*

A state "without a Mate"—and thus purged of the troubles caused by love, society, temptation, and mortal toil—is a possibility canceled at the beginning of human history, or rather canceled so that human history could begin. The tone of witty exaggeration which characterized the first four stanzas reappears as mock arrogance, and its absurdity is a measure of the poet's new detachment: "How silly of God and Adam to conspire in producing the useless Eve. The indiscretion has made us all miserable, and the whole affair might have been better managed had I been God and Adam."

---

[50] Perhaps also the Platonic heaven is felt as one of the "Far other" worlds created by the human mind. There is ample precedent for such an irony in the English poetic and philosophical tradition.

[51] The emblematic function is conveyed by the vaguely localized "Here . . . / Or" of the opening couplet. We are directed not to the sensuous immediacy but to the symbolic suggestiveness of "sliding foot" and "mossy root." Marvell is not simply presenting a scene here but translating a "text" into visual equivalents. See Toliver, *Marvell's Ironic Vision*, 149f.

The "historical" speculation is itself dissolved in the subjunctive and counterfactual mood of the final couplet, which gives way to the brilliantly muted here-and-now of stanza nine:

> How well the skilful Gardner drew
> Of flow'rs and herbes this Dial new;
> Where from above the milder Sun
> Does through a fragrant Zodiack run;
> And, as it works, th' industrious Bee
> Computes its time as well as we.
> How could such sweet and wholsome Hours
> Be reckon'd but with herbs and flow'rs!
>
> *(65–72)*

We are, I think, to visualize a real garden surrounding the poet, not a metaphoric, emblematic, or fantastic pleasance inhabiting his mind.[52] The tone of casual observation and reflection, the relative simplicity of statement, and the calm, equally simple delight of the final couplet must issue from the real poet or subject-self—not from the "Marvell" projected by the former into the first person of stanzas two, three, and five, the object-self whose arguments and gestures of withdrawal were represented by Marvell with increasing amusement. Now for the first time he frames his meditation in the actual occasion which prompted it; for the first time the demonstratives of place scattered through the poem (*here, this lovely green, hither, in this*) are definitely grounded in such a framing occasion; for the first time he conveys the impression of standing or strolling in a distinctive garden whose objects he notices and indicates. The first-person plural either draws him closer to us or suggests he is not alone. We are suddenly and belatedly made to feel that this scene supplies the full context which had been working on the poet from the very beginning.

To move thus out of a mental and into an actual garden is to step back still further from the green world, for the second world of the poem now includes those external conditions that prompted the meditative withdrawal of the previous stanzas. Obviously, he can leave *this* garden any time he so desires, and the mood of the final couplet—"How *could* they be reckoned," not "How *can* . . ."—suggests that he is placing the experience behind him. The ninth stanza thus emphasizes the recreative

---

[52] In taking the first four lines as literal reference to an ingenious sundial made of flowers in the image of a zodiac, with signs for hours, I follow Bradbrook, "The Poetry of Andrew Marvell," 201.

and temporary character of the poetic withdrawal from the perspective of a mind which has effectually disengaged itself, a mind in process of returning to the world, all witty passion spent. The stanza is remarkable for its quality of dénouement; the unknotting of thought leaves the poet relaxed yet alert to his surroundings, in a mood quite different from the manic languor of stanza five.

It is even more remarkable for the way Marvell combines this muted tone with explosive symbols: the iconography of dial, gardener, and bee stores the charges built up during the previous stanzas. Gardener and bee are, in fact, a little too explosive and defy the effort to establish precise references—partly because the poet has not limited the ways in which they may be related to himself and to each other, partly because they are already familiar emblems which Marvell may have wished to use as figures of his own activity in *The Garden:* the gardener conventionally symbolizes the artist vexing nature; the bee, the poet among the flowers of the Muses. It is unclear, for example, whether as emblems they represent different components of the poetic process (e.g., rational and instinctive) or different perspectives on it (the poet as gardener or as bee) or whether, on the other hand, they are in some way contrasts to the poet.[53]

A sharper focus might be achieved by considering the more manageable image of the flowery dial. Though it has practical value as a time-telling symbol, its sensuous immediacy lures the mind away from that symbolic function; it persuades us to forget time and lose ourselves in thyme, since there are no clocks in the green world. Even as a clock, it playfully deceives us, pretending to be a zodiac, offering us World enough and Time: it stretches a normal day to a green year and a garden plot to a universe. Yet it excludes the less sweet and wholesome hours of the great world so that, as in Appleton House, "Things greater are in less contain'd"—possessed, controlled, and enjoyed in relative security where time and space exist only as flowers. All this pretense is manifestly play and not illusion. The zodiac with its green year is imaginary, a recreative ornament which does not attempt to hide the essential fact that the fragrant miniature is more short-lived than most dials.[54] Though the

---

[53] The uncertainty is further complicated by what appears to be a genuinely unresolved crux in syntax: "as it works" may mean either "as the sun works" or "as the bee works." Even if one feels that the phrase must belong to the bee because of "works," there is still a problem about the antecedent of "its time." This opens the way to too many possible readings to justify the ambiguity on new-critical grounds.

[54] R. M. Adams's gloss does violence to the poet's directions: "While the growth and decline of the garden measure the passage of time, the sun, a milder clock, runs through

dial is, in Sidney's phrase, a zodiac of the poet's or gardener's wit, it differs from other dials in depending for its life and beauty on a light source coming from outside the garden and outside the mind. This gift is repaid with interest; as if in metabolic interchange, the dial transforms what it takes and returns it to the sun, enhanced by fragrance, color, and significant pattern.

The same interchange occurs at the level of instinctive purpose in the bee and at the level of rational purpose in the gardener. However self-delighting and self-sufficient their activity is, it begins and ends beyond the self. In its solitary work among flowers, the bee is responsible to the hive. The gardener—who in this poem is not, let us hope, Lord Fairfax—exercises his skill for his master, at once enhancing his pleasure and measuring his day. Both processes assist or improve nature; both are ultimately social and less valued for themselves than for their products. Neither is esteemed as an expression of its creator, the creative act, or the creative pleasure. In this sense both are perhaps ironic models of the poet whose subject has consisted of his own experience and reflections. And both are models for the poet, oblique reminders that the imaginative act is to be consummated not in an unshared garden fantasy but in a verbal artifact.

The irony takes on a certain tartness, I think, in view of Marvell's having published only his political verse during his lifetime. If the pursuit of poetry is itself a withdrawal from public problems to private pleasures, then is the product mainly of personal value, is it too personal to be communicated, or is it simply that the product is anticlimactic to the act of making? Perhaps Marvell's attitude toward the poetic pleasure was similar to his attitude toward drinking, as reported by Aubrey:

> Though he loved wine he would never drinke hard in company and was wont to say that, *he would not play the good-fellow in any man's company in whose hands he would not trust his life.*
> He kept bottles of wine at his lodgeing, and many times he would drinke liberally by himselfe to refresh his spirits, and exalt his muse.[55]

Perhaps also it is only in the transition from wine to the muse that Marvell played "the good-fellow" even in his own presence, letting go not in

---

the zodiac, or constellation of the seasons," *Norton Anthology of English Literature* (New York: Norton, 1962), I, 862. But Marvell writes: "Where [i.e., in "this Dial new"] from above." And there would not be much point in making the heavenly constellations fragrant.

[55] *Brief Lives . . .* , ed. Andrew Clark (Oxford: Clarendon Press, 1898), II, 53–54.

his study but in imagination where, secure and amused, he staged such orgies as are recorded in *The Garden* and *Upon Appleton House*. The self divided between private and public image, between the urge to escape and the urge to participate, between the voices of the pure Poet and the pure Politician—these are the tensions which the great poems reflect and attempt to resolve. Something of the concealed private life comes through in the Oxford edition portraits: the hint of a suppressed or inward smile playing over the sensual mouth, and the half-guarded, almost blankly shadowed, expression of the eyes. We see a man whose discretion is self-consciously manifest, almost to the point of being a joke on the observer: he has had his world "as in his time," but such delicious secrets are no concern of ours.

Marvell's Upon Appleton House:
An Interpretation

In this great poem the speaker enacts the process of withdrawal and return in a manner which is traditional when seen against the background of pastoral literature but unique when explored in other contexts. One such context is that of the lyric or first-person poem, especially as we find it in the late Renaissance or trace it through the line of great English poets from Chaucer. Another context is the "baroque" interest in theatricality and role playing. For in this as in other poems, the experience about which Marvell writes is identical with the experience the speaker is at once uttering and undergoing, i.e., *what happens* in *Appleton House* happens *now* in and to Marvell while he "says" the poem. And the peculiar tone Marvell imparts to this experience, a tone at once engaged and detached, sensuous and wittily disengaged, is closely connected to Marvell's staging himself, trying on (and trying out) certain conventional "roles"—attitudes, gestures, habits of mind—and delighting in his play both as participant and audience.

But these contexts are too purely esthetic to allow us to do justice to other aspects of the poem, and I should like to approach my interpretation by way of another, wider, corridor, over whose entry might be inscribed, *"Thinking* reed and thinking *Reed."* The necessary interdependence of these contrary emphases is a commonplace. The great seventeenth-century versions of the commonplace are distinguished by their dialectical and disjunctive stresses and by their concern with the antipathy of inside to outside or of small to large. Thought is opposed to extension, time to space, spirit as psyche to matter as nature, interpretation to phenomena, conscience to authority, soul to state, substance as inner force or process to substance as something static, bounded and extended. The traditional axis of hierarchy—*up-down*—tends to be replaced by, or defined in terms of, two other axes, *in-out* and *before-after*. Kant's systematic analysis of inner-temporal and outer-spatial intuitions concludes an epistemological revolution to which Marvell and Rembrandt and Milton contributed as much in their own way as did Descartes and Leibniz and Newton. In defining space as the order of coexistence, Leibniz discloses the new center of value, the new criterion of reality, for "the order of coexistence" is a *temporal* concept, i.e., simultaneity.

"It is not from space," remarks Pascal's thinking reed, "that I must seek my dignity, but from the government of my thought. I shall have no more if I possess worlds. By space the universe encompasses and swallows me up like an atom; by thought I comprehend the world." Seventeenth-century statements of the Pauline and Augustinian tenet "No one will be good who was not first of all wicked" differ from their early Christian predecessors in treating *conversio* as a moment or gesture which is externally a *contractio*, inwardly a *complicatio*. The more bounded man's nutshell, the vaster his empire. An interesting corollary is that during the seventeenth century, political thought returns to the Platonic assumption that the state is less real, or on a lower plane of reality, than the soul.

From St. Paul to Dante the notion of mystical community and divinely ordered society prevailed to sustain belief in a socio-political environment whose spiritual substance was interinvolved with that of the souls which constituted it. The aggregate, or macrocosm, is no less real than the individual, or microcosm, which it "places," envelops, and defines: membership in the group is an intrinsic attribute of the soul. But by the seventeenth century, historical and intellectual changes across the whole field of European culture had operated so as to produce a new set of assumptions. Basic to the historical consciousness of the time is the premise that civilization develops by moving toward increasingly smaller and more intricate units of order. *Now,* if not *then* (in medieval and classical times), the human condition tends toward structures which are primarily microcosmic or atomistic, so that the criterion of human culture must (now) be the extent to which it encourages or allows a high degree of intensive, rather than extensive, organization. One virtue of this premise, understood as a normative account of cultural history, is that it can explain the large-scale disorders of the century. If the world is not what it once was, if there is darkness and chaos all around us, it may well be the natural consequence of the development of civilization toward an optimal state of inwardness and spirit. In the modern age, the seventeenth century, we should expect civil and religious disorder, since extensive forms of organization weaken as the locus of human order is displaced from outside to inside. Furthermore, since the individual soul is more real than any aggregate of souls, men can no longer be expected to form themselves naturally into hierarchies, classes, churches, etc.; macrocosmic structures must be artificially established. Hence the attention to Leviathan, to the social contract, to utopias, to the problems of international law.

The sense of the individual soul's burden and responsibility increases with the sense of its power and importance. Civil and social disorder become explicitly the extended forms of failure in the individual soul. Problems are to be confronted by withdrawal into the self. The dangers, stresses, and complications of the great world are to be reproduced within the little world of soul, mind, garden, estate, etc. They are to be activated in play form and contained in experiments, poems, models, and miniatures. But withdrawal into the self is fulfilled only by return to the world; otherwise it becomes escape. A similar rationale governs what appears to be a contrary impulse—not withdrawal into the self but temporary self-expansion which, in like fashion, is fulfilled in new gestures of self-limitation.

Such an act of return and self-limitation is fulfilled in the brilliantly muted here-and-now of the last stanza of *The Garden*, which I discussed earlier. By framing himself *in* an actual garden which the poem has transformed to a symbol (or a set of symbols), Marvell asserts at once the true power of the mind and the proper use of gardens. The poetic act is not an escape to free fantasy but an interpretation of the actual or real existence which the mind does not create. The gesture of return is enacted when the poet *re*-creates within his second world the image of the first; when this occurs, the second world displays its greenness and is voluntarily dissolved, sealed off, or transcended. This is the road not taken by the complaining nymph but taken in the *Drop of Dew*, and it is a road which Marvell concisely maps towards the end of *Fleckno:*

> I, finding my self free,
> As one scap't strangely from Captivity,
> Have made the Chance be painted.

> *(167–69)*

The perversion of this occurs when the mind collapses distinctions between inside and outside; projecting its fantasies as realities, the expanding self tyrannizes nature, seduces or forces it to a monstrous hybrid which is neither art nor nature, mind nor world. *The Mower against Gardens* complains of "Luxurious Man" that his lustful curiosity led him to tamper directly with the physical world and reduce it to an extension of his vice. There is nothing wrong with being a gardener, but there is something wrong with luxurious man who can assert himself, like a gardener, only by direct action on external nature, who lacks the discipline to move inward, like a poet, and act on the second nature.

As Marvell phrases it in *Upon Appleton House*, luxurious man "unto Caves the Quarries drew, / And Forrests did to Pastures hew." He is bad enough as a gardener, worse as an architect who annihilates all that is made to "Marble Crust,"

> Who of his great Design in pain
> Did for a Model vault his Brain,
> Whose Columnes should so high be rais'd
> To arch the Brows that on them gaz'd.
>
> *(5–8)*

As the ellipsis suggests, he no sooner conceives his *disegno interno* than it appears before his eyes, and a moment later the projected pomps of his airy brain become his house and world:

> Why should of all things Man unrul'd
> Such unproportion'd dwellings build?
> The beasts are by their Denns exprest:
> And Birds contrive an equal Nest;
> The low roof'd Tortoises do dwell
> In cases fit of Tortoise-shell:
> No Creature loves an empty space;
> Their Bodies measure out their Place.
>
> But He, superfluously spread,
> Demands more room alive than dead.
> And in his hollow Palace goes
> Where Winds as he themselves may lose.
> What need of all this Marble Crust
> T'impark the wanton Mote of Dust,
> That thinks by Breadth the World t'unite
> Though the first Builders fail'd in Height?
>
> *(9–24)*

The whole problem is contained in that brilliant line, "The beasts are by their Denns exprest." The beast builds only for use—hiding and sleeping—not for beauty; like an Aristotelian envelope of place, his snug home expresses his shape, signifies the rudimentary nature of animal withdrawal and therefore virtually squeezes him into the open. The tortoise secretes only enough of itself to produce what for man's body would supply a coffin. We must realize that though these stanzas offer man a genuine model of constraint and humility, the tone is subtly contaminated by the voice of the Body. Animals are neither constrained nor humble; "Nature" does their work for them or impels them to secrete just enough shell, collect enough straw, or scoop out enough dirt for a bare fit. Were man to follow this model, he could save himself a good deal of trouble and at the same time lay claim to simple and primitive, stoic and unaspiring virtues. But this bucolic rationalization will scarcely do. If we did not remember what happened to Spenser's contented rustic, Melibee, when the robbers got hold of him (*Faerie Queene* VI.xi.18), Marvell reminds us later of the dangers of the "equal nest":

> Unhappy Birds! what does it boot
> To build below the Grasses Root;
> When Lowness is unsafe as Hight,
> And Chance o'retakes what scapeth spight?
> And now your Orphan Parents Call
> Sounds your untimely Funeral.
>
> *(409–14)*

Clearly if man is not to be ex-pressed from his den, he will need not only stronger walls but more room, and this room will have to extend further in as well as further out. He learns from the animals, for example, not by imitating them literally and physically but by converting the model to a mental figure, by reflecting on the differences and correcting the model as needed. That was no foxhole Fairfax built, and even if, as Don Cameron Allen remarks, it was relatively modest "by seventeenth-century aristocratic standards,"[56] it was elegant enough to impress an early eighteenth-century (perhaps middle-class) antiquarian.[57] The scale of the human house is determined by its relation to its owner's mind and soul, not his body:

[56] *Image and Meaning*, 116.
[57] Ralph Thoresby, whose diary entry for October 16, 1712, Margoliouth quotes, "saw the old house pulled down, and a stately new one erected by Thomas Lord Fairfax, the

> But all things are composed here
> Like Nature, orderly and near:
> In which we the Dimensions find
> Of that more sober Age and Mind,
> When larger sized Men did stoop
> To enter at a narrow loop;
> As practising, in doors so strait,
> To strain themselves through *Heavens Gate.*
>
> *(25–32)*

> Yet thus the laden House does sweat,
> And scarce indures the *Master* great:
> But where he comes the swelling Hall
> Stirs, and the *Square* grows *Spherical;*
> More by his *Magnitude* distrest,
> Then he is by its straitness prest:
> And too officiously it slights
> That in it self which him delights.
>
> *(49–56)*

The inner man measures out his place or "secretes" his shell, and it is in relation to the inner man that the shell is at once protective, functional, and expressive—to use Sir Henry Wotton's more Vitruvian terms, firm, commodious, and delightful (*Elements of Architecture,* 1624). But since this is so, cannot a poem also serve these needs, and does poetry not in fact fulfill them more completely? There is a shadow of double reference in lines 49–50 above, and more than a shadow in the sixth stanza:

> *Humility* alone designs
> Those short but admirable Lines,
> By which, ungirt and unconstrain'd,
> Things greater are in less contain'd.
> Let others vainly strive t'immure
> The *Circle* in the *Quadrature!*
> These *holy Mathematicks* can
> In ev'ry Figure equal Man.
>
> *(41–48)*

General, and now the most of that pulled down, and a much more convenient (though not quite so large an one) erected by Mr. Milner." *The Poems and Letters of Andrew Marvell,* 2 vols., ed. H. M. Margoliouth (Oxford: Oxford University Press, 1927), I, 231.

If house and garden express their owner, it takes a poet to say so and to articulate the inner connections. Only in Marvell's verbal world is the physical ambience created by Fairfax rendered fully transparent as a gesture of the human spirit.[58] The poem is a more inward *and* a more expressive medium than house and garden; the inner man *speaks* the poem, while house and garden bespeak their owner in a more metaphoric, less immediate way. Not until Marvell's mind has played over and penetrated the possibilities suggested by the house does every architectural figure equal Man:

> So Honour better Lowness bears,
> Then That unwonted Greatness wears.
> Height with a certain Grace does bend,
> But low Things clownishly ascend.
> And yet what needs there here Excuse,
> Where ev'ry Thing does answer Use?
> Where neatness nothing can condemn,
> Nor Pride invent what to contemn?
>
> A Stately *Frontispiece of Poor*
> Adorns without the open Door:
> Nor less the Rooms within commends
> Daily new *Furniture of Friends.*
> The House was built upon the Place
> Only as for a *Mark of Grace*;
> And for an *Inn* to entertain
> Its *Lord* a while, but not remain.
>
> *(57–72)*

By the final couplet, even *Inn* assumes its original prepositional force and the house is contained in the soul.

Upon Appleton House is surely one of the most remarkable poems of the seventeenth or any century, breathtaking in the virtuosity of its detail but much more impressive in the way Marvell sustains and modulates the lyric experience of withdrawal and return. This experience, not the house, is Marvell's real subject, and it is also the real model of all the themes on which he discourses. I think it is useful at this point to introduce a general description of this experience by Ortega y Gasset since his comparison of man to animals is similar to Marvell's and perhaps,

---

[58] Among Marvell's improvements is his rewriting of a Fairfax stanza at lines 71–72. See Margoliouth, *Poems*, I, 231, for the original.

from the zoological standpoint, equally out of date. Ortega remarks that the ape

> cannot take a stand within itself. Hence when things cease to threaten it or caress it; when they give it a holiday; . . . the poor animal has virtually to cease to exist, that is: it goes to sleep. Hence the enormous capacity for somnolence which the animal exhibits, the infrahuman torpor which primitive man continues in part. . . .
>
> . . . if man enjoys this privilege of temporarily freeing himself from things and the power to enter into himself and there rest, it is because by his effort, his toil, and his ideas he has succeeded in retrieving something from things, in transforming them, and creating around himself a margin of security which is always limited but always or almost always increasing. This specifically human creation is technics. Thanks to it, and in proportion to its progress, man can take his stand within himself. But conversely, man as a technician is able to modify his environment to his own convenience, because, seizing every moment of rest which things allow him, he uses it to enter into himself and form ideas about this world . . . , to form a plan of attack against his circumstances, in short, to create an inner world for himself. From this inner world he emerges and returns to the outer, but he returns as protagonist.[59]

This is a virtual description of what Marvell does during his poem and also a description of what he counsels Fairfax to do, although, as we shall see, the poet's retirement differs considerably from the lord's.

Appleton House provides Marvell with an external margin of security, but it becomes questionable whether the inner world he creates is one which could be shared or appreciated by Fairfax or any other upstanding man of affairs. The general's retirement is conceived merely as a temporary contraction of interest to the more manageable and orderly, the more exemplary, compass of his domestic microcosm. But Marvell's retirement turns into what can only be called imaginary *implosion*. He expands inwardly as he moves further away from the house—through garden, meadow, and wood. With the ocean and forest of his mind he creates far other worlds, perspectives in perspectives. His imagination does for him what "Multiplying Glasses" were doing at about the same time for Robert Hooke:

> By this means the Heavens are open'd, and a vast number of new Stars, and new Motions, and new Productions appear in them, to which all the antient

---

[59] "The Self and the Other," trans. Willard Trask, in *The Dehumanization of Art* (Garden City: Doubleday, 1956), 168–69.

Astronomers were utterly Strangers. By this the Earth it self, which lyes so neer us, under our feet, shews quite a new thing to us, and in every little particle of its matter, we now behold almost as great a variety of Creatures, as we were able before to reckon up in the whole Universe it self.[60]

But Marvell's experiments are less innocent and not marked by the scientific ideal of "objectivity." His *indecus* behavior in the forest mocks the very order—sober, constrained, and neat—which protects him from the world. By the time he has assumed the role of *"easie Philosopher"* (561) conversing with birds, his retreat is scarcely motivated by concern "for some universal good" (741). He sees himself as a grotesque lord of misrule: "Under this *antick Cope* I move / Like some great *Prelate of the Grove"* (591–92), a primitive and comical celebrant to and through whom Nature unmediated speaks. His special immunity—that of priest, fool, poet, or madman—gives him licence to war on the World, and one feels that Marvell, evoking this particular mood, would not exclude his equestrian lord and beautiful pupil from the World:

> How safe, methinks, and strong, behind
> These Trees have I incamp'd my Mind;
> Where Beauty, aiming at the Heart,
> Bends in some Tree its useless Dart;
> And where the World no certain Shot
> Can make, or me it toucheth not.
> But I on it securely play,
> And gaul its Horsemen all the Day.
>
> *(601–8)*

Such recklessness would seem in fact the point of the joke, the climax of the imaginative orgy in which a moment later the poet offers himself as a willing prisoner or sacrifice to the woods, a sylvan Christ shading off into Bacchus and Merlin.

Having thus "privately" let go, he can move back, refreshed, toward society, and he does this by imagining another person, one who stands for the very order he has just upset—Miss Maria, the embodiment of rules, external constraint, domestic and social decorum. In effect his mind constrains itself by projecting the image of the censor; therefore Maria is clearly a pattern or Idea, as Allen has acutely observed.[61] The mind's holiday is over and the orderly pattern, temporarily denied and

---

[60] Preface to *Micrographia* (London, 1665), fol. a2v.
[61] *Image and Meaning*, 148–53.

mocked, appears more sympathetic after the poet's anarchic release. In her character and appearance, in her relations to Fairfax and to the poet, Maria embodies all the attachments by which Marvell is bound to his fellow men, and she embodies them as something fresh and new, something now acceptable and even attractive. Maria turns the poet's wild nature into an aristocratic ménage, and her image is thus anticipated by two stanzas which indicate how the poetic orgy has refreshed him and prepared him to face the world:

> For now the Waves are fal'n and dry'd,
> And now the Meadows fresher dy'd;
> Whose Grass, with moister colour dasht,
> Seems, as green Silks but newly washt.
> No *Serpent* new nor *Crocodile*
> Remains behind our little *Nile;*
> Unless it self you will mistake,
> Among these Meads the only Snake.
>
> See in what wanton harmless folds
> It ev'ry where the Meadow holds;
> And its yet muddy back doth lick,
> Till as a *Chrystal Mirrour* slick;
> Where all things gaze themselves, and doubt
> If they be in it or without.
> And for his shade which therein shines,
> *Narcissus* like, the *Sun* too pines.
>
> *(625–40)*

Like the seventh and eighth stanzas of *The Garden*, the last four lines characterize the poet's previous behavior in an epitome and thus remove it to a distance. His exotic world fades, the cosmos shrinks to the familiar local scene, his orgy has not been a new Fall but a playful swim in the mind's ocean, and he can now revest himself with social thoughts. The final stanza of solitude may faintly suggest that he is turning in mystic fashion into the landscape, but it also presents us with the most familiar and local of images:

> Oh what a Pleasure 'tis to hedge
> My Temples here with heavy sedge;
> Abandoning my lazy Side,
> Stretcht as a Bank unto the Tide;
> Or to suspend my sliding Foot
> On the Osiers undermined Root,

                    And in its Branches tough to Hang,
                    While at my Lines the Fishes twang!
                    (641–48)

Both the pose and the implied "unity with nature" convey the new sense
of ease and relaxation. Communion with the depths is at once expressed
and attenuated in the amused figure of the final line. Nobody, the tone
implies, nobody would suggest what cosmic mayhem has been let loose
inside the mind of this lazy angler—unless, unlike Miss Maria, he had
just read the previous *Lines*. Nobody, that is, except Sir Izaak Walton,
who knew that angling was like poetry, that it was at once contemplative
and active as well as "honest, ingenuous, quiet and harmless," that it was
not only an escape from "the press of people and business and the cares
of the world" but also a source of revelation:

> The great Naturalist Pliny says, "That nature's great and wonderful power is
> more demonstrated in the sea than on the land" . . . doubtless this made the
> Prophet David say, "They that occupy themselves in deep waters, see the
> wonderful works of God"; indeed such wonders and pleasures too as the land
> affords not.[62]

But there is a time for all things, especially since the different sides of
the mind see the world in different ways, so that the right side might
disapprove of what the left side was doing:

                    But now away my Hooks, my Quills,
                    And Angles, idle Utensils.
                    The *young Maria* walks to night:
                    Hide trifling Youth thy Pleasures slight.
                    'Twere shame that such judicious Eyes
                    Should with such Toyes a Man surprize;
                    She that already is the *Law*
                    Of all her *Sex*, her *Ages Aw*.

                    See how loose Nature, in respect
                    To her, it self doth recollect.
                    (649–58)

The different sides of the mind to which Marvell gives play during
the poem are concisely, if perplexingly, focused in the final three stan-

<hr>

[62] *The Compleat Angler* (London, 1960), 37–40, 44, 48. Marvell's reference to hooks
and *quills* (floats, plectrums, pens) at line 649 further encourages the fishing/poetry/
music collocation suggested by the fish-twanged lines of 648.

zas. After his praise of Maria he turns and apostrophizes the estate, exhorting it to follow her example and be the best in its class:

> For you *Thessalian Tempe's Seat*
> Shall now be scorn'd as obsolete;
> *Aranjuez,* as less, disdain'd;
> The *Bel-Retiro* as constrain'd;
> But name not the *Idalian Grove,*
> For 'twas the Seat of wanton Love;
> Much less the Dead's *Elysian Fields,*
> Yet nor to them your Beauty yields.
>
> 'Tis not, what once it was, the *World;*
> But a rude heap together hurl'd;
> All negligently overthrown,
> Gulfes, Deserts, Precipices, Stone.
> Your lesser *World* contains the same.
> But in more decent Order tame;
> *You Heaven's Center, Nature's Lap.*
> *And Paradice's only Map.*
>
> But now the *Salmon-Fishers* moist
> Their *Leathern Boats* begin to hoist;
> And, like *Antipodes* in Shoes,
> Have shod their *Heads* in their *Canoos.*
> How *Tortoise like,* but not so slow,
> These rational *Amphibii* go?
> Let's in: for the dark *Hemisphere*
> Does now like one of them appear.
>
> *(753–76)*

Antipodes has two different meanings which are actualized in the poem: (1) the same form but upside down, as when one sees one's reflection in the surface of the water; here, it may be observed, the surface conceals the depths in functioning as a mirror; (2) opposite in form, as when one diving through that watery mirror with its "orderly and near" images comes on a strange undersea wilderness—"such wonders and pleasures too as the land affords not," or, as William Empson, who might have been paraphrasing Walton, put it, "all land-beasts have their sea-beasts, but the sea also has the kraken; in the depths as well as the transcendence of the mind are things stranger than all the kinds of the world." [63] As a rational amphibium, man lives both in the "land" which surrounds him

---

[63] *Some Versions of Pastoral,* 126.

and in "the Mind that Ocean" which he contains; as a *rational* amphibium, he lives a double life within the mind, oscillating between extremes of extravagance and constraint, wilderness and neatness, nature and art, fantasy and science, contemplation and action, poetry and politics, passionate surrender and rational control, delicious solitude and social demand, self-expansion and self-limitation, love of anarchy and love of law.

These extremes are problematically related by the ambiguous syntax connecting lines 761 and 762: (1) "The world is no longer the rude heap it once was"; (2) "The world is no longer what it once was; now it is a rude heap and the paradisaic order of a Former Age is all negligently overthrown." The previous stanza, with its suggestion that the latest is the best, would opt for Baconian optimism, while the political chaos of Marvell's time would encourage chiliastic pessimism. Does civilization gradually improve nature and move through myth and history toward an apex in Appleton House, and is Appleton House a microcosm of a developed culture which is the daughter of time? Or is Appleton House a small and precious exception to the work of *tempus edax*, an oasis in the Modern Wilderness? The paradox is only apparent, for each is a familiar extreme, a one-sided response of the mind, and the solution lies in the two meanings of *contains:* in its "more decent Order tame" the lesser world possesses and controls the disordered greater world.

As an escape from contemporary chaos, the lesser world of Appleton House chastens down the wilderness, brings time to a standstill ("*Admiring Nature* does benum" 672)[64] and revives the disciplined ideal of an older, purer age when Nature mirrored Reason. One thinks of Roman, especially Virgilian, appeals to the ancient Italian *frugalitas*, not only because of the general tone and the specific reference to Romulus and "his Bee-like Cell" (40) but also because of a distinct echo of *Aeneid* VIII. 362 in which Evander describes how Hercules stooped to enter his humble palace:

> haec, inquit, limina victor
> Alcides subiit, haec illum regia cepit.
> aude, hospes, contemnere opes, et te quoque dignum
> finge deo, rebusque veni non asper egenis.
> dixit et angusti subter fastigia tecti
> ingentem Aenean duxit . . .

---

[64] See also the poet's express motive at lines 81–82: "While with slow Eyes we these survey, / And on each pleasant footstep stay." The first two stanzas of *Musicks Empire* support this reading.

> that more sober Age and Mind,
> When larger sized Men did stoop
> To enter at a narrow loop . . .
>
> Things greater are in less contain'd.
>
> Yet thus the laden House does sweat,
> And scarce indures the *Master* great.[65]

Restraint was natural to uncorrupted man, who did not therefore require great space or *opes;* recognizing his own gulfs, his stony and desert places, he bound them in. It was through slackening that the lesser world spread superfluously into the greater, drew the quarries to caves, and expressed its unruled pride in rude heaps of marble crust. In Marvell's hands this arcadian commonplace, however stoic, fits easily with the Mower's Epicurean argument. For example:

> Nature here hath been so free
> As if she said leave this to me.
> Art would more neatly have defac'd
> What she had laid so sweetly wast;
> In fragrant Gardens, shaddy woods,
> Deep Meadows, and transparent Floods.
>
> *(75–80)*

It is in this context that *Antipodes* means mirror-image: nature mirrors reason, earth mirrors heaven, the estate gratefully gives back to Maria "that wondrous Beauty" which "first she on them spent" (689–702).

If, then, the estate is viewed as a restoration of the Former Age, the poetic perspective which so views it may be an even more complete withdrawal from contemporary darkness. Appleton House is at most a garden wilderness, like that of the complaining nymph. The poem describing it describes a Reason which has already been externalized as Nature, and this mirroring surface screens out the other antipodes which lie "behind" or "beneath" it. Of the three scenes which Marvell stages in the meadow (385–417, 418–40, 441–64), the first two conclude the "bloody" lessons of history with funeral images, but the third wipes these out: it "brings / A new and empty Face of things" (441–42), makes a passing reference to the Levellers, and shifts to the more distant perspectives of art and science; the immediate problems are dissolved in

---

[65] Allen has discussed the Virgilian atmosphere and echoes, *Image and Meaning*, 144–46 and 149–53. The figure is also a Christian commonplace.

microscopic and telescopic vistas; here disorder is flealike and order cosmic. The green-world attitude is implicit in the fact that history, insofar as it is admitted, is negative.

This reading of lines 761–62 is counterbalanced by the other: "The world is no longer the rude heap it once was." Civilization is ideally a gradual refinement of matter by mind and flesh by spirit; as human organization increases, it should therefore ideally contract into forms which are less extensive, more complex and intricately structured, capable of giving play to a richer and broader variety of experience within a smaller or finer expressive compass. But this means that a microcosm is more than merely a miniature of whatever macrocosm it reflects. Its very compression and inwardness, the degree to which it transforms what it reflects into the higher order of spirit or mind or psyche, makes it by definition superior to the macrocosm. Here "Gulfes, Deserts, Precipices, Stone" would seem to suggest primitive and barbaric nature rather than moral chaos;[66] the suggestions of physical extension and force are more literal in such a context, and we are clearly in the presence of what will later be called the sublime; the relation of lesser to greater world is not so much that of domestic order to political chaos, or of individual to state, but that of civilized man to unimproved nature. The cataclysmic and irrational energies of raw nature are contained as vestiges in the mind; they are the underwater antipodes of that reason which is reflected by nature's cultivated surfaces, of that restraining art through which domestic and social orders are stabilized. When these titanic energies erupt, when they are solicited or succumbed to, they produce esthetic and ethical *indecencies*; lust and pride with their various weapons and structures, war and violence, civil and religious cataclysm, division in friendship, family, sect, and state.

The obvious way to contain these energies is to recognize them for what they are and discharge them in play. Rather than allow eccentric, antisocial, anarchic, Dionysiac, etc., impulses to explode in martial or sexual excess, in socio-political or autoerotic irresponsibility, Marvell practices poetic implosion. As we have seen, he does not abandon himself to the wild and primitive antipodes of reason; he conjures them up, not as immediate orgy or fantasy but as phases of a formal poetic meditation. Where else but in a poem can the mind creatively let go, annihilate all that's made in what William James has called "the exuberant excess," the "quest for the superfluous," which distinguishes man from brutes? "Prune down his extravagance," James said, "sober him, and you undo

---

[66] The word *rude* ("rude heap") seems here to be used with the same double meaning as in *The Garden* ("Society is all but rude").

him." [67] For Marvell, however, man must return to sobriety and to the limits imposed by his own reason, the limits symbolized in *Appleton House* by the patron and his family. One prunes down extravagance homeopathically, by being extravagant, and one justifies the restraint and decency of reason by the same technique. In this the estate and the poem are differently inflected, the former toward order, the latter toward energy, and they thus serve the two sides of the mind in a dialectical manner. Like Fairfax's flowery fort, the precipices and gulfs of the estate are scaled down; they are physically contracted to the dimension of toy models, but not yet expanded by imagination. Using these physical models as starting points, Marvell projects his own vaster and less decent allusions to chaos:

> And now to the Abbyss I pass
> Of that unfathomable Grass,
> Where Men like Grashoppers appear,
> But Grashoppers are Gyants there:
> They, in there squeking Laugh, contemn
> Us as we walk more low than them:
> And, from the Precipices tall
> Of the green spir's, to us do call.
>
> To see Men through this Meadow Dive,
> We wonder how they rise alive.
>
> *(369–78)*

The progress of implosion in the poem is straightforward: it moves from world to self, from similes based in observation of landscape to metaphors expressing participation, from Apollonian distance to Dionysiac involvement. The distance, however, is sustained in relation to the greater world and its warfare, while the involvement is in the unreal world of the poet's own making. The most sinister echoes occur in the first meadow scene, as noted above, when Marvell converts the tawny mowers to Israelites and then, by implication, to soldiers who massacre the grass and murder defenseless birds. [68] Because the bird is imme-

---

[67] James's statements are cited by Edgar Wind in an essay relevant to this discussion, "Every Artist Needs a Hard-boiled Patron," *Harper's Magazine* 228, no. 1366 (March 1964): 108.

[68] The echoes are attenuated by a brilliant and characteristic flash of nonsense: the "bloody Thestylis" is allowed to overhear Marvell's analogy of mowers to Israelites and is aggrieved; she discharges her choler on an available bird, and the indefinite pronoun suggests that her prey is a poor scapegoat for Marvell: "on another quick She lights, / And cryes, he call'd us *Israelites*" (405–8).

diately made an emblem—"Lowness is unsafe as Hight"—the transition to the second meadow scene suggests an actual image of the effects of the Civil War:

> Or sooner hatch or higher build:
> The Mower now commands the Field;
> In whose new Traverse seemeth wrought
> A Camp of Battail newly fought:
> Where, as the Meads with Hay, the Plain
> Lyes quilted ore with Bodies slain:
> The Women that with forks it fling,
> Do represent the Pillaging.
>
> *(417–24)*

For a moment we feel the extraordinary pressures of the time; the naturally peaceful countryside becomes a scene of carnage. But only for a moment: Marvell turns the image to a happy rural conclusion, separates the heroic from the rustic and, even while keeping the reminders of war, removes them to a distance:

> And now the careless Victors play,
> Dancing the Triumphs of the Hay;
> Where every Mowers wholesome Heat
> Smells like an *Alexanders sweat*.
> Their Females fragrant as the Mead
> Which they in *Fairy Circles* tread:
> When at their Dances End they kiss,
> Their new-made Hay not sweeter is.
>
> When after this 'tis pil'd in Cocks,
> Like a calm Sea it shews the Rocks:
> We wondring in the River near
> How Boats among them safely steer.
> Or, like the *Desert Memphis Sand*,
> Short *Pyramids* of Hay do stand.
> And such the *Roman Camps* do rise
> In Hills for Soldiers Obsequies.
>
> *(425–40)*

The playfulness is reasserted because the two sides of the analogies spring apart; the pastoral scene is felt as a contrast to the ancient wonders and horrors of the great world. The powerful and dynamic ellipsis of the final couplet, together with the local tumuli to which it alludes, points toward the cynic's view of history: "Imperious Caesar, dead and

turned to clay, / Might stop a hole to keep the wind away." The contrast
suggests how much of the great world the lesser world of Appleton
House excludes. The lessons of history are scarcely evident in that time-
less bucolic retreat until the poet warily projects them there; the landscape knows only the recurrent rhythms, the slow and certain English
seasons, of an order in which "nature" and "society" are harmoniously
fused. In so secure a retreat, the mind may safely make chaos come again
without excessive risk. The only risk derives from those "creative obstacles" inherent in the very forms which offer the margin of security:
the patrons and their vitrified nature, the poet's prudence and his verse.

From this oblique meditation on man as the destroyer of nature and
man, Marvell withdraws in thought to a scene more innocent, creative
and artificial:

> A levell'd space, as smooth and plain,
> As Clothes for *Lilly* strecht to stain.
> The World when first created sure
> Was such a Table rase and pure.
> Or rather such is the *Toril*
> Ere the Bulls enter at Madril.
>
> *(442–48)*

Though man's bloodlust is chastened to game and art in the "more decent
Order tame" of the bullring, it is still present, and I think the modu-
lation through the Levellers (449–50) to the villagers who "in common
chase / Their Cattle, which it closer rase" (451–52) is meant to refer
this sophisticated form of violence to the utopian or communistic aims of
the Levellers. This violence, as Marvell knew, would reduce us all to
cattle—a "Universal Heard"—and the strategy he himself immediately
adopts is precisely the contrary: where utopians would try to realize their
dreams by imposing them on the world around them, Marvell withdraws still further within himself. He appeals to the common topos of
the flood to create an *imaginary* destruction of the existing order
(465–80), after which he creates his own new world, his own magical
and wish-fulfilling utopia:

> But I, retiring from the Flood,
> Take Sanctuary in the Wood;
> And, while it lasts, my self imbark
> In this yet green, yet growing Ark.
>
> *(481–84)*

He plays not only Noah but Adam and Eve, running away from trouble *in medio ligni paradisi*, which meant, as St. Augustine pointed out, retiring *ad seipsos*,[69] i.e., to a green thought in a green shade within the *hyle* of imagination.

Here life's problems are diminished to the problems of birds and trees, while history is blurred by being viewed in a cosmic perspective, as when the trees momentarily assume genealogical significance:

> On one hand *Fairfax*, th' other *Veres:*
> Of whom though many fell in War,
> Yet more to Heaven shooting are:
> And, as they Natures Cradle deckt,
> Will in green Age her Hearse expect.
>
> *(491–95)*

Here chaos is easily and effortlessly transformed to architecture, not by drawing quarries to caves but by a mere focus of the magic eyebeam:

> Dark all without it knits; within
> It opens passable and thin;
> And in as loose an order grows,
> As the *Corinthean Porticoes*.
>
> *(505–8)*

Here too lowness is as safe as height, the nightingale has Orphean influence rather than an "Orphan Parents Call," her prophetic voice is heeded by Elders, as by the plant previously used to symbolize the prickling leaf of Conscience, "which shrinks at ev'ry touch" and is too rare on earth (355–58):

> The *Nightingale* does here make choice
> To sing the Tryals of her Voice.
> Low Shrubs she sits in, and adorns
> With Musick high the squatted Thorns.
> But highest Oakes stoop down to hear,
> And listening Elders prick the Ear.
> The Thorn, lest it should hurt her, draws
> Within the Skin its shrunken claws.
>
> *(513–20)*

---

[69] *De Genesi Contra Manichaeos*, Patrologia Latina, XXIV, 208.

Only in a delightfully incredible world where plants replace men is such harmony possible.[70] Here finally the high seriousness of original sin is thrown away on some insights into the local ecology of woodpeckers:[71]

> the Tree . . . fed
> A *Traitor-worm*, within it bred.
> As first our *Flesh* corrupt within
> Tempts impotent and bashful *Sin*.
> And yet that *Worm* triumphs not long,
> But serves to feed the *Hewels young*.
> While the Oake seems to fall content,
> Viewing the Treason's Punishment.
>
> *(553–60)*

In this section the symbolic echoes, such as the allusion to the fall of the royal oak, are brilliantly in evidence, but again in a disjunctive manner characteristic of green-world withdrawal: by concentrating on the natural vehicle, shifting away from the human tenor, the poet turns his world into an animated cartoon. What is more logical than that he himself, in the next phase of retreat, should become the arm-flapping conductor of his own Silly Symphony?

> Thus I, *easie Philosopher*,
> Among the *Birds* and *Trees* confer:
> And little now to make me, wants
> Or of the *Fowles*, or of the *Plants*.
> Give me but Wings as they, and I
> Streight floting on the Air shall fly:

---

[70] Allen's description of this phase (*Image and Meaning*, 143–44) illuminates Marvell's green-world strategy. For example: "First, he is shown the lovelorn nightingale, then the married doves, then the 'thrastles' begetting a family, and, finally, the heron sending its mature offspring into the world. The nightingale answers his questions about the profession of poetry; she sits low, but her singing is harkened to by noble oaks and venerable elders." The nightingale stanza, if taken as political allegory, might suggest a utopian harmony between royalist-Scottish and liberal ("Low Shrubs," "squatted Thorns") factions.

[71] Allen again makes all the important points in his brief iconographic survey of the woodpecker (144–46), though he perhaps fails to see Marvell's general drift: the analogy of the poet to Aeneas focuses on *difference* rather than similarity, i.e., on the ease and inconsequence of the present "Virgilian" quest. This is parody rather than straight allusion. Marvell's *pious* does not innocently symbolize *Picus* or the human woodcutters and rangers; he replaces them so that their more considerable functions are here reduced to playful hyperboles describing a bird.

Or turn me but, and you shall see
I was but an inverted Tree.

Already I begin to call
In their most learned Original:
And where I Language want, my Signs
The Bird upon the Bough divines.

(561–72)

In the next stanza, he attains, predictably enough, to historical omni-
science, though the object of his knowledge is a cabbala of his own
devising:

Out of these scatterer'd *Sibyls* Leaves
Strange *Prophecies* my Phancy weaves:
And in one History consumes,
Like *Mexique Paintings*, all the *Plumes*.
What *Rome, Greece, Palestine*, ere said
I in this light *Mosaik* read.
Thrice happy he who, not mistook,
Hath read in *Nature's mystick Book*.

(576–84)[72]

Total control of this sort means externalizing one's wishes not only as
Nature's mystic book but also as "Chance": "see how Chance's better
Wit / Could with a Mask my studies hit!" (585–86). Having thus
completed the work of creation and supplied his own apocalypse, the
poet reclines into a well-deserved sabbath:

Then, languishing with ease, I toss
On Pallets swoln of Velvet Moss;
While the Wind, cooling through the Boughs,
Flatters with Air my panting Brows.
Thanks for my Rest ye *Mossy Banks*,
And unto you *cool Zephyr's* Thanks,
Who, as my Hair, my Thoughts too shed,
And winnow from the Chaff my Head.

How safe, methinks, and strong, behind
These Trees have I incamp'd my Mind.

(593–602)

---

[72] Allen (146) discusses the pun on "Light *Mosaick*" but ignores the most immediate
sense, "easy," "not serious." This is a more painless way to "learn history" than submit-

Since the above passages have as their object the poet in his sylvan activities, I think it worthwhile to repeat that it is not *there* in the woods but *now* in the course of poetic utterance that Marvell lets go. The descriptive references are general rather than singular: "I confer among the *birds* and *trees*," "I toss on *pallets*," "I gaul the world's horsemen *all the day*." The focus of concrete experience is on the poet *as he imagines* these generalized situations; it is therefore his activity of imagining, as manifested in the play of his rhetoric, analogies, and syntax, which constitutes the return to chaos. His own violence discharges itself as wit; his own pleasure principle, with its archaic inheritance, pursues its leveling and utopian, its destructive and creative, tendencies in the controlled form of symbolic play. Into the more "private" and subjective mode of the lyric poem Marvell brings a dominantly theatrical institution, the Vice, on whose saturnalian functions C. L. Barber's study of Shakespeare has thrown much light—as in the following statements, which might have been made with Marvell's reveler in mind:

> Clowning could provide both release for impulses which run counter to decency and decorum, and the clarification about limits which comes from going beyond the limit. . . .
>
> . . . the energy normally occupied in maintaining inhibition is freed for celebration. . . .
>
> . . . the clown or Vice . . . was a recognised anarchist who made aberration obvious by carrying release to absurd extremes.[73]

Barber's comments on the double plot, inspired by Empson, also illuminate the poem, since Marvell's implosion is largely a parody of what those in social, political, and intellectual authority do—or try to do—in the great world of affairs. Shakespeare uses clowns in a traditional way,

> to present a burlesque version of actions performed seriously by their betters. . . . In the early plays, the clown is usually represented as oblivious of what his burlesque implies. When he becomes the court fool, however, he can use his folly as a stalking horse, and his wit can express directly the function of his role as a dramatized commentary on the rest of the action.[74]

---

ting to the whole classical and biblical inheritance. Also, like a Mexican painting, it is more innocent and brilliant, a *tour de force* from the sinless new world. Here the birdlike poet sits on his branch and weaves the various light of fantasy in his plumes.
[73] *Shakespeare's Festive Comedy* (Cleveland: World, 1963), 5, 7, 13.
[74] Ibid., 12–13.

Marvell, of course, is the court fool playing the naïf. Having clarified the limits by going beyond them, he returns, as I have already suggested, and willingly accepts the rule-making and inhibiting impulses of the mind. These are projected in the pleasant symbol of Mary Fairfax, "the *Law* / Of all her *Sex*, her *Ages Aw*." Similarly the Nature surrounding Maria is made visually to objectify the present poetic state of mind: "See how loose Nature, in respect / To her, it self doth recollect." The poet recollects himself and his loose thoughts by an act of symbolic compression embodied in the *streightness* of the image: Maria is an epitome of the domestic order around her, which is in turn an epitome of the social and natural order around it, etc.[75] If nature was previously a fluid imaginative medium, an ocean of mind, it is now contracted and solidified to the familiar surfaces of Fairfacian decorum. It is a nature which aspires to the condition of household art so as both to mirror and to protect its fair paradigm. Thus "the gellying Stream compacts below, / If it might fix her shadow so," fishes hang stupidly like "*Flies* in *Chrystal* overt'ane" (675–78), by Maria's flames "in *Heaven* try'd, / *Nature* is wholly *vitrifi'd*" (687–88). Furthermore,

> 'Tis *She* that to these Gardens gave
> That wondrous Beauty which they have;
> *She* streightness on the Woods bestows;
> To *Her* the Meadow sweetness owes;
> Nothing could make the River be
> So Chrystal-pure but only *She*;
> *She* yet more Pure, Sweet, Streight, and Fair,
> Then Gardens, Woods, Meads, Rivers are.
>
> Therefore what first *She* on them spent,
> They gratefully again present.
> The Meadow Carpets where to tread;
> The Garden Flow'rs to Crown *Her* Head;
> And for a Glass the limpid Brook,
> Where *She* may all *her* Beautyes look;
> But, since *She* would not have them seen,
> The Wood about *her* draws a Skreen.
>
> *(689–704)*

[75] Maria is not visualized as present; Marvell meditates on her general presence and effect, but she certainly does not "approach" (Summers, Introduction to *Marvell*, Laurel Poetry Series, 23). This is important when we try to keep our gaze on the *now* as the dramatic focus.

This gradual re-collecting and voluntary straitening is made possible only by utilizing the mind's expanding inward spaces. The poem offers itself as a model or exemplum of this essential human activity. Showing how the domestic order may provide a screen when the social order fails, it doubly glorifies the house. It provides both the answer and the explanation to the question asked in the third stanza:

> What need of all this Marble Crust
> T'impark the wanton Mote of Dust,
> That thinks by Breadth the World t'unite
> Though the first Builders fail'd in Height?

The answer is inherent in the concluding image of the salmon-fishers shod in their canoes: to say that "the dark *Hemisphere* / Does now like one of them appear" is simultaneously to contract the hemisphere and expand the tortoise-like fishermen. The object is not only a boat sustaining them above the flood while they fish in the depths; it is also a shoe, a hat, a head, a tortoise-like house, a hemisphere—in short, an *antick cope*. Man's house, his *oikos*, can ultimately be nothing smaller than the universe he creates. A world view or world order is the only magnitude sufficient to contain the wanton mote of dust; it is as natural to man to create, clothe himself in, and inhabit a cosmos as it is for a turtle to secrete a shell, and in fact the image suggests that this alone can preserve man on the flood or chaos of his historico-natural environment. Such a *cope*, embracing the universe, occupies very little space. But man's first tendency—the primitive response of the child or of archaic civilization—is always a step in the wrong direction, an attempt to express this impulse in sensuous and extended forms, or to misconstrue the interior constitutive functions of mind as the external functions of nature. The proper response is demonstrated in *Appleton House*, where the poet's wanton wit spans the poles, makes contact with the antipodes, connects the world of fleas and the world of stars, recovers the primal wilderness and the archaic mind, and recognizes through all this business at once the reality of the world-making process and the fictive absurdity of the products.

One might expect, from this interpretation, to find the poem resolving its problems in clear-cut fashion, to find the poet emerging at the end and fulfilling the rhythm of withdrawal and return. This is indeed the dominant shape of the poetic experience, yet the details make it more tenuous and complicate the movement with hesitations. For example, consider the final couplet: the sense of the great world as a dark hemisphere may well have been attenuated by the work of the poem until that hemisphere is reduced to the more reassuring silhouette of a salmon-fisher. But on the other hand, the lines may be read this way: "The salmon-fishers appear now, and so does the dark hemisphere. Therefore let's in." "Let's in" is a conventional way to conclude eclogues, and it frequently signifies a new withdrawal after the temporary and often limited resolution achieved within the eclogue. Marvell's image is brilliantly vague and menacing, and his gesture of withdrawal seems more urgent because it includes *us*. It is a gesture which acknowledges the limits of control through the inner discipline of poetry, a discipline which may sustain the self but cannot be expected to renovate the world. The gesture signifies the poet's return from delicious solitude because it implies a sense of the common cause and the common danger—an awareness of human frailty, of the consequent need for human solidarity and thus for political as well as poetical action. Marvell is a little like Prospero who, having gradually surrendered his magic power and prepared to leave his magic island, comes forward to find himself "in this bare island"—this bare platform in England, England as a bare stage—and asks to be released; to be "sent to Naples" is to move back to the redeemed image of actuality in the second world where Prospero has had good effect, and this seems preferable to being trapped in the actuality of the first world, no wonder-working Duke of Milan. Here, this side of the second world where fictions vanish, the poet, like the actor and playwright, is no longer a god but a man among men. He relies on their good will, assistance, and esteem; his pleasure and security are mutually bound up with theirs. Yet he comes forward guardedly and hesitantly—long enough to register that the darkness, though moral and political, looms and gathers inevitably as evening. With this, he seems on the verge of retiring once again.

The drift of the ambiguous syntax of this couplet is very much like that of lines 761–62, "'Tis not, what once it was, the *World* . . ." In both cases the poet seems to waver between feeling better and feeling worse; to the extent that his thoughts about Appleton House have made the outside world seem darker and ruder by comparison, he invokes the house even more insistently: "*You Heaven's Center, Nature's Lap. / And Paradice's only Map.*" More interesting is the projection of this vacillation, or perhaps we should call it vibrational equilibrium, into the structure of the poem. Marvell's own withdrawal, occupying the center of the poem, is flanked on the one side by the retirement of the nuns and of Fairfax, on the other by that of Maria. Each is more satisfactory than the one it precedes, and the example of Maria obviously provides a healthy contrast to that of the nuns. Yet the cases of both Fairfax and Maria are affected by the poet's ambivalent feelings, and Marvell's treatment of each figure reveals the pressure of his feelings.

When General Fairfax, resigning his command, withdraws to his manor, "His warlike Studies could not cease," and therefore he "laid . . . Gardens out in sport / In the just Figure of a Fort." The poet immediately converts this miniature to a model of a different kind—"with five Bastions it did fence, / As aiming one for ev'ry Sense" (284–88)—but then goes on to develop the lord's martial conceit in four stanzas of recreative fancy, in a delighted tone which suggests that although he takes his cue from his patron, he is less interested in playing war than in the poetic play of analogies. The brief glance at the castle of the body connects Fairfax's miniature with that fortress which the nuns had yielded to Created Pleasure, and Marvell subsequently relates it to the general's principled rejection of power:

> he preferr'd to the *Cinque Ports*
> These five imaginary Forts:
> And, in those half-dry Trenches, spann'd
> Pow'r which the Ocean might command.
>
> For he did, with his utmost Skill,
> *Ambition* weed, but *Conscience* till.
> *Conscience*, that Heaven-nursed Plant,
> Which most our Earthly Gardens want.
> A prickling leaf it bears, and such
> As that which shrinks at ev'ry touch;
> But Flowers eternal, and divine,
> That in the Crowns of Saints do shine.
>
> *(349–60)*

The moral is that external political chaos is caused by defective cultivation of the world within; there are too few virtuous men in public life and the reformer's first job must be to retire and set his own house in order. In drawing this moral and making Fairfax a model of proper reform activity, Marvell exemplifies his own relation to the general: the poet depends on his patron not only for his margin of security but also for the subject matter which he then develops according to his own inclination; in return, he carries the patron's model-making tendencies much farther, converting house, garden, and owner to figures of thought.

But while praise for Fairfax is the dominant note, the stanzas preceding the above lines (349–60) suggest the presence of another feeling. In elaborating on his patron's toy fort, Marvell describes soldierly bees and

flowers safe in a world of "known Allies" and discharging the functions
of a guard of honor—colors, salute, parade (289–312). There is little
chance of war in the garden. Secured by the vigilance and power of cosmic ministers, the sentinel bee has an easy time of it:

> But when the vigilant *Patroul*
> Of Stars walks round about the *Pole,*
> Their Leaves, that to the stalks are curl'd,
> Seem to their Staves the *Ensigns* furl'd.
> Then in some Flow'rs beloved Hut
> Each Bee as Sentinel is shut;
> And sleeps so too: but, if once stir'd,
> She runs you through, or askes *the Word.*
>
> *(313–20)*

It is only between stars and bees, in the intermediate world of men, that
war is real. Marvell's flight of fancy seems to bring on a genuinely
rueful moment, a brief surrender to the longing for escape. The miniature paradise is pressed into the service of this wish, and from such a
perspective Fairfax's retirement may be felt as premature:

> Oh Thou, that dear and happy Isle
> The Garden of the World ere while,
> Thou *Paradise* of four Seas,
> Which *Heaven* planted us to please,
> But, to exclude the World, did guard
> With watry if not flaming Sword;
> What luckless Apple did we tast,
> To make us Mortal, and The Wast?
>
> Unhappy! shall we never more
> That sweet *Militia* restore,
> When Gardens only had their Towrs,
> And all the Garrisons were Flowrs,
> When Roses only Arms might bear,
> And Men did rosie Garlands wear?
> Tulips, in several Colours barr'd,
> Were then the *Switzers* of our *Guard.*
>
> The *Gardiner* had the *Souldiers* place,
> And his more gentle Forts did trace.
> The Nursery of all things green
> Was then the only *Magazeen.*
> The *Winter Quarters* were the Stoves,
> Where he the tender Plants removes.

> But War all this doth overgrow:
> We Ord'nance Plant and Powder sow.
>
> And yet there walks one on the Sod
> Who, had it pleased him and *God*,
> Might once have made our Gardens spring
> Fresh as his own and flourishing.
> But he preferr'd to the *Cinque Ports*
> These five imaginary Forts.
>
> *(321–50)*

One feels a bare hint of censure: perhaps instead of peaceably playing war in his garden, Fairfax should have remained in public life and militantly resisted further Parliamentarian aggression; perhaps at that moment the sick commonwealth needed more tilling and weeding than the exemplary private man. The conduct of toy forts and imaginary wars should be left to poets, not to generals. Marvell's earlier words may, from this vantage point, seem admonitory rather than descriptive: "for an *Inn* to entertain / Its *Lord* a while, but not remain."[76] Thus in taking leave of Fairfax and turning to imagine the meadow—the stanza on conscience is the last sustained reference in the poem—he projects scenes of carnage as if to remind his patron that real war is going on elsewhere and that soldiers may perhaps someday replace mowers even here. This questioning of the wisdom of a retirement which is premature or too final leads into Marvell's own escape and ultimately to its climax:

> Bind me ye *Woodbines* in your 'twines,
> Curle me about ye gadding *Vines*,
> And Oh so close your Circles lace,
> That I may never leave this Place.
>
> *(609–12)*

There is more irony in the implied advice, "Send the general out, let the poet retire" ("Send the general out *so that* the poet may safely retire," cf. the *Horatian Ode*) than Allen's summary would seem to allow:

When Marvell leaves the wood to sing the future of his patron's race, he has, I think, solved his own problem to his immediate satisfaction. He will be the

---

[76] This interpretation follows Allen's, 139–40 and 146–47. In presenting his pageants of war on the meadow, Marvell may well be attempting to persuade his patron—i.e., "How would you like to have war here?" or "If it is peaceful here, there is war elsewhere."

nightingale singing among the lowly thorns. This is the place he hopes "he may never leave." He has advised his patron against retirement as best he can, holding up to him his magisterial duties, the excellence of his qualifications, the urgent necessities of the state of England, and the spiritual impotence and danger of withdrawal from the active life. He knew in his heart of hearts that Fairfax would remain aloof; so he makes his last effort . . . the fortunes of the House of Fairfax depend on Mary.[77]

If the advice is also aimed at the latent politician in Marvell, the poet in him is not prepared to accept it. It is the return to action which seems premature to the poet, who may well claim that the imaginative exercise productive of the sylvan stanzas is the poet's way of weeding Ambition and tilling Conscience, which shrinks at every touch. The return from the woods to Maria is like a return from the voice of the Body to the voice of the Soul, and it is thus a compromise. It may be incumbent on Fairfax to hurry back into action, but his daughter is, after all, only twelve years old; she may legitimately remain home a few more years at least, during which time she will need tutoring. If she represents the claims of social and rational order, she does so in a domestic rather than a political context and she symbolizes the halcyon calm of Paradise's only map. To move from the image of Fairfax to that of Maria is therefore a retardation in the rhythm of return. The felt disparity between the young Mary Fairfax and the symbolic Maria, noted by Allen and Joseph Summers,[78] contributes to this effect: safe within this friendly and excellent lesser world, the poet may deal with heaven and hell, with war and politics and passion, *in parvo*. He prefers to manipulate symbols rather than directly to confront their referents.

Allowing for the particular differences of tone, the return to Maria is somewhat like the return from Eveless Eden to the flowery dial in *The Garden*. The urge to withdraw from time to thyme is still present, but sharply qualified by the poet's self-consciousness, his acknowledgment *that* the urge is still present. We sense, I think, more resolution and control in the shorter poem, and perhaps the longer poem is longer in part because it dramatizes the mind's vacillation at closer range, shows Marvell moving toward a resolution again and again yet never quite letting himself achieve it. Thus while he reveals a coyness in his own nature by picking Mary Fairfax as symbol, he self-consciously projects his reticence onto the symbol: since Maria would not have her beauties seen, "The Wood about *her* draws a Skreen."

[77] *Image and Meaning*, 146–47.
[78] *Image and Meaning*, 148, 153; Summers, 14–15.

> For *She*, to higher Beauties rais'd,
> Disdains to be for lesser prais'd.
> *She* counts her Beauty to converse
> In all the languages as *hers;*
> Nor yet in those *her self* imployes
> But for the *Wisdome,* not the *Noyse;*
> Nor yet that *Wisdome* would 'fect,
> But as 'tis *Heavens Dialect.*
>
> *(705–12)*

This is not only a contrast to the nuns but also an echo of the poet as "*easie Philosopher.*" The ideal order of Appleton House is to be viewed by Maria as preparation for her proper functions in the great world, not as an escape from the dangers attendant on true fulfillment. Yet again, while Marvell contrasts this fulfillment to the perverted self-love of the nuns, his exhortation echoes with images from the sylvan retreat—the *antick cope,* the prelate of the grove, the "double Wood of ancient Stocks":

> This 'tis to have been from the first
> In a *Domestick Heaven* nurst,
> Under the *Discipline* severe
> Of *Fairfax,* and the starry *Vere;*[79]
> Where not one object can come nigh
> But pure, and spotless as the Eye;
> And *Goodness* doth it self intail
> On *Females,* if there want a *Male.*
>
> Go now fond Sex that on your Face
> Do all your useless Study place,
> Nor once at Vice your Brows dare knit
> Lest the smooth Forehead wrinkled sit:
> Yet your own Face shall at you grin,
> Thorough the Black-bag of your Skin;
> When *knowledge* only could have fill'd
> And Virtue all those *Furrows till'd.*
>
> Hence *She* with Graces more divine
> Supplies beyond her *Sex* the *Line;*
> And, like a *sprig* of *Misleto,*
> On the *Fairfacian Oak* does grow;

[79] One wonders whether the pun on Vere is matched by a pun on Fairfax—fair *fas* or fax? Line 743, "And make their *Destiny* their *Choice,*" might argue a play on *fas.*

Whence, for some universal good,
The *Priest* shall cut the sacred Bud;
While her *glad Parents* most rejoice,
And make their *Destiny* their *Choice*.

                    (721–44)

This is a curiously strained passage, at once very emblematic and very physical, both decorous and unpleasantly suggestive. It is as if Marvell feels the difficulty of what he is urging, since few eyes are without the wanton mote. As in *The Picture of Little T. C. in a Prospect of Flowers*, the green prospect is shown to idealize love but also to oversimplify its dangers and obligations. By making his green metaphor seem a little insistent, a little inappropriate, Marvell suggests, on the one hand, the frustration and prudery related to the fear of exposing oneself to one's sexual and social fate and, on the other hand, a love which may be reduced to genealogical husbandry. Maria's retired life in the harmoniously responsive world of Appleton House is fulfilled only when she leaves it behind to open herself to the promising yet uncertain future, the great world, "*some* universal good." After registering the risk as well as the promise, Marvell turns his thought from the image of Maria, which has served its purpose, and he moves in the next Stanza from future problems to present joys, from the exemplary human flower to the real plants around him—"ye Fields, Springs, Bushes, Flowers, / Where yet she leads her studious Hours."

In this way, as the poet moves from the nuns to Fairfax to Maria, the representations of the retired life at Appleton House become increasingly attractive. Though the general drift of the poem is a praise of Appleton House as a *temporary inn*, the impulse to confront the world is countered by new urges to withdrawal. And as the poem reaches its inevitable conclusion, these countermovements seem to be intensified. From the moment Marvell introduces Maria, they knot together in more frequent and compact juxtapositions. Of course the poem as a whole is characterized by a dominant rhythm of alternating systole and diastole which affects both spatial and temporal prospects: Marvell's attention sweeps from the house out to the estate and back to the house ("Let's in"); his meditation moves from the physical presence of "this sober Frame" back in time to the nuns, forward to his patron, inward to the more personal and immediate present of his own withdrawal, outward again to Maria—Thwaites *rediviva* as symbol of the future—and finally, after the brief glance at *her* future, back to the present tense and place, the poet surrounded by the estate and retreating into the house from the approach of darkness. But these vibrations are most drastically compressed at the end: in the "rude heap" stanza, where the poet's focus rapidly widens and narrows, while his temporal prospect seems at once to extend backward and forward in search of paradise; in the restlessness of the final stanza, as his imagination darts from meadow and river to the antipodes, then to tortoises and finally to the dark hemisphere which seems both to expand and contract; in the syntactical alternatives of the "rude heap" and "dark Hemisphere" passages; in the way the brief closing figures—salmon-fishers, antipodes, tortoises, and rational amphibii—recollect and epitomize the oppositions generated through the entire poem.

The work of the poem has led Marvell to sharpen the distinction, which also confronted Prospero, between his reformed symbol or image of actuality and the dark actuality itself; between the lesser world and the rude heap, the friendly family as social microcosm and the chaotic society of which it is a microcosm, the poem as experience and the experience beyond the poem. A controlled return to actuality leads inevitably to a disjunction, to a sense of the gap between the inner and outer orders.[80] If the ambience from which the poet retreats is gradually readmitted into the lesser or second world, it is also tempered. He may not want to step out too far and too hastily into the first world where he is helpless and alone. Yet he knows that ultimately he must, that only the ultimate gesture fulfills the imaginative withdrawal and creation by marking off its limits. Like the return to the flowery dial of *The Garden*, the last section of *Appleton House* is a tempered surrender, a compromise, *which makes itself known as such*, and it is this added dimension of self-awareness, this frame of ironic self-diminution, which constitutes the *real* return. Man's *oikos* may expand to a universe, a plurality of universes, yet be no bigger than his head. And though it houses heaven and hell, it may nevertheless prove inadequate for its humble primary function in the struggle for existence: to protect man against the dark contingencies—or certainties—of Weather.

[80] "What one finds intimated at large in the prose, and more intensely focused in the poetry is a special version of the relationship between microcosm and macrocosm which is antagonistic rather than concentric. It is a puritan point of view: the inviolate soul confronting the social world with its power and law" (MacCaffrey, "Some Notes on Marvell's Poetry," 261). The version is not, however, so special; I have tried elsewhere to show some aspects of its development from the fifteenth century on, and this disjunctive relation becomes a commonplace of seventeenth-century thought, of which the puritan point of view is one instance.

Paradise Lost Evolving, Books I–VI: Toward a New View of the Poem as the Speaker's Experience

As MANY COMMENTATORS have suggested, *Paradise Lost* is presented by Milton as the unfolding and changing experience of a particular consciousness—the speaker's—at a particular moment in history. Since in the present reading the perspective of interpretation will focus squarely on this relation between speaker and poem, it might be fashionable to call it an essay in phenomenological criticism. The organizing principle in which this relation develops may be conveniently expressed as a version of Haeckel's familiar axiom: cultural history is recapitulated in personal history. The dialectical pattern underlying both is enacted in the dynamic unfolding of *Paradise Lost*. Here I would like to amplify the relation between Milton's semantics and cosmologies as an index to the developing consciousness of the speaker. By way of underlining the importance of this relation, I shall begin with a brief comparison between Dante and Milton.

I

Dante's experience in the *Commedia* is charted along a preestablished visual and spatial course which we understand to be a *copy*, a verbal rendering of an already existing universe. We follow the past experience and the present narrative together. The poem is shaped largely by the influence of the world system and cosmic structure which Dante inherits and accepts—even if his own versions of Hell and Purgatory are literary, they are treated as literal, as actual places in the spherical world visualized by the poem. His explicit contribution is to re-present the traditional order in its traditional clarity, to show how it may explain and justify human experience on earth, in Europe and in Florence. His poem is, in other words, a Bonaventuran *reductio*, in every sense a leading-back to God.

The copy situation manifests itself in another way: there are three Dantes in the poem. Dante the pilgrim and Dante the poet-speaker are present to the reader; Dante the maker is not—or rather pretends not to be, since the poem is presumptively about an actual visionary experience. Dante assumes a clear distinction between the exercise of the poet's art in rhetoric, in the craft of persuasive narration, and the world created by God, not Dante, the vision received from God by Dante. Thus we have a poet *now* and a pilgrim *then;* the poet "copies" the past visionary experience so as to share it, make it vivid, disclose the way of salvation to other wayfarers; the focus of the poem is on the *then* rather than on the *now,* though the poet frequently lets it be known that he would like us to appreciate the greatness of his achievement as a poet. The relation between the *now* and the *then* is fundamental but not static. Toward the end of each canticle the speaker becomes more involved and excited; he is pulled back into the past experience as its vividness overcomes him now in the act of writing or speaking.

The reasons are different in each canticle. In Hell, for example, the poet as well as the pilgrim betrays a morbid interest in suffering, a morbid gratification at having his pity stirred, an anger which is not at all proper Christian indignation but rather a strain of pessimism, frustrated idealism, seeing the whole world as evil because it is not perfect, giving up on life as it is. Most important, he reveals a morbid interest in the physical and literal spectacle of hell during the late cantos. Dante the maker presents Dante the speaker as excessively fascinated by the tabloid details immediately before him rather than by the total plan. We see this first, perhaps, in the slapstick Malacoda cantos, where the narrator gives himself to the scene in such a way that it is hard to keep attention on what is important—the spiritual torment, the inner pain and distortion of self, the privation of good. Similarly, in presenting the metamorphoses of the thieves in Canto xxv, Dante seems more interested in his descriptive virtuosity and allegorical ingenuity than in the larger ethical significance. This is all shadow action, a kind of poetry which, as he reminds us (xxv.94), is borrowed from the pagans, yet the scene clearly grips the poet now as well as the pilgrim then. It is this very sense of being imposed on, obsessed, tyrannized by the past, of being unable to transform and creatively redirect past experience, which characterizes the infernal condition; this tyranny is the perverse form of the true copy situation in which the traditional order and past experience are recovered, rendered newly significant and functional as part of the present quest of the living soul.

In *Paradise Lost* the relation between the past experience and the present narration is totally different. Here is the actual sequence of events in the past experience: creation of the Son; revolt, defeat, and fall of angels; building of Pandemonium; creation of earth and man; ascent of Satan to Eden; Raphael's visit with Adam and Eve; temptation and fall; reeducation by Michael; exile. Here, on the other hand, is the narrative sequence: fall of angels to Hell; building of Pandemonium, conclave, etc.; ascent of Satan to Eden; Raphael's visit and his account of the creation of the Son, the revolt and war in Heaven, and the creation of the earth; temptation and fall; reeducation and exile. The original temporal flow is sustained only in the last four books. Thus in *Paradise Lost*, unlike the *Commedia*, our attention and understanding are guided largely by the present rearrangement of inherited materials which Milton orders according to his own poetic plan and vision.

Milton calls this rearrangement an *argument*. In *The Art of Logic* (translated by A. H. Gilbert) he defines an argument as

> *that which has a fitness for arguing something* . . . that is for showing, explaining, or proving something . . . the proper and primary potency of a simple argument is to explain and prove how one thing follows or does not follow from another; that is, it is judged that when one thing has been laid down as true something else is or is not also laid down originally. Our Bacon . . . rightly suggests the same thing about induction: "By one and the same operation of the mind the thing in question is both invented and judged." . . . An argument in the proper sense of the word is not a word or a thing, but a certain fitness of something for arguing; this . . . can be called *reason*.

The poem is a fictional argument, a manifestation of hypothetical causes one function of which is to make sense of disjointed modern times. Considered tonally and dynamically as *utterance*, the poem is a sustained *arguing* in the present tense. But more conventionally, as exemplified by the *arguments* preceding each book (and not included in the first edition), the ways of God and tradition are causally justified by the new arrangement of events, the shape and plan whereby the ancient wisdom is revived and reordered to express the new Idea of *this poet*. If the preliminary arguments are like blueprints articulating the basic plot of each

book, they are also reminders of the extent to which Milton has transformed what he has inherited. Where Dante treats traditional culture
and cosmology as *exemplars* by which to order his poem, Milton appeals
to them as *models*. He uses mythic and cosmographic data like stage sets
which give the reader initial directions and visualize the ethico-spiritual
polarities of the argument. The elements or episodes of the original
events, the traditional sequence of Sacred History, are not assigned any
structural value in themselves. Since the tradition has become a source of
skepticism rather than of dogma or belief, the poet feels compelled to
justify God in his own way; he brings out God's order by rearranging
the received elements in a narrative scheme which alone will restore
them to their persuasiveness as "causes," explanations, simple arguments. Thus where Dante stylistically subordinates the poet's *now* to the
pilgrim's *then*, Milton's argument, voice, and verse make it clear that
the most immediate experience of *Paradise Lost* is not the *then* being recalled, but the very free treatment of it in the *now*.

If our main response to Dante is *seeing the image*, to Milton it is *hearing the voice*. For *voice* is the externalization of that moral energy which
Milton calls right reason, and right reason may, without too much lati-
tude, be defined as uncloistered consciousness testing its own quality and
that of the norms imposed on it by subjecting them to the continual play
and pressure of experience. The essential form of moral energy is not
action in the world but the inner conflict, the struggle toward decision,
which precedes this action. Such a principle is not conceived as requiring space, or as existing *in* space and time; it creates time by its very
nature, since it unfolds in the order of succession. Its most appropriate
expressive medium is therefore the discursive instrument of language,
and the most important elements of that language are not nouns, which
name what is already in existence, but verbs and prepositions, through
which the mind defines, controls, creates, destroys, and re-creates the
relations and therefore the orders which constitute its world.

Milton's treatment of Creation and of the cosmic effects of the Fall
suggests that the phenomena of nature and history are externalizations or
embodiments of moral force. His view of the cosmic continuum of Book
V suggests that this energy is the highest and most real form of existence,
the condition to which other forms strive and which they, in so striving,
sustain. Thus physical energy appears as either the primitive or the degraded form of moral energy; as energy moves down the continuum,
it becomes increasingly volcanic, uncontrolled, and self-destroying, increasingly brute and blind. The denser the matter, the more volcanic the
force, the more compelling the sensuous image—the more primitive

(premoral) or degraded (immoral) the energy. In all this Milton leans
heavily on the new dissociation of spiritual from physical hierarchies developed in different ways by the Florentine Platonists and by Calvin.
His own treatment is a way of provisionally solving the dilemma perceived by Donne in the *First Anniversary*, the "weakness in the want of
correspondence of heaven and earth." The physical size and place of the
earth are of little consequence in themselves, since the earth is important
as the node and center of a continually developing spiritual or moral universe which has no fixed physical character. Cosmological theories are
finally to be judged not by their scientific accuracy but by their usefulness
in serving the needs of moral symbolism, e.g., "for the Heav'n's wide
Circuit, let it speak / The Maker's high magnificence" (VIII.100–101).

In *Paradise Lost*, when the spatial environment has served its symbolic purpose, it is retracted, dissolved, or turned more patently into
emblem and artifice. The various bridges and routes leading the cosmic
warriors—Satan, Sin, Death and the Son—into the soul may be destroyed or discarded when they have served their functions. In Kantian
terms, Milton uses the forms of the external intuition to visualize aspects
of inner process, and he frequently reminds us of their hypothetical nature by presenting his universe, in whole or in part, as an artifact, a toy
model, or the locus of a literal melodrama somewhat absurdly acted out
as physical spectacle. The very absurdity of the war in Heaven implies
the great gap between visual symbol and spiritual referent and shows
the need of the new symbolic relations developed in the second half
of the poem.

In human experience, at both the individual and the historical levels,
moral development proceeds through a dialectic of self-expansion and
self-limitation, a dialectic which Milton imitates in his poetic narrative.
He begins with vast, extensive, and externally epic gestures, criticizes
his own scope and ambitiousness at the beginning of Book VII, and
promises to limit himself to the tiny earth. He then expands the earth
"inwardly" by making it the new moral center of the universe. The
moral gesture of self-limitation cannot take place until the mind has first
probed its expansive powers, has tried to fulfill its wishes by making the
whole universe its place. Similarly the physical, the external, and the
sensuous cannot be controlled so as to express inner moral force until
they have first been experienced, enjoyed, evaluated in and for themselves. The appeal to sensuous experience and sensuous modes of imagining is partly an attempt to make the self passive to its fantasies, to withdraw into some idyllic cloister. The appeal to spatial experience and to

visualizing techniques of imagination is partly an effort to negate the irreversible pressure of time, for time is the true medium of moral force and moral force thrives on inner conflict.

II

Two aspects of the relation between poet and poem are embodied in the double invocation toward which the opening lines of *Paradise Lost* tend:

> Sing Heav'nly Muse, that on the secret top
> Of Oreb, or of Sinai, didst inspire
> That Shepherd, who first taught the chosen Seed,
> In the Beginning how the Heav'ns and Earth
> Rose out of Chaos: Or if Sion Hill
> Delight thee more, and Siloa's Brook that flow'd
> Fast by the Oracle of God; I thence
> Invoke thy aid to my advent'rous Song,
> That with no middle flight intends to soar
> Above th' Aonian Mount, while it pursues
> Things unattempted yet in Prose or Rhyme.
> And chiefly Thou O Spirit, that dost prefer
> Before all Temples th' upright heart and pure,
> Instruct me, for Thou know'st; Thou from the first
> Wast present, and with mighty wings outspread
> Dove-like satst brooding on the vast Abyss
> And mad'st it pregnant: What in me is dark
> Illumine, what is low raise and support;
> That to the highth of this great Argument
> I may assert Eternal Providence,
> And justify the ways of God to men.

(1.6–26)

The relation to Urania has to do with Milton as public poet rather than with Milton as private man; with Milton as an essentially passive (inspired) medium of communication rather than with Milton as active moral agent; with poetry as something akin to prophecy or revelation rather than with poetry as fable, fantasy, or inner edification. The divine prospect connected with Urania is at once more external and more remote than that connected with the Spirit. The associations of the first section are historical, cultural, and institutional, while the rhetoric with which Milton describes his purpose is that of the heroic poet who hopes to continue and transcend the great tradition.

The transition from the first to the second part is thus very much like that from the first to the second half of *Paradise Lost*. The expansive and extensive character of "advent'rous Song" and "Things unattempted yet" gives way to the more intimate appeal, the more austere humility, of Protestant heroism. Milton's thought moves from the tops of actual, if remote, mountains to the inner height of *this* great argument. He asks the Spirit for assistance which is at once poetic and ethical: since "Instruct me" can mean "build within me" or "build me up within" as well as "teach me," will and mind are involved together. The Spirit is to preside over Milton's ethos and over his poem, and we may speculate that the development of one is inseparable from that of the other. Perhaps one of the "Things unattempted yet" for which the Spirit is chiefly responsible is this identity of poetry with moral action. Making and uttering the poem seem presented to the reader partly as the manifest working of the Third Person in the soul, partly as the response of the soul, the arduous effort to meet so great a charge and privilege.

That the Spirit demands more active participation than the Muse, that the writing of a poem may involve a risk which is ethical as well as esthetic, is suggested by the vague image which hovers over lines 19–22—hovers after, if not before, we have read further in the first two books. It is the image of Satan, who also sat brooding over a vast abyss and who illumined Hell by raising Pandemonium. The same association is more explicit in the invocation to Book III in which Milton, after describing Satan's flight from Hell, applies it as an image to his own activity:

> Thee I revisit now with bolder wing,
> Escap't the Stygian Pool, though long detain'd
> In that obscure sojourn, while in my flight
> Through utter and through middle darkness borne
> With other notes than to the Orphean Lyre
> I sung of Chaos and Eternal Night,
> Taught by the heav'nly Muse to venture down
> The dark descent, and up to reascend,
> Though hard and rare. . . .
>
> *(III.13–21)*

Milton of course distinguishes his source from that of Satan, who had proclaimed himself at II.975 as "Alone, and without guide," though by the beginning of the ninth book the poet seems less sure that an appeal to the Muse will automatically procure inspiration: "*If* answerable style I can obtain / Of my Celestial Patroness," he will succeed, but not "if all be mine, / Not Hers who brings it nightly to my Ear" (IX.20–21, 46–47). The message may be obscured by other forces and motives within his soul. The fear that the poem may be nothing more than a self-created fantasy echoes in a different mood Satan's fatuous speculation that the angels were "self-begot, self-rais'd / By our own quick'ning power" (V.860–61).

What Milton actually thought about his poetic activity and its sources is irrelevant here. What he *presents* is a poet aware of the satanic possibility, a poet who knows that if the soul is a battlefield for the cosmic struggle, it may well be deceived by Satan posing as muse. The poetic act, like every human act, every creative decision and assertion of will, involves a calculated risk. How can the poet really be sure whether the vision he "receives" comes from heaven or hell, whether it is a truly inspired justification or merely a presumptuous fantasy, the working of original sin within him? *If* the muse descends, then the poem may be a symbol of what is substantially real, more real than itself; it will be, for all its size, like a sacramental ark. If the muse does not descend, the poem may be a vast and glittering Pandemonium, an externalization of the satanic forces within the poet's soul. A poem, a verbal artifact, is a more inward, personal, and therefore "evolved" expression than a visual and architectural object, but it may be evil as well as good which has evolved to a subtler, because invisible, fabric. The *man* who makes a poem does and reveals much more than the *men* who made the Tabernacle; both as a mortal and as an individual, his role is greater, his experience and perspective more important. But he is bound by the same principle of self-constraint raised to a higher power: like the sanctuary and ark, the poem is framed by God's prescript, and in the poem "his Testimony, / The Records of his Cov'nant" (XII.251–52), the covenant between muse or Holy Spirit and the inward heart and pure.

Contrary to this is the merely organic impulse to projection, self-expansion, and endless (because unregulated) creative complication. It is the tendency expressed by the adornment of the "Fabric huge" of Pandemonium, by the wanton growth of cosmological fantasies "scribbl'd o'er" God's "Fabric of the Heav'ns" (VIII.75ff.), by Adam's early response to Eve's physical beauty ("Too much of Ornament, in outward show / Elaborate," VIII.538–39), and by Belial's men "in wandering mazes lost" (II.561). There is no doubt that Milton in his poem takes a deliberate step in this direction, that he gives play to fabulous and rococo impulses within himself, that he consciously experiments with satanic and archaic modes of imagination as a prelude to containing and transcending them.

Thus the critical event and enveloping action of the first six books is the revolt of the angels, presented in heroic or chivalric terms by a poet who easily slips into an angelic persona and anthropomorphizes heaven. Blending heaven and earth together, converting spiritual motive to physical image, he lowers the former and raises the latter. By rearranging the plot and placing the first event—the war in heaven—last, he not only produces a circular or time-abolishing effect but also concludes the first half of *Paradise Lost* with a Happy Ending: good and evil are clearly separated, evil clearly defeated and cast out by means of a single cosmic combat. After the heroic test of arms, the good angels will presumably live happily, the demons unhappily, ever after. If the angelic revolt and fall is a paradigm for man, it is cast in a Homeric or chivalric mode—the wrath of stern Messiah, the "long and tedious havoc" of "fabl'd Knights in Battles feign'd" (IX.30–31). As presented in V and VI, the warring angels *do* seem fabled and feigned, the product of human invention rather than revealed knowledge. The invention is hyperbolic and broad planed rather than subtle; it is "archetypal" in the sense of being both grand and a little fusty, the simplified and archaic image of a recurrent human concern. If we did not feel this while reading Book VI, Milton reminds us of it when in the invocation to VII he reverses his direction, and also in the invocation to IX where he in effect cites the antique source and model of the war in Heaven. We can hardly read this last invocation without being newly struck by the poet's having himself extended the subject and style of heroic imagination from earth to heaven, by his presenting himself to us as recognizing this fact and correcting himself. He reminds us that real human evil demands a paradigm totally different from the war in Heaven, something less grand and cosmic, less literal and external, less simplistic in its image of the central polarities.

I believe this is why Milton does not allow either of his two primary figures—God and Satan—to be entirely satisfactory as embodiments of pure good and evil. The poem represents as one of its dramatic issues the problem of establishing a creature sufficiently *other* in relation to God to allow him meaningfully to act on and interact with that creature. Such a creature will be man, not Satan. Narcissism is a threat to the poet's early anthropomorphic image of God as it is a threat to all other figures in the poem. A tyrannical God who runs the whole show cannot fulfill himself by simply reduplicating his image in defective and inferior creatures lacking true independence. Satan is not sufficiently other to God for a number of reasons: first, because he is simply God's instrument and his behavior, as I shall show, is determined from the outside. The other reasons are all founded on a fact critics have long noticed but failed to understand: that the satanic trinity is an infernal parody of the divine Trinity. The terms in which I have just stated that fact reflect the basis of misunderstanding: if we take the temporal sequence of the poem seriously, we shall be more inclined to say that the divine Trinity emerges as an image of the satanic trinity. God and Satan *are* too much alike in early stages of the poem. The need for revised images of God and his Son becomes obvious when we realize that Satan's characterizations of them as thunderer and warrior *are* accurate. There can be no meaning, no fulfillment, for God in a victory over Satan, or in a punishment which so disables man after the Fall that no good could possibly originate from his will (the image of man delineated by God in Book III). It is only from within the consciousness of a human creature who has real alternatives (Satan or God), who can really suffer and lose, who can initiate action, can make demands on God and even change his relation to God as he himself changes through history—only from within such an *other* set in some way over against God can the divine point of view be fulfilled.

We might ask to what extent Milton conceives Satan as an actual figure in cosmic history, to what extent as a complex personification of certain human tendencies. If primarily the former, then his myth must be construed as aetiological—i.e., what Satan did in prehistory partly caused and explains the way man has always behaved in history. If primarily the latter, then his myth does not seriously pretend to record prehistory or provide a real causal explanation; the myth of Satan is an analogy, a fictional or hypothetical cause devised *ex post facto* to make sense of the divine and human behavior revealed in history and in experience. My own interpretation leans toward the latter account, since I assume that in the character of Satan, Milton has abstracted and externalized what he believes to be the essence of human evil. And this, if we stop to consider it, leads to a peculiar situation: Milton's Satan is more like an *effect* of human behavior than a *cause;* Satan is a fictive visualization who plainly manifests what is already the case within the human soul but is seldom so visible in ordinary life.

Yet he appears in the poem as an archetypal cause. I think we are supposed to be sensible of this discrepancy. We are to look on the character of Satan as an invention of a certain kind, as the product of a particular imagination. He seems conceived as a sometimes pathetic, sometimes melodramatic and moustache-twirling personification of evil projected at the level of mythic fairy tale. This is, again, a relatively childlike view which Milton first gives play to and then transcends: Satan is dangerous not as a warrior or bogeyman but as a sophist; his mission is fulfilled when his bad influence is infused *in* the human soul—when Eve is *impregn'd* by his false dialectic—and when his effects, Sin and Death, establish themselves on earth not as personifications but as human conditions. The poetic justice accorded the fictional character Satan in Hell (X.504–84) is clearly a secondary consideration. The personification of evil who is periodically transformed into a serpent, who occupies a particular place furthest away from God in a cosmos which to the educated minds of Milton's age was mythic or fictitious—this remote and easily identified figure of evil is presented by Milton as being controlled within the fabulous prehistory of his feigned world but not in the actual world of fallen men where his bad influence abides. Milton has, after all, delineated his father of evil in the antique and primary mode of early culture, after the heroic and stark imagination of pagans and Hebrews. His concluding account of Satan in effect returns the character to his sources, fades him out, as it were, until he recedes to the distances of old beliefs and traditions:

> Thus were they plagu'd
> And worn with Famine long, and ceaseless hiss,
> Till thir lost shape, permitted, they resum'd,
> Yearly enjoin'd, *some say*, to undergo
> This annual humbling certain number'd days,
> To dash thir pride, and joy for Man seduc't.
> *However some tradition they dispers'd*
> *Among the Heathen* of thir purchase got,
> And Fabl'd how the Serpent, whom they call'd
> Ophion with Eurynome, the wide-
> Encroaching Eve perhaps, had first the rule
> Of high Olympus, thence by Saturn driv'n
> And Ops, ere yet Dictaean Jove was born.
>
> *(X.572–84, italics mine)*

The demons, that is, persuaded the ancients to view the conquest of evil in heroic and conclusive terms, externalizing it as a military campaign and projecting it back into archaic times. Evil as Satan has fulfilled its function in Milton's argument. Evil internalized as sin makes itself felt in the lines which immediately follow.

III

There is, then, something of the satanic as well as of the archaic in the expanding, soaring, outward-bound vision of the first six books. The triumphant movement, the confident visualization of the spiritual, the clear exorcism and defeat of the enemy through the panacea of personification and allegorical vision—all these belong to the native assurance Milton knew in his earlier years and thus to the habit of imagination he ascribes to the early phases of culture. The youthful vitality and beauty of that vision still draw him, even as he recognizes its dangers. We see not the youthful assurance itself but a late autumnal portrait of it, a portrait which gives that earlier and still vivid sensibility its play while containing and evaluating it, a portrait which shows how far it can go, where it must stop, to what it may lead, and thus how it may be fulfilled in being rejected, or at least sharply tempered.

To focus the satanic aspect more clearly, we must recognize a more complex representation than that of the figure of evil on which I have been dwelling. The image of Satan is simplistic insofar as it is unrelievedly negative, one side of human nature abstracted from the richer mixture. But the evil which Milton abstracts and portrays is itself complex, familiar, and central to the Western literary tradition. It is the Kierkegaardian sickness unto death which Milton could have found in Dante, Chaucer, or Spenser—that syndrome of which pride and despair are two aspects, each entailing the other, pride the surface and despair the ground. Its basis is in pain and self-hatred; its effects are the various forms of escape from pain, self, or God; its ultimate aim is the transformation of self into God, the delusive hope of absolute power or pleasure. The satanic condition is so obsessively bound to the wheel of an original choice that it cannot control the outward thrust of mind objectifying itself into its own place and prison.

The fall of the angels was qualitatively complete in Satan's first moment of revolt: "fraught / With envy against the Son of God," he

> could not bear
> Through pride that sight, and thought himself impair'd.
> Deep malice thence conceiving and disdain,
> Soon as midnight brought on the dusky hour
> Friendliest to sleep and silence, he resolv'd
> With all his Legions to dislodge, and leave
> Unworshipt, unobey'd the Throne supreme,
> Contemptuous. . . .
>
> *(V.664–71)*

We see first his misguided and weak nature—the sight he could not bear, the envy and pride which overwhelm him as *affects*, the erroneous sense of injured merit ("thought himself impair'd"). The phrase "thence conceiving" suggests a response which seems half-deliberate, the not quite involuntary assumption of a fixed emotional role—malice and disdain—by an actor who might have chosen otherwise. His next response is symbolic rather than tactical: having decided on malice and disdain, he resolves to externalize them in a gesture of contempt; spatial distance is simply the visual display of the new inner withdrawal. His warfare and fall to Hell are not a new phase of his condition but a symbolic game, a pageant or manifestation which publishes and fulfills on the graph of external action what had already happened within the demonic soul. Thus God to Abdiel:

> Servant of God, well done, well hast thou fought
> The better fight, who single has maintain'd
> Against revolted multitudes the Cause
> Of Truth, in word mightier than they in Arms;
> And for the testimony of Truth hast borne
> Universal reproach, far worse to bear
> Than violence. . . .
>
> *(VI.29–35)*

"The easier conquest now remains," i.e., the physical warfare and violence which are mere effects of the fixed malice and disdain. In Book VI the demons not only gravitate toward their new home but register the stages of gravitation as God lets them externalize their inherent tendencies. They shift from words to deeds, turn heaven into earth (even into an analogue of hell, VI.472–91), and invent an instrument, the cannon, which precisely expresses the nature of satanic energy, as Milton himself had characterized it in previous passages, e.g.:

> his dire attempt, which nigh the birth
> Now rolling, boils in his tumultuous breast,
> And like a devilish Engine back recoils
> Upon himself. . . .
>
> *(IV.15–18)*

The mechanic fury and violence with which the satanic mind is driven to objectify itself is suggested in our very first view of the arch-demon:

> But his doom
> Reserv'd him to more wrath; for now the thought
> Both of lost happiness and lasting pain
> Torments him; round he throws his baleful eyes
> That witness'd huge affliction and dismay

> Mixt with obdurate pride and steadfast hate:
> At once as far as Angels ken he views
> The dismal Situation waste and wild,
> A Dungeon horrible, on all sides round
> As one great Furnace flam'd, yet from those flames
> No light, but rather darkness visible
> Serv'd only to discover sights of woe.
>
> *(I.53–64)*

Witness'd may mean both "saw" and "revealed"; we see first the inward prospect of satanic pain, brought even closer to us by Milton's shift from the narrative past to the historical present (expressing Satan's limited view of himself as in midcareer), and we then watch that mental anguish *thrown*, as it were, from his eyes to the surrounding dungeon. The ambiguous phrase "to discover sights of woe" completes the projective movement and confirms the correspondence of inner and outer Situations. From this moment on the colonization and organization of hell, the exfoliation of Satan's soul, takes place with the speed and ease of fantasy. Like Dantesque sinners, the demons instinctively create around them a world, shadowy yet real, which is the effect and extension of the prison of self, which both symbolizes their existing pain and causes them new pain:

> Abhorred Styx the flood of deadly hate,
> Sad Acheron of Sorrow, black and deep;
> Cocytus, nam'd of lamentation loud
> Heard on the rueful stream; fierce Phlegeton
> Whose waves of torrent fire inflame with rage.
>
> *(II.577–81)*

Apart from the actual plot situation, or containing it, there is a verbal or rhetorical "plot" binding the first two books together into an epitome of satanic process as it spreads out from the center of self, divides into simple components (as in the rigged parliament in which each speaker voices one aspect of the total satanic attitude), thins away into the distortions of self which Satan fathered (Sin and Death, more purely allegorical, therefore shadowy, than Satan), and finally spends itself in a Chaos whose swirling fragments are so described as to recall previous moments of description (e.g., II.888, 898, 905, 933). Like the *Inferno*, Books I and II are visualized and voiced in an essentially archaic mode, in "pagan" imagery and rhetoric which suggest the speaker's affinity to the impulses he knows he must contain.

Milton and Satan are closer in these books than they are later; by Book VI Satan as warrior hero has become a slightly comic figure. He has in fact been too easily exorcized and labeled, too easily diminished in stature, by both God and the speaker. If we see from I to VI a gradual "rejection" of Satan and the satanic imagination on the speaker's part, I think we are also expected to see another and more insidious danger: Milton playing Raphael, trying out the exalted and panoramic perspective of good angels with which it is tempting to identify oneself. It is obviously easier to detach oneself from a bad angel, however heroic, than from a good one. And to assume the persona and vision of the good angel is to risk seeing things too clearly—compare the murk, the fluid and volatile shifting of shadowy forms, which characterizes the brilliant vision of hell, with the all-too-lucid and literal view of the war in heaven. (I should emphasize here that I am speaking not about a defect in the poem but about a defect in the speaker's assumed point of view, a defect which is a phase in the unfolding experience of narration.) From III through VI there is a double effect of spreading out from the center—the earth—and squeezing together the extremities of the world. The following discussion will examine some aspects of this process.

IV

Some of the limitations which Milton deliberately adopts in early sections of the poem may be seen at work in Book III. In the invocation, he employs a simplistic version of the paradox that one can gain power by giving it up. He uses his blindness and alienation, his helplessness as a man, to assert his inspired power as a poet. His nostalgia for the lost sweetness of visible nature and "the cheerful ways of men" is balanced by assurance that the loss is prelude to a greater gain. Having been deprived of his common humanity and of the external world, he offers himself as a purged vessel. He would like the divine light to fill him, to make him godlike or angelic in his breadth of prospect:

> Celestial light
> Shine inward, and the mind through all her powers
> Irradiate, there plant eyes, all mist from thence
> Purge and disperse, that I may see and tell
> Of things invisible to mortal sight.
>
> *(51–55)*

Aiming higher than the muse, Milton begins by directly hailing the creative light which is the Second Person, not the Third Person invoked in Book I:

> Hail holy Light, offspring of Heav'n first-born,
> Or of th' Eternal Coeternal beam
> May I express thee unblam'd? since God is light,
> And never but in unapproachéd light
> Dwelt from Eternity, dwelt then in thee,
> Bright effluence of bright essence increate.

(1–6)

The height toward which he reaches is increased by the chiastic play of thought over the possible alternatives of filiation and identity ("off-spring . . . Coeternal . . . God is light . . . Bright effluence"). So to obscure the divine relations helps affirm God's ineffability but also implies that the poet wants to be inspired by a totally ineffable and unapproachable godhead. Greedily, he wants the whole Trinity to bear in on him. This differs in two important respects from the more conventional Protestant appeal to the Holy Spirit: first, the Protestant appeal involves a clearer distinction between the portion of divinity which makes itself available to man and that which is absolutely beyond him. Second, the descent of the Spirit entails an active moral response. Milton's comparison of himself to a nightingale at III.37 suggests that he has in mind a more passive and intuitive state, a state whose magical ease and potency are to be guaranteed by the most primitive form of participation—"Then *feed* on thoughts." The blind ravished bard and the warbling bird of night figure two sides of the same condition: they express the wish for an enthusiasm which the mature Milton understands as at once too high and too low for man. This situation reflects Milton's view of the paradoxical state of unfallen man in Books IV through IX and of archaic man in the ancient history of XI and XII: in the state of innocence, in the fantasies characteristic of personal or cultural childhood, man imagines himself as at once too close to God and too far from him. God is too indulgent a parent and too stern a tyrant. Adam is confined to a mountaintop nursery where he has everything he wants and where his obvious godlike capabilities fust in him unused.

God's attitude toward man in the third book is unimaginable, a parody of Lutheran pessimism far from Milton's true idea of this attitude. While he defines his relation to ingrate man, God circles repetitively back—as if in morbid fascination—to the ignominy of the Fall and his own freedom from blame in the matter. This repetition lends his statement of the traditional paradoxes about fate, providence, and free will an air of rationalization—"After all, *I* had nothing to do with it." He speaks a little petulantly, like a frustrated parent whose good plans and intentions are about to be spoiled by a nasty child. And though he speaks of man's freedom, the two kinds he suggests are both prelapsarian: the relatively unhampered liberty of garden life and the freedom to fall. If after man has failed nothing which derives from him alone can be other than evil, then fallen man is not really free: "Man shall not quite be lost, but sav'd who will, / Yet not of will in him, but grace in me" (173–74).

Because time and its tenses do not exist for God, his larger prospect is shown in III as oddly limited. His chief concern is the clear and simple outline of universal history, the single great pattern framed by the Fall and the Last Judgment. Emphasis naturally falls on the intercession of the Second Person in cosmic history rather than on the ingression of the Third Person into the individual soul. The divine overview, remote from man, is free of the clutter and detail, the diversity and untidiness, which characterize history from the existential perspective. In using the word *Man*, rather than *Adam* or *men*, and in referring indiscriminately to Adam's original sin and the sins of fallen men, God reads history as Adam's fall writ large, or as a series of archaically determined repetitions of the first fatal act. Everything Milton readmits into the history which concludes *Paradise Lost* is carefully screened out of the divine preview in III.

The one-sidedness of the divine prospect is almost irritatingly evident in the words of approbation God addresses to his Son. After outlining the contrast between evil man and good Son, God is less interested in man's redemption than in assuring the Son that everything will turn out well. The Son did not need this moral support since his own offer reveals that he expects at most to be mildly and temporarily inconvenienced by his sacrifice. In Book III, although the Son stands over against the Father in affirming his future role as intercessor, his viewpoint is dominated by that of the Father. His offer presupposes that man is all bad and God all good, man helpless and God omnipotent. To ask that the Father's anger be deflected from man to Son is therefore to invoke the *deus ex machina* from the human as well as the divine standpoint. Not only will the Son's triumph over Death be absolute and easy but miserable man is in effect urged to luxuriate in his helplessness. Since he *can* do nothing, he *need* do nothing. The work of salvation will be taken entirely out of his hands and carried on at that divine level on which the Happy Ending is assured. As the Son looks forward to his final triumph, his voice takes on the militant ring of a pagan deity moved by *phthonos*, or of Messiah scourging those enemies with whom the chosen people are too weak to deal. This view of the Protector as Pantocrator is reassuring for passive, childlike man: he may surrender his responsibility with his power, his control of his future with his capacity for good. In thus relieving himself of moral efficacy and effort, in charging God with the good fight, man complements God's disengagement from human evil.

The implied relation between man and God is thus very much like the relation between poet and God suggested in the invocation to Book III. It is also like the relation sketched out in Books XI and XII between God and primitive man. In all three cases we see God primarily as the Father. For Milton the Age of the Old Law was a paternal age; in this period man conceived of his relation to God on the simple and inadequate model of patriarchy—stern father, and children who tend to waywardness. Such a relation, or rather such an image of relation, puts a strain on both parties. Adam cannot understand why God is willing to spend time among a race of sinners, and by the time of the Mosaic era the sinners themselves want greater distance between themselves and their thundering Father. The Hebrew image of God as an authoritarian First Person was too inflexible and external to allow a true filial response. Since there was more justice than mercy, more anger than love, the divine image was too easily effaced in man. But when, as in Book III, the early patriarchs act effectively, they are depicted by Milton not as independent spirits but as passive vessels of divine power.

The New Law fulfills the Old through a process of internalization which places greater stress on man's capacity for positive response— "From imposition of strict Laws, to free / Acceptance of large Grace, from servile fear / To filial, works of Law to works of Faith" (XII.304– 6). But this new possibility depends on a change which affects God as well as man's image of God: though the attributes of the Father remain in force, those of the Son and Holy Spirit must be given greater play. An image of God restricted to the First Person is no less imperfect than an image of religion restricted to the Law, its works and covenants. The Hebrews envisaged their deity as human in behavior but remote from man in attitude—like the God of Book III. The Incarnation reverses this view: the three-personed God is mysterious and remote from man in behavior, much closer to man in the manifestation of his love. On the one hand, he withdraws from men, places the teaching of his Word in their hands, endows them with greater power and independence, therefore greater responsibility. On the other hand, his union in love and sacrifice signifies a new relation which renders obsolete the pure exteriority of the Age of Law and which promises man a share in a much greater future. But this development from the Old Law to the New, and from the Father to the Son to the Holy Spirit, is one in which problems as well as promise move inward to the "upright heart and pure" of each soul. Problems will change, not vanish. The effects of the Sacrifice are mystical and moral, not magical. It is therefore to be expected that the more God requires man to rule himself from within, the greater will be the risk that man may not be able to support his new burden.

The development from the childlike to the mature image of relationship demands both greater independence and a more profound basis of interdependence. All the figures involved must divide from each other— the three Persons, God, man, woman, and garden. There must be creation, voluntary self-limitation, separation, alienation, expulsion, a new and more diversified assignment of functions. The *other* must be seen as truly other; the urge to absolute union, whether of man with God or man with woman, must be transformed into an urge for communion.

This process not only is depicted at work in Creation, Fall, and history but is imitated in the poem itself. The poet begins with vast epic gestures, criticizes his own scope and ambitiousness at the beginning of Book VII, and promises to limit himself to the tiny earth. The moral gesture of self-limitation cannot take place until the mind has probed its expansive powers, has tried to fulfill its wishes by making the whole universe its place. Trying to raise itself to God, the poet's mind finds in Book VI that it can only lower heaven to earth and visualize spiritual warfare as Homeric or chivalric bombast. But this error is necessary: the poet must first have uncloistered himself and indulged his titanic impulses so that he may experience his limits; it is through this dialectic that the mind refreshes its awareness of God's distance and transcendence.

V

In moving into Book III from Book II, Milton gives us a sense of the vastness of the cosmos, emphasizing the great physical and spiritual gap separating heaven from hell. Satan, at II.1047ff., beholds

> Far off th' Empyreal Heav'n, extended wide
> In circuit, undetermin'd square or round,
> With Opal Tow'rs and Battlements adorn'd
> Of living Sapphire, once his native Seat;
> And fast by hanging in a golden Chain
> This pendant world, in bigness as a Star
> Of smallest Magnitude close by the Moon.

Here, though we are aware of distances, especially of Heaven's distance from Satan, the cosmos is small and toylike, or rather jewellike—a gem for Satan to pluck from the ear of Night. After his invocation to the holy light in III, the speaker's imagination leaps to heaven and assumes the divine perspective, God's "prospect high, / Wherein past, present, future he beholds" (III.77–78):

> Now had the Almighty Father from above,
> From the pure Empyrean where he sits
> High Thron'd above all highth, bent down his eye,
> His own works and their works at once to view:
> About him all the Sanctities of Heaven
> Stood thick as Stars, and from his sight receiv'd
> Beatitude past utterance. . . .
>
> *(III.56–62)*

From III.80 to 343, the poet impersonates Father and Son in a dialogue which emphasizes God's repeatedly affirmed distance from the evil in his creation. This is followed by a description of cheering angels which is simple, unguarded, and childlike in its literalness:

> The multitude of Angels with a shout
> Loud as from numbers without number, sweet
> As from blest voices, uttering joy, Heav'n rung
> With Jubilee, and loud Hosannas fill'd
> Th' eternal Regions; lowly reverent
> Towards either Throne they bow, and to the ground
> With solemn adoration down they cast
> Thir Crowns inwove with Amarant and Gold,
> Immortal Amarant, a Flow'r which once
> In Paradise, fast by the Tree of Life
> Began to bloom, but soon for man's offence
> To Heav'n remov'd where first it grew, there grows,
> And flow'rs aloft shading the Fount of Life,
> And where the river of Bliss through midst of Heav'n
> Rolls o'er Elysian Flow'rs her Amber stream;
> With these that never fade the Spirits elect
> Bind thir resplendent locks inwreath'd with beams,
> Now in loose Garlands thick thrown off, the bright
> Pavement that like a Sea of Jasper shone
> Impurpl'd with Celestial Roses smil'd.
> Then Crown'd again thir gold'n Harps they took,
> Harps ever tun'd, that glittering by thir side
> Like Quivers hung. . . .
>
> *(III.345–67)*

The only rhetorical qualifiers which might indicate this as a human image, and not the reality, are displaced: "as from" does not mean "as from *voices*," but "as from very *many* and very *blest* voices." The pavement *like* a sea and the harps *like* quivers direct our attention to sensuous comparisons and reinforce the literal vividness of the scene. Though these are painted or theatrical angels, they are imagined and presented with ingenuous directness. Milton raises no questions here, as he does later, about the language of accommodation. If the pagan elements of the image suggest childlike fantasy, the scriptural echoes suggest apocalyptic vision, as if the poet's plea to the holy light had been answered and he had become a vessel of God:

> Shine inward, and the mind through all her powers
> Irradiate, there plant eyes, all mist from thence
> Purge and disperse, that I may see and tell
> Of things invisible to mortal sight.
>
> *(III.52–55)*

Toward the end of their hymn the angels slip into the first person singular ("thy Name / Shall be the copious matter of *my* Song," III.412–13); Merritt Hughes remarks that "throughout *P. L.*, as the invocations to the Heavenly Muse imply, Milton regards himself as almost a member of the choir of angels."* *Throughout* and *almost* are misleading, but certainly in this part of the poem Milton displays a confidence in his visionary or visualizing power which he will later question. Because he does not here bring the issue of angelic perspective into view as a dramatic fact, the reader tends to accept the scene at face value. If we are disturbed by Book III, we should consider that Milton himself later brings the source of disturbance out into the open—I think we should not be disturbed *by* him because we are meant to be disturbed *with* him.

It is interesting that critics disturbed by the poet's attitude toward God in III should not be equally disturbed by his treatment of the garden in IV. For this book has aptly been described as a sustained act of "narrative inattention" (I borrow the phrase from H. M. Leicester, who remarked in a personal communication that Book IV is "thrown" on the narrative just as the mountain and garden are thrown "upon the rapid current" of the "River large" that runs southward through Eden). Milton's treatment of the garden suggests that it is a place of withdrawal for him as well as for Adam. What it embodies is not so much an ideal as an idyll, and the poet's lavish rhetoric makes it clear that he is gratifying his own

---

*John Milton, *Paradise Lost*, ed. Merritt Y. Hughes (New York: The Odyssey Press, 1935), 94, n. on l. 413.

wishes in describing paradise. If he gives play to this urge, however, he
does so only while adopting the perspective of Satan, from whose *pros-pect* most of the garden is viewed. He is aware, like Satan, that the garden is not for him; he is also aware that Satan's envy of paradise and
man's nostalgia for the "lost" green world may be intertwined. The desire to escape from oneself and one's painful condition is pathetic in Satan
but dangerous in man, and Milton allows his very act of describing the
garden to be associated with Satan's seeing it:

> Beneath him with new wonder now he views
> To all delight of human sense expos'd
> In narrow room Nature's whole wealth, yea more,
> A Heaven on Earth. . . .
>
> *(IV.205–8)*

Satan had earlier been compared to "a Thief bent to unhoard the cash /
Of some rich Burgher" (IV.188–89), and we are certainly allowed to
feel that too much of nature's wealth is *hoarded* in too narrow a room;
earth under the aspect of garden is too heavenly. Milton sees the garden
as offering or *exposing* itself like a temptress:

>   the flow'ry lap
> Of some irriguous Valley spread her store,
> Flow'rs of all hue, and without Thorn the Rose:
> Another side, umbrageous Grots and Caves
> Of cool recess, o'er which the mantling vine
> Lays forth her purple Grape, and gently creeps
> Luxuriant; meanwhile murmuring waters fall
> Down the slope hills, disperst, or in a Lake,
> That to the fringed Bank with Myrtle crown'd,
> Her crystal mirror holds, unite thir streams.
> The Birds thir quire apply; airs, vernal airs,
> Breathing the smell of field and grove, attune
> The trembling leaves, while Universal Pan
> Knit with the Graces and the Hours in dance
> Led on th' Eternal Spring. . . .
>
> *(IV.254–68)*

The image, growing cosmetic and literary, has more in common with
Spenser's Bower of Bliss than with his Garden of Adonis, for here all
things *conspire* in a single display of pleasure, a display which is as controlled and deliberate as a dance. There is no need of time or change or

larger space because, as Milton later shows, the whole world reaches itself into Eve's hands,

> Whatever Earth all-bearing Mother yields
> In India East or West, or middle shore
> In Pontus or the Punic Coast, or where
> Alcinoüs reign'd, fruit of all kinds. . . .
>
> *(V.338–41)*

The poet's own response to Adam and Eve contains within its complex
structure a satanic element. He envies mainly the ease and simplicity of
their innocent—i.e., immature—love:

> into thir inmost bower
> Handed they went; and eas'd the putting off
> These troublesome disguises which wee wear,
> Straight side by side were laid, nor turn'd I ween
> Adam from his fair Spouse, nor Eve the Rites
> Mysterious of connubial Love refus'd:
> Whatever Hypocrites austerely talk. . . .
>
> *(IV.738–44)*

The "I ween" reminds us that the poet is speculating from the distance,
perhaps, of his own disappointment. His subsequent praise of "wedded
Love, mysterious Law" appears at first to continue the description of
Adam and Eve (750–52) but changes to the different praise of postlap-
sarian marriage. The rarity and difficulties of this ideal are shadowed in
the references to hypocrites and harlots, to "Court Amours,"

> Mixt Dance, or wanton Mask, or Midnight Ball,
> Or Serenate, which the starv'd Lover sings
> To his proud fair, best quitted with disdain.
>
> *(IV.767–70)*

From this he turns sharply away, escaping back to the vision of paradisaic love, and seeks refuge in a brief counterfactual wish:

> These lull'd by Nightingales imbracing slept,
> And on thir naked limbs the flow'ry roof
> Show'r'd Roses, which the Morn repair'd. Sleep on,
> Blest pair; and O yet happiest if ye seek
> No happier state, and know to know no more.
>
> *(IV.771–75)*

This is not, as we know, Milton's reasoned feeling; it represents a moment of weakness. His total response is radically different from Satan's, yet he reveals in both voices a dangerously common emotional ground, and he might well have assigned some of Satan's sentiments to himself. For example:

> Ah gentle pair, yee little think how nigh
> Your change approaches, when all these delights
> Will vanish and deliver ye to woe. . . .
>
> *(IV.366–68)*

> And should I at your harmless innocence
> Melt, as I do, yet public reason just,
>
> · · · · · · · · · · · ·
>
> . . . compels me now
> To do what else though damn'd I should abhor.
>
> *(IV.388–92)*

> Knowledge forbidd'n?
> Suspicious, reasonless. Why should thir Lord
> Envy them that? can it be sin to know,
> Can it be death? and do they only stand
> By Ignorance, is that thir happy state,
> The proof of thir obedience and thir faith?
> O fair foundation laid whereon to build
> Thir ruin! . . .
>
> *(IV.515–22)*

Again in the ninth book, to suggest a similar moment of weakness, Milton laments, "O much deceiv'd, much failing, hapless Eve" (IX.404) and nostalgically reiterates the catalogue of gardens, reminding us at the same time that such literal garden images (his more delicious than others) are escapes from pain and meaning unless spiritualized by allegorical revision:

> Spot more delicious than those Gardens feign'd
> Or of reviv'd Adonis, or renown'd
> Alcinoüs, host of old Laertes' Son,
> Or that, *not Mystic*, where the Sapient King
> Held dalliance with his fair Egyptian Spouse.
>
> *(IX.439–43, italics mine)*

And in the next line the city-dwelling poet's perspective merges with Satan's, or rather catches up the satanic longing, in a comparison which is itself—local, familiar, ages removed from that terrible threshold of history—a brief holiday from the painful narrative, a brief withdrawal which delays the climax:

> Much hee the Place admir'd, the Person more.
> As one who long in populous City pent,
> Where Houses thick and Sewers annoy the Air,
> Forth issuing on a Summer's Morn to breathe
> Among the pleasant Villages and Farms
> Adjoin'd, from each thing met conceives delight,
> The smell of Grain, or tedded Grass, or Kine,
> Or Dairy, each rural sight, each rural sound;
> If chance with Nymphlike step fair Virgin pass,
> What pleasing seem'd, for her now pleases more,
> She most, and in her look sums all Delight.
> Such Pleasure took the Serpent to behold
> This Flow'ry Plat, the sweet recess of Eve
> Thus early, thus alone; her Heav'nly form
> Angelic, but more soft, and Feminine.
>
> *(IX.444–58)*

There is an echo of that critical moment described a little earlier in which Eve withdrew her hand from Adam's "and like a Wood-Nymph light . . . / Betook her to the Groves" (IX.386–88), and another, even more revealing of Milton's response, of Adam's excessive love of Eve's physical beauty: "what seem'd fair in all the World, seem'd now / Mean, or in her summ'd up" (VIII.472–73). Thus Milton depicts himself projecting and virtually falling in love with his own images: yet at the same time, by qualifying the images, he contains and evaluates his response.

VI

The same technique is evident in Book V. Describing Eve's culinary art, Milton makes her appear a little too curious and "exact of taste," a little too anxious to please her angelic visitor's palate, yet the passage is voiced in the nostalgic tone of one who himself lingers over the lovely age of green or gold when all things reached themselves into the hand:

> She turns, on hospitable thoughts intent
> What choice to choose for delicacy best,
> What order, so contriv'd as not to mix
> Tastes, not well join'd, inelegant, but bring

> Taste after taste upheld with kindliest change,
> Bestirs her then, and from each tender stalk
> Whatever Earth all-bearing Mother yields
> In India East or West, or middle shore
> In Pontus or the Punic Coast, or where
> Alcinoüs reign'd, fruit of all kinds, in coat,
> Rough, or smooth rin'd, or bearded husk, or shell
> She gathers, Tribute large, and on the board
> Heaps with unsparing hand; for drink the Grape
> She crushes, inoffensive must, and meaths
> From many a berry, and from sweet kernels prest
> She tempers dulcet creams, nor these to hold
> Wants her fit vessels pure, then strews the ground
> With Rose and Odours from the shrub unfum'd.
>
> (V.332–49)

This tone continues in the lines immediately following:

> Meanwhile our Primitive great Sire, to meet
> His god-like Guest, walks forth, without more train
> Accompani'd than with his own complete
> Perfections, in himself was all his state,
> More solemn than the tedious pomp that waits
> On Princes, when thir rich Retinue long
> Of Horses led, and Grooms besmear'd with Gold
> Dazzles the crowd. . . .
>
> (V.350–57)

It is a nostalgia not only for a simpler, more unencumbered time, but also for an easier, more indolent time—not only a critique of decadence and aspiration but also an antiheroic (and anti-Miltonic) praise of cloistered and effortless existence. The sentiment penetrates Adam's greeting to Raphael, who deigns to visit those two

> who yet by sovran gift possess
> This spacious ground, in yonder shady Bow'r
> To rest, and what the Garden choicest bears
> To sit and taste, till this meridian heat
> Be over, and the Sun more cool decline.
>
> (V.366–70)

And it also resonates in the angel's answer, as he refers to the nearness of men and heavenly beings:

>   nor art thou such
> Created, or such place hast here to dwell,
> As may not oft invite, though Spirits of Heav'n
> To visit thee; lead on then where thy Bow'r
> O'ershades; for these mid-hours, till Ev'ning rise
> I have at will. . . .
>
>   *(V.372–77)*

Later, after his famous stage direction, "No fear lest Dinner cool" (V.396), and after Raphael's short introductory account of angelic feeding habits (V.426–33), Milton allows himself a last wistful glance backward before the long day's talking:

>   Meanwhile at Table Eve
> Minister'd naked, and thir flowing cups
> With pleasant liquors crown'd: O innocence
> Deserving Paradise! if ever, then,
> Then had the Sons of God excuse to have been
> Enamour'd at that sight; but in those hearts
> Love unlibidinous reign'd, nor jealousy
> Was understood, the injur'd Lover's Hell.
>
>   *(V.443–50)*

But this response, sensuous and verging on sensual, had been preceded by a passage in which the poet's feeling, though present, was contained within a perspective which was tonally and rhetorically more complicated:

>   So to the Silvan Lodge
> They came, that like Pomona's Arbour smil'd
> With flow'rets deck't and fragrant smells; but Eve
> Undeckt, save with herself more lovely fair
> Than Wood-Nymph, or the fairest Goddess feign'd
> Of three that in Mount Ida naked strove,
> Stood to entertain her guest from Heav'n; no veil
> Shee needed, Virtue-proof, no thought infirm
> Alter'd her cheek. On whom the Angel Hail
> Bestow'd, the holy salutation us'd
> Long after to blest Mary, second Eve.
>   Hail Mother of Mankind, whose fruitful Womb
> Shall fill the World more numerous with thy Sons
> Than with these various fruits the Trees of God
> Have heap'd this Table. Rais'd of grassy turf
> Thir table was, and mossy seats had round,

> And on her ample Square from side to side
> All Autumn pil'd, though Spring and Autumn here
> Danc'd hand in hand. . . .
>
> *(V.377–95)*

Eve's nakedness symbolizes her innocent truth and virtue, her obviously good intentions, but something else is suggested in the classical analogies: though she is fairer than a dryad or Venus or Ida, there are ways in which she may not be very different from them. As the Pomona of Paradise she is justly proud of her domain, confident of its—and her—ability "To entertain our Angel guest" (V.328). But she is closely interinvolved with her garden. This is suggested by Raphael's salutation "Hail Mother of Mankind, whose fruitful Womb . . . ," which echoes the poet's recent reference to "Earth all-bearing Mother" (V.338). It is more pervasively suggested throughout the poem in phrases which by implication transfer attributes back and forth between Eve and her flowers, fruits, and trees—especially the tree and fruit of knowledge (e.g., IV.269–70 and IX.424–32, IX.794–804 and 834–38, 849–52 and 892–901, 1100–1107). The Narcissa passage, in which Eve longs for her image in the lake "that to me seem'd another Sky" (IV.456–80), may be seen as a synecdoche of her situation: she loves not only her garden per se but her image in the garden, her self as reflected in her domain; thus even at the end it takes some effort to pry her loose from her native soil and persuade her to follow her husband (XI.268–92). All this seems to be packed into the transition from Pomona's arbor through the wood nymph to Venus trying to impress the connoisseur on Ida and win the prize, and the transition in turn colors the phrase "Stood to entertain." *Entertain* is elsewhere used by Satan with explicit irony (IV.382, V.690, VI.611), and here it is made to betray intentions of which Eve is unaware, intentions all the more dangerous because unconscious: she receives Raphael as a guest, tries to amuse, please, and divert him, perhaps also to hold him a willing captive in her garden (*inter-tenere*) as long as she can. In her own person as in her property and domestic skill, she would like him to feel "that here on Earth / God hath dispenst his bounties as in Heav'n" (V.329–30). If we admit the associations clinging to the wood nymph, we are reminded of a figure whose virgin independence, or *daunger*, is a function of her first love, her loyalty to the region from which she is by nature inseparable, the region which protects, expresses, and belongs to her, as she in turn protects and personifies it. Venus striving on Ida suggests a more self-conscious figure putting her physical charms (and those of her garden) to use. Eve's whole performance, as Milton describes it, comes close to a display of primping, but here the very ingenuousness and misplaced confidence which later cause trouble enhance her charm for the poet. When the latent dangers are about to become actual just before the fall, Milton echoes, expands, and varies two of the pagan analogies:

> from her Husband's hand her hand
> Soft she withdrew, and like a Wood-Nymph light,
> Oread or Dryad, or of Delia's Train,
> Betook her to the Groves, but Delia's self
> In gait surpass'd and Goddess-like deport,
> Though not as shee with Bow and Quiver arm'd,
> But with such Gard'ning Tools as Art yet rude,
> Guiltless of fire had form'd, or Angels brought.
> To Pales, or Pomona, thus adorn'd,
> Likest she seem'd, Pomona when she fled
> Vertumnus, or to Ceres in her Prime,
> Yet Virgin of Proserpina from Jove.
>
> *(IX.385–96)*

There is something comico-pathetic about the way her self-deception is heightened by the substitution of rude gardening tools for the goddess's noble weapons; having just asserted her "Virgin Majesty" and haughtily proclaimed herself above temptation, she emulates the virgin goddess but lacks both her divine immunity and her weapons.

As the allusion to Ceres and Proserpina belies Eve's pose, so in the earlier passage Milton's reference to Mary and Raphael's salutation sounds the shallows of her cloistered condition, consciousness, and virtue. The true Venerean purpose is stated in "Mother of Mankind"— Venus Genetrix, not the Idaean goddess whose narcissism helps initiate the Trojan War. The serial change from virgin to mother will be transcended by the *hortus conclusus* of the second Eve, who is both at once. The fruitfulness of the garden becomes momentarily a figure of the fruitfulness of Eve, which in turn prefigures the fruitfulness of Mary. Yet if historical continuity and typological development are suggested here, the tension between figure and fulfillment is just as clearly implied. The spatial enclosure and sensuous fullness of the paradisaic present, the ingenuous complacency and self-sufficiency of the first Eve, stand in the way of the fullness of time. Everything in Milton's portrait of Eve so far points toward her resisting a fate which would involve expulsion, alienation, and sacrifice—the only entry into the worlds of birth and rebirth. As William Madsen has put it: "Only by an act of sin that destroyed the Garden could the Garden come to be seen as a type of the spiritual life" ("Earth the Shadow of Heaven: Typological Symbolism in *Paradise Lost*," *PMLA*, 75[196]: 524).

In Book VIII (253–314) Milton has Adam make the fairly important yet often neglected point that he was *not* created in paradise but below in the plain of Eden. God takes him up the mountain from the wide earth to the narrow room of paradise, less for temporal or spatial *prospect* than for a life which is complete, self-enclosed and self-contained, a life which does not need the rest of space and history. The experience in the garden is limited and repetitive: Adam and Eve do little else but celebrate God and Creation, make love, amuse themselves and tend plants. Surely Man as Gardener, *Homo Horticultus*, is not Milton's ideal *imago Dei*, and one senses throughout the poem a critique of the commonplace pastoral arguments against aspiration, a critique similar to those of Spenser, Shakespeare, and Marvell. Thus Adam's second mountain ascent in Books XI and XII is presented as a contrast and corrective. Under Michael's direction, he learns that God's presence is not "to these narrow bounds confin'd / Of Paradise or Eden" (XI.341–42). The experience echoes that of Spenser's Redcross being enjoined by Contemplation to leave the Faerie he had been lost in and to return to history:

> only add
> Deeds to thy knowledge answerable, add Faith,
> Add Virtue, Patience, Temperance, add Love,
> By name to come call'd Charity, the soul
> Of all the rest: Then wilt thou not be loath
> To leave this Paradise, but shalt possess
> A paradise within thee, happier far.
> Let us descend now therefore from this top
> Of Speculation; for the hour precise
> Exacts our parting. . . .
>
> *(XII.581–90)*

It is time to leave the green world of sensuous and contemplative fulfillment, time to justify withdrawal by a return to action.

VII

By the end of Book IV Milton is hardly ready to return to the tragic action of the Fall. He "withdraws" in a different way for four more books, the "large day" of discourse which moves in a parabola up to heaven and back down to earth. Here the issue of angelic perspective becomes central. The poet shifts from the naive imagining of III to a more sophisticated view because the dramatic situation embodied in the descent of Raphael allows him to place before us the problem of accommodating divine to human vision:

> Sad task and hard, for how shall I relate
> To human sense th' invisible exploits
> Of warring Spirits. . . .
>
> *(V.564–66)*

Exploits derives from *explicare:* the invisible conflict will seem to *unfold* into visible warfare. The question Raphael subsequently asks will receive an implicitly affirmative answer in the action of the sixth book:

> what surmounts the reach
> Of human sense, I shall delineate so,
> By lik'ning spiritual to corporal forms,
> As may express them best, though what if Earth
> Be but the shadow of Heav'n, and things therein
> Each to other like, more than on earth is thought?
>
> *(V.571–76)*

Later, when Michael and Satan are about to stop boasting and start fighting, Raphael seems less sanguine about the possibility of likeness:

> Unspeakable; for who though with the tongue
> Of Angels, can relate, or to what things
> Liken on Earth conspicuous, that may lift
> Human imagination to such highth
> Of Godlike Power: for likest Gods they seem'd,
> Stood they or mov'd, in stature, motion, arms
> Fit to decide the Empire of great Heav'n.
>
> *(VI.297–303)*

But the effect is actually to increase rather than diminish our sense of Heaven's earthliness: the things on earth to which Raphael likens the angels are the pagan images of divinity. Raphael is not saying, "How they transcend the reach of human sense!" but rather, "How immensely big and strong they are!" Here as everywhere in V and VI, the difference is one of degree, with the implication that heaven is only a bigger, better, and slightly more rarefied version of earth, e.g.:

> Ev'ning now approach'd
> (For wee have also our Ev'ning and our Morn,
> Wee ours for change delectable, not need). . . .
>
> (V.627–29)

> the face of brightest Heav'n had chang'd
> To grateful Twilight (for Night comes not there
> In darker veil). . . .
>
> (V.644–46)

> darkness there might well
> Seem twilight here. . . .
>
> (VI.11–12)

> So under fiery Cope together rush'd
> Both Battles main, with ruinous assault
> And inextinguishable rage; all Heav'n
> Resounded, and had Earth been then, all Earth
> Had to her Centre shook. What wonder? when
> Millions of fierce encount'ring Angels fought
> On either side, the least of whom could wield
> These Elements, and arm him with the force
> Of all thir Regions. . . .
>
> (VI.215–23)

> (. . . Earth hath this variety from Heav'n
> Of pleasure situate in Hill and Dale).
>
> (VI.640–41)

These explanations not only keep the semantic problem before us but also force on us a particular cosmological theory, so that when Raphael concludes, "Thus measuring things in Heav'n by things on Earth" (VI.893), we feel that the measurement has real, and not merely rhetorical, justification. Raphael has been describing levels of existence whose main difference is expressed in his choice of prepositions: *in* the fluid ethereal medium of Heaven, *on* the solid, compacted earth.

The theory behind this view is not *the* cosmology of *Paradise Lost*, but one of a number of world models put forward in sequence and according to dramatic necessity. The action of the poem is not to be construed as occurring *in* a particular universe but as *creating* and *using* cosmic ambients which symbolically manifest its phases. In Book III there is a gap, as it were a layer of insulation, between the spiritual and cosmic regions,

and the latter is an inorganic or mechanical double of the former. The
angels sing "in Heav'n, above the starry Sphere" while the "first con-
vex" of

> the firm opacous Globe
> Of this round World . . . divides
> The luminous inferior Orbs, enclos'd
> From Chaos and th' inroad of Darkness old.
>
> *(III.418–21)*

This globe, we remember, was first depicted from Satan's viewpoint
as hanging from a golden chain, while above it God was "Thron'd above
all highth" and "About him all the Sanctities of Heaven / Stood thick as
Stars." The analogy is completed at III.577–87, when Milton describes
the "golden Sun in splendor likest Heaven":

> Aloof the vulgar Constellations thick,
> That from his Lordly eye keep distance due,
> Dispenses Light from far; they as they move
> Thir Starry dance in numbers that compute
> Days, months, and years, towards his all-cheering Lamp
> Turn swift their various motions, or are turn'd
> By his Magnetic beam, that gently warms
> The Universe, and to each inward part
> With gentle penetration, though unseen,
> Shoots invisible virtue even to the deep:
> So wondrously was set his Station bright.

The last three lines but one echo two previous passages, the first connected with Satan's approach from Chaos and the second with Milton's
plea for the *holy*–i.e., spiritual—light from God's "sovran vital Lamp":

> But now at last the sacred influence
> Of light appears, and from the walls of Heav'n
> Shoots far into the bosom of dim Night
> A glimmering dawn. . . .
>
> *(II.1034–37)*

> So much the rather thou Celestial light
> Shine inward, and the mind through all her powers
> Irradiate, there plant eyes, all mist from thence
> Purge and disperse. . . .
>
> *(III.51–54)*

On the one hand, Milton seems deliberately to conflate spiritual and physical light—at III.22–26, for example, he glides without warning from divine to visual light and from spiritual to physical blindness; the distinction between upper and inner worlds is blurred, while the poet asks for a sharper distinction between inner and outer worlds. On the other hand, although one process is carried through at all levels, there is a clear separation between the empyreal and physical orders; the latter resembles the former because the effect is so completely determined from the outside (from above) by its cause. There is something like a quantum jump between God and the cosmos that embodies his order in its mechanico-chemical intricacies. At the same time, as we have seen, the poet of Book III visualizes the empyreal world in a naively perceptual manner.

In Book V the quantum-jump view is replaced by a Neoplatonic image of existence as a vertical continuum. This cannot be taken as a mere amplification of the former view; it is a contradiction: the mechanistic and deterministic relation of spirit to matter is replaced by one which is organic and vitalistic:

> one Almighty is, from whom
> All things proceed, and up to him return,
> If not deprav'd from good, created all
> Such to perfection, one first matter all,
> Indu'd with various forms, various degrees
> Of substance, and in things that live, of life;
> But more refin'd, more spiritous, and pure,
> As nearer to him plac't or nearer tending
> Each in thir several active Spheres assign'd,
> Till body up to spirit work, in bounds
> Proportion'd to each kind. So from the root
> Springs lighter the green stalk, from thence the leaves
> More aery, last the bright consummate flow'r
> Spirits odorous breathes: flow'rs and thir fruit
> Man's nourishment, by gradual scale sublim'd
> To vital Spirits aspire, to animal,
> To intellectual, give both life and sense,
> Fancy and understanding, whence the Soul
> Reason receives, and reason is her being,
> Discursive, or Intuitive; discourse
> Is oftest yours, the latter most is ours,
> Differing but in degree, of kind the same.

(V.469–90)

The context of this explanation affects its meaning. Raphael has assured Adam that human food is not "ingrateful" to angels, and part of his assurance consisted in describing the Great Chain as held together by cosmic digestion and assimilation:

> food alike those pure
> Intelligential substances require
> As doth your Rational; and both contain
> Within them every lower faculty
> Of sense, whereby they hear, see, smell, touch, taste,
> Tasting concoct, digest, assimilate,
> And corporeal to incorporeal turn.
> For know, whatever was created, needs
> To be sustain'd and fed; of Elements
> The grosser feeds the purer, Earth the sea,
> Earth and the Sea feed Air, the Air those Fires
> Ethereal, and as lowest first the Moon.
>
> *(V.407–18)*

The moon, Raphael continues, exhales nourishment to the higher orbs, the sun exchanges light for humid exhalations, "his alimental recompense," and though the menu in heaven is superb,

> yet God hath here
> Varied his bounty so with new delights,
> As may compare with Heaven; and to taste
> Think not I shall be nice. . . .
>
> *(V.430–33)*

This leads Milton to a brief but admiring aside on the real (not illusory) appetite of angels and on the "concoctive heat" whereby their systems alchemically transmute waste matter to intellectual spirit. His next stage direction is turned by a pun into a comic exemplification of the process just described:

> Thus when with meats and drinks they had suffic'd
> Not burd'n'd Nature, *sudden mind arose*
> In Adam, not to let th' occasion pass
> Given him by his great Conference to know
> Of things above his World. . . .
>
> *(V.451–55, italics mine)*

Dinner is thus the occasion, the model, and even the cause of Raphael's Neoplatonic account, itself a refined and generalized version of the passage on digestion. Mind and matter, knowledge and appetite, spiritual and physical beings, angels, men, and elements—all are parts of a single cosmic organism to whose functions they contribute. So far as rank and differentiation are concerned, the digestive model places emphasis less on various forms or degrees of substance and life than on density and rarity: to be higher and better is primarily to be "more refin'd, more spiritous, and pure." Thus, as in the famous analogy of the flower ("So from the root . . . ," V.479–83, the *so* ambiguously meaning "as" and "thus"), any lower and perceptually more available object can give accurate information about objects above it on the scale and can, as *pars pro toto*, give accurate information about the whole process. As object it contributes to the life, and as symbol to the knowledge, of higher beings. The emphasis on the dense-to-rare continuum as the criterion of rank and diversity produces a corresponding emphasis on a unity ("one first matter all") which is more than analogical and which is attributed to Being, not merely to Thought. This entails two consequences: beings may be ontologically translated up or down the scale, a process which seems mainly to involve adjustment of the dense-rare proportion; and rational beings may learn about the Whole accurately and absolutely (while remaining in place) by contemplating its microcosmic reflection in themselves or in other available members of the continuum. These consequences are drawn, the first by Raphael and the second by Adam, at the conclusion of the cosmological discourse:

> time may come when men
> With Angels may participate, and find
> No inconvenient Diet, nor too light Fare:
> And from these corporal nutriments perhaps
> Your bodies may at last turn all to Spirit,
> Improv'd by tract of time, and wing'd ascend
> Ethereal, as wee, or may at choice
> Here or in Heav'nly Paradises dwell;
> If ye be found obedient. . . .
>
> *(V.493–501)*

> O favourable spirit, propitious guest,
> Well has thou taught the way that might direct
> Our knowledge, and the scale of Nature set
> From centre to circumference, whereon

> In contemplation of created things
> By steps we may ascend to God. . . .
>
> *(V.507–12)*

The Fall not only cancels the first possibility; it leads to a rearrangement of the universe which will greatly diminish the ease of access and intercourse between different ranks. Emphasis will shift from likeness to difference and from difference in degree to difference in kind. Though Adam's statement of the familiar ladder theory of knowledge may still be valid, it will have to be reinterpreted—reinterpreted, that is, in the light of what follows, for Milton uses the theory in Books V and VI to make heaven a mere rarefied shadow of earth.

VIII

Thus Milton's use of the Neoplatonic continuum in this part of the poem encourages a self-expansive optimism which will be checked and criticized in the second half. It may well be that he, like More, Spenser, Shakespeare, Donne, Marvell, and others, intends to suggest the limits of that idyllic or green-world idealism associated with the Florentine Academy and its influence. At any rate, he uses it to support a deliberate move in the wrong direction, the move toward the war in heaven which—with the continuum in mind—we can but interpret as literal description. The very arrangement of episodes and topics in Books IV–VI enforces this movement, characterizing it as an anthropomorphic extension of ideal earthly experience to the realm of spirit. The poet's detailed and loving treatment of the dense earthly garden is recalled by numerous rarefied echoes in Raphael's account of heaven. The fifth book opens with an anticipation of the digestive continuum—note how the poet begins with a large-scale horticultural image and then moves up close to his subject:

> Now Morn her rosy steps in th' Eastern Clime
> Advancing, sow'd the Earth with Orient Pearl,
> When Adam wak't, so custom'd, for his sleep
> Was Aery light, from pure digestion bred,
> And temperate vapours bland. . . .

Exhorting Eve to awake, he concludes his reference to the garden with an epitome of the process to be dilated throughout the book until it embraces the whole world:

> Awake, the morning shines, and the fresh field
> Calls us, we lose the prime, to mark how spring
> Our tended Plants, how blows the Citron Grove,
> What drops the Myrrh, and what the balmy Reed,
> How Nature paints her colours, how the Bee
> Sits on the Bloom extracting liquid sweet.
>
> *(V.20–25)*

After this there is a pivotal movement from the cosmology of Book III to the continuum model. Adam's explanation of reason and fancy (V. 100 – 113) looks backward, both to the interrupted narrative of temptation in IV and to the quantum-jump hierarchy of III, here extended to psychic faculties. The two main points of transition are the hymn of Adam and Eve and Raphael's descent from heaven. The hymn begins by distinguishing the Creator from his works and by echoing the description of angels in III:

> Unspeakable, who sit'st above these Heavens
> To us invisible or dimly seen
> In these thy lowest works, yet these declare
> Thy goodness beyond thought, and Power Divine.
> Speak yee who best can tell, ye Sons of light,
> Angels, for yee behold him, and with songs
> And choral symphonies, Day without Night,
> Circle his Throne rejoicing, yee in Heav'n,
> On Earth join all ye Creatures to extol
> Him first, him last, him midst, and without end.
>
> *(V.156–65)*

The analogy of stars and angels is then echoed, but here with a slight satanic tinge in the indirect reference to Lucifer:

> Fairest of Stars, last in the train of Night,
> If better thou belong not to the dawn,
> Sure pledge of day, that crown'st the smiling Morn
> With thy bright Circlet, praise him in thy Sphere.
>
> *(V.166–69)*

This is followed by praise of the "Sun, of this great World both Eye and Soul," the moon, the planets "that move / In mystic Dance not without Song," and the elements, "the eldest birth / Of Nature's Womb," which by metamorphosis describe their own "Perpetual Circle, multiform."

Paradise Lost *Evolving*

The hints of personification (Sun and Nature) are broadened and sustained in the following apostrophes:

> Ye Mists and Exhalations that now rise
> From Hill or steaming Lake, dusky or grey,
> Till the Sun paint your fleecy skirts with Gold,
> In honour to the World's great Author rise,
> Whether to deck with Clouds the uncolour'd sky,
> Or wet the thirsty Earth with falling showers,
> Rising or falling still advance his praise.
> His praise ye Winds, that from four Quarters blow,
> Breathe soft or loud; and wave your tops, ye Pines,
> With every Plant, in sign of Worship wave.
> Fountains and yee, that warble, as ye flow,
> Melodious murmurs, warbling tune his praise.
> Join voices all ye living Souls, ye Birds,
> That singing up to Heaven Gate ascend.
>
> *(V.185–98)*

This image of an animate universe is produced by transfer of terms from soul to world, and the first part may remind one of Satan at Eve's ear trying "to reach / The Organs of her Fancy," to see if,

> inspiring venom, he might taint
> Th' animal Spirits that from pure blood arise
> Like gentle breaths from Rivers pure, thence raise
> At least distemper'd, discontented thoughts.
>
> *(IV.804–7)*

But apart from such particular echoes, the entire process embodied in the hymn suggests how the human soul (Ficino's *nodus et vinculum mundi*) binds together the unspeakable and the mute levels of existence by treating them all on the model of organic human activity. The seen and the unseen are linked through *words;* the images of physical and visible nature are made to *bespeak* God in being converted to symbols or changed by metaphoric attribution. Thus a growing fluidity characterizes the relations of upper to lower and inner to outer as we approach the visit of Raphael and the interpenetration of angelic and human sensibilities.

Raphael's descent is visualized in a passage in which Milton has heightened "the demonic insidiousness of his language," to borrow a phrase from Thomas Greene's brilliant interpretation of V.219–300 in *The Descent from Heaven* (New Haven: Yale University Press, 1963). As

Greene shows, the murky syntax and imagery of the passage enforce the distinction between Raphael's clear and our obscure vision. But we should remember that *our* includes the fallen poet's vision and that a reflexive analogy may lurk in the analogues of Galileo and the pilot:

> As when by night the Glass
> Of Galileo, less assur'd, observes
> Imagin'd Lands and Regions in the Moon:
> Or Pilot from amidst the Cyclades
> Delos or Samos first appearing kens
> A cloudy spot. . . .

> *(V.261–66)*

The earlier Galileo references sharpen the analogy: Satan's shield, described as he is about to set up his domain on the "shore" of Hell, is compared to the moon,

> whose Orb
> Through Optic Glass the Tuscan Artist views
> At Ev'ning from the top of Fesole,
> Or in Valdarno, to descry new Lands,
> Rivers or Mountains in her spotty Globe.

> *(I.287–91)*

At III.588–90, Satan landing on the sun is described as

> a spot like which perhaps
> Astronomer in the Sun's lucent Orb
> Through his glaz'd Optic Tube yet never saw.

There is of course the implied danger of merely physical or scientific exploration in a universe whose essential character is moral. More relevant is the danger of projecting from the near to the remote, from the familiar to the unfamiliar, so as to extend the limited categories of fallen human experience to an area which may indeed be different from or transcendent of these categories. Galileo *imagined* lands and regions; he viewed the moon to *descry* new lands, rivers, *or* mountains (the *or* suggests that he is looking for something familiar, though he is not certain what he will find). Thus peopled by human conjecture, the new regions may remain unknown; thus leading our fantasy into possibly false surmises, spiritual powers may hide their true natures from us. As Satan colonizes hell and Galileo the moon, perhaps also Milton colonizes—or is about to colonize—heaven. For Milton, too, is an explorer: if, looking through his glass, he brings heaven and the angel nearer so that they

can be seen more clearly, he also allows us to wonder whether anthropomorphic preconceptions do not travel in the other direction, from
mind through eye and glass to heaven. He may want us to entertain the
possibility that the necessary limit expressed in the phrase *in aenigmate* is
not being honored as it should.

There is no apparent difference between Raphael as described in
heaven and on earth, though at two points Milton's rhetorical shifts
smoke the edges of the figure. The first is Raphael's departure:

> nor delay'd the winged Saint
> After his charge receiv'd; but from among
> Thousand Celestial Ardors, where he stood
> Veil'd with his gorgeous wings, up springing light
> Flew through the midst of Heav'n. . . .
>
> (V.247–51)

Partly because of the image suggested by *Ardors,* partly because of the
way the penultimate line delays yet leans on the final phrase, *light* seems
momentarily to function as a noun, the subject of *Flew.* As in the sentence, so in the image, the angelic form is briefly blurred; this baroque
touch not only conveys sudden speed and power but also dematerializes
and dehumanizes the form. The second, more puzzling, passage first
compares Raphael to the phoenix—"to all the Fowls he seems / A Phoenix" (V.271–72)—"He lights, and to his proper shape returns / A
Seraph wing'd" (V.276–77). It is as if the appearance, the simile, has
become the reality. The poet moves from a tentative and conjectural
to a definite literal description. The angelic form, once flickering and
blurred because of the way it was visualized, now appears solid and more
precisely human in detail. At the same time it is more artificial—more
painted, as it were—and symbolic:

> six wings he wore, to shade
> His lineaments Divine; the pair that clad
> Each shoulder broad, came mantling o'er his breast
> With regal Ornament; the middle pair
> Girt like a Starry Zone his waist, and round
> Skirted his loins and thighs with downy Gold
> And colours dipt in Heav'n; the third his feet
> Shadow'd from either heel with feather'd mail
> Sky-tinctur'd grain. Like Maia's son he stood,
> And shook his Plumes, that Heav'nly fragrance fill'd
> The circuit wide. . . .
>
> (V.277–87)

Shade means both "to conceal" and "to figure forth": what seem to be concealed are simply the "lineaments Divine" of his human body. What is figured forth, on the other hand, is the hierarchic universe: the upper pair of wings manifests the regal ornament suggestive of Raphael's rank and his relation to God; the middle pair connotes the higher region of the heavens associated with fixed stars; the third pair seems to indicate the lower region of the *sky* occupied by birds. As Milton describes him, he becomes not only more human but more pagan in his heroic quality, and by the time we get to his winged feet, we are prepared for the reference to Hermes. Perhaps we are expected to think that the pagan image of the heavenly messenger was a distorted version of this "real" angel. But perhaps we are also to remember Milton's classical sources—perhaps, that is, the allusion is to the process of borrowing and imitating—and to note that the poet has reverted to an older mode of visualization. *Hermes*, at any rate, means—and is—"the interpreter," and Raphael descending on a hermetic mission bears the upper reaches of the universe *in propria persona* and makes them available to Adam in the garden.

The descent is thus a dramatic symbol of and prelude to the lowering of heaven and the anthropomorphic mingling of divine and earthly orders which is about to unfold in the continuum model and in the war in heaven. And the scene which follows the descent reveals how that process is rooted in the dense, compact earthly center of the garden, within the idyllic context of dinner and infinite leisure—the process is rooted here, and in expanding outward it carries the garden imagery with it. The angel wanders through the chaotic plenty of the green world, "A Wilderness of sweets" which expresses Eve as well as Nature:

> Nature here
> Wanton'd as in her prime, and play'd at will
> Her Virgin Fancies, pouring forth more sweet,
> Wild above Rule or Art, enormous bliss.
>
> *(V.294–97)*

The sun "Shot down direct his fervid Rays, to warm / Earth's inmost womb" (V.300–301) while, as Adam remarks,

> Nature multiplies
> Her fertile growth, and by disburd'ning grows
> More fruitful, which instructs us not to spare.
>
> *(V.318–20)*

Eve's response concludes with the leitmotif which will echo throughout the ensuing narrative:

> Adam, earth's hallow'd mould,
> Of God inspir'd, small store will serve, where store,
> All seasons, ripe for use hangs on the stalk;
> Save what by frugal storing firmness gains
> To nourish, and superfluous moist consumes:
> But I will haste and from each bough and brake,
> Each Plant and juiciest Gourd will pluck such choice
> To entertain our Angel guest, as hee
> Beholding shall confess that here on Earth
> God hath dispenst his bounties as in Heav'n.
>
> *(V.321–330)*

We should remember that the premise underlying both this sentiment and the entire angelic narrative through Book VI has already been introduced in an episode which qualifies them from the start: Eve's evil dream (V.28–93). Though the dream makes her uncomfortable, its influence lingers. The magical idea that total knowledge, experience, and power can be gained by eating is echoed in the assumption that it can be gained *while* eating and extends further in the notion that it can be embraced on the model of nourishment. At one point in her dreams Eve remembers,

> Forthwith up to the Clouds
> With him I flew, and underneath beheld
> The Earth outstretcht immense, a prospect wide
> And various. . . .
>
> *(V.86–89)*

A version of this experience is imitated vicariously through the medium of angelic disclosure in Books V–VIII, but with this central difference: Raphael's account describes a parabola which crests at Book VI and arcs downward in VII and VIII; earthly categories are "outstretcht immense" until they embrace heaven but are retracted in VII. Eve's sudden fall when her guide abandons her (V.90–92) contrasts with the controlled descent of Milton's angelic discourse.

The apogee of the discourse is the appearance and triumph of the Son, who is presented not as the self-sacrificing Savior but as a Jovian Messiah. Here Milton conflates Hebraic and pagan modes of imagination—Ezekiel's vision applied to Messiah's chariot and the warrior-god accoutred with an eagle-winged Victory, a bow and arrows, and thunderbolts—to produce a distinctly archaic episode, marked by two noteworthy characteristics. First, after the visionary and symbolic aspects are stressed, Milton puts those objects literally into play as military functions. In Ezekiel, the vision gradually materializes through the first chapter, never crystallizing into a definite chariot image; the element of visionary appearance is always kept before us ("the appearance of the likeness of the glory of God"); and the total image, which serves only as a prelude to God's spirit entering the prophet, is left behind, to be restated among other symbolic visions (Ezek. 10). While Milton encourages us to think of this context, he immediately *de-sophisticates* the vision by applying it to an object which, however mystical, is real enough to hold a passenger, is located in a precise narrative situation requiring literal activity:

> the third sacred Morn began to shine
> Dawning through Heav'n: forth rush'd with whirl-wind sound
> The Chariot of Paternal Deity,
> Flashing thick flames, Wheel within Wheel, undrawn,
> Itself instinct with Spirit, but convoy'd
> By four Cherubic shapes. . . .
>
> *(VI.748–53)*

The Messiah is crowded into his chariot along with a variety of objects which seem at first to symbolize attributes but which harden into useful implements after Raphael makes it clear that he is picturing the event as it occurred:

> Hee in Celestial Panoply all arm'd
> Of radiant Urim, work divinely wrought,
> Ascended, at his right hand Victory
> Sat Eagle-wing'd, beside him hung his Bow
> And Quiver with three-bolted Thunder stor'd,
> And from about him fierce Effusion roll'd
> Of smoke and bickering flame, and sparkles dire;
> Attended with ten thousand thousand Saints,
> He onward came, far off his coming shone,
> And twenty thousand (*I thir number heard*)
> Chariots of God, half on each hand were seen.
>
> *(VI.760–70, italics mine)*

> At once the Four spread out thir Starry wings
> With dreadful shade contiguous, and the Orbs
> Of his fierce Chariot roll'd, as with the sound
> Of torrent Floods, or of a numerous Host.
> Hee on his impious Foes right onward drove,
> Gloomy as Night; under his burning Wheels
> The steadfast Empyrean shook throughout,

> All but the Throne itself of God. Full soon
> Among them he arriv'd; in his right hand
> Grasping ten thousand Thunders, which he sent
> Before him, such as in thir Souls infix'd
> Plagues; they astonisht all resistance lost,
> All courage; down thir idle weapons dropp'd;
> O'er Shields and Helms, and helmed heads he rode.
>
> *(VI.827–40)*

As in the description of Raphael descending, the shift from scriptural to pagan imagery and from rough to precise notation converts transcendent vision into the kind of heroic image which would appeal to a child: the wheels make a whirring noise, the ground shakes, the angelic victims have not only helms but helmed heads.

Second, if the apocalyptic connotations are retained, they serve another purpose, which is suggested in William Madsen's statement that "Raphael's account is not a moral allegory, nor is it primarily a metaphorical description of what happened a long time ago in heaven. It is a shadow of things to come, and more particularly it is a shadow of this last age of the world and of the Second Coming of Christ" ("Earth the Shadow of Heaven," p. 525). Madsen, however, reads it as a serious typological prophecy, whereas I think it is one of a number of wish-fulfilling moments which give the sixth book its primary character. In looking simultaneously back to the Old Testament and forward to the Second Coming, Raphael's overview suggests the same circular time-abolishing vision as that produced by the narrative arrangement of the first six books. The vision in fact overleaps the "shadow of this last age" to resolve all problems in the finality of the Happy Ending. Both the millennial quality of the vision and its historical limitations are suggested in Milton's use of the name Messiah. The physical violence of Messiah's triumph, the forceful projection and separation of good and evil into two armies, the single encounter which resolves all difficulties, the irrevocable exorcism whereby Heaven is easily "disburd'n'd"—all this suggests the play of an imagination impatient of actual conditions, giving vent to utopian impulses, vicariously chastising evil and concluding with a great visionary sigh of relief:

> Sole Victor from th' expulsion of his Foes
> Messiah his triumphal Chariot turn'd:
> To meet him all his Saints, who silent stood
> Eye-witnesses of his Almighty Acts,
> With Jubilee advanc'd; and as they went,

> Shaded with branching Palm, each order bright,
> Sung Triumph, and him sung Victorious King,
> Son, Heir, and Lord, to him Dominion giv'n,
> Worthiest to Reign: he celebrated rode
> Triumphant through mid Heav'n, into the Courts
> And Temple of his mighty Father Thron'd
> On high; who into Glory him receiv'd,
> Where now he sits at the right hand of bliss.
>
>   *(VI.880–92)*

All that remains—an anticlimax, perhaps, from the heavenly perspective in which the final triumph is assured and is recurrently foreshadowed both in history and in *Paradise Lost*—all that remains is the sum total of human vicissitude. In the closing verse paragraph of Book VI Raphael frames Messiah's blissful *now* in the other blissful *now* of the garden discourse, reminds Adam of the trouble ahead, and thereby reminds us that the poem is but half complete. As I suggested above, we might see this performance as a critical staging by Milton of his own youthful optimism as well as an enactment of an imaginative mode indigenous to an older time, the youth of civilization. It is a necessary phase of consciousness which must be experienced to be understood, must be given its head to be controlled and transcended. Madsen suggests this but does not draw the proper conclusion:

> When Abdiel's "noble stroke" sent Satan back recoiling, one can imagine the youthful Milton in the very forefront of the angelic host, filled with "Presage of Victory and fierce desire / Of Battle" . . . , just as he had been in the forefront of those who saw in the Puritan Revolution a presage of the Millennium. But Abdiel was wrong: his reason did not overcome Satan's might, and the first blow struck against evil did not end the war. From the reader's point of view the outcome of the struggle is never in doubt because he is privileged to see it under the aspect of eternity (526).

To see it under that aspect is clearly, for Milton, the easy way out; what really matters to him is not the heavenly war and the angelic vision but the much more limited and embattled prospect of the human and historical present. For the concrete individual, the outcome *is* in doubt, and Milton's appeals to the larger view, the divine plane of events, seem to function largely as moments of temporary escape, relief, clarification of issues, unguarded optimism, or impatience with limited mortal solutions. If, as Madsen states, "the principal lesson that Raphael's narrative inculcates is the lesson of patience" (525), this is clearly a lesson shown to apply to the speaker himself as well as to Adam.

PART FIVE

Art

L. B. Alberti on Painting: Art and Actuality in Humanist Perspective

I

THIS ANALYSIS OF Leon Battista Alberti's *Della Pittura* (1435) grows out of the rudimentary sketch of the theory and practice of rational perspective which I gave in "The Renaissance Imagination" (reprinted in this volume). That sketch was largely a summary of the interpretations made by art historians since the early decades of this century.[1] Its aim was to slant their conclusions toward my own topic, the second world, and to suggest how the Renaissance interest in creating a heterocosm permeates the style and practice as well as the theory of the period. I now want to carry this discussion further by examining at closer range certain theoretical assumptions and technical details of Alberti's method. I shall first examine the art theory in the treatise and then its literary structure, and I shall conclude with some generalizations about the early, or humanist, form of Renaissance imagination.

In "The Renaissance Imagination" I described Alberti's interest not only in the self-sufficient second world of painting and its relation to the first, or actual, world but also in the imaginary or hypothetical nature of the second world (pp. 17–25). I discussed his concern for the reality of make-believe in relation to his faith that the hypothetical or mind-made image corrected the actual world of which it was an image. Its superiority was seen to result in part from the synthetic embodiment and uni-

[1] See note 18 of "The Renaissance Imagination" for a select bibliography.

fication in a painting of a more or less rigorous analysis of visual experience. In concluding my discussion of perspective, I suggested that in many of Alberti's descriptions of procedure "the notions of difference from and superimposition on actual experience are extended to matters of technique, to the relation between painter and observer, to the creation of a new world not simply *on* the picture plane but on both sides of it" (p. 25).

This is curiously apparent in Alberti's treatment of optical theory. His translator, John Spencer, interpolates two Latin passages into his version of the Italian text,[2] passages which indicate that Alberti was familiar with classical theories about the actual psychology and physiology of vision but that he did not consider them relevant to his current undertaking:

> Among the ancients there was no little dispute whether these [visual] rays came from the eye or the plane. This dispute is passed over easily and is useless for us.

> Nor is this the place to discuss whether images rest on the juncture of the interior nerve, as it is called, or whether they are represented on the surface of the eye as on a living mirror. Nor is reference made here to the work of the soul or eye in vision. It will be enough in this brief commentary to demonstrate only things which are essential. (46–47)[3]

Purely objective or subjective conditions are ignored because they are not directly pertinent to those aspects of vision connected with pictorial construction. What Alberti stresses are "facts" like these: "Some . . . rays strike the outline of the plane and measure its quantity. . . . The eye measures these quantities with the visual rays as with a pair of compasses" (46). The rays are like threads bound tightly within the eye; the eye, like *un nodo*, sends its shoots to the intersecting surface. If this is playful and metaphoric, it is also extremely important because it shows Alberti raising on the objective platform of geometry a purely hypothetical or imaginary theory of vision which yet affirms the subjectivist principle. The picture embodies the particular experience of a particular artist; it is seen from a particular standpoint, yet it has been scientifically stabilized and rendered universally valid: each observer can replace the artist before the painting and in effect see what he "saw." While claim-

---

[2] Leon Battista Alberti, *On Painting*, trans. J. R. Spencer (New Haven: Yale University Press, 1956). All page references will be to this edition.

[3] Codex Vat. Ottoboniani Latini 1424, fol. 2v & 3v. The passage seems to be copied from Vitruvius, VI.ii.3.

ing a philosophical or mathematical basis for painting, the theorist is on the way to a distinction later codified by Pomponius Gauricus as that between "natural" and "graphic" perspective. In transferring his topic from the realm of perceptual fact to that of pictorial representation, from seeing actual images to making hypothetical images, Alberti is aware of the differences and of the need to correct the data. In his imaginary psychology of vision, the artist becomes the model for the observer, and making a picture becomes a model for seeing an image. The hypothetical character of the undertaking is frankly expressed much later by Andrea Pozzo (1693) in a statement not unlike Sidney's "The Poet . . . nothing affirmes, and therefore never lyeth": "Since Perspective is but a Counterfeiting of the Truth, the Painter is not oblig'd to make it appear real when seen from Any part, but from One determinate Point only."[4]

A significant aspect of Alberti's hypothetical theory of vision is his distinction between strong and weak rays. The former are the extreme and central rays, the latter the median rays:

> With the extreme rays quantity is measured. All space on the plane that is between any two points on the outline is called a quantity. The eye measures the quantities with the visual rays as with a pair of compasses. (46)

> The central ray is that single one which alone strikes the quantity directly, and about which every angle is equal . . . the most active and the strongest of all the rays . . . tightly encircled by the other rays, it is the last to abandon the thing seen, from which it merits the name, prince of rays. (48)

> Median rays, that multitude in the pyramid . . . within the extrinsic rays, . . . behave . . . like the chameleon, an animal which takes to itself the colours of things near it . . . these rays carry both the colours and the lights on the plane from where they touch it up to the eye . . . through a great distance they become weakened. I think the reason may be that weighted down with light and colour they pass through the air, which, being humid with a certain heaviness, tires the laden rays. From this we can draw a rule: as the distance becomes greater, so the plane seen appears more hazy. (48)

The most important and active rays are those which have geometrical functions and are therefore connected with what later came to be known as primary qualities; the more passive median rays are connected with secondary qualities. Alberti speaks of the active rays as if they traveled unidirectionally from eye to plane and of the median rays as if they trav-

[4]Quoted in Timothy K. Kitao, "Prejudice in Perspective: A Study of Vignola's Perspective Treatise," *Art Bulletin* 40 (1961): 189–90.

eled unidirectionally from plane to eye. As his rhetoric clearly shows, this theory of rays is not an attempt to deal with optics at the level of fact; rather, the optical "facts" are used to "explain" some of the data and processes of representation in a way that places them on a more "scientific" footing. The theory also gives symbolic expression to more general and epistemological relations between mind and matter, art and nature, thought and perception, and the like. Among other things, it exemplifies the Florentine predilection for linear rather than coloristic elements in design, and it helps redefine the medium in dominantly intellectual terms. Color is connected to what comes to the mind from the material world, and it is perhaps by way of emphasizing its subordinate function that Alberti appeals to the medieval identification of the four "true" colors with the four elements.

Alberti's treatment of the measuring and color rays is not an isolated pattern; it is an epitome of his way of thinking and finds a parallel in his general procedure. He describes the process so as to make it seem that the active measuring rays first go out and the passive color rays then return. The mind, working through the eye, selectively abstracts the appropriate mathematical forms and then fills them out with the sensuous data which render the scene vivid and lifelike. The plan for the whole treatise follows a similar pattern:

> You will see three books; the first, all mathematics, concerning the roots in nature which are the source of this delightful and most noble art. The second book puts the art in the hand of the artist, distinguishing its parts and demonstrating all. The third introduces the artist to the means and the end, the ability and the desire of acquiring perfect skill and knowledge in painting. (40)

> To make clear my exposition in writing this brief commentary on painting, I will take first from the mathematicians those things with which my subject is concerned. When they are understood, I will enlarge on the art of painting from its first principles in nature. . . . Mathematicians measure with their minds alone the forms of things separated from all matter. Since we wish the object to be seen, we will use a more sensate wisdom [*più grassa Minerva*]. (43)

The treatise begins by withdrawing to the universal and quantitative schemata of geometric form, the special province of the mind, and goes on to readmit into this prepared space the local qualifications—light, shadow, human gesture, and action—through which a significant moment of life is visually rendered. The plan and treatment of the second book reveal a similar movement:

Painting is divided into three parts; these divisions we have taken from nature.

Since painting strives to represent things seen, let us note in what way things are seen. First, in seeing a thing, we say it occupies a place. Here the painter, in describing this space, will say this, his guiding an outline with a line, is circumscription.

Then, looking at it again, we understand that more planes of the observed body belong together, and here the painter drawing them in their places will say that he is making a composition.

Finally, we determine more clearly the colours and qualities of the planes. Since every difference in them is born from light, we can properly call their representation the reception of light.

Therefore, painting is composed of circumscription, composition and reception of light. (67–68)

We should note the causal inversion: "let us note in what way things are seen" explains the previous phrase, "taken from nature," but it is actually *modeled after* Alberti's description of the way things are to be represented; nature implicitly equals art. And with Alberti, as has often been pointed out, the idea of art is partly dissociated from its traditional connection with—rather, reduction to—*craft* and elevated to an intellectual discipline. This is well exemplified in the treatment of color. Where Cennino, in his *Libro dell'Arte* (1437), discusses color in terms of pigment, of material sources and their preparation, of application *to* the opaque surface, Alberti considers color along with light and shade as aspects of the imaginary three-dimensional field seen *through* the transparent surface. For a late-medieval sensibility like Cennino's, color is a material component of the first, or actual, world, whereas Alberti treats it as having another existence in the second world. Cennino does not substantially differentiate black and white from the other colors, but Alberti reminds the painter that "white and black are not true colors but are alterations of other colors," by which he means that in the heterocosm they are the means of conveying light and shade, the values which qualify a colored object because of its situation in a visual field.

Alberti considers not only the formal beauty *of* the second world but also the beauty and significance of what is *in* the second world—i.e., the *istoria*. As Spencer remarks, this term is difficult to translate with precision, but it refers to "monumentality and dramatic content": "The *istoria* advocated by the treatise . . . is directed towards the expression of a new humanist art which will be capable of incorporating the finds of the literary and theological humanists while at the same time satisfying the demands of the artistic humanist" (23–24). *Istoria* does not refer to subject matter in a strictly narrative, historical, or iconographic sense. If *istoria* adds to Alberti's concern for significant form, a more embracing concern for the image of man, the emphasis on *man* is not to be isolated from the emphasis on *image*. Through the concept of *istoria* Alberti unites formal and affective considerations under a single rubric: *istoria* is discussed in the section on composition as its most important aspect, indeed its end, and composition-as-*istoria* is treated in its relation to the beholder. For example:

> Composition is that rule of painting by which the parts of the things seen fit together in the painting. The greatest work of the painter is not a colossus, but an *istoria*. *Istoria* gives greater renown to the intellect than any colossus. Bodies are part of the *istoria*, members are parts of the bodies, planes part of the members. (72)

> The *istoria* which merits both praise and admiration will be so agreeably and pleasantly attractive that it will capture the eye of whatever learned or unlearned person is looking at it and will move his soul. (75)

> The *istoria* will move the soul of the beholder when each man painted there clearly shows the movement of his own soul . . . we weep with the weeping, laugh with the laughing, and grieve with the grieving. These movements of the soul are made known by movements of the body. (77)

> We painters who wish to show the movements of the soul by movements of the body are concerned solely with the movement of change of place. (79)

If in these passages visual form subserves human content, there are a few other places in which the relation is reversed:

> In every *istoria* variety is always pleasant. A painting in which there are bodies in many dissimilar poses is always especially pleasing . . . to each one is given his own action and flection of members. (76)

> Since man is the thing best known to man, perhaps Protagoras, by saying that man is the mode and measure of all things, meant that all the accidents of things are known through the comparison to the accidents of man . . . no matter how well small bodies are painted in the picture they will appear large and small by comparison with whatever man is painted there. . . . Here I determine as it pleases me the sizes of the men in my picture. I divide the length of this man in three parts. These parts to me are proportional to that measurement called a *braccio*, for, in measuring the average man it is seen that he is about three *braccia*. With these *braccia* I divide the base line of the rectangle into as many parts as it will receive. . . . Then . . . I make a point which occupies that place where the central ray strikes. For this it is called the centric point. This point is properly placed when it is no higher from the

base line of the quadrangle than the height of the man that I have to paint there. Thus both the beholder and the painted things he sees will appear to be on the same plane. (55–56)

The ascending series planes-members-bodies-souls is reversible so that the artist may just as easily consider the human figure and the expressions of soul as means to an esthetic end and effect; this emphasis is subordinate in the *Della Pittura*, but we see it actively competing with a more representational and humanist impulse certainly no later than in Raphael's Eliodoro phase.

Alberti's concept of *istoria* is much like Aristotle's concept of *muthos*, or plot:

> most important . . . is the structure of events. For tragedy is an imitation not of men as such but of an action . . . and the end of the story is a certain action, not a quality . . . the course of events, the plot, is the goal of tragedy. . . . (*Poetics* 1450a, 15–24, trans. Gerald Else)

Both are concerned with a self-sufficient heterocosm, with a visual medium in which movement and moment are to express actions of the human soul. As Aristotle subordinates *opsis* to *muthos*, the spatial to the temporal component, so Alberti treats the formal, spatial, and generally spectacular elements of painting as instruments of *istoria* or *muthos* and yet, like Aristotle, does not think of *istoria* as a thing apart from its formal constituents. Like Aristotle, Alberti considers composition and istoria in their effect on the audience and treats the emotions, gestures, and actions of painted figures as homeopathic models for the beholder's responses. Finally, Alberti, like Aristotle, is concerned to coordinate a unified action—a fictional *now*—with the particular standpoint of the beholder.[5]

Most interesting among these aspects is the manner in which Alberti both sustains and transforms the unity of pictorial object and perceiving subject from the purely geometrical context of spatial diagram to the more sensuous context of representation. His peculiar use of a "distance point" illuminates his purpose. He remarks as an aside in the first book that "a painted thing can never appear truthful where there is not a definite distance for seeing it"; then, after stating how orthogonals are to be established by drawing lines from baseline divisions to the centric point, he describes another diagram for determining relations among transverse lines:

[5] Noted by Luigi Mallé in the introduction to his edition of the Italian text, *Della Pittura* (Florence: Sansoni, 1950), 15.

> Placing a point at a height equal to the height of the centric point from the base line, I draw lines from this point to each division scribed on the first line. Then I establish, as I wish, the distance from the eye to the picture. Here I draw . . . a perpendicular cutting whatever lines it finds. (57)

That is, if we imagine ourselves facing the diagram, this point is placed somewhere to the left of the centric point and on a line with it. The perpendicular represents the profile of the picture plane, and Alberti seemingly treats it as the variable, locating it *quanto io voglia* between the previously established eyepoint and the extreme left baseline division.[6] The diagonals from baseline divisions to eyepoint intersect the perpendicular at points which mark where the transversals are to be drawn on the vertical panel. The next step implied but not stated by Alberti involves superimposing the second, or transversal, diagram on the first, or orthogonal, diagram: "The intersection of this perpendicular line with the others [i.e., with the diagonals] gives me the succession of the transverse quantities. In this fashion I find described all the parallels, that is, the squared *braccia* of the pavement in the painting." (57)

It has often been pointed out that this is not the easiest way to determine the sequence of transversals: it can be done more simply—without a second diagram and without the use of a perpendicular—by what is called the three-point or distance-point method of construction. Reduced to its essentials, this method establishes the vertical sequence by running a diagonal from one corner of the baseline up through the orthogonals to a lateral vanishing point placed outside the picture, a point that corresponds with but is not conceived as the optical viewing point posited by Alberti. Whatever Alberti's reasons may have been for failing to use the simpler device, the apparently impractical addition of the perpendicular is essential if one wishes to diagram the distance-depth profile of the visual system. The second diagram merely isolates and emphasizes this view. The positive value, in fact the historical importance, of the distance-point construction has been well defined both by John White, who reminds us that the distance-point construction "by-passes the whole conception of the visual pyramid and its pictorial intersection," and by W. M. Ivins, who shows how the view "from the side lines" is necessary

---

[6] W. M. Ivins, Jr. (*On the Rationalization of Sight* [New York: Metropolitan Museum of Art, 1938], 26), and Mallé (73) discuss the peculiarity of this passage, which presupposes a sliding picture panel. In fact it is not really variable if we infer from Alberti's previous instruction—"this base line of the quadrangle is proportional to the nearest transverse and equidistant quantity seen on the pavement" (56)—and assume the second diagram to be a profile of this. Ivins (26) and Spencer (112) misunderstand this.

Phrases like "quanto io voglia" are not infrequent in Alberti, and they remind us of the creative freedom of artist and theorist in choosing his view or diagram.

to a proper representation of an "object as seen through the beholder's eyes."[7] Alberti's main interest is not simply in the practicality or coherence of a geometrical system—his two diagrams are implicitly unified, but it remained for Piero and Leonardo to incorporate them explicitly; his main interest is in the coherence of an *optical* system which will support his concept of *istoria*, and to achieve this he indulges in various shifts which may be unsatisfactory from a purely technical and geometric standpoint.

Neither the bifocal method apparently developed in the Trecento nor the three-point method described by Viator reveals an interest in the human observer as an element to be considered and manipulated along with the more objective components of pictorial representation. Concerned with the technical problem of creating an accurately foreshortened object or space, these methods presuppose the factor "from a certain viewpoint," but they do not explicitly deal with it. As Ivins says: "Until Alberti's time the problem seemingly had been confined to a simple two-term relation between the beholder and the single object, in which the beholder saw only the object and no one saw the beholder."[8] In this connection, we should bear in mind that the conversion of lateral points to distance points is by no means inevitable. Viator does not exploit the convertibility whereas Vignola does, and this does not seem to make much difference so far as constructive techniques and diagrams per se are concerned. But it makes a great deal of difference as soon as we take into account the wider intellectual contexts inferred from these two methods. The bifocal and three-point methods are preoccupied mainly with what is seen, with optical illusion within the framed area, with making what happens *on* a surface look as if it is happening *behind* the surface. A wholly different mode of thought and frame of reference are involved when one *begins* with the view *through* the transparent surface and reads diagrams as descriptions of a rectangular box *within one end of which* the

[7] John White, *The Birth and Rebirth of Pictorial Space* (London: Faber & Faber, 1957), 122, and Ivins, 32.

[8] Ivins, 32. Ivins, however, treats Viator as if he were in Alberti's camp, though there is no evidence, either in Viator's text and diagrams or in Ivins's commentary, that this is the case. Viator's central point and two lateral points are, in Ivins's words, "located on a line at the level of the eye," but there is no indication that the lateral points are convertible to distance points. In Viator's statement that his two *tiers points* are "equedistans du subiect" (48), the word *subiect* refers to the central point ("le point principal . . . assis au nyveau de lueil").

Panofsky remarks of High Gothic art that in general its pictorial world is "constructed without reference to the visual processes of the beholder and even without reference to his very existence" (*Early Netherlandish Painting: Its Origins and Character* [Cambridge: Harvard University Press, 1953], I, 16–17).

observer is situated. Alberti thinks in architectural, Vignola in theatrical, terms, which means that both mentally walk around the object to
be depicted and then reduce the derived system of total possible views to
the limited aspect perceptible from a point at one end of the rectangular
box. A hypothetical object of vision is measured as if it existed before
being seen and treated as if the problem were to make what happens behind the picture plane visible to a subject standing at a certain distance
from the other side of the plane.[9] Here the hypothetical or imaginary
locus is not restricted to the picture plane, as it is in the bifocal and
three-point methods; it embraces the entire rectangular box containing a
"real" observer on one side of the plane and a "real" object on the other.
Viator presupposes an actual observer but does not include him as a measurable factor in the imaginary world. Alberti's second diagram, with its
perpendicular representing a profile of the picture plane placed at a certain distance from the eye, reveals his interest in *creating* a second, or
hypothetical, observer. Where Viator's observer in effect stands outside
the rectangular box and, like the figures in woodcuts, looks through a
peephole, Alberti's observer begins outside the box and is led into it at
the proper time.

We cannot appreciate the significance for Alberti of painting and of *a*
painting unless we remember that the world painting "imitates" is the
world within the rectangular box, that this box is a hypothetical world
superimposed on an actuality from which it differs and that only within
the imaginary volume of this *as if* world are the elements so sharply articulated and distinguished, so firmly stabilized and controlled. On the
one hand, Alberti emphasizes the independent reality of the perceivable
object from its painted image and the perceiving subject; since Alberti
asks the painter to imagine and measure the object (solid or space) as a
thing in itself before reducing it to the partial image seen on the plane,
the object has an "otherness" built into it. On the other hand, this very

---

[9]Apropos Alberti's second diagram: if, as Ivins does, we take literally the direction
"quanto io voglia" and posit a variable picture plane, then it might occur to us that Alberti has two relations in mind: (1) that between eye and "actual object behind" the plane
and (2) that between eye and foreshortened image of that object *on* the plane. This would
entail a fixed relation between eye and object, which in turn would entail a variable relation between eye and image *so that* the painter would have some freedom in choosing his
view. What is significant about this possible interpretation is again Alberti's tendency to
take the imaginary world seriously, to act as if there *really were* an objective three-
dimensional world to be reduced to its optical equivalent. In the sequence articulated by
the diagrams, the eye-object relation comes first, the eye-picture relation after. Alberti
could just as easily have dropped the perpendicular first *and then* established the eyepoint
and drawn the diagonals. Piero della Francesca, for example, describes first the object
and then the panel.

independence from plane and perceiver increases the importance of the subject's point of view: to conceive of a "real object" behind the plane is to imagine something which cannot be seen all at once and which does not present itself with equal advantage from every aspect. The subject is therefore obliged *to choose* his viewpoint, and—especially when the target is an *istoria* with certain foci of significance—to choose with care: "the painter . . . in painting this plane, . . . places himself at a distance *as if searching* [*quasi come ivi cerchi*] the point and angle of the pyramid from which point he understands the thing painted is best seen" (51, italics mine). Within the *quasi* world of the box, the picture plane relates subject and object, observer and *istoria*, by keeping them apart. Their increased interdependence is a function of the increased independence of each, which merely illustrates the epistemological commonplace that subject and object are functions of each other and are grasped as distinct in a single recognition. A depicted event need not be an object in this sense, and it *is* not if it is thought to have its real existence in heaven, or the Bible, or the past rather than in the rectangular box. The box, as I am using it, provides a symbolic or diagrammatic statement of the phenomenological situation underlying Alberti's instructions to the painter. This situation allows the painter to operate on a level higher than that of the craftsman who *makes* a sensuous artifact; *making* is now understood as *interpreting what is seen;* the imagination posits the *what*—the act traditionally known as *inventio*—and then "responds," "as if searching the point . . . from which . . . the thing painted is best seen," a response which may be compared to the rhetorical function of *dispositio*. The limited decorative originality allowable to the medieval artist is now transformed to an act of cognitive discovery. Painter and beholder share this act, which is essentially the act of interpretation and which therefore by its very nature acknowledges both the otherness and the objectness of the thing interpreted. As in the painting acts of souls are interpreted by movements of bodies, so in the rectangular box these movements exist for and are fulfilled by new acts of soul: seeing, or interpreting. It should be noted that the hypothesis of the rectangular box helps explain how Alberti can set up an imaginary field without resorting to the then-suspect appeal to "creation."

II

The terms *heterocosm* and *second world* are both dialectical in implication in that they suggest or demand a first world, *this one* as opposed to the *other*. Whatever the particular relation between them, there *is* a relation of worlds built into the very notion of second world. More specifically, this means that any awareness of, any attention to, the imaginary hetero-cosm entails at the same time an awareness of audience, of artist, of self, of the actual world and time within which the heterocosm is located. But the last phrase is inaccurate: the preceding section has shown that we can conceive of such components of the first, or actual, world *within* the het-erocosm (the rectangular box); the second world painted on the panel generates a new and hypothetical actuality on both sides of the panel. The elements of style which characterize the painted panel are conditioned by involvement in an experience more comprehensive than that which the panel confines. The idea of mimesis may be extended not only objec-tively to include a more fully represented "nature" but also subjectively to include the genetic and affective context within which the esthetic ex-perience takes place.

The relation between the two worlds, between artwork and audience, now comes within the purview of the esthetic experience. The degree to which the relation is stressed will vary from work to work, as will the elements of tension and distance which characterize the relation. The present section will consider how this relation is dialectically embodied in Alberti's treatise—not in the theory and method described in it but in its literary structure. I shall be concerned with the author's shift of atten-tion *from* the method and theory of painting in themselves *to* the audi-ence to whom the treatise is addressed. There is a doubling here: the relation between a painting and its spectators is one thing, that between a treatise about painting and *its* audience another. But, to violate geo-metrical logic, I hope to show that the two relations are curiously parallel and interinvolved. First, however, I should like to restate certain con-clusions from the last section to show their bearing on the new topic.

Alberti's rectangular box bounds an area within which we find a con-structive analysis of visual experience. The analysis is itself an experi-ence which differs from the original, or given, experience, for Alberti has separated the components of the original into "clear and distinct ideas." As a corrected version informed by a method and controlled by a purpose, the analysis is hypothetical. Alberti brushes aside the theories and controversies of contemporary optics because he is less interested in "what is actually the case" than in "given such and such a purpose, let us act as if such and such were the case." One may, but one need not, justify the *as if* clause as truer or better in itself; one may also justify it on prag-matic grounds, in which case one may adopt a more tentative attitude toward the *as if*, treating it as experimental; again, one may, but one need not, consider *ideal* and *experimental* as mutually exclusive charac-terizations of the hypothetical experience. In any event it is clear to him that this experience represented by the rectangular box is not the real thing but a model of the real thing.

Now in Alberti, as in many other Renaissance thinkers, there is a tension or ambivalence in the idea of "seeing x as a model." On the one hand, "x is emphatically, triumphantly, a model, an improvement over mere life and nature, the achievement of the human mind and its instruments, a technique of discovery, an approach to reality." On the other hand, "x is *only* a model, an artifact, an interpretation, something I have made, neither life in itself nor reality in itself; since making the model absorbed me and delighted me as play does, I must justify the energy and pleasure spent in this way by trying to show I have done something useful, something instructive or moral." As I hope to show, the dialectical relation between these two attitudes is usually one of mutual entailment: each may be given full play only if the other is present in the background as a counterpoise. For on the one hand, if what we really like best is the immediate activity of game playing, model or theory building, experimenting, picture making, story telling, versifying, and so on, all for their own sakes, we can best justify this pleasure by showing it to be useful in some social or ethical or scientific or philosophical context. Artists, for example, have frequently progressed by developing a guilt complex about their delight in the esthetic activity per se, so that since they have not the slightest intention of giving it up, they have had to make themselves take nonesthetic "subject matter" more seriously; in many great artists, the preceding clause is itself one of the topics present in their work. On the other hand, if we really want to take something— ourselves, for example—seriously and are not sure of the consequences, we can always take x seriously in quotation marks, which resembles what is popularly known as kidding on the square. The controlling awareness *that* one is only playing provides a frame within which one can abandon oneself to the pleasure or to the seriousness all the more intensely.

If the ambivalent attitude toward art and its products is transposed to a sequential or dialectical form, it may be found to underlie two familiar patterns of experience: the pattern—more familiar to scholars as a dated esthetic debate—of pleasure and profit and the pattern of withdrawal and return. The present section attempts to show how these patterns inform the *Della Pittura*. Luigi Mallé has suggested as a literary precedent for Alberti's tripartite essay the traditional division of the Hellenistic-Roman poetic treatise into a section dealing with *poiēin*, subdivided into two parts—*poiēsis* and *poiēma*, e.g., and a third part dealing with *poētēs*.[10]

---

[10] Introduction to *Della Pittura*, 9–10.

Poiēsis is concerned with *inventio*, the finding of arguments, and thus comprises the study of matter or content; *poiēma* is about *dispositio* and *elocutio* and comprises the study of stylistic or formal devices and techniques; *poētēs* considers the poet—his sources, character, sensibility, education, function, culture, and environment. Mallé points out that Alberti's sequence—*Rudimenta-Pictura-Pictor*—involves a reversal in the traditional order of the first two terms with the effect noted above, that content and form, *istoria* and *compositione*, are much more closely identified. *Rudimenta,* or *poiēma,* considers stylistic elements in such a way that, as Mallé puts it, "content is annulled as such and becomes form." *Pictura* is then amplified to include these stylistic elements under the aspect of content, and in this way *la forma*, which is for Alberti *essenziale*, is welded to *istoria* as its embodiment rather than treated as a separate category of ornamentation.[11] The third book follows its classical models more closely, especially in reverting to themes discussed in earlier books but treating them now from the standpoint of the painter's culture and education—e.g., composition and *istoria* are now viewed as problems in humanistic invention.[12] This book is very brief and adds little to the theoretical material which is the heart of the treatise. There are obvious motives for its inclusion: the exaltation of the painter to the status of an intellectual is one; another is the literary pleasure in the skill of imitation, which requires, according to the classical theory, as H. O. White has put it, "that individual originality be shown by choosing and using models carefully, by reinterpreting borrowed matter, and by improving on those models and that matter."[13] With its simultaneous appeal to a modern theme and an ancient formal precedent, the third book may be seen as the crown of a successful mimetic venture in which the old and the new, the conventional and the personal, exist in close harmony, if not in a unison.

As to the structure of the treatise, I have already noted that Alberti's method embodies a version of the familiar withdrawal-return pattern. He begins by turning his back on content, then moves from geometry through composition, and returns to content in the discussion of *istoria*. Similarly, the second book moves from the relatively abstract or geometrical problems of circumscription (drawing planes and outlines) through the central discussion of composition-*istoria* to the topic of the

---

[11] Ibid., 11.

[12] Ibid., 11–12.

[13] H. O. White, *Plagiarism and Imitation during the English Renaissance* (Cambridge: Harvard University Press, 1935), 18.

reception of light. Reception of light has, for Alberti, partly the ornamental function of heightening the appeal of the *istoria* and partly the
mimetic function of heightening the actuality of the *istoria* by adding to
significant form the local and concrete accidents of situation. Two features of this progression in the second book should be emphasized. (1) In
moving from the abstract consideration of planes and outlines to the sensuous consideration of light and color, the middle term provides a pivot
which makes the whole progression seamless or continuous; circumscription shades into the composing of planes, and the discussion of
three-dimensional form becomes a discussion of humanly significant
form.[14] (2) Considering the first phase as withdrawal to "the forms of
things separated from all matter," we may see that Alberti's return to the
più grassa Minerva of sensuous representation occurs in two steps: the
treatment of *istoria* returns to the human image, approaching the vividness and dignity of form as an expression of the soul in action; the treatment of light and color carries the return beyond this union of form and
soul into the more immediate physical actuality of bodies modeled by
light and shade (underpainting with white and black) and into the
affective or sensuous actuality of local-color harmonies considered as elements of design.

With qualification, both these features appear in the order of the
treatise as a whole. The desire for continuity is at least nominally indicated in the brief argument which concludes the prologue. The first
book is "*tutto mathematico*," the second "*pone l'arte in mano allo artefice*,"
and the third tells the artist how he can and ought to acquire "*perfecta
arte e notitia*." The passage from *ars* to *artifex* is smoother here than in
the Hellenistic scheme, and it is essentially a passage from abstract to
concrete, theory to practice, the ideal and impersonal realm of mathematics to the actuality of the painter's life. Again the middle term is used
as a pivot: the geometrical roots of art come to life as an objective set of
procedures, "*l'arte in mano*," which are finally viewed from the subjective standpoint of the artist who must learn them.

This transition is not as smooth as I made it out to be. If we take
seriously as an instrument of analysis the distinction between the actual,
or first, world and its image in the second world, then we must see that
the second and third books embody two different phases, two kinds of
return from the realm of pure mind. Book II deals with the readmission

---

[14] That Alberti's treatment of the third topic also reinforces the continuity is borne out
by the practice of underpainting, which is a function of both composition (black and
white used for modeling) and light (black and white used for degrees of intensity).

of content, life, soul into the prepared space of the picture. Book III moves from the actuality within painted space to the actuality around it. There is a distinct analogue here to Alberti's readmission of the observer into the rectangular box; the third book, in readmitting the painter and his environment, surrounds the world on the picture plane with the more complicated, the less ideal, social actuality which confronts the man who would be a painter and which Alberti describes from the would-be painter's perspective. The character and tone of the third book seem to me both interesting and important: they reveal things about Alberti himself—i.e., about the "intention" or attitudes embodied in the treatise—which throw light on some of the human conditions taken account of by a Renaissance perspectivist. More specifically, they illuminate a form of withdrawal-and-return which we shall come on again and again in the products of Renaissance imagination.

The third book begins by focusing on a familiar Renaissance motif:

> Ma poi che ancora altre utili cose restano affare uno pittore tale che possa seguire intera lode, parmi in questi commentarii da non lassarlo. (Mallé, 103)

> But since there still remain other useful things to make a painter capable of achieving complete praise, they must not be left out of this exposition.[15]

Alberti then characteristically backtracks to summarize the subjects of the previous books and catch them up in the new context of the painter's concern:

> Dico l'oficio del pittore essere cosi: descrivere con linea et tigniere con colori, in qual sia datoli tavola o parete, simile vedute superficie di qualunque corpo che quelle, ad una cierta distanza et ad una cierta positione di cientro, paiano rilevate et molto simili avere i corpi. La fine della pictura, rendere gratia et benivolenza et lode allo artefice molto più che richezze. Et seguiranno questo i pittori ove la loro pittura terrà li occhi et l'animo di chi la miri. . . . piacerammi sia il pictore, per bene potere tenere tutte queste cose, huomo buono et docto in buone lettere; et sa ciaschuno quanto la bontà del huomo molto più vallia che ogni industria o arte ad acquistarsi benivolenza da ciptadini et niuno dubita la benivolenza di molti molto all'artefice giovare a lode insieme et al guadagnio; et interviene spesso che i ricchi, mosso più da benivolenza che da maravigliarsi d'altrui arte, prima danno guadagnio a costui modesto et buono lassando a drieto quell'altro pittore, forse migliore in arte, ma non si buono in costumi. (Mallé, 103)

---

[15] From here on I supply my own translations because in some places my interpretations and, therefore, my renderings differ considerably from Spencer's.

I say that the function of the painter is this: to represent with lines and tint with colors, on any given panel or wall, the imitated [*simile*] visible planes of any body so that, from a fixed distance and a fixed central position, they seem to have relief and almost to have bodies. The end of painting is to bring the painter favor and goodwill and praise rather than riches. And painters will achieve this provided that their painting holds the eye and soul of whoever sees it . . . it would please me if the painter, in order to be well able to grasp all these matters, were a good man and learned in literature; and everyone knows how much more effectual than any industry or art a man's goodness is for attaining the goodwill of the citizens, and no one doubts that the goodwill of the many greatly helps the artist to both praise and gain; and it often happens that the rich, motivated more by benevolence than by admiration of any art, give reward sooner to this man who is honest and good, leaving behind that other painter who is perhaps better in art but not so good in his habits.

If the painter presents himself as civil—*molto porgersi costumato*—and especially as possessed of *humanità et facilità*, the goodwill he gains thereby will be a firm defense against poverty.

Of Alberti's statement that painters should seek praise rather than riches, Mallé remarks that for Alberti *la gloria* is "the natural end of every human act."[16] But *la gloria*—the fame and "immortality" accruing from solid artistic achievement—is only one aspect of the *intera lode* discussed here. It is true that a good portion of the third book consists of helpful hints to the painter qua painter: on the usefulness of a broad humanistic culture (or an acquaintance with poets and orators) in helping compose a beautiful *istoria*, "*di cui ogni laude consiste in la inventione*"; on learning painlessly but patiently and thoroughly; on selective imitation, the proper use of nature and models; on developing good habits of mind and hand in practice. But these matters only fulfill half the program of the third book as outlined in the prologue: "*El terzo instituisce l'artefice quale et come possa et debba acquistare perfecta arte e notitia di tutta la pittura.*" The frame and nominal focus of the book is not "*quale . . . possa . . . acquistare . . . arte,*" but "*come . . . debba acquistare . . . notitia,*" and *notitia* adds to *lode* a sense which differs substantially from *gloria*. *Lode* is at once *dolce et utile*: if it is more satisfying to the ego than riches, it is not entirely irrelevant to staying alive and comfortable. Alberti acknowledges the perennial compromise artists must make in playing up to the nonesthetic motives of their public, especially a Quattrocento public consisting of unpredictable patrons and hard-bitten *fio-*

---

[16] *Della Pittura*, 103, note 1.

rentini. The artist is his own image maker, and painting may be only part of the image; since praise and gain are functions of public *benivolenza*, it may be more exigent to be—or rather to display oneself as (*porgersi*)—a good man, thus avoiding poverty.

Alberti's advice may seem cynical, but it is only realistic, an acceptance of commonplace insights about a world in which fire must be fought with fire, *ars longa vita brevis*, etc. In an uncertain social atmosphere dominated by *condottieri*, bankers, and other adventurers, the artist had to accommodate himself to the rationale of self-interest and expediency. One might choose to overstress these elements in the third book and ask whether Alberti wants a man with artistic aptitude to take up painting as a means to fame and fortune or whether the effort to please is simply the necessary condition without which the artist is not free to pursue his artistic passion. In the light of the whole treatise, the second alternative is too obviously the case; yet within the more limited context of the third book, Alberti presents the painter with motives sufficiently blurred to allow at least a glimpse of the first alternative. An interesting example of this ambiguity occurs near the very end of the book. Advising the painter to take the advice of friends and also, since his work aims to please the multitude, to hear and respect the *sentenzia della moltitudine* whenever possible, he cites Apelles, who hid behind the panel so that he could absorb the freely uttered praise and blame of unwitting observers:

> Così io voglio i nostri pittori apertamente domandino et odano ciascuno quello che giudichi et gioveralli questo ad acquistare gratia. Niuno si truova il quale non estimi honore porre sua sententia nella fatica altrui. Et ancora poco mi pare da dubitare che li invidi et detrattori nuocano alle lode del pictore; sempre fu al pittore ogni sua lode palese et sono alle sue lode testimoni cose quale bene arà dipinte. Adunque oda ciascuno et inprima tutto bene pensi et bene seco ghastighi et quando arà udito ciascuno creda ai più periti. (Mallé, 113)

> Thus I wish that our painters would openly ask, and hear everyone who makes a judgment, and this will help them acquire favor. There is no one who does not esteem it an honor to render his opinion on the work of others. I think there is little doubt that the envious and the detractors hurt the painter's reputation; to the painter his own full worth was always evident and the things he has painted well are testimonies to his merits. Therefore listen to everyone but first judge and correct everything justly within yourself, and when you have heard everyone, believe the most expert.

The introductory *così* is deceptive, since Alberti's application turns the Apelles example upside down. The painter is not to hide behind the panel gathering frank opinions useful to him as a painter; he is to flatter his public and safeguard himself against ill will by openly asking for judgments which, privately, he may feel free to ignore. The more friends, the fewer detractors. We might recall Burckhardt's characterization of Italy as a school for scandal, rich with targets for the *detrattori:*

> celebrities of every kind, statesmen, churchmen, inventors, and discoverers, men of letters, poets and artists. . . . This host existed in the fifteenth and sixteenth centuries, and by its side the general culture of the time had educated a poisonous brood of impotent wits, of born critics and railers, whose envy called for hecatombs of victims; and to all this was added the envy of the famous men among themselves. In this the philologists notoriously led the way . . . while the artists of the fifteenth century lived in peaceful and friendly competition with one another.[17]

But in the third book we have brief anticipations of that concern for techniques of survival which was to dominate Cellini's consciousness.

In view of Alberti's awareness of the *detrattori*, it seems possible to read into two familiar motifs cited early in the third book the more or less sophisticated function of allegorical allusion. These motifs are introduced as examples of *la bella inventione*, which has such power that it can please without being seen. The first example is Lucian's description of the Calumny of Apelles: Ignorance and Suspicion (*due femine*) on either side of a man with large ears; Calumny holding a burning torch and dragging a young man by the hair; her guide Envy and servants Deceit and Fraud; finally, Penitence in funereal robes followed by a shamefast and chaste young woman named Truth.[18] One may read the image as a temporal and causal sequence, in which case the final appearance of Truth symbolizes the vindication of Calumny's victim, but one may read it another way which I find more congenial to Alberti's description: Penitence, "*quale . . . tutta stracciava*," and Truth, in spite of her "*vergogniosa et*

---

[17] *The Civilization of the Renaissance in Italy*, trans. S. G. C. Middlemore (New York: Phaidon, 1950), 98.

[18] Panofsky's inference that Alberti "already imagined Truth as a naked figure of the 'Venus Pudica' type" seems unwarranted. He argues that Alberti would not call Truth "shamefaced and bashful"—*vergogniosa et pudica*—unless he thought of her as nude (*Studies in Iconology* [New York: Oxford University Press, 1939], 158–59). But (a) *vergogniosa* can certainly describe Truth's response to the shameful treatment of the young man by Calumny, and (b) *vergogniosa* may be understood as "shamefast," which indicates a disposition (see St. Thomas Aquinas, *Summa Theologica* II-II, 144) rather than "shamefaced," which indicates a passing response. Panofsky would like to connect the nudity with the familiar representations of Truth unveiled by Time. My motive for rejecting this implication of nudity, and for rejecting Panofsky's inference, appears above in the next sentence.

pudica" character, drag along behind the others, helpless to assist. Like the unfortunate *garzonetto* dragged by Calumny, Alberti's Truth is only a *fanciulletta*, not an oracular Botticellian nude in her late thirties. One requires more intrinsic skill and virtue to compete with the multitude of bitter, weak, or vicious spirits who monopolize the large ears of the public.

What the painter needs to survive is symbolized by the second *invenzione*, which follows immediately after the first:

> Piacerebbe ancora vedere quelle tre sorelle a quali Hesiodo pose nome Eglie, Heufronesis et Thalia, quali si dipignieano prese fra loro l'una l'altra per mano, ridendo, con la vesta scinta et ben monda, per quali volea s'intendesse la liberalità, ché una di queste sorelle dà, l'altra riceve, la terza rende il beneficio; quali gradi debbano in ogni perfetta liberalità essere. (Mallé, 105)

> It would also be pleasing to see those three sisters to whom Hesiod gave the names Aglaia, Euphrosyne, and Thalia, who are depicted taking each other by the hand, laughing, with robes unbound and very clean, and through whom liberality is signified, since one of these sisters gives, the other receives, the third returns favor; these degrees ought to be in all perfect liberality.

These inventions, especially if taken in sequence, are so apposite to the lurking image of society which Alberti seems to presuppose in the third book that it is tempting to construe them as condensed and crystallized — if indirect—references to the painter's actual conditions. And this would certainly be in keeping with the ideal of literary imitation embodied in the treatise: the classical motifs are both activated and transformed; they have at once an esthetic and a moral function, providing models to the man-as-painter and warnings to the painter-as-man. Alberti is careful to accompany each example with assertions about its esthetic relevance. Of the first, he remarks that it will not be *aliena* to his subject to warn painters in what matters, concerning invention, it behooves them to be vigilant. And, after describing the three Graces:

> Adunque si vede quanta lode porgano simile inventioni al artefice, pertanto consiglio ciascuno pittore molte si faccia familiare ad i poeti, rethorici et ad li altri simili dotti di lettera, sia che costoro doneranno nuove inventione o certo aiuteranno abbello componere sua storia, per quali certo adquisteranno in sua pictura molte lode et nome. (Mallé, 105)

> One sees then how much praise similar inventions may bring to the artist; thus I advise every painter to familiarize himself with poets, rhetoricians and others equally learned in letters, for they may give new inventions or indeed help in beautifully composing his *istoria*, through which means they will certainly purchase much praise and fame for his paintings.

In making inventions, painters should be vigilant of Calumny and cultivate the Graces, which may be done by joining hands with poets, orators, and other humanists—Alberti's language elicits a curious inter-penetration or blurring of esthetic with practical motives, even while he indicates the purely artistic aim of the discussion. In fact, he uses his two examples as he would want a painting to be used: *la forma* of the in-vention lends its inherent significance to the *istoria* of Book III. And the relation between the two inventions illustrates an important aspect of our general topic. In the first exemplary panel is the image of the brazen actuality with which the painter must cope; in the second is an image of that ideal mythic or golden world justified not only explicitly for its beauty as invention but also implicitly for the potential usefulness it de-rives from the presence of the Calumny. What makes the vision of the Graces in art more than a symptom of escapism, what makes the cult of the Graces in behavior more than merely courtly ornament, what gives both vision and cult a purpose beyond even that positive function of sup-plying "a daily beauty" which refreshes life as it is and points beyond it to life as it might be—what gives added point to vision and cult is the omnipresence of Spenser's Blatant Beast of Slander with its jaw full of ill-assorted teeth: *calumnia, ignorantia, sospezione, livore, invidia, in-sidia*, etc. Thus we see within the "second world" of the *invenzione* an epitome of the dialectic, the mutual entailment, of the actual and the ideal. But we may also see another epitome of the relation of the *inven-zioni* to the third book: an epitome of the way art functions as a selective, simplified, intensified, and beautified image of life; it is at once different from life in its concise emblematic *forma* and involved with life in re-flecting the concerns which actuality forces on the painter.

Thus the third book, insofar as it treats of art in the context of actu-ality, may be seen to exist in a tensional or disjunctive relation to the first two books, which consider actuality only as it may be admitted into the second world of the painting and rectangular box. I am sure Alberti, for all his civic-mindedness, did not feel that the "disinterested" attention to theory and method in the first two books was permissible only if justified by the implied moral context of the third book, nor do I think he in-tended to identify the conditions within which the painter must operate with the subjects to be painted. But if the painter can hardly expect to find his ideal in the world of the third book, if he can pursue it only by withdrawing to the circumscribed area of the first two books, he is yet responsible to the imperfect world. He lives in it; he must keep up his guard even while doing mathematics; what he is and makes are ulti-mately incomplete until submitted to the wills of those others who com-prise audience, patrons, friends, and enemies. If the inherent urge of the man as artist is godlike, to create and control a universe all his own, the inherent need of the artist as man is to learn to live well in a common world he has not made and cannot control, a world run by politicians rather than artists. Like the Complete Art, the Complete Artist must make the best of two essentially irreconcilable worlds, must not stray too far from either, yet must inhabit and explore the second world as far as is consistent with the demands of survival and morality imposed by the first.

In the remarks to his readers which conclude the treatise, Alberti hits off with great precision the guarded and shuffling tone essential to the artist who, wishing to make his way in such a world, must commend himself without offending others. He begins by saying that if his work has been useful to painters, he asks only one reward—that they paint in their *istoria* a comely image of him in an attitude *"studioso dell'arte."* The request takes on resonance if we remember some advice given earlier in the third book, advice meant to illustrate the advantage of painting *dal naturale*, i.e., from life:[19]

> Ove . . . in una storia sarà uno viso di qualche conosciuto et degnio huomo, bene che ivi sieno altre figure di arte molto più che queste perfette et grate, pure quel viso conosciuto ad sé imprima trarrà tutti li occhi di chi la storia raguardi. (Mallé, 108)

> Where . . . there is in an *istoria* the face of some well-known and worthy man, although other figures may be much more finished and favored by art than his, the well-known face immediately draws to itself the eyes of all those who behold the *istoria*.

Alberti appeals to the symbiosis which will keep the community of artists healthy: he will show them how to make an *istoria;* they will immortalize him as a student of art; both for himself and as a representative of all artists, he will assume the role of well-known and worthy man; his well-known and worthy image will supply painters and spectators with a center of local interest.

Alberti continues to walk the courtly tightrope up to the last word:

> Et se meno satisfeci alle loro aspettationi, non però vituperino me se ebbi animo trapendere matera si grande et se il nostro ingegnio non à potuto finire

[19] The advice to follow nature has, in the second book, a generalized and cognitive significance; here, in accordance with the different atmosphere of Book III, it is local and affective. The criteria of Book II are derived from the second world of geometric form and noble actions, those of Book III from the first world of social form and noble patrons.

quello che fu laude tentare; pure solo il volere nei grandi et difficili fatti suole essere lode. Forse dopo me sarà chi emenderà e nostri scritti errori et in questa degnissima et prestantissima arte saranno più che noi in aiuto et utile ad i pictori; quale io, se mai alcuno sarà, priego et molto ripriego piglino questa fatica con animo lieto et pronto in quale essercitino suo ingegnio et rendano questa arte nobilissima ben governata. Noi però ci reputeremo ad voluptà primi avere presa questa palma, d'avere ardito commendare alle lettere questa arte sottilissima et nobilissima. In quale impresa difficilissima se poco abbiamo potuto satisfare alla expettatione di chi ci à letto, incolpino la natura non meno che noi, quale impose questa leggie alle cose: che niuna si truovi arte quale non abbia avuto suoi initii da cose mendose; nulla si truova insieme nato et perfetto.

Chi noi seguirà, se forse sarà alchuno di studio et d'ingegnio più prestante che noi, costui quante mi stimo farà la pittura absoluta et perfetta. (Mallé, 114)

And if I have done less than satisfy their hopes, let them not blame me for having had the courage to undertake so great a subject; and if our wit was not able to finish what it was praiseworthy to try, perhaps only the will should be praised in great and difficult matters. Perhaps one will follow me who will correct our written errors and will be of more help and use to painters in this most worthy and excellent art; if anyone ever does, I beg and entreat that they begin this labor gladly and apply their wit readily and make this noblest art well governed. Nevertheless we would reserve to ourselves the pleasure of having first carried off this palm, i.e., to have dared to commit this subtlest and noblest art to writing.[20] If in so difficult an undertaking we were but little able to satisfy our readers' expectations, blame nature no less than us, for she imposes this law on things: that there is no art which has not had its origins among errors; nothing is born and perfected at the same time.

Whoever follows us, if by chance he should be superior to us in diligence and ability, will in my opinion render painting absolute and perfect.

That the passage is a tissue of familiar rhetorical devices, studded with what Curtius has called *modesty topoi,* increases rather than diminishes its peculiar force; by their very conventionality the classical postures cut down the stridor of self-assertion. Alberti is in fact quoting traditional formulas by way of reminding his audience that he has just rendered

---

[20] Spencer replaces this sentence with one translated from the Latin (in ms. Codex Vat. Ottoboniani Latini 1424)—"However, I was pleased to seize the glory of being the first to write of this most subtle art" (98)—because he finds the latter "more in keeping with the context of the remainder of the passage than is the weaker and more confused Italian" (136). But since Alberti wrote the Latin version first and the Italian version after, the change may have been deliberate. For, inasmuch as the Italian is more cautious and periphrastic, it accords better with the politic tone of the peroration as a whole.

traditional methods of painting obsolete. And his deference to his successors is a way of marking out his own historical significance.

This carefully controlled presentation of self dramatizes his own caveat, that the artist should "*molto porgersi costumato.*" Though only a
fragment, it has interest as a practical application of a rhetorical stance
made available largely through the efforts of Petrarch and Boccaccio: the
public and literary expression of one's private self, not simply as the act
of communicating one's ethos (a program described in Aristotle's *Rhetoric*) but as the act of seeing self and *oeuvre* each in the context of the other
and of viewing both in historical perspective. Petrarch's "private self,"
for example, is illuminated both by the *Rime* in connection with the *Se-
cretum* and by the letters to ancient authors in connection with the letter
to posterity. The latter is an autobiographical portrait which begins with
the admission that it is unlikely future readers will have ever heard of
him, but if by any chance they have, they may want to know what sort of
person he was. Here, as more casually in Alberti's peroration, the author
attempts to project a persona, to see himself as others may see him so as
to anticipate and influence the response of posterity. Such a strategy was
to become a way of life for Montaigne, who knew that published meditation on one's insufficiency was not only a means to self-knowledge—"Il
faut voir son vice et l'estudier pour le redire. Ceux qui le celent à autruy,
le celent ordinairement à eux mesmes"—but also a way to control public
and future opinion: "Je suis affamé de ma faire connoistre; et ne me
chaut à combien, pourveu que ce soit veritablement; ou, pour dire
mieux, je n'ay faim de rien, mais je crains mortellement d'estre pris en
eschange par ceux à qui il arrive de connoistre mon nom."[21]

Alberti's peroration modestly steers his audience toward contemplation of his *usefulness*—a *utilità* which is to be judged primarily in relation to *la vita civile e attiva*. *Utilità*, the driving impulse behind all
Alberti's work, is an esthetic as well as an ethical motive. For since, in
following this principle, he returns from private to public interests,
from self to others in the present and future, from art to society, the
principle imposes a shape and structure on the work. The reentry is no
radical act, since the withdrawal was tempered—not the gratuitous flight
into metaphysics or into the past for which Alberti censured the idle *in-*

---

[21] Book II, Chapter 5; *Essais*, ed. M. Rat (Paris: Editions Garnier Frères, 1958), III,
64, 65. Some formal and rhetorical strategies of self-presentation were discussed in an
illuminating paper by Richard M. Douglas, "Self-Knowledge, Ingenium, and the Humanist Vocation," delivered on May 4, 1963, at the New England Renaissance Conference held at Brandeis University.

daginatore but the solid withdrawal into art performed in the first two books of *Della Pittura*. What Alberti shows us is not a moral tension between art and life—this does not really become a problematical issue until the time of Reformation and Puritan controversies—but rather what might be called mimetic collaboration: as in art there is a withdrawal to theory and a return to practice, so in life there is a withdrawal to art and a return to society. The treatise on painting, which stands between and mediates the two processes, shows how each depends upon the other.

The novelty of the Albertian form of withdrawal-and-return may be focused by a glance at the background which Hans Baron has exhaustively explored in tracing the way political experience (the Milanese threat at the turn of the fifteenth century) transformed Florentine thought from "an abstract classicism" to "civic Humanism." [22]

The repeated pattern of Trecento humanism is characterized by Baron as "a discord between recent experience and traditional conviction, producing inner unrest and intellectual struggles, and followed by submission to or a compromise with the powers of the past" (95). But by the time Alberti's generation was active, the shift in the other direction had already occurred. Abstract classicism, the worship of antiquity for its own sake, the urge not only to unearth and revive but to relive the past: these could be assigned a purely negative position in the dialectic—that of obsessive withdrawal or escape. This urge and pursuit had to be justified by moral reference to the demands of the *now*; in itself *dolce*, it was not inherently *utile* until the mere passion for antiquity had been mastered by rational concern for its relevance. But when Alberti in effect assigns the withdrawal position to art, he replaces the passion for antiquity with a pursuit which adds technique to passion, which has its own built-in criteria of *utilità*, its own relation to classicism, and its own phase of withdrawal to abstract principles. At the same time, it is art and not history which occupies the withdrawal position: a much more completely and explicitly hypothetical domain. The *now* of the second world and the *now* of the first world have greater independence; the charges at both poles are more nearly equal; because art is both rational and confessedly hypothetical it can be more fully explored in and for itself with greater freedom of conscience. And whereas in art it is obvious that the second world is a construct, a conscious externalization of self and its vision, it is much less clear—and not discovered until much later than

[22] *The Crisis of the Early Italian Renaissance* (Princeton: Princeton University Press, 1955), see especially vol. I, 295–96, 92.

Alberti's time—that the pursuit of historical antiquity is actually a selective and constructive art, the projection of one's image, vision, and ideals onto the past, the effectual creation of a second, or hypothetical, world. What emerges clearly for the first time in Alberti's studies of the arts, and primarily in the *Della Pittura*, is the dialectical significance of fiction, the counterfactual, as a central mode of human withdrawal which is inherently practical and moral, a mode which, merging the passion for the antique with the passion for art, allows the former to be at once fully and legitimately indulged.

III

In the previous sections of this essay, Alberti's assumptions about the heterocosm and his employment of the withdrawal-return pattern were explored in the particular contexts of artistic theory and literary structure. In this final section, I should like to draw on those explorations to get at something more general—something which might be called a preface to the phenomenology of the humanist imagination. This preface will concern itself with the rationale of imitation or emulation, with some of the motives behind the humanist interest in art and antiquity.

Alberti's use of history as well as nature—especially in his ten books on architecture—is directed by the same habits of thought which inform his method of art. This is obviously true at the general level of the imitation process: the old idea that art improves nature is readily transferable to history when historical data consist for the most part of ruins, fragments, and textual sources which are limited and not overly accurate. History and nature alike provide cues which stimulate the imagination, cues which in fact demand to be completed and placed in a new context. What is obviously important and desirable to the great humanists is not that the past be revived for its own sake with archeological objectivity— this attitude, familiar to the strain of humanism which Baron calls abstract classicism, is not lacking in Alberti, though it exists in solution with more significant aims. What is important is the element of *distance* or *objectivity* per se. Alberti is never interested in true historical understanding, even if he thinks he is. He does not have a weak theory of history; he has no theory of history in any proper sense, for historical exploration is not his object. It is true that the critical attitude toward sources and remains—the attitude which a real historiography presupposes—is itself dependent on the general establishment of that sense of distance known as historical perspective. But as has often been pointed out, historical perspective by itself arises from an attitude similar to that which produces pictorial perspective. It was at best but dimly understood that the humanist reconstruction of history was largely hypothetical, that *invenire* involved invention or projection as much as—if not more than—it involved discovery. The humanist method is more proper to artistic *production* than to historical or scientific *investigation*, and perhaps it was necessary to bring it out into the open *as* a method of art before the approaches to history and nature could develop on their own terms, using or discarding the elements of artistic method as their disciplines required.

At a much more specific level, Alberti's method of art provides a model of the humanist approach to history. This may be evident if we recall the double value of the picture plane, at once a window on a self-sufficient world and an idealizing mirror of the observer. In history as in art a unified hypothetical field is at once projected *onto* an actual superficies and treated as if it were in some sense there, *behind* the superficies. The humanist can find his own preferred image of man in the past, his own preferred image of rational order in nature, only if he has first established the otherness of past and nature. Thus at some implicit level the imagination must have transformed the actual medium—plane surface, history as ruins and monuments and texts, nature as phenomena—into the new frame of a heterocosm; there the historian or scientist may project his golden world of human or cosmic order, converting the heterocosm into a mirror. As in the case of painting, the surface is only *hypothetically* a second world, or mirror: the past, or nature, assumes the double status of object and reflection only within that imaginary frame.

Only when this basis in art becomes a conscious issue, when the tension between the critical and the didactic attitudes toward history emerges into clear view from its matrix in the sense of historical distance, does historiography achieve independence as a method.[23] Similarly, in the approach to nature, only when the power of hypothesizing—of imagining second worlds within which experiments may be tried—has been clearly perceived and evaluated, does what C. S. Singleton calls "the perspective of art" become the doorway to scientific method.

To Alberti's theory of painting also belong the criteria of generalization, simplification, and selectivity which influence the approaches to history and nature and, along with these criteria, that paradoxical identity of impulse which binds together the tendency toward greater pic-

---

[23] See Myron P. Gilmore, "The Renaissance Conception of the Lessons of History," in *Facets of the the Renaissance*, ed. W. H. Werkmeister (New York: Harper & Row, 1963), 85.

torial realism with the tendency toward greater reliance on artifice and idealization. In this context, observation of detail is always preceded and controlled by conscious formulation of the frame of reference—i.e., the total field which is viewed and the point from which it is viewed. The *objective* is not defined in terms of *things, objects,* qualified substances, but in terms of *placement,* of location and relation within a self-sufficient field; not in terms of individual percepts but of unifying concepts. Looking beyond Alberti, we may see this shift of emphasis operating in a number of different areas: in the distinction between Flemish and Florentine styles of painting; in that between Quattrocento and Cinquecento styles analyzed by Wölfflin; in Huizinga's general distinction between medieval and Renaissance "realism" and Chabod's application of it to the "photographic realism" and "conceptual realism" of medieval and Renaissance historians; in the new criteria of experimental method analyzed by many historians of science, but perhaps most lucidly by Herbert Butterfield and A. C. Crombie.[24]

Alberti's use of antiquity is strikingly demonstrated in the prologue to the *Della Pittura:*

> Io solea maravigliarmi insieme et dolermi che tante optime et divini arti et scientie quali per loro opere et per le historie veggiamo chopiose erano in que virtuosissimi passati antiqui, ora così siano manchate et quasi in tucto perdute; pictori, sculptori, architecti, musici, geometri, rethorici, auguri et simili nobilissimi et meravigliosi intellecti oggi si truovano rarissimi et pocho da lodarli. Onde stimai fusse quanto da molti questo così essere udiva, che già la Natura, maestra delle cose, fatta anticha et straccha, più non producea chome né giganti così né ingegni quali in que suoi quasi giovinili et più gloriosi tempi produsse amplissimi et meravigliosi.

> I used to be at once astonished and sad that so many supreme and divine arts and sciences which—as we see through their products and through records—abounded in that most virtuous antique past, may now be lacking and almost totally lost; painters, sculptors, architects, musicians, geometers,

[24] Heinrich Wölfflin, *Classic Art,* trans. Peter and Linda Murray (London: Phaidon Press, 1952); J. Huizinga, "Renaissance and Realism" (1929), in *Men and Ideas,* trans. J. S. Holmes and H. van Marle (New York: Meridian Books, 1959), 288–310; Federico Chabod, *Machiavelli and the Renaissance,* trans. David Moore (Cambridge: Harvard University Press, 1958), 176ff. H. Butterfield, *The Origins of Modern Science* (New York: Free Press, 1965), especially chapters 1 and 5; A. C. Crombie, *Medieval and Early Modern Science* (Garden City: Doubleday-Anchor, 1959), especially vol. I, chapter 1, and vol. II, chapters 1.1, 1.4, 1.5, 2.1, and 2.8. See also A. R. Hall, *The Scientific Revolution, 1500–1800* (Boston: Beacon Press, 1956), chapters 1, 5, and 6. For a brilliant general discussion of this topic see S. Sambursky, *The Physical World of the Greeks* (New York: Macmillan, 1962), chapter 10.

rhetoricians, seers, and intellects equally noble and marvelous are very rare today, and there are few to praise them. Whence I thought it was—as one has often heard—that Nature, mistress of things, now grown old and weary, no longer produced either giants or geniuses such as she brought forth so copiously and wonderfully in those her more youthful and glorious days.

The point of view is established with the first word, the familiar dialogue—*Io / passati antiqui*—with the first sentence. The *Della Famiglia* (1437–1438), which opens with a similar *ubi sunt*, uses the relation in a more complicated way, treating the illustrious Roman past both as historically remote—outside *Io*—and as part of *Io*, its ancestral heritage. The ancient remains—*loro opere*—stand as symbols of the lost culture, and in the *Della Famiglia* the catalogue of *intelletti* is replaced by a list of illustrious Roman families: Fabii, Drusii, Decii, Gracchi, etc. But insofar as the *opere* are effects of *virtù* and *umanità*, they point to something which is always recoverable, which *fortuna* can not permanently exile because it is a power intrinsic to the *natura* of *Io*. The prologue to the *Della Famiglia* moves from the ancient families to their modern counterpart, *nostri passati Alberti*.

Thus in the next section of the prologue, Alberti shifts the balance from past to present, supplying a curiously apposite parallel—one might almost wish to say allegory—between the revival of *ingegno* and the return of the Alberti:

Ma poi che io dal lungo exilio in quale siamo noi Alberti invecchiati, qui fui in questa nostra sopra l'altre ornatissima patria riducto, chompresi in molti ma prima in te, Filippo et in quel nostro amicissimo Donato sculptore et in quelli altri Nencio et Luca et Masaccio, essere a ogni lodata cosa ingegnio da non postporli acqual si sia stato anticho et famoso in queste arti. Pertanto m'avidi in nostra industria et diligentia non meno che in beneficio della natura et de tempi, stare il potere acquistarsi ogni laude di qual si sia virtù. Confessoti se a quelli antiqui, avendo quale aveano chopia da chi inparare e imitarli, meno era difficile salire in cognitione di quelle supreme arti quali oggi annoi sono fatichosissime ma quinci tanto più el nostro nome più debba essere maggiore se noi sanza preceptori, sanza exemplo alchuno, truoviamo arti et scientie non udite et mai vedute. (Mallé, 52–53)

But since, from the long exile in which we Alberti have grown old, I have been led back here into this our *patria* embellished above all others; I have discerned in many, but especially in you, Filippo, and in our dearest friend Donato the sculptor, and in those others, Nencio and Luca and Masaccio, a genius for every praiseworthy thing, such that they should not be ranked behind anyone ancient and famous in these arts. Hence I have decided that in our industry and diligence, no less than in the generosity of nature and of the times, resides the power of winning all praise for any accomplishment. I own indeed that if it was less difficult for those ancients—since they had much from which to learn and copy—to leap to knowledge of those supreme arts which are today very hard work for us, then our name should afterwards be so much the more exalted, since without teachers, without any model, we discover arts which have never before been known or seen.

Alberti goes on to praise Brunelleschi for his *Duomo*, "large enough to cover with its shadow all the Tuscan people," and for its method of construction, "made without any center-beam support or any great supply of wood," an achievement incredible in these times and thus, no doubt, far beyond the limits of ancient science and knowledge. He points out that he has translated his treatise into the *volgare* in Brunelleschi's honor and then, after profiling the argument of the three books, concludes with a request to the architect, whose substance anticipates, though with emphasis slightly modified by context, what we have seen in the third book:

> Piacciati adunque leggiermi con diligentia et se cosa vi ti par da emendarla correggimi. Niuno scriptore mai fu sì docto al quale non fussero utilissimi gli amici eruditi et io in prima datte desidero essere emendato per non essere morso da detractori. (Mallé, 54)

> May it please you therefore to read me with diligence, and if anything here seems to you to need emending, correct me. No writer was ever so learned that erudite friends were not most useful to him, and I desire above all to be emended by you so as not to be bitten by detractors.

For us, the most immediately significant aspect of the prologue as a whole is Alberti's handling of the ancient-modern relation. The classical heritage is first established as the product of an age when there was not only an abundance of genius but a more vigorous Nature and men lucky enough to have behind them a developed cultural tradition. When Alberti describes how the evidence of Florence revived his spirit, he tacitly allows the common opinion about "*Natura . . . fatta anticha et straccha*" to stand so that the modern ethos, confronted by greater odds, may be rendered more heroic. In the prologue to the *Della Famiglia*, wishing to affirm the general superiority of *virtù* over *fortuna*, Alberti minimizes the influence of the latter: without good fortune virtuous men can seize fame; with it they can attain glory. But in the *Della Pittura* the argument requires the difference to be stressed, so that the modern artist may be shown not only to recover the ancient *virtù* but to transcend it. Alberti asserts both the excellence of the past and contemporary hard times to augment the glory of the *Io* and *noi* and to locate their historical significance. The Florentine *now* is the moment of *rinascimento*, but this means not the mere rebirth of antiquity but the transference of *virtù* from old to new, and consequently the outmoding of those very models which are being freshly unearthed and imitated.

As in Alberti's description of relations in painting the eyepoint shoots out to the centric point and then rebounds, so here the attention of *Io* shoots backward to antiquity and rebounds to the observer's present. The transfer of *virtù* from old to new, the transfer of attention and praise from ancients to moderns, the shifting function of antiquity from an exemplar to something which is transcended—this process, with its embodiments in the different treatments of art, nature, and history, bespeaks a fundamental dialectic of experience. In the humanist sensibility epitomized by Alberti is a new dawning awareness *that* a single dynamics—the continually changing dialectic between the self and its models—underlies all relations. This dynamics finds expression in the interplay of the esthetic and utilitarian motives as analyzed above in Alberti's work, and since it is a peculiarly widespread phenomenon of Renaissance culture, I should like to conclude this essay on Alberti with a general description.

The proper activity of the self when confronted by models is not *imitation* but *emulation*. Emulation is aggressive imitation, an agon between the emulating self and its rival, the model. The self tries to reach the level embodied in the model, tries not only to surpass it but also to replace it. If it succeeds, it will have rendered the model obsolete: the form and content of the original will have been drastically altered by the pressure of new experience. The emulator hopes to assimilate not the model but rather its power and excellence. The model is like a lodestar, a fixed point of orientation, which serves the self as a guide rather than as a goal. Therefore the model is to be kept at arm's length. Both as a rival and as a guide, the model must stand fast *there*, over against the self, so that the self may continue the agon and journey of its own development. The self measures its progress by observing its changing relations to its models.

This means that the term *model* does not take a stable reference, nor can it be simply located as the name of a particular object. *Model* specifies certain functions which anything may acquire by virtue of its relation to an interpreter or user. These functions may include visualizing, symbolizing, making believe—the functions of image and fiction—but to these the concept *model* usually adds the implications of doing, experimenting, using, teaching, or learning. Furthermore, the history of the term reveals a basic ambiguity in usage: at one extreme *model* is construed as an exemplar, something to be copied; at the other extreme it is construed as the copy. Exemplar and copy are two sides of the same situation, for if we think an original is exemplary, we would want to reproduce it as exactly as we can: the exemplar as a prior model is considered to be fulfilled when it is accurately reproduced so that it exists as the prototype of a class, the *primum in aliquo genere*. The relation between copy and exemplar is asymmetrical in that the mind tends to move from copy to exemplar as from an effect to a cause or from a symbol to its referent. For one who emulates, however, the model is not reducible to either extreme, exemplar or copy, though it may appropriate their functions at different moments. In early phases of the emulator's experience, an object becomes a model when it is assigned the normative role of exemplar: it is a guide to be studied and scrupulously copied, for it is felt to embody a significant level of achievement which transcends the particular historical conditions of its genesis. In more mature phases, the emulator departs from the exemplar, freely varies it, drastically alters it, or leaves it behind altogether—overgoing the model, he substitutes his own work or self as the new model. Thus the relation between old and new model is more symmetrical and dynamic than that between exemplar and copy. The exemplar in emulation is ultimately a blueprint or platform fulfilled by the new work which, it is hoped, will strip the prior model of its status as exemplar.

The difference between exemplar-copy and model-model situations is a useful touchstone for distinguishing characteristic attitudes in a period imagination. As we know from the history of the concept *Idea*, especially its passage from Plotinus to St. Augustine, and as we know from the scholastic thinkers' addition to Aristotle's four causes of a primary *causa exemplaria*, exemplar-copy thinking was the normal or at least normative mode of medieval imagination. This is to be expected in a culture whose interests are best served by concealing the extent to which its world consists of models projected from mind to God. For centuries the paradigmatic image of man was that of *homo scribens*, man as scribe, copyist, glossarian; the more creative power he exorcised from himself and projected upward, the more validly and fully he could reassume that power felt as divine influx; human creativity in its own name was restricted to what the rhetoricians called amplification and abbreviation. On the other hand, the Renaissance imagination characteristically declares that God wants man to make models; in this climate of awareness, the feeling develops that the tentative and experimental creation of models is the chief role of interpretation, the surest discovery procedure. One way to throw off the onus of certainty, custom, and atrophied tradition is to turn away and make a model, adopting a wait-and-see attitude. This turning away is initiated by an act of choice, in which the self selectively isolates those achievements of the past which best conform to its needs and ideals. Thus arises the explicit concern for—and the many Renaissance debates over—the methods of finding (*invenire*) and emulating suitable models drawn from history and nature.

I have just used the term *model* in a somewhat devious way, referring it indiscriminately to two different contexts which are often felt to have nothing to do with each other: the model as something to be imitated and the model as a construct or artifice. But I think we can now say that these are closely related usages. Whoever constructs a model aims at making it in some sense an ideal, an exploration which will clarify, simplify, or show us something new about the original, whether this original is something in nature, in antiquity, in the mind, in heaven, etc. The second world, the perspective field, the painted image are all in this sense models as artifice. It is less clear that a model understood in its exemplary meaning of a guide is a construct or artifice. But this becomes apparent as soon as we recognize that a model found in ancient Rome is no less a construct than is an exemplar found in the mind of God; both are equally projections from the mind of the *Io*, though they embody radically different impulses and lead to radically different responses. With varying degrees of awareness, the early humanists were moving toward a new, constructive, view of historiography as soon as they took it upon themselves to question not only aspects in their medieval heritage but also interpretations of the past made by their medieval predecessors. Insofar as the past was seen as subject to reinterpretation according to the needs of the present, antiquity for the Renaissance imagination was no less a construct, no less a heterocosm, than the world within a painting. Explicitly the humanists sought their image *of* the past; implicitly they sought their image *in* the past. But to do this and believe in what they did, they had to feel that historical interpretation was *not* creation or artifice but discovery of what was actually the case *in illo tempore*. They could validate their own ideals only if they found them objectively embodied *elsewhere*. Thus for the Renaissance imagination antiquity became a Hegelian *other*, a self-there to which the modern, or self-here, could appeal. What was truly found—dug up from the earth or shipped over from Constantinople—had a status equal to that of a painter's model: it was raw material accorded the function of a blueprint; something ideal was "seen in it," abstracted "from it," isolated and heightened and framed in the mind's reconstruction. The ultimate purpose of finding/implanting that ideal in the past was to win it back for the

present. Conversely, we might infer as a tacit impulse the urge to separate it from the defects and uncertainties of the actual present, not only to
reinforce its objectivity as an "ideal-there" but also to safeguard it. Thus
the repertory of models which the Renaissance imagination built up into
the field or system called antiquity was useful both as an ideal and as an
other place, a heterocosm.

As a prototype of this dynamics, we may look back to Plato's theory
and enactment of self-motion, articulated especially in the *Phaedrus*. Defining soul as that which is capable of self-motion, he describes this
activity as a continual oscillation out from the self and back. It is an
activity which leads the mind, on the one hand, to commit itself to something beyond itself and, on the other hand, to keep itself free of fixation,
free of obsessive commitment to some single action or object which stops
forward movement. The description of love in the *Phaedrus* is based on a
complex psychology of projection, and on a distinction between consciousness and *nous*, the latter conceived as operating behind individual
consciousness and as being a generic, even a cosmic, force inhabiting the
psyche: the lover *thinks* he is being drawn to another person, but what
really happens is that his own *nous* projects and embodies a beautiful image of itself and its god (i.e., its ideal generic type) in the beloved; the
lover is thus unwittingly filled with eros for *nous*, his own best part, and
at the same time his longing sets him in forward motion toward an object
outside himself (*Phaedrus* 252c–255e).

A classic Renaissance statement of the process, in Shakespeare's *Troilus
and Cressida*, describes it as a more completely conscious pattern: Ulysses, trying to rouse Achilles to action by appealing to his self-esteem,
pretends to read the opinions of "a strange fellow," whom some commentators have identified as Plato but who is really Ulysses himself:

> "That man, how dearly ever parted,
> How much in having, or without or in,
> Cannot make boast to have that which he hath,
> Nor feels not what he owes, but by reflection;
> As when his virtues shining upon others
> Heat them and they retort that heat again
> To the first giver."
>
> ACHILLES: This is not strange, Ulysses.
> The beauty that is borne here in the face
> The bearer knows not, but commends itself
> To others' eyes; nor doth the eye itself,
> That most pure spirit of sense, behold itself,
> Not going from itself; but eye to eye opposed

Salutes each other with each other's form;
For speculation turns not to itself,
Till it hath travell'd and is mirror'd there
Where it may see itself. This is not strange at all.

ULYSSES: I do not strain at the position,—
It is familiar,—but at the author's drift;
Who, in his circumstance, expressly proves
That no man is the lord of any thing,
Though in and of him there be much consisting,
Till he communicate his parts to others;
Nor doth he of himself know them for aught
Till he behold them form'd in the applause
Where they're extended. . . .

(III.iii.96–120)

In the humanist version of the dialectic which is epitomized by Alberti, nature, antiquity, contemporary society, and the future provide the termini, the *others*, on which the self tacitly ("unconsciously") projects itself or to which it consciously appeals for recognition, correction, and justification. Thus Alberti views both nature and antiquity in the same double perspective and uses both in the same way: each is at once an exemplary guide to be imitated and a matrix of forms and processes which, however excellent, are relatively incomplete, unperfected, in need of revision. To objectify one's ideals in an external guide, a natural or historical exemplar, is to validate them as ultrahuman or ultrasubjective norms which the mind may discover and to which it must conform. Having thus placed limits upon itself, the mind may shift the emphasis to its own power and excellence, its freedom from the bonds of nature and the past, its obligation to improve, revise, move forward creatively toward new discoveries and achievements. For this assertion, it is necessary to establish nature as inferior to man and antiquity as inferior to the present. But this assertion must in turn be validated by a new appeal beyond the self, to one's contemporaries and successors. If one can communicate one's parts, project one's image and ideals on others, one will have attained a new objectivity and self-transcendence. To become thus "immortal" is to replace and outmode the antique models. And if one is guided by the fate of the ancient models vis-à-vis oneself, one will recognize the peculiarly limiting conditions of one's own immortality as model: to be altered, corrected, revised, and rendered obsolete is not the kiss of death but the mark of vitality and influence, the sign of enduring historical significance. Alberti treats himself and the ancients in the same manner. The honor of serving as models/guides is first accorded to the ancients, then to the moderns, finally, and hesitantly, to Alberti himself. And as the ancients fulfill themselves in the moderns who replace them, so Alberti hopes that his trailblazing effort will be corrected, emended, revised, and in that way both rendered obsolete and kept alive, accorded a place and function in the cultural sequence. As a model, one claims to be an exemplar for only a limited time. At the end of the *Della Pittura*, Alberti submits himself to the public and to the future—to others in space and time—and while reminding them that he has made a difference, he acknowledges the extent to which he depends on them for goodwill, for cooperation, for judgment of his *utilità*. If the conclusion is conventional, and as I have suggested it is a pastiche of rhetorical commonplaces, this merely proves the point. The conventions are blueprints and models which are at once justified and transcended in that very moment when the new text, the new experiential context, fills them with its life. Perhaps it is not entirely ingenuous to wonder whether the author can be conventional and "sincere" at the same time, for this puzzle has the virtue of keeping before us the ambiguous quality, the brief and precarious equilibrium, of this moment. He is, of course, both conventional and sincere because he is sincerely conventional and, in the best sense, conventionally sincere.

Leonardo da Vinci:
The Influence of World View
on Artistic Style

I

Leonardo painted the *Mona Lisa* and *St. Anne* after 1500, during his sixties, and in both pictures the harmonious counterpoint between foreground and background has often been remarked. Comparison with an earlier painting, *Adoration of the Magi*, will show how much sharper and more deliberate the counterpoint is in the later works. The present essay will explore this difference in terms of the following hypothesis: Leonardo's development as a painter may in large part be accounted for by important aspects of his world view which affect the stylistic organization of the later work. I shall discuss the relevant features of the world view before looking at the paintings, and I should like to begin by converting one of Vasari's anecdotes into an allegory.

Leonardo was something of a practical joker, and Vasari tells us that he often had the guts of sheep or cattle carefully cleaned, "and in this way made so fine, that it could be held in the palm of the hand. He fixed one end to a pair of bellows in the next room and blew the intestines up until they filled the room, which was very large, so that whoever was there was forced into a corner." In our allegory, let the original room with its occupants be the actual world in which Leonardo finds himself, the mundane existence he confronts. Let his bellows and lung power represent the force of his imagination, and let the guts stand for

Leonardo's universe, his second world or nature. The motives for creating and expanding this universe vary; they may include sheer fun and entertainment; the gratuitous pleasure in imaginative and technological virtuosity; a more ironic or sardonic humor; finally a serious need to cope with the actual world by keeping it at a distance. We should note that he moves into the empty adjacent room only to do something to—or for—the occupants of the first room.

The allegory suggests a radical or primitive attitude toward the actual world and, in reaction to this attitude, a response which discloses not only a quirky and creative mind but one which is independent, critical, energetic, and productive. Leonardo is no less practical as a visionary than he is as a joker. He is eccentric but not misanthropic, hermetic and eremitic yet humane and intensely aware of the world about him. The essence of his primitive or natural attitude is a distaste for close contact with the daily world of men and affairs, also a more general distrust of human and natural forces. There is both a positive, contemplative side and a negative, ethical side to Leonardo's diffidence: He needed to be left alone to think and work; he felt that few men could be counted on to understand or appreciate what he was doing; at once idealistic and self-critical, he knew his own failures and limitations, and knew also that he had only to multiply these by an exponential factor to find the measure of the majority of men who remain in the first room.

In his fables, prophecies, allegories, and bestiaries Leonardo's natural attitude modulates from hardheaded Florentine skepticism to downright bitterness, and we often hear the acerb and styptic chuckling of the solitary crank. Kenneth Clark notes this frame of mind in the fables:

> The animals, plants or inanimate objects who are the heroes of the fables, are no sooner confident of success and security than they are utterly destroyed by some superior and usually unconscious agency. If they avoid one misfortune, they immediately fall victim to a far greater as a result of their previous cunning. We see reflected Leonardo's view of contemporary politics, and indeed of life in general, where nature only allows man to reach some pinnacle of self-esteem in order to deal him a more shattering blow.[1]

Leonardo contemplates a world where time continually crumbles or dissolves the forms produced by nature and man, a world where creaturely consciousness is too narrowly focused on self, pleasure, and the main chance and thus too exposed and fragile:

[1] Kenneth Clark, *Leonardo da Vinci* (Harmondsworth: Penguin Books, 1958), 68–69.

Supreme happiness will be the greatest cause
of misery, and the perfection of wisdom the
occasion of folly.

O Time, thou that consumest all things! O envious age,
thou destroyest all things and devourest all things
with the hard teeth of the years . . . in slow
death! Helen, when she looked in her mirror
and saw the withered wrinkles which old age had
made in her face, wept, and wondered to herself
why ever she had twice been carried away.

Man and the animals are merely a passage and
channel for food, a tomb for other animals,
a haven for the dead, giving life by the
death of others, a coffer full of corruption.

While I thought that I was learning how to live,
I have been learning how to die.

O human stupidity! Do you not perceive that
you have spent your whole life with yourself
and yet are not aware of that which you have
most in evidence, and that is your own
foolishness?[2]

However conventional these aphorisms may sound, they assume special importance if taken to express the natural attitude which sets off the reactions (or abreactions) known as the works of Leonardo da Vinci. I shall now arrange some of these reactions in a hypothetical sequence based on the familiar withdrawal-return pattern. The logical first moment is a step back—withdrawal *from* a dangerous, obstructive, or merely annoying actual world; withdrawal *toward* a more comprehensive vantage point. Leonardo places greater distance between himself and the actual world not merely to escape from contact but also to see more and see better. And his seeing takes on different modes. I shall call these modes the panoramic, the analytic, the analogical, the apocalyptic, and the artistic. My treatment of the first four modes will differ considerably from my treatment of the fifth—that is, the discussion of the artistic mode will consist of the formal analysis of the paintings because the notebooks and drawings manifest Leonardo's withdrawal into the second

---

[2] Leonardo da Vinci, *Notebooks*, trans. Edward MacCurdy (New York: Reynal & Hitchcock, n.d.), I, 67, 69, 71, 89.

room, whereas the paintings embody in a special way the return to the first room.

The essence of the panoramic mode is *observation*, the act of perceiving and noting large- and small-scale forms of the universe as they appear to the eye. The essence of the analytic mode is *penetration* beneath the diversity of forms in search of basic causes or principles. The essence of the analogical mode is the *coordination* of forms and causes into a dynamic and implicitly systematic vision of existence; in this vision, a few basic natural processes operating throughout space-time produce similar effects in the most diverse phenomena and events. The essence of the apocalyptic mode is the *fascination* with destructive power; here, the aphoristic pessimism of Leonardo's natural attitude is directed away from its proximate causes, is magnified, intensified, and universalized into a vision of elemental fury and cosmic doom. The following remarks, accompanied by examples from the drawings and notebooks, will suggest at greater length the character of each of the first four modes.

II

The panoramic vision is bipolar. Divided between telescopic and microscopic perspectives, it shifts back and forth between the bird's- or god's-eye view of space and time and the close, loving observation of detail. It is expressed not only in Leonardo's aerial views of valley and mountain ranges but also in his drawings of plants, hair, and drapery; it apprehends not only the musculature of the earth but also that of the human body:

> (a) The sea shuts itself in among the great valleys
> of the earth; and this earth serves as a cup for
> the sea. . . . (I, 361)
>
> Lacking the weight of the waters of the Mediterranean
> which had been diminished the earth rose and changed
> in itself its centre of gravity. (I, 339)
>
> (b) The figure of the foam which . . . remains behind in
> the wave is always triangular, and its angle is made
> up of the first foam and that in front of the course
> where the wave first descended. (I, 335)
>
> (a) The surface of the earth was from of old entirely
> filled up and covered over in its level plains by
> the salt waters, and . . . the mountains, the bones

of the earth, . . . penetrated and towered up amid the air. (I, 335)

The body of the earth like the bodies of animals is interwoven with a network of veins [rivers] which are all joined together . . . they originate in the depths of the sea, and there after many revolutions they have to return through the rivers formed by the high burstings of these veins. (I, 368)

(b) The vein is one whole, which is divided into as many main branches as there are principal places which it has to nourish. (I, 105)

The colon in the old becomes as slender as the middle finger of the hand, and in the young it is equal to the maximum breadth of the arm. (I, 144)

The veins . . . within the cranium . . . produce an imprint of the half of their thickness in the bone of the cranium, and the other half is hidden in the membranes which clothe the brain. (I, 164)

(a) The fact of the summits of the mountains projecting so far above the watery sphere may be due to the fact that a very large space of the earth which was filled with water, that is the immense cavern, must have fallen in a considerable distance from its vault towards the centre of the world. (I, 372)

(b) The leaf always turns its upper side towards the sky so that it may be better able to receive over its whole surface the dew which drops down with the slow movement of the atmosphere. (I, 320)

These notes do not record mere descriptions but rather a complex tissue of experiment, inference, speculation and comparison. They presuppose, though they do not insist on, a rational relation between perceived forms and the forces which caused them or the functions they fulfill. Ernst Cassirer remarks "that Leonardo's ideal of science aims at . . . the perfection of seeing" in which "abstraction and vision" collaborate, and this seeing—at once scientific and artistic—discerns the essence of things "in visible and graspable forms."[3] Leonardo does not perceive these

---

[3] Ernst Cassirer, *The Individual and the Cosmos in Renaissance Philosophy*, trans. M. Domandi (New York: Barnes & Noble, 1963), 158, 157.

forms as mere immediacies, surface appearances. He perceives them as effects and manifestations—that is, physical shape (or visual form) embodies the force or function by which it is activated. Whether telescopic or microscopic, his act of seeing is tinged with the awareness of underlying causes and relations.

III

Panoramic vision gives way to the analytic mode when this awareness becomes central. The following two passages will demonstrate the transition and also the essential features of the new mode. Notice in the first how the aerial viewpoint affects not only the scale of spatial imagining but also the way the activity of aeons is compressed or sped up and felt as a dynamic process:

> The summits of the mountains in course
> of time rise continually. . . .
> During the same period of time the valleys
> sink much more than the mountains rise.
> The bases of the mountains are always
> drawing closer together.
> As the valley grows deeper so its sides
> become worn away in a shorter space of time.
>
> *(I, 344)*

In this as in many similar visions, Leonardo feels the inexorable, deterministic workings of nature on a spatio-temporal scale compared with which the dimensions of the merely human are dwarfed. Yet at the same time, such descriptions are often phrased in terms which imply rationality and purpose. Our next passage suggests how in the act of explaining what is observed, he tends to fuse the rationality of mental process with that of natural process:

> The surface of the watery sphere is always
> more remote from the centre of the world:
> *This comes about by reason* of the soil
> brought by the inundations of turbid rivers.
> These deposit the soil which causes their
> turbidity on the shores of the ocean and so
> narrow the sea beach; beside this they raise
> their bed and so *of necessity* the surface of
> this element comes to be raised.
> The centre of the world continually changes

> its position in the body of the earth fleeing
> towards our hemisphere.
> This is shown by the above-mentioned soil which
> is continually carried away from the declivities
> or sides of the mountains and borne to the seas;
> the more it is carried away from there the more
> it becomes lightened and *as a consequence* the
> more it becomes heavy where this soil is deposited
> by the ocean waves, *wherefore it is necessary*
> that such centre changes its position.
>
> *(I, 344, my italics)*

In passages of this sort, phrases which take the form "by reason of" usually have the same value as the formula "of necessity." Notice also how the qualities of the subject matter control Leonardo's attention and permeate his style: the restlessness, the continual pulsing of natural forces, the endless metamorphosis of natural forms—these are felt in the rapid scanning thoughts that move from event to event, image to image, and clause to clause; felt also in the way Leonardo nervously and repeatedly refers back to the antecedents to carry them forward in the causal sequence. Whether deliberate or accidental, this blending of style and content, mind and nature, epitomizes the new alignment of reason and necessity which Cassirer ascribes to Leonardo: "Hitherto," he writes, "as the *regnum naturae*, necessity had been the opposite of the realm of freedom and of mind; but now it becomes the seal of mind itself."[4] And it is preeminently in those passages which exhibit the analytic mode that we sense the dynamic convergence of forces and reasons.

Penetrating beneath the observed world, Leonardo's analytic glance falls not on the traditional system of nature, the hierarchy of substantial forms, but rather on a *process*—a process in which forces interact with bodies, and in which the forces are more basic than the bodies. In his most general definition, force is "a spiritual power, incorporeal and invisible, which with brief life is produced in those bodies which as the result of accidental violence are brought out of their natural state and condition. . . . [it is] of brief duration because it desires perpetually to subdue its cause, and when this is subdued it kills itself" (I, 74):

> It lives by violence and dies from liberty.
> It transforms and constrains every body with
> change of position and form.

---

[4] Cassirer, 159.

Great power gives it great desire of death.
It drives away with fury whatever opposes
its destruction.
Transmuter of various forms.
Lives always in hostility to whoever controls it.
Always sets itself against natural desires.
From small beginnings it slowly becomes larger,
and makes itself a dreadful and marvellous power.
. . . dwells in bodies which are kept away from
their natural course and use.

(I, 530)

Nature is driven by the interplay and conflict between opposing forces, between forces and elements, or between force and form. Some examples:

Many times one and the same thing is drawn
by two violences, namely necessity [here,
need] and power. . . . the earth absorbs it
[water] from necessity of moisture; and the sun
raises it up not from necessity but by its
power.

(I, 73–74)

Intellectual passion drives out sensuality.

(I, 72)

Movement of earth against earth pressing down
upon it causes a slight movement of the parts struck.

Water struck by water creates circles at a
great distance round the spot where it is
struck; the voice in the air goes further,
in fire further still; mind ranges
over the universe but being finite it does
not extend into infinity.

(I, 77)

Heat and cold produce the movement of the
elements.
No element has of itself gravity or levity.

Gravity and levity . . . arise from the movement
of the element . . . in its rarefaction and
condensation. . . .

Levity is born of gravity and gravity of levity;
repaying in the same instant the boon of their

creation they grow the more in power as they
grow in life and have the more life in proportion
as they have more movement, in the same instant
also they destroy one another in the common
vendetta of their death.

(I, 82−83)

There cannot be any sound where there is no
movement or percussion of the air. There cannot
be any percussion of the air where there is no
instrument. There cannot be any instrument
without a body. . . .

And if any should say that through air being
collected together and compressed a spirit may
assume bodies of various shapes, and by such
instrument may speak and move with force, my
reply to this would be that where there are
neither nerves nor bones there cannot be any
force exerted in any movement made by
imaginary spirits.

(I, 74)

What is . . . the cause of so great a force of
arms and legs which is seen in the actions of
any animal? . . . it is the skin which
clothes them; . . . when the nerves of sensation
thicken the muscles these muscles contract and
draw after them the tendons in which their
extremities become converted; and in this process
of thickening they fill out the skin and make it
drawn and hard; and it cannot be lengthened out
unless the muscles become thinner; and not
becoming thinner they are a cause of resistance
and of making strong the . . . skin, in which the
swollen muscles perform the function of a wedge.

(I, 121)

In these passages Leonardo presupposes the principle of equilibrium,
but if he describes force as an intrusive and unnatural power, he feels it
to be no less fundamental than natural energy. The dialectic between
constraining force and natural tendency drives the universe through its
career, imposing on it, and on each of its parts, the same irreversible
pattern. We are familiar with the subject of Leonardo's apocalyptic vision, his increasingly obsessive fantasies of the end of the world. These

are but the logical conclusion of the pattern he sees as following an ancient principle, that of the economy of nature. Let me cite two brief notes stating the principle in its conventional form, and then a third, more interesting, variation applied to human psychology:

> Every action done by nature is done in the
> shortest way.
>
> *(I, 79)*
>
> Every part of an element separated from its
> mass desires to return to it by the shortest
> way.
>
> *(I, 71)*
>
> [The longing for death] is in its quintessence
> the spirit of the elements, which finding
> itself imprisoned within the life of the human
> body desires continually to return to its
> source.
>
> *(I, 81)*

The analytic vision justifies the death, flux, dissonance, and chaos of the actual world by raising them to a cosmic level and conceiving them as a phase of nature. But they constitute only one phase: nature's orderly process is form producing as well as form destroying. And these two phases occur not only in the normal temporal sequence; they may overlap in confusing ways, they may occur simultaneously at different levels of organization, and they may work to sustain some forms while destroying others. So in the next two passages Leonardo's emphasis falls first on the metamorphic and then on the constructive aspects of nature's power:

> The streams of rivers move different kinds of
> matter which are of varying degrees of gravity,
> and they are moved farther from their position
> in proportion as they are lighter, and will
> remain nearer to the bottom in proportion as
> they are heavier, and will be carried a greater
> distance when driven by water of greater power.
>
> But when this power ceases to be capable of
> subduing the resistance of the gravel this gravel
> becomes firm and checks the direct movement of
> the water which led it to this place. Then the
> water, as it strikes on the gravel which has
> been increased in this manner, leaps back

crosswise and strikes upon other spots to
which it was unaccustomed, and takes away
other deposits of soil down to their foundations.
And so the places where first the said river
used to pass are deserted and become silted
up anew by a fresh deposit from the turbid
waters, and these in due course become choked
up in these same places.

(I, 327)

The creature that resides within the shell
constructs its dwelling with joints and seams
and roofing and the other various parts, just
as man does in the house in which he dwells;
and this creature expands the house and roof
gradually in proportion as its body increases
and as it is attached to the sides of these
shells.

Consequently the brightness and smoothness which
these shells possess on the inner side is somewhat dulled at the point where they are attached
to the creature that dwells there, and the hollow
of it is roughened, ready to receive the knitting
together of the muscles by means of which the
creature draws itself in when it wishes to shut
itself up within its house.

When nature is on the point of creating stones
it produces a kind of sticky paste, which as it
dries, forms itself into a solid mass together
with whatever it has enclosed there, which,
however, it does not change into stone but
preserves within itself in the form in which
it has found them. This is why leaves are found
whole within the rocks which are formed at the
bases of the mountains, together with a mixture
of different kinds of things, just as they have
been left there by the floods from the rivers
which have occurred in the autumn seasons; and
there the mud caused by the successive inundations
has covered them over, and then this mud grows
into one mass together with the aforesaid paste,
and becomes changed into successive layers of
stone which correspond with the layers of the mud.

(I, 331)

IV

In turning from the analytic to the analogical mode of vision, I shall first identify a boundary area in which Leonardo fluidly blends causes and effects, forces and forms. The analogical mode was defined above as concerned with the coordination of forms and causes, and with the production of similar effects in the most diverse phenomena and events. In the boundary region, the so-called elements of water, wind, and fire are treated by Leonardo as graphic embodiments of force:

> The water that falls back into the sea . . .
> penetrates through the pores of the earth . . .
> rises anew with violence . . . descends in its
> accustomed course, . . . then returns. Thus
> adhering together and united in continual
> revolution it goes moving round backwards and
> forwards; at times it all rises together with
> fortuitous movement, at times descends in
> natural liberty. Thus moving up and down,
> backwards and forwards, it never rests in
> quiet either in its course or in its own
> substance: . . . it has nothing of itself but
> moves or takes everything, and is changed to
> as many different natures as the places are
> different through which it passes.
>
> *(I, 345–46)*

Leonardo's separate descriptions of force and water are so often shaded toward each other that water moved or taken by force becomes identical with force—or, to put it the other way, force materializes in and as the local form of water, so that water is a paradigm as well as an instance. Fire, because distinct from water, offers a slightly different paradigm of the force-form relation:

> Flame has its beginning and end in smoke. . . .
> Flame is condensed smoke. . . .
>
> The blue smoke is the transit of the material
> nutriment that is the grease that is in the
> candle. The white smoke that surrounds the
> vestige of the flame is the spiritual transit
> of the flame of this candle. . . .
>
> Fire comes into existence in the upper part of
> the blue spherical flame . . . the roundness of

which immediately undergoes . . . extension and
assumes the shape of a heart, of which the point
is turned towards the sky. And this shape
immediately and with swift dilation overcomes
the power that feeds it, and penetrates the air
which serves it as a covering.

(I, 402–3)

A more complicated paradigm, perhaps a special case, is Leonardo's description of a forcing garden, or garden of Adonis. I quote this at length partly because so many of the more interesting features of the analogical perspective are packed into it but partly, too, because it looks toward the apocalyptic vision and suggests the relation between the analogical and apocalyptic modes:

Instances and Deductions as to the Earth's Increase
Take a vase, fill it full of pure earth, and set
it up on a roof. You will see how immediately
the green herbs will begin to shoot up, and how
these, when fully grown, will cast their various
seeds; and after the children have thus fallen at
the feet of their parents, you will see the herbs
having cast their seeds, becoming withered and
falling back again to the earth, and within a
short time becoming changed into the earth's
substance and giving it increase; after this you
will see the seeds springing up and passing through
the same course, and so you will always see the
successive generations after completing their
natural course, by their death and corruption
giving increase to the earth. And if you let
ten years elapse and then measure the increase
in the soil, you will be able to discover how much
the earth in general has increased, and then by
multiplying you will see how great has been
the increase of the earth in the world during
a thousand years. Some may say that this
instance of the vase which I have mentioned
does not justify the deduction based upon it,
because one sees in the case of these vases
that for the prize of the flowers that are
looked for a part of the soil is frequently
taken away, and its place is filled up with
new rich soil; and I reply to them that as the

soil which is added there is a blend of rich
fat substances and broken bits of all sorts
of things it cannot be said to be pure earth,
and this mass of substances decaying and so losing
in part their shape becomes changed into a rich
ooze, which feeds the roots of the plants above
them; and this is the reason why it may appear
to you that the earth is lessened; but if you
allow the plants that grow in it to die, and
their seeds to spring up, then in time you will
behold its increase.

For do you not perceive how, among the high
mountains, the walls of ancient and ruined
cities are being covered over and concealed
by the earth's increase?

Nay, have you not seen how on the rocky summits
of the mountains the live stone itself has in
course of time swallowed up by its growth some
column which it supported, and stripping it
bare as with shears and grasping it tightly,
has left the impress of its fluted form in
the living rock?

(I, 337–38)

His form of statement modifies the experiment it records. The forcing garden by itself demonstrates cosmic processes in miniature; like a good scientist, Leonardo creates a hypothetical testing ground and, in dealing with objections, acknowledges its difference from actuality only to assert the isomorphism between them. The message of the experiment is that small observable events can be made to illuminate large events which are otherwise unobservable; what makes this credible or probable is belief in a single structure of activity underlying both sets of events. Such a message affirms not only the unity and continuity of nature throughout space and time but also the triumph of the human mind in discovering and establishing this unity.

Leonardo's account is peculiar in that it fights with that message. He begins with a sharply focused set of instructions, but as he proceeds his statement is poetically colored by an Ozymandian mood. The mood flickers tentatively in the metaphor of parents and children; disappears with the positive statement of the parallel between generations of plants and terrestrial millennia; is covertly sustained in subtle variations of rhetoric ("the prize of flowers, this mass of substances . . . becomes changed into a rich ooze") even while the experimenter busily and successfully refutes objections; then, as if the mood has been building up until it can no longer be suppressed, there is a sudden and rhetorically heightened lifting of the eyes, and the long elegiac view of the ruins of time gives way to a final moment of vague terror as man's works are seen to be devoured not by abstract time but by the primeval living growing rock. Against this background the brief foreground moment in which the flowerpot, the experiment, and the statement are interlocked assumes a paradoxical meaning: it is a vanity, an example of man's pride and insignificance; but it is also a precious mote of insight and vision wrested from the onslaught of hungry rock. The course of this feeling through the statement may be described in a phrase which Leonardo applies to force: "From small beginnings it slowly becomes larger, and makes itself a dreadful and marvellous power." And this power, toward the end of Leonardo's life, will give birth to his most intense expressions of the end of the world.

But in the other, more positive, aspect we find the essence of the analogical vision. From his Archimedean viewpoint, Leonardo "sees" (imagines, conceives) similar processes going on at different places, on different scales, and at different rates of time:

> As water flows in different directions out of a
> squeezed sponge, or air from a pair of bellows,
> so it is with the thin transparent clouds that
> have been driven up to a height.
>
> *(I, 400)*
>
> As the natural warmth spread through the human
> limbs is driven back by the surrounding cold
> which is its opposite and enemy . . . so the
> clouds being made up of warmth and moisture,
> and in summer of certain dry vapours, and
> finding themselves in the cold dry region,
> act after the manner of certain flowers and
> leaves which when attacked by the cold hoar-
> frost press themselves close together.
>
> *(I, 401)*
>
> As man has within himself bones as a stay and
> framework for the flesh, so the world has the
> rocks which are the supports of the earth; as
> man has within him a pool of blood wherein the

lungs as he breathes expand and contract, so
the body of the earth has its ocean, which also
rises and falls every six hours with the breathing
of the world.

(II, 21)

As the blood from below surges up and then falls
back should a vein burst in the forehead, so the
water rises from the lowest depth of the sea to
the summits of the mountains, and . . . is poured out
through them and returns to the depths of the
sea.

(I, 345)

To see nothing more than "old and quaint beliefs untested by experience" in such analogies is to misunderstand the way Leonardo deploys
them.[5] Again and again, oscillating between minute and gigantic events
or phenomena, he discerns similarities of form and function which
he reads as evidence of a single force of nature operating throughout
the whole range of the spatio-temporal scale. The world seen in paradigmatic perspective has a unity different from that of the extensive
spherical cosmos. Its unity is that of the single intensive process which
produces and destroys these paradigms or variables, which continually
seeks new manifestations and is thus the artist working through time to
shape—*disegnare*—the visible world. What is real and basic is no longer
the substantial form (*ousia*) but the dynamic relations and analogies
binding substances together.

V

The fourth and most dramatic mode is the apocalyptic vision exemplified
by the famous storms and deluges. Here Leonardo's pessimism is magnified and transfigured in fantasies which, whether in word or image,
reveal him more exhilarated than horrified by the prospect of cataclysm.
In his book on landscape, Richard Turner calls the late drawings and
descriptions Leonardo's "concluding unscientific postscript": "Because
Leonardo had seen all, recorded all, and now left it behind, his empirical mind shifted wholly into the limitlessness of the imagination
where it was free to envision the chaos of doom." And in these visions, a

---

[5] A. Richard Turner, *The Vision of Landscape in Renaissance Italy* (Princeton: Princeton
University Press, 1966), 31.

good part of the exhilaration must derive from the free release of esthetic energy, the effortless control of visual and verbal form evident in the most Dionysiac images of dissolving natural form. It is the ultimate triumph of art that it can visualize and hence formalize the enemy of form and art.

VI

This concludes my discussion of the first four modes of vision, and I now turn to the fifth, the artistic vision. As I noted above, my illustration of this mode will consist of the major paintings themselves as I suggest how features of Leonardo's stylistic development may be partly accounted for by the world view we have just explored. I have treated these modes as reactions to the natural attitude, and to some extent as strategies—or better, as life responses—of the mind. Painting in itself was for Leonardo an esthetically self-sufficient pleasure, one of the noblest skills of mind and hand. But as a mode of vision it is more than that; Leonardo comes to see it as the most perfect embodiment of form, the most meaningful visualization of the form-force relation, and the creative activity in which the impulses of the other modes of vision are ultimately fulfilled. I said that he *comes to see it* this way, and I mean that the influence of world view is registered less fully in his earlier than in his later paintings. The counterpoint between background and foreground provides a simplified model in which to trace the changes. In the later paintings, it represents a counterpoint between nature and man, but this is not the case in the relatively early and unfinished *Adoration of the Magi,* of 1481–1482 (Figure 3). Here, foreground and background are emphatically bound together, as Sidney Freedberg has shown, by two intersecting diagonals which run "through the oblique directions implied in the contrapposto of the Virgin" and "bind together all the elements within the composition."[6] Freedberg notes that this linking depends not on a perspective structure but on the subordination of the varied natural forms to harmonious geometrical vectors of design. The upper and lower parts of the design are clearly distinguished, both in values and in the counterplay of the overall formal patterns. Yet there is a kind of sluice up the left side of the panel, a flow of bright figures swirling around from the central figure into the distance, and this disperses the human elements upward and downward across the clearly de-

[6]Sydney Freedberg, *Painting of the High Renaissance in Rome and Florence* (Cambridge: Harvard University Press, 1961) I, 8.

fined boundary line. In this way, Leonardo arrives at a new treatment of the conventional binary schema, distinguishing yet harmonizing foreground and background, the lower and upper halves of the panel, the elements of design and those of representation. But this solution is *purely* formal, which is to say that the problems the *Adoration* seems to disclose and confront are, in the main, esthetic problems having little or nothing to do with Leonardo's thought or world view. What this means may better be grasped by comparison, first with the earlier *Annunciation* and then with some of the later works.

Compared to the *Adoration*, the Uffizi *Annunciation* (c. 1472, Figure 4) is less unified and mobile, more awkward and artificial. We feel the conflicting claims of isolated episodes, each with its own insistence on some virtuoso item, such as the painstaking antique design of the lectern; the use of architectural coigning to accentuate the perspective; the Flemish delight in minutiae and in the busy middle distance. These reveal the young artist perfecting himself in the vocabulary of accepted visual conventions which belong to the earlier Quattrocento manner; for this reason the painting was long thought to be the work of an artist like Ghirlandaio. Yet the sharp contrast between the two paintings only makes the similarities of intention stand out more clearly. It is true that the cleavage between foreground and background is marked by a number of devices: the dominant lateral organization; the sharp outlining of forms, which stresses their confinement in the plane; the low wall; the relation of the two figures. There is, nevertheless, an attempt to break down the division. Instead of the rhythmic sluicing effect, we have the wall opening which frames the angel's upraised hand. The garden area seems to continue beyond the formal barrier. The orthogonals implied by the coigns lead swiftly back into the distant landscape, and this effect is intensified by the smooth, broad, and irrationally drawn top of the wall (seen from too high a viewing point). Finally, the background contains human as well as natural elements, so that the cleavage is not yet felt by Leonardo in an intelligible or symbolic manner. The world of man and his works is depicted on both sides of the barrier. The world of nature is defined either as a minor mood-making feature of the background, or else it appears domesticated by man in gardens, trees, horses, and waterways. The mobility which informs the whole of the *Adoration* design is visible here only in one passage, the flowers in the foreground, of which Kenneth Clark writes: "Leonardo has given to his flowers and grasses something of the turbulence which he felt to be the essence of nature. They twist and surge like little waves over the space between the angel and the Madonna, giving vitality to what would otherwise have

3. *Adoration of the Magi.* Uffizi, Florence.

been a dead area in the composition."[7] Mountain ranges rather than grasses will provide the later graphs of this turbulence.

The world of nature as such is virtually ruled out of *The Last Supper* (Figure 5). Through the windows at the rear we glimpse the remains of a vaguely specified scene whose primary function is to set off the head of Christ. (A drawing of *The Last Supper*, made before 1800, shows buildings in the distance.) As in the *Adoration*, though in a very different manner, the entire background is dynamically organized by and around the central figure. The visual movement pulses outward from the hands of Christ, catches up the figures and tapestries at the wings of the picture, then closes in and embraces him once more. The balances and tensions reveal not merely the vital movement of organic forms but the

[7] Clark, *Leonardo da Vinci*, 27.

4. *Annunciation.* Uffizi, Florence.

5. *The Last Supper.* S. Maria delle Grazia, Milan.

psychological action of human souls. Unlike the *Adoration*, in which the geometric design is produced by the treatment and disposition of figures, here it is produced by the organization of space—that is, by a linear perspective system whose vanishing point is located in the head of Christ. The recession into depth is thus suggested and at the same time attenuated, so that it serves primarily as the visual reinforcement of Christ's influence (and only secondarily as a way to create the illusion of depth).

In his writings on perspective, Leonardo describes three methods by which the illusion of depth may be produced: diminishing the size of bodies, diminishing their color, and diminishing their distinctness of form. Of these, he remarks, the second and third derive from the atmosphere, but "the first has its origin in the eye." That is, only rational, or linear, perspective is a function of the human mind using geometrical measurement to clarify the spatial relations among objects. Unlike Alberti and Piero della Francesca, Leonardo does not envisage the geometry of perspective as a body of axioms to be employed for static architectonic or mathematical construction. In the *Notebooks* he speaks of geometry as a dynamic field of rectilinear forces and motions where the *ragione* of mind apprehends that of nature.

These notions play an important role in the pictorial conception of *The Last Supper*. The space-making function has been preempted by linear perspective. Except for the landscape beyond the window, the two atmospheric methods have been ignored, and the details in the rear of the room are as distinct as those in the foreground (for example, the pediment or lintel over the window). The tautness of Leonardo's conception suits the subject of the painting: where the *Annunciation* and *Adoration* are somewhat diffuse efforts—pretenses, really—to depict historical events, *The Last Supper* is sharply centered on a single moment, contracted in focus and purely mental or psychological in its form of action. The link with physical activity in *The Last Supper* is less immediate than that in either the *Annunciation* or the *Adoration*. The dynamism of natural forces is manifest, but in its most rational aspect. The perspective space is mobile and optical rather than static and architectural. Its sharp lateral thrust from wings toward center is the visual equivalent of the contracted temporal focus. The counterthrust from the vanishing point through the hands of Christ and outward visualizes the moment in which the news of his betrayal radiates like a shock wave not only through his companions but also through history. As in Leonardo's geometry the point compresses within itself the line, plane, and pyramid which it will generate, so this moment contains the betrayal, the crucifixion, and all that follows.

Different in every respect are the next two paintings, the *Mona Lisa* and *The Virgin and Child with St. Anne* (Figures 6 and 7). From the volumes of comment devoted to them, I choose a few sentences which illuminate the present topic. First, Richard Turner on the *Mona Lisa* landscape:

> The land seen from on high . . . is an expansive vista on a heroic scale, carved from the raw rock of young mountains, and softened by a layer of atmosphere. . . . the winding road and stone bridge . . . are forlorn signs of man's presence in a barren landscape. . . . Glacial in its icy damp, this is a forbidden land where . . . one stands in wonder, but dares not go on.[8]

Mona Lisa, Pater remarked in his famous description, "is older than the rocks among which she sits," and of Leonardo's rocky landscapes Kenneth Clark has much to say: Leonardo saw in landscape "the wildness of nature, the vast untamed background of human life. . . . Rocks were not simply decorative silhouettes. They were part of the earth's bones, with an anatomy of their own, caused by some remote seismic upheaval."[9]

They have been called "petrified deluges" (A. E. Popham), and Clark describes a series of drawings at Windsor (c. 1508–1510) in which Leonardo studies

> outcrops and disturbed stratification, where the rock has broken through the comfortable humus, and reveals the ancient, grim foundations on which living things have their precarious existence.
>
> This sense of the world as a planet, seen from a point of distance at which human life is no longer visible, is given final expression in the background of the Virgin and St. Anne.[10]

There is a tendency among commentators to accentuate the pervasive harmony of atmosphere or mood which unites this landscape with the foreground figures. And it is true that such a harmony is to be found—in the value of light, in the dispersion of similar color tones, and in the repetition of forms. But these serve primarily to establish a

[8] Turner, *The Vision of Landscape*, 27–28.
[9] Clark, 113.
[10] Clark, 135–36.

6. *Mona Lisa*. Louvre, Paris.

7. *The Virgin and Child with St. Anne.* Louvre, Paris.

counterpoint. Heinrich Wölfflin has pointed out that the *Mona Lisa* landscape is "of a different order of reality from the figure and this is . . . a means of increasing the apparent solidity of the figure."[11]

In its broadest aspect, this contrapuntal relation sets the universe of nature over against that of man. The landscape discloses the world without life, the world before or after civilization, the primeval or cataclysmic scene where nature plays her recurrent drama. The foreground is given to the immensely complicated, the solid yet vital, structures of the human form and psyche—structures so recent to the earth and, in these images, so tenuously (perhaps briefly) poised in their improbable existence. In contrast, the panorama of desolation behind them spreads out its confusion of relatively shapeless and repetitious forms.

Leonardo stresses this counterpoint further in two ways. First, the human figures are not blended into the background by *sfumato*. Smoked edges occur within the contours of the figures and, with a different effect, in the landscape. But the figures are held apart, contained firmly within themselves, by color contrast and by occasional use of the artifice of the outline. Since in nature force is more basic and longer lasting than form, since natural forms continually dissolve in flux, the artist is not merely to imitate nature in his formal paintings, even though precise imitation may be his chief object in the observation that fills the *Notebooks*. The second nature of art imprisons the pressure and shape of force in the presumptive artifice of its monumental forms.

Second, the radical contrast of scale similarly underscores the counterpoint between nature and man: the human figures are seen from relatively close up and are caught in a particular moment of repose or activity; behind them, the panorama contains echoing details in a different context—note the similarity of wrinkles in the drapery and in the mountains, an effect which Leonardo seems particularly concerned with in the later work (the rocky mass beside St. Anne's head, the movement of drapery on the Virgin's right shoulder repeated in the swirl of rock behind her to the left).

The *St. Anne* goes far beyond the *Mona Lisa* in the way Leonardo has diversified the binary pattern. To the contrast in scale, for example, is added a contrast in the implied modules of temporal duration: in the background, the sweep and desolation of aeons; in the foreground, the figures varied within the complex articulation of a moment. The foreground movement begins slowly with the brooding matrixlike figure of St. Anne and comes to a climax in the more concentrated activity and the

---

[11] Heinrich Wölfflin, *Classic Art* (London: Phaidon, 1952), 32.

more intense chiaroscuro of the child and lamb. This variation in activity and light is enforced by a similar variation in the treatment of the size and gaze of each figure. By her monumental size as well as her veiled, unfocused expression, St. Anne would seem to belong to the primordial landscape no less than to the foreground incident her form encompasses. The Virgin's eyes are dreamily fixed on the child and lamb, who look upward in a more direct manner. Interrupted in their casual play, they are entirely absorbed in the present instant, but the women in different degrees seem to be looking before and after.

The most striking feature of the painting is the combined effect produced by the situation of the figures and the irrational foreshortening. We look down on the Virgin from above and up at St. Anne from below. Since they are grouped on the edge of a precipice, a disturbing tension arises between St. Anne, leaning slightly backward in relatively secure balance, and the Virgin, for whom there is a distinct possibility of pitching forward over the brink. The precipice reveals those stratified rocks which according to Leonardo were "created in the vast depths of the sea" from mud deposited on the bottom by storms and lying motionless until petrified (I, 370). Thus the figures are dubiously poised in a high and narrow zone of life curving back toward the trees at the right, a zone flanked by a lifeless or life-imperiling topography.

Leonardo had used the precipice in an earlier painting, the Paris *Madonna of the Rocks* (c. 1483–1485) (Figure 8). Wölfflin notes "how diffuse the earlier work looks beside the compressed riches of the *St. Anne*";[12] he sees in the change a paradigm of the development from the style of the Quattrocento to that of the Cinquecento. If Leonardo follows this pattern, he does it in his own way and for his own reasons, and the change reflects the growing interpenetration of intellectual and esthetic tendencies. The Paris *Madonna* reveals no contrapuntal design, no intention to mass the elements of nature over against those of humanity. The figures are absorbed into the mysterious landscape by atmosphere, by the twilight play of light and shadow, by the diagonal recession from the angel toward the distant rocks vanishing to the left of the Virgin's head. The laminated shale precipice is less threatening than theatrical. Theatrical also are the conventional gestures of the Paris painting: they combine with the placidity of pose and with the somewhat languorous expression of the Virgin and the heavy-lidded angel to suggest a feeling of timelessness or immobility which persists under the coruscations of surface detail.

---

[12] Wölfflin, 33.

8. *Madonna of the Rocks* (1483). Louvre, Paris.

When Leonardo and his assistants returned to this theme some twenty years later, in the London version of 1506–1508, the influence of his changed vision produces striking departures (Figure 9). The whole group has been moved to the front; the rock formation closes in more aggressively; the poses have been rearranged, the pyramidal volume flattened forward, the figures nearer the edge of the shelf more insecurely situated; a hash and waxen light of death suffuses the masklike faces. These faces are more sinister, and the lamialike Virgin looms larger— like the rocks behind her—over the scene, closer to the abyss; this effect is reinforced by the addition of the halo, and by its position. The precipice in the earlier picture is a solid ground of stratified shale, but the London precipice is rendered as soft crumbling rock. The changes in figure grouping are all in the direction of subtler animation connected to the more precarious placement. The child's hand is slipping over the edge; the angel is turned around so as to offer more support; St. John is foreshortened so as to face more directly toward the abyss; the Virgin's hand, her fingers no longer languidly curved, reaches tensely over the child and thrusts almost through the picture plane; what was a gesture of benediction in the earlier painting is now an anticipatory gesture of protection. Finally, we sense a sharper division between foreground and background. The openings in the rocks are larger; there is less graduated shading, less dramatic chiaroscuro in the distant rocks; the cold blue background is more evenly lighted, more visible as a unit, more flatly contrasted with the foreground rock structure. The Paris picture, with its smaller aperture, leads us back into depth because sizes and intensities are more finely graded so as to prevent us from easily separating the nearer and more distant rocks. But the London arrangement is more planar by implication: the rocks form a screen which is the rear boundary of the foreground, and we sense a horizon of desolation stretching across the rear plane of the landscape. In all these details, the London Madonna is pervaded by the feeling that informs *St. Anne* and the *Mona Lisa*.

The Paris *Madonna* is the antithesis of the *Last Supper*. There the world of nature was excluded, here the human world. There, *linear* perspective dominated the space with a simplifying "masculine" vigor; here, the sensuous atmosphere is filled by heavy irregular forms and given depth by the two methods of *atmospheric* perspective. There, an event which alters history is compressed in a single point of action; here, the slow and dreamlike tempo of the event is enhanced by its being iconographically rather than dramatically specified. Thus in these two paintings we have, so to speak, the simple opposites which Leonardo

9. *Madonna of the Rocks* (1507). National Gallery, London.

brings together in dramatic and dialectical interplay in the *Mona Lisa* and the *St. Anne*.

Judging from their expressions, the figures in the *Mona Lisa* and *St. Anne* do not seem cognizant of the anomalous world behind them or of the abyss before them. An iconographer might see an ironic comment on mortal pride and frailty in this precarious location of human forms which are otherwise solidly modeled, geometrically stabilized, and self-contained in graceful yet monumental repose. But the ultimate comment embodied in these great paintings is perhaps more detached and wide angled. They tell us that nature's process is an Empedoclean tug-of-war in which forms are perpetually being created and destroyed, contracting into the dense microcosm of form, life, and culture, expanding into the volatile cosmos of jagged or oozy remains ruled by elemental forces. They show us the systolic moments of this process in the foreground, the diastole in the background. In scale, the foreground is adjusted to the scope and dimensions of man. But seen from the greatest distance, spreading out in the enormous temporal and spatial reaches of the background, mere nature appears dominated by the catabolic process, and against this dominance of destructive force humans must pit their mental, creative, and constructive energies—must capture, harness, embody, and visualize force in form:

> *Against.*—Why nature did not ordain that one animal should not live by the death of another.
>
> *For.*—Nature being capricious and taking pleasure in creating and producing a continuous succession of lives and forms because she knows that they serve to increase her terrestrial substance, is more ready and swift in creating than time is in destroying, and therefore she has ordained that many animals shall serve as food one for the other; and as this does not satisfy her she sends forth frequently certain noisome and pestilential vapors and continual plagues upon the vast accumulations and herds of animals and especially upon human beings who increase very rapidly because other animals do not feed upon them; and if the causes are taken away the results will cease.
>
> *Against.*—Therefore this earth seeks to lose its life while desiring continual reproduction for the reason brought forth, and demonstrated to you. Effects often resemble their causes. The animals serve as a type of the life of the world.
>
> *For.*—Behold now the hope and desire of going back to one's own country or returning to primal chaos, like that of the moth to the light, of the man who with perpetual longing always looks forward with joy to each new spring and each new summer, and to the new months and the new years, deeming

that the things he longs for are slow in coming; and who does not perceive that he is longing for his own destruction. But this longing is in its quintessence the spirit of the elements, which finding itself imprisoned within the life of the human body desires continually to return to its source.

And I would have you to know that this same longing is in its quintessence inherent in nature, and that man is a type of the world. (I, 80–81)

Conspicuous Exclusion in Vermeer: An Essay in Renaissance Pastoral

IN A CORNER of one of those flowery Gothic paradises framing the Virgin and child, a tiny dragon lies helplessly on its back, pierced through the middle. This pathetic salamander is all that remains of evil in the redeemed garden. Its associations are nevertheless obvious; we recognize the symbol of sin and of the second death. But the token of danger has been so chastened in form that our recognition is disjunctive; what the dragon conventionally represents is to be found everywhere else in this fallen world, but not there.[1] It seems too good to be true: the source of all our trouble no longer abroad, no longer fearsome or monstrous, but trapped, visualized, and dismissed as a toy dragon—a dead pet. The referent separated from its symbol, evil from the dragon, is shut outside the garden wall, outside the boundaries of the image. This is no casual exclusion. It is stressed and rendered conspicuous by the incongruous portrayal of the dragon. Our normal expectations are not fulfilled by conventional imagery; being checked, they are replaced by the response "too good to be true." Part of this response consists in our remembering what is true, namely, that what the dragon signifies flourishes on our side of the garden wall. And here in our world it assumes the subtler forms of the spirit, not of the body; the forms of man, not of monsters.

---

[1] These comments paraphrase some ideas suggested many years ago by Martin Price.

No doubt all painted or literary dragons are potentially symbols of this sort. That is, any symbolic dragon is capable of reflecting back to us the deep psychic exorcism by which we have transferred the sources of evil from ourselves to external scapegoats and charged a monster with powers for which we are properly responsible. We have excluded evil from ourselves, and the artist may return the compliment by excluding evil from the monster, i.e., by portraying the dragon in a manner which will make it difficult for us to take it seriously as the source of all our woe. This is less likely to happen when the treatment of the symbol is conventional and when piety or esthetic admiration, rather than self-awareness, is all that is asked of us. But when the artist stresses the incongruity and makes it clear that his image is too good to be true, he may make us question our magical or childlike urge to exorcise and localize evil. As in Uccello's delightful St. George paintings, the ritual slaying of evil in single encounter is relegated to the radiant world of fantasy and fairy tale. The possibility of our identifying ourselves with the hero is conspicuously excluded.

Conspicuous exclusion makes us attend to what has been left out; the omitted item is not merely missing but *present-as-missing*. It is one thing for an artist merely to omit, exclude, forget, or ignore something. But it is another for him to make a point of his omission, directing our attention to it. Conspicuous exclusion is a technique especially useful in the sophisticated pastoral art which makes a practice of what in our Gothic garden may have been an exceptional or accidental effect. This art identifies *conventional* pastoral with the impulse to escape from life; it identifies a human with an artistic motive and contains them (*contains* in both senses) in its critical perspective. It does this by purging its world of darker shadows so that we take note of their absence; it presents a world which seems excessively overordered and idyllic and which, at the same time, displays incongruities—tokens of what has been purged—similar to the toy dragon in the redeemed garden.

The art of Vermeer is self-conscious pastoral of this sort; and it pivots on his varied employment of the technique of conspicuous exclusion. The following essay supports this assertion by a "close reading" of three of his works.

The Allegory of the New Testament, *or* of Faith

I begin with a copy of Vermeer's most blatant allegory and least popular painting (Figure 10) because of the problems it has posed for critics analyzing Vermeer's treatment of visual symbols; it makes the relation of

10. *Allegory of the New Testament*, or *of Faith*. Metropolitan Museum of Art, New York.

symbols to referents questionable at best, and at worst incongruous and indecorous. The thesis which I somewhat hesitantly put forward is that Vermeer anticipated his critics; therefore although their descriptions of the problematic passages are accurate as descriptions, they are wrongly converted to negative evaluations of the painting.

Descargues observes that Vermeer "has neatly introduced, without disturbing the tidiness of the room, such symbols as the apple of sin lying

444 Conspicuous Exclusion in Vermeer
on the well scrubbed tiling and the serpent of evil writhing in agony under a providential stone." This juxtaposition of "so neat a middle-class interior" with the symbols of original sin produces "a bizarre effect," heightened because the "woman in ecstasy . . . would be more at home in the sumptuous setting in which Bernini, Domenichino, and Le Brun usually represent the Faith."[2] Furthermore, the terrestrial globe serving as a footstool "obliges triumphant Faith to strike a rather uncomfortable attitude." Goldscheider is more outspoken: "This personification of Faith is a fat, female figure with large feet and hands, and a head like an Easter egg; she is tightly swathed in her silk Sunday-best dress, blue and white and very shiny. Her attitude is almost indecent. Jan Steen's *Drunken Woman* has exactly the same pose."[3] The pose is also to be found in Steen's *Lovesick Maiden*, hanging next to Vermeer's painting in the Metropolitan Museum: there the symbolic globe underfoot is replaced by a footwarmer (see also Metsu's *Music Lesson* for another of the not infrequent instances of this pose). Thus at least the bottom half of Vermeer's figure belongs to the family of profane genre motifs. The top half, on the other hand, is a standard devotional motif sometimes used to represent St. Catherine, as in the version by Raphael, or by Bernardo Cavallino, also in the Metropolitan, which is similar in pose to Vermeer's: "hand clasped over her bosom to indicate where the true and living Faith exists."[4]

The worlds of profane and sacred love, of Dutch genre and Italianate devotion, of Protestant bourgeois interiors and counter-Reformation iconography are sharply juxtaposed in a single figure, and in the painting as a whole. The Crucifixion in the background is by Jordaens, a pupil of Rubens, and may have been done after his conversion to Calvinism around 1650. There are Mannerist touches in the treatment and proportions of the Virgin, in the hard angular planes of St. John, and in the facial types, all of which combine with the lurid chiaroscuro (more impressive for its diminished range of values) to frame our heroine in a penumbra of spirituality. And she is clearly trying to make the most of it. Her left contour accentuates the diagonals of the painted figures behind her, and her upper half leans back into that context; but the effect is contrastive in subject matter as well as lighting. Her relation to the small crucifix on the table echoes that of the Virgin to Christ in the painting,

[2] Pierre Descargues, *Vermeer*, trans. James Emmons (Geneva: Skira, 1966), 69, 136.
[3] Ludwig Goldscheider, *Johannes Vermeer*, 2d ed. (London: Phaidon, 1967), 27.
[4] Hans Koningsberger, et al., *The World of Vermeer, 1632–1675* (New York: Time, 1967), 167.

though her glance is directed melodramatically upward and comes to rest on the hollow glass sphere, which appears to have been improvised for the occasion—affixed by the artist to the ceiling. And there she sees, perhaps, the same reflection of the windows and light source that we see. We shall never know, but we can at least hope that she is moved by an ardor more spiritual than ours—that the cause of her admiring gasp is the light of God rather than that of Vermeer. She seems to be trying unsuccessfully to imitate or reenact the experience of the painting. One reason for her failure is that her posture seems even more askew when compared with that of the relatively well-planted figure of Mary. The strong lighting and pronounced gesture, the highlights on pearls and coiffure, the slashing contrasts on skirt and bodice all conspire to make her, in her opulence, overdo the more stark and constrained gesture of Mary. The chief physical cause of her animated gesture is the world beneath her foot. The globe is as big as a beach ball; but it is no substitute for a homelier, more comfortable, and stable footstool or footwarmer. Its high finish and rich decoration suggest those cartographic works of art, flat and spherical, for which Dutch artisans and mapmakers were justly famous. This globe is less notable for what it might symbolize— e.g., the world subdued by faith—than for what it is: a smooth and lovely miniature, a chastened model of earth,[5] appealing to the fingers (or toes) and delighting the eye. Gleaming between the tapestry, chair, and cushion in the left foreground and the ornate screen in the right background, it helps situate the woman in a diagonal recession which tends further to unsettle her head and upper torso toward the clutter of redemptive symbols, while her feet and the globe appropriately describe a more mundane triangle with the symbols of evil and sin.

In all these respects, visual and iconographic, there is an element of *conspicuous allusion* which makes the clash and incongruity of different contexts hard to ignore.[6] I find it difficult, therefore, to see how the devotional "intent" of the picture can be taken at face value. It seems rather to be the subject of parody. Koningsberger remarks that "aside from telling its allegory about the triumph of the faith and of good over evil, the work has little to say, at least for a Vermeer" (150). But what the

[5] Is the globe terrestrial or celestial? Cesare Ripa's instructions specify the earth, but it resembles the globe in Vermeer's *Geographer* which, despite the painting's title, critics generally assume to be celestial. (Ripa's influential *Iconologia*, published in Italy in 1603, was translated into French in 1636 and into Dutch by Dirck Pers in 1644. The texts relevant to this painting appear on pages 147–48 of Pers's translation.)

[6] On conspicuous allusion, see my essay "The Discarding of Malbecco: Conspicuous Allusion and Cultural Exhaustion in *The Faerie Queene* III.ix–x," *Studies in Philology* 66 (1969): 135–54.

painting has to say is that it is not telling its allegory, or not telling it straight. The triumph is, visually, a Pyrrhic victory, and it is not clear how long the woman's right foot will be able to keep the earthly beach ball from rolling off. This effect of instability is visual rather than actually physical: she is not losing her balance; we know this because her left arm is relaxed rather than tense. But the disposition of limbs, skirt, and globe set in the strong recessive thrust from chair to screen conveys the sense that she cannot keep her pose very long. These visual suggestions challenge or undercut the presumptive subject of the painting—the permanence and stability of faith's triumph over the temptations of the world. Faith is "the substance [the support] of things to be hoped for, the evidence of things not seen." But in the painting what is seen preempts our attention and at the same time raises questions about the permanence of Vermeer's leaning Faith.

These questions are not in themselves at the level of religious allegory. They are directed against the religious subject matter not qua religion but qua subject matter. Why should painting subordinate itself to religion, the art of the visible to the mysteries of the invisible? Why shouldn't it purify itself of all but the joy of making and seeing? Why shouldn't the painter withdraw from the demands of actuality and reality, from the mundane world and the spiritual warfare—withdraw into the sunlit pastoral cube protectively framed by walls, floors, windows, tapestries, and picture frames? Why not an eternal return to the sheltered seclusion of the kitchen, the virginals, the sunlit parlor, domestic mornings by windows that magically transform daylight into a garden radiance, excluding dirt, noise, and the contingencies of the busy street? Why not Huizinga's Vermeer?

> All the figures seem to have been transplanted from ordinary existence into a clear and harmonious setting where words have no sound and thoughts no form. Their actions are steeped in mystery, as those figures we see in a dream. The word realism seems completely out of place here. Everything is of unrivalled poetic intensity. If we look carefully, we see that Vermeer's figures are not so much Dutchwomen from the sixteenth century as figures from an elegiacal world, peaceful and calm. Nor do they wear the costume of a particular period; they are dressed like visions, symphonies in blue, green and yellow. . . . It may be rather bold . . . to say that Vermeer fails precisely when he depicts holy scenes. . . . For it is not with the Gospel story itself that he is primarily concerned; rather does he treat the subject as a brilliant exercise in colour. (J. H. Huizinga, *Dutch Civilization in the Seventeenth Century and Other Essays*, trans. Arnold J. Pomerans [New York: Harper & Row, 1969], 85)

This last statement, in the case of the *Allegory of Faith*, would wish away the embarrassment of richly symbolic objects which has offended some critics. For example: "The symbolic allusions . . . are perhaps a little too explicit";[7] Vermeer "is somewhat at a loss with the subject, which looks contrived."[8] Once again, the critics have observed accurately but have prematurely converted their observations to evaluations. The painting is conspicuously contrived, the allusions resoundingly explicit, and whatever the real Vermeer may have had in mind, the artist paralogically created by this painting was not at a loss. The subject, as we know, is in all respects but one (the Jordaens painting) copied from the description of Faith in Ripa's *Iconologia*. Yet it is also "a brilliant exercise in colour," light, and representational virtuosity, though not a gratuitous exercise. If Vermeer executes the pastoral withdrawal from life to art, from subject matter to pure form, he shows us at the same time what he is withdrawing from. Serious commitment to allegory may be conspicuously excluded partly because the allegory itself is conspicuously included.

Because of the manner in which allegory is included, invisible realities are at once shadowed and overshadowed by their visible symbols. The symbolic blue, the globe, the chalice, the Bible, and the crucifix divert us on two levels of art: as beautifully crafted objects in the imaginary room and as beautifully painted images on the canvas; the former may reflexively symbolize the latter with no less immediacy than they objectively symbolize the triumph of faith. The apple is finely modeled and its hues enhance the bright red of the snake's blood, which stands out by its contrast to the cooler grays, greens, and blues that surround it. These splendid objects are gathered into the varied patterns and textures of the richly adorned interior, and there they contribute more to a display of the triumphs of bourgeois materialism than to the allegory of spiritual warfare.[9] If the world, the flesh, and the devil have been ritually exorcised by the allegory and esthetically reduced to their innocuous lovely symbols—the globe, the apple, and the dead or dying snake—they may still linger on in a modest, domestic, venial way in the complacency and conspicuous consumption of the interior. This is by no means

[7] Jean Leymarie, *Dutch Painting*, trans. Stuart Gilbert (Geneva: Skira, 1956), 188.

[8] Jakob Rosenberg, Seymour Slive, and E. H. Ter Kuile, *Dutch Art and Architecture: 1600–1800* (Baltimore: Penguin Books, 1966), 123.

[9] "We can hardly share the taste for allegory which Holland pursued to such incongruous extremes—where else did a man arrange to be painted with his betrothed as the Archangel Gabriel and the Virgin Annunciate?" (Lawrence Gowing, *Vermeer* [New York: Beechhurst Press, 1953], 50).

a new allegory, but it is a qualification of motive which affects our response to the allegory of faith. It suggests something about the people who commission such paintings as the Jordaens to adorn interiors such as this. The Crucifixion, dimly lit, relieves the blankness of wall and signifies a pious investment in culture. Scholars who dislike this painting assume it must have been commissioned. But it is just as easy to assume that it is a painting about certain kinds of commissioned paintings. In a vague and distant manner, a whole set of anecdotal, allegorical, and narrative values hovers about Vermeer's painting. But none of them is firmly developed, articulated, or nailed down. They merely linger, so to speak, around the frame as unactualized possibilities, and all of them are to some degree present-as-excluded.

The painting is further complicated by the interplay between the realistic depiction of objects and the theatrical overstatement of theme. P. T. A. Swillens criticizes the painting because the lady's gesture is "little elegant, her glance theatrical, her posture clumsy," and because the dais beneath her is covered by a carpet "which taken by itself is beautiful, but which despite all this rather reminds one of the painter's atelier than of an abstract scene." [10] Denatured of their critical intent, these remarks contain genuine insights. For among the possible narratives suggested by the painting is one which tells us that the artist has dragged every religious prop he owns out of the storeroom, set them carefully in place, helped the burgher's daughter arrange herself on her stage, and done his best to make her reenact the mystery framed in the painting behind her. The curtain is then drawn aside to reveal a comic *compositio loci*, a *tableau vivant* which simultaneously depicts the typical bourgeois interior and the typical religious allegory. Perhaps the most peculiar props are the crystal sphere and the serpent. The sphere has been attached to the ceiling by a length of symbolically blue ribbon. This motif echoes, and possibly alludes to, the symbolic egg which, for example, hangs above the Virgin in Piero della Francesca's Brera Altarpiece. No doubt it may, like the egg, be a symbol of eternity or resurrection ("things to be hoped for"), since the heroine eyes it longingly. But as noted above, the light it reflects comes more directly from the windows than from heaven and the sphere seems primarily there as a witness to the painter's skill.

That her pose is clumsy; that the sphere seems, like all the other symbols, positioned for this particular occasion; that the objects are realisti-

---

[10] *Johannes Vermeer, Painter of Delft, 1632–1675*, trans. C. M. Breuning-Williamson (New York: Studio Publications, 1950), 98.

cally imaged—these impressions oddly qualify our response to the serpent who has just been brained by what Descargues calls "a providential stone" and others call a "cornerstone."[11] The oddness comes out in the verb tense I used: "has just been brained." For whether newly dead or near dead and writhing, the snake's aspect implies a sequence of prior moments—another potential anecdote. Among all those inert and credible objects this is the one prop which can't be conceived as having been kept in the painter's storeroom and sited for this occasion (unless it is a toy snake). The appearance and demise of the serpent pose no problem at the mediated allegorical level, but at the more immediate and realistic level—that of the bourgeois interior—we wonder how it got there and who dropped a brick on it. Its head gleams and from open jaws its bright translucent blood trickles across the marbled floor, which will have to be scrubbed again. In the painter's atelier decked out as a burgher's parlor, the snake must be construed as an uninvited visitor from the outside world (the painter's or burgher's garden?). Though it looks sinister enough to play its part as the symbol of primal evil, its more immediate threat is mundane and local: snakebite at worst, more likely the impact on squeamish sensibilities of "a horrible thing that doesn't belong in here." A beautifully ugly boundary breacher, a little wild life intruding into the domestic fortress, the snake offends against the sense of order and neatness and arouses perhaps a touch of puritan horror.

Having just given the anecdotal impulse its head, I want to neutralize—at least in part—what must appear as an overscrupulous reading. As I observed earlier, the painting abounds in possible but unactualized episodes. We view the painting within an ambient manifold of stories, meanings, and action sequences wreathed in soft focus, like a frame around the image. Some of these possibilities clash and qualify each other, but to none can we give decided preference. None is sufficiently worked out; not enough clues are given; we are not, therefore, in a position to select one or two of them and say, "These are present, the others absent." On the other hand, we violate the painting if we screen them out entirely and consider them nonexistent;[12] they are rather present-as-undeveloped or present-as-excluded. In the same manner, the sense of

---

[11] Ripa's instructions call for "a book which lies on a firm Cornerstone, i.e. Christ. . . . Under the cornerstone lies a crushed Snake, and Death with his arrows broken" (quoted in Goldscheider, *Johannes Vermeer*, 134). Vermeer's cornerstone is not under the book, and it seems less an emblem of Christ than a mere dropped brick.

[12] R. H. Wilenski observes that "as social descriptions the pictures in many cases are not only eccentric but definitely 'bizarre'" but converts this insight into a criticism of the *Allegory*, which he finds obscure. Therefore he screens out narrative possibilities: "Such

life's action, its richness, its uncertainties and complexities is conspicuously excluded. The strange stillness of the Vermeer world vibrates with these excluded presences and possibilities even here, where the world is tuned in a comic key. As is the case with the heroine's clumsy pose and instability, this suggests a moment of suspended animation. However frozen and stilled, the pose belongs to an unactualized sequence of prior and subsequent poses, of possible motions and changes of position which are also present-as-excluded. This is why the heroine and the painting as a whole strike the observer as visually uncomfortable, and to this effect we owe much of our refusal or inability to take the scene seriously as the spiritual allegory it comically claims to be. Those conspicuously irrelevant details, which in a genuine allegory would be played down, smoothed out, and shown as merely conventional, are here pushed in our faces in a way which dispels the inattention evoked by conventional appearances.[13]

Girl Interrupted at Her Music

Gowing's general thesis seems to be beyond improvement and must inevitably provide the starting point of any further reading of a painting such as *Girl Interrupted at Her Music* (Figure 11).[14] The paradox inherent in great pastoral is based on the conflict between an interest in art and an interest in life. It also depends on the way the individual work displays both the image of an art that mimetically opens and subordinates itself to life and the image of a more virginal, self-enclosed art that domesticates life to pure form and design, to an esthetic paradise of color, light, music, geometry, to the flowers of rhetoric. Gowing analyzes the paradox dynamically by treating shifts in the relations between the polar terms in the context of the artist's development: those paintings that admit life more directly are earlier, the others later. In view of the paucity of information about Vermeer—only one painting is dated[15]—it is gratuitous to

---

considerations, which would be appropriate in the case of descriptive works by Jan Steen or Van Ostade, are obviously quite beside the point in front of such pictures by Vermeer" (*Dutch Painting*, 2d ed., rev. [London: Faber & Faber, 1955], 186).

[13] Here I disagree with Gowing, who dismisses the painting as "a grandiose religious *Allegory*, arranged on the most conventional lines and as conventionally represented" (*Vermeer*, 57).

[14] This painting is small (14.5 × 16.5") and its size is obviously important to its effect.

[15] The attribution of this painting, *The Procuress*, to Vermeer has been challenged by Swillens.

11. *Girl Interrupted at Her Music.* The Frick Collection, New York.

convert what is fundamentally an analytical range or continuum into a chronology. But outside the context of art history, that is a relatively minor point; Gowing's subtlety and persuasiveness in showing how the "later" or more withdrawn works indirectly admit the life they seem to exclude deserve our gratitude. He notes the increasing prevalence of the *gallant* genre among Vermeer's contemporaries, and the inclusion of the courting motif in Vermeer's blatant *Couple with a Wine Glass* at Brunswick in comparison with the more tempered treatment in *Interrupted Music* at the Frick:

> Over the seated lady whose eyes meet ours in the conversation-pieces there bends a man, an assiduous visitor, in the picture at Brunswick odiously attentive, breaking in upon the quiet life of the room. . . . We are informed only obliquely, though none the less certainly, of the errand which brings this gentleman to the *Girl Interrupted at Music.* We learn it through the medium of the picture, Cupid as a messenger, which hangs behind him on the wall. The possessive hand no longer finds its way to the girl's breast

[as in *The Procuress*], no money is offered, but the motif of interruption in these pictures remains the civilized descendant of that which appeared in *The Procuress*. . . . Yet the emotional content is far from weakening. It seems that the essence of Vermeer's subject extends beyond its exterior happenings. (*Vermeer*, 49)

Growing finds the symbolism of the painting of Cupid direct, its erotic emphasis "no subtler than that which similar pictures serve in the works of Jan Steen" (51). But the subtlety resides in other elements.

The cursory treatment which Gowing has observed in the figures of Vermeer's *Couple* is more marked in the *Interrupted Music:* "There is something ill at ease in the artist's handling of these figures. . . . where the human detail emerges the style becomes evasively general, even primitive" (116). In the painting at the Frick, this affects not merely hands and faces but the whole right side of the painting, i.e., the main subject of interest; Eros, the man, and the girl are all summarily painted in relatively soft focus and low intensity in the gray area of the value scale. Gestures are toned down, his attention is ostensibly displaced from her to what is probably—but not necessarily—a sheet of music (the shading at the bottom suggests staves), and hers is displaced from the sheet to us. The influence of Cupid, dim and barely visible on the back wall, seems almost dissipated by the time it reaches the picture plane.

The erotic motif remains diffused in the composition: detail is more sharply articulated on the left, where objects catch the light. From foreground chair to window to birdcage to painting, the perspective play of varied rectangles creates a semihexagonal space which then narrows and flattens toward the right, where the figures are. This joins with other aspects to enforce a convergence of the man's plane with the girl's: the similar tone and intensity of her skirt and his cape, the more complex and animated modeling of the cape, and the flattening of her left shoulder and sleeve produced by the summary treatment of texture and volume. The effect is one of crowding and encompassment. He has perhaps just left the chair in the background and moved forward to join her in reading. His forward motion can be most clearly felt in the relation of his foreshortened right hand to her left shoulder (the hand seems irrationally close to the picture plane) and in the steadying function of his left hand, which allows him to lean over the page. She is thus formally stabilized and framed in place by the concave forward swirl of the cape, the left sleeve of which threatens to swallow her chair. But unlike the figures in the *Couple*, neither of these figures seems to be paying attention to their all-but-physical contact.

The move toward encompassment in *Interrupted Music* is opposed in three ways: first, the girl's position on the chair is uncomfortable and not clearly depicted, but Vermeer's treatment of her back and knee makes her appear, to some extent, to be shifted to the left of the chair, closer to us. Second, and most obvious, like the girl in the *Couple* she makes eye contact with whoever stands on the other side of the picture plane, but her expression is much more ambiguous. Gowing's response to the girl posing as Clio would seem applicable here: "She both invites the painter's attention and as tenderly wards it off" (54). She seems neither displeased nor overjoyed by whatever is happening at her right (the man) or her left (us). Third, her shawl seems too large for her head, especially when contrasted with her small and delicate features. Its size, modeling, and defined contour bring it forward from the cape in which it is framed. The shawl swathes and encompasses her, a frame within a frame, protecting her not only from dust but also from him. If their hands share the music, their divergences of attitude and attention are emphasized by the barrier of the shawl.

The use of the shawl exemplifies a repeated theme in Vermeer's work: frames and their functions. A frame is a boundary, border, or enclosure separating what it contains from what is around it. Its significance may vary from disjunction to conjunction: it may be a barrier, a transition, or a connecting bond, but the disjunctive function must come first. Two things have to be separated before they can interact. Boundaries cannot be crossed or violated until they exist. The significance of such trespassing presupposes the existence of the frame. The frame of a painting considered as a two-dimensional design is simply its literal border. But the frame of a three-dimensional image includes the picture plane and the "window glass" through which we look. In the Vermeer world windows, pictures, doors, mirrors, maps, curtains, and even tables are frames or serve framing functions. They articulate relations of *within* and *beyond*. The window frame delimits the measured access to and from the outside world; the window as a whole is part of the frame enclosing the room. Closed, it shuts out noise and dust and filters light. Partly open, it lets in air and stronger light along with the possibility of noise and dust. Seen from the outside, as in *Street in Delft* (see Figure 15) windows offer no access; they are blind panels, backed by dark interiors protected from our view. In only one painting, the *Girl Reading a Letter*, in Dresden, is the casement wide open. Otherwise windows are closed or only partly open. The degree to which this appears to be significant or symbolic or to serve merely compositional and illuminative ends varies from painting to painting. The window as a transparent membrane, a medium, visually incarnates Vermeer's pastoral paradox, at once admitting and excluding the life outside. The picture plane and frame, the fourth wall as window, are no exception, and the paradox is heightened in intensity when there is eye contact with the observer.

In the *Interrupted Music* the birdcage to the right of the window metaphorically extends the motif of the frame as an enclosure. Even if, as some scholars maintain, it was a later addition, its conventional symbolism is in agreement with the rest of the painting. Delicately barred and dark within, its form and color echo those of the chairs. Are the chairs, the music, and the room altered in meaning if seen under the aspect of the songbird's cage? Has the meaning of the caged bird, as of the framed Eros, "escaped" from its enclosure to permeate the scene? Have they, like the man, moved forward? Is she moving forward toward us? Are they out of bounds? All the suggestions are clearly there, and are as clearly unresolved. They are questions asked and left unanswered. The focus is soft; the light falls placidly with a hint of evening, gathers reassuringly on the stoppered Delft jug, touches the (untasted?) wine, strengthens the contour of the shawl, and picks out the ubiquitous finials whose lionheads guard the maiden—or do they threaten her? Whatever their attitude means, they are domesticated and neutralized as *objets d'art*; unlike the *Allegory of Faith* with its serpent, this painting conspicuously excludes animals as such—conspicuously because their crafted symbols are present in the room.

Officer and Laughing Girl

Also in the Frick, this painting (Figure 12) is at once more straightforward in its anecdotal content and more subdued. I find it hard to agree with Gowing that it is "marked by an unhappy jocularity" (*Vermeer*, 89) and that the painter "is never quite at ease" with drinking scenes of this sort (104). But in the following comment Gowing assembles the elements that, for me, make the image compelling:

> The incident . . . is drawn from the common stock; in the early fifties it was a typical subject of De Hooch. It is a legacy of the wars, the entertainment of foraging soldiery in a house that is more or less of a tavern, a scene in which the extent of the hospitality that will be exacted of the agreeable hostess is rarely open to doubt. In Vermeer's picture the subject is . . . rendered with the perfect mildness of his method; its intention might well escape us if we had not his prototypes. Its essence remains. This subject with its delicate hint of erotic *force majeur* is a translation into the domestic idiom of the formal theme of venal love. (*Vermeer*, 48)

12. *Officer and Laughing Girl*. The Frick Collection, New York.

I would prefer to say that this theme and Vermeer's prototypes are present mainly by contrastive allusion; that is, they are distanced, virtually—but not quite—excluded by Vermeer's concentration of light upon the girl and by her expression. She looks not at us but at the officer. She leans slightly toward him, but in a measured rather than relaxed manner. Her left hand rests on the table in a quietly eloquent gesture, her arms and the glass presenting, as it were, an instinctive barrier; the hand is half relaxed, half opened toward him in an equally instinctive attitude which reflects her expression; tightly swathed in her gleaming protective linen, she sits absorbed. Her face and listening smile reflect both the light streaming in through the half-open window and the worldly attention with which the officer temporarily brightens her.

At the same time, the officer temporarily darkens the room. He is too large for it, and in his huge, faintly sinister hat he looks even larger, cutting off part of the window and the map. He serves as a *repoussoir* figure—red coat darkly shaded by the black hat and sash—making the room at once brighter and deeper (because the girl is smaller) by contrast. Whatever reason one gives for the "strong perspective divergence"—whether photographic distortion or the proximity of the painter to his subject—the effect is not the one discerned by Swillens (76), i.e., to give the spectator the illusion that he is in the room itself. The effect is rather to assimilate the officer more closely to our space and remove the girl in her radiant cubicle further from us: perhaps the room is not deeper for his presence but simply smaller and further away. With his body shifted toward us and slightly flattened against the picture plane, his pose is conventionally rakish but a little cramped. In all these respects he appears as an interloper, a visitor from the outside world.

The map is another token of the outside world. "The figure of the laughing girl, dressed in yellow and blue, is seated before a white wall beneath a bright coloured map of Holland—the country, and the whole world is open to her."[16] Gowing, alert for the erotic motif, wonders whether "the broad lines of the map . . . do not add something to our impression of the soldier's bold plan of campaign" (51). This is too direct, but the ships on the map do suggest a general and diffuse connection. Some are small, others large; some seem grouped in convoys of flotillas, others possibly in combat. The map is the locus of activity in the otherwise still scene. Politics, warfare, trade—the life of risk and action, the outer world containing the room that contains the map—are vaguely adumbrated in delicate, harmless miniatures which adorn the wall. Love is only one of the passions that animate the actual world—but this world hardly seems "open to her." The map frames and chastens it, admitting only the artistic symbols, conspicuously excluding the reality.

The map at once symbolizes and distances the world from which the officer came and to which he belongs. As in the *Interrupted Music*, the left side of the painting is semihexagonal in composition, and each of the three planes admits some aspect of the outer world: the seated soldier, the half-open window, and the map. In that order, they diminish both in size and in the immediacy of intrusion. Each plane is a frame within which there is controlled access or reference to the world beyond; all are visually linked or breached by the overlapping of hat, window, and map and by the interplay of thematic suggestions. The intrusive elements

---

[16] Goldscheider, *Johannes Vermeer*, 19.

communicate across the frames within which they are carefully enclosed, offer the possibility of penetrating into the purified domestic idyll and making "one little roome an everywhere." The half-open planes surround the girl, but ultimately they remain in place, withholding their potential *force majeur* and respecting the luminous space in which she is sealed.

If Vermeer has echoed the genre convention of carousing, card-playing, or flirting soldiers, and if he has borrowed a compositional motif—most probably from De Hooch—these are not merely casual sources but conventions and motifs to which the painting conspicuously alludes. Reminded of them, we think perhaps of the possibility of venal or casual love, and this possibility hovers among the others that vaguely threaten or qualify the scene before us. Not simply present, not simply excluded, but present-*as*-excluded, it contributes to the precariousness that edges the pastoral stillness and thus adds a delicate poignancy to her expression. Yet her pastoral magic prevails. Bundled in clean linen, gathering the warmth and brilliance of sunlight about her, she disarms the threat. For Vermeer has departed from most of his prototypes in leaving his shadowy officer's motives and actions in doubt and in making the girl not merely one of the ingredients of a pleasant evening but the interpretive center of the scene. We read his intentions only in her visible response—the receptive smile and half-open hand, gestures instinctively subdued yet warming to an attentiveness, sympathy, or delight much more personal than physical. So mirrored, the officer's motives are, at least for the suspended moment of this painting, purified of their conventional associations.

To say this, however, is to say something different from the form-over-content assertion characteristic of those who want to claim Vermeer as a property of the modern cubist age, e.g.: his men "are much less clearly defined than the women; in fact they are not much more than background figures placed there because the subject matter requires them. Vermeer never sought to explore the depths of human nature and he shows very little interest in the expressions of the men."[17] Gowing's basic insight, poised against this formalist interpretation, seems much more adequate to what we see: "The remarkable order which he extracts from the world" is at the same time an "elaborate evasion of its human claims," and these together "suggest the imminent possibility of opposite qualities, a fearsome anarchy" (60). This is rhetorically overstated, and

---

[17] A. B. de Vries, *Vermeer* (New York: B. T. Batsford, 1967), 14. See also Leymarie, *Dutch Painting*, 187.

Gowing would not apply it to the *Officer and Girl* except as criticism, yet I think the basic insight is relevant to that painting. It helps us see that Vermeer shows *considerable* interest in concealing or blurring the officer's expression and defining him less clearly than the girl. To carry the insight further, if human claims are *elaborately* evaded, this can only be the result of their being in some manner carefully admitted so that the evasion may be visualized. If Vermeer is, like so many of his admirers, tempted to escape into art, determined "to transform the setting of his daily life into a dream palace of light and color,"[18] this temptation is itself one of his themes and not merely one of his weaknesses.

Conclusions: Vermeer and Renaissance Consciousness

My approach to this interpretation of Vermeer was guided by some working hypotheses which I would now like to make explicit. They derive from a general model of "Renaissance consciousness"—more accurately, postmedieval or Renaissance-to-modern consciousness—some versions and aspects of which I have discussed elsewhere.[19] These hypotheses center on the notion of heterocosmic thought and the second world. The heterocosmic attitude posits the commonsense world as only one among a number of possible worlds and assumes that the proper way for the mind to explore reality is to leave the *given* world of perception, nature, and common experience temporarily behind and to generate an alternative universe which will provide the field of play, thought, or experiment. Heterocosmic thinking is abstractive and disjunctive: it withdraws from the given world to alternate frames of reference which are characterized more by difference or otherness than by similarity—hence the term "heterocosm." This withdrawal or abstraction is framed within a governing awareness that actuality is being left behind, that its claims persist and must be settled, acknowledged, or evaded. Such an awareness imposes the pressure to return on every act of withdrawal; it imposes on every visionary of other worlds the need to convert the heterocosmic vision to a program of action in this world.

It is not enough for the heterocosmic thinker to proclaim, with Milton's Satan, that the mind is its own place; nor is it enough to proclaim it in

---

[18] Descargues, *Vermeer*, 108; cf. Koningsberger, *The World of Vermeer*, 157.

[19] See the following essays, all in this volume: "The Renaissance Imagination: Second World and Green World," 3–40; "The Ecology of the Mind: The Concept of Period Imagination—An Outline Sketch," 41–62; "Pico and Neoplatonist Idealism: Philosophy as Escape," 189–228; and "L. B. Alberti on Painting: Art and Actuality in Humanist Perspective," 373–408.

Satan's tone of dogmatic (because desperate) certainty. The heterocosmic mind has first to create a matrix for its second world by marking off an imaginary time and space, and it has to begin by sweeping the matrix clean of actuality. But the mind has then to remain tentative and provisional in its commitment to imaginary worlds if it is to avoid being trapped or paralyzed within the pool of Narcissus. The imaginary world must be made secure for the systole of withdrawal but not secure enough to discourage or prohibit the diastole of return. This measured commitment is dramatized in a number of ways: first, the imaginary world is both disjunctive and hypothetical. It is *not* real life but art or artifice; *not* actuality but fiction, hypothesis, or make-believe; not merely an imitation of the world God has made and placed us in but a new and different world created by the mind. Both its autonomy and its limits are indicated by some original framing gesture intended to show that the second world is, at least initially, contrary to established fact; only after it has been framed as counterfactual is it allowed to hold the mirror up to nature and readmit into its cleared space the elements of actuality. Second, the imaginary world is tonally presented in an attitude of serious playing; *serio ludere* means playing seriously with full knowledge; however seriously you play, you are only playing. It is "only a game," but a game which (like all games) is to be played or taken with dead seriousness while it is going on. Carefully framed within this attitude, the mind may abandon itself with intensity to the pleasure or seriousness of its second world. Third, the preceding features entail a significant tendency toward self-reference, or reflexive awareness. By this I mean both conspicuous artifice, through which any work points to itself *as* a work and, closely related to this, increased attention to and exhibition of the mastery of craft and technique, of medium and methodology. Through such reflexive display the second world may be offered simultaneously as *only* a work of art and as *triumphantly* a work of art. Artist and observer may give themselves to the second world without forgetting that it is second, not first. The temptation to make it absolutely autonomous, a perfect and eternal retreat, produces what has been called the green world of pastoral escapism (as well as the golden world of heroic escapism and the black world of satiric escapism).

For the artist, the crucial aspect of this equilibrated attitude is likely to be found in his gratuitous or recreative delight in the processes of art: in technique, virtuosity, and the creative experience; in pigment, light, color, form, and design; in other painters and paintings; in the very smell and feel of his craft. The immense deepening of technical knowledge from the time of Giotto on, the climate of experiment, the growing attention to the interrelations between theory and practice, the consequently quickening rate of stylistic change and innovation—these all testify less to the mimetic than to the recreative impulse. For many painters, the imitation of nature would almost seem to provide a convenient excuse to explore and exhibit the techniques of painting. The recreative interest develops into a "science." It generates its own literature, traditions, and academies. With the spread of Mannerism, it even becomes a legitimate subject of painting.[20]

Vermeer is a direct inheritor, and a sometimes ironic and witty beneficiary, of all these developments. Both the paradoxes of framing and the technique of conspicuous allusion imply as their precondition the heterocosmic relation between the world within and the world beyond the picture. The relation need not be rendered explicit; it may remain a latent possibility. But in Vermeer's hands it becomes manifest and, furthermore, becomes a central theme. His portrayal of the ambivalent relations between art and life, the second and first worlds, is additionally complicated by a salient recreative interest which makes the work of art vibrate between the status of a second world and that of a green world. That is, the work lures the observer into it by offering him pure pleasure, relief from life's problems, and a chance to give himself up to the magic of color, light, and "abstract" patterns. It offers him a recreative escape parallel to that cherished by the artist. The purely formal idyllism is doubled by the idyllic choice and treatment of subject matter. Thus our first response to a Vermeer is most likely to be a response to the small size of the painting, the radiance of the light, the purity of the color, and the quiet cloistered reticence of the represented world. But once the observer is pastorally engaged, he comes up against unexpected details: incongruities, allusions, motes of actuality, and the shades of life's perplexes and risks are present-*as*-excluded.

Finally, to return to the allegory with which I began, Vermeer's ironic use of symbolism suggests still another connection between heterocosmic thought and conspicuous exclusion. I have distinguished elsewhere between two kinds of symbolic reference, based on the degree to which any symbol claims our attention for its own sake rather than for the sake of its referent.[21] An *iconic* symbol moves the observer beyond itself with relatively greater speed because it is simpler and less articulated— perhaps more stylized—as an immediate form; it relies on hieratic conventions that tell us to look beyond it toward what it represents. An

---

[20] See John Shearman, *Mannerism* (Baltimore: Penguin Books, 1967), 44ff.
[21] See "Theater, Drama, and the Second World," in this volume, 111–29.

imagistic symbol encourages us by its complexity and formal interest to look within rather than beyond it for clues to its meaning and reference; it asks us to explore its immediate visual or literary configuration not merely as an index of its transcendent referent but as a new interpretation of it. Imagistic symbols create tension between the *within* and the *beyond*, direct us toward a disparity between symbol and referent which can be resolved only by paying closer attention to the former. This is a familiar and peculiar effect of much postmedieval art, encouraged by the fusion of the heterocosmic attitude with the recreative delight in technique.

In the case of the *Allegory of Faith*, the imagistic play element does not gracefully yield primacy to allegorical reference. Yet the symbols are conspicuous as symbols. Vermeer includes iconographic elements but makes it hard for us to view them iconographically. The visible symbols bumptiously interfere with our conventional impulse to look through them toward their invisible referents. As the painter's displayed virtuosity proclaims its affinity for the clarified forms and colors of the visible world, so his treatment of the subject proclaims a commitment to the bourgeois actualities of his secular environment. Art affirms its self-sufficiency by remaining within the visible confines of *the image*—its proper home—and by rendering modest or homely subjects whose notability resides less in themselves than in the virtuosity with which they are represented. But this affirmation is given its emphasis by the underlying heterocosmic structure of the imagistic symbol: Vermeer accentuates his allegiance to this world of painting (and Delft) by reminding us of other worlds whose claims on art are rejected—not only the world of the next life but also that of the Italianate baroque, considered as a genre of painting, a form of religion, and a way of life.

Some Vanity of His Art: Conspicuous Exclusion and Pastoral in Vermeer

"OF ALL THE painters whose work we value highly, Vermeer is perhaps the hardest to come to grips with. He thwarts our curiosity about his personality, his struggles with his work and with his life." So John Walsh begins his valuable essay in mildly plaintive tones, expressing a bafflement common in the Vermeer literature. It is not that the evidence is insufficient, but that it is *almost* sufficient; not that Vermeer seems carelessly to have neglected the image he left posterity but that he seems cunningly to have abridged it. Walsh astutely picks out the one detail that best embodies the painter's aggressive coyness: "When Vermeer paints an artist at work, it is an artist, not Vermeer himself. . . . His back is turned to us." Strange, then, that in his next phrase Walsh articulates a lack of concern which might well have disappointed the artist: "It is not the man's character or personality that matters to Vermeer, but his activity as an artist."[1] Walsh refuses to be teased; what we do not see—rather, what we see we are not being shown—should not matter. And this refusal epitomizes too much Vermeer commentary. But what

---

[1] John Walsh, Jr., "Vermeer," *The Metropolitan Musem of Art Bulletin* 31 (Summer 1973), no pagination. Though this brief set of comments comes to no startling conclusions, it is a convenient and intelligent summary of opinion current at the time it was written. Future quotations from this issue will be attributed in my text to Walsh without further elaboration.

we see we are not being shown matters a great deal. The life excluded so archly, so conspicuously, vibrates in every glowing inch of paint, transforms the art to a protective screen tempting us to penetrate to the secret beyond it. Yet there is no secret *beyond* it, only the blank back of panel or canvas. The secrets are all *within* the painting.

In the preceding chapter I described conspicuous exclusion as a device by which a work of art makes us attend to something it led us to expect but does not let us find. The absence of the omitted item is indicated in the work; the item is not merely missing, but *present-as-missing*.[2] This effect is nicely illustrated by Walsh's remarks on the Dresden *Woman Reading a Letter*. Vermeer emphasized "the privacy and self-absorption of the act. Small in relation to the setting, the girl is shown in pure profile, removing much possibility of expression—only the mouth might reveal something, and the mouth is carefully hidden in the image reflected in the window." This reticence, characteristic of so many paintings, is rendered conspicuous by another consideration. In his earliest known painting, *Christ in the House of Martha and Mary*, Vermeer had accentuated the very aspects of human interaction which his subsequent work was to present evasively or indirectly:[3]

> Our interest is directed entirely to the people, and like a skilled director Vermeer gives his actors expressive poses: Martha, who thinks she is doing her duty to Christ by bustling about, pauses for a moment at the table; Mary, who ignores the housework in order to listen, sits in rapt attention; and Christ, explaining that "Mary has chosen the better part," links the two women with his gaze and broad gesture. (Walsh, "Vermeer")

It is as if he had prepared us in advance by showing us how much he could directly express if he wanted, whetting our expectation for what would henceforth be withheld.

My interpretations in the preceding chapter were intended to support the thesis that in Vermeer's art conspicuous exclusion is the sum product of two contrary pressures: the pressure to escape to the purified domain of light and color, to give oneself up to the pleasures of one's art, and the

---

[2] "Conspicuous Exclusion in Vermeer," 441–61 in this volume. Like the painter's art in *Artist's Studio*, the lacework we do not see in *The Lacemaker* and the music we do not hear in *The Concert* are examples of conspicuous exclusion.

[3] This statement does not apply to *The Procuress* or to the Brunswick drinking scene. A handful of paintings with strained facial expressions are difficult to assess because of the problems posed by repainting as well as by our poor knowledge of physiognomic or pathognomic conventions.

counterpressure to take note of what has been left behind in the back-wash of escape. On the one hand, the art expresses the desire to focus all attention on the still center of the brilliant pastoral cube of the depicted interior; on the other hand, it expresses the desire to breach that closed world, open it up to a life which may render it less perfect but more significant. On the one hand there is the splendor, simplicity, and sus-pended animation of sheer visibility; on the other, the unresolved com-plexities of ongoing life, complexities which can never be fully captured and domesticated within the limited confines of the visual image.

Vermeer is oddly like Rembrandt—oddly, because no two *oeuvres* could differ more in scope, tone, and sensibility. Yet both painters dis-play the same fundamental concern and a common theme. This theme may best be approached from a literary perspective because it involves an element of reflexivity more easily manifested in verbal than in pictorial art. It may be figured, for example, in the amused ambivalence of Andrew Marvell, partly embracing and partly exorcising the ardor of the garden visitor whose mind withdraws into its happiness from pleasure less. It is more explicitly figured in Shakespeare's enisled magician whose words articulate the theme: "I must / Bestow upon the eyes of this young couple / Some vanity of mine Art" (*Tempest* IV.i.39−41). This is spoken·to Ariel in a tone that attempts reluctance and self-deprecation while be-traying Prospero's eagerness to continue his *tours de force* at any price, his growing unwillingness to surrender the pleasure and power of magic art. Miranda's betrothal provides the excuse that legitimizes his obses-sion: "I *must*" because "it is my promise, / And they expect it from me." Prospero's delight in art is presented to us as an escape from the difficulties of life, a misanthropic idyllism that continually distracts him from his ethical purpose, making him sacrifice plot to spectacle and drama to the-ater. This allure, this temptation, this vanity of art, vibrates in the works of Rembrandt and Vermeer. And the resonance is ambivalent: the vanity is not merely to be transcended; it must first be bestowed upon the eyes; it must be present, but present-as-transcended. Their two vanities, how-ever, are played in different registers: Rembrandt's richer, more tur-bulent harmonics are closer to Shakespeare's, Vermeer's—more secretive and flutelike, with fewer partial overtones—closer to Prospero's. This is an invidious comparison which expresses what too many observers have felt about Vermeer, i.e., that he never really consented to leave his magic island, and one purpose of this essay is to move him a little nearer to the Shakespearian pole in value and complexity, if not style.

The theme of vanity is marked by a tension between the claims of art and those of life, more specifically, between the delight in painting and the rights of the painted. The United States Department of Health, Education, and Welfare has an Office of Protection from Research Risks, which sends out periodic bulletins specifying the precautions to be taken in research or experiments using human subjects. I contend that Vermeer (like Rembrandt) internalized an office of protection from research risks as his artistic conscience. This office sends out bulletins which touch on two particular aspects of the artist's experiments with human subjects.

First, though Prospero is a Milanese, the spirit of *Vanitas* is wafted from a birthplace closer to the Orient. *Vanitas* is *Venitas*, more Venetian than Venerean, more sensuous than sensual, and the Northern European painter must continually send himself bulletins against the dangers of Venice. For the soul trapped in "Venice" inhales the splendor and abundance of surfaces, the richness of shape and color and texture, the vibrant radiance that ripples from sky and sea across flesh, jewels, robes, façades, and pillowed rooms. "Venetians" are slaves of that glittering world, and the voyeurism induced by its burnished light can penetrate into art. Paint may enhance the worldly allure and become a surrogate for jewelled appearances. Paint threatens the best painters more insidiously than inferior artists because the former may succumb to their own virtuosity and remain trapped in the visual limits and technical pleasures of the medium. For in dematerializing the world, paint does not necessarily spiritualize it. On the contrary, it may increase the world's sensuous allure and reduce the observer's sensorium to famished eyes by abstracting the precious appearances of things from matter and dullness. Artistic *vanitas* surrenders to the natural gravitation of the medium toward delight in the esthetically beautiful for its own sake and in the manipulation of paint and its qualities for their own sake. This gravitation must be overcome so that the painter, mastering the appeal of visible and painted surfaces, may push his art beyond its natural boundaries toward those private, inward worlds which paint can only imperfectly express.

Second, experiments with human subjects are especially risky when sitters are pulled in from another room of the house, or off the street, to pose for friendship or money. Max Friedländer has observed that the job of commissioned portraits "entails something akin to obsequiousness" in the painter. Apart from the limits which the demand for accurate description imposes on his freedom and imagination, "the portraitist is quite specifically in a subservient position to the patron—who, even if he does not consider himself knowledgeable in matters of art,

still thinks he knows himself better than the artist and therefore feels
entitled to pronounce judgment on the portraitist's performance."[4] But
compensation for the artist is built into this contractual or symbiotic relation. In the process of fulfilling the terms of his commission he may
fulfill his own artistic urge with the help of what is accidentally a living
subject but substantively an esthetic object. The contract is his passport
to Clio. Titian paints Titians and Rembrandt Rembrandts, and while the
Paul III's and *Jan Six*'s are hardly anonymous, they are less representative of themselves, their tribes, and their milieux than they are of their
painters. Hence the office of protection from research risks has to remind the painter of his obligation to transform objects to subjects and
personages to persons.

Great painters in the nature of things overcome the threat to their dignity and independence by making their subjects extensions of their art.
Real personages can take care of themselves. But only the greatest painters can protect against the danger of vanity in the anonymous portrait,
the picture of some nobody chosen to model a personage or hold a pose
for a study. Here, where the sitter is subservient to the painter and
where no demand for accurate description interferes with artistic vision,
the lowly sitter may expect to vanish into paint. Scholars have admired
the handiness with which Rembrandt availed himself of a houseful and
cityful of models to feed his insatiable easel. If this did not solve his
financial problems, it dispelled the pressures of patronage that inhibit
the artist's freedom and power. Beginning thus from strength in the
anonymous portrait, Rembrandt found his way by heeding the voice of
the office of protection. He overcame his painterly domination of his
models, gave them back to themselves, rewarded them with being, and
transformed nobody to somebody.

We are all familiar with this achievement. But we are less willing to
acknowledge it in the more quiet and modest *oeuvre* of Vermeer than in
Rembrandt's *oeuvre*. The vanity of Vermeer's art is such that it would be
difficult to find many critics who would not second Ludwig Goldscheider's judgment: "Vermeer, the antithesis of Rembrandt, had no
message to proclaim, except that of the beauty of colored surfaces, 'the
deeds of light'. . . . For him, as an absolute artist, reality and his own
life were 'purely matters of form'."[5] Lawrence Gowing is a notable exception, though his example has not generally been followed. It is time

---

[4] *Landscape, Portrait, Still-Life*, trans. R. F. C. Hull (New York: Schocken Books,
1963), 232–33.
[5] *Johannes Vermeer*, 2d ed. (London: Phaidon, 1967), 26.

to return to Gowing's vision by showing that the office of protection has confronted the spirit of Vermeer's vanity and left its traces in his work. I shall approach this task cautiously, beginning with some technical problems connected with paintings in which human significance seems to interfere very little with the deeds of light, then moving gradually toward works that vibrate with the tension between those deeds and the deeper research into human subjects.

The Camera Obscura and the Vanity of Art

"Vermeer's evasiveness and his resistance to direct human response": this leading motif of Gowing's study seems inapplicable to *Woman Pouring Milk* and *The Lacemaker* (Figures 13 and 14), and Gowing's own comments indicate this, although in both cases he stresses the sense of distance.[6] The "bare notation of tone with which her head and arms are stated" creates for the pouring woman "a distant world of her own. Her act is simple, customary, unrevealing," and "her only life is that which she shares with the matter about her." She receives the light "with a passiveness remote from time and personality" (40–41). Similarly, "*The Lacemaker* bends intently over her pursuit, unaware of any other happening. It is perhaps the fact that she is so absorbed, enclosed in her own lacy world, that allows us to approach her so close" (145):

> Weight and volume, the lovely bulk of the head, seem in their lucent translation almost within our measure. Yet her distance remains; with gentle firmness the impartial tones convey it. Tangled defences are woven about her. (46)

Each woman, totally absorbed, is an extension of the still-life phenomena that possess her consciousness: the massive form of the milkmaid echoes those of the pitchers and bowl and seems made of the same solid stuff; the lacemaker's head and hands are planed smooth as the frame on which she works. Neither suggests by her expression even the possible trace of diverted attention or concern. Like the filtered light, the women's beings are concentrated in the small brilliant cubes of domestic pastoral. Self-sufficient and narrowly focused, they approach the condition of objects, solidly filled with and in the present, giving off no sense of other worlds or missing contexts. They reflect the painter's own pastoral concentration as he makes them centers of radiant color and light.

---

[6] *Vermeer*, 2d ed. (London: Faber & Faber, 1970), 41.

13. *Woman Pouring Milk.* Rijksmuseum, Amsterdam.

Some of the compelling strangeness of these images may owe to effects attributed to Vermeer's use of the camera obscura. The sense of distance, for example, may be partially explained by Daniel Fink's hypothesis that at any instant the lens of the camera obscura "is critically focused on only one plane, known as the principal plane of focus," and that Vermeer generally located this plane "parallel or nearly parallel to the far interior wall depicted":[7]

---

[7] "Vermeer's Use of the Camera Obscura—a Comparative Study," *Art Bulletin* 43 (1971): 495.

14. *The Lacemaker.* Louvre, Paris.

In the *Lacemaker* . . . the effect of the principal plane of focus intersecting the far wall is pronounced. Surface defects describe the intricate surface of the far wall. Beginning with this plane of sharpness and proceeding to the threads spilling from the girl's sewing box in the foreground one sees a gradual increase in the size of the circles of confusion, until the foreground skeins of thread are almost totally abstract.

Several nails and many chips in the rear wall shown in the *Maidservant Pouring Milk* are painted as if in focus, but the objects on the table are formed by highlights as if out of focus. . . . The plane of focus is the rear wall. Small circles and ellipses intersect and touch to form the character of the objects on the table. (496)

Fink's observation that "the wall is more clearly defined than the principal figure in many of Vermeer's paintings" (496) to some extent fits these two pictures and should be considered together with another peculiarity he attributes to the use of the camera obscura:

> The still-life portions of the paintings of Vermeer are drawn and painted at least as well as the principal figures and in many cases are handled in more detail. The amount of detail in the still-life portions of the paintings runs contrary to the procedure followed by most artists of the period. An inherent limitation of the camera obscura prevents the device from being much help with moving subjects. . . . Vermeer's figures generally hold comfortable, relatively stable, immobile positions, which can be maintained for some length of time. . . . Despite these rigidifying positions of the figures, however, the still-life portions of the paintings are even more highly detailed. (502)

One could infer from this statement that Vermeer at times relegated human figures to the position normally held by *nature morte*, and since faces are not pears, nor figures pitchers, this might arouse our curiosity. Why should he flaunt his technique in rendering objects and be technically evasive in rendering faces? Why should the splendor of those two deeds of light, *Woman Pouring Milk* and *The Lacemaker*, be marred by the cursory drawing of the lacemaker's bowed head, and by the "bare notation" of the milkmaid's head, "the omission of drawing at the base of the nose and across the expanse of shadow" (Gowing, 109)? Vermeer might be accused of a lack of human concern which, together with his technical ardor, would endanger the autonomy of any subject who agreed to contribute her person to his optical experiments. Fink could easily answer our questions by explaining that the heads are out of the principal plane of focus, and he could then go on to defend Vermeer against charges of inhumanity ("cold as crystal"—Goldscheider, 25) by suggesting that he painted the faces quickly to avoid inconveniencing the sitters.

Fink's response, as modest as it is economical, is characteristic of those who speculate about Vermeer's use of the camera obscura. Their analysis of optical phenomena provides essential and valuable material for interpretation. We miss, however, any sense of connection, of *rapprochement*, between their technical interests and the more "humanistic" orientation of, e.g., Gowing's analysis. In the articulation of human content they are no less reticent than the painter to whom they seem electively affined, though their modesty often masquerades as confidence. The camera obscura theorists appear convinced that their hypothesis can, in A. Hyatt Mayor's words, "explain a number of peculiarities" in Vermeer's art,[8] and indeed many of the ten phenomena analyzed in Fink's essay would lend support to the thematic interpretation exemplarily practiced by Gowing. To those already discussed I shall add two which, when liberated from the theorists' framework of modesty or confidence, may contribute to the reading of the works considered in the present study.

The first of these two "peculiarities," both mentioned by Mayor, is that "the highlights on objects in the immediate foreground—the carved lion-head of a chair or the bright threads of a tapestry—break up into dots like globules of halation swimming on ground glass" (20). R. H. Wilenski, also struck by the "vitreous quality" of Vermeer's images, attributed it to the use of mirrors.[9] The second peculiarity is the absence of what psychologists call "constancy scaling": both geometrical and photographic perspectives produce much sharper diminution of size as objects recede from the eye because unlike visual consciousness, they do not compensate with knowledge of actual size. The camera image resembles the preinterpreted retinal image and, in addition, it resembles only one retinal image: the unconscious convergence of the eyes in binocular vision also contributes to the constancy effect. Mayor speculates that "if Vermeer were painting from an image seen in the camera obscura, his eyes would not converge more for a near object than for a far one and he would tend to paint near objects bigger and far objects smaller than if he were painting direct from nature" (20).

Facility and precision are adduced as reasons for using the camera. Fink notes that it "offers a precision of operation" which could not be matched by the rational techniques introduced by Italian painters and carried northward by Dürer. Charles Seymour, Jr., cites as the advantage of the camera obscura, distortions aside, its ability to perform an automatic "reduction of a view of the three-dimensional 'natural' world to a two-dimensional image which could be traced or otherwise imitated without much recourse to a complex mathematical perspective construction."[10] But suppositions of this kind naturally produce uneasiness, and even Fink, while paying homage to Vermeer's mechanical triumphs with

[8] "The Photographic Eye," *The Metropolitan Museum of Art Bulletin*, n.s., 5 (Summer 1946): 20.
[9] *Dutch Painting*, 2d ed., rev. (London: Faber & Faber, 1955), 191.
[10] "Dark Chamber and Light-filled Room: Vermeer and the Camera Obscura," *Art Bulletin* 46 (1964): 326.

the vaguest critical bromides, finds himself obliged to apologize: "Vermeer was not a slave to the camera obscura but used it technically much as he used his brushes, paint, or eyes" (504).

The trouble with these explanations is perhaps too obvious. The camera obscura theorists confine themselves to reductive efficient- or final-cause explanations, i.e., they attribute the phenomena to the limitations of primitive lenses, or they posit as the painter's aim the attempt to produce "esthetically" pleasing technical effects, many of which are consonant with what we would now call "photographic realism." For Fink, the peculiarities "*can be satisfactorily explained* in terms of the behavior of optical phenomena" (496, my italics). Seymour attributes the use of "the mechanical eye" to a Cartesian quest "for visual truth": "the most faithful instrument for discerning and recording . . . perceptions, as far as purely sensory accuracy goes, is necessarily in Descartes' logic mechanical: *oculus artificialis*" (331). Mayor concentrates on the technical motive: "By throwing near-by objects out of focus, as it were, Vermeer suggested depth with a device more subtle than the standard practice of making them markedly lighter or darker than what is behind" (20).

To see how much is being explained away rather than explained, we have only to look again at *The Lacemaker*, and especially at the threads in the foreground, which are thrown out of focus because, according to Fink, they are so far from the principal plane of focus at the rear wall. Fink describes them as "almost totally abstract," and we may seize on the evasiveness of "abstract" to note that it need not be synonymous with "out of focus"; the foreground threads are "abstract" in the sense of "painterly"; they dissolve into light and paint. This effect begins to become meaningful only when we contrast it to the more subdued but graphically more precise rendering of the V-shaped thread between the lacemaker's hands. If we assume that the theme of the painting is adequately expressed by its title, we understand why the *compositional* elements conspire to fix our attention on the woman's working hands. The varied foreshortenings of table, book, pillow, and lowered head center the hands in a concave semicircular frame; our glance is funneled upward between the "barrier" in the left foreground and the wooden support post; the slight turn and flattening of the figure toward the right combine with the treatment of the background to bring the wall forward and to accentuate the profile of her left hand. Outlining their contours tends to still the hands, but their shading and position suggest the complementary tension and movement demanded by the lacemaker's work. Reasons may now be offered for the muted handling of the face. We could say that its chief purpose is to direct our eyes (following her eyes) down to the work, and we could say that the facial blur combines with the free lock of hair to supply optical cues to movement. Since her face and thought, like the painting, subordinate themselves to the sharp, precise working of her hands (confined within their outlines), we may infer that the movement is rapid and assured.

This account of the composition, however, is inadequate because it abstracts from the effects produced by light and color. Warmth and brilliance concentrate chiefly in the left foreground, centering on the cascade of white, the fluent flowering of red, the touches of yellow chroma and brightening green that float on the edges of the tablecloth, all intensified by the contrasting depths of blue and green shade. Against this aggressive interplay of values, the subdued tonality of the lacemaker further recedes and diminishes. The material she works on is bleached pale by the contrast. The tasseled and pillowed volume of the workbox pushes her backward against the wall and implies a cramping of her arm to fit her narrow space.

No merely optical analysis can account for these effects, nor can it begin to approach a statement of the theme of the painting. For this we must turn to the painterly, or textural, elements: the flower of thread sending out shoots of red paint; the thinly painted areas bringing out the weft of the canvas so that it merges with the textures of tablecloth and wall, producing ambiguous cues to the source of light, since we expect tablecloth and wall to reflect the fictive source but canvas the actual source outside the painting. The signature helps transform the lovely muted variations of the background from wall to canvas. We may say of these elements that they signify the presence of the painter. The middle distance of the painting "belongs" to the lacemaker, but the foreground and background "belong" to the painter. The chromatic drama condenses in what is nominally the mere frame of the subject; the lacemaker's jacket provides a complementary background to the blue workbox.

On the basis of these remarks I propose that the title of the painting be changed to *Painter Against Lacemaker,* or *The Conflict of Two Crafts,* or *The Stolen Thread,* with the expressive center of the conflict located in the contrast between the foreground thread transformed to paint and the fine but tensile, pale but sharply focused V of thread being transformed to lace. The painter reduces the space in which his subject works, appropriates her materials, challenges her claim to the title. It will not do, then, to criticize Vermeer for subordinating the life of his subjects to his art until one has at least recognized his own express recognition: the vanity of his art is conspicuously included, is thematized in the optical distortions, the chromatic and textural diversions, that threaten the graphic autonomy of the subject. The question whether this inclusion constitutes a self-criticism presupposes another question: Is the vanity of art not merely represented in the painting but represented as overcome? Does the painter finally reinstate the lacemaker, reaffirm his allegiance to the human subject against the seditious and seductive claims of art?

Because of its proximity, distortion, and tonal contrast, the left foreground presses almost too importunately on our attention, and this may set off a psychological recoil in the observer, may move him to adjust by mentally stepping back or peering over the workbox to survey the scene as a whole in order to put the foreground in its proper perspective. This response brings into play other compositional possibilities. The diagonal recession from the left foreground toward the wall that outlines the lacemaker's left hand generates a depth, a spatial envelope, within which the other hand—already animated by vivid shading—may move. The left tassel and the wooden knob form the base of a hollowed pyramidal motif which, tilting up and back toward the right, at once centers attention on the lacemaker's head at its apex and turns the figure slightly away from us. Intensified by the jutting table and the canted planes of workbox and book, that subtle torsion returns us to the person in the figure. Both head and hands, drawn together by identical tonality, are poor in structural information but rich in expressive force. This torsion, poverty, and richness combine in two interrelated effects: distance and animation. Partly shielded by furniture, protectively cupping her work, communing through lowered eyes with whatever pattern materializes under her hands, the figure suggests that her remoteness and privacy are the counterpart of total concentration. But this attention, though quiet, is active. Her stillness is midmotion; it breathes with the rhythm, the continuity, of prior and consequent movements. The sequential representation denied to painting here is not passively surrendered but conspicuously excluded. Head, eyes, mouth, fingers, the lock of hair, the bobbins of taut thread, the restless light: all conspire in a visual "rhetoric of temporality," compelling us to infer what we cannot see and thus to acknowledge the consciousness that works successive bobbins of time into its fabric.

"It is perhaps the fact that she is so absorbed, enclosed in her own lacy world, that allows us to approach her so close." Gowing's speculation is reversible: because we seem to be so close, our failure to penetrate the lacemaker's privacy or disturb her concentration signifies her withdrawal into the happiness of art. When our visual perambulations bring us back to her face, it is with a new sense that she is rapt, if not enraptured. We sense loving care that flares into delight—a sense all the more poignant because the face by itself does not quite yield it up. Like one of Vermeer's circles of confusion, the face initially asks us to bring it into focus so that we can read it and then prevents us from doing so, diverting us to the hands, to the figure as a whole, and to the foreground territory claimed by the painter. Only then do we notice that the shadow on her face (as on her hand) assimilates and subdues the foreground tints; touches of blue and green and a trace or two of red give life and luster to the shade that flickers across, rather than models, her cheek and wrist—as if the painter had subdued his vanity so that it might vivify her sober delight. Perhaps his own delight and self-absorption are modestly mirrored in hers; but perhaps not. It is her face we almost see, not his. On the other hand, his work is visible, while hers is not. What lies lacily among the pegs between her hands is withheld—the cause of her quiet intensity, the effect of her art, the quality of her work. At the center of his art, in the dialogue of the lacemaker's hands, is the mystery of hers: a small mystery, a mere domestic trifle. Yet it includes her life, closes in her consciousness, partly by closing us out. That mystery is what Vermeer's brilliant foreground both celebrates and protects as it invites us to draw near and fends us off. At the center of the lacemaker's art, in the distanced dialogue of face with hands, is the mystery of Vermeer's.

By looking through the camera obscura, art historians have found evidence of Vermeer's reliance on a mechanical device which could help him produce strange optical and perspective effects, effects that still human life, throw it out of focus, vitrify it, trap it in amber or glass. But the historians have not tried to assimilate these effects to some general project of meaning. They have accepted the subordination of life to art as a given, and although their researches have lent support to Gowing's thesis, they have not themselves drawn the connection: if the convergent optical effects suggest a painterly design to master life, evade it, or exclude it, we shall never arrive at that theme, much less wonder about its status, by looking through the lens of camera obscura theory.

One reason for this is the theorists' reluctance to consider their findings in the light of the full range of representational systems or emphases available to the painter. Their optical emphasis is too exclusive: painting things *as they are seen* is only one of three systems available to the painter. There is also the graphic system, painting things *as they are known to be,* and the textural system, which accentuates the qualities of paint and the presence of the painter's hand. And there is, finally, the articulation and modification of *theme* produced by the fluent interactions among the three systems. Historically, the graphic system is the first to provide the dominant emphasis. The microscopic detail of distant objects in Flemish painting is graphic, as is the concern for the detailed articulation of anatomical or architectural structure familiar in Florentine art. In graphic depiction line, color, light, and shade are used to model and describe the known features of texture, surface, and structure. The graphic impulse may manifest itself in linear emphasis, bounded contours, uniform local color, and smooth finish, all of which may contribute to "the perception of individual material objects as solid, tangible bodies" (Wölfflin) or as sensuously textured surfaces.

By contrast, the optical system fixes on the portrayal of objects under the conditions and limitations of vision, and this may imply interest in the quality of light; in a particular "moment," situation, or time of day; in the movement caused by the varying play of light and shade as they affect, dissolve, or reveal plastic form; in the motions of the objects themselves or the focus and movement of the eye. Rembrandt and others used the tonal system of black/white or dark/light to overcome the local color and structure of substantial forms in order to suggest the subject's momentary life situation, to heighten dramatic effect, add mystery, or evoke a more active interpretive response from the observer. Finally, the textural emphasis brings new stylistic elements into play: the quality of brushwork and surface relief; the contours of paint as substance or its hues as chroma; the physical character of glazing and scumbling as their vibrations strike the eye. Though the expressive and thematic possibilities of the textural system were fully appreciated only by Rembrandt, its sensuous possibilities had been valued and featured by Venetian painters active in the early sixteenth century. In Vermeer's time elements of the three systems could be variously combined according to dictates of taste or habitual reflexes of style. But they could also be deployed in the interests of thematic interpretation, as I have tried to suggest in discussing *The Lacemaker*.

Some of the optical effects described by Daniel Fink appear in *Woman Pouring Milk* to contribute to subtle ambiguities produced by their conflict with graphic and textural passages. It may seem at first that Hans Koningsberger's judgment of this painting is adequate: "There is little contemplation, but great stillness. . . . It shows only a maid pouring milk into a pot: a physical presence recorded by the artist, a capturing of reality that even includes a nail hole in the wall."[11] But this impression begins to change as soon as we take into account Fink's observation that the details of the rear wall "are painted as if in focus, but the objects on the table are formed by highlights as if out of focus." Yet are they unambiguously highlights? The famous *pointillés*, or discs of confusion, on

[11] *The World of Vermeer, 1632–1675* (New York: Time, 1967), 148.

the bread may also be read as nubbles on the crust. The trickle of milk converges with highlights around the edge of the pitcher which may also be read as white paint. The stippling on the wall translates fairly simply as graphic detail, the marks of wear, but on the woman's face it may be the modeling light, or roughness of skin, or the texture of paint.[12] A similar ambiguity invests her right sleeve, her pouring hand, and the apron gathered at her waist. The conflict of optical, graphic, and textural emphases is no doubt quieted by the simplicity of primary and complementary harmonies. But it is not entirely dispelled, for—like the ambiguous cues of the Necker cube—these emphases are disjunctive alternatives; at any moment we are forced to choose one or the other, and this sets up an oscillating or vibrating field which may be temporarily *re*solved but not permanently *dis*solved.

The tranquillity of the painting is finally imposed on, or wrested from, a multitude of minor motions and tensions. It is hard to estimate the depth or height of the room or the precise viewing point established by the composition. We see little floor and no ceiling. The pouring pitcher is viewed from the right while the two nails projecting from the rear wall are viewed from the left. The angle of the nails implies a lower viewing point which—together with the height of the table relative to the woman's waist, and the apparently high window—makes the woman seem taller. So also does the low and relatively small footwarmer, a crucial element in the painting because it enters into various dialogues which at once enhance the pouring figure's volume and imperil its poise: it enhances volume by joining the two wicker baskets in a pyramid that both confirms the recession of the table and frames the figure in a deeper space; it imperils poise by turning its open face obliquely away from the pitcher's mouth to accentuate the Raphaelesque twist of the woman's apron against the turn of her upper torso.[13]

These dialogues create a field of forces, a play of torsions and *contrapposti*, that redefine the figure's quiet attitude. Thus, for example, the tilt

---

[12] See Hubert von Sonnenburg's "Technical Comments" following Walsh's essay in *The Metropolitan Museum of Art Bulletin:* "In the still life in the foreground, the paint is more thickly applied: it is gradually built up into an almost tactile relief. Vermeer suggests the roughness of the bread by combining this relief with a scintillating surface created by a wide variety of touches of thick light paint."

[13] The object of the floor is variously described as a footwarmer and a mousetrap. The latter would be more appropriate to the iconography of *Temperantia* sometimes postulated for this image of "domestic virtue," but the color and shape of its contents suggest glow and, perhaps, stone. For its small size, compare the footwarmer in Steen's *Lovesick Maiden* and in the drawing *Maidservant Warming Her Feet*, bearing Vermeer's signature, in the Weimar Schlossmuseum.

of the head is rhythmically enlivened by that of the hanging basket while the asymmetry of the white coif accentuates the turning of the face in the direction of the apron. The interplay of arms and sleeves echoes this movement: the graphic clarity of the green upper sleeve closest to us reinforces the stillness of the supporting arm; the optical/textural treatment of the other sleeve and foreshortened arm conveys movement to the pouring arm, movement which seems to be pushed by the pan on the wall forward and downward through an arc that bends the pitcher toward the apron.[14] The expressive brow and mouth challenge the sculptured roughness of the face with life and breath; they signify the woman's absorption in her task as she holds still to steady the pitcher against unwanted movement. The heavy hang of the blue cloth on the table creates an impression of possible (if not impending) slippage. Finally, the angle of the projecting nails conspires with the disposition of head and shoulders and with the slope of floor, footwarmer, and table to tilt the standing figure slightly forward in space—a threat of imbalance which is, however, neutralized by the columnar stability of her red skirt.

These hints of motion and imbalance produce in the observer a vague sense of *vertige,* which is intensified by the vibration of optical/textural/graphic ambiguities. The woman's monumental pose is jeopardized on all sides by the activity it so conspicuously excludes. It is not still life but stilled life—a precarious stillness compact of kinetic pulls and pushes, twists and stresses. We feel both gravity and the resistance to it in the slope of surfaces, the sag of the hanging basket and blue cloth, the vertical folds of the skirt. We see the marks of wear, the work of time, on the walls and floor (and on the woman's face?). Against this, like new life replacing the old, the bread warms freshly into light, and the turning rope of luminous white paint drops or hangs from the pitcher. All the motion and motionlessness of the captured moment press into, find their center and resolution in, that suspended milky fall. The woman's heroic stature, her robust plasticity, pay tribute to the painter's wit—to the incongruous translation of majestic Renaissance form into a Dutch corner. But the wit deepens into sympathy and admiration for his subject. Her firmness withstands the pressures of gravity and time, and her attentive care for the prosy needs of life earns the painter's radiant praise. She is durable; she weathers well; she provides.

---

[14] The effect of motion is accidentally increased by the *pentimenti,* which suggest that Vermeer repositioned the arm to bring it forward and closer to the body, making the *contrapposti* more dramatic.

15. *Street in Delft*. Rijksmuseum, Amsterdam.

Landscape as Stilled Life: The Camera Obscura Revisited

Street in Delft (Figure 15) is inhabited by four figures: a woman cleaning in the alley, another sewing in the doorway, a man (?) and woman kneeling before the house. The monocular flatness of the alley tends to contradict the sharp orthogonal recession and brings the bending woman forward as if she were framed in a mirror or painting. The visible activities, cleaning and repairing, establish the theme of the painting, while the flat light, empty street, and small faceless figures establish its mood. The painting gestures toward anecdotes it never discloses. We cannot tell whether the kneeling figures are scrubbing, cleaning, repairing, reading, or playing, since what they are doing is hidden from us, and while this secret is hardly pulse quickening, it speaks to us (like the dark windows and the shadowy shape behind the sewing woman's head) of ongoing life withheld from view. The painting also gestures toward a history to which these self-contained lives contribute. Whitewashing was begun but was not—or has not been—completed. About the ground story it gives way to cracks, flaws, and mended places. The marks of decay give meaning to the human activities. The actors do their best to keep things clean and mended. But they are small and few, and their efforts are narrowly focused. They cannot compete with industrious time, which works away at whole façades. Hence the painter intervenes on their behalf.

The whitewashed areas provide a clean frame or backdrop for his cleaning figures. Rectangles flatten out. The cobblestones of the street dissolve into calligraphy (Gowing's term). The decaying brick and mortar are so finely patterned, so painterly in their animation, that the esthetic moment triumphs and decay becomes design.[15] The painter momentarily brings the aging world under the rule or vanity of art. But if he regulates and briefly neutralizes the decay, he does not try magically to dissolve it. He allows the darker theme to murmur against its conspicuous exclusion. Time's vestiges justify the need for scrubbing, sewing, painting, renovating, and revising even as they argue their insufficiency. The house is assumed by scholars to be one which was pulled down in 1661, which could not be long after it was painted. Thus another aspect of the vanity of art is thematized: the painter keeps alive in pictures what must surely die in life.

Street shares with *View of Delft* (Figure 16) qualities which turn commentators' thoughts, once again, to the camera obscura. Seymour thinks it conceivable that this device enabled Vermeer "to achieve the remarkably casual effect of exactness in the middle distance" of the *View*, and he notes that this work "most closely conforms in program to the run of seventeenth century texts dealing with the possibilities in using the camera obscura. They most often stress its usefulness in depicting large stretches

---

[15] Von Sonnenburg remarks of the brick wall that the highlights "make the eye move over its surface at the same time as they suggest the distance and atmosphere separating it from the observer. This network of highlights is omitted on the whitewashed portions, since a white surface in sunlight tends to look flat and dazzling."

16. *View of Delft*. Mauritshuis, The Hague.

of nature in panoramic or 'chorographic' views" (326). This emphasis accords with the general premise of his essay, which is that the use of the camera obscura was encouraged by interest in the conscientious observation and recording of nature. Speculating on the significance of the camera obscura hypothesis, he tentatively associates it with "three concepts characteristic of the seventeenth century, but all with Renaissance roots: 1) the expansion of 'natural philosophy,' 2) the concept of nature as both work of art and artist, and 3) the ennoblement of the so-called mechanical arts by mechanizing organic functions" (331).

There are problems with this statement at the level of intellectual history—another view of the Renaissance might uncover different roots flowering into different characteristic concepts—but the imputation of this motive (the "search for visual truth") to Vermeer concerns me at this point. Since the burden of Seymour's demonstration is that Vermeer's camera obscura effects resemble blurred or distorted phenomena, his conclusion seems less than persuasive. Clearly the visual truth apprehended by the human eye differs considerably from that apprehended by

a primitive mechanical eye, and unless the painter's effects show him trying to be "scientific," trying to transcend "subjective optics" and explore
"objective optics," there is little warrant for this conclusion.

Seymour refers in passing to Gowing's having connected Vermeer's
use of the camera with "his poetic richness of content" (323), but he does
not confront the implied contradiction between Gowing's view and his
own. Gowing assimilates the hypothesis to his central argument, which
is that Vermeer, for reasons both of temperament and of technique, es-
chewed naturalistic representation and, among other things, set himself
against the insistence of the *trompe l'oeil* tradition on "the credibility of
visual perception" (25). Vermeer, he claims, is alone in putting the camera "to the service of style rather than the accumulation of facts" (23):

> For him the play of light upon form not only conveys its substance but also
> subtly denies it. The illusion which he seeks is not closeness but distance. . . .
> Immediacy, touch, are excluded; his subject is the immutable barrier of
> space. It is for this, for the impalpable veil which it implies, that visual im-
> pression in all its genuineness is so precious to him. There is in his thought,
> the paradoxical accompaniment of its clarity, a deep character of evasiveness,
> a perpetual withdrawal. (25)

The limitations of the camera are obviously congenial to this project,
and it is natural to see its influence in the flatness and impalpability of the
Street. Monocular vision impedes the perception of volume, which is
produced by the blending of the slightly different images registered by
each of the two eyes. As an object recedes and decreases in size, the angle
of vision narrows so that both eyes report a similar frontal image, and
this diminishes the stereoscopic impression of volume and thickness as
well as detail. In the tonal field of monocular vision, shadow tends to
emphasize chromatic values at the expense of plastic values. It has been
suggested that Giorgione treated proximate objects in this manner, in-
vesting them with an intangibility which poignantly enhances their visionary remoteness. Vermeer chose what Gowing terms "the optical way"
(24) for similar pastoral reasons.

Gowing thinks the camera may have been responsible for the optical
pastoral of the two Delft landscapes: "The bluntly undramatic slice of
life presented, the ruthless revelation of the physical insignificance of
people beside the world which they inhabit, both recall it" (128). He
extends his comments on *The Music Lesson* to the *View:* everything

> is more visible than humanity; we are left to contemplate an accumulation of
> geometric intersections. . . . It is the signifying detail of life that Vermeer

resists. He relegates it to the distance; *The Music Lesson* and its pendant [the Boston *Concert*] recall the great monument of this phase of his thought, the *View of Delft*. In the landscapes the very absence of human tension allows a whole material poetry, a poetry of brick and vapor, of resistance and penetration to develop. We see in it how much is excluded by the terms of Vermeer's dilemma. Yet it was the human problem that he pursued to the end. (38)

It is a pity that Gowing did not himself pursue "the human problem" which presents itself by conspicuous exclusion in the *View*, for his distinction between distance as a human theme and as an esthetic reflex depends on it. If human tension is simply absent, then it is hard to avoid conflating his judgment of the *View* with those of less discerning observers:

> Though contemporary with Bernini and Rembrandt, Vermeer has no Baroque spontaneity or sensuality, no kinetic energy or dramatic action. The *View of Delft* is undramatic, passionless, remote and detached; a studied, static performance rendered through an impersonal mastery of technique. Vermeer's great qualities are harmony, serenity, sensitivity and clarity of vision; and the motionless tranquillity of the landscape is expressed in the smooth, enamel-like surface of the painting.[16]

In the face of such a painting, the pursuit of the human problem necessarily begins with speculative and impressionistic responses. This is presumably an early-morning scene—the clock on the central building, the Schiedam Gate, reads 7:10—and I am reminded of Wordsworth's Westminster Bridge sonnet by the ships and towers lying "silent, bare," and open "to the sky; / All bright and glittering in the smokeless air." Yet Gowing's observation makes a difference. The "ruthless revelation of the physical insignificance of the people," their number, size, and disposition, especially the isolated apparitions on the quay across the water, affect me with a feeling which I do not think a cityscape altogether without people would have produced: a compelling sense of emptiness, loneliness, and passivity. The brooding middle distance suggests why this is so, and as we rub the dewy dreamlike splendor of the image out of our eyes, as we remember that Wordsworth's city only wore its bareness, "the beauty of the morning," "like a garment," the freshness gives way to an architectural vista with buildings crowded together, their patchy walls compressed between dark reflections and an uncertain sky—compressed, also, in a chilly, even light between a more radiant fore-

---

[16] Jeffrey Meyers, "Proust and Vermeer," *Art International* 17 (1973): 69.

ground and background. The forms are cheerless. Their drowned doubles push back the buildings, intensify the sense of the city as a wall. The ships, shorn of sails, lie hulking and inert. Dark windows and archways suggest reserve, inwardness, seclusion. The wall that fortifies the buildings packs them tightly against each other, the heavy sky weighs them down, and if "the very houses seem asleep," the more oppressive qualities and guarded attitudes of city life have not been forgotten, are only "lying still."

This horizontally stressed mood is, however, relieved by the repeated play of verticals. Masts, posts, and towers move up from the city toward the sky, the church tower catches the sun, and the trees accentuate the break in the wall. Two crossing diagonals inflect the countermovement of relief and release: one moves from the yellows of the lower left foreground to the sunlit buildings; the other moves from the boats on the right, along the buildings, through the bridge, over the trees, and into the background, opening distances and breaching the insistent city wall. Sky and water, light and shade, weather the man-made world, wash and erode its surfaces. The pastoral of open spaces, of nature's free and flowing rhythms, plays its life against the huddled geometry of Delft.

There is, however, another kind of pastoral, one which is more absolute than nature's, which promises not renewal but suspension. When we focus on the detail of the surfaces, especially from center to right, the heavy inertness gives way to the galaxy of *pointillés* coruscating like dewdrops. The scars of age are sparkling and picturesque. If we estimate distance by the relative sizes of figures on both sides of the canal and compare that estimate to our rough guess of the distance across it; if we notice that only the two women in the foreground have the barest suggestion of plastic form; if, finally, we respond to the essential flatness of the city façade, the volumes and textures of which dissolve into tonal patterns, then our view of Delft becomes not so much one of densely crowded buildings packed against and behind each other in space as one—more a vision than a view—of a strangely distant and intangible town projected in two dimensions. Its values are chromatic rather than plastic or stereoscopic. Even the diagonal structure on the right tends toward flatness, and the more plastic modeling of the boat seems to intensify this effect by contrast. What appear at first to be carefully observed descriptions of textural detail turn out to be vague, and when we realize this, the façades recede and flatten still further. Brickwork and patchwork metamorphose before the eyes into pure esthetic patterns, variations of color and light that animate the forms.

This visionary sense of distance and intangibility may well owe much to the camera obscura. Its uncompensated and monocular perspective may account for the impression of an urban middle distance which seems in some respects to be farther away than it should be, judging from the apparent width of the canal and the apparent clarity of what are at first glance minute details of texture. Whether or not Vermeer actually used the mechanical eye, these effects contribute to the ambiguous statement which the painting makes. For the appearance of fine detail first draws us across the canal to explore at closer range the human and social implications of the urban image: crowding, disrepair, dungeonlike arches, dark interiors behind windows, isolation, a quiet but oppressive and fortified gloom. Vermeer's optical pastoral then attenuates this moment. It chastens the city by flattening and distancing, which push it back into the tranquil embrace of sky and water. The motion of clouds, the waver of reflections, the dramatic chiaroscuro, the hands of the clock, the etching of time—the scene with all its implied activity is resolved into the stillness of suspended animation. The gloom of the city and the activity of nature are at once implied and overcome, are present but present-*as*-excluded. *View of Delft* is almost, but not quite, the view of a vitrified world. Its glassy veil shimmers with "the very absence of human tension." It teases us out of thought by inviting us to pass through the looking glass while blocking the way. Vermeer never lets us reach the end of "the human problem that he pursued"; he only invites us to pursue it.

Obscurity in the Light-Filled Room: The Question of the Face

His theme [in *The Music Lesson*] is purged of its grossness, its importunity. But so long as Vermeer has a positive subject, his subject remains the attention that man pays to woman. . . . We find, looking back to the conversation-pieces, even to *The Procuress*, that what is most memorable, most lasting in their drama is the part which has been played in it by the lady. Under the pressure of male attention, neither resisting nor complying, she has remained of her nature intact. There is inherent in her being an inviolable status, a separateness. In Vermeer's maturity the subject of the conversation-pieces is incorporated in a single body, the standing figure of a woman. (Gowing, *Vermeer*, 52–53)

What is either a picture or a novel that is *not* of character? What else do we seek in it and find in it? It is an incident for a woman to stand up with her hand resting on a table and look out at you in a certain way; or if it be not an incident I think it will be hard to say what it is. At the same time it is an expression of character. If you say you don't see it (character in *that—allons donc!*), this is exactly what the artist who has reasons of his own for thinking he *does* see it undertakes to show you.[17]

In art, persons do not inevitably deign to enter and inhabit the faces or figures that represent them. But when they do, the iconography of life is activated, for in life the face or body is an embodiment: something more than meets the eye always meets the eye. Unlike the iconography of art, which raises questions about the sufficiency of a visual image only to answer them, the archive of the iconography of life is not voluminous and promises few answers. Faces are hard to read, even when we know the physiognomic and pathognomic conventions behind their expressions, yet in our researches using human subjects we expect to find meaning centered in the attitude of the face and haloed in the disposition of body, limbs, and (especially) hands. If some paintings or kinds of painting neither arouse this ready expectation nor impose on us (what the French might call) the question of the face, others do both, and it is to these that we may accord the term *anecdote* in its more profound etymological sense, i.e., something "not given out." In this sense the word refers to "secret or hitherto undivulged particulars of history or biography." The focus of an anecdote falls upon an incident, and the convergence of these two notions of anecdote brings out the implications of James's usage: not merely, as the dictionary puts it, "a definite, distinct occurrence; an event"; but also, "an event that is subordinate to another," "something contingent upon or related to something else"—in itself, perhaps, "a relatively minor occurrence," but something that obscurely shadows (*in aenigmate*) and conspicuously withholds secret particulars.

In certain paintings Vermeer's treatment of faces is especially enigmatic because of the refusal either to articulate features or to commit them to an easily identifiable expression. This effect is increased by the contrast between the understated face and the brilliant clarity of its surroundings. The contrast at once commands attention and arouses frustration, for since the ambience of still life is readily ceded to us, we are tempted all the more eagerly to appropriate the face. The promise held out to us is the fullness of presence, the apocalypse of perfect embodiment, the charismatic unveiling of what was "hitherto undivulged." But the promise is held out only so that it may be broken, only so that the wish concentrated in the definition's "hitherto" may be stated and then

---

[17] Henry James, "The Art of Fiction," in *"The Art of Fiction" and Other Essays*, ed. Morris Roberts (New York: Oxford University Press, 1948), 13.

canceled out. In the frustration or surrender of the wish *the other* emerges as an absent presence and the figure becomes a person.

Perhaps Lawrence Gowing's most important and original contribution to the study of Vermeer lies in his eloquent (if somewhat repetitive) enactment of the dynamic of *alienation*, or *making other*, generated in the interplay between the interpreter and Vermeer's paintings of women. If the present essay owes much to Gowing's monograph, the precise nature of the debt has not been fully articulated because I have not yet stated the reservations which lead me to carry his approach in a direction somewhat different from that which he himself might wish. The reservations cluster around a slippage in his use of critico-interpretive language: his terms sometimes waver between descriptive and evaluative statement, and this irresoluteness is complicated by his not distinguishing clearly at other times qualities attributed to Vermeer's paintings from those attributed to his psyche. I shall illustrate these problems with a passage which will also introduce us to the question of the face.

In discussing the Berlin *Drinking Scene* Gowing (30–31) notes Vermeer's failure to extend to "human detail" the care he lavishes on "the transcription of still-life" and contrasts this to "the genial breadth of Metsu's grasp of feature and furnishing alike in one equable and unexacting rhythm," a unity which "makes all the clearer the dislocation to which Vermeer's approach is subject." This is less unfavorable to Vermeer than it seems, since elsewhere in his study Gowing contrasts "genial" and "unexacting" to Vermeer's higher "standard of genuineness," the "exacting quality" of his "self-criticism," and his "finer," if "narrower," understanding. "Understanding," which is also Gowing's term, arouses uncertainty: is it a literal reference to the painter's mind ("a naturally more profound intelligence") or a metonymic displacement from producer to product? It is Vermeer's *approach*, not necessarily his pictures, which is subject to dislocation. Gowing's language gravitates toward the terminology of genetic explanation and, more specifically, of psychological analysis: "It seems as if the very efficiency of his still-life method were a symptom in itself, as if the quality of surface observation sought to compensate for some deep impediment." The evasion of human detail which accounts for the relative disunity of Vermeer's work in esthetic terms is thus grounded in shortcomings which are at once technical and temperamental: Metsu's attitude toward life "is generous, relaxed; his gentle picturesque rhythm has a quality of sympathy, the quality of a caress. Throughout his life this gesture remains beyond Vermeer's power."

The "deep impediment" which Gowing pursues through his monograph is both an erotic block associated with Vermeer's ambivalence toward women and a more general reticence to deal directly with human life:

> For all the stature with which he endows the inhabitants of his world, indeed perhaps because of it, Vermeer stops short of humanity. The lack of facility in dealing with human issues, which emerges side by side with the elemental clarity of vision and which is its counterpart, is the fundamental factor *in the formation of his style*. . . . Vermeer's distinction is that . . . he accepted this part of his nature as a basis of the expressive content of his style. The instinctive seriousness of his assent to the requirements of his temperament is the sign of his genius. The lack of facility corresponds to a depth of feeling; his diffidence in dealing with the aspect of humanity is the measure of the meaning he attaches to it. The virtue in an artist is often like a bare nerve; sensitivity may not only qualify but disable. (31, my italics)

Gowing's balanced assessment of achievements and limitations is intended to establish the uniqueness, the peculiarity, of Vermeer's vision. The precarious balance at which he aims, however, is subject to continual local pressures so that he seems sometimes to praise and at other times to dispraise the same effect—sometimes "qualify but disable" tips the balance, sometimes the equivalent of "disable but qualify." At times his interpretation appears primarily descriptive of effects in the painting, at other times primarily critical, and this oscillation of modes is not clearly flagged. Similarly, the inference from style to psyche, the hypostasis of a causal temperament, makes it difficult for Gowing's reader to pinpoint the precise location assigned by his monograph to Vermeer's themes. Insofar as his account is genetic, in fact, the themes seem to be those elicited by Gowing rather than those displayed by Vermeer. Diffidence combined with clarity is stated to be "the fundamental factor" not in his style but "in the formation of his style." It is never clear whether the genetic attributions are meant as figures of speech, periphrastic ways of describing the work, or as literal psychological inferences.

To sharpen the distinction between formal and genetic concerns, I have put the term *conspicuous* into play. To call an effect conspicuous is simply to say that the work "intends" us to take note of it and wonder about it: whether or not the artist intended what he can be shown to have achieved is irrelevant to this consideration. The exacting self-criticism Gowing attributes to Vermeer may be more effectively defended on these grounds, for we can now ask whether his "diffidence in dealing with the aspect of humanity" is something that flaws his work, something for which he is to be criticized, or is something to which the work itself directs attention, something it thematizes, perhaps a part of the artist's self-criticism projected into his work. Viewed in this light, Gowing's account of the development of one of Vermeer's principal themes may be given a more formal emphasis, which at the same time makes contact with significant changes in artistic representation occurring in Vermeer's time—changes recently identified and conceptualized by Svetlana Alpers, to whose analysis I shall return in the next section of this essay.

Gowing traces Vermeer's transformation of the theme of venal love, first announced in *The Procuress:*

> At the outset it is the single and conspicuous subject of a great masterpiece. In succeeding pictures it is progressively refined into subtler and more elusive forms. Finally it is seen, as if in a marginal note, only as a picture hanging on his wall: it is a *Procuress,* a work painted early in the century by the Utrecht artist Baburen, that appears as a decoration, a collector's piece, behind *The Concert* and the *Lady Seated at the Virginals.* (49)

Gowing speculates that "the manner of Utrecht" may have interested Vermeer "as much in its invariably lascivious application as in any deeper quality of style" (50), but he goes on to describe the complexity and ambivalence of that interest as represented in the Brunswick *Drinking Scene* (Figure 17):

> The theme which has engaged his taste proves also, subtly, to offend it. . . . The man . . . bends over the lady in his customary fashion: we feel for her. A second glance shows that Vermeer himself now stands aside from the presentation. The serpentine attentions of this cavalier are openly contrasted with the upright, ideal man, painted in the style of Palamedesz, on the wall. The calculation is a nice one. The suitor is transfixed. This perfect objectivity holds the possibility of mockery: we may view him as we please, lusty or ridiculous, and the situation is saved. And looking closer, it is seen that the cavalier, rendered in so simplified a pattern, is no more than a figment of the man he seemed, the man who pays his court in the works of Vermeer's simpler contemporaries. (51–52)

The ambivalence is further marked by the figure in the window, closer to us and more colorful: an old man bearing what appears to be a scythe with serpentine attachments; his *carpe diem* message swings forward, catches the light, and clashes against the somber puritan in the background painting. Vermeer's theme is broadly overstated: the cavalier flaunts his gallantry; the woman appears to flaunt her conquest (though her grimace seems to have resulted from restoration); the man at the table flaunts his boredom; in the passages of still life the painter flaunts

17. *Drinking Scene*. Herzog Anton Ulrich-Museum, Brunswick.

his descriptive skill. The superficiality of the conflict between pleasure and virtue is matched by the thematic irrelevance or triviality of the clash between description and narration. If pleasure conquers the woman and description the observer, or if description "saves" the figure of the woman and mocking disapproval (along with the tipped-up ground plane) elevates the observer above the actors, it is at the expense of a more subtle, more complex integration of style with theme and of pleasure with virtue.

Gowing sees this work as marking the point "at which outward events, real happenings, ceased to hold the painter's imagination" and

Vermeer turned to explore subtler motifs in apparently more "undramatic" subjects like *The Concert* and *The Music Lesson*. The thematic reversal in the paintings within the paintings testifies to this change: to replace the "upright, ideal man" of the Brunswick painting with Baburen's *Procuress* is to shift from an ethical commonplace to a psychological tension. In *The Concert* Baburen's three figures "supply an ironic commentary on the performance of the trio in front of them; its immobility, its very innocence, gain a curious significance" (52). And in the London *Woman Seated at the Virginals* (Figure 18), the erotic theme has similarly been chastened to a hint, a remote possibility. The musician is almost, but not quite, puppetlike. She makes eye contact with someone on this side of the picture plane and establishes a relation with—whom? The painter? The cellist? A caller? The observer? The porcelain mask of her face and reticent turn of her head communicate something more than still life: perhaps a vague uneasiness at being interrupted, or visited, or on display. But if her relation to the theme of the Baburen painting is marked, it is also markedly indefinite. Is music the food of love, or is love the food of music?[18] Does the Baburen represent anything more than her taste in art? Or is its theme present as a canceled possibility, a displacement, the vestige of a world which everything in the woman's room is calculated to exorcise and defend against? Here, where narration appears at first glance to be reduced to, supplanted by, description, it gradually emerges as something merely repressed and therefore returns, but in a form which teases rather than fulfills our expectations.

This ambiguity is most compellingly depicted in *Woman Standing at the Virginals* (Figure 19). Gowing is struck by "her unshrinking nature, her . . . delicacy. . . . Her presence has the force of a challenge" (61). Both Cupid and the lady look at us, Cupid more intensely, the lady more placidly or perhaps guardedly. The darkening sky around the Eros figure is enhanced by the black frame and set off by the coruscating carved and gold-leaf frame of the smaller landscape to the left. The bright frame makes the duller-toned landscape recede, while the larger, brighter Cupid moves forward, becomes bolder and more sinister, and plants his bow in the woman's head. The three paintings surround her with windows on other worlds. In each, the ground swells up toward the right in a loose and free echo of the rigidly formal pattern of Vermeer's picture—i.e., the woman and the virginal together compose into a more rectilinear analogue of the rounded swell and fall at the right of the land-

[18] If Gowing is correct in associating this motif with the iconography of St. Cecilia (*Vermeer*, 156–57), the narrative possibilities are further complicated.

18. *Woman Seated at the Virginals*. National Gallery, London.

scapes, and, as in the room, the free space at the left of each painting stresses the crowding at the right. How shall we interpret this formally insistent connection between the room and the landscapes? The rural scenes of uncivilized nature, the domain of passion and Cupid, are set over against the extremely civilized formality embodied in the woman's dress, her pose, her activity and in the squares, frames, art, craftsmanship, and stately music of this domestic pastoral. But again, although the contrastive relation is marked, its meaning remains indefinite.

Some critics have conjectured that the Cupid symbolizes the woman's engagement or a proposal of love. But the point is that while any number of narrative possibilities clearly exists, the painting opts for no one in

19. *Woman Standing at the Virginals*. National Gallery, London.

particular and leaves them all in abeyance. The woman does not help us resolve our doubt. The masklike quality of her face is preserved by its porcelain or alabaster paleness; soft fallible flesh has been consigned to the personification of desire, and hers is a less penetrable covering. Protectively sheathed in porcelain, sleeve, dress, and chair, she poses with restrained confidence. Her hands suggest either playing or pretending to play, and what she communicates to me is a slightly amused awareness of something on this side of the picture—perhaps our desire to penetrate the mask and discover whether *she* knows Cupid has triumphantly claimed her head or knows he makes direct contact with us from behind her. But neither she nor the painting as a whole gives anything away.

The questions are conspicuously posed, their answers just as conspicuously excluded.

The theme of conspicuous exclusion may be harder to sustain before what is one of the loveliest deeds of light by Vermeer or any artist, *Woman with Water Pitcher*, in the Metropolitan Museum (Figure 20). Here, if anywhere, daily life is transformed into "a dream palace of light and color." Here there is surely no elaborate evasion of human claims. There is scarcely even a defined subject. Gowing's general insight, drawing its full meaning from a survey of many paintings, could apply to this one only if the cumulative evidence were somehow read into it:

> Around his central subject, the figure of a woman, to which he makes so many approaches, each complicated by a simultaneous gesture of withdrawal, an enigmatic meaning accumulates. The woman's detail, the complexity of her being, conceals a disturbing element. Examined too narrowly she will become a source of danger. The painter's style develops along a line of self-preservation; its infinite ingenuity is all directed to isolating from these latent, intimate perils the visible beauties among which they hide. (60–61)

This passage is directed specifically to his account of *Woman Standing at the Virginals*, and the erotic accent Gowing places on it further disables it as a comment on the Metropolitan painting. No matter how narrowly we examine the woman with the pitcher, she will not become a source of danger, and it will be necessary to generalize Gowing's theme to make it speak to this work. The erotic relation is only a special (if central) case of Vermeer's pastoral paradox, his interest in depicting the tensions between the claims of life and those of art, between the urge to approach life and the urge to avoid its impact, between the escapist fear of encounter and the sophisticated awareness that this temptation, made more alluring by the pastoral fusion of idyllism with art, is to be resisted.

The limitations of Gowing's thesis make themselves felt in the language with which he describes Vermeer's painting of the woman. He observes that although "the lustrous handling and neatly accented tonal divisions are clearer than ever,"

> Vermeer's method . . . still falters when the crucial detail is reached. The head is a conventional summary and a far from confident one, but it is *at least* without any obtrusive expression. *There remains a certain uneasiness.* . . . [But a positive sign of development, appearing in the] arm passing behind the window frame, displays Vermeer's innovation in another aspect. It is a statement of tone as unsubstantiated as it is decisive. . . . Here descriptive line and the detail of life are finally cast off. (130–31, my italics)

20. *Woman with Water Pitcher.* Metropolitan Museum of Art, New York.

Here again Gowing wavers between descriptive and evaluative responses. "A certain uneasiness" is a technical criticism of the painting of the head, and it recalls a comment made earlier about the Berlin *Drinking Scene:* "Where the human detail emerges the style becomes evasively general," and this is a function of the painter's "profound resistance to the naturalistic description of life," especially in the depiction of human relations (116). In these instances the artist's resistance is made to account for technical deficiencies, but when Gowing describes the arm, the same technique is praised as contributing to the theme of escape—casting off the detail of life—and the italicized "at least" suggests a sense of relief in the critic which merges with and intensifies the relief he finds in the artist. Is the arm good because the understatement and avoidance of detail are decisive, and is the head bad because its simplified treatment is too indecisive—i.e., gives rise to unresolved suggestions of human meaning? As I noted earlier, it is often hard to decide on what basis Gowing treats Vermeer's uneasiness sometimes as the product of artistic or psychological defects and sometimes as a theme within the painting which is to be considered as contributory to its meaning.

The woman's head is a conventional summary until it is more narrowly examined in relation to the window, the light, and her stance. One commentator, writing more recently than Gowing, has noted that "something or someone outside seems to have caught her attention," and remarks that "Vermeer has done more than paint a woman standing arrested on the spot, but instead has observed her and depicted her in action" [19]—more accurately, in arrested action, a moment which conspicuously suggests and excludes prior and succeeding moments. It is unclear whether she is merely holding the casement in place or is about to open it or close it. What is clearer is that her head seems cocked to her left either to see something better or to avoid being glimpsed (like someone peering sidelong from behind a drape), or both. She is protectively swathed in linen, and although her headdress reflects light, we feel its translucency: it seems to transmit a measured amount of light and even the vaguely articulated impress of form. She can hide within it—can even turn her head within it—and yet be warmed by direct, filtered, and reflected light. The subdued tonality of her face seems partly an effect of the head's deep nesting. Its planes are smoothed by filtered shadow as well as filtered light. The face is half withdrawn into flatness.

These details accommodate themselves to "the crucial detail," over which Vermeer does not, in my opinion, falter: the woman's slow, secret, distant, musing, and reticent look, interested and attentive but not deeply involved. The tilt of her body and her grasp on the pitcher incarnate a possibly divided attention, arrested between the world within the room and that outside the window. Once again a map accompanies a half-opened casement. A portion of Europe squares the upper right-hand corner; its duller tones set off her luminous modeled form and her relation to the window; the mapstick helps lock her in place; the barely discernible cartographic details distract us from the virtuosities of the table enough to make the eye return to the standing figure. Again we encounter those unresolved anecdotal possibilities which occasionally

[19] Emil R. Meijer, *Dutch Painting: Seventeenth Century* (New York: McGraw-Hill, 1962), 39.

tempt the critic to round off one or another narrative. But this painting helps us out less than others. Even the following account goes too far: "First the woman opened the window, then she took hold of the handle of the jug. What she did next we shall never know, for we cannot decipher the action with any certainty."[20] The editor of the Classici dell-Arte *Vermeer* somewhat scornfully alludes to another interpretation: "The need for a narrative pretext made people suppose that the lady is on the point of watering flowers."[21]

Yet we may legitimately ask whether the undefined narrative "pretext" in any way affects or is affected by the more immediately striking qualities of the painting: the shimmering reflections on metal, the detail of the carpet, the pure glints of primary harmonies, the gradations of light, and above all the spectrum of blues interanimating all surfaces, spreading from blue-colored areas to the windowpanes, the off-white wall, the white linen, the yellow bodice, the grey-ochre map, the pitcher, the bowl, and the red ground and blue and yellow floral designs of the tapestry.[22] If each object is "framed" and bounded in its own contours and clearly separated from the others, these boundaries are breached by the manifold bleeding and reflecting of blue, by the shadowed lights and illuminated shadows, and by the vibrant chromatic interchanges throughout. The paradox of the frame—its function as both an isolating enclosure and a medium of communication—is conspicuous at the purely formal level of design. And over against this interpenetration stand the clear outlines and "geometrical purity" of the larger forms, the measured and subdued gestures, the simplified structure of the standing figure. The picture abounds in borders that accentuate and isolate the objects: framing edges on the window, bodice, map, folded headdress, jewel box, the left side of the tapestry, the rim of the bowl, and the studs of the chair.

In its present condition, the picture reveals three main light sources: the sunlight passing behind the casement and diffusely reflected from the wall is primary and the reflecting metal surfaces tertiary; the headdress is

---

[20] *Meijer,* 39. Pierre Descargues, on the other hand, dismisses the possibilities: "Note the rather unnatural stance of the woman; she is not so much performing a household task as simply linking the window to the jug" (*Vermeer,* trans. James Emmons [Geneva: Skira, 1966], 130).

[21] *L'opera completa di Vermeer,* pres. di Giuseppe Ungaretti, apparati critici e filologici di Piero Bianconi (Milan: Rizzoli Editore, 1967), 90.

[22] This effect is probably more striking in the picture's present state than originally, since, as Goldscheider notes, "all the blue tones . . . have turned stronger and independent" (129).

the secondary source. Because the light on the wall appears, by its de-saturating effect, to be diffused and because the window glass is blue in tint, there seems to be relatively little direct and highly selective sun-light. What there is gathers and concentrates on the white headdress, which effectively becomes a primary source. It is a hub to which lumi-nous pencils of light radiate from the window, traveling up the figure's right sleeve between the black stripes (visible under the linen), around the folded edge of the headdress, down her left sleeve and spilling across her wrist into the reflecting bowl and onto the table. The main source of shadow illumination, placed across the picture from the window, is the blue material bunched on the right and enriched by its accord with the blue amplitude of skirt. As this is pasteled by the window light and re-flected white linen, so it gives back its blue to the headdress, the pitcher, and the woman's bodice; blue also tints the mapstick and the map; the same pastel glows in the flowers of the tapestry foreground, suggesting still another reflecting source of lower intensity. Looking at the picture, one finds it difficult after a while not to see the window glass as a reflector of blue shadow rather than a bluish transmitter of white light. Amid these vital interchanges of white light and blue, the woman stands as an intermediary, both reflecting or refracting and radiating, her bodice providing, at the same time, the main source of color contrast, gathering light from the edge of the window frame and establishing the chromatic value varied in the bowl and pitcher, the table top, the gilt and tiny bal-usters of the jewel box, and the map.

In the preceding two paragraphs I have described the painting in purely formal terms, ignoring the narrative context, or pretext. In these terms the woman is indeed a puppet, a wax model entirely subordinate to painterly motives—of no interest either as a woman or as a human being. And *Woman with Water Pitcher* is certainly among those paintings of Vermeer's in which the pastoral escapism of art seems most to domi-nate the subject matter. How, then, are we to rehabilitate the human content of the picture before us and integrate it with its lights and forms and colors? The forms themselves will help us: the central feature, the headdress, frames within it the human center, the face. The uneasiness that disturbed Gowing arises from the contrast between the brilliant treatment of the tonality of the linen and the pale, flat, summary treat-ment of the face. But the contrast serves to draw attention to the question of the face; the flaws in workmanship lead to the main source of meaning in the picture and to the one element that will transform all the others.

The hues of the face, which may themselves be a source of distur-bance, are muted echoes of the surrounding context: a suggestion of blue in the shaded areas and an ivoried hint of the tones of the bodice, map, and bowl where diffuse highlights bring out the structure of the face. In spite of the protective linen frame, the woman's features are barely but visibly touched by everything around her, even though the enclosed face is withdrawn from all the chromatic and luminous activity to which the woman unknowingly—by her mere physical presence—contributes so much and of which she is part. Her attention, her consciousness, her inner life are veiled by the receding face. But the veil, like the head-dress, is partly translucent. We intuit something behind the face, but we cannot make it out. The face becomes opaque, reflecting back our intrusive glance. But if we try again and return to the atmosphere that surrounds her, opening ourselves to the tones of light and color, taking in the "poetry of the scene," the picture may disclose itself to us under the aspect of "mood." The mood is blue: subdued, cool, shaded amid radiance—a musing meditative blue. Admittedly this is a metaphoric and literary response, and also an arbitrary reading of "blue." The suffusion of blue seems nevertheless to enhance the particular quality of the woman's arrested motion as she watches something beyond the window and draws away from it while her body appears to anchor itself of its own accord to the lovely familiar objects of her cloistered world. Her arms and hands embrace that world, caress the heightened purity of its textures and hues; within the nunlike linen, her eyes are slowly, coolly, and reticently—yet definitely—drawn beyond. The blue of azure distances, of close corners, of shaded retreats, of rich material surround her with all their vague indications of mood accruing either through association or psychological mechanism. Under the aspect of mood, another boundary is breached: the blue suffusion of the room penetrates or externalizes this distant shadowed moment of her inner life.

The Vanity of Judgment: A Descriptive Anecdote

The development from explicit to implicit narration traced by Gowing charts a course which stresses Vermeer's increasing reliance on devices that produce the effect of conspicuous exclusion. It is neither necessary nor useful to anchor this course in actual chronology, given the paucity of evidence; the continuum is equally available in abstraction from chronology. If all Vermeer's paintings had been miraculously completed at one moment, we could still arrange them according to the same scheme. Even if they are dissociated from Vermeer's life and psyche, the scheme and the continuum remain explicable on other historical grounds. These grounds have been articulated in Svetlana Alpers's stimulating essay,

"Describe or Narrate? A Problem in Realistic Representation."[23] Beginning with a reference to similarities in paintings by Caravaggio and Courbet—"a deliberate suspension of action achieved through a fixity of pose and an avoidance of outward expression" (15)—Alpers goes on to argue that what distinguished Renaissance and seventeenth-century artists from those of the nineteenth century was an unquestioning (or at least less questioning) commitment to "the representational possibilities inherent in art" (37). Within that commitment, narration and description constitute two divergent modes, with the former preceding the latter as the normative mode by which Renaissance artists and theorists asserted their claim to be inheritors of the art of antiquity. What Alpers finds new in paintings by some of the great seventeenth-century realists is "the decision to emphasize description rather than narrative action" (18), but—and this is the novelty of her thesis—she is at pains to argue, with reference to Velázquez's *Water-Seller,*

> that Renaissance artistic practice and Renaissance assumptions about art—the concern for the imitative nature and fictive presence of art—contained within them the possibility for making such an apparently unprecedented image. In turning an anecdotal genre scene into a portrait, Velázquez is treating with profound seriousness the descriptive instead of the narrative aspects inherent in the scene. . . . Like certain other great realist works of the seventeenth century, the *Water-Seller* is rather produced out of a concentration on that imitation which is recognized as the basis of all styles in the Renaissance view of art. I am in effect proposing another dimension in which to consider the conventions of Renaissance art: as a commitment to representation as such which cuts across the hierarchy of styles without, as it were, disposing of them. (21)

As Alpers clearly indicates, this approach enables us to see the dialectical value of description as a *counternarrative mode* which conveys the implications of narrative in a new manner. Comparing Rembrandt's two versions of *Saul and David,* she views the later image "less as a retreat from outward dramatic action . . . than as a kind of description. Intensely described though his figures are, Rembrandt . . . does not still their action in the interests of surface description" but suggests psychological depth "by a new kind of pictorial depth." In redefining "what it is to represent, suggesting things that lie beneath the surface," he is also suggesting "that this in-depth portrayal must replace narration as the expression of serious human interest" and, therefore, "that narration as conceived of by Renaissance art is impossible" (24).

<hr>

[23] *New Literary History* 8 (1976): 15–41.

Alpers believes that in this respect Rembrandt goes beyond Caravaggio, Velázquez, and Vermeer, all of whom "produce paintings which avoid narrative action to concentrate on imitation without questioning the basic commitment to narration" (24). I think, however, that if by "basic commitment to narration" Alpers means the pictorial telling of specific stories—"susceptibility to . . . narrative verbal evocations" (17)—this opinion cannot be applied to Vermeer without some minor revisions. The line of interpretation which Gowing has taught me to pursue suggests that Vermeer uses description to evoke such narrative expectations only to question the ability of conventional narration to convey "things that lie beneath the surface." His counternarrative effects indeed rely on those expectations, evoking them to criticize, foil, and revise them, as the world of *The Procuress* and the Brunswick *Drinking Scene* is evoked and revised in the music scenes or *Officer and Laughing Girl*.[24] This may be tested by a glance at the painting which Alpers uses to illustrate her thesis, *Woman with Scales* (Figure 21).

Alpers sensibly challenges the view that

this picture of such considered formal perfection, representing a woman absorbed in a task specifically characterized by an absence of self-regard or pride, is a representation of vanity. Is vanity intended by a mirror not looked at, or pride by jewels displayed but left untouched on the table? We note the care with which the left hand steadies the weight of the woman's body and the grace with which the glance attends to the hand so delicately balancing the scales. . . . Is Vermeer's still, subtly balanced figure intended as an image of radical imbalance, of sin? (25)

Furthermore, as Arthur K. Wheelock, Jr., has argued against Albert Blankert's interpretation of this as the picture of a gold weigher, microscopic examination indicates that neither gold nor pearls are in the balance pans, the white spots therein visible being highlights.[25] This finding would seem to lend support to Alpers's statement that "the painting of the *Last Judgment* on the wall" behind the woman should be understood not "as rendering a judgment" on her but as reinforcing what "her action . . . and the order of the composition suggest," namely, "that she herself is a just judge":

A most common image of justice is, after all, a woman holding scales. The Christ in the painting, on the other hand, is represented with the other traditional image of justice, the raised sword. Far from judging this woman, the

---

[24] For comments on *Officer and Laughing Girl*, see pages 454–58 above.
[25] Review of Blankert's *Johannes Vermeer van Delft*, *Art Bulletin* 59 (1977): 440.

21. *Woman with Scales*. National Gallery of Art, Washington, D.C.

painting on the wall would appear to assist us in seeing the woman herself as the kind of justice (justness) possible on this earth, in the Dutch home, of the woman. (26)[26]

I am more sympathetic to her criticism of the negative interpretation than to the definiteness with which she maintains the positive reading. Not that the latter is absent but that one would not want to insist on it as the only alternative. A possibility which would complicate either reading is introduced by those commentators who assume that the woman is

[26] Gowing arrived at much the same conclusion (*Vermeer*, 53).

pregnant. John Walsh, for example, observes that Vermeer's contemporaries "could have recognized a bit of folk medicine, the use of scales for divining the sex of an unborn baby" ("Vermeer"). It may be risky to assume here, as in the Amsterdam *Woman in Blue*, that the swelling shape indicates pregnancy rather than a dress fashion,[27] but even without this complication the problem remains. Is the painting emblematic or is it not? Must one decide whether the image signifies vanity or justice? Is it not "possible simply to enjoy the exquisite play of colors as one would delight in the sight of a field of flowers"?—this from Hans Koningsberger (*The World of Vermeer*, 148), who nevertheless succumbs to the lure of conspicuous allegory a few pages later and orchestrates the "incidental elements" of the painting into his own final judgment.[28]

Alpers's thesis leads her to waver uncertainly between these two different questions: Anecdote of vanity or of justice? Anecdote or description? She uses the painting to illustrate the historical point that "the disengagement from narrative action" which "played a significant role in the engagement with realistic description" was not complete, was "still understood as connected in some way to the narrative concerns of art" (25). The connection is elucidated in the following passage:

It is true that in the past few years more and more women in Dutch genre paintings have turned out to be whores or at least guilty of promiscuous thoughts or letters. Vermeer, however, though he repeatedly starts from such anecdotes of sin, permits his representation of the women involved to take over from these essentially narrative points. . . . The mistake in the interpretation of the *Woman with Scales* has been to interpret the presence of the pearls and the painting on the wall, against the evidence of the entire work before our eyes, as a fixed clue to the meaning rather than as a part of the process of pictorial invention. In this work (as in others by Vermeer) emblematic elements like the scattered pearls and the mirror are vestiges of narrative action or anecdote which Vermeer's representation replaces. In a most profound way his art, but of course also his view of women and life, replaces

---

[27] I owe this cautionary note to my former colleague, Eleanor Saunders.

[28] "The key that unlocks the allegory is the scene of the Last Judgment in the background. Immediately an analogy becomes apparent between God judging the just and the unjust and the woman weighing gold. The gold and pearls spilling from the strongbox now acquire another meaning: they represent everything that mortal man values and tries vainly, in the face of his mortality, to hold on to." Koningsberger goes on to observe that since the woman is pregnant, the painting is "filled with hope" despite its depressing message and celebrates "life everlasting" (152). He has touched all bases.

On the vexed question of the iconography of pearls, see E. de Jongh, "Pearls of Virtue and Pearls of Vice," *Simiolus* 8 (1975/76): 69–97, and especially 84. De Jongh follows Gowing (135) and Blankert in assuming that pieces of gold (not pearls) are in the scale.

an anecdotal action with description and leaves us with that powerful, self-contained presence which is so characteristic a feature of the seventeenth-century realistic mode. (26)

Yet by what criterion do we decide that the emblematic value of the scales is somehow less vestigial than that of the other elements? And if the scales are a vestige, not a fixed clue to meaning, why should we see the woman as a kind of justice rather than a kind of vanity? Ornaments, pearls, and coins *are* on the table, the woman *is* in the middle of an action, the painting is somber in tone, and the image reeks of iconography: it virtually dares us not to wonder about the meaning of her action. Hence the idea of a *vestige*, a nonfunctioning anecdotal element left over in "the disengagement from narrative action," seems inapplicable here. The emblematic elements are not so much vestiges as *seeds* of narrative action or anecdote, conspicuous tokens of things not given out, "things that lie beneath the surface."

This alternative is embedded in Alpers's own argument and is in fact (as I see it) proof of the high generative value of her hypothesis. Her revision of the anecdotal sense of the painting is based on her perception of the "still, subtly balanced figure" and of the "absence of self-regard" that characterizes the task in which the woman is absorbed. In itself this is not a telling point against the conventional *vanitas* interpretation, because the conventional painter and observer may depict and see the human figure as merely the vehicle rather than the object of the moral lesson. But when a critic with Alpers's discernment directs our attention toward visual effects we might otherwise have taken for granted, the conventional reading is placed in jeopardy. It is not necessary, however, that it give way to a meaning which puts the woman on the side of the law as a just judge. Alpers's insight can just as easily lead toward a less conventional and much more interesting treatment of *vanitas*.

"I had not known sin but for the Law," St. Paul wrote, and we could infer from the woman's composed and absorbed attitude, her apparent innocence of the sin she represents, that she has not yet been blessed with that painful enlightenment. This would constitute an especially poignant rendering of the *vanitas* theme. The same is true of *Woman with Pearls*—situated in the same room, before the same mirror and window, but with no painting on the wall—which John Walsh calls "a masterpiece of concentration; a few key elements of traditional Vanitas imagery and the poetry of Vermeer's light and color combine in an image of worldly pleasure that is wonderfully seductive. As so often in Dutch art, the celebration and the warning are one."

That Walsh responds more fully to the celebration than to the warning may dramatize his insistence that the warning is there. The response alerts us to the danger of being seduced by what we know is vanity. Vermeer's symbolism would then be "cleverly disguised" (as Walsh argues) in making vanity seem more appealing and innocuous without hiding its true significance from us. And if we cannot dismiss Vermeer's women by reducing them to iconic vehicles of moral disapproval or to painterly deeds of light, the human problem delineated by these paintings becomes dramatically more striking. Confronted by the composure of the woman with the scales or the gravely quizzical self-contemplation of the woman with the pearls, observers sensible of the moral meaning might be prompted to repeat Gowing's words: "We feel for her." For those who insist on reading the images as "anecdotes of sin," Alpers's fine description suggests a profound and compelling narrative concept: "these quiet, self-absorbed, self-possessed women, who are the center of their pictorial worlds, so present to our sight but somehow so inviolate behind the barricade of objects and space with which Vermeer removes them from our touch" (26).

I am not saying that this is the case, only that such an interpretation remains possible, is decisively canceled out neither by Alpers's appeal to figural attitude nor by her selective identification of relevant emblems. I think the double question—vanity or justice, anecdote or description— is thematized by the painting. It presents itself as a puzzle, perhaps as the puzzle inherent (if inexplicit) in all such allegories, and it drives us to seek help from the usual source whence all help comes, the woman's facial expression. But the face is understated, shaded, and slightly out of focus. We might read it in a number of ways: as the face of one meditating, daydreaming, inattentive to what she is doing; or as the face of one musing over whatever significance the scales and the weighing have for her; or as the face of one completely absorbed in the act of testing itself, waiting for the balance to settle and stabilizing herself with her left hand to prevent unwanted disturbance; or as the face of one half dreamily enjoying the sensation of the slight pendulum motion; or, finally, as the face of a patient model holding a pose in a somewhat portentous iconographic setting which, carefully arranged by the painter, has nothing to do with her.

Her expression, then, refuses to provide the key that would resolve our uncertainty even as its veiled quality draws us toward it in the hope of a modest apocalypse. The *Last Judgment* on the wall has much to do with this controlled arousal and checking of our expectations. Conceivably the iconographic consensus of Vermeer's age would have made the *vanitas* theme perfectly evident without it—as seems to have been true of *Woman with Pearls*. The addition of the painting on the wall does not, therefore, confirm the iconography. It exaggerates it, renders it inescapable and somewhat oppressive. It transforms the moral theme from a convention, easy to accept and gloss over, to an interpretive problem. Its brooding presence asks us to make a final judgment about the meaning of the woman's act and then conspires with her face, her attitude, and her action to prevent us from making it. And since we are not allowed to judge the meaning or quality of the woman's act of judgment, this uncertainty permeates our response to Christ's act of judgment. Perhaps his judgment is irrelevant in this case; perhaps it is inconclusive; perhaps, like a map, it is no more than a wall ornament, the painted figment of human imagination, a tribute to the vanity of art. And perhaps, ironically, it represents a conspicuous investment in culture, exemplifying the very *vanitas* against which it warns. To the extent that the woman draws my attention as a protagonist, a human presence ("quiet, self-absorbed, self-possessed"), I want to know how to respond to her, and I experience a curiosity which can only be called anecdotal. But Christ's judgment, the woman's judgment, and my judgment are called forth only to be held in abeyance. Should the painting, should all of Vermeer's paintings, be entitled *Suspended Judgment?*

The consistent appearance of paintings within Vermeer's pictures inevitably raises the reflexive question, as I just implied. Like the *pointillés*, like the flowering paint in the foreground of *The Lacemaker*, it draws attention to the painter and his art. In a brief and tantalizing note Alpers refers to Vermeer's peculiar way of rendering the works of art found on the walls in his paintings: "the actual rendering of the paint—often applied so as to emphasize the artifice involved," "the attention to the very presence of paint on his painted surfaces" (40). These paintings formally accentuate or complement the human figures they embellish, and they often qualify or complicate them in an anecdotal manner. That is, in their functions they are always ornamental and descriptive, and occasionally narrative. Gowing imaginatively explores, through a number of Vermeer's paintings, the hypothesis that "whenever an artist represents as part of his subject a work in which we can construe another, an image within an image, we may expect that the conjunction will prove significant" (49–50). Will the conjunction direct any significance toward the relation between the first-order image and its maker or observers?

There is no way of deciding whether those second-order paintings that could conceivably tell stories *on* the human figures—the Baburen *Procuress*, the *Cupid*, the religious paintings, the *Roman Charity* partly visible in *The Music Lesson*, the upright man in the Brunswick *Drinking Scene*—also tell stories *to* them. But I think it is safe to assume that they convey primarily the decorative taste of their owners, for whom they have the same value as tapestries, Delftware, maps, chandeliers, gold picture frames, and other lovely artifacts. If they were designed as narratives, their exposure to the culture market transforms them into background embellishments and tokens of conspicuous consumption. We may speculate that they speak most forcefully to the inhabitants of Vermeer's interiors as deeds of light. In this respect, the shift from narrative to adornment resembles the "disengagement from narrative action" discussed by Alpers.

The artist's compromise with his clientele is in the mode of *Vanitas* and *Venitas:* the fame and fortune he settles for are won by his descriptive and decorative prowess. The work variously entitled *Allegory of Fame, Allegory of Painting,* and *Artist's Studio* (Figure 22) makes an ironic feint toward an anecdotal representation of the act of painting. But everything in it conspires to exclude the reality of the act from the observer encouraged to look for it: the painter's back, his unlikely garb, his bulbous hand, and his procedure (he begins improbably at the top and, impatiently, with the laurel crown, the symbol of fame, and he uses the mahlstick when there appears to be little need for it). It is a message not only to but also about his clients: "Let's show them what *they* want painting to be"—a message which has often been validated by critics, e.g.: "The map of Holland, emblazoned with coats of arms . . . and replete with the ships that had helped make the country rich and a home of art, suggests that the Lowlands had become the new Parnassus, and that because of the achievements of Dutch artists, Fame, wearing a laurel, has taken up her residence there. But in the end, it is not the allegory that makes the painting unforgettable but the picture's clean, clear light, its beauty of color, and the insouciance of the young girl who serves as the model" (Koningsberger, *The World of Vermeer,* 165). The image of the painter, described by commentators as "wearing a gala costume" (which, like the map, is about eighty years out of date), "a gloriously dressed-up model who has posed for Vermeer," contributes to the same idealizing, or idyllizing, effect. It is a description pretending to be an anecdote. Gowing's comment catches the irony:

> It is improbable that Vermeer yields, in any simple sense, information here of the way he worked. It would be unlike him to do so. There is something in the stolid, ingenuous manner in which this artist sets about his canvas to suggest that his purpose, as usual, was nearer to dissimulation. (141)

22. *Artist's Studio*. Kunsthistorisches Museum, Vienna.

Throwing its curtain aside as if to make a full disclosure of the painter's mystery, *Artist's Studio* arouses and foils our voyeuristic impulse by offering us only a mirror of our own desires. A description which conspicuously excludes the anecdote to which it pretends, it tells us (tells on us) a story of another kind. Thus the initial feint toward narrative becomes a feint toward description, and Vermeer reestablishes on his own terms the deeper narrative value of all his art. If we accept it either as a conventional anecdote or an "insouciant" description, we equate ourselves unwittingly with the figures who inhabit his paintings.

In our effort to escape from the more complex task to which, by conspicuous exclusion, he enjoins us—the interpretation of "the human problem"—we consign ourselves to the lovely fate and vanity of his creatures, inhabitants of Miranda's rare and "wond'red" island, or of Marvell's garden:

> Mean while the Mind, from pleasure less,
> Withdraws into its happiness:
> The Mind, that Ocean where each kind
> Does streight its own resemblance find;
> Yet it creates, transcending these,
> Far other Worlds, and other Seas;
> Annihilating all that's made
> To a green Thought in a green Shade.

INDEX

Page numbers in *italics* denote illustrations.

Designer: Janet Wood
Compositor: G & S Typesetters, Inc.
Text: 11/13 Caslon Old Face #2
Display: Caslon Old Face #2